GENERAL JOHN POPE

General John Pope

A LIFE FOR THE NATION

Peter Cozzens

UNIVERSITY OF ILLINOIS PRESS • URBANA AND CHICAGO

Ⓧ This book is printed on acid-free paper.

The Library of Congress cataloged the cloth edition
as follows:
Cozzens, Peter, 1957–
General John Pope : a life for the nation / Peter Cozzens.
    p.   cm.
Includes bibliographical references and index.
ISBN 0-252-02363-3 (alk. paper)
I. Title.
I. Pope, John, 1822–1892.
2. Generals—United States—Biography.
3. United States. Army—Biography.
4. United States—History—Civil War, 1861–1865—Campaigns.
E467.1.P76C68   2000
973.7'092—dc21   99-006848
CIP

PAPERBACK ISBN 978-0-252-07259-8

For Issa and Ismael

Contents

Maps

Illustrations

Acknowledgments

Conducting research while abroad on diplomatic assignments with the U.S. Department of State presents unique challenges. It also makes the assistance of archivists and librarians crucial. I am pleased to acknowledge several persons who were particularly helpful.

Alan C. Aimone and the staff of the United States Military Academy Archives, West Point, New York, brought to my attention several collections containing material pertinent to my research.

Gary Arnold of the Ohio Historical Society, Columbus, and Nan Card of the Rutherford B. Hayes Presidential Center Archives, Spiegel Grove, Ohio, continue to be of incalculable help to me; both are consummate professionals with whom it is a delight to work. Gary alerted me to a large collection of Pope letters acquired during the course of my research; Nan sifted through the Hayes collection for correspondence of the former president and General Pope.

Timothy H. Bakken of Clarendon Hills, Illinois, gave me transcripts of several Pope letters sold by the Abraham Lincoln Book Shop, Chicago, Illinois, in recent years.

Megan Hahn of the Manuscripts Department of the New-York Historical Society, New York City, reproduced for me the contents of the society's John Pope Papers.

Lisa Ann Libby, curator of rare books at the Huntington Library, San Marino, California, provided me with photocopies of numerous letters, pamphlets, and other scarce material pertaining both to General Pope and to the Fitz John Porter proceedings.

Gary Lundell of the University of Washington Manuscripts Archives, Seattle, Washington, assisted me with the Manning F. Force Collection.

Gail R. Redmann and Ann Sindelar of the Western Reserve Historical Society, Cleveland, Ohio, combed their collections for material on John Pope and Second Manassas.

E. Cheryl Schnirring of the Illinois State Historical Library, Springfield, has been most helpful in providing information from the library's superb Civil War manuscript collections for use in each of my six books.

The staff of the Periodicals Department of the Wheaton, Illinois, Public Library located for me many obscure journal articles through interlibrary loan.

Others whose help I wish to acknowledge are Chuck Barber, manuscripts librarian at the University of Georgia, Athens; Gene DeGruson, curator of special collections at Pittsburg State University, Pittsburg, Kansas; Margaret R. Goostray, curator of special collections at the Boston University Library; Casey Edward Greene, head of special collections at the Rosenberg Library, Galveston, Texas; Steve Nielsen, reference associate at the Minnesota Historical Society, Saint Paul; Sandra Owens, head of the newspaper department at the Free Library of Philadelphia; Tony Saxe, archivist at the Chicago Historical Society; and Jennifer Songster, curator of audiovisuals at the Ohio Historical Society.

I also am indebted to the historians John Y. Simon and Jeffry D. Wert, both of whom read the manuscript and made numerous well-considered suggestions and comments. Two close friends—Robert I. Girardi, my coeditor for *The Military Memoirs of General John Pope,* and Greg Phillips, a Foreign Service colleague—also read the manuscript and made astute observations and helpful suggestions.

My most sincere thanks to my mother, for submitting innumerable requests for interlibrary loan material on my behalf. Finally, I wish to thank Richard Wentworth and Carol Betts of the University of Illinois Press for their continuing confidence in, and enthusiasm for, my work.

Prologue

The war had been good to John Pope. In December 1860 he had been designing lighthouses on Lake Erie, an obscure Regular Army captain toiling in a drafty Cleveland office. Fifteen months later he was a major general of volunteers, commanding an army of thirty-two thousand men. In April 1862 Pope captured Island No. 10 after a nearly bloodless campaign that opened the Mississippi River down to Memphis, Tennessee. That victory brought him national acclaim. In May and June, during the otherwise lifeless siege of Corinth, Mississippi, Pope displayed a zest for battle that cemented his reputation as a fighter of the first order.

Pope was pleased with both the plaudits and his station. As an Illinoisan with a strong sense of state loyalty, he was drawn naturally to service in the West. Among his division commanders were friends from the Regular Army and Republican stalwarts like himself, and two successful campaigns had fostered a deep mutual esteem between Pope and his men. The Army of the Mississippi "had already done great things under my command," said Pope, "and was capable of still more distinguished achievements, with which I could not bear to be disconnected."

But in late June 1862 Pope received from Secretary of War Edwin M. Stanton an enigmatic summons to Washington, D.C. "If your orders will admit," wrote Stanton, "and you can be absent long enough from your command, I would be glad to see you at Washington." Nothing more. When Pope hesitated, Stanton ordered him east. Pope returned to his army just long enough to relinquish command and bid his brother officers farewell. Everyone was sorry to see Pope go; all felt he was headed for trouble. As Pope left a final gathering with his lieutenants, Brigadier General Gordon Granger dampened an already dismal proceeding by hollering regretfully, "Good-bye Pope, your grave is made." Seldom were more prophetic words spoken.[1]

1 The Approbation of My Own Conscience

John Pope was born on March 16, 1822, in Louisville, Kentucky, and raised in Kaskaskia, Illinois, where he grew up privileged and well-placed socially, enjoying the finest a half-settled prairie had to offer. His mother, Lucretia Backus Pope, had a college education and came from a New England family with roots in America reaching back two hundred years: one ancestor, the Reverend William Hyde, was cofounder of Hartford, Connecticut; a second, John Haynes, governed the Massachusetts Bay Colony in the 1630s.

John Pope's paternal lineage was equally distinguished. His uncle, John Pope, for whom he was named, was a United States senator from Kentucky. His grandfather, William Pope (the family seems to have eschewed middle names for their male offspring), served in the colonial army and married the aunt of Ninian Edwards, a future governor of Illinois. Young John's first ancestor in America, Nathaniel Pope the elder, owned the land on which Robert E. Lee was later born and had a daughter who married George Washington's great-grandfather. John's father, the younger Nathaniel Pope, was one of the most illustrious men in Illinois.[1]

Nathaniel Pope had come to Kaskaskia from Kentucky at the turn of the nineteenth century, having attended Transylvania University at Lexington for one year and read law in his brother John's office. Nathaniel moved easily in the pio-

3 •

neer community, and in 1809, when Congress authorized the organization of the Illinois Territory, he was appointed territorial secretary. That year also he married Lucretia Backus.

Although Nathaniel owed his appointment to the influence of his brother John and of Henry Clay, he proved worthy of the job. When the new governor, his cousin Ninian Edwards, was detained several months in Kentucky, it fell to Pope to organize the territory. He drew county lines, settled boundary disputes, and appointed territorial officials. Six years later, under the authority of the legislature, he revised the *Laws of the Territory of Illinois,* a massive two-volume work that became known simply as *Pope's Digest.*[2]

Pope's popularity won him election as territorial delegate to Congress in the fall of 1816. In Washington, he became an aggressive champion of statehood for Illinois. When in 1818 the territory petitioned for admission to the Union, Pope was asked to draw up the necessary resolution. In doing so, he turned what might have been a prosaic parchment into a dynamic entreaty for Illinois's preeminence in the Northwest Territory.

The fifth article of the Ordinance of 1787 had stipulated that there should be formed from the Northwest Territory no fewer than three nor more than five states, and the ordinance proceeded to define the boundaries of the future states of Illinois, Ohio, and Indiana. Troublesome to Pope was a proviso that permitted Congress to "form one or two states in that part of said territory which lies north of an east and west line drawn through the southerly bend of Lake Michigan." As Wisconsin had applied for statehood north of that line, Pope realized Illinois would be deprived of access to Lake Michigan; specifically, it would lose control of the tiny settlement of Chicago. Enlisting the help of his brother John and of Henry Clay, and displaying what the distinguished early Illinois lawyer Thomas Hoyne called "the forecast of a truly great statesman," Pope induced both houses of Congress to agree that the ordinance of admission he had drawn should supersede the provisions of the Ordinance of 1787. Pope's ordinance drew the northern boundary of Illinois at its present 42°70' latitude. To the chagrin of Wisconsin's less-enterprising delegates, Illinois was admitted to the Union with Chicago snugly inside its boundaries. Thomas Hoyne summarized the debt Illinois owed Pope when he observed, "No prescience could have supposed that in sixty years the part of Illinois included by that change of boundary, would have given her the fourth largest city of the Union, and that in the fifteen counties, organized out of the territory then taken from Wisconsin, there would be a majority of the population of this state, by the census of 1880, while three-fourths or four-fifths of all the wealth of the state would be found north of the southern bend of Lake Michigan."[3]

Impressive too were Pope's efforts on behalf of public education. Ordinarily, states carved from the Northwest Territory were granted 5 percent of the revenue from the sale of public lands to finance road building. But Pope won an exception. Certain that roads would be built with or without state aid, he convinced Congress to allow the state of Illinois to retain 3 percent of land-sale proceeds for the furtherance of learning. Pope also laid the foundation for an educational grant that gave the state government the thirty-sixth section of land in every township of Illinois, which might then be sold or rented for the benefit of a general school fund. For this too Thomas Hoyne paid tribute to Pope: "The organization and support of schools was with Judge Pope and the men of that day, one of the primal objects secured to the state, through their efforts, for posterity. The people of this generation owe them the acknowledgment of that service."[4]

Unfortunately, the gratitude of Nathaniel Pope's own generation proved fleeting. A year after he had shepherded Illinois's application for statehood through Congress, the voters of his home county rejected Pope's bid to return to Washington as their representative, giving him only 175 of 775 ballots cast in the November 1818 election. Rejected by the plain folk, Pope allied himself with the aristocracy of learning. He and Ninian Edwards became Whig opponents of Andrew Jackson and vigorous champions of John Quincy Adams for president.

Aligning himself with the Whigs sealed his fate, insofar as elected office was concerned, as the overwhelming majority of voters in southern Illinois were Democrats. Pope defended his Whig politics in a distinctly Johnsonian manner. "Sir," he told a young Democrat lawyer of whom he was fond, "I despise a young man who is not a Democrat; but a man of forty who is not a Whig I also despise."

Cast aside by the electorate, Pope accepted an appointment as United States district judge in 1819. For the next nineteen years, Pope would be the only federal magistrate in Illinois. The entire state was his circuit, and he spent a good deal of his time on the road, traveling from one rough, log courthouse to another. His visits were big events. "The court-rooms in those days were always crowded. To go to court and listen to the witnesses and lawyers was among the chief amusements of the frontier settlements," explained the jurist Isaac N. Arnold. "The judges and lawyers were the stars; and wit and humor, pathos and eloquence, always had appreciative audiences." Relations between the bench and bar were free and easy, said Arnold. "The judge usually sat upon a raised platform, with a pine or white-wood board on which to write his notes. A small table on one side for the clerk, and a larger one, sometimes covered with green baize, around which were grouped the lawyers, too often I must admit, with their feet on top of it," recalled Arnold. "From one to another of these rude court-rooms the gentlemen of the Bar passed, following the judge in his circuit from county to county, traveling, generally on horseback, with saddle bags for a clean shirt or two, and perhaps one or two elementary law books."[5]

Not surprisingly, given the hardships of travel in pioneer Illinois, Judge Pope preferred to leave the rambling, frame family home in Kaskaskia as seldom as possible. Nine children were born to Nathaniel and Lucretia Pope under its puritanical roof. John was the fourth child to enter the Pope household. Siblings William, Penelope, and Elizabeth preceded him; his sisters Lucretia and Cynthia came at close intervals thereafter. Three more daughters, all of whom died in childhood, were born to the Popes. When John was just seven, William left home to join the navy, and John became the principal object of attention of his mother, four sisters, and the black nursemaid who cared for him.[6]

Although he professed antislavery sympathies, Judge Pope was never active in the cause, and he retained slaves until slavery was outlawed in Illinois. At heart a Kentucky aristocrat, Nathaniel Pope prided himself on his erudition and ancestry, and it most certainly had been this arrogance that cost him the 1818 congressional election. Although he founded Bible societies in Jackson County, donated land for the county courthouse, contributed money to the first Kaskaskia public school, and built the first bridge over the Kaskaskia River, frontier democracy passed Nathaniel Pope by, and his judgeship proved the zenith of his public career. In 1824, Pope tried unsuccessfully to obtain a vacant seat in the United States Senate, and he spent the winter of 1826 in Washington, vainly seeking a place on the United States Supreme Court.[7]

The ingratitude of the electorate infuriated John Pope. Too young to understand the rough machinations of frontier politics, John nonetheless felt acutely his father's anguish. In a letter to his married sister, Penelope Pope Allen, fourteen-year-old John excoriated as satanic buffoons the garrulous, illiterate men who attacked Judge Pope. By contrast, their father was the Angel Gabriel come to earth.[8]

John both admired and feared his father, and from the judge and his progenitors he inherited traits that helped both to make and ultimately to break him. The Pope men were a curious mix of erudition, ambition, and braggadocio. Born to command, learned but gruff, outgoing but bookish, more than a bit sloppy with the truth, a Pope male would exaggerate a story or a claim as much from enthusiasm as mendacity. Or, as a close friend of John Pope later put it, "Those who thought that, because he was so sanguine to florid in statement, he was not careful and accurate in determining what was essential, entire[ly] mistook the man." And a Pope male would roar, swagger, and posture—invariably more threatening in speech than deed.

All these qualities were bound up in the looming and turbulent presence that was John Pope's father. The judge cut a contradictory figure. Said his intimate friend, the attorney Usher F. Linder, "Judge Pope's physical form was not very remarkable; he was rather above than below the medium height, and rather corpulent, [but] a man could not look upon him without thinking that he was a man of considerable intellectual power." Stephen T. Logan, a law partner of Abraham Lincoln and one of the preeminent lawyers in the young state, shared Linder's high opinion of Nathaniel Pope's intellect, calling him "a man of the finest legal mind he ever knew." Judge Joseph Gillespie, who began his legal career practicing before Pope, carried Logan's estimate a step further; to him, Nathaniel Pope was simply "one of the ablest men of the nation."[9]

Judge Pope's emotions were always close to the surface, and he was so blunt as to strike many as rude. In one case before his court, Judge Pope's reply to an argument of counsel was simply, "This is preposterous." An Illinois attorney said of Nathaniel Pope, "He had a head like a half-bushel, with brains enough for six men. He had a wonderful knowledge of human nature and was utterly without fear." Judge Pope's son, the attorney added, had many of the father's qualities.[10]

Easily angered, Nathaniel Pope could also be gracious, even tender, with those of whom he was fond. Usher F. Linder was one upon whom he bestowed special favor. "I was a young man at the beginning of my acquaintance with Judge Pope, and a sort of pet of his," remembered Linder, "and he used to scold me for not coming to his room more often than I did." Abraham Lincoln was another favorite. Judge Pope knew Lincoln well and over the years developed a deep affection for him. Crusty in the courtroom, the judge softened when Lincoln argued a case. Lincoln, in turn, came to understand and appreciate Judge Pope, and later his son. "The judge was rough toward everyone, but his roughness toward Lincoln had a touch of tenderness in it," remembered a fellow circuit-riding lawyer. "He would sometimes rebuke him, but in a sort of fatherly way. . . . Many people wondered at the favor shown to John Pope by Mr. Lincoln during the war. . . . Lincoln understood the sort of roar in John Pope's proclamations which many people thought gasconade. That roar he got from his gruff old father; it was the roar of the lion and Lincoln had heard it a thousand times."[11]

Besides bombast, John Pope inherited something of his father's genius and a good deal of his tendency toward overweight. Judge Pope also imparted to his son Republican ideals, a deepening abhorrence of slavery, a love of learning, and a splendid family library in which John might indulge his considerable intellectual curiosity. What he could not instruct his son in was the managing of money. He admonished John to practice economy and "always be ahead of your business," but he failed to benefit from his own teachings. Land speculation was the accepted way for early state officials to supplement their salaries, but while Ninian Edwards and others grew rich off their dealings, Nathaniel Pope's ventures not only refused to return a profit but also wiped out his savings. John had prepared for college, and his mother wanted him to attend school in the East, but there was no money for tuition. So Judge Pope traveled to Washington to ask a favor of his friends. Ninian Edwards, then a United States senator, agreed to champion John's appointment to West Point, as did Congressman William R. May. Pope also called on Henry Clay and John Quincy Adams, both of whom pledged to help. On March 20, 1838, at the age of sixteen, John was accepted into the Military Academy, to graduate, if all went well, with the class of 1842.[12]

At first, nothing seemed to go well. Cadet Pope arrived at West Point on July 1, 1838, and with the other plebes went into summer camp, where he was miserable.[13] He got into some minor trouble, apparently with girls, and his father had to cancel a planned visit to the academy, which meant Pope would not see his parents for two years, when cadets were granted their first leave. Guard duty was interminable, the heat oppressive, and, Pope told his mother, the stiff, gray-wool uniform coat that cadets wore buttoned to the chin chafed his neck and spoiled his good looks.

Cadet Pope was under great pressure to succeed. Judge Pope expected his son to finish first in his class, nothing less. Six months before John was accepted at West Point, Nathaniel had admonished him "to do things right and in apt time. If you hear a man say he is hurried and his business is behind hand and apologize for doing a thing incorrectly because he was too much hurried, you may be sure that he is very lazy or deficient in systematic arrangement. Hence, do your work and then play."

The odds seemed against Cadet Pope. The West Point of 1838 was dominated by New Englanders and was, in terms of educational standards, an extension of the New England prep school. Most of the faculty were Yankees, and nearly half the entering class was from the northeastern or mid-Atlantic states. Poorly prepared by western schools, a disproportionate percentage of midland cadets— particularly Illinoisans—washed out.

But years of his father's tutelage and the resiliency of youth enabled Pope to adapt rapidly to the curriculum. By mid-September, he was near the head of his class in French and mathematics. Quite pleased with himself, Pope told his mother, "I have not only the approbation of my own conscience . . . but also when a person is transferred up it is published before the whole Corps of Cadets at the evening parade, and I assure you it is a great deal of satisfaction for one to hear himself praised."[14]

Praise was scarce after the first semester, as Cadet Pope slipped in the class standing. His classmate James Longstreet thought he knew the reason: Pope had plenty of ability but "did not apply himself to his books very closely." Perhaps to defuse his father's predictable rage at his failings, John preferred to blame the system. Class standing was "very foolish," he hastened to assure his mother after she saw the monthly results for October 1839; "they are of no manner of use, and there is no justice whatever in them." Nevertheless, he promised to do his best.[15]

And he did reasonably well. A graceful rider, Pope stood first in his class in horsemanship. Remembered Longstreet, "He was a handsome, dashing fellow, a splendid cavalryman, sitting his horse beautifully." Overall, Pope ranked seventeenth in his class of fifty-six at graduation: high enough to allow him to choose his branch of service—he selected the topographical engineers—but not good enough for Judge Pope, who flew into a rage when he learned his son had not graduated first. Nor was it good enough to keep John Pope from leaving the academy with a chip on his shoulder that grew weightier with time.

Brevet Second Lieutenant Pope's ninety-day West Point graduation leave ended on October 5, 1842, when he was ordered to active duty at Palatka, Florida. His first commander was Captain Joseph E. Johnston, also an engineer officer. Although Johnston was just thirty-five, the young lieutenants looked upon him "as rather a venerable man" of wide experience with the ladies. "I don't know how such an idea originated," confessed Pope, "but it prevailed among us and invested its object with a halo of romance which constantly attracted our curiosity and interest."[16]

Certainly there was little in Pope's assigned duties to hold the interest of a vigorous twenty-year-old. Several months before Pope arrived, the First Seminole War ended. To induce settlers back into the region, Congress offered 160 acres of land to anyone who would homestead it. Army engineers were called on to survey the public lands and lay out roads and canals to ease access to them. Pope spent several long months traipsing across Florida with his compass, rods, chains, and notebooks. Perhaps boredom drove Pope to misbehave, because for some reason he and Johnston grew to dislike one another intensely. Disdainful of his commander and weary of the company of alligators and rattlesnakes, in early 1843 Pope went to Washington to lobby for a better assignment. This irregular course was the first display of an independence of mind that led Pope to numerous acts early in his career that, if not openly insubordinate, at least reflected poor judgment.

Pope was not unique among young Regular Army officers in blowing his own horn, just unwise in the way he did so. Promotions in the antebellum army came with glacial slowness; ten years as a lieutenant was typical for a line officer, and topographical engineer officers usually had to wait twenty years for a permanent promotion to captain. Those unable to cultivate high-ranking advocates had little hope of advancement. Ten years after Pope's first gambit for a better assignment, Brevet Major Isaac I. Stevens addressed a memorandum to Congress, demanding that engineers receive more equitable consideration in promotions—he suggested fourteen years to captain as not unreasonable.[17]

No better satisfied with his next posting, which was to the genteel Southern port city of Savannah, Pope stepped outside military channels and wrote to Senator James Semple of Illinois for help in securing an assignment to Louisville, Kentucky. Pope hoped to serve near family and under the command of Major Stephen Harriman Long, a noted explorer and the army's preeminent engineer officer.

Pope miscalculated badly. Senator Semple only compounded his troubles by writing directly to Colonel John James Abert, chief of the Corps of Topographical Engineers, on behalf of Pope. Though placid by nature, Abert could not let pass a breach of military etiquette so egregious as circumventing one's superior officers to lobby politicians. Not only did he refuse the Illinoisan's request for a transfer, but Abert also admonished Pope's commanding officer to discipline him.[18]

Whatever action Pope's commander took failed to impress him. Several months later, he bypassed the engineer corps and asked the adjutant general of the army for three weeks' leave to attend to "business of a personal and private nature." When Abert saw Pope listed on the leave rolls, he exploded. This time, Abert chose to rebuke Pope himself. Abert had just received a request from Major James D. Graham, the senior army representative to the American-Canadian Boundary Survey, for a topographical engineer to help mark the northeastern border. Abert was delighted to comply; perhaps Lieutenant Pope would prefer snow to Florida swamps. On October 23, 1844, Abert ordered him to report to Major Graham in far-off Maine.

Pope was in a quandary. The private business that had taken him from his post was a bad case of syphilis. Judged temporarily unfit for active duty by the family physician, Pope had to tell Colonel Abert of his problem. He did so with typical Pope temerity, appending a plea for reassignment to Louisville to his request for additional leave. An exasperated Colonel Abert replied, "In reference to your leave of absence, allow me to say that the issue of these indulgences in your case already exceeds that of any officer in the Corps who has been as short a time in commission as yourself." And, no, Pope would not be going to Louisville. He was to leave for Maine as soon as he was fit.

Pope went to Louisville anyway, to visit the Kentucky Popes and, evidently too embarrassed to share his medical woes with his parents, recuperate there. Around his relatives, Pope proved an able thespian, as no one apparently suspected his troubles. His Uncle Curran wrote Judge Pope that John looked well and "appeared to be in good standing with the War Department."[19]

Pope's true standing in Washington was as low as the temperature at his new post, which was thirty degrees below zero when Pope arrived in January 1845. For eighteen months, Pope lived in a tent and tramped over the northeastern backcountry, marking the international boundary. When the work of Major Graham's team was done, Pope wrote a "memoir" of his part in the survey, which he sent over Graham's head to Colonel Abert. Sputtering about "proper channels" and "irregularity," the colonel returned Pope's missive to Major Graham.[20]

The outbreak of war with Mexico spared Pope a second reprimand, or worse. Mexico had broken off diplomatic relations with the United States in late 1845, after negotiations over an American purchase of California and New Mexico collapsed. President Polk responded by sending a small army under General Zachary Taylor to the Rio Grande. Sharp battles with Mexican forces occurred north of the river in the spring of 1846, after which Taylor crossed the Rio Grande, captured the border city of Matamoros, and made ready to march on Monterrey, 150 miles from the Texas border. Volunteers flocked to his camp by the thousands, and a small coterie of Regular Army officers followed. Lieutenant Pope was among them, one of eight topographical engineers assigned to field duty with Taylor's army.[21]

Logistical problems delayed Taylor's expedition, giving Pope time to acquaint himself with his fellow officers, many of whom would rise to prominence in the Civil War. Jefferson Davis commanded a Mississippi regiment, Braxton Bragg led a Regular artillery battery, and Ulysses S. Grant was a lieutenant of infantry. Captain Robert E. Lee and Lieutenant George Gordon Meade, the opposing commanders at Gettysburg, were among the engineer contingent, which was led by Brevet Major Joseph Mansfield, who would die at Antietam.

Pope took to Mansfield at once. His "Dr. Jekyll and Mr. Hyde personality" amused the lieutenant. In camp, Mansfield was "fussy and fond of meddling with his subordinates." But in battle, said Pope, he "visibly swelled before your eyes; his face flamed out with fiery ardor, and his whole figure and his every movement seemed filled with a sort of terrible passion. He pervaded all places of danger, and everywhere put himself in the forefront of the battle. . . . I never yet have seen a man so regardless of his personal safety or so eager to imperil it."[22]

Pope first saw Mansfield under fire at Monterrey. Beginning his advance in late August, Taylor arrived before the Nuevo León capital with the vanguard of the army on the morning of September 19, 1846. As the remainder of his troops came up, Taylor ushered them into camp, while Major Mansfield and his engineers reconnoitered the Mexican defenses. All day long on the nineteenth, and throughout the morning of the twentieth, they surveyed the dusty plains and barren mountains around Monterrey for the best approach to the city before settling on the Saltillo road, which debouched from a deep gorge west of Monterrey. Lieutenant Pope had been assigned the northeastern approach to the city, and he made his observations under a steady fire from Mexican sharpshooters posted in outlying forts. General Taylor planned his attack from the information Mansfield's engineers gathered, splitting his army into two attacking columns to take the Mexican garrison in a double envelopment from the northeast and the west.

Major Mansfield and his engineers were attached for the assault to the northeastern column, comprised of the divisions of Brigadier General David E. Twiggs, temporarily led by Lieutenant Colonel John Garland, and of Major General William O. Butler. At dawn on September 20, Garland and Butler formed their troops on the arid plain northeast of Monterrey, while the engineers reconnoitered the northeastern approach to the city. Commanding the ground over which the Americans must pass were a series of fortified buildings, the most formidable of which was El Fuerte de la Teneria.[23] Mansfield made the fort the object of a personal reconnaissance. While the major took in its defenses, General Taylor told Colonel Garland to "lead the head of your column off to the left, keeping out of reach of the enemy's shot, and if you think (or you find) you can take any of them little forts down there with the bay'net you better do it—but consult with Major Mansfield. You'll find him down there."[24]

Garland and Mansfield conferred briefly. Mansfield bade him proceed with the attack, and while Garland formed the eight hundred men of the First Infantry, Third Infantry, and the Maryland and District of Columbia Battalion on the broken plain northwest of El Fuerte de la Teneria, Mansfield rode ahead to have a closer look at the northeastern edge of the city. With him rode Lieutenant Pope and Captain William George Williams, also of the engineers. Satisfied the city defenses could be breached, Mansfield granted Pope the privilege of ordering Garland forward. As it swept past La Teneria from the west, Garland's column was raked by a horrible enfilading fire. The Maryland and District of Columbia Battalion disintegrated, but the remainder of the division kept on. At the head of the column were Mansfield, Williams, and Pope. Into town they spilled with the attacking infantry. In their headlong dash through the streets, the Americans stumbled upon a masked battery, which raked the column with grapeshot. The infantry gave back, reformed amid the low adobe houses, and charged again. Mansfield, Williams, and Pope were still out in front on horseback. A withering fire of musketry erupted from the housetops above the battery. Two bullets clinked against the scabbard of Pope's saber. A single round bore through Mansfield's calf. Another bullet shattered Williams's skull. As bullets peppered the dusty street, Pope dismounted and carried Williams into a nearby house, where the captain died. Mansfield crawled into the house after them, had his leg bound up, then returned with Pope to the fight.[25]

The battle was going badly for the Americans. The narrow streets were barricaded at every turn, and each house concealed a squad of Mexican infantrymen. In an effort to break the deadlock, General Taylor sent forward Braxton Bragg's battery of Regulars. The limbered guns rattled into town, only to be brought to a halt by an abatis of dry brush and branches. While the battery waited in column amid a hail of bullets, Lieutenant Pope and a handful of pioneer troops tore at the scrub. Pausing a moment to glance behind him, Pope caught a glimpse of a burly young mounted officer at the head of the column—Lieutenant George H. Thomas, a section commander in Bragg's battery. Pope took the measure of the man in a moment: "He was, as always, tall and stalwart, but in those days he had not put on the flesh which rather disfigured him in later years. Even then he wore the impassive, unmoved countenance in dangerous places which became during the Civil War so marked a characteristic." At Pope's behest, Thomas sent up a cannoneer with a lighted port-fire to ignite the brush. The abatis burned quickly, and the battery rumbled past.[26]

Pope's efforts at the abatis availed little. Bragg's cannon made no impression on the Mexican defenses, and on the recommendation of Mansfield, who surveyed the scene from a stretcher, Garland quit Monterrey. Brigadier General William J. Worth's division fared no better, having stalled on the dusty hills west of town.

Taylor rested his army on September 22. General Worth resumed the battle west of town on the twenty-third with a daring, predawn surprise attack that eventually took his division into the heart of the city. To the east, Major General John A. Quitman's brigade of Twiggs's division cautiously probed Monterrey's outer defenses until night put a close to the fighting. Pope played no appreciable role in the battle of the twenty-third, nor would he have a chance at further glory at Monterrey. Mexican resistance collapsed overnight, and the garrison surrendered on September 24.[27]

Monterrey was a decisive if bloody victory that made the reputations of a number of junior officers, Pope among them. Major Mansfield told Taylor that "Lieutenant Pope executed his duties with great coolness and self-possession and deserves my highest praise." Lieutenant Colonel Garland, whose division Mansfield and his engineers had helped forward on the first day, reported that Pope "deported himself as a gallant soldier under the heaviest fire of the enemy."[28]

At last someone apart from Pope himself was singing his praise, and the young lieutenant made the most of it. He appended Garland's and Mansfield's tributes to his own highly embellished account of the battle, which he mailed to Illinois newspapers. Pope's self-promotion paid off. Perhaps with Judge Pope's prodding, the General Assembly of Illinois resolved to present Lieutenant Pope with a sword, "as a testimonial of the high estimation in which are held his gallant conduct, noble bearing and important services in the battle of Monterrey."[29]

His fellow engineer officers were surprised to read of Pope's manufactured exploits. As Lieutenant Meade said in a letter home, "I regret also to state that Lieutenant Pope, of my corps, *did not discover a battery one day, and lead the col-*

umn of attack the next,[30] and that, if 'his gallantry was the theme of admiration of the whole army,' the army never knew it till after the letter so stating the fact came back in the papers. . . . Pope behaved very well and did his duty," Meade conceded, "but nothing more than all the rest of the army did."[31]

Although impressed with Pope in battle, the officious Major Mansfield could not condone his behavior in camp during the long season of inactivity that followed the capture of Monterrey. Pope and Meade became messmates, sharing a wealthy Mexican's home and generally living like lords. "We each of us have our own servants, one of whom is a cook, the other hostler, the third plays waiter; so that we are quite comfortable, and, from our luxurious quarters, the envy of the army," said Meade. To his retinue Pope added a fourteen-year-old Mexican girl, whom Braxton Bragg said he had "kidnapped" to satisfy his carnal cravings; as if that were not enough, Pope rode openly about town with her.[32]

Pope soon fell into disfavor with Mansfield. As an insubordinate twenty-four-year-old subaltern of robust libido and defiant mien, Pope felt wronged by the major. Although he conceded Mansfield to be a "man of kindly disposition and very just," Pope felt "tormented and persecuted unwarrantably" for his off-duty dalliances. No matter; Pope's easy living ended on February 22, 1847, when a large Mexican army attacked Taylor's army on a high plateau near the hacienda of Buena Vista. The first day's fight was inconclusive, and Taylor temporarily left the conduct of the battle to his second-in-command, Brevet Major General John Wool, while he looked to the security of the army's rear. While Taylor was away, the Mexicans struck a blow at dawn on February 23 that crushed the American left.

Wool was helpless to reverse the disaster, said Pope, because the troops despised him as an unfeeling martinet. By the time General Taylor and Pope, who was on temporary duty with Taylor's staff, reached the field at 9:00 A.M., the retreat of the left had deteriorated into a near rout. Taylor and Pope rode up an arroyo and onto the plateau at the extreme left of the line. With the help of Jefferson Davis's Mississippi Rifles, Taylor checked the Mexican onslaught and reformed his left a half-mile to the rear of its first position.[33]

The battle resumed shortly after noon with another strong Mexican attack. Taylor set up headquarters behind Captain J. M. Washington's battery on the Saltillo road and for the remainder of the afternoon busied himself with countering the numerous Mexican assaults. He employed Pope in carrying orders to his troop commanders and in bringing back information on the progress of the fight. When not relaying messages, Lieutenant Pope stayed near two Illinois regiments that were in the heart of the action.

Pope rejoined Taylor in time to witness the climactic moment of the battle, as the united remnants of three Mexican divisions, having repelled a counterattack by the Illinoisans, swept across the plateau toward the Saltillo road from the southeast, threatening to enfilade Taylor's entire line. As the Illinoisans stumbled past, Taylor wheeled around all available guns to meet the Mexicans, but their fire was insufficient to stop the attackers. To Pope, the situation seemed hopeless: "The plain in front of us seemed to swarm with Mexicans, pressing forward to what, unless they were instantly checked, was certain and complete victory." Pope fixed his gaze on Taylor. Having witnessed Taylor's irascible nature in camp, when he would fly "into passion on the most trifling causes," the young lieutenant feared the general would come apart then, "in this crucial moment of his life when the next ten minutes would settle the question whether he was to be a victorious or dishonored general." Instead, he saw a man in absolute control of his emotions: "As I looked at him I was struck with surprise and admiration. He sat on his horse in an easy careless attitude, with no sign of excitement about him, and with an expression of countenance as placid and pleasant, and a manner as composed and quiet as if he had just risen from a very satisfactory dinner."[34]

The Mexicans were less than four hundred yards away, and "an advance of 200 yards further would have placed them so . . . they could have turned the rear and completely destroyed our right wing also," remembered Pope. At that instant, Braxton Bragg appeared at the head of his battery. Prodding their tired horses with sabers, the drivers steered the guns up the wall of the arroyo and onto the plateau. Bragg reported to Taylor for orders, and Pope eavesdropped on their discussion. Taylor told Bragg to unlimber his guns and go into action, to which Bragg remonstrated, "General, if I go into battery here I will lose my guns." Taylor remained adamant: "If you do not, the battle is lost."

Bragg complied at once and loaded his guns with double-shotted canister. Captain Thomas W. Sherman brought his battery into line alongside Bragg's, and together they roared a salvo that staggered the Mexican line. "The effect was simply amazing," said Pope, who sat on horseback behind the right section of Bragg's battery. Salvo after salvo was poured into the Mexican ranks, piling the dead and wounded "into heaps on the plain. It was a dreadful sight, but the work was effective and settled the issue of the Battle of Buena Vista."[35]

And Buena Vista effectively settled the war in northern Mexico. Peace came to Mexico five months later, with the Treaty of Guadalupe Hidalgo.

2 The Most Ridiculous Assumption of Position

The end of hostilities in Mexico brought the Corps of Topographical Engineers a project of unprecedented scope and responsibility—the survey of the boundary between the United States and Mexico. Assignment to the survey commission carried young engineer officers far beyond routine duties of mapping and marking a border; they were called upon to pass judgment on issues critical to the settling of the Southwest and with implications for rising sectional rivalries within the Union.[1]

Perhaps recalling the past indiscretions of young Pope, now a brevet captain, Colonel Abert shipped him far from the controversial southwestern frontier to Fort Snelling, Minnesota, and the border with Canada. There topographical engineers were charged with the important but far less career-enhancing task of locating an appropriate site for an army post on Minnesota's Red River, near the border settlement of Pembina, to keep troublesome Indians in check and Hudson's Bay Company fur traders from hunting and trapping on American land.[2]

Pope reported to the commander of the expedition, Brevet Major Samuel Woods, on May 22, 1849. Two weeks later, escorted by a company of dragoons, Woods's party started north. Heavy rains soaked the virgin prairie so badly it took the expedition fifty-six days to hike 420 miles.

Apart from being plagued by mosquitoes and nearly struck by lightning, Pope found that the trip was without adventure. He succeeded, however, in making a nuisance of himself. As the party's only topographical engineer, with orders emanating from Washington, Pope behaved as if he were accountable only to himself. He wandered off constantly, supplementing his soundings of the Red River, calculations of distances, observations of wildlife and vegetation, and map drawing with extensive interviews of fur trappers, voyageurs, settlers, and government agents. He became familiar with the region's Indian population and agricultural potential, about which he declaimed in high style. Most annoying to Major Woods, Pope had the audacity to challenge the correctness of the Canadian-American boundary survey done by Major Stephen Harriman Long in 1823. A friend of Colonel Abert, Long had sunk a post at the forty-ninth parallel to mark the boundary. Pope wanted to resurvey the line, and he entered into correspondence on the subject with a representative of the Hudson's Bay Company. Pope even crossed the border to question British soldiers on the matter, until Woods ordered him to desist.[3]

Having barely prevented Pope from instigating an international incident, Major Woods was only too pleased to grant Pope's request that he be permitted to make his own way back to Fort Snelling and even allowed him the company of another officer; "I did not think their presence with the command would be of any service to it," reported Wood laconically. Engaging twelve French mixed bloods and a thirty-three-foot canoe, Pope departed Pembina on August 20. Continuing his methodical observations of the waterways and wildlife of the Minnesota Territory, Pope made his way leisurely back to Fort Snelling. During his journey, he drew maps of the major bends and islands in the Red and Crow Wing rivers, as well as of the numerous lakes encountered along the way, and kept notes on the navigability of each body of water. On September 27, Pope reached Fort Snelling, nearly two weeks after Woods had returned. Without informing Major Woods, Pope left for Washington to brief Colonel Abert on the expedition. From there he went to St. Louis, where his original orders permitted him to write his report.

Woods was incensed. In his report of the expedition, Woods told Congress, "Brevet Captain Pope joined the expedition, continued with it, and left it, with the most ridiculous assumption of position, which he endeavored to maintain by misrepresentation and a wasteful extravagance of public monies placed at his disposal. His duties were neglected and he left his post [Fort Snelling] without authority."[4]

Pope penned his report during an extended leave of absence, taken in part to visit his gravely ill father, who died while he was home. Eschewing the "spritely narrative or the recital of wild adventure" that characterized what he implied were the self-aggrandizing reports of earlier expeditions written by John C. Frémont, Major Long, and Colonel Abert, Pope hoped "to accomplish the more useful object of placing in the hands of the hardy pioneers, in the settlement of a mighty state, all the information which I possess as to its character and resources."

Pope accomplished that purpose through painstaking descriptions of the Indian populace and of the land and the quality of its soil, waterways, and portages. But he compromised the integrity of his report by making broad policy recommendations—to include the abandonment of Fort Snelling—that exceeded his authority. With characteristic ebullience, Pope claimed for Minnesota a limitless future. "I am at a loss to express myself with sufficient force to do justice to the beautiful country embraced within this division, which is perhaps the most remarkable in the world for its peculiar conformation and vast productiveness." That it had not been exploited was the fault of the government. "I can only attribute to ignorance of its great value the apathy and indifference manifested by the government in failing as yet to extinguish the title of the Indians, and to throw open to the industry of the American people a country so well adapted to their genius and their enterprise." Pope repeated his complaint in a letter to the Minnesota *Chronicle and Register.* He discussed his report with Illinois congressmen and Minnesota territorial legislators before submitting it to the Topographical Bureau and privately arranged for Senator Stephen A. Douglas to call for it in the Senate, and for Congressman Henry H. Sibley to do the same in the House.[5]

Published in March 1850, Pope's report neither impressed Colonel Abert nor won Pope friends in the corps. That Pope had resumed of his old habit of bypassing the army bureaucracy in favor of conversations with congressmen angered Abert. Indignant too over Pope's swipe at his own work and his unsolicited counsel on national affairs, Colonel Abert slapped the brevet captain down sharply. He reprimanded Pope for buying a chronometer for the expedition with army funds after he had told Pope to rent one. More important, Abert accused Pope of having plagiarized a map of Minnesota done by Joseph N. Nicollet twelve years earlier. Although Pope seems to have erred only in failing to credit Nicollet's work as a base map for his own, his occasional carelessness in map making, as well as the florid tone of his report, fed his growing reputation in the army as a liar and braggart. William T. Sherman later said his Minnesota report was the principal cause of Pope's bad standing among his brother officers, who would only grudgingly concede him "to be a man of ability in certain directions."[6]

Their opinion of him would have suffered even more had they known that his motives in trumpeting Minnesota's virtues, and in recommending large federal expenditures in the territory, may have been partly personal. Before leaving Minnesota, Pope had purchased several choice lots near Fort Snelling. There was nothing improper in his doing so, and the purchases may have simply reflected

Pope's enthusiasm for the region's potential, but knowledge of them undoubtedly would have raised eyebrows in the corps—and irritated Colonel Abert.[7]

While en route to St. Louis to write his report, Pope stopped off in Springfield, Illinois, to receive the sword the state assembly had voted him two years earlier "as a testimonial of the high regard which your native state entertains of your services and your bravery" in the Mexican War. The governor presented Pope with the sword in a ceremony held on October 30, 1849.[8]

Twelve years would pass before he was again honored for military exploits. The intervening years were for Pope marked by frustrated grabs for small glory and incessant wrangling with his superiors. Pope hoped to return to Minnesota and in his report pled for a second assignment there: "I have become so much interested in the country, and so fully convinced of the rapid progress it will make in wealth and population, that it would not only be a high honor but a deep gratification to me should I be selected for the purpose of continuing the explorations yet to be made within its borders." He repeated his plea in an ill-considered letter to Colonel Abert. The territorial legislature of Minnesota demanded his presence to advise them on needed internal improvements, Pope informed Abert imperiously. He sought Abert's permission not only to return to Minnesota, but also to make public his report.

Pope's appeal fell on deaf ears. Major Woods, in command at Fort Snelling, did not want the supercilious captain back in his district. And Pope's arrogance so infuriated Abert that he immediately ordered him to duty in Texas under Joseph E. Johnston, now a colonel.[9]

If Abert thought he had dispensed with Pope by returning him to duty under a commander who detested him, the colonel was mistaken. Johnston wanted nothing to do with Pope and insisted Abert take him back. And Pope used complications arising from the settlement of his late father's estate as an excuse to demand a lengthy leave of absence in St. Louis. With temerity remarkable in a junior officer but typical of Pope, he reminded Abert of his dislike for Colonel Johnston: "My relations with Colonel Johnston are and have been such for some years that it would be exceedingly unpleasant to serve with him. . . . As Texas is a pleasant station I have little doubt that any officer of the corps would be glad to exchange Oregon, New Mexico, or California for that station."[10]

Abert acquiesced and ordered Pope to the New Mexico Territory as chief topographical officer. Pope was delighted. After arranging for the sale of his Minnesota lots, he left St. Louis the first week of May 1851.

Pope took an immediate liking to his new commander, Colonel Edwin V. Sumner, a sentiment Sumner apparently reciprocated. And Pope found the arid beauty of the New Mexico Territory enchanting. Thirty-seven years later, suffering through a St. Louis blizzard, Pope would "sigh for the balmy breezes and bright sunshine of New Mexico," which he thought had been "the best station and the most agreeable duties" he had ever had.[11]

Pope met Colonel Sumner at Fort Leavenworth, Kansas, and set out for the New Mexico Territory with Sumner's mixed command of infantry and dragoons on May 28. Traveling the long and tortuous Santa Fe Trail, Sumner's column was nearly two months in reaching the new headquarters of the Ninth Military District at Fort Union, just east of Santa Fe.[12]

No sooner had the command arrived at Fort Union than Sumner ordered Pope back over the trail to find an easier way to Fort Leavenworth. Sumner charged Pope with charting a route that circumvented the two most difficult stretches of the Santa Fe Trail. The first was fifty-eight miles long, running from the Cimarron Crossing of the Arkansas River (near the site of Fort Atkinson) to Lower Spring on the Cimarron River. Devoid of water nearly yearly round, this stretch crossed a barren desert and had claimed countless lives; wary travelers christened it the Jornada del Muerto. Better watered but a hundred miles longer, with high, craggy passes, was the Mountain Route through Colorado. Colonel Sumner ordered Pope to blaze a trail midway between these stretches, from McKnee's Crossing and Big Timbers, Colorado.[13]

With Edward M. Kern, a prominent civilian artist who had accompanied John C. Frémont's Third Exploring Expedition, and a small detachment of soldiers, Pope started on August 9. He and Kern got on well. Pope superintended the expedition and mused over better ways of subduing hostile Indians, although Pope's party met with nothing more threatening than a band of Arapaho who stampeded their pack animals. Kern was the true map maker, taking elaborate field notes, recording courses and distances, and sketching landmarks.

On September 6, Pope and Kern reached Missouri and, apparently without authority, went on to St. Louis, where they drafted a map based on Kern's field notes. Had Pope left off simply with the map Colonel Abert had requested, he would have spared himself the severest reprimand of his young career. But the irrepressible brevet captain could not resist trumpeting his accomplishments and offering gratuitous advice on matters of policy. Sumner had charged him, Pope reminded Abert in a lengthy epistle written September 18, 1851, with finding a route that followed the valleys of streams, avoided "all mountain passes and heavy sandy country," and shortened the traveled distance. "In accomplishing all these objects I have been successful beyond my most sanguine expectations," said Pope. He would have had even greater success had it not been for the "entirely inaccurate and useless" map of the Arkansas River Valley made some years earlier by Captain John C. Frémont.

After dispensing with Frémont, Pope went on to criticize the long-standing policy of concentrating troops in large garrisons in territorial towns like Taos and

Santa Fe. Better to disperse them in small posts throughout the Indian country, thus compelling Indians "who may be disposed to commit depredations upon the inhabitants to pass a military post both in going and returning." Colonel Sumner, Pope hastened to add, also subscribed to this view.[14]

Accustomed though he was to Abert's censure, Pope was startled by the coldness of the colonel's response. In a letter dated October 2, Abert not only upbraided Pope for his slight of Frémont, who happened to be a personal friend, but also rejected his claim of having opened a new trail. "The route which you described has been previously indicated in print," said Abert, which suggested Pope was "taking to himself a credit which does not belong to him." But, Abert concluded, that was no more than might be expected of Pope, who had plagiarized Nicollet's map of the Red River region, made sloppy observations while in Minnesota, and written an unauthorized memoir while in Maine.[15]

Pope shot back with a letter that might have earned him a court-martial. "If the route from the Big Timbers of the Arkansas has ever been explored, it will be news to the people of New Mexico," he sneered. And Frémont's map was disgracefully inaccurate. As for Maine, Colonel Abert himself had sanctioned Pope's memoir. "I have only to say," Pope concluded, "that as I have always endeavored to do my duty without fear and without favor, the compliments or censures of any officer of the corps are alike indifferent to me."[16]

Remarkably, Abert chose to forgive Pope his letter, dismissing it as "more thoughtless than deliberate." Henceforth, Abert would simply ignore the sharp-tongued twenty-nine-year-old subaltern, who in nine years of service, through arrogance and clumsy efforts at self-promotion, had succeeded in alienating three colonels and a host of lesser officers.[17]

But John Pope also had friends, both in the army and in the government. Colonel Sumner had complete confidence in Pope, and together they would conspire to bring the much-debated Pacific railroad through New Mexico. Also, Pope was a favorite of Illinois Whigs. While in St. Louis he had cultivated several Missouri congressmen, and he continued to enjoy the nonpartisan support of Minnesota's territorial legislators.

Most officers who actually served with Pope found him a congenial companion. His raucousness and raunchy wit made him a favorite at mess. David Sloane Stanley recalled one joke that nearly brought Pope and Captain Gordon Granger to fisticuffs:

> Granger was very much in love with Miss Sally Strother of Louisville and as the lady expected to have a big fortune, Granger's motives were suspected. Someone said to him, "What do you wear black gauntlets for?" "Oh!" said he, "I am wearing mourning for my mother-in-law." Granger's suit fell through

and Sally married a German baron. One evening, in our fun, Pope turned to Granger and said, "Count (his nickname was Count), what has become of that husband-in-law of yours?" "Who do you mean?" said Granger. "Why that Dutch baron who married Sally," answered Pope.[18]

In early 1853, Pope's career took a turn for the better. Isaac Stevens's memorandum on promotion inequities led Congress to pass a law that year giving "relief for the old lieutenants" in the engineer, topographical engineer, and ordnance services. Captaincy now came in fourteen years, and second lieutenants of long standing were advanced one grade. Thus on March 3, after eleven years of service, Pope received his first permanent promotion, to the rank of first lieutenant, and with Sumner's help, a choice assignment to the Pacific railroad surveys.[19]

Before leaving the Ninth Military District, Pope burdened Colonel Abert with another long epistle, in which he again proffered solutions to territorial problems. As the eminent western historian Robert Utley has conceded, Pope's plan "revealed he was an acute observer capable of formulating well-reasoned military plans." It also showed him to be a close student of Indian society and sympathetic to the plight of native peoples. Understanding the loose nature of Navajo government, in which tribal obligations were second to clan loyalty, Pope saw the difficulty in negotiating lasting treaties. "In such a state of things," he observed, "it is impossible to make a treaty with them which is not likely to be violated, and it appears unreasonable and unjust to punish a whole tribe for the depredations of a few."[20]

When he thought it warranted, Pope criticized brother officers freely. Fort Union was poorly situated and proper lines of communication across the territory had been neglected, he explained, assigning the cause to the ignorance of those who had come before him: "I am fully aware that the views I have expressed are, in many respects, opposed to the experience of old officers who have served long and intelligently in the Indian country, but it must be remembered that the circumstances which have prompted them are wholly foreign to our history and to the experience of our citizens."[21]

Pope's polemics earned him no reprimand from Colonel Abert. In keeping with his resolve to let the brevet captain annoy him no longer, Abert passed Pope's plan on to bureau file clerks.[22]

— ✦ —

The Pacific railroad surveys were the product of political necessity. The nation could afford to build at most two transcontinental lines, but sectional interests in Congress offered up nearly a dozen possible routes. As an historian of the surveys explained, "the Pacific railroad surveys were an attempt to break a political and economic deadlock over the proper location of the first transcontinental railroad . . . to substitute the impartial judgment of science for the passions of the politicos and the promoters." In March 1853, the outgoing Thirty-second Congress authorized surveys along eight parallel routes, to be conducted by army engineers.[23]

As secretary of war, Jefferson Davis was broadly responsible for the surveys. But their actual conduct rested with Colonel Abert. Hardly an impartial administrator, Abert strongly endorsed the proposed route along the thirty-second parallel through Texas, a line naturally favored by Southern interests, including Secretary Davis. Colonel Abert apparently held Pope's work in higher regard than he let on, because he selected him to conduct the survey of the most critical section of his preferred route. On February 12, 1854, Brevet Captain Pope set out from Doña Ana, New Mexico, the central point of the proposed thirty-second-parallel line, with a large party to survey the eastern half of the route, from the Rio Grande to the Red River.[24]

Escorting Pope's party was a twenty-five-man detachment led by Lieutenant Louis H. Marshall of the Third Infantry. In the course of the survey, Pope and Marshall became fast friends. Although a Virginian and a nephew of Robert E. Lee, Marshall was loyal to the Union. As a member of Pope's staff during the Civil War, Marshall would learn that even the general's closest friends were not immune to his humorous barbs. David Stanley recalled how Pope enjoyed goading the Virginian, who had been "elected colonel of an Ohio regiment but, political wrangling arising, was successively reduced from colonel to lieutenant colonel and then to major, whereupon he quit the regiment in disgust and took a place on Pope's staff. Referring to his experience, Pope said to him, 'Lou, that was a singular career you had in that regiment. If you had gotten another promotion you would have landed in the penitentiary.'"[25]

Broadly speaking, Pope was charged with two tasks: locating a pass through the Guadalupe Mountains of New Mexico suitable for a railroad and exploring the Llano Estacado, a vast desert lying between the Pecos and Bravos rivers. Neither job proved difficult. Pope readily found a route through the Guadalupe Mountains, and he painstakingly recorded both the challenges and opportunities the Llano Estacado presented.[26]

In his report of the survey, Pope praised the thirty-second-parallel route and the country it traversed as lavishly as he had the Red River Valley of Minnesota, calling the land east of the Llano Estacado, later known as the Cross Timbers, "the richest and most beautiful district" he had ever seen. The key to developing the area from the Arkansas to the Rio Grande, both commercially and for military purposes, was procuring water on the Llano Estacado. Pope believed this obstacle surmountable, at "so little expense, that it cannot weigh as a feather in the balance against the unrivalled advantages of this route."

Pope proposed boring four artesian wells at regular intervals across the 125 miles of the Llano Estacado through which the thirty-second-parallel railroad route passed. His study of the geology of the Llano Estacado convinced Pope that deep springs lay beneath the upper strata of the plain, and he endorsed a civilian report which held that by "boring . . . on any point of the Llano, abundant columns of water would be found to gush out over this immense plain." Pope calculated it would take eight months to complete the wells.[27]

In the end, the railroad surveys of Pope and other engineer officers suffered from the very political antagonisms they were supposed to reconcile. No survey offered conclusive proof that only one—or no more than two—"practicable and economical" railroad routes existed to the Pacific. Every surveying officer recommended his route. The growing sectional strife that rent Congress also removed any hope for a federally sponsored transcontinental railroad until after the Civil War.

Although Congress tabled the Pacific railroad project, the recommendations Pope made in his report were to shape his duties for the next four years. Intrigued with Pope's arguments on the feasibility of watering the Llano Estacado—and the promise it held for military operations in the southwest—Davis convinced Congress to appropriate $100,000 for "the experiment of testing the practicability of procuring water by artesian wells on the arid plains of the interior." He selected Pope to lead the expedition, which was comprised of seventy-five soldiers and eighty civilians, the largest command Pope had yet enjoyed.[28]

Using drills and a pump powered by a steam engine that was itself fueled with mesquite wood, Pope made his first dig in June 1855 along the thirty-second parallel, fourteen miles east of the Pecos River. In 100 days he bored a well 641-feet deep. At 360 feet he struck pure, clear spring water, which rose 70 feet in the well. Two hundred feet farther down he again found water, but upon boring a third time the well caved in. Undaunted, in November Pope began boring a second site near Doña Ana over the objections of his geologists, who argued the rock strata and regional dip were all wrong for artesian wells. After four months with no sign of water, Pope shifted back to the Pecos River, resuming operations five miles east of the first test site. In May 1856, he found water at 675 feet before running out of boring rods.[29]

Confident "a large supply of water overflowing at the surface would have been found" had he had sufficient equipment, Pope went to Washington to help Davis lobby Congress for more funds. While there, he received a permanent promotion to captain. Pope returned to the field in September 1857 with an additional $50,000 in public monies, new equipment, and a party that had grown to 100 soldiers, 42 teamsters, and the best crew of drillers in the West. Hopeful of success, the War Department also assigned Harry S. Sindall, a promising young artist, to dramatize on canvas the exploits of the second expedition.

All the expense availed of nothing. For ten months Pope labored vainly to find water near the falls of the Pecos. One problem after another plagued his efforts: an unusually harsh winter drove his crews indoors, pipes sheared off, the boring apparatus broke down, the steam boiler became clogged with lime, the strata crumbled, scurvy broke out, and the men grew mutinous.

In June 1858, after having bored one thousand feet without finding water, Pope called a halt. "I am constrained to say after ten months of very severe and unremitted labor that, I fear that, without greater facilities and more extensive preparations than could have been secured under the appropriation, it will be impracticable to overcome the mechanical and physical difficulties of the work," Pope confessed to the War Department. Encouraged by Secretary of War John Floyd, Pope tried again at a new site in December 1858. At 1,301 feet he found water, which natural pressure forced to within twenty feet of the surface. It was a technical success, but one that exhausted the money allocated for the venture. Caught in the national tailspin toward disunion, Congress refused to consider further funding for a project that would benefit only one section of the country. Pope was compelled to abandon his work on the Llano Estacado, much to the amusement of his brother engineers; even the most sympathetic observer "conceded that the experiment [had] yielded more romance than water." In the early fall of 1859 Captain Pope was reassigned to Cincinnati to plan lighthouses for the Great Lakes, his first permanent duty station off the frontier in seventeen years.[30]

3   *A Favorite Son of Illinois*

Duty in Cincinnati brought Pope a wider circle of political patrons and a wife. On September 15, 1859, he married Clara Pomeroy Horton, eldest daughter of Congressman Valentine B. Horton, at their family home in Pomeroy, Ohio.

The couple had met in Washington while Pope was lobbying for the artesian well project. He was thirty-seven when they wed; she twenty-four, well bred and well educated, of delicate health but every bit as strong-willed as her husband.

Pope had married into a family as distinguished as his own, and a good deal wealthier. One of southern Ohio's most aggressive businessmen, Congressman Horton owned several coal mines and a fleet of river towboats. A man of remarkable breadth and vision, Horton, who was born in Windsor, Vermont, on January 29, 1802, had attended the Partridge Military Academy; when the school moved from Windsor to Middletown, Connecticut, Horton went along as an instructor. In Middletown, Horton also studied law and in 1830 was admitted to the bar. While yet a law student, Horton became interested in the coal deposits of the Ohio country. He traveled to Ohio to see the veins for himself and carried samples of the coal to Boston, where he interested his elder friend Samuel W. Pomeroy, from whose land he had extracted the coal, in a joint mining venture.

In 1833, Horton married his partner's twenty-nine-year-old daughter, Clara Alsop Pomeroy. They made their home first in Pittsburgh, where Horton practiced law briefly, then in Cincinnati, and finally in Nyesville, Ohio, which Horton renamed Pomeroy.[1]

As the driving force behind the coal business, which had expanded to include Pomeroy's two sons and a second son-in-law, Charles W. Dabney, as partners, Horton grew wealthy. He added to his fortune by inventing the first towboat to ply inland waters. When Horton and Pomeroy set up business, the transport of coal had been clumsy and expensive. Coal extracted in Ohio was loaded on rafts and sent down the Ohio River. Because the current was too strong for the rafts to return upriver, new rafts had to be built for each trip. Annoyed with this added expense, Horton devised a single-engine, side-wheel towboat to tow empty rafts back upriver. From this invention Horton profited immensely.

Not content with the profits from coal and from his boat patent, Horton availed himself of the numerous salt wells in southern Ohio to enter into the salt trade. In 1851 he organized the Pomeroy Salt Company, which would yield ten million barrels over the next forty years.

Horton and his wife were of a deeply religious, generous nature. Of Clara Alsop Horton, an early chronicler of Meigs County wrote, "Her courteous manners and fine intellectual equipment made her the peer of any lady in any land. Her gracious charity and broad views of life gave her influence with the best class of people in social, civil, or religious life. She was a wise, exemplary wife and mother." A devout Episcopalian like his wife, Horton donated the land upon which the Episcopal Church of Pomeroy was built, and he defrayed most of the costs of its construction. He also took a great interest in public education, serving for forty years as a trustee of Ohio University and as the first president of the board of trustees of Ohio State University. In gratitude for his many services, the people of his district elected him as a Whig representative to Congress in 1855 and again in 1857. A close friend of the self-styled head of the Republican Party, Governor Salmon P. Chase, Horton became a Republican himself in 1859.

In view of his own Whig politics and military education, Congressman Horton undoubtedly approved of his daughter's marriage to Captain Pope. He certainly had a hand in his son-in-law's assignment so near the family home, as Pope's orders were dated nineteen days after the wedding.

Pope enjoyed his assignment. Designing lighthouses was pedestrian work, but the proximity to his in-laws, with whom Pope got along well, and to his friend from academy days, William Starke Rosecrans, who had quit the army to go into the coal-oil business, compensated greatly. Pope shared in the antislavery Republicanism that dominated Cincinnati politics. He cultivated friendships in polite society and indulged his broad intellectual interests, joining the Literary Society of Cincinnati and becoming an honorary member of the Academy of Natural Science of Philadelphia and that of St. Louis. Gratifying too was the election of his father's favorite circuit-riding lawyer, Abraham Lincoln, as president in 1860, the return of Valentine Horton to Congress, and the election of Salmon P. Chase to the United States Senate. For the first time in Pope's career, it appeared playing politics might pay off.[2]

From Cincinnati, Captain Pope passed what Henry Adams termed the "Great Secession Winter of 1860–1861" pondering the fate of the nation and his own military future. Designing lighthouses for frigid northern lakeshores when the country was tumbling toward disunion struck Pope as a waste of his talent, and he told Lincoln as much. In a didactic, seven-page letter to the president-elect, dated January 27, 1861, Pope also cautioned Lincoln not to presume all officers were loyal: high-ranking officers in key posts might be secessionists. Prudence dictated Lincoln require every officer to renew his oath of allegiance. Those who refused must resign; those who temporized should be transferred to a harmless, far-away post, such as Puget Sound. Pope gave the president-elect advice on civil matters as well. "There should be no effort to conciliate until rebellion is at end and secession as a right explicitly abandoned," insisted Pope. "The fact whether we have a government, and whether it has the right to enforce its laws and protect its officers, must be brought to speedy issue." The thirty-nine-year-old captain would treat secessionists as his father had warring Indians in Illinois: they were lawbreakers for whom no punishment was too severe.[3]

Lincoln read the letter at his home in Springfield, as he prepared for the inaugural trip to Washington. Lincoln evidently took no offense at Pope's rather impudent epistle, because he invited the judge's son to make the trip to the capital with him.

It was a high honor and, more important to the ambitious captain, a chance at intimacy with the president-elect's inner circle. Norman B. Judd of Chicago and Judge David Davis of Bloomington, Illinois, two of those most responsible for "making" the president, were among the party, as were private secretaries John Nicolay and John Hay, prominent state Republicans Ozias M. Hatch and Jesse Dubois, and Lincoln's trusted friend, Ward Hill Lamon. The small military escort consisted of Pope's former commanding officer, Colonel Edwin V. Sumner, Major David Hunter, and the president-elect's young favorite, Elmer Ellsworth.[4]

The presidential train left Springfield on the morning of February 11, 1861; Pope joined it in Indianapolis that evening. "Then," recalled Pope, "I became a member, though a very insignificant one, of the party which surrounded and, in a sense, guarded Mr. Lincoln in that most wonderful journey, the like of which has never been made before or since."[5]

Pope had come to know the president-elect eleven years earlier in Chicago, where Pope had gone to visit some old friends; Lincoln happened to be in town for a gathering of the state bar. Knowing the judge's son had fought and, as Pope put it, made a "small reputation" in a war he himself had opposed in Congress, Lincoln paid him a call. Captain Pope saw Lincoln as most others did: "a tall, gaunt, angular man, very homely and awkward, but with a very intelligent and kindly face. He appeared to be in high spirits, and was overflowing with humor. He told a number of very funny stories which kept everybody laughing, and appeared to be a man altogether happy and without a care." Being garrulous of a kind (though Lincoln had greater tact), the two got on nicely.

When Pope boarded the train at Indianapolis, he found the president-elect markedly different from the Lincoln he had known in Chicago. "Whilst his outward appearance was much the same, his face had strangely lost that look of careless humor which I remembered. Already a shade of care had begun to creep over his countenance and dim its joyous expression."[6]

Lincoln had good cause for worry. From the eastern newspapers came fantastic stories of revolution, of plots to seize Washington, burn public buildings, obstruct the counting of electoral votes, and prevent the inauguration of the new president. With each passing mile, Lincoln grew more despondent, the "harassed and worried look wholly uncommon to him" more pronounced. But throngs of well-wishers and the curious, of city fathers and political patrons met the train at every stop, demanding a speech. They wanted "assurances [Lincoln] could not give and encouragement he could not honestly offer."

The strain played hard on Lincoln. "Through this vast multitude, whose continuity was scarce anywhere broken, Mr. Lincoln pursued that memorable journey, unrelieved by any of the cheerfulness and enjoyment usually attendant upon such occasions," said Pope. "Oppressed with care and with the awful responsibilities imposed upon him, suffering from fatigue and loss of sleep, called for by excited and anxious people at all hours for assurances he could not give and encouragement he would not honestly offer, he underwent tortures which lined his face."[7]

Everywhere Lincoln's words were measured and vague. In Indianapolis, apart from conceding that marching an army into South Carolina would constitute unlawful invasion, he said nothing concrete: "Fellow-citizens, I am not asserting anything; I am merely asking questions for you to consider." In Columbus, Ohio, he defended his reticence on the grounds that the crisis was not yet acute, and he assured state legislators "there is nothing that really hurts anybody. We entertain differing views upon political questions, but nobody is suffering anything."[8]

Pope disagreed publicly. While the president spread salve on the sectional discord, Pope proclaimed the inevitability of war. Availing himself of an overnight train stop in Cincinnati, Pope addressed his friends at the literary society on "Our National Fortifications and Defenses." It was a long discourse, reminiscent of the ponderous briefs he had sent to Washington from the frontier. This time, Pope had an audience for his pronouncements, which were egregious. Everything he said contradicted the assurances of the president-elect. Lincoln had promised to work toward "peaceful settlement of all our difficulties. . . . In my view of the present aspect of affairs, there is no need of bloodshed and war." But Pope, repeating sentiments expressed in his letter to Lincoln of January 27, told the literary society that secession was a "revolutionary measure" that demanded the "inevitable penalty of revolution." The president must purge the military of disloyal officers, call out the militia, recover federal property appropriated by the seceded states, and defend that which remained. The coastal fortifications—in particular Fort Sumter—must be "reinforced at all hazards, and should be held as long as there is a man to raise an arm in their defense."

Not content to dictate government policy, Pope castigated President James Buchanan for his inaction. Only Major Robert Anderson, the defender of Fort Sumter, had shown backbone in dealing with secessionists. Said Pope, "His prompt and soldierly conduct was the first exhibition of patriotism, the first evidence of any honorable sense of duty on the part of the executive department. . . . It roused the President from his lethargy, opened his eyes to the treasonable conspiracies of his associates and advisers, and broke up his corrupt and infamous cabinet." Pope's sharp words were repeated in the *Cincinnati Gazette* and circulated in pamphlet form.[9]

Lincoln probably knew what Pope was about. In the cramped quarters of the presidential passenger car, Pope could not have disguised his work on the literary society lecture. Having read Pope's letter of January 27, and knowing the tendency of the Popes toward intemperate speech, Lincoln probably suspected what Pope would say, yet apparently neither he nor his advisers tried to dissuade him.[10]

Pope continued with the party on their journey eastward, taking every opportunity to ingratiate himself with Norman Judd, Ward Hill Lamon, and Judge Davis. As the presidential train neared the nation's capital, "rumors of insult and violence to the president increased in violence and directness." While in Philadelphia, the party received word from William Seward of a plot to assassinate Lincoln when the train reached Baltimore, and Pope was one of the few consulted on what steps should be taken to safeguard the president-elect. It was agreed Lincoln and Lamon would change trains and travel to Washington incognito, while the rest of the party completed the trip on the presidential train.

The need for Lincoln to pass secretly through Baltimore and enter Washington furtively was debated then and after. To Pope, the precautions seemed warranted. At the Baltimore depot, he watched with concern as a mob gathered around the train that presumably carried the president-elect. People stared into the windows, searching for Lincoln. "I myself heard a number of ugly expressions and saw many scowling faces," recalled Pope. "No violence was committed, though the crowd pressing upon our car consisted precisely of the people capable of outrage, and none of us were sorry when the train moved out of the station."[11]

Something more personally threatening than Baltimore thugs greeted Pope in Washington. A week after his arrival, Pope was served with a special order summoning him before a general court-martial. The charge against him: violating the Fifth Article of War; the specification: making derogatory remarks about President Buchanan in his speech to the Literary Society of Cincinnati. By his indiscretion, Pope had positioned himself to pass the impending war in a military prison.

Remarkably, President Buchanan spared Pope. A second special order scrubbed the court-martial; the outgoing president had "expressed to the [War] Department his conviction that the language of the said Captain Pope . . . would not in any manner affect him injuriously."[12]

Pope later claimed he had refused the demands of a cabinet officer, acting on the president's instructions, that he publicly apologize for his words against the government, and that the administration backed down in the face of his principled intransigence. In truth, Postmaster General Joseph Holt, a friend of the Kentucky Popes, intervened on his behalf, for which Captain Pope was forever grateful privately, if not publicly.

This near brush with disgrace made no impression on Pope. Before leaving Washington, he had asked Judge Davis to use his influence with Secretary of War–designate Simon Cameron to obtain for him the position of inspector general of the army. When that gambit failed, he again went outside channels, asking Ward Hill Lamon to arrange his appointment as Lincoln's aide and military secretary. Who better to look after the president than a Regular Army officer from Illinois who supported the Union categorically and took to heart the president's personal and political welfare, Pope asked rhetorically. Lamon passed the letter on to Lincoln. The president forwarded it without comment to Secretary of War Cameron, who endorsed the note sardonically, "The Secretary of War thinks this is a *very* modest request."[13]

Nothing came of Pope's petition. The Confederates opened fire on Fort Sumter on April 12, 1861, the day after Pope posted the letter to Lamon. With war at hand, Pope set his sights on higher honors. Before sundown on the twelfth, Pope wired Governor Richard Yates of Illinois to offer his services "under the banner of my own state." Yates accepted and asked Pope to come to Springfield immediately, to help organize the thousands of volunteers expected soon to converge on the state capital. Before leaving Cincinnati, Pope had the good sense to request a one-year leave of absence from the Regular Army. And he asked, and received, the president's permission to go to Springfield.[14]

His Illinois assignment pleased Pope. Governor Yates accorded him "a most cordial reception," telling Pope the arrival of a Regular Army officer removed "a prodigious load from his shoulders." Pope, in turn, was quite taken with Yates: "He had a handsome face, with the kindest and most engaging expression, and a manner full of genuine good feeling for all the world. He was in his ways and his power and devotion of attachment, as well as his great modesty and gentleness, more like a woman than a man, though he was a man of iron nerve and unshakable resolution. All in all, I think he was one of the most lovable men I ever met. I was greatly attached to him and to this day cannot think of him without a tender feeling."[15]

Pope went to work at once for Yates, mustering and organizing Illinois's contingent of six thousand volunteers, which had rendezvoused in Springfield at the governor's behest. Captain Pope performed his duties with dispatch. As quickly as they marched into Springfield, the unorganized regiments of recruits were directed to the state fairgrounds, where barns, display booths, sheds, and cattle stalls had been appropriated to military use and named Camp Yates. There the first group formed ranks for Captain Pope on the morning of April 25. He passed before each volunteer—a tall, somewhat portly Regular Army captain with jet black hair and beard, soft features, and lively, piercing eyes—and in an instant settled the man's fate: fit for army service, or rejected. Pope yanked from the ranks and sent home as unfit so many men that some companies lost a third of their number before the recruits had raised their right hands to take the oath of allegiance. "Ten companies of us, numbering from 93 to 125 men each, were trimmed down to 77 rank and file, each. This created considerable dissatisfaction and made a deal of very wicked swearing," remembered Charles Wills, who passed muster. "Some of the men who were turned out of our company threatened to shoot our captain."

Before noon on April 25, Captain Pope had mustered in the remainder of Wills's and the other nine companies as the Seventh Regiment of Illinois Volunteer Infantry. That afternoon he repeated the process with the recruits who were to comprise the Eighth Illinois Infantry. On April 26 he mustered in the Ninth Illinois; on April 29, the Tenth Illinois; on the thirtieth, the Eleventh Illinois, and on May 2, the Twelfth Illinois.[16]

Pleased though he was with his duties, Pope wanted more for himself, and quickly, before promotions and choice troop commands were exhausted. On May 8, less than three weeks into his Springfield assignment, Pope wrote Senator Lyman Trumbull of Illinois, asking him to use his influence with the president to secure for Pope a brigadier general's commission. A week later, Pope appealed directly to Lincoln, both for the commission and, in keeping with "the sentiments of the State of Illinois," field command of the Illinois regiments he had mustered in.[17]

Although confident Lincoln would favor him, Pope did not let matters rest. A brigadier general's commission in itself was not enough. As a career officer, Pope needed to secure the highest possible rank in the Regular Army; for when the war ended and the volunteers went home, those who had left the Regular Army to accept volunteer commissions would either revert to their highest Regular rank or be discharged. At first, Pope was prudent enough not to push for too much himself. Instead, he enlisted his father's former political allies and Lincoln's Illinois friends to make the request for him, which they did. In late May, Lincoln assured Governor Yates, Senator Lyman Trumbull, and Colonel John McClernand (an influential Illinois War Democrat) he intended to accord Pope one of four brigadier general's commissions approved for a Regular Army that was to expand by eleven regiments, and he authorized Trumbull to so advise Pope.[18]

But Lincoln had not yet mastered his willful cabinet, and they thwarted his promise. Attorney General Montgomery Blair and Secretary of War Cameron were locked in a battle of wills over army appointments. Blair demanded wholesale acceptance by the federal government of elected officers and commissions—Regular and volunteer—for "political" generals. Cameron preferred to elevate Regular officers (particularly those of his home state of Pennsylvania) and opposed the appointment of political generals. In the compromise they struck, Pope lost out. The lone Regular major general's commission went to George B. McClellan, and one of four Regular brigadier general's commissions went to Joseph Mansfield; both men were Pennsylvanians. To mollify Blair, twelve of fifteen volunteer brigadier general's commissions were given to volunteer officers.[19]

Under such circumstances, Pope might have considered himself fortunate to come away with even a volunteer commission. Instead, he railed against the president's apparent perfidy. "My juniors in rank and civilians without number from Ohio and Pennsylvania have been promoted over my head in the Regular Army and I live to see what I never expected in this earth, myself driven out of the [Regular] army by a president from Illinois," Pope told Senator Orville Browning. Although Pope had decided to "cheerfully accept" the volunteer commission, "believing that I can be of more service to my native state in that capacity than by holding my present commission," he wanted it understood his grievance was real. "Perhaps you will think that I feel this too deeply," Pope continued, "but when you consider the pride every good soldier must feel in his profession, and the sting which neglect or injustice inflicts upon him, you will find excuses for my feeling bitterly in this subject."[20]

Browning and other prominent Illinois Republicans not only excused Pope's indignation, they also interceded with the president to right the wrong done Pope and the honor of Illinois. Pope's political views found favor among party leaders, and his military presence captivated them. "Elegant in deportment, charming in manners, with the bearing of a trained soldier, we regarded Captain

Pope as a favorite son of Illinois, destined for a grand career," recalled Republican boss Clark Carr. William Butler, Jesse Dubois, and Ozias Hatch insisted Pope be granted a Regular commission and given command of Illinois as a separate military department. "Our people without exception expect and demand it," they advised the president by telegram. Governor Yates added a peremptory appeal of his own.[21]

The president was unmoved. He had "raised no one from a captain to a general in the Regular Army; and the officers of the army are not willing that he should." Pope's volunteer army appointment, dated June 14, would stand.[22]

Governor Yates resigned himself to Lincoln's decision; Pope did not. In a curt postscript to a letter that could have cost him not only his general's commission but his career, Pope called the president a liar. "Governor Yates has just shown me your dispatch stating that you had not appointed any captain to general—McDowell was only a brevet major . . . Meigs was a captain of engineers," said Pope. "I would much prefer taking a colonelcy in one of the new regular regiments than to be a brigadier-general of volunteers. I could not with honor hold my commission after being thus oversloughed [sic] by my juniors and civilians for what seems to me no better reason than that they are personal or political friends of the Secretary of War."[23]

Lincoln neither obliged nor disciplined him. After one last outburst to Senator Trumbull on the subject, Pope dropped the matter. He accepted the volunteer commission and turned his energies to securing a field command.

Apart from letter writing, Pope had been idle since May 4, when he completed the mustering-in of Illinois volunteers and Ulysses S. Grant replaced him as commanding officer at Camp Yates. Unlike Captain Pope, who had a Regular rank and the support of Springfield's leading men, Grant had come to the state capital an obscure civilian. "I had known him slightly at West Point, where he was in no sense a man of mark, either with cadets or professors," Pope recalled. "I met him afterward in the service during the Mexican War, and subsequently I saw him frequently in St. Louis after he was out of the army and in extreme poverty. Whilst I never was intimate with him in those days, I yet knew him very well, and often talked with him, and from these conversations I knew that he was profoundly discontented and unhappy."[24]

Having a good opinion of Grant, Pope offered to help him secure a volunteer command befitting his fourteen years of Regular service. But Grant declined Pope's offer—rather brusquely, as Grant told it. "On one occasion [Pope] said to me that I ought to go into the United States service," remembered Grant. "I told him I intended to do so if there was a war. He spoke of his acquaintance with the public men of the state, and said he would do all he could for me. I declined to receive endorsement for permission to fight for my country."[25]

Pope decided to help Grant anyway. He suggested to Governor Yates "how desirable it was, in the dearth of military men and knowledge, to secure the services of such a man as Grant." Yates agreed and appointed Grant first to his personal staff and then to command Camp Yates.[26] For Pope himself, getting a responsible field command proved nearly as difficult, and initially as humiliating, as his futile efforts at securing a Regular commission. The officers of the six volunteer regiments Pope had mustered in were permitted to elect their commanding general. They chose Benjamin Prentiss, a prominent and popular Illinois Republican, over Pope, leaving Pope to sulk about Springfield with a star on his shoulder but not a single troop to command. To Valentine Horton, Pope confessed he had felt more useful mustering troops as a captain than he did now as an unemployed general. Only the presence of Clara and her younger sister Catherine made life in Springfield tolerable. Clara was in unusually good health, for which Pope was most grateful, and she and her sister took frequent buggy rides in the country. Cheered by Clara's presence, Pope hastened to assure his father-in-law, "I shall enter upon my duties with zeal and cheerfulness and don't doubt that matters will come straight in the end."

They did, and sooner than Pope had expected. Shortly after his unseemly petition to President Lincoln regarding his brigadier general's commission, Pope had a command thrust upon him. On the Fourth of July, Major General George B. McClellan, commander of the Department of the Ohio, which embraced Illinois, ordered Pope to proceed from Springfield to the Mississippi River town of Alton and take command of six Illinois regiments gathered there. Pope saw Clara and Catherine off to Cincinnati and repaired at once to Alton.[27]

It was a portentous transfer. Alton lay just upriver from St. Louis; on the opposite bank was the rich, rolling farmland of northeastern Missouri. The bucolic vista belied a sectional hatred that had turned the state into what Captain Charles Morton, a Missouri Yankee, called "a cauldron of seething desperation." The coming of war ripped apart Missouri more fiercely than any other state, unleashing passions neither faction could control. Decamping with public funds, records, and most of the militia, Governor Claiborne Jackson and General Sterling Price began recruiting an army to free Missouri from Federal control. The powerful Blair family (represented in Lincoln's cabinet by Postmaster General Montgomery Blair and in Congress by his son Frank) and their military champion, Captain Nathaniel Lyon, rallied the pro-Union element against Jackson and Price.[28]

Into this region of churning "confusion and uncertainty" came Pope on July 17, at the head of his Illinois volunteers. Nathaniel Lyon had marched on Springfield with most of the organized Union forces in the state, leaving St. Louis unprotected and northern Missouri prey to marauding ruffians. The adjutant general in St. Louis, Chester Harding, begged Pope to cross the Mississippi to help restore order. Pope in turn sought the permission of Major General John C. Frémont (commander of the newly constituted Department of the West, which embraced Missouri) to take charge in northern Missouri. Frémont was in New York City, unaware of the problems his department presented; Pope, no better informed, assured Frémont "a vigorous campaign of a week will settle secession in North Missouri, and leave the troops at your disposal for other service." Frémont told him to go ahead.[29]

Forty-eight hours after crossing the Mississippi River, Pope proposed sweeping measures to rectify a problem he scarcely understood. But, as Pope correctly deduced, time was at a premium; if northern Missouri were to escape bloody anarchy, measures decisive and drastic had to be taken quickly. Captain James Foley of Frémont's Body Guard seconded Pope's appraisal: "Outbreaks of serious character were occurring at short intervals in the northern part of Missouri. . . .

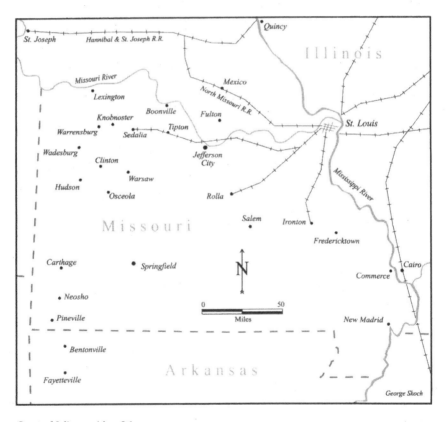

Central Missouri in 1861

There was no pretense at civil government. Neighbor was arrayed against neighbor, each prepared to kill or destroy the property of the other. The bonds of civil society were dissolved."[30]

Pope endeavored to reknit them. But first, he had to secure his lines of communication, "so that in case other measures of pacification failed, military operations could be conducted with convenience and rapidity." Two railroads bisected the district: The North Missouri Railroad, which ran northward from St. Louis to Hudson, and the Hannibal and St. Joseph Railroad, which ran westward from the Mississippi River. Pope lacked the troops needed to protect the entire lines, so he posted his command at critical points and devised a unique plan for guaranteeing the integrity of the remainder: he would make the people living along the railroads responsible for their protection.[31]

After a cursory investigation of recent depredations to the north Missouri road, Pope notified the residents of towns and stations along the road they would "be held accountable for the destruction of any bridges, culverts, or portions of the railroad track within five miles on each side of them. . . . Without conclusive proof of active resistance on the part of the population . . . the settlement will be held responsible, and a levy of money or property sufficient to cover the whole damage done will be at once made and collected." The people, Pope added, knew the marauders; should they choose to indulge them "in committing these wanton acts, and to shield them from punishment, they will hereafter be compelled to pay for it."

To carry out his plan, Pope had the railroad divided into administrative divisions, with civilian superintendents selected from the community "without regard to political opinions, who will be held responsible for the safety of the railroad track within their specified limits."[32]

It was a novel idea, eliciting the cooperation of secessionists to protect Federal railroads, particularly in a region where opinion was so inflamed, but it worked. Depredations dropped off sharply, and Pope imposed the same solution along the Hannibal and St. Joseph line.

Satisfied he had the solution to northern Missouri's woes, Pope next sought to allay the wider "excitement among the people, and as far as practicable [restore] quiet and sense of safety." General Frémont arrived in St. Louis on July 25 and at once confirmed Pope as de jure commander of all forces north of the Missouri River. Armed with this authority, Pope served a second notice to the people of his district, designed to "compel the people of property, discretion, and influence to act together, irrespective of their political sympathies, to enforce the civil law and preserve peace among themselves" without recourse to martial law. (Pope's pronouncements amused Confederate leaders; they nicknamed him "Proclamation Pope.") "I was well satisfied," Pope later told Congress, "that less arbitrary measures would best secure peace in north Missouri." Placing responsibility for domestic order on those who stood to lose most from disorder would prevent his troops from themselves sinking to the level of guerrillas and free them up for field duty.[33]

In a letter to the president of the North Missouri Railroad, family friend J. H. Sturgeon, Pope elaborated on his purpose: "I was, and am satisfied, that the people of the counties in North Missouri are abundantly able to keep peace among themselves, and this is all I ask or exact from them. . . . I believed that as soon as it was felt that, only by preserving peace and quiet among themselves, and not molesting public or private property, there would immediately result security of person and property, and the power to pursue unmolested their several avocations, Union men and Secessionists would alike engage in putting a stop to lawless and predatory bands."[34]

Pope was unwilling to disperse troops to keep order for another reason, one that he was careful to keep private, perhaps because it sounded self-serving at best and secessionist at worst. As he told Senator Trumbull in a private letter before entering Missouri, Pope wished to unite the regiments from Illinois, which constituted most of the force then on guard duty throughout Missouri, into a powerful command led by an Illinoisan and fighting for Illinois interests. Scattered about, Illinois regiments had been compelled "to serve with the forces of other states, where they do only the least conspicuous and the most odious duties. . . . The men are discouraged and dissatisfied and the regiments less fit for service." What was needed was an Illinois Napoleon, who could lead the state's twenty thousand troops serving west of the Alleghenies on a march of conquest. "If this force can be kept together and properly commanded," said Pope, "upon Illinois will devolve largely the reconquest of the Valley of the Mississippi. Where she moves, with such a force, she will of necessity stand first and hers will be the voice which controls the warlike operations in this valley." Of course, added Pope, a force of this size should be commanded by a major general, preferably of Regular Army rank. It was an appeal for promotion unusually transparent, even for Pope, evidence he had learned little from Colonel Abert's admonitions against playing politics for military gain.[35]

— • —

Pope issued his second proclamation on July 31, 1861. Before removing troops from their stations, Pope intended to appoint local committees of public safety, comprised of persons—Unionist and secessionist alike—with "social, domestic, and pecuniary interests at stake" to "maintain peace and order in their respective counties." Should they fail, or be unwilling, to keep the peace, Pope would send in soldiers at the community's expense. Exhorted Pope, "To preserve the peace is the duty of all good citizens, and as all will suffer alike from the breach of it, men of every shade of political opinion can act cordially together in the discharge of a duty as full of interest to one as to another." Pope expected good results. As he assured Robert T. Van Horn, "I am satisfied that peace can be kept if the people will interest themselves in keeping it and I have therefore furnished them a very strong inducement to do so."[36]

To carry out their temporary police duties, Pope reorganized his forces. He placed Brigadier General Stephen Hurlbut, an Illinois War Democrat who also was a notorious drunkard, in command of the length of the Hannibal and St. Joseph Railroad, stationed regiments at Warrenton, Renick, and Sturgeon, and set up his own headquarters at Mexico, the midway point of the North Missouri Railroad. To command the forces at Mexico, Pope assigned Colonel Ulysses S. Grant of the Twenty-first Illinois.[37]

Grant had obtained a commission without Pope's help, and Pope was pleased to have him in Missouri. Ignoring his Regular Army reputation for irresponsible drinking, Pope introduced Grant to Frémont as "an old army officer, thoroughly a gentleman and an officer of intelligence and discretion." And when Hurlbut bungled his duties, Pope asked permission to replace him with Grant, telling Frémont: "Grant is a soldier by education and experience and a discreet, prudent man who is eminently needed now for immediate supervision of the disaffected counties north of the Hannibal and St. Joseph road."[38]

Frémont agreed. Grant performed his duties in northern Missouri so well that in late August Frémont assigned him to command in the state's troubled southeastern counties. Before he left Pope's district, Grant rectified most of the ills of Hurlbut. Under Hurlbut, soldiers "had been in the habit of visiting houses without invitation and helping themselves to food and drink. . . . They carried their muskets while out of camp and made every man they found take the oath of allegiance."[39]

Although Grant stopped the abuses in his sector, they went on elsewhere in northern Missouri. There, soldiers looted homes, raped slave women, stole horses, and carried off farm produce. The populace came to fear the soldiers as much as the ruffians they were supposed to police. Prominent Unionists called on Frémont and on the authorities in Washington to dismiss Pope, whom they derided as a "tyrant and a madman," or, at a minimum, rescind his policies. They resented measures placing them on the same footing with secessionists, whom they insisted should alone be subject to Pope's general orders. They even believed Pope countenanced the depredations of the drunken and lawless among the Federal ranks.[40]

Meanwhile, guerrilla bands kept up their midnight raiding. Judging the moment right to test Pope's resolve, in mid-August marauders in Marion County fired into a passenger train, wounding several women and children. Another band fired on a troop train, killing one soldier. A third group raided the telegraph office in Palmyra, the county seat. Pope immediately called on the county committee of public safety to take action. When the committee declined to act, he dispatched a brigade to Palmyra, announcing he would levy $10,000 against the county and $5,000 against the town to quarter the troops. That, wrote Pope, "brought the matter to an issue."[41]

Pope lost. Not only did Frémont repeal Pope's policies, but he also placed the state under martial law. He decreed the property of Confederate sympathizers—slaves included—subject to forfeiture seizure and promised to shoot any armed civilians found within Union lines. Pope remonstrated angrily. His network of public safety committees had kept the peace and prevented Rebel guerrillas from making inroads in his district. Only in Marion County had Pope had to enforce his policies, and he was sure a brief military occupation of the county seat would suffice to bring peace; "where outrages are so expensive, they will not be repeated." Pope implored Frémont not to override him, "lest a much worse thing befall the people hereafter." Martial law, Pope warned, would bring "an uprising in every county against the Union men."[42]

Which is what occurred. However, Pope too had failed to pacify northern Missouri, and not simply because Frémont thwarted him. Pope's policy of public self-protection floundered because factional hatred went too deep for Missourians to work together. Also, his soldiers' bad conduct made them as repugnant as the guerrillas. People whose homes Yankee troops had ransacked were hardly inclined to cooperate with Federal authorities. Though his program was fatally flawed, Pope preferred to blame its collapse on Frémont, whom he had come to loathe.

Relations between the two had never been warm. They first met at Colonel Abert's District of Columbia home in 1845, when Brevet Captain Frémont, recently returned from his Rocky Mountain explorations, was the toast of the capital. Although he pretended to admire Frémont, Pope more probably envied his fame; he certainly paid Frémont no deference. In the self-congratulatory report of his 1851 expedition along the Santa Fe Trail, Pope said he could have done even more, had he not been hindered by Frémont's inaccurate maps, which erred in locating several important landmarks. Criticism of a national hero cost Pope whatever favor his efforts might have won him. Once again, it fell to Colonel Abert to scold Pope. Not only had Pope himself made mapping errors far more egregious than Frémont's, Abert reminded him, but he also had publicly condemned a superior officer on questionable grounds.[43]

Perhaps recalling that slight, after assuming command in Missouri Frémont let two weeks pass before summoning Pope, who was next in rank, to St. Louis for consultations, an episode Pope recounted with great humor to readers of the *Na-*

tional Tribune. "I reached St. Louis at night, and early next morning repaired to his office" in the large and stately mansion of Colonel J. B. Brant, a relative of his wife, Jessie. Under its roof was housed the entire administrative apparatus of the Department of Missouri. In a large room on the second floor were desks for Frémont and his senior staff officers; on the first floor, the offices of subordinate staff. In the basement was a veritable arsenal, with arms and ammunition stored for emergencies. Sentries were posted at every approach. Gaudily dressed Hungarian and Garibaldian officers shielded Frémont from outsiders, John Pope included.

Two sentries with crossed sabers denied Pope access through the front entrance, directing him instead to the basement door. In submitting to the affront, Pope began a dizzying odyssey in search of an audience with the commanding general. Throwing open the door, Pope found the basement hall "filled with people— jammed in fact—from all classes and conditions of society, struggling and pushing for no visible purpose or result, unless ill-temper and bad words be result."[44]

Pushing his way into a side room, Pope encountered "two aides-de-camp of General Frémont fortified behind a sort of counter." Pope stated his business to the senior aide, Colonel Isaiah C. Woods, who insouciantly informed him that the general was "very much engaged." Pope again yielded: "I seated myself and watched with some amusement, but more impatience, the mixed and apparently half-crazy crowd that still struggled and crowded each other in the hall." When the humor of the situation wore off, Pope grabbed the officious Woods and told him he must see Frémont at once. As Woods protested, Pope ascended the basement stairs. The main floor was vacant and the doors to the inner rooms thrown open. Pope found Frémont in the parlor, "quite alone, as he had apparently been for some time."

Pope was hardly overawed. "In most respects General Frémont appeared much as I expected to find him. He appeared dazed with the confusion and excitement around him, and but imperfectly to realize the situation and its necessities. One may look in vain for evidence he possessed that robust common sense characteristic of his countrymen and essential in his position."

No doubt the disdain was mutual; nonetheless, Frémont received Pope "very pleasantly and cordially. We had half an hour's conversation about affairs in my own command and the general situation in Missouri. [Confederate General Sterling] Price was slowly advancing toward the Missouri River at Lexington from the southwest, and General Frémont appeared to be satisfied that the measures he had taken to prevent the success of such a movement would be effectual, though what those measures were I did not quite make out."[45]

Nor did Pope find them clearer in the weeks that followed. From St. Louis came pronouncements that spread chaos and consternation. Pope saw his public-security regime dismantled and provost marshals descend on his district "with their armies of assistants and followers. [They] ruled supreme, and being in authority, above and beyond the reach of any civil process, exercised their full pleasure."[46]

To catch guerrillas and help the provost marshals administer the martial law that Pope found so abhorrent, his command was scattered across northeastern Missouri. As Pope had feared, their efforts were wasted. "The moment it was known that my order would not be executed, all the violent and reckless elements in north Missouri at once resumed full sway," he later told Congress. "Bands of secessionists and of Union men were organized all over that section of the state, and commenced an indiscriminate warfare upon each other and the people. Distress and dismay invaded every fireside for four long years."[47]

Pope's disgust with Frémont led him to lash out at the Lincoln administration. While believing in the president himself, Pope detested everyone in his cabinet except Salmon P. Chase. From St. Louis on August 22, Pope lamented to his father-in-law, Congressman Horton, that "the Administration will do in a different manner what Jeff Davis is doing directly[;] that by neglect, corruption, and outrage, the states of the West will be driven to join together and act without reference to the authority of the central government. Yet it seems impossible for Mr. Lincoln to make up his mind to consult with anybody except the miserable herd around him." Pope considered Secretary of War Simon Cameron the cabinet's principal malefactor, assuring Horton, "Everybody in this wide land knows him to be corrupt and dishonest, a public plunderer and an unprincipled politician."

Pope's immediate worry was the bad effect Frémont's martial-law regime had had on morale. Indifferently trained and led by green colonels, Illinois and Iowa regiments had been dispersed across Missouri "as soon as they are arrived, without anyone to receive or control them," Pope told Horton.[48]

Active operations interrupted Pope's ruminations. In early September, Frémont directed him and Brigadier General Samuel D. Sturgis to track down and destroy the mounted regiment of Martin Green, the most successful Rebel guerrilla commander in the state. Pope and Sturgis each led a brigade by separate routes toward Shelbina, where Green had been recruiting volunteers. Poor direction from department headquarters not only prevented Pope and Sturgis from cooperating effectively, but also left them in the dark as to one another's locations. Tipped off to Pope's approach and under orders to join Price's army, Green decamped from Shelbina before Pope and Sturgis were able to effect a junction. Without waiting for Sturgis, of whose movements he could get no reliable information, Pope gave chase with the Sixteenth Illinois and Third Iowa regiments. Entertaining no real hope of catching Green's mounted men with his infantry, Pope planned to pursue for two or three days, then leave for Keokuk, Iowa, in compliance with earlier orders from Frémont to muster new Iowa troops into the service.[49]

While Pope chased Green across northern Missouri, a greater threat developed south of the Missouri River. Sterling Price was back, marching northward from Springfield to retake the state. His immediate destination was the river town of Lexington, where Colonel James A. Mulligan's Irish Brigade and several hundred members of the loyal Missouri Home Guard had occupied and fortified the Masonic College. Upon word of Price's approach, Mulligan called in his troops, buried $900,000 from the local bank under his tent, then sent to Frémont for reinforcements.[50]

With barely enough troops to suppress secessionist sympathizers in St. Louis, a Confederate army menacing Cairo, Illinois, and Washington demanding five thousand of his infantry for duty in Virginia, Frémont had little to offer Colonel Mulligan. Free-wheeling subordinates and his own ambivalence frustrated what he did attempt. Colonel Jefferson C. Davis, in command of a small force at Jefferson City, confirmed reports circulating in St. Louis newspapers that Price was moving on Lexington in considerable force and asked for instructions. Frémont told him to send two regiments toward Lexington at once, but Davis demurred, instead turning his attention toward Martin Green, whom Pope had pushed to the Missouri River, near Glasgow. Although Davis ignored repeated appeals to reinforce Mulligan, Frémont himself seemed uncertain. On September 13, one day after Price's vanguard clashed with Mulligan's skirmishers on the outskirts of Lexington, Frémont ordered General Sturgis to meet an expected Confederate attack on Boonville—nearly 100 miles east of Lexington. The next day, he countermanded the order, telling Sturgis to march to Jefferson City, then revoked the latter instructions a few hours later, ordering Sturgis to march directly on Lexington instead. To Pope, whose two regiments were much closer to Lexington than Sturgis's, Frémont said nothing.[51]

Pope learned of the threat to Lexington by chance, during a train stop at Hudson, Missouri, on September 16, while en route to Keokuk. Pope had left the Sixteenth Illinois and Third Iowa near Glasgow, after Martin Green crossed the Missouri River and eluded his grasp, with orders to acting commander Colonel Robert Smith to sweep the railroad clean of Rebels as far as St. Joseph, then turn south and clear the Missouri River. Availing himself of the layover to read the post telegrapher's traffic and catch up on department happenings, Pope found Frémont's telegram ordering Sturgis to Lexington. Disgusted at having been left out, Pope scribbled a sardonic message to Frémont: "Presuming, from General Sturgis's dispatches, that there is [an] imminent want of troops at Lexington, I have dispatched Colonel Smith to move forward to that place with [the] Sixteenth Illinois and Third Iowa and three pieces of artillery from Liberty as soon as he completed the object of his expedition." Continuing on to Palmyra that evening, Pope learned the gravity of Mulligan's predicament. Again, he wired Frémont: "From papers just handed me I learn for the first time that important matters are occurring at Lexington. The troops I sent to Lexington will be there day after tomorrow, and consist of two full regiments of infantry, a reinforcement of four thousand men. Do you wish me to come down to St. Louis or go to Canton and Keokuk to finish matters in that section?"[52]

Frémont told Pope to go on to Iowa. Undoubtedly affronted by the intimation that Frémont could manage without him, Pope unburdened himself to Orville Browning, with whom he spent the night of September 16 in Quincy, Illinois. Browning pressed him for news from Missouri. There would be no more trouble along the Hannibal and St. Joseph Railroad, Pope assured the senator—he had been out as far as St. Joseph and pacified the country; what's more, Pope added, "there was not a rebel in North Missouri except a few hundred about Canton." And what of Lexington? The troops there probably were already captured, Pope snarled. Abruptly changing the subject, Pope complained that the government boat he had requisitioned to carry him to Keokuk never appeared. Angry with the idiocy at department headquarters, Pope refused Browning's offer of a place on a regular river packet, preferring to sulk about Quincy until *his* boat arrived.[53]

The comedy about Lexington continued in Pope's absence. Frémont addressed a telegram to Sturgis at Lexington on September 18, under the mistaken impression he had reached that place with his brigade. Frémont told him Davis, with five thousand men, and Jayhawker James Lane, with his irregulars, were en route to Lexington to join Sturgis in a "combined attack upon the forces now surrounding Lexington."[54]

But Sturgis was stuck on the opposite bank of the Missouri River, five miles from town and ten miles from the nearest ferry. Pope's two regiments had made no move toward Lexington; the courier carrying Pope's order had, inexplicably, returned to St. Joseph without delivering the message. Not that the presence of Pope's men would have made a difference. The Rebels had gathered in every boat in the vicinity of Lexington capable of ferrying troops across the Missouri, leaving the Federals with no means of reaching the garrison. Sturgis did not stand on ceremony but decamped at once after local slaves warned him of a Confederate column making to attack his brigade from behind.[55]

The fall of Lexington on September 20 caused a clamor for Frémont's removal. Demanding to know why Frémont had been unable to get reinforcements to Mulligan, the press insisted on prompt measures to retrieve the disaster. So too did President Lincoln, who expected him "to repair the disaster at Lexington without loss of time." In response to press and presidential pressure, Frémont began to assemble his army west of Jefferson City for an advance against Price. "I am taking the field myself, and hope to destroy the enemy, either before or after the junction of the forces under McCulloch," he hastened to assure the president.[56]

Few besides Frémont himself and his obsequious staff of foreign officers believed his bold assurances. As Pope saw matters, it was Frémont's Army of the West, rather than Price's command, that was about to be destroyed. Moreover, Pope feared his paltry command would be the first annihilated. As soon as Pope returned from Iowa, Frémont had sent him with two regiments to reinforce the garrison at Boonville, which lay on the southern bank of the Missouri River, between Lexington and Jefferson City. Reaching Boonville on October 1, Pope was shocked to find the town empty of Federal troops; Frémont apparently had recalled the garrison. As he made ready with twenty-four hundred men to meet Price's entire army, Pope complained bitterly to his father-in-law of Frémont's incapacity and of the cheap politics that sustained him. "I am heartsick and discouraged and at the same time indignant that mere party claptrap should thus hazard the lives of brave men and the best interests of the country," wrote Pope. "Frémont shows his inefficiency more and more every day and walks about at Jefferson City with his hands to his head as if he were on the verge of insanity. There are no plans and no hope of any that are intelligible."[57]

Concluding Frémont's days to be numbered, Pope began a painfully transparent campaign to replace him. To political benefactor and family friend William Butler, Pope expounded on what must be done. Secretary of War Cameron would try to replace Frémont with an eastern general; that must be prevented at all costs, argued Pope. "It is quite time that Illinois should assert her right in a voice and manner not to be denied," he contended. "She furnishes nearly all the troops for the West. It is her right and her privilege to name the man who shall command in the West." Demand for Illinois that she shall have Frémont's successor and insist positively upon it."[58]

Pope's letter revealed not only an unslaked thirst for high command, but also a marked aversion to eastern officers. That he harbored such strongly sectionalist sentiments as he asserted in his letter to Butler, and in earlier letters to Valentine Horton, is unlikely; as he had done so often in the past, in employing hyperbole to further his own interests, Pope sounded a bit ridiculous. Nothing came of Pope's maneuver, and for the moment, John C. Frémont remained in command of the Department of the West. Pope resigned himself to Frémont's presence and hoped for a speedy conclusion of the fall campaign: Clara was expecting their first child, and she had agreed to move from Pomeroy, Ohio, to St. Louis, to be near her husband when the baby came.[59]

After assuring Lincoln he would move against Price, Frémont organized his Army of the West into five division-sized elements: a right wing of 9,220 men under Pope, and a center, left wing, advance guard, and reserve. With headquarters at Boonville, Pope deployed his forces in a line paralleling the Missouri River, from Boonville to Chillicothe. The remainder of the army formed an arc extending from Boonville to Versailles. Scouting parties were sent into the countryside to gather information on Price's whereabouts. Not that Price was concealing his movements. On the contrary, Pope said, he "was moving south from Lexington very deliberately and much at his ease, inviting all those well disposed to the South to join him."[60]

Although he may have agreed on the need for action, Pope did little to help Frémont. He and his Regular Army friend, Major General David Hunter, who commanded the left wing, regarded the planned campaign with contemptuous wonder. To begin with, said Pope, few of the units Frémont hastily assembled as an army had served together, even at brigade level. Many were poorly trained and inadequately armed, and none had wagons enough for a march across half the state. Hunter concurred, and he and Pope grumbled at each misstep.[61]

As did the administration. Although strongly inclined to remove Frémont, President Lincoln decided to give him a hearing, and in mid-October he sent Secretary of War Cameron and Adjutant General of the Army Lorenzo Thomas to make a personal inspection of affairs in Missouri, with authority to dismiss Frémont if matters warranted.

Cameron found matters much as Pope and Hunter saw them. In the neighborhood of Frémont's headquarters, Cameron told the president, he found "forty-thousand troops, of which only one division was fit for duty; all the others were poorly supplied with munitions, arms, and clothing." Cameron showed Frémont his discretionary order to remove him. Frémont begged the secretary to permit him to complete the campaign, which he was sure would result in the destruction of Price's army. Cameron agreed to withhold the order until he returned to Washington, giving him "the interim to prove the reality of his hopes."[62]

In his memoirs, Pope feigned innocence in the unseemly proceedings against Frémont. "I only know what occurred, either of conversation or of action, as I heard it from others. I remained at my own headquarters and called upon neither of these high officials [Cameron and Thomas], as I had nothing to say of value to them, and preferred to say nothing."[63]

Not directly, perhaps, but Pope made certain his views were made known; indeed, his contempt for Frémont was an open secret in the Department of Missouri. Frémont's staff thought Pope jealous of the general's prewar accomplishments and envious of his elevation to high command. Frémont himself knew Pope was intriguing against him; Jessie Benton Frémont complained of Pope's caballing in a letter to a friend, saying of Pope's lack of fidelity to her husband, "Pope is of that inferior nature of man which runs to the rising sun."

Pope sent General Hunter, with whom Cameron and Thomas were to meet, a frank letter relating his disgust with Frémont, which Hunter was free to share with the secretary and adjutant general. "I received at one o'clock last night the extraordinary order of General Frémont for a forward movement of his whole force," began Pope. "The wonderful manner in which the actual facts and condition of things here are ignored stupefies me. . . . There is not transportation enough to move this army one hundred yards; in truth, not one solitary preparation of any kind has been made to enable this advance movement to be executed. I have never seen my division, nor do I suppose you have seen yours. I have no cavalry even for a personal escort, and yet this order requires me to send forward companies of pioneers protected by cavalry." What was Frémont's game, Pope wondered aloud? "Is it intended that this order be obeyed, or is the order only designed for Washington and the papers? How in the face of the fact that [Frémont] knew no transportation was furnished . . . he should coolly order such a movement, and expect it to be made, I cannot understand on any reasonable or common-sense hypothesis."

Hunter showed Pope's letter to Cameron and Thomas, adding that he too felt Frémont was unfit for command. Brigadier General Samuel Curtis, in command at St. Louis, gave an equally discouraging view of things. Frémont, said Curtis, was vain, quixotic, and unapproachable; he should be relieved at once.

Armed with the opinions of three professional soldiers, whose views coincided with the general drift of complaints received from civilian officials and ordinary citizens, Lincoln decided on October 24 to relieve Frémont and replace him with Hunter until a satisfactory permanent replacement could be found; unless, that is, Frémont was engaged in or in expectation of battle when the courier reached him.[64]

Someone tipped Frémont off to the order for his removal, and on October 26 he ordered his division commanders to make a forced march on Springfield. Believing the enemy's line of retreat would pass near Springfield, Frémont intended to strike Price before he slipped into Arkansas.

Pope was incredulous. He forwarded his copy of the movement order to Hunter, along with his candid opinion of Frémont's plan. Franz Sigel's and Alexander Asboth's divisions, which had already started for Springfield, were living on quarter rations with no prospect of resupply, Pope told Hunter, and seemed to him "doomed to destruction, or to such suffering as would make death grateful." Furthermore, "Price is doubtless in Arkansas, as he was at Neosho five days ago still moving south. When our forces have succeeded in reaching Neosho, or Arkansas itself, what is to be accomplished, or rather what does any sane man suppose will be the result? The prospect before us is appalling, and we seem to be led by mad men. Of course, General Frémont and the men around him, whose official existence depends upon his not being superseded, are desperate. I think Frémont crazy or worse."

Pope had no intention of allowing his men to suffer merely to save the "official lives" of Frémont and his "gorgeous staff" of European dandies. Nor did Hunter, and between themselves they agreed not to move until adequately supplied; in other words, to disobey Frémont's orders.[65]

Frémont was not crazy, as Pope alleged, but rather a poor judge of combat intelligence. Shortly before daylight on October 24, while reconnoitering ahead of the army, Frémont's gaudily dressed bodyguard, commanded by one of his European dandies, Major Charles Zagoni, had come upon a Rebel foraging party, eight miles north of Springfield. Zagoni continued on to Springfield, where he dispersed a small Rebel force after a running fight through town. From Zagoni's clash, the notoriously unreliable attestations of Confederate prisoners, and reports from his own scouts, Frémont concluded that the united Confederate armies of Sterling Price and Benjamin McCulloch were marching from southwestern Missouri to attack Springfield.

Frémont ordered Hunter and Pope to push forward at once, but despite repeated prodding, not until November 1 did they deign to advance. Sharing her husband's frustration at the apparent insubordination of his generals, Jessie Benton Frémont wrote Ward Hill Lamon on October 30 that "Hunter is waiting his authority to order the army back." When at last Hunter did move, he had a personal reason for making haste—President Lincoln had dismissed Frémont and elevated Hunter temporarily to department command. Pope hurried along to help his friend.[66]

Five miles short of Springfield, Pope made camp for the night. When he rode into town the next morning, November 2, he was surprised to find the army preparing for battle. A group of officers from Sigel's and Asboth's divisions greeted him, all "much excited by the prospect of immediate battle, and congratulated me on being in time to take part in it."

More amused than alarmed, Pope asked them who they intended to fight. "Price, of course," the officers replied. "I told them that of course it might be so, but that according to my impression, drawn from reliable scouts, there was no enemy within fifty miles of Springfield to fight with," remembered Pope. Continuing on to Frémont's headquarters, Pope found the general roused and ready for action: "He had abandoned the idea of relinquishing command until General Hunter's arrival, and appeared to be preparing for battle in all seriousness."

Riding out to have a look himself, Pope found Sigel's and Asboth's divisions aligned smartly on an open plain. Batteries were hitched up and ready to move; beyond them, the cavalrymen stood "booted and spurred, ready to mount and charge the enemy." Pope hailed their commander, Colonel Eugene Carr, who proved no less mystified. "He told me that he was only obeying orders, and had been ready for battle for more than 24 hours, but knew nothing of the enemy or where any was to come from."[67]

That evening, Frémont called his generals to a council of war. The discussion grew animated, with Sigel and Asboth (the two foreign-born generals who, alone among the division commanders, remained loyal to Frémont) offering their suggestions. The absurdity of it all was beyond Pope's limited tolerance. "It might be best, before deciding upon a plan of battle, to know whether there was any enemy to fight," he interjected. Frémont seemed startled. He was ready to argue with Pope, when the door swung open and General Hunter strode in. "Good evening, General," stammered Frémont. "Good evening," replied a travel-worn Hunter. Did the general intend to relieve him, asked Frémont? He did. When? "Now," said Hunter. With that, said Pope, the council of war dispersed.

The next morning, Frémont left for St. Louis, and Hunter sent the cavalry to reconnoiter far beyond Springfield. As expected, they reported the country clear of the enemy; nor, residents reported, had there been a Rebel in the area for six weeks. On November 8 Hunter withdrew the army from Springfield to Rolla, the westernmost railroad terminus south of the Missouri River. Eleven days later, with half the army distributed along the railroad from Jefferson City to Sedalia, he yielded command to Major General Henry Halleck.

Pope later would conclude the timorous Halleck was singularly unsuited to command an army in the field, but for the moment, his delight in being rid of Frémont led him to overlook Halleck's faults. Also gratifying was Halleck's estimate of affairs in Missouri: he saw matters precisely as did Pope and Hunter. "Affairs here in complete chaos," he told General-in-Chief George B. McClellan. "Troops unpaid; without clothing or arms. Many never properly mustered into service and some utterly demoralized. Hospitals overflowing with sick." To what extent Frémont, as opposed to Pope and the other division commanders, was responsible for these deficiencies is an open question; what is important is that everyone from President Lincoln to General Halleck placed sole blame on him.[68]

Pope began in the good graces of the new commander of the Department of Missouri, so much so that Halleck placed Pope in charge of the forces along the railroad and created the District of Central Missouri around them. But differences surfaced when Pope dismissed scouting reports that had Price marching in force on central Missouri—"in my opinion," said Pope, "there is not the slightest prospect of his attempting to come north."

Ever cautious, Halleck discounted Pope's views, instead crediting erroneous reports that Price and McCulloch were moving on Rolla and Springfield in large numbers. Pope wanted to cross the Osage River and clean up the small, demoralized recruiting detachments that he believed to be the only Rebels in the region. After rebuffing several strong pleas from Pope, Halleck at last acceded to his request—in a manner. He authorized Pope to move, but away from rather than toward Price's detachments. Pope wanted to march southwest, toward Osceola, where the bulk of Price's troops had gathered after Hunter withdrew from Springfield; Halleck, however, directed him to march northwest from Sedalia to capture recruits bound for Osceola. When Pope objected, Halleck allowed him to march west to intercept the Rebels between the Missouri and Osage rivers.[69]

Pope had read the situation in western Missouri correctly. Ben McCulloch's troops were posted at Carthage in southwest Missouri. Price's army lay encamped near Osceola, on the banks of the Osage River. From there, he had sent out the recruiting parties Pope's scouts had reported seeing, and he had detached one division north of the Osage, leading Southern sympathizers to believe he would retake Lexington in a winter campaign. Pope was not deceived, and his continued presence at Sedalia caused Price to fear Pope would intercept a large, poorly armed detachment of recruits then coming from northern Missouri to join his army. To see them through to Osceola, Price sent out an 1,100-man mounted escort. The Confederate troopers met the recruits, 2,500 strong, at Lexington, and on December 13 turned south for the hundred-mile return march.

From spies and scouts, Pope knew both their numbers and their route of march. He also knew that the secessionist population of Sedalia would pass on word of any movement to intercept the Rebel column. To deceive the watchful civilians, Pope let slip his destination to be Warsaw, a settlement on the Osage River due south of Sedalia. To lend credence to the ruse, on December 15 he took the southwest road out from Sedalia at the head of two brigades of infantry, under Colonels Jefferson C. Davis and Frederick Steele, and portions of four regiments of cavalry. The next morning, the Federals turned due west for their true destination: the town of Warrensburg, on the south bank of Blackwater River. As Pope's cavalry combed the snowy prairie for Confederates, the weather turned miserable. A harsh wind whipped over the open prairie, stinging the soldiers with needles of snow. The temperature hovered near zero, and the ground was frozen so hard the men could not pitch tents.[70]

After a forced march of thirty miles, at sunset on the sixteenth the Federals bivouacked astride the Clinton and Warsaw road, midway between the two towns. Before bedding down the command, Pope pushed his advance guard, consisting of four companies of the First Iowa Cavalry, up the road two miles to the crossroads hamlet of Chilhowee, where they captured a Rebel picket post. From the startled Confederates they learned what Pope had suspected: some two thousand Southerners, mostly unarmed recruits, were encamped six miles to the north. Pope planned to attack at dawn on December 17, but the Rebels, forewarned of his presence, slipped around his left flank and took flight for Osceola under the cover of darkness.

The Seventh Missouri Cavalry of Lieutenant Colonel E. B. Brown galloped off in pursuit. For the next thirty-six hours the Yankee troopers chased the enemy column, pressing the recruits so closely that they abandoned their supply wagons and broke up into small detachments, some to make their way to Price's army, others to return to their northern Missouri homes.

Brown's cavalrymen rejoined the main body on the morning of December

18 near Clinton. Supposing more Southern recruits lay to the north, Pope had remained at Chilhowee while Brown scoured the countryside to the south.

He guessed correctly. On December 18, scouts reported two large Southern contingents—comprised of portions of two regiments of infantry, three companies of cavalry, and several hundred recruits—marching south from Arrow Rock and Waverly, which probably would make camp together that night at the mouth of Clear Creek, a mile south of Milford and ten miles northeast of Warrensburg. Pope hurried his command northward under a light snowfall. The next morning he deployed his infantry between Warrensburg and Knobnoster, astride the Rebel line of march, and sent Davis with the cavalry to turn the enemy's left and rear. The movement worked perfectly. Davis came upon the Rebels encamped in wooded bottomland between Clear and Blackwater creeks and immediately charged. Finding their line of retreat blocked and exhausted from a forty-mile march the day before, the Southerners surrendered after delivering a single, ragged volley that struck just ten Federals. Davis captured 1,300 men, 500 horses and mules, and 73 fully loaded wagons. There were more Rebels nearby, but a blizzard compelled Pope to return with his prisoners to Sedalia.

Although a small victory, in the absence of other Federal successes the affair at Blackwater Creek received wide newspaper coverage. The *Cincinnati Commercial,* a Republican paper always friendly to Pope, extolled the expedition as a "most glorious and successful campaign—the most glorious in results, and the lightest in casualties, which has thus far signalized our success in arms." A delighted Pope staged a grand review of his command.[71]

Pope's foray devastated secessionist morale in Missouri. Price felt compelled to abandon his plans for a return to Lexington; the disappointment that engendered, along with the risk of being captured by Pope's wide-ranging Federals, caused most of the remaining Rebel recruits north of the Missouri River to return home. Halleck and Pope, however, read too much into Price's discomfiture. Taken in by their own press, they concluded the Blackwater River foray had frightened Price back into Arkansas, when in fact he had fallen back no farther than Springfield. Under that mistaken assumption, in early January 1862 Halleck sent three divisions under Brigadier General Samuel Curtis to pursue Price. Curtis eventually penetrated the wild mountains of northwest Arkansas, where in April he defeated Price in the strategically important Battle of Pea Ridge.

Blackwater Creek proved to be Pope's only real action in Missouri. After the affair, his command was broken up to support operations elsewhere. With few troops at his disposal and the guerrillas in his district relatively quiescent, at year's end Pope applied for leave to visit Clara, who was three months pregnant with their first child, in St. Louis.[72]

4 *You Deserve Well of Your Country*

For John Pope, the war seemed about to end before it really had begun. As much as he craved high rank and glory, family meant more to him. In early February 1862 Clara's precarious health weakened under the strain of her first pregnancy, and Pope became despondent. With his command broken up and no prospect of an active campaign before him, Pope gave serious thought to resigning his commission and returning with Clara to Pomeroy, where she might recover in the company of her parents. The prospect of a visit from Mrs. Horton, while easing his mind, did not, as Pope saw it, remove the fundamental source of woe for Clara. "She is so far away from her home and her life must under the circumstances be so unsettled and uneasy that it fills me with anxiety for her," Pope told his father-in-law.

Melancholy moved Pope again to lash out at President Lincoln. He dismissed the advice of both J. H. Sturgeon and Congressman Horton that he press William Butler, now Illinois state treasurer, and Governor Yates to renew their efforts to gain him a Regular Army brigadier general's commission. "This I cannot do," Pope wrote Horton on February 14. "My self respect is already startled at what I have done in the matter and I cannot go farther. Mr. Lincoln's treatment of me has been so shabby that I would feel almost humiliated today to receive an appointment from him."[1]

Four days after this disconsolate confession, Pope was handed a chance at an independent campaign against a foe far more formidable than recruits and guerrillas; an undertaking that, if successful, would make a Regular commission a merited promotion, rather than an empty benefaction. Ironically it was the success of Grant, whom Pope had helped rescue from obscurity, that now spurred Pope's career. Grant's capture of Forts Henry and Donelson earlier in the month had turned the Confederate flank on the Mississippi River, compelling theater commander General Pierre G. T. Beauregard to evacuate Columbus, Kentucky, an important river stronghold from which Halleck long had feared an attack on the Union depot at Cairo, Illinois. Some weeks before the fall of Forts Henry and Donelson, Beauregard had charged Major General Leonidas Polk, the commander at Columbus, with selecting a fall-back position from which to block any further Federal progress down the Mississippi River. Polk chose Island No. 10—a marshy, mile-long, 450-yard-wide island nestled in the Madrid Bend, a large twist in the Mississippi that touched the borders of Missouri, Kentucky, and Tennessee—and began transferring troops and heavy guns there.[2]

Island No. 10 owed its prosaic name to its location; it was the tenth island in the Mississippi River, counting southward from Cairo. Six miles farther downriver, at the northern extreme of the Madrid Bend, lay the town of New Madrid, Missouri. At New Madrid, the river turned first to the south, then curled to the southeast above Tiptonville, which rested on the east bank of the Mississippi River, nine miles from New Madrid. That bend put Tiptonville just five miles from Island No. 10 by land, but twenty-seven miles by water.

Halleck was quick to seize the opportunity Grant's victories provided to plunge Federal armies deeper into the Confederacy. Immediately after Fort Donelson capitulated, Halleck redirected all troops bound for Tennessee to Commerce, Missouri, which he intended to use as a staging area for operations against Island No. 10 and New Madrid. Halleck hoped to open the Mississippi River as far as Memphis and to cut off the retreat of Polk's garrison from Columbus. He recalled Pope to St. Louis and offered him command of the enterprise.[3]

With Clara's assurance she would be all right in his absence, Pope accepted. He paused at Cairo just long enough to confirm that Polk had no designs on the river town, then set off in a steamboat, with his staff and two companies of infantry, for Commerce, forty miles distant. That act—going forth "ahead of his army"—won him the instant admiration of the officers and men who arrived afterward.[4]

Pope reached Commerce on the evening of February 22; two nights later he had assembled sixty-five hundred men, nearly all raw recruits who had "arms placed in their hands for the first time when they embarked to join me. Very few of them had ever served at all," noted Pope. "Even those which had served had done so separately, and had never been even assigned to brigades." More such men were

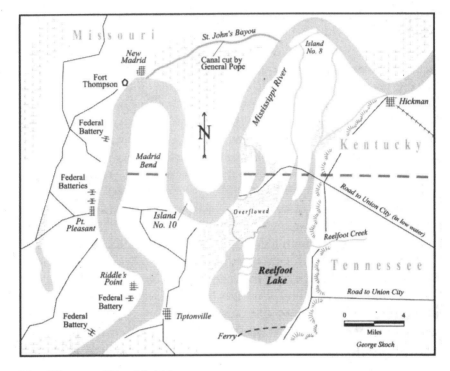

Island No. 10 and New Madrid

on the way; Halleck promised to send reinforcements as quickly as they could be found. "If necessary I will sustain you with five, fifteen, or even twenty thousand," he assured Pope. "The object must be accomplished if it requires 50,000 men."[5]

Appreciative as he was of Halleck's willingness to help, Pope was not one to tarry, even when the majority of his troops were little removed from civilian life. Ably aided by four of the finest generals then in the West—Schuyler Hamilton, David S. Stanley, John M. Palmer, and Gordon Granger—Pope organized his green regiments into brigades, gave the men rudimentary drill and target practice, and had them ready to march on February 27, a mere five days after he had disembarked at Commerce.

Not that locals or the Confederates tucked behind their fortifications at Island No. 10 and New Madrid believed an army could march from Commerce to New Madrid. It was an odd and ominous land, hardly propitious for a march or a battle. Once fertile prairie, the country around New Madrid had been shaken into dank, alluvial bottomland by the great earthquake of December 6, 1811, which had its epicenter near New Madrid. Thirty thousand square miles of land sank to depths of five to fifteen feet, creating huge bayous and swamps. Among the largest was the Great Mingo Swamp, which extended from Commerce to New Madrid. A second, deeper swamp, named Reelfoot Lake, began just south of Island No. 10, on the east side of the Mississippi, and ran far below Tiptonville. Interminable swamps snaked southward from New Madrid for sixty miles, along both banks of the Mississippi. The only large, normally dry expanse near Island No. 10 was the peninsula created by Reelfoot Lake and the Mississippi River, between New Madrid and Tiptonville. And even that was moist. Melting snows farther north and heavy area rains had caused the Mississippi to overflow its banks. The whole country for thirty miles west of the river was submerged from one to ten feet, and the sole road between Commerce and New Madrid, an old corduroy byway that ran atop a sandy embankment, was broken in a hundred places.[6]

Undeterred, Pope split his eight thousand infantry into two march columns comprised of two small divisions each: the first column under Brigadier General Schuyler Hamilton, brother-in-law of Henry Halleck, and the second under Brigadier General John M. Palmer, an Illinois Republican who had seen service in Missouri. Pope entrusted the cavalry to Gordon Granger, a friend from frontier days. Pope had kept his own counsel, and not until the evening before the planned movement had his division commanders learned of the object of the campaign. At dawn on February 28, an unseasonably warm day, Hamilton's division set out along the corduroy road, with Palmer trailing. The raw troops marched too fast, and the veterans plodded along behind, some nearly naked. "The hard field service had reduced the contents of our knapsacks to one worn-out blanket and part of an overcoat," said an Ohio veteran. "Our clothing, rank and file, was worn to rags, blouses were sleeveless, and pants in many cases legless and seatless." Sun and sand slowed the new men, so that by late afternoon, all marched in a soft shuffle.[7]

Overnight the temperature plummeted. A drenching rain mixed with snow fell the next day, turning the sandy road into an obstinate paste that sucked down wagon wheels at every turn. March 2 was worse than the day before. Rain yielded to snow, whipped about the swamps by a harsh winter wind. "We waded and trudged for three of the most disagreeable days I ever passed," said Pope. "The men and animals were cased in mud more inches in thickness than I would venture to tell, and if there had been any way of melting them out of their mud envelopes without breaking the casing, we could have presented a complete and striking collection of dirt-colored statues of the Army of the Mississippi." Pope suffered as acutely as his men. The first day out, he was struck by an attack of "camp measles." Wrapped in blankets, he alternated between his horse and the headquarters ambulance. "At length," Pope recalled, "on March 3, after nearly four days wading and dragging wagons and artillery by hand, we debouched on the dry lands and corn fields near New Madrid."[8]

An imposing array of Rebel earthworks greeted the Army of the Mississippi. West of New Madrid, hugging the bank of the river and surrounded by a necklace of abatis, was a fourteen-gun redan built of dirt and sacked corn named Fort Thompson. Two infantry regiments and two artillery companies manned it. Four hundred yards east of town, near the mouth of Wilson's Bayou, stood a seven-gun work called Fort Bankhead, garrisoned with three infantry regiments. A line of entrenchments connected the forts. A flotilla of six gunboats lay just offshore. Commanding the combined forces was Brigadier General John P. McCown, a fidgety, easily frightened former Regular.[9]

Pope grasped the situation clearly. Estimating the enemy force at five thousand, he dismissed a direct assault as futile: "I can take the work by much loss and without the result desired," he explained to Halleck, "as the gunboats, owing to the extraordinary high water, could drive us out immediately." With no sign of Commodore Andrew Foote's gunboats, which had been promised him, Pope begged Halleck for heavy siege guns to combat those of the enemy. In the meantime, he would conduct feints and forced reconnaissances around New Madrid—"as much to accustom our troops to act promptly and coolly under fire as for any harm to the enemy." More important, he would move to close the river to Rebel supply boats, without which the garrisons at New Madrid and Island No. 10 could not long endure.

With the ground between Reelfoot Lake and the Mississippi River ten feet under water, the Confederates had only two lines of retreat: the Mississippi itself and, by means of a small ferry boat unsuited for large-scale transport, Reelfoot Lake.[10]

On March 4, Pope detached a third of his army under Colonel Joseph B. Plum-mer to occupy Point Pleasant, a river hamlet nine miles south of New Madrid, from which the Federals could seal the Mississippi. After a two-day fight, Plummer's command drove away two Confederate gunboats anchored offshore, then dug rifle pits and cannon emplacements. While assuring Halleck that the river between New Madrid and Point Pleasant had been closed to Rebel navigation, Pope warned that enemy reinforcements arriving from above Island No. 10 made victory uncertain. Reinforcements would continue to reach the island from the north, Pope added, until Foote reported in from Cairo with his gunboats.

As Halleck had said he could count upon fifty thousand troops, should such numbers be needed to take Island No. 10, Pope not surprisingly expected the department commander would push Foote, weakened by wounds received during the Donelson campaign, off the Cairo docks. Instead, Halleck temporized. On March 3, he told Brigadier General George Cullum, the commander at Cairo, to order Foote underway at once. When Foote refused, Halleck not only backed down but also called on Pope to withdraw.

On March 7, Halleck's messenger carrying the recall order left St. Louis for the field. The next day, Pope's messenger bearing word of the capture of Point Pleasant reached Halleck's headquarters. Halleck pondered and wrote Cullum: "This may change the program and it may be advisable to remain."

Halleck's indecision was of little moment to Pope. Ignoring the recall order, Pope pushed on with his preparations to reduce New Madrid. He sent Colonel Josiah Bissell, commander of his engineer regiment, to Cairo to procure siege guns and pricked the Confederate defenses with skirmishers. In his correspondence, Pope conveyed a calm certitude as to the outcome. Rebel reinforcements, which had brought the two armies to near parity, troubled him not. All he required were siege guns, Pope told Cullum; "when they arrive and are placed in position we will be able to drive off the gunboats, and it will then require but a short time for us to carry the entrenchments."[11]

Before his troops, however, Pope wore a harried and excitable demeanor. His wonderful temper often got the better of him. Charles Adkins of the Twenty-seventh Ohio happened across Pope's path at one such moment. Pope had issued orders against foraging or looting so strict that most soldiers dismissed them as absurd, as for instance: "In gathering firewood for the use of the troops only the top rail must be taken." The men laughed and obeyed the order literally; each took one rail from the top until the plundered fence disappeared. Regrettably for Adkins, his comrades had piled their rails in a wagon he and another soldier were driving. As they returned to camp, Adkins and his accomplice were overtaken by Pope's ambulance. "With a volley of unprintable words, he invited Tom and me to get in his private conveyance and ride with him; which we did, he adding that in the interest of having his orders obeyed he would have both of us court-martialed and shot as an example to the thieving volunteer hounds," recalled Adkins. "On reaching headquarters he gave us another blast of threats, and then the sergeant put us in the guardhouse with a lot of rebel prisoners, in the custody of Regular Army guards, which made our chances for escape very discouraging and our minds burdened with anxiety as to the outcome." The next morning, the sergeant of the guard called them out and, "in the stern dignity of a Regular," told them to report to their company. Adkins and his companion learned what the western soldier later would commonly understand: Pope's words were far more menacing than his actions.[12]

No number of threats, it seemed, could start Commodore Foote before he was ready. Having retracted the recall order to Pope, Halleck complained to Cullum: "Why can't Commodore Foote move? By delay he spoils all my plans." Cullum had no greater success with Foote, who refused to leave Cairo until the damage done his gunboats at Fort Donelson was repaired.

Fortunately for Pope, there was someone then in Cairo able to prod Foote.

Assistant Secretary of War Thomas A. Scott, responsible for all government railways and transportation lines, sympathized with Pope. Although Scott had only advisory power, his title sufficed to intimidate Foote. Against his better judgment, Foote agreed to move against Island No. 10 and New Madrid with seven gunboats and ten mortar boats.

Unaware of Scott's and Halleck's efforts on his behalf, Pope wrote off Foote and concentrated instead on getting the siege guns; "with them," he told General Cullum, "I can settle matters without the aid of the gunboats from Cairo."

He was right. Colonel Bissell returned with four heavy guns on March 12. Under the cover of darkness, Pope had the cannon run to within eight hundred yards of Fort Thompson. Shortly before dawn on March 13, two Federal regiments swept the ground between the guns and the fort clean of Rebel pickets. At daybreak, the cannon opened fire. All day long, Pope's four guns dueled with the Rebel gunboats and the batteries of Fort Thompson. By nightfall, several Rebel transports had been shot apart and most of the Rebel gunboats damaged. Pope lost one siege gun to a direct hit and one man killed and a dozen wounded by bounding or ricocheting solid shot.[13]

A garbled order nearly cost him far more. During the cannonade, Pope had directed Brigadier General Eleazer A. Paine to demonstrate against Fort Bankhead and Stanley to advance his lines nearer to Fort Thompson. Pope briefly contemplated a full-scale attack, until John Palmer made it clear he would not cooperate in what he considered a suicidal proposition. Pope readily relented, but at least one of Stanley's regimental commanders, Colonel John Groesbeck, understood he was to charge the fort. Colonel Groesbeck had led his Thirty-ninth Ohio out of camp before dawn, through a dark, dense fog. The Ohioans felt their way into place to the right of the siege guns and behind a tall fence. To everyone's surprise, Groesbeck ordered the fence torn down and the men forward in line of battle. As Groesbeck was about to give the order to charge, General Pope galloped up and demanded an explanation for the colonel's action. He was going to charge the fort, Groesbeck replied. "Charge hell, there are not men enough in the army to take that fort," Pope bellowed, then loosened a stream of obscenities on Groesbeck, pausing just long enough for the colonel to stammer that Stanley had ordered the assault. Stanley appeared, and Pope redirected his tirade. Undoubtedly, the hot-tempered Stanley replied in kind. Pope waved the Ohioans back, and no harm was done, except perhaps to Colonel Groesbeck's nerves.[14]

Pope intended to renew the cannonade at daybreak on March 14. Just before midnight, a furious thunderstorm swept over the swamps, turning the night black as pitch. With the dreary dawn came a squad of wet Rebels under a flag of truce, who announced that General McCown had abandoned New Madrid.

"To my utter amazement," Pope confessed to Halleck, "the enemy hurriedly evacuated the place last night, leaving everything. They were landed in the woods opposite and dispersed." Everywhere Federal troops found evidence of a "hasty and disgraceful flight," said an Illinoisan. "The heavy guns had been imperfectly spiked, and were not rendered useless; a large amount of fixed ammunition and quantities of small arms, as well as a number of field guns, were left behind . . . and the knapsacks of the men, in large quantities, were lying in the unstruck tents."[15]

Pope had confounded the Confederate generals. Believing it impossible to bring siege guns through the swamps, they were dumbstruck when the Yankee cannon opened up on March 13. Commodore George N. Hollins feared for his gunboats, and Pope's demonstration against Fort Bankhead convinced McCown a general assault was forthcoming. Under cover of the storm, he removed the garrison to the Tiptonville peninsula.

General Halleck was elated. "I congratulate you and your command on the success which has crowned your toils and exposures," he wrote Pope. "You have given the fatal blow to the rebellion in Missouri and proved yourselves worthy members of the brave Army of the West." And to Secretary of War Stanton, Halleck wired: "This was the last stronghold of the enemy in this state. There is no rebel flag now flying in Missouri." Wonderful praise, but as Pope knew, it came prematurely. Halleck technically was correct—there were no more Rebel troops in Missouri; but Hollins's gunboats, the batteries on Island No. 10, and the nine thousand soldiers whom McCown was reorganizing opposite New Madrid were as great a threat to river navigation as Forts Thompson and Bankhead had been. As Pope saw it, only the "first phase of the problem was solved." Island No. 10 must be reduced and the Confederates on the Tiptonville peninsula defeated.[16]

On March 15, Foote's flotilla anchored above Island No. 10 and the next day began what Pope thought a useless barrage. "All the bombardment in the world could not have reduced Island Number Ten," he wrote. "To do that it was necessary to either starve out its garrison by cutting off its supplies or to find some means to cross the river with sufficient force to overcome resistance. How to do this was the question."[17]

Pope perceived that the easiest and least costly way of capturing the island was to get in its rear, but he was at a loss how to do so. At a council of war, General Hamilton proffered a solution. As the ground was too spongy to admit of a road, Hamilton suggested a canal be dug from some point above Island No. 10, across the bayou to New Madrid, which would permit steam transports to join Pope's command without hazarding the island batteries. Pope might then ferry his army across the peninsula and come upon the island from behind. Pope scoffed at the notion of clearing a canal through country deep under water. But Colonel Bissell, who had explored the land north of Island No. 10 himself, agreed with Hamilton. He showed Pope the most promising ground on a map and said he could complete the task in two weeks; it would be largely a matter of cutting away tree stumps and widening preexisting channels. As a former engineer Pope found the plan intriguing, and he directed Colonel Bissell to reconnoiter a suitable canal route at once.

To succeed, Hamilton's plan demanded the cooperation of Foote. The Confederates were planting batteries at every possible river crossing from New Madrid to Tiptonville. Without gunboats to neutralize them, the Rebel guns would blow apart the transports. It was impossible to dig a canal deep enough for the gunboats, so Pope begged Foote to run two or three past Island No. 10.

Foote refused. Thoroughly nonplussed, the commodore wrote Halleck that the island "is stronger and even better adapted for defense than Columbus ever was. Each fortification commands the one above it. We can count forty-nine guns in the different batteries, where there are probably double the number, with 10,000 troops." Nonsense, Pope told Halleck. Nothing but the gunners themselves and a handful of infantry remained on or near the island. The rest of the Rebel forces, Pope believed, were dispersed along the river or congregated near Tiptonville. He assured Halleck that, with the shore batteries silenced, he could cross the river and "bag the whole of them." Foote had little to fear, Pope added; at night, he might safely run gunboats past Island No. 10. In any case, Pope concluded, "surely such a risk is much less than will be that of crossing a large force in frail boats over a wide, swift river, in the face of an enemy, and without anything to cover the landing."

Pope and Foote had presented their cases to Halleck for decision. Instead, he waffled. "I heartily approve of your plan," he told Pope. "If you can in this way turn and capture the enemy, it will be one of the most brilliant feats of the war. I will not attempt to hamper you with any minute instructions." Neither would he help Pope. "I am very glad that you have not unnecessarily exposed your gunboats," he assured Foote, whom he left to do as he pleased.

Pope kept up the pressure, bombarding Halleck with appeals while Foote's gunboats shelled space, until the harried department commander suggested Pope call the whole thing off and send his troops up the Tennessee to join Grant's army. As he had before New Madrid, Pope ignored Halleck's pusillanimous suggestion. "Your dispatch of the 24th received. Will take Island 10 within a week. Trust me," Pope replied. If Foote wouldn't risk a gunboat or two, then they should be turned over to him; he would place a crew of infantrymen aboard and bring them down himself. "I can get along without them, but will have several days' delay. . . . I am confident of success and shall carefully provide against any danger in crossing the river."

In strength of character, Halleck was no match for Pope, and he again conducted a volte-face. To Foote, he wrote on March 28: "General Pope is confident that he can turn the enemy's position by crossing below. Give him all the assistance in your power by the use of your gunboats. I think that by a combined operation the object can be accomplished. One or two gunboats are very necessary to protect his crossing. Assist him in this if you can." With that, Halleck removed himself from the picture.[18]

Pope's anxiety to press operations had puzzled Halleck. Pope had established a heavy battery at Riddle's Point, opposite Tiptonville, which closed the last means of resupply to the island. Cut off as it was from resupply, it seemed to Halleck that time alone would compel the garrison to capitulate. But time was something Pope did not have in abundance. Encamped in soaked fields, his troops were falling ill by the score. Smallpox broke out at the end of March, sweeping away a half dozen a day in each regiment. With only corn for feed, horses grew weak and died—ten a day in the Seventh Illinois Cavalry, said a trooper. If a way were not found to get below Island No. 10 rapidly, disease, rather than Halleck's indecision, would compel Pope to break off operations.[19]

Fortunately, Pope was well served by Colonel Bissell's engineers. In a superb bit of engineering, they cut a channel from Island No. 10 to New Madrid in fewer than three weeks. Following the trace of a submerged wagon road, Bissell first opened a two-mile course through sunken cornfields and thick forest to Wilson's Bayou. His men worked atop floating platforms mounting huge swinging saws to cut out the innumerable trees that blocked their path. "When we reached the bayous," said Bissell, "the hard and wet work began. The river had begun to fall, and the water was running very rapidly." Precariously perched on slippery logs, the engineers cleared heavy driftwood from an eight-mile course through the bayou that emptied into the Mississippi just east of Fort Bankhead. General Pope watched admiringly as the work went on. "An avenue was made through heavy timber for six miles with incredible labor and by men wet to the skin in the cold month of March from morning to night. At the end of the six miles of swamp the so-called canal intersected the course of the large bayou which enters the Mississippi at New Madrid. The bayou was everywhere full of snags and dead trees embedded in the mud. These had to be hauled out to leave a channel wide enough for the boats, and the labor in this part of the canal was not appreciably less than it was in the swamps," he recalled. "Nineteen consecutive days were spent in this tremendous work by Colonel Bissell and his engineer regiment, at the end of which time he reported to me that not only was the canal finished, but his regiment was finished also. Of the 700 or 800 men with whom he began the work scarcely a score were fit for duty at the end."

While most of Bissell's engineers sawed and hauled timber, a small detachment began work on a three-gun floating battery, improvised from coal barges. With or without Foote's gunboats, Pope was determined to cross the river. "I have no doubt that these batteries would have answered their purpose," Pope averred. "My whole command volunteered to man them."[20]

On March 30, the day before the channel was completed, Commodore Foote consented to run a gunboat past Island No. 10 on the first foggy or rainy night. For "this delicate and somewhat hazardous service" he chose the USS *Carondelet,* commanded by Commodore Henry Walke. On the storm-wracked night of April 4, as Pope had predicted, the *Carondelet* steamed past Island No. 10 undamaged. The following morning, Pope exhorted Foote to send a second gunboat: "I am urgent, sir, because the lives of thousands of men and the success of our operations hang upon your decision. With the two boats all is safe; with one, it is uncertain." Again, Assistant Secretary Scott came to Pope's assistance. Reaching New Madrid on April 5, Scott wired Stanton the next morning, asking him to intercede with the secretary of the navy to order the boat down "and thus relieve a flag officer from a responsibility he is not willing to assume." That evening, the *Pittsburgh* passed the island unscathed.[21]

With two gunboats now on hand, Pope moved quickly. Already he had selected a crossing site—Watson's Landing—and had concentrated his heavy cannon on the near bank. General Paine's division, which was to cross first, lay encamped behind the battery. Pope ordered down the transports, which were hidden near the mouth of St. John's Bayou, and directed the crossing to begin on April 7, as soon as Commodore Walke silenced the Rebel batteries at Watson's Landing.

The operation came off perfectly. At daybreak, Walke's gunboats began shelling the Rebel gun emplacements. By noon, they had wrecked nearly every gun and sent the crews and their infantry support scattering into the forest. Paine's division, which began crossing immediately thereafter, met not a single Southern soldier at the landing.

Pope had intended to cross his entire army before moving on Island No. 10. But a reliable spy, who came over from the peninsula on one of Walke's gunboats, reported the Rebels had abandoned the island and all their shore batteries and were in full retreat toward Tiptonville, more concerned with finding a way across Reelfoot Lake than in fighting Yankees. Pope changed his plans accordingly. He sent word to Paine to march on Tiptonville at once; Stanley and Hamilton would follow as soon as they were over.[22]

Shaking out skirmishers, Paine started his four regiments toward Tiptonville, expecting at any moment to meet heavy opposition. After slogging two miles through the swampy forest, Paine's advance ran up against a strong Confederate line of battle, drawn up across the only wagon road on the peninsula. The Yankees hastened to deploy, but before they fired a shot, the enemy disappeared into the timber. Paine pursued. Again he met the enemy, and again they dispersed. Paine halted at nightfall, having closed to within a few hundred yards of Tiptonville without losing a man.

Although he lost touch with Paine, Pope was not troubled. "Everything will be over by 12 to-night," he wrote Halleck before sunset. "All goes well and everybody in fine spirits. Think we shall bag the whole force." Scott agreed, wiring Stanton: "The whole movement has been a grand success. By to-morrow night General Pope will have the enemy completely caged."[23]

Pope guessed wrong as to the hour of victory, but he properly divined the denouement. The Confederates never contemplated resistance. After Walke's gunboats destroyed the Watson's Landing defenses, Brigadier General William Mackall, who had replaced McCown the week before, ordered Island No. 10 and the nearby batteries abandoned. He intended to make a stand in the woods behind the landing, but his officers betrayed him. When the Federal transports started across the river, regimental and company commanders, believing all hope gone, passed the word for "each man to take care of himself." Every effort by Mackall at rallying them failed. Seeing no way over Reelfoot Lake in the dark and knowing the Yankees would attack at first light, Mackall offered to surrender unconditionally. Paine passed on the message to Pope, who had crossed the river during the night and made camp behind his division. Pope agreed to accept Mackall's surrender at 6:00 A.M.[24]

April 8 dawned clear and frosty. From his forest encampment, Pope waited impatiently for word of the Confederate surrender. Six o'clock came and went, and seven was announced, with no news from the front. Wondering if he had been cozened, Pope was quick to credit the report of "two or three busy bodies . . . that the rebels were escaping over Reelfoot Lake," remembered Oliver Nixon, then medical director of the Army of the Mississippi. Pope immediately ordered General Paine to hurry his division to the designated surrender spot and open fire on the fleeing enemy. Thirty minutes later, Mackall's chief of staff rode into Pope's camp to report the Confederates ready to surrender; the men had lashed their stacked arms to tree trunks and were merely awaiting orders. General Mackall, it seemed, had not entirely understood the arrangements made during the night.[25]

Pope was horror-stricken: his bloodless triumph might end with a massacre. With the rest of the staff away on errands, Pope begged Nixon to "mount the first horse I could reach and run him for life until I overhauled General Paine and recalled him." Nixon "made the best time ever made through the mud of the Mississippi bottoms" and caught up with Paine's second brigade. But his first brigade had double-quicked into line of battle opposite the gathered Confederates, wheeled a battery into place, and made ready to shoot. Those few Confederates yet armed quickly grounded their rifles, and the encounter ended quietly. At that moment Pope galloped up, swearing violently at every field-grade officer he could find. Needless to say, this brush with ignominy never found its way into Pope's report.[26]

So Pope was credited with a brilliant and bloodless victory. He claimed 7,000 prisoners (the actual number was closer to 5,000), including the unfortunate General Mackall, 123 pieces of heavy artillery, 35 field pieces, and a huge quantity of supplies and ammunition. Commodore Foote accepted the surrender of the corporal's guard stranded on Island No. 10. Not a man had been lost in the river crossing or pursuit, and the toll for the entire campaign was just 32 killed, wounded, or missing, a fact Pope reported with "profound satisfaction" and his soldiers blessed. Recording their common sentiment, Surgeon Nixon wrote that Pope "could have stormed the fort at New Madrid and captured it the first week of his arrival with the cost of perhaps a thousand of his brave men. But he did not, and the results proved his wisdom and exhibited his humanity, which no general of the United State army held to a larger degree than General Pope." Lieutenant Colonel Alfred W. Gilbert of the Thirty-ninth Ohio thought others in high command might benefit from Pope's compassion. "Had he ordered an assault at the fort and works we should have taken them, but would have lost many lives, yet the glory to him would have been perhaps much greater in the *newspapers,*" noted Gilbert. "Had General Pope been at Fort Donelson and in chief command, I have no doubt that stronghold would have been taken at much less loss of life."

A delighted General Halleck waxed eloquent in his praise of Pope: "Your splendid achievement excels in boldness and brilliancy all other operations of the war. It will be memorable in military history and will be admired by future generations. You deserve well of your country." And Assistant Secretary Scott promised Stanton that with enough transports Pope could capture Memphis in ten days and then join Grant in crushing secession.

His ego swelled to a new extreme, Pope scratched out a telegram to his political benefactor, William Butler, renewing his campaign for a Regular Army promotion. "You will see from the papers and Halleck's dispatch that we have now a great success. I think if the governor [Richard Yates] and yourself will telegraph Lincoln at once he will now promptly transfer me as major general to the Regular Army," he told Butler, adding a promise to reward his aide-de-camp, William Butler's son Speed Butler: "Independent of the gratification of myself it will enable me to give my staff increased rank if Lincoln is telegraphed in the spur of this victory."[27]

Widely praised and poised to push down the Mississippi River Valley, Pope seemed likely to earn for himself and for Illinois the glory he had told Senator Trumbull was due the state.

— ♦ —

William Butler and Governor Yates backed Pope's renewed bid for high Regular rank. They appealed to Lincoln to "transfer Major General John Pope to Regular

Army with his present rank as a token of gratitude to Illinois. Give one of her sons a position in the U.S. Army who has so gloriously achieved the just reward we ask for him." Accustomed now to Pope's relentless ambition, President Lincoln felt free to deny this latest plea openly and with humor. "I fully appreciate General Pope's splendid achievements with their invaluable results," he assured Yates and Butler, "but you must know that Major Generalships in the Regular Army are not as plentiful as blackberries."[28]

Pope suffered a second disappointment a few days later, when his tenure in independent command ended abruptly. Far from being ready to join Pope's Army of the Mississippi in crushing secession, Grant's command lay recuperating from its own near destruction. On April 6, as Pope perfected plans to capture Island No. 10, the Confederate Army of Tennessee under General Albert Sidney Johnston had attacked Grant's sprawling, unprepared forces at Pittsburg Landing in southwestern Tennessee, nearly pushing them into the Tennessee River. Reinforced during the night, Grant counterattacked on April 7, compelling the Confederates, now led by Pierre G. T. Beauregard, to fall back to Corinth, Mississippi. Grant had won, but at a horrible cost, and his stock with Halleck plummeted. Hurrying from St. Louis to Pittsburg Landing, Halleck assumed field command himself. He had intended for Pope to invest Fort Pillow, Tennessee, the next Confederate bastion on the Mississippi, but the near defeat at Shiloh and rumors Beauregard had been reinforced at Corinth caused Halleck to concentrate his armies at Pittsburg Landing.

Pope reached Pittsburg Landing late on April 21. What he saw—and smelled—stunned him. "Practically the camps occupied almost the exact positions of the troops during the battle, and it may certainly be said that more uncomfortable quarters have seldom been occupied by troops," averred Pope. "The deep, tenacious mud made it difficult to walk even a few yards from the tents, and the atrocious and sickening smells arising from a battlefield where the dead had of necessity been thrown into shallow trenches and barely covered over, so poisoned the atmosphere that no air could be breathed not contaminated by this horrible alluvium of animal decomposition."

While his troops remained aboard their transports, Pope disembarked to find Halleck. "I climbed the steep bank at the landing in . . . clay so deep that I was in danger every moment of having my boots dragged off my feet; indeed, it was only by the greatest care that I avoided such a catastrophe. Boots in those days by no means grew on trees." Stumbling about in the dark, Pope at last chanced upon "General Halleck in a tent planted in the mud, and lying on a cot with as woebegone countenance as I ever saw. After some conversation I returned to my steamboat to wait till morning and learn our destination."[29]

Halleck had gathered the largest force ever assembled on the continent—three armies totaling nearly 100,000 men. With it, he intended to capture

Corinth, which he considered the "great strategic point of the war." To prevent an attack on an isolated wing, Halleck would march with his forces well-concentrated. Army commanders Pope, Don Carlos Buell, and Grant were enjoined to keep in constant communications with him and with one another, avoid a general engagement at all costs—"it is better to retreat than to fight," cautioned Halleck—and to entrench at every halt. Defeating Beauregard's army was of little concern.[30]

Halleck's leviathan moved on May 1. Grant's Army of the Tennessee constituted the right wing, Buell's Army of the Ohio held the center, and Pope's Army of the Mississippi made up the right wing. Progress was slow. Recent rains had beaten roads to paste and flooded the surrounding country. Wagons and gun carriages sunk to their axles, and marching soldiers were sucked into the "almost fluid earth." Pope pushed twelve miles in two days before pausing in front of Farmington, four miles east of Corinth and just two miles short of the Rebel entrenchments.[31]

In advancing so quickly, Pope had disregarded Halleck's stricture that he move no faster than Buell. The Army of the Ohio was eight miles behind Pope's command, and Halleck himself had not yet left Pittsburg Landing. Pope went farther astray, attacking Farmington's forty-five hundred defenders with Paine's division. At a cost of two killed and twelve wounded, the Federals swept Farmington clean of Confederates. Leaving thirty dead on the field, along with their tents and baggage, the Rebels "fled in wild confusion" onto their breastworks before Corinth. Pope pursued with cavalry and swung Paine southward to tear up the Memphis and Charleston Railroad. Anxious to press his advantage, Pope planned to bring up his entire army to Seven-Mile Creek, on the outskirts of Farmington. "If you do not approve, please telegraph me immediately," Pope wired Halleck on the night of May 3, "as my arrangements are all made to move in the morning."

Not only did Halleck not approve, but he also directed Pope to fall back four miles and form on Buell's left. Then, amidst growing criticism, Halleck dug in across his entire front. The press pilloried Halleck as "a vacillating coquette . . . a born conservative who lags rather than keeps pace." William T. Sherman, whose division held the extreme right, complained that the march on Corinth was "provokingly slow." General Grant, whom Halleck had bumped up to the empty position of second-in-command of the combined armies, thought Corinth could be taken in a two-day campaign. General Edward Bouton remembered that "it was the generally expressed opinion at the time, that had Pope been allowed to do so, he would have effected the capture or compelled the evacuation of Corinth in two days." As the weather had improved, Pope also questioned the long delay in closing on Corinth: "I did not then and do not now know either why we moved when we did, nor why we halted. Certainly the reason was not to be found in anything the enemy did or even threatened to do."[32]

Nearly everyone complained, but only Pope acted. He wheedled Halleck with regular reports of low Confederate morale, frequent desertions, and the impending evacuation of Corinth until, on May 7, Halleck granted him permission to reconnoiter the main line of Southern entrenchments. Interpreting his orders loosely, the next day Pope pushed two divisions beyond Farmington to within a mile of the Rebel works. But Buell had not supported him. A huge gap yawned between Pope's right and Buell's left division, several miles to the rear, and Halleck lost his nerve. He reminded Pope to stay clear of a general engagement and ordered him back to his camp east of Seven-Mile Creek.

Pope complied, for the most part. Loathe to abandon the town he had twice captured, Pope left Brigadier General John Palmer's brigade on the eastern edge of Farmington, intending to relieve Palmer in twenty-four hours. It was an exposed position, but Palmer was certain he could hold the town "against the world, the flesh, and the devil." Pope was satisfied; "I am not likely to be taken at a disadvantage and trust you will not be uneasy about us," he told Halleck on the night of May 8.[33]

Pope and Palmer were about to pay for their reckless confidence. The dormant Confederates could not ignore so inviting a prize as an isolated brigade, and General Beauregard ordered Earl Van Dorn to march his entire corps out on the morning of May 9 to destroy it. Arraying Brigadier General Daniel Ruggles's division on the main road west of Farmington and holding Sterling Price's division in reserve to Ruggles's right and rear, Van Dorn advanced into Farmington shortly before noon. He easily brushed aside the Federal advance guard, but obstacles Palmer had thrown across the roads in town contained Ruggles until mid-afternoon. When he broke clear, Ruggles found twice the expected number of Yankees, in line of battle behind a wooded road bank.[34]

Fortunately for the Federals, Van Dorn's attack had come at the very hour Pope was relieving Palmer with Plummer's brigade. Palmer and Plummer elected to fight it out together, a decision Pope heartily endorsed when he reached the front at 4:00 P.M. Dismounting, Pope climbed a tall tree that overlooked the battlefield. From his high perch, he shouted orders down to his staff. Pope deployed his army in the line of battle behind Seven-Mile Creek and kept a weather eye on his right flank, which Buell's continued lassitude left exposed. Having heard nothing from Buell, Pope concluded to obey Halleck's admonition against general engagements, and he withdrew Palmer and Plummer across the creek at nightfall, having lost 178 men in holding off a Confederate corps. Van Dorn returned to the Corinth entrenchments, leaving Farmington once more between the lines.

Dawn of May 10 revealed the Confederates gone, and a sanguine Pope pushed his cavalry through Farmington. He was all for a general advance, which Assistant Secretary Scott proposed on his behalf. But Halleck refused. "Don't let Pope go too far ahead," he told Scott. "It is dangerous, and effects no good." Buell eventually closed the gap with Pope's right along Seven-Mile Creek, and a sultry, Southern-spring stalemate set in.[35]

Again it was Pope who broke the impasse, perhaps in a play to public opinion. Halleck had run horribly afoul of the press. Impatient with the reporters who loitered about headquarters asking why "we were putting up breastworks every hundred yards between Shiloh and Corinth," on May 13 Halleck issued an order expelling "unauthorized hangers on" from his army; anyone seeking to evade the order would be put to work on the entrenchments.

Having won the favor of the press, Pope was reluctant to ban newspapermen from his camp. A man like Pope, who enjoyed boasting of himself and gossiping about others, needed an audience for his self-praise and fulminations—the wider the better. His verbal indiscretions were so egregious as to startle even veteran journalists. Said Henry Villard, "[Pope] was, no doubt, an able man and good soldier, but he talked too much of himself, of what he could do and of what ought to be done; and he indulged, contrary to good discipline and all propriety, in very free comments upon his superiors and fellow-commanders."

The press corps delighted in Pope's open needling of the newspaper-phobic Halleck. First, Pope inquired what the commanding general meant by "unauthorized" personnel. Halleck dodged the question by replying that "the regulations fully explain that point." Perhaps with the connivance of friendly reporters, Pope demanded a clarification, asking Halleck: "Do you include newspaper correspondents among the unauthorized hangers on?" Halleck was forced to admit he did.

The departure of the reporters in no way denied Pope access to the public. Uniformed correspondents simply took their place, and reports of Pope's exploits continued to find their way into print. Said Doctor Oliver Nixon, now both chief surgeon of Groesbeck's brigade and field reporter for the *Cincinnati Commercial:* "General Pope's little army have been chafing and edging up toward the enemy, several miles in advance of the main column. It is rather a remarkable fact that our army should have come from Fort Pillow all the way to this place, and then be ready for action so much in advance of the main army—which was said to be ready before we left the Mississippi River."[36]

General Grant chafed too. Thinking the Confederates might be maneuvered from Corinth far more quickly than Halleck's anaconda tactics could squeeze them out, he suggested the Army of the Mississippi be withdrawn from its place on the left, where Phillips and Bridge creeks and numerous swamps impeded forward movement, and marched to the right, where the ground was dry and relatively open. From there, Pope might sweep "to the south of Corinth on the enemy's communication and flank Beauregard out of Corinth or make him come out and fight." But Halleck silenced Grant "so quickly that I felt that possibly I had suggested an unmilitary movement."

Rebuked unfairly and denied a meaningful role at headquarters, Grant grew morose. With little else to do, he came often to visit Pope. Recalling Grant's anguish, Pope later wrote, "He had his personal camp in a thick grove to the rear of the right of the line, and lived there in perfect solitude, except for the companionship of his personal staff and a few friends who sought him out in his seclusion. His mortification was excessive. . . . He came a number of times to my camp, on the left of the line and three or four miles from his, and would spend nearly the whole day lying on a cot bed, silent and unhappy. I never felt more sorry for anyone."[37]

After ten days of military inactivity, Pope tried to stir up the Confederates. He sent his cavalry ranging beyond the Memphis and Charleston Railroad, pushed skirmishers a mile beyond Seven-Mile Creek, and called up heavy artillery to shell the Rebel earthworks. After a brisk skirmish on the evening of May 10, Pope retook Farmington. This time Halleck let him stay. Rather than reining in Pope, Halleck exhorted his other commanders to complete their forward entrenchments and make ready for battle. "There are very important reasons," he told Buell," why an attack should not be delayed many days."

Pope agreed. The enemy seemed to be stirring south of the Memphis and Charleston Railroad, and Pope feared an attack on his left flank to be imminent. None came, but Pope chafed nonetheless. While Halleck gently nudged Buell forward, Pope planned a daring enterprise of his own. Halleck's armies had Corinth hemmed in from three sides, but the southern way out of town remained open. Although he lacked the men needed to close it, Pope could disrupt the chief line of escape in that direction, the Mobile and Ohio Railroad. On the evening of May 27, Pope ordered Colonel Washington L. Elliott to take two regiments and strike at the railroad forty miles south of Corinth. Elliott was to tear up the track, destroy any stores in the vicinity, and generally wreak as much havoc as possible.

Elliott succeeded handsomely. For the expedition he chose his own Second Iowa Cavalry and the Second Michigan Cavalry, commanded by an obscure colonel named Philip H. Sheridan. Crossing the Memphis and Charleston Railroad at Iuka, the Federal troopers traveled through enemy country so rapidly that the inhabitants at first supposed them to be Rebel cavalry. At Booneville, about eighteen miles below Corinth, they captured two thousand convalescent Confederates and seized an ordnance train bound for Beauregard's army. After paroling their prisoners and burning the train, Elliott's men returned to Farmington, having lost just nine men. Then and after, Pope was proud of Elliott's expedition, later writing, "I organized and sent out the first cavalry raid ever made by our troops, or I think the Confederates, and it was well-conducted and successful."[38]

By the time Elliott returned on May 31, Beauregard had abandoned Corinth. Journalists saw Elliott's success as ample proof the enemy could be bested by prompt action. The immediate advance of "a large portion of this army with hot haste on the fleeing Rebels" was imperative, said a New York correspondent.

Pope agreed. He had entered Corinth on the morning of May 30, full of fight and eager to push on. While in town, Pope released a bit of his anxiety on a fellow Federal general. Crossing the abandoned Confederate earthworks just behind the vanguard of his army, Pope and his escort had galloped ahead, through smoldering ruins and over streets sticky with spilled molasses and putrid with spoiled beef, to watch the major of the Thirty-ninth Ohio raise the regimental and national flags over the courthouse. But an Illinois regiment from Major General William "Bull" Nelson's division of Buell's army had arrived first. The Illinois major dismounted at the courthouse with the regiment's banners, and the two majors fell into a quarrel.

General Nelson arrived next. He settled the dispute by having the Ohio major arrested. Up rode Pope. Why had the major been arrested, he wondered? "For getting my flag up first," answered the Ohioan. Pope flew into a rage. A soldier of the Thirty-ninth Ohio noted, "Those of you who have served under Pope know what a universal knowledge he had of cuss words and with what artistic ease, grace, and vim he could use them. . . . He turned to Nelson and hurled such a torrent of abusive epithets at him that it seemed he must soon exhaust the entire vocabulary." The soldier recalled, "On this occasion he seemed to surpass any former effort of his left, and he seemed to enjoy it too. I know the boys did. General Nelson sat on his horse as immovable as a statue and never replied. . . . When Pope got tired of the fun he rode off. Our major resumed his place in the regiment and we took up our line of march." The exchange mortified General Stanley, who blamed both Nelson and his friend Pope for their scandalous "cursing match" over who should have "the empty honor to enter first the miserable little town of Corinth."

Pope and Nelson parted bitter enemies. Some four months later, Nelson was murdered by an enraged Brigadier General Jefferson C. Davis, whom he had insulted. Nelson's demise moved Pope to write: "The only surprise felt by those who knew him was that some such fate had not befallen him some time before. He was the most tyrannical, arrogant, and abusive officer to those junior to him in rank that I ever saw."[39]

As Pope was nearest the line of Confederate retreat, Halleck charged him with leading the pursuit. Reinforced by one division from Buell, Pope had his army on the road to Booneville shortly after noon on May 30. By nightfall he had pushed seven miles and gathered in two thousand Southern stragglers. The next day Pope's command pressed on vigorously, his cavalry snapping at the Rebel rear guard and sweeping the woods for stragglers. Hundreds surrendered willingly. Three days later his advance, consisting of two divisions under Brigadier General William S. Rosecrans, reached Booneville.

Pope was not present to witness the deterioration of Beauregard's army. A severe attack of diarrhea had compelled him to remain at Danville, ten miles from Halleck's headquarters at Corinth. For three days, he lay on a cot, too ill to do more than forward reports from the front. Pope rejoined the army late on June 4, in time to accompany it twenty miles farther to Baldwyn. Although the Confederates continued to give ground without a fight, Pope agreed with Halleck that further pursuit would only attenuate his already strained lines of supply. On June 11, he withdrew to Camp Clear Creek, near Corinth.[40]

Perusing a Northern newspaper the day after his return to camp, Pope was stunned to read a bombastic, and completely false, report attributed to him by Halleck. From his sick bed on June 3, Pope had forwarded, under his own name, a report from Gordon Granger that the road from Baldwyn was "full of stragglers from the enemy, who are coming in squads. Not less than 10,000 men are thus scattered about, who will come in within a day or two." Somehow Halleck interpreted this to mean Pope's command already had captured 10,000 Confederates, and he told the War Department, "General Pope, with 40,000, is 30 miles south of Corinth, pushing the enemy hard. He already reports 10,000 prisoners and deserters from the enemy and 15,000 stand of arms captured. Thousands of the enemy are throwing away their arms."

Pope was furious. He had not tried to bring in the Confederate stragglers who choked the roads and filled the forests; Pope's generals assumed they would come in of their own accord. When few did, the press pilloried Pope as a braggart and a liar. Pope's predicament garnered the sympathy of his fellow generals, most of whom probably expected him to demand a retraction from Halleck, but Pope was denied a chance to clear the record. Claiming that a sense of higher duty caused him to keep silent, Pope later told Congress, "I had resolved when this war began that I would never during its continuance resort to the newspapers for any justification of myself from charges or statements made against me, and never suffer myself to be drawn into personal controversy with other officers which might impair my usefulness or theirs, or in any other manner obstruct, in the slightest degree, the prosecution of the war."

But the truth was less flattering; Pope would manipulate the press to his advantage. It was not propriety that caused him to defer a rebuttal to Halleck, but rather an enigmatic telegram from the secretary of war, received on June 19, while Pope was visiting his family in St. Louis. "If your orders will admit," said Stanton, "and you can be absent long enough from your command, I would be glad to see you at Washington."[41]

Pope was bewildered. On a short leave of absence to visit Clara, who had just given birth to their first child, a daughter they named Clara Horton, he had neither the time nor the inclination for a trip to Washington. Pope advised Halleck of Stanton's summons; should he go? Absolutely not, Halleck replied. "The Secretary of War can order you to Washington if he deems proper; but I cannot give you leave, as I think your services here of the greatest possible importance," he told Pope. Stanton sent a second telegram, ordering Pope to Washington.[42]

Although Stanton said nothing of his reasons for summoning him, Pope expected he was being transferred to duty in the East. No doubt he was as reluctant to leave the Army of the Mississippi as he later claimed to have been. Pope's disdain for McClellan and his eastern generals was exceeded only by his esteem for his own western subordinates. Pope, Gordon Granger, and David Stanley had served together on the frontier and were on intimate terms. They were of a kind: gruff, bombastic, and foul mouthed; direct in their speech and decisive in their actions. William Starke Rosecrans, an Ohioan and also a Republican, was garrulous and blunt, like Pope. Hamilton and Plummer were as affable and boisterous as the other division commanders. Together, Pope and his generals formed "a very pleasant and social set who sat around the campfires in the evening and talked about things old and new," remembered Stanley. They all liked Pope greatly; he was, Stanley said, "a very agreeable and a very witty man and often turned the laugh on his staff officers and others."

Among the high command of the Army of the Mississippi only John M. Palmer disliked Pope, more from a general disdain for West Point officers, whom he considered "profligate and wicked and profoundly ignorant of everything other than their profession," than from any trait of Pope himself, save the same general "flabbiness of character" Palmer saw in all former Regulars. Palmer also felt Pope had slighted him in his report of the New Madrid operations and in brigading the best regiments under Regular Army chums. Despite his aversion to Pope personally, Palmer respected his abilities and as a fellow Illinois Republican at least shared his politics.[43]

In marked contrast were the senior generals of McClellan's Army of the Potomac. Like their commander, they were politically conservative and socially circumspect; preferring parlor intrigue to public bombast. Neither McClellan nor his principal lieutenant, Major General Fitz John Porter, cared much for Pope. They remembered only his Regular Army reputation as a braggart and liar of modest accomplishments. "Pope could not quote the ten commandments without getting ten falsehoods out of them," sneered Porter. He was a "low, dishonest, untruthful man" to whom Porter would concede only a certain "shrewd ability." Pope thought little better of Porter.[44]

Most of Pope's generals regretted his departure—Gordon Granger's prophetic warning of "Good-bye Pope, your grave is made" expressed their shared concern—but what about the subordinate officers of the Army of the Mississippi? How did they regard Pope? Their first impression of him had been unfavorable. Most resented his harsh discipline and seeming contempt for the volunteer soldier, leading one Illinoisan to deride Pope as "the little dandy mustering officer" from Camp Yates. Others decried his bad manners and rough language. Captain Cyrus Carpenter, an Iowa Republican who would one day become governor, termed Pope "pugnacious and confident and conceited. I do not think much of General Pope as a man, yet I consider him a good general." As Commissary of Subsistence for the Army of the Mississippi, and a fellow Republican, Carpenter expected better treatment than he received, leading him to traduce Pope as "a wicked profane and overbearing old scallawag." Colonel Robert Ingersoll of the Eleventh Illinois Cavalry, who would become one of America's most illustrious orators, the "great agnostic" to whom nothing was sacred, dismissed Pope as "an incompetent squirt" who, like all West Pointers, need be kicked out of the army before the Rebellion could be suppressed. Commodore Foote thought Pope "a good man for a dash" but not up to a major command.[45]

Whatever they might think of his deportment, Pope's refusal to shed blood needlessly at New Madrid won him the gratitude of the infantry, just as the capture of Island No. 10 and his aggressiveness before Corinth won their esteem. Said Captain Oscar Jackson of Fuller's brigade, "It is with regret we parted with Pope, who for so long a time had held our entire confidence as a commander." The cavalry appreciated his daring use of the mounted arm for independent missions. Pope reciprocated their regard, moving an orderly to write, "General Pope, as I saw him, appeared to me like another one of those sound-minded, honest, patriotic and well-informed soldiers. What I learned about him caused me to believe that he understood his business and attended to it. General Pope possessed the right conception of the American soldier, that is to say, he thought the men in ranks to be the real heroes of the war." An Iowa sergeant agreed: "To be sure he is given to blowing a little, but he is a stirring man, and one the Rebs feared, and hated, more than anyone else."[46]

5 A Moral Odor of Sewer Gas

John Pope arrived in Washington, D.C., on June 24, 1862, to what the pro-administration *Philadelphia Inquirer* termed an "enthusiastic welcome." Although clad in civilian dress, he was recognized everywhere. Well-wishers, gossips, and hangers-on thronged his room at Willard's Hotel. From them Pope came away with much unwanted advice on how to run the armies, and a general revulsion. "I think I received more suggestions and advice during that afternoon and evening at Willard's than in all my life together, and the advice was, perhaps, the more valuable because it was given by people who had no knowledge of me whatever, nor of the business which brought me to Washington," sneered Pope. "As I was myself quite as ignorant as the least-knowing one among them of the subject of my appearance at the capital, I neither relished nor even appreciated the banquet of good advice and wise suggestion to which I sat down." Pope was incredulous: "The air of mystery worn by everyone, accompanied by the knowing look, which intimated how much could be told if it were wise to do so, and especially the predominance of personal over public interests, which I could not avoid noticing, and which was so different from my experience in the West, all left an unpleasant impression of intrigue and plots extremely disagreeable in itself and unpromising for the success of the cause. In fact, there was a sort of moral odor of sewer gas in the air, which left a bad taste in the mouth, from which even a good night's sleep did not altogether relieve me."[1]

Although John Pope did not yet know why he had been called east, Clara Horton Pope was "perfectly convinced" her husband would not return to the West. "I am almost sure that you now will have Banks and Frémont's and perhaps McDowell's departments and that you will then take the field against Jackson," she wrote John from St. Louis. "It is possible that you may supersede McClellan, but I do not with my present light on the subject consider it likely."[2]

From his first interview with Secretary Stanton on the morning of June 25, Pope learned nothing, nor would he until President Lincoln, who had gone to West Point to consult with General Winfield Scott about the administration's plans for Pope, returned that evening. He did, however, come away with a vivid impression of the secretary of war. Pope had been swept into Stanton's office amidst a throng of favor-seekers, office-seekers, disgruntled soldiers, and army contractors of dubious integrity, quite reminiscent of St. Louis.

Stanton stood behind a high, slightly inclined table—the only furniture in the room—with a piece of paper before him and a pencil in his hand. "Around the room stood his visitors, who stepped up one by one to this high table, stated his business as briefly as possible and in the hearing of everybody, and received a prompt and final answer as rapidly as words could convey it."

Pope saw the wisdom of Stanton's abrupt and public manner with "self-seekers or those in search of favors for others. The necessity of taking a whole room full of strangers into their confidence much abbreviated all such communications, and whilst the secretary's popularity among these people and their followers was not successfully established by such methods, there is no doubt that the public interests were greatly subserved."[3]

The next morning, in his private chambers at the War Department, Secretary Stanton revealed to Pope the purpose of his summons to Washington. For three months, a small Confederate army under Stonewall Jackson had been wreaking havoc with three independent Federal commands in the Shenandoah Valley, diverting Union reinforcements from McClellan and throwing the Northern capital into a panic. For much of the fiasco, Stanton conceded himself and the president to blame. Having placed political patrons in command of the forces opposing Jackson, they then had tried to regulate their movements from the capital. Disarray and disaster resulted. After Jackson thrashed his opponents at Cross Keys and Port Republic in early June, the president bowed to Treasury Secretary Salmon P. Chase's suggestion that the two armies then in the valley and Irvin McDowell's widely scattered corps be united under one commander, whose threefold mission it would be to protect Washington, defend the Shenandoah Valley, and disrupt the Virginia Central Railroad in the neighborhood of Charlottesville and Gordonsville. By threatening this vital Rebel rail link with the valley, the administration hoped to compel the Confederates to draw off much of Robert E. Lee's Army of Northern Virginia from the defenses of Richmond, thus easing McClellan's way into the city. Stanton told Pope he had been called east to carry out these tasks.

A long silence followed. "General, you don't seem to approve the arrangements I have outlined to you," said Stanton.

"Mr. Secretary, I entirely concur in the wisdom of concentrating these widely scattered forces in front of Washington and using them generally as you propose, but I do certainly not view with any favor the proposition to place me in command of them."

Visibly annoyed, Stanton said he should have thought Pope would be flattered at so high an expression of the government's confidence in him. Yes, Pope answered, he was gratified by the gesture, but he gravely objected to the station. Stanton insisted he explain why. Pope did, at length. He pointed out that the three generals whose armies were to be united under Pope were his senior in rank and would naturally feel humiliated and resentful, sentiments they undoubtedly would convey to their troops. That Pope had been summoned from another theater would only add to their anger. Under the best of conditions, Pope added, it would take far more time properly to organize and discipline his new command than circumstances permitted. "In short," quipped Pope, "I should be much in the situation of the strange dog, without even the right to run out of the village." And for this, the command "of a forlorn hope under the most unfavorable conditions possible for success," Pope was asked to leave a western army of equal size, to which he was greatly attached.[4]

Stanton was unconvinced but agreed to refer the matter to President Lincoln. Both Pope and Stanton conferred privately with Lincoln, who in the end concluded Pope must stay in the East. With a promise to do his best "with cheerfulness and zeal," Pope assumed command of the newly christened Army of Virginia on June 27.[5]

Stanton had told Pope the official reason he had been summoned to Washington; how much the secretary divulged of his personal motive for beckoning Pope is an open question. Pope said Stanton made clear "without unfriendly criticism" the administration's discontent "with the lame results accomplished by the great army under McClellan's command"; from that Pope might draw his own conclusions.

Although there was much in Pope's military record to recommend him for the command, President Lincoln, at the insistence of Stanton and Chase, had chosen Pope more for political purposes than for his battlefield abilities. Weary of McClellan's demands for more troops, suspicious of his conservative, Democratic politics, and exasperated with his kid-glove treatment of Southern non-combatants, Stanton and Chase wanted a general who would fight their war—a hard, relentless contest, unsparing of the Southern populace, especially in Virginia. Chase argued for Pope primarily on policy grounds, with a bit of old-fashioned patronage thrown in. But Stanton wanted Pope in the East specifically to humiliate McClellan, whom he detested personally and actually believed a traitor. In an unguarded moment during the Second Bull Run campaign, Stanton would expose to Secretary of the Navy Gideon Welles the intensity of his feelings against McClellan. Welles also wanted to see McClellan removed, but he objected to the manner in which Stanton wished to proceed; the secretary of war had gotten up a petition demanding McClellan's dismissal that he wished to present to Lincoln in cabinet as a fait accompli. When Welles refused to sign the petition, Stanton flew into a rage. The secretary of war, recalled Welles, "said he knew of no particular obligations he was under to the president, who had called him to a difficult position and imposed upon him labors and responsibilities which no man could carry, and which were greatly increased by fastening upon him a commander who was constantly striving to embarrass him in his administration of the department. He could not and would not submit to a continuance of this state of things."

But President Lincoln was not yet ready to relieve McClellan. He not only recognized his enormous popularity within the Army of the Potomac but also was somewhat fond of the man, despite Little Mac's thinly veiled bouts of insubordination. Lincoln recognized, however, that McClellan was the man neither for general command in the East nor for overall command of the Union armies. And he also thought well of Pope. So he consented to Chase's recommendation that the Shenandoah Valley armies be united under Pope, just as he would later agree to Winfield Scott's suggestion—strongly seconded by Pope—that Henry Halleck be called to Washington as general-in-chief. For the moment, Stanton satisfied himself with having McClellan's antithesis appointed to command the forces in northern Virginia.[6]

In this sense, Pope was not merely the right but perhaps the only man for the job. Unlike most of his brother officers of the Regular Army, who were either apolitical or conservative, Pope was decidedly and outspokenly Republican. He declaimed against slavery and favored "using every instrument which could be brought to bear against the enemy," to include inducting slaves as army laborers. He was quite willing to bring the war home to the civilian populace, as his policies in Missouri demonstrated. Pope was as aggressive as McClellan was cautious. The New York Tribune assured its readers that Pope was "not the type of man to sit around and wait . . . he is a man of action, a man of bold dash and bayonet," and the Philadelphia Public Ledger predicted he would speedily "bring order out of the late chaos in the Shenandoah Valley and be ready at once for offensive service." Unlike McClellan, a successful Pope would pose no political threat, indebted as he was to Lincoln and Chase.[7]

The same traits that made Pope appealing politically guaranteed that he and McClellan would be unable to cooperate militarily. The two did not disguise their mutual antipathy. McClellan confessed his "plain dislike" of Pope and hoped to see his "bubble collapsed." Pope questioned both McClellan's military judgment and his loyalty. But while McClellan contented himself with quiet remarks to his lieutenants and private slander in letters home, Pope took his calumny public. On June 26, just two days after his arrival in Washington, Pope told the House of Representatives that McClellan had exaggerated the strength of the foe defending Richmond, much as Halleck had inflated Rebel numbers at Corinth. Pope believed Lee's army to be half what McClellan reported. In the same imprudent speech, Pope engaged in a bit of foolish braggadocio, claiming to have captured not ten thousand men after Corinth as Halleck had reported, but a full thirty thousand Southerners, most of whom he paroled. The House was "struck by Pope's frankness and ability"; McClellan undoubtedly was enraged at his accusations.[8]

Pope freely expressed his contempt for McClellan to the administration. The defeat of McClellan before Richmond during the last days of June and his withdrawal toward the James River fundamentally altered the strategic situation in Virginia. President Lincoln called Pope to a cabinet meeting to obtain his views on appropriate measures to assist McClellan, who was loudly crying for reinforcements.

Pope spoke bluntly. McClellan's withdrawal toward the James River was a grave error and should be halted, Pope told the cabinet, as it would place the Rebels squarely between his own army and that of McClellan, allowing the enemy to attack either at will. Pope was loathe to succor McClellan. "I considered it my duty to state plainly to the president that I felt too much distrust of General McClellan to risk the destruction of my army, if it were left in his power, under any circumstances, to exhibit the feebleness and irresolution which had hitherto characterized his operations," he recalled. Only peremptory orders to McClellan to renew the offensive against Richmond could induce Pope to act. Under the circumstances, Pope concluded, he would prefer to return to the West.[9]

Lincoln again refused Pope's request. Saddled with the command, Pope made an overture of mutual cooperation to McClellan. On July 4, Pope assured McClellan of his "earnest wish to cooperate in the heartiest and most energetic manner with you. . . . There is no service, whatever the hazard or the labor, which I am not ready to perform with this army to carry out that object." But circumstances mitigated against his taking the offensive. The small armies he had inherited were "much demoralized and broken down, and unfit for active service at the present."

A march on Richmond was impossible. "Were I to move with my command direct on Richmond, I must fight the whole force of the enemy before I could join you, and at so great a distance from you as to be beyond any assistance from your army," he explained. A water-borne expedition to reinforce McClellan was also impractical. It would uncover the capital, allowing the "enemy to be in Washington before [Pope's army] had half accomplished the journey." Until "some well-defined plan of operations and co-operation can be determined on," the best Pope could do was to take up a defensive position east of the Blue Ridge Mountains, harass the Virginia Central Railroad, and, as he told the Joint Congressional Committee on the Conduct of the War on July 8, "lay off on [Lee's] flanks and attack him day and night," should he march against Washington.[10]

There was nothing untoward in Pope's letter. He laid out his situation honestly, and his offer of cooperation, while far less enthusiastic than he allowed, was nonetheless real. McClellan's reply of July 7 was a polite mix of contradictions. He applauded Pope's intention to concentrate his forces but offered no thoughts on what Pope should do with them. His own army was anxious to resume the offensive at once, which in one breath he intimated he would do. But in the next he expressed a fear for his lines of communication so great as to have obliged him to take up strong defensive positions. McClellan thanked Pope for his offer of cooperation without reciprocating, except to say he would advance on Richmond if the enemy abandoned their capital to attack Pope. The same day he wrote Pope confidently, McClellan handed Lincoln, who was visiting his headquarters, a letter informing him that the enemy was preparing to overwhelm his army "by attacking our positions, or reducing us by blocking our river communications"; consequently, McClellan could not "but regard our condition as critical."[11]

Pope certainly read both letters. Concluding from their contradictory and bizarre tones that "harmonious and prompt cooperation" with the Young Napoleon was impossible, Pope pointedly asked the president to relieve McClellan. When the president demurred, Pope suggested he place Henry Halleck in "general command of all the operations in Virginia, with power to enforce joint action between the two armies." Lincoln agreed only to summon Halleck, leaving uncertain the question of unified command. Until Halleck arrived, Pope would act as the president's de facto military adviser.

With uncustomary diffidence, Pope accepted as his Washington office the upper floor of a modest brick house near the War Department. Army clerks appropriated the lower floor, which resounded with pleas of people seeking passes through the lines—sutlers, relic-hunters, idlers, and displaced Virginians. Through the throng pushed the young journalist George Alfred Townsend, anxious for the pass that would allow him to travel with the army. Ever ready to curry favor with the press, Pope obliged Townsend with pleasure. The general and he "chatted pleasantly for a time," recalled Townsend. While Pope talked on, Townsend took the measure of the new commander of the Army of Virginia. "He was dark, martial, and handsome—inclined to obesity, richly garbed in civil cloth, and possessing a fiery black eye, with luxuriant beard and hair," said Townsend. "He smoked incessantly, and talked imprudently. His vanity was apparent, and although he was brave, clever, and educated, he inspired distrust by his much promising and general love of gossip and story-telling. He had all of Mr. Lincoln's garrulity and none of that good old man's unassuming common sense."[12]

Pope should have protested the president's request he remain in Washington. Poorly led and indifferently supplied, the three corps of the Army of Virginia badly needed his presence. Pope had spoken truthfully when he told McClellan his inherited command was "much demoralized and broken down, and unfit for active service." The sound thrashing Stonewall Jackson had dealt the Federals in the Shenandoah Valley, particularly at the Battles of Cross Keys and Port Republic, shattered their morale. They saw Jackson as an invincible genius and their own leaders as "played out and down forever." Enlisted men deserted at the rate of four hundred a day, and hundreds of officers were absent without leave.[13]

There was little in their commanding officers to inspire confidence. A more worthless set of corps commanders than those with whom Pope was saddled can hardly be imagined. German emigré Franz Sigel assumed command of the First Corps after John C. Frémont, who had led it in the valley, resigned rather than serve under Pope. For all their mutual ill will, Pope would have preferred Frémont to Sigel. Frémont was "not a bad man nor dishonest," Pope told a staff officer, but "simply foolish." But Sigel, with whom he had served in Missouri, Pope rated as miserably inept, an opinion seconded by most of the German's brother officers. He also thought Sigel "the God damndest coward he ever knew" and swore to his newly formed staff that he would "arrest Sigel the moment he showed any signs of cowardice."

Sigel returned the compliment. "John Pope," he later wrote, "was an imbecile and a coward . . . affected with looseness of the brains as others [are] with looseness of the bowels." Sigel resented Pope's elevation over him nearly as much as did Frémont, yet he was too enamored of military life to resign and too uncertain of his standing with Lincoln to request a transfer.[14]

Sigel hated fellow corps commander Irvin McDowell as thoroughly as he detested Pope. But then, nearly the whole army despised McDowell, whom the nation yet held responsible for the debacle at First Bull Run the year before. Arrogant and easily excited, a martinet of little human warmth, McDowell had alienated nearly everyone but Pope. Perhaps recognizing something of himself in the man, Pope not only liked McDowell but regarded him as his principal adviser on command matters.

That role would give McDowell far more influence at headquarters than those who did not know Pope well might expect. For behind his facade of conceit and windy self-assurance was a man quite willing to accept advice from those he respected. Although he grossly distorted this aspect of Pope's nature to traduce the man, Brigadier General George H. Gordon did capture something of his character when he wrote, "Fortunate indeed it was for us that pompous utterances and empty boasts were indulged in by Pope only in fair weather, when gentle breezes and quiet waters gave no token of a coming storm. In an angry ocean Pope was a different being. He was silent, even despondent at times, leaning on stronger men for counsel." Whether McDowell would measure up to the part remained to be seen.[15]

Pope's third corps commander, Major General Nathaniel Banks, owed his commission to purely political considerations. The former Speaker of the House had been Jackson's primary victim in the Shenandoah Valley. But he was a brave, if not prudent, commander and a loyal subordinate. He and Pope respected one another, and relations between them were cordial.[16]

That cordiality was severely tested during the early days of Pope's tenure. Banks, Sigel, and even McDowell all proved vexatious to Pope as he sought to unite his widely scattered forces east of the Blue Ridge. Although he well understood his army's problems, as his letter to McClellan evinced, he sought to remedy its ills and orchestrate its movements with telegraphed orders from Washington, rather than his presence in the field. The results were predictable. Marching orders were ignored, deadlines missed, and phantom enemy legions spotted at every turn. General Banks pleaded for more time to take up his assigned position near Little Washington, because "the insecurity of our position [in the valley] has prevented the accumulation of supplies upon our line." Brigadier General Robert Schenck, acting First Corps commander pending Sigel's arrival, told Pope on June 28: "I do not find on my accession to the command that things are in a good condition in this corps for immediate movement." Two days later, Sigel gave an even more dire report: "I assumed command this morning. . . . The troops forming the First Corps are not in good condition; they are weakened and poorly provided. The organization is not complete, and the whole cavalry force consists of not more than 800 effective men and horses . . . scarcely sufficient for picket and patrol duty." Matters were no better a week later. "The corps [is] in a very bad condition in regard to discipline, organization, construction of divisions and brigades, equipment, and to a great extent, demoralized," said Sigel.

Rufus King's and James B. Ricketts's divisions of McDowell's corps, at Fredericksburg and Manassas Junction, respectively, were in good condition. But James Shield's division, on detached service in the valley, was "in a bad state, morally and materially—officers resigning and even men deserting," said McDowell. And

McDowell's cavalry brigade commander, George Bayard, reported his troopers in "no condition to move at present. Shoes, boots, haversacks, canteens, poncho-tents, and wagon wheels, which are absolutely indispensable," were all wanting. Chasing Stonewall Jackson up and down the Shenandoah Valley had so used up his brigade, Bayard wrote home, that "I need two weeks' rest at least for my horses" and six hundred fresh mounts to replace those broken down. "There was scarcely a horse in the brigade with a full set of shoes left upon his feet," said a war correspondent, "some of them, as well as the men, had gone two and three days at a time without a mouthful of subsistence."

Conditions in the Army of Virginia were so bad that Brigadier General Jacob D. Cox, in far off West Virginia, offered Pope the services of his division: "In view of the report that disciplined troops are wanted at the East, I call your attention to the fact that my division is among the best-seasoned and oldest troops in the field, and . . . are desirous of joining the principal column."[17]

Equally troubling to Pope was the extent to which Jackson had cowed his generals. Stonewall and his army had quit the Shenandoah Valley on June 18, bound for Richmond. But four days later, frightened Federal commanders believed him still in the valley and heavily reinforced. As late as June 26, Frémont credited rumors that troops from the Western Theater had united with Jackson and were preparing to attack Winchester from the north, and Banks meekly offered that he "could defend against any force the enemy can bring, if no other movement is made." No one wanted to move without guaranteed lines of retreat. "Each order to move through a pass of the Blue Ridge to the position required was apt to be followed by a query as to what should be the line of retreat or what should be done in case an enemy was found to dispute their advance," recalled a member of Pope's staff. "Do?" exclaimed Pope in reply to one such query from Robert Schenck on July 9, "Do? Fight 'em, damn 'em, fight 'em!"[18]

To prevent the Confederates from moving with impunity, as Jackson had in the Shenandoah Valley, Pope issued from Washington a stream of orders admonishing his timid subordinates to be aggressive in gathering intelligence on the enemy. Unlike McClellan, who relied almost exclusively upon Allan Pinkerton and his inept cadre of detectives, Pope would cast a wide net for information. "Spare no means through spies and others to inform yourself of the movements of the enemy's cavalry in the valley," he told the panicky Robert Schenck. He likewise instructed Sigel, McDowell, and Banks to employ scouts, spies, and every other means possible to collect intelligence in their sectors.

At the same time, Pope kept pressing his generals to expedite their own movements. "The critical condition of affairs near Richmond and the danger of an advance of the enemy in force on Washington make it necessary that your movements be made with all dispatch," he told Banks on July 5. Sigel and Schenck got similar prodding.

With each passing day, Pope admonitions became more curt. Their tone perhaps had less to do with tactical imperatives than with Pope's own distracted mind. Back in St. Louis, his infant daughter was desperately ill. The strain of a sickly child undoubtedly played hard with Clara's delicate constitution, which always concerned Pope.[19]

More than a week passed before Banks was in place, and Sigel did not even leave the valley until July 14. That same day, Pope learned that Brigadier General John Hatch, leading a cavalry force he had directed Banks to send forward to occupy Culpeper, had taken it upon himself to burn bridges in the neighborhood, including the critical railroad bridge over the Rapidan River. Pope had intended Hatch to seize Gordonsville and, if possible, continue on to Charlottesville to tear up the track of the Virginia Central Railroad; instead, Hatch behaved as if he were covering a withdrawal. Pope was furious, and he vented his anger on Banks. His duty was to preserve the road, not burn bridges. "We are advancing and shall continue to advance, and the roads must be preserved for our use," Pope reminded Banks. "I again beg you to dismiss any idea that there is any purpose whatever to retreat from the positions which you are instructed to take."[20]

Pope had had enough. Rampant desertion from the ranks, widespread absenteeism among officers, the timidity of Hatch, the lassitude of Sigel, the trepidation of Brigadier General A. Sanders Piatt, who believed that unnumbered Rebel hordes were about to sweep down on his garrison at Winchester, and the terror the mention of Stonewall Jackson inspired drove Pope to lash out at his new command in what was perhaps the most ill-advised military proclamation of the war. Written in longhand by Pope himself, it read as follows:

> By special assignment of the President of the United States, I have assumed the command of this Army. I have spent two weeks in learning your whereabouts, your condition, and your wants; in preparing you for active operations, and in placing you in positions from which you can act promptly and to the purpose. These labors are nearly completed, and I am about to join you in the field.
>
> Let us understand each other. I have come to you from the West, where we have always seen the backs of our enemies; from an Army whose business it has been to seek the adversary and to beat him when he was found; whose policy has been attack and not defense. In but one instance has the enemy been able to place our western armies in defensive attitude. I presume that I have been called here to pursue the same system, and to lead you against the enemy. It is my purpose to do so, and that speedily. I am sure you long for an opportunity to win the distinction you are capable of achieving. That opportunity I shall endeavor to give you. Meantime I desire you to dismiss from your minds certain phrases which I am sorry to find much in vogue amongst you.

I hear constantly of taking "strong positions and holding them," of "lines of retreat," and of "bases of supplies." Let us discard such ideas. The strongest position a soldier should desire to occupy is one from which he can most easily advance against the enemy. Let us study the probable lines of retreat of our opponents, and leave our own to take care of themselves. Let us look before us, and not behind. Success and glory are in the advance; disaster and shame lurk in the rear. Let us act on this understanding, and it is safe to predict that your banners shall be inscribed with many a glorious deed, and that your names will be dear to your countrymen forever.

Pope told his staff that he cared not whether the army "should receive this declaration as an assurance that Southern troops could be beaten or whether they should feel stung by it as a taunt." His object, which was to instill a fighting spirit in the men, "would be attained in either case."[21]

But Pope miscalculated terribly. Before his proclamation, the Army of Virginia generally was well disposed to Pope. Most officers had sincerely hoped he would be succeed. "We hail the coming of General Pope with much satisfaction," said Rufus Dawes of the Sixth Wisconsin on July 1. Pope's reputation preceded him, said Brigadier General Cox, but on the whole it was a favorable one: "No one who had any right to judge questioned Pope's ability or his zeal in the national cause. . . . His reputation . . . was that of an able and energetic man, vehement and positive in character, apt to be choleric and even violent toward those who displeased him." Pope's was a temperament of the sort old soldiers understood, and which Cox came to appreciate: "I remember well that I shrunk a little from coming under his immediate orders through fear of some chafing, though I learned in the army that choleric commanders, if they have ability, are often warmly appreciative of those who serve them with soldierly spirit and faithfulness."[22]

The Northern volunteer, however, took taunts poorly. Some liked the aggressive sound of Pope's words. "He is a man of action," said one of McDowell's men, "and will take advantage of any circumstance to strike a blow." Although put off by much of the verbiage, John Gould of the First Maine gave Pope credit for "one paragraph which every one of us will say was well-written: 'Success and glory are in the advance; disaster and shame lurk in the rear.'"

But most deprecated the proclamation, which became known among the enlisted men as "Pope's Bull." Some soldiers thought Pope's remarks "unjust and cruel reflections on the conduct" of their corps commanders in the valley. The majority probably cared little for their generals but thought the tenor of the proclamation unbecoming in an army commander. Said a soldier of the Thirteenth Massachusetts, after passing by Pope in review, "A handsome man, but I don't see the major general."[23]

Among the officer corps, whose leadership the address impugned far more than it did the fighting ability of the men, reaction was almost universally hostile. Wrote Rufus Dawes, "General Pope's bombastic proclamation has not tended to increase confidence, indeed the effect is exactly contrary." Marsena Patrick, a crotchety brigade commander in McDowell's corps, called Pope's address "very windy and somewhat insolent." Lieutenant Robert Gould Shaw, the Boston aristocrat who was to die leading black soldiers at Battery Wagner, dismissed both the man and his proclamation: "His personal appearance is certainly not calculated to inspire confidence or liking. He looks like just what we have always understood he was—a great blow-hard, with no lack of confidence in his own powers." Brigadier General George H. Gordon, a brigade commander in Banks's corps, wondered if Pope was simply "a weak and silly man." The German immigrant Brigadier General Carl Schurz, whose political sympathies were similar to those of Pope, conceded that the Illinoisan had "managed to make an unfavorable impression by one of those indiscretions which an untried leader should be most careful to avoid. . . . There was in this [address] a good deal of boasting not altogether well founded, and some almost contemptuous criticism of Eastern officers and soldiers not altogether merited, and likely to stir up among these a feeling of resentment."[24]

None were more offended by Pope's address than George B. McClellan and his generals. Pope later claimed his aggressive words were directed solely at his own army; that Secretary Stanton had dictated passages censorious of the Army of the Potomac's leaders over Pope's objections that they "were not quite in good taste." The secretary, Pope said, urged such public declarations so strongly that he felt constrained to go along. Salmon P. Chase believed President Lincoln may also have read and approved the proclamation, which would have left Pope even less able to object to its language. Certainly Pope himself had reason enough for deprecating such phrases as "taking strong positions and holding them," "lines of retreat," and "bases of supply," which littered the official correspondence of his own timorous subordinates. But such admonitions were also in vogue at McClellan's headquarters. Given Pope's openly expressed contempt for McClellan, it is no surprise that the Army of the Potomac took umbrage at his address.[25]

McClellan, who had been courteous in his communications with Pope previously, now railed against the "paltry young man who wanted to teach me the art of war" and privately expressed his hope that Pope would be "badly whipped." And Fitz John Porter told his friend J. C. G. Kennedy, the chief of the Census Bureau, on July 17, "I regret to see that General Pope has not improved since his youth and has now written himself down as what the military world has long known, an ass. His address to his troops will make him ridiculous in the eyes of military men abroad as well [as] at home, and will reflect no credit on Mr. Lincoln, who has just promoted him. If the theory he proclaims is practiced, you may look for disaster." While conceding Pope's apparent criticism of McClellan's leadership to be warranted—Little Mac was an incompetent coward who should be shot—Major General Philip Kearny took umbrage at the implied slur of the fighting men of the army. "This insolent appeal in orders by Pope [was] a base lie, for the Western fighting has been child's play," he told a friend. Although more circumspect in his remarks, Major General Ambrose Burnside was no less disturbed: "I do not think it was the impression with the officers generally that General Pope, notwithstanding he was a talented officer, was fully up to the task of conducting so large a campaign."[26]

The soldiers of the Army of the Potomac also resented Pope's thinly veiled slurs against their commander. Practically as a unit, said Jacob Cox, the officers and men united in an "intense dislike and distrust" of Pope. "No personal vilification was too absurd to be credited, and no characterization was too ridiculous to be received as true to the life. It may be that this condition of things destroyed his possibility of usefulness in the East," concluded Cox.

Neither did the proclamation play particularly well in the press. Salmon P. Chase's organ, the *Philadelphia Inquirer,* chose to say nothing about it, and the staunchly Republican *Philadelphia Public Ledger,* while sympathetic with the tone of the message, regretted its contents: "It is not good for a general, just taking the field, to indulge in this kind of public display. The promises are likely to beget large expectations that cannot be lived up to [and] produce dissatisfaction . . . and bitter dissension."[27]

Pope's haughty proclamation proved merely the prelude to a barrage of general orders from his headquarters that would rock the conservative military establishment and set a new tenor for the conduct of the war in the East. The first of these, General Order Number Five, issued July 18, directed the Army of Virginia to "subsist upon the country in which their operations are carried on." Officers would superintend the foraging and provide vouchers to local farmers, who would be reimbursed at the war's end upon proving their loyalty during the conflict. Pope supplemented the order with a directive ending McClellan's practice of posting guards over homes and private property.

The second order, General Order Number Seven, was reminiscent of Pope's practices in Missouri. Local civilians were to "be held responsible for any injury done to the track, line, or roads, or for any attacks upon trains or straggling soldiers by bands of guerrillas in their neighborhood." The final order, General Order Number Eleven, called for the arrest of all disloyal male citizens within army lines. Those unwilling to take an oath of allegiance would be "conducted South beyond the extreme pickets of this army." If caught again within Union lines, they would be considered spies and hung. Anyone found violating his oath would be shot and his property seized.[28]

Enlisted men and most regimental officers delighted in the general orders, which went far in restoring the faith in their new commander that his July 14 proclamation had shaken. Lieutenant Colonel Wilder Dwight of the Second Massachusetts was especially pleased. Only weeks before he had complained, "We are the most timid and scrupulous invaders in history, [the] velvet-footed advance" of the army "keeps the men in a state of chronic contempt." The regiment's chaplain, the abolitionist Alonzo Quint, agreed: "Every one feels that we have played at war. War is to destroy, not protect an enemy." Said an Ohio officer, "I am proud to be under the command of a man who understands how to deal with rebels, and who has the grit to do what he thinks is right, notwithstanding the terrible wincing and wriggling of rebel sympathizers in the North and South." And James Gillette of Sigel's staff said Pope's "great orders are objectionable only in so far as they are not literally and completely enforced."[29]

Particularly popular was the order that sanctioned foraging. The men milked local cows dry, slaughtered sheep and swine indiscriminately, and stripped farms of their vegetable crops. Returning from one such expedition, Lieutenant Robert Gould Shaw had only praise for Pope. "Our boys are growing enthusiastic in the prospect of a general who has a little life," said Shaw, who insisted the general orders were "carried out in good faith, and, so far as I know, no abuse has been perpetrated." "The army is enthusiastic in its praises and adorations of our commanding general," agreed an Ohio officer. "He is the man for the times, a man who comprehends the wants of the loyal North, the magnitude and nature of this rebellion, and the best and most speedy way to crush it."[30]

Senior officers responsible for good order and discipline disagreed. Sharing the conservative philosophy of war practiced by McClellan, most deplored war against civilians. Expressing sentiments similar to those of Brigadier General Isaac I. Stevens, on whose staff he served, Captain William Lusk labeled "Pope's orders the last nuisance. We are henceforth to live on the enemy's country. . . . Do you know what the much applauded practice means?" he asked rhetorically. "It means to take the little ewe-lamb—the only property of the laborer—it means to force from the widow the cow which is her only source of sustenance. . . . The last thing needed in our army is the relaxing of the bands of discipline." General Stevens not only ignored the proclamation but punished those who used it to straggle and plunder.

"The resulting effects of these orders were, to license the brutality of our soldiers toward their victims; pillage and arson ceased to be crimes," said Captain James S. Lyon of Franz Sigel's staff. Brigadier General Marsena Patrick concurred: "Our men know every house in the whole country, and they now believe they have a perfect right to rob, tyrannize, threaten and maltreat any one they please. . . . This order of Pope's has demoralized the army and Satan has been let loose. I do not like his orders—they are the orders of a demagogue."

Patrick was wrong in ascribing authorship to Pope. Far from being the mad manifesto of a renegade, Radical general, the general orders were, as the historian John Hennessy observed, "a calculated outgrowth of the Federal government's changing approach to the war . . . made necessary by the failure or, at best, stalemate on the battlefield. The goal: To bring the hard edge of war to the Southern people as a whole."[31]

Nothing better than these general orders demonstrated that John Pope was first and foremost a political weapon wielded by the administration against McClellan and the conservative approach to war-making he personified. Secretary of War Stanton in part had authored and President Lincoln had approved the orders. Three days after they were issued Lincoln brought them before the cabinet, for discussion on the propriety of applying similar measures in all theaters of the war. Correctly deducing that "Lincoln himself probably saw and OK'd the orders," the New York Tribune speculated that Pope's declarations were "the first draft of a declaration of war against the Rebel states," one that would culminate in the Emancipation Proclamation. The Southern press also recognized the political undercurrents at play in Pope's appointment, labeling him a "convenient instrument for the work of villainy and brutality with which [Washington] proposed to resume the active campaign in Virginia."

As one of the few Republican stalwarts in the army high command, Pope was brought east to orchestrate the new policies in Virginia. Unlike Radical generals John C. Frémont or Benjamin Butler, he could be counted on to implement politically charged instructions without exceeding them. Being indebted to Lincoln and Chase, Pope also could be relied upon to take public criticism of them upon himself. That he was also a competent field commander was a decided bonus.[32]

Between the issuance of General Orders Six and Seven there occurred an event that made Pope regret his presence in Virginia more passionately than pride would permit him to reveal, then or later. On July 19, Clara Horton Pope died, aged two months. Family came first for John Pope. He had been content to win his laurels in the West, in the company of generals he liked and men he understood, and close to family and friends. Now he was in command of a patchwork army less than a month old, sniped at by hostile subordinates, lost in sorrow for his dead child, and longing to be with his grieving wife. Duty demanded, however, that he forget all that and make ready to match wits with the South's finest generals, in command of the Confederacy's best army.

Perhaps Pope read the issue of the Pomeroy Weekly Telegraph that told the residents of Clara's home town of the death of her infant daughter. If he did, one cruelly ironic detail could not have escaped his notice. In the column of print opposite the obituary was an editorial reminder that the public expected a soldier to sublimate personal tragedy to the national interest. "It is not to be denied that the eyes of the loyal people are just now directed with interest to General Pope and his proceedings," said the *Telegraph*. "Whether he is the coming man who is to immortalize his name and save the country, remains to be developed. . . . For the sake of our bleeding, betrayed, and almost ruined country, we earnestly pray that he may prove equal to the hour."[33]

— • —

Thomas J. "Stonewall" Jackson, the Confederacy's hero of the hour, was about to sound the depths of Pope's abilities. General Lee had hoped to postpone fighting Pope until after he had dispensed with McClellan, who clung to his supply base on the Peninsula, near the mouth of the James River. But when Pope occupied Culpeper, twenty miles from Gordonsville and the Virginia Central Railroad, Lee was compelled to act to preserve his communications with the Shenandoah Valley. Keeping most of his army near Richmond to confront McClellan, on July 13 Lee sent Jackson with two divisions to Gordonsville to check Pope.

Jackson reached Gordonsville on July 19. His presence, and the bungling of Brigadier General John Hatch, who disregarded Pope's orders that he move rapidly on Gordonsville, foiled Pope's first attempt at wrecking the Virginia Central Railroad. When Hatch failed again three days later, Pope replaced him with Brigadier General John Buford. The only command appointment Pope was to make, it proved a most fortunate choice, as Buford's sterling service at Gettysburg was to demonstrate.[34]

McClellan's torpor allowed Lee to reinforce Jackson with a third division under Ambrose Powell Hill. No specific instructions came with the additional troops, only a brusque admonition that Jackson "suppress" Pope.

Apart from the threat the Army of Virginia posed to his communications, Lee had personal reasons for wanting Pope eliminated. Like nearly everyone in the South, Lee found Pope's general orders reprehensible, the brainchild of an uncivilized brute. And the presence of his nephew, Colonel Louis Marshall, on Pope's staff was cause for chagrin. "I could forgive [him] fighting against us," Lee told his daughter, "if he had not joined such a miscreant as Pope."[35]

The arrival of Hill at Gordonsville on July 29 coincided with Pope's departure from Washington to join the Army of Virginia. Henry Halleck had been installed as general-in-chief with a mandate so vague that Pope left for the front assuming "Old Brains" would take field command of his and McClellan's armies when the two were united. But Halleck had no such intention. He accommodated Pope's wishes only insofar as he ordered McClellan to abandon the Peninsula and unite the Army of the Potomac with the Army of Virginia. What would happen then, and who would command, was left uncertain.

Halleck intended for McClellan to disembark his troops at Aquia Landing and the armies to meet along the Rappahannock River, north of Gordonsville. Until the Army of the Potomac arrived, Pope was to keep a strong front along the Rapidan and Rappahannock Rivers and maintain communications with elements of Major General Ambrose Burnside's corps at Fredericksburg.

The objectives of Pope's campaign were limited. They were, said Pope, "to cover the approaches to Washington from any enemy advancing from the direction of Richmond, and to oppose and delay its advance to the last extremity so as to give all the time possible for the withdrawal of the army of the Potomac from the James River." If the enemy did not move north, he was "to operate on their lines of communication with Gordonsville and Charlottesville, so as to force Lee to make heavy detachments from his force at Richmond and facilitate to that extent the withdrawal of the Army of the Potomac."[36]

Pope would describe his journey from Washington to the front in bucolic terms, suggesting an aspect of quiet confidence. But inwardly, Pope was in turmoil. His carefully constructed facade of self-assuredness, built upon bluster and boasting, had cracked under the lesser pressures of the Island No. 10 campaign; with the personal tragedy of his daughter's death and the strain of a field command that brought him up against the South's best, it collapsed.

David Hunter Strother, a Virginian, a journalist of national renown, and a skilled topographer who joined Pope's staff in early July, recorded Pope's changing demeanor in his diary. Pope had impressed Strother when they first met at Willard's Hotel on June 30. "He is a stout man of medium height, [of] prepossessing manners and appearance," observed the Virginian. And the following day, as Strother watched Pope discuss strategy and generalship: "He reads character and talks like a keen, cool man of the world, kindly withal. Pope is a much cleverer man than I at first took him for." But on August 2, three days after Pope took to the field, Strother found him dramatically changed. "General [Henry] Prince says he never saw Pope in such a jaded and irascible condition as he is now." Strother, whom Pope had upbraided over a minor topographical error, agreed: "His whole deportment is different entirely from when I first met him."[37]

That Pope had cause to feel overused was abundantly clear to Major General Philip Kearny, a savage fighter who chafed under the yoke of McClellan's inactivity. "How do they expect Pope," he wrote on August 4, "to beat, with a very inferior force, the veterans of Ewell and Jackson? Get me and my fighting division with Pope. . . . With Pope's army I would breathe again."[38]

Pope certainly faced a foe superior in morale, leadership at all levels, and discipline. But numerically he enjoyed a distinct advantage. The Army of Virginia numbered between 48,000 and 52,000 men present, nearly 20,000 more than Jackson mustered. Pope's army was badly scattered between Culpeper and the

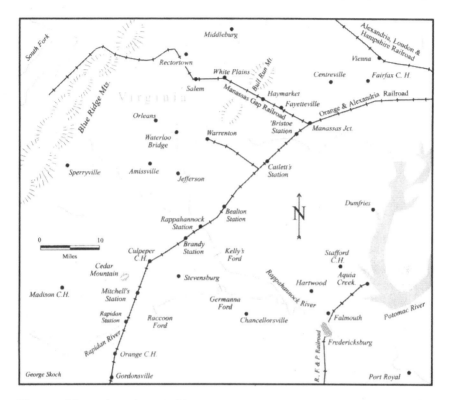

Theater of Operations, August 1862

Blue Ridge Mountains, however, while Jackson had his three divisions well in hand. Learning of Pope's predicament on August 7, Jackson struck north from Gordonsville.[39]

Pope was at Sperryville on August 7, inspecting Sigel's corps. Banks's corps was strung out on the march, between Sperryville and Culpeper. During the day, scouts brought Pope word of Jackson's march toward the Rapidan River. Returning to Culpeper at 10:00 the next morning, Pope found only Samuel W. Crawford's brigade of Banks's corps and James B. Ricketts's division of McDowell's corps. Jackson was coming, but from what direction and in what strength was unclear. Bayard's cavalry brigade, which was falling back on Culpeper, reported the enemy to be advancing in force along the Orange and Alexandria Railroad. Buford's command, posted further to the west, reported a heavy Rebel column marching on Madison Court House. In view of Halleck's instructions that he interpose his army between the enemy and the lower Rappahannock, Pope decided to concentrate at Culpeper. To help Bayard develop the strength and intentions of the enemy, Pope sent Crawford forward to Cedar Mountain, a commanding elevation six miles southwest of Culpeper, shortly after noon on August 8. He ordered Banks to bring the remainder of his corps to Culpeper; similar instructions went to Sigel.[40]

Pope was "self-confident and clearheaded" that day, said Strother, who watched him closely. He dined heartily with McDowell and their staffs. But by nightfall Jackson's proximity and Sigel's apparent ineptitude had reduced him to sharp-tongued irascibility. Despite high temperatures and oppressive humidity, Banks marched his men into Culpeper before midnight. Sigel, however, never got started. Pope received a message from the German, dated 6:50 P.M., inquiring by which road he should march from Sperryville. "As there was but one road between those two points [a macadamized turnpike]," noted Pope, "I was at a loss to understand how General Sigel could entertain any doubt as to the road by which he should march." Pope first dictated a harsh dispatch to the German peppered with obscenities, but his better judgment prevailed. Anxious to "keep his relations with his corps commanders as harmonious as possible," he softened the language to a simple admonition that Sigel "march direct to Culpeper Court House by the turnpike."

Pope had counted on the presence of Sigel that evening, presumably to throw at least a portion of his corps forward to cover the river crossing near Madison Court House. But it was mid-afternoon on August 9 before Sigel reached Culpeper. His troops arrived exhausted and hungry; despite explicit orders to the contrary, they had come without rations. Any remaining respect Pope may have had for Sigel undoubtedly vanished that day.[41]

Pope's instructions to Sigel for August 9 were unequivocal; those to Banks, ambiguous at best. On the morning of the ninth, Pope sent Banks forward with the remainder of his corps to join Crawford at Cedar Mountain. In his official report, Pope said he intended that Banks take up a strong position beside Crawford, in order to "check the advance of the enemy, and to determine his forces and the character of his movements as far as practicable." Before the Joint Congressional Committee on the Conduct of the War, Pope grew more specific: "I directed [Banks] when he went forward from Culpeper Court House, if the enemy advanced to attack him on the strong position which I had instructed him to take up, that he should push his skirmishers well to the front and notify me immediately." In the *National Tribune,* Pope expanded further on his plans, saying he meant to reinforce Banks with Ricketts's division, which was posted three miles behind Banks, and with Sigel as soon as he came up. In the meantime, Banks was to hold at all costs.[42]

Pope dispatched Colonel Marshall to give General Banks his orders. If Pope wished Banks to act as he later alleged, he did not make clear his intentions to Colonel Marshall. Banks and his adjutant general, Lieutenant Colonel Louis H.

Pelouze, said Marshall told Banks "to move to the front immediately, assume command of all the forces in the front, deploy his skirmishers if the enemy approaches, and attack him immediately as soon as he approaches, and be reinforced from here."

Marshall challenged Banks's and Pelouze's claim, insisting the exact language he used to Banks was as follows: "The general commanding directs that you move to the front and take up a strong position near the position held by General Crawford's brigade; that you will not attack the enemy unless it becomes evident the enemy will attack you; then, in order to hold the advantage of being the attacking party, you will attack with your skirmishers well to the front." Marshall understood that Pope wished Banks to hold the enemy in check without bringing on a general engagement until the remainder of the army came up and to attack with his skirmishers only.[43]

To attack with skirmishers alone was unorthodox, if not foolish. All Banks could hope to accomplish in sending one-tenth of his command to certain death or capture was to check the enemy's skirmish line a few moments, until the Confederate main body came up. Banks should have known this, if Pope did not. Lieutenant Colonel Thomas C. H. Smith, an obsequious staff officer who considered Pope a military genius without peer, later excoriated Banks for not sending one-third of his force out as skirmishers to develop the Rebel position. But standard doctrine called for just one company in ten to man the skirmish line. Meant as a defense of Pope's order, Smith's criticism revealed merely his overweening desire to protect his chief.

A much more convincing defense of Pope was made by Brigadier General George H. Gordon, who had no special love for either Pope or Banks. "There can be no doubt that [Pope] did not authorize or expect [Banks's corps] to attack, single-handed, the whole of Jackson's army," he told survivors of the Second Massachusetts eleven years after the war. And did Pope communicate his intentions clearly to Banks? Without question he did, concluded Gordon.

Pope's single error was to entrust oral orders to a staff officer with a hazy memory, rather than reduce them to writing. It was an oversight hard to pardon, as Pope's staff to date had proven notoriously unreliable. The month before, Chief of Staff George D. Ruggles had wrongly castigated Banks for missing a movement. When Banks confronted him with the facts, Ruggles blamed staff bungling for his error: "The retained copy of the dispatch is not in my handwriting, and there may have been a mistake in copying the original," said Ruggles. "I can only account for such carelessness on account of the hurry and confusion of organizing my office for an early departure to the field." To a similarly unfair rebuke, General Schenck retorted, "I am not a little astonished at the contents and tone of your telegram . . . and I ask for the fullest and strictest inquiry into my conduct." Nor did Pope and Ruggles get along particularly well, often squabbling over trivia. The petulant General Patrick expected no better, as Pope had scraped together a staff of "boot licks, toadies, politicians, and rowdies who are anything but soldiers."[44]

But any doubt as to the meaning of the order Marshall conveyed probably was cleared up an hour after it was delivered, when Banks left the head of his march column to visit Pope's headquarters in Culpeper. In congressional testimony three years after the events, when neither Pope nor his staff was present to refute him, Banks insisted no mention was made of the orders Marshall had carried; Pope merely said, "I have sent an officer acquainted with the country who will designate the ground you are to hold, and will give you any instructions he may deem necessary." That neither Pope nor Banks would have brought up the 9:45 A.M. order is hard to conceive; more credible is Pope's own testimony, given before the Irvin McDowell court of inquiry in late 1862. "On the morning of August 9, in a personal interview at my headquarters at Culpeper, I gave Banks instructions," Pope said. "I told him if the enemy advanced to attack him, he should push his skirmishers well to the front, and notify me immediately, it being my wish to gain all the time possible to concentrate our forces at Culpeper Court House."[45]

The officer Pope sent forward to assist Banks was Brigadier General Benjamin S. Roberts, his inspector general and chief of cavalry. A fifty-one-year-old Regular officer of mediocre ability and elastic scruples, Roberts would prove most useful as a uniformed cat's-paw for Secretary Stanton and congressional Radicals. What he told Banks this day is uncertain. Having been over the ground two days before, Roberts was able to point out to Banks the most defensible terrain, which he did. But Banks had no intention of waiting to be attacked, said Roberts. After a two-hour-long, desultory artillery duel in which the Federals were notably worsted, Banks decided to attack alone. Few Rebel infantry were visible, so Banks concluded he could take the enemy guns easily. Roberts said he tried to dissuade Banks: "I was convinced that the batteries . . . were supported by heavy forces of infantry massed in the woods. He expressed a different opinion. He told me he believed he could carry the field."

Not surprisingly, Banks told a different story. Far from restraining him, Banks said, Roberts had shamed him into attacking. In a mocking tone, Roberts declared repeatedly during the artillery duel, "There must be no backing out this day." Roberts's barb mortified Banks. "I made no reply to him at all, but I felt it keenly, because I knew that my command did not want to back out; we had backed out enough." At 5:00 P.M., Banks threw Brigadier General Christopher C. Augur's division against the Rebel cannon.[46]

In Banks's confession is the one certain kernel of truth to the controversy.

Having been bested repeatedly by Jackson in the Shenandoah Valley, Banks undoubtedly felt compelled to prove himself to a commander who had "only seen the backs of his enemies," and who believed "the strongest position was that from which the soldier could most easily advance upon the enemy." Failing to dissuade Banks, at 4:30 P.M. Roberts scribbled Pope a note, "telling him that a general battle would be fought before night, and that it was of the utmost importance that General McDowell's corps should be at once sent to the field."

That Pope did not mean for Banks to bring on a battle was also evident from Pope's demeanor. During much of the afternoon, said a quartermaster officer who happened to be nearby, Pope lay in the grass "smoking a cigar with as much sangfroid as if the country was at peace." Beside him sat McDowell, contemplating the ground. A member of Sigel's staff encountered Pope "domiciled in a comfortable mansion, lolling on this hot August morning in a rocking-chair, smoking a very fragrant Havana—General McDowell keeping him company."

Roberts's note brought Pope and McDowell at once to their feet. Minutes later, they and Pope's picaresque cortege were galloping toward the front. Shortly after 5:00 P.M., the generals were stunned by a sudden thunder from the direction of Cedar Mountain. Rattling volleys of musketry, mingled with the deep pounding of cannon, confirmed Roberts's fears. When Pope and McDowell reached the battlefield at sunset, said Colonel Strother, "the roughly handled brigades and batteries of Banks' divisions were slowly retiring." Pope found Banks, attended by a single aide, on a gentle ridge, beyond which was a forest from which "large numbers of disorganized troops were emerging."[47]

"What does this mean, General Banks? Those troops are in retreat," bellowed Pope. To his own staff, he shouted, "Ride in here, gentlemen, a dozen of you—rally these men." Then, the general who condemned retreat made his first battlefield decision, "selecting a position to take in case Banks should be forced back." George Gordon rode up a moment later, furious his brigade had been slaughtered for no apparent purpose. "General, this battle should not have been fought, sir," he growled. "I never ordered it fought," rejoined Pope. Gordon cast a glance at Banks, who stood beside Pope. To Pope's response "Banks made no reply, no retort or remonstrance."[48]

The throng of soldiers that had prompted Pope's rhetorical question to Banks was a shattered fragment of the eight thousand men Banks had thrown against Jackson's seventeen thousand. Nearly a third of his corps fell before the battle sputtered out at dusk.

As the moon rose and the brigades of Ricketts's division arrived on the field, Pope shepherded them into position along the ridge to the right of his headquarters entourage. They were to replace the exhausted survivors of Banks's right-flank units, which Pope ordered consolidated on the center. Cheering Pope as they came on the field, Ricketts's infantrymen attracted the attention of William Pegram's Virginia Battery, which opened fire on the ridge. Colonel Strother, who happened to be reclining in the grass, watched as a half-dozen shells, "hissing, screaming, and bursting," scattered fragments "in nervous contiguity, some striking within ten feet of where I lay." Unfamiliar with the ground and disoriented in the darkness, Pope assumed the battery to be friendly, and he at once dispatched a staff officer to silence it. Pope himself retired from the exposed brow and with his staff sat down to watch the remaining pyrotechnics. The unfortunate staff officer drew rein before the barrels of Pegram's battery, but he had the presence of mind to bark out an order to cease firing. In the darkness his identity remained a secret. The Confederates obeyed and drew off their cannon, and the field fell silent. "When it was over," recalled Strother, "I felt relieved and observed the party generally more excited and cheerful than during the operation."[49]

No sooner had they resumed their places on the ridge than a regiment of Virginia cavalry under Colonel William E. "Grumble" Jones trotted out of the forest to their left, which Pope had assumed to be picketed by friendly infantry. He and most of his staff, along with Generals Banks, Gordon, and Alpheus Williams, were resting in the grass when they noticed the Southern troopers, just forty yards away. The Rebels paused to size up their foe, which Jones thought merely a small body of Yankee cavalry, then charged full tilt, yelling and pouring a volley of carbine and pistol fire on the headquarters assemblage and toppling two members of Pope's escort. "We mounted in hot haste," said Strother. Despite the danger, General Williams found the spectacle of the commanding general and his retinue scrambling for their horses hilarious. As they ran, "bullets hissed through the bushes, sparkled in the darkness as they struck the flinty road, or singing through the tree-tops, covered Pope and his officers with leaves and twigs." Banks went down, kicked in the hip by a wounded horse. Colonel Ruggles lost his mount when a nearby Federal regiment fired blindly into the group. General Pope "stuck his head down, and, striking spur, led off at full speed," said Colonel Strother, who watched the flight of half a dozen staff officers interrupted by a rail fence: "They rushed on without checking and some half dozen of them crashed together on the fence, broke it down, and tumbled one upon another." Regrouping two hundred yards farther to the rear, the Yankees stopped "to count noses." Among the missing was General Pope. "I thought for a while that Pope was killed or taken and the game was up," said Strother, who found Pope sometime after midnight, sitting on a pile of fence rails with Banks, McDowell, and Sigel.[50]

The next day, Colonel Strother again happened upon Generals Pope and McDowell. The two were sitting on some boxes under an apple tree, near a large mansion that served as their headquarters and as a hospital, watching a burial detail. As a pair of soldiers lifted the dead man onto a litter, Pope remarked, "Well, there seems to be devilish little that is attractive about the life of a private soldier." To which McDowell replied, "You might say, General, very little that is attractive in any grade of a soldier's life."[51]

Certainly Pope's life had become less agreeable. Jackson withdrew across the Rapidan on August 11, leaving Pope the victor of sorts in a battle even ardent Republican newspapers could call only drawn at best. But Pope was shaken. The bold promises of his earlier dispatches were gone, replaced by hesitation and doubt. The day after Cedar Mountain, Pope told Halleck the enemy was "in very superior force and endeavoring to interpose between me and Fredericksburg. I will do the best I can, and if forced to retire will do so by way of Rappahannock Crossing." Also on August 11, Pope implored Halleck to "please make McClellan do something to prevent reinforcements being sent here."[52]

Halleck also was troubled. Cedar Mountain demonstrated that Lee would not wait idly for the two Federal armies to unite, and McClellan had shown little inclination to move. Instead, McClellan insisted Halleck permit him to remain on the Peninsula. Halleck had countered on August 6 with a long epistle explaining why McClellan must move. After Cedar Mountain, he pelted McClellan with dispatches urging haste and told Pope his "main object should be to keep the enemy in check till we can get reinforcements to your army." Wisely discarding the plan to lay off the enemy's flank from the Blue Ridge he had trumpeted before Congress in July, Pope agreed to take up a strong blocking position along the Rapidan, with the hope the Army of the Potomac would arrive before Lee joined Jackson.[53]

6 The Enemy's Purpose Is Not Easy to Discover

Pope and Halleck had surrendered the initiative to Robert E. Lee, who was quick to accept it. Determined to crush Pope before McClellan joined him, on August 13 Lee directed Lieutenant General James Longstreet to start his corps for Gordonsville. Once united, the Army of Northern Virginia would cross the Rapidan River on August 18 to attack Pope and wedge its way between Pope's left and Fredericksburg, where Pope expected Federal reinforcements to arrive.[1]

While Pope waited, morale plummeted. The apparent timidity of its commanding general played a part in dampening the army's ardor. A misplaced belief that they had been "needlessly sacrificed" at Cedar Mountain because McDowell had refused to support them estranged the officers and men of Banks's corps from Pope and his despised lieutenant. The soldiers of Sigel's corps also were down on Pope for having slandered them. Exasperated by their absence from the Battle of Cedar Mountain, Pope reputedly had snarled, "They must march, because they will not fight unless they are tired and cannot run." Particularly deleterious was Pope's liberal foraging policy. Taken by many as "a general license to pillage, rob, and plunder," General Order Number Five demoralized whole regiments. After watching the Twenty-first New York steal horses and loot homes, General Patrick was "so utterly disgusted that I [felt] like resigning and letting the whole thing go. There has never been such a state of things before, in any command."[2]

Reluctantly, Pope agreed. He had never intended his orders to be a license to plunder and had himself on numerous occasions shown great kindness toward the residents of northern Virginia. On August 14, Pope issued a general order expressing his "great dissatisfaction that General Order Number Five has either been entirely misinterpreted or grossly abused" and threatening to punish severely anyone caught pillaging.[3]

General Patrick was pleased with the "most stringent character" of the order, but for the men in ranks it merely fed the grumbling that empty stomachs occasioned. Foraging had been poor in any case—roasted corn and potatoes were all there was to be had—and after Cedar Mountain regular issues of rations stopped suddenly. Pope tried to blame the railroads, but the fault was his. Over General McDowell's strenuous objections, upon assuming command Pope had dismissed Colonel Herman Haupt, the talented superintendent of army railroads in northern Virginia, thinking his services unnecessary. Railroad operations fast deteriorated. By mid-August, traffic on the Orange and Alexandria Railroad, the army's lifeline, had ground to a halt. Pope confessed his error and begged Haupt to return at once.[4]

Yet another grave problem was the sorry state of the cavalry. Wisely ending McClellan's practice of using the cavalry parsimoniously, Pope had consolidated the mounted arm into three brigades, one brigade being assigned to each infantry corps. But better organization did not immediately yield greater efficiency. Pope had inherited cavalry nearly used up by hard service in the Shenandoah Valley and hampered by a lack of equipment. Little had changed since George Bayard declared his brigade unfit for duty at the end of June. Men and horses were better rested, but horseshoes, wagon wheels, boots, haversacks, and canteens were all wanting, and forage was poor. Pope would contribute to the problem, pushing his cavalry harder than they were accustomed in the coming days.

The cavalry performed one truly worthy act before succumbing. Although Pope's administrative grasp over the army had grown uncertain, his tactical sense remained sharp. He recognized the vulnerability of his left flank, a critical concern because of Halleck's insistence he keep connected with Fredericksburg until all of Ambrose Burnside's corps from North Carolina (two divisions under Jesse Reno already had joined the Army of Virginia) and McClellan's troops from the Peninsula had disembarked at Aquia Creek. Wary of a Rebel turning movement, Pope sent two regiments of Buford's brigade splashing across the Rapidan on August 17 toward Louisa Court House to gather intelligence.[5]

The Federal troopers did well, capturing a staff officer carrying an order from Lee to Major General J. E. B. Stuart detailing the plan for attacking Pope's left, which had been delayed two days, and also nearly bagging Stuart himself. However, their efforts paled beside that of Thomas O. Halter, a former trooper in the First Indiana Cavalry. Franz Sigel had detailed him for espionage detail in late July, in response to Pope's demand for better intelligence on the enemy. Falling in with Longstreet's corps during its march to Gordonsville, Halter mingled freely with the garrulous Southerners. He slipped away on the morning of April 18, swam the Rapidan, and delivered to Pope word of Confederate intentions. Later that morning, a second spy returned with corroborating information.[6]

Colonel Haupt was at army headquarters when Pope learned from Halter of Lee's program for his destruction. The general had ridden off to review a corps, said Haupt, "but returned in haste in about an hour with the information that the enemy was in full force in front and advancing rapidly." Invoking the same hyperbole of which he accused McClellan, Pope announced Lee was coming with an army of 150,000 (Lee actually had 55,000 men, roughly the strength of Pope's command). Pope begged Haupt to help remove the army stores from Culpeper and ordered a retreat to the north bank of the Rappahannock, between Rappahannock Station and Kelly's Ford, a prudent move that placed him on the same side of the river as Burnside at Fredericksburg.[7]

A traffic snarl in Culpeper, upon which the corps of both Sigel and McDowell converged, disrupted Pope's timetable. Swearing like "a Mississippi stevedore," he spent the night personally sorting out jumbled wagon trains until, on the morning of August 19, the congestion eased and the army resumed its march. Pope was furious with one and all, but he reserved his special rage for the men of Sigel's corps, whom he greeted "by a salutation of profanity," said a member of Sigel's staff, of a style wholly unbecoming a major general. By midnight, most of the Army of Virginia was over the Rappahannock.

Endorsing Pope's decision to retire behind the river, Halleck on August 18 also enjoined him to "stand firm on that line until I can help you. Fight hard, and aid will soon come." Three days later, Halleck repeated himself: "Dispute every inch of ground, and fight like the devil, till we can reinforce you. Forty-eight hours more and we can make you strong enough. Don't yield an inch if you can help it."[8]

Although he wanted to fall back farther north to meet reinforcements, dutifully Pope spread out his army to defend the crossings of the Rappahannock, setting up his headquarters tent at Rappahannock Station, a short distance from the river. Again Pope anticipated Lee's actions correctly. He expected Lee would sidle upstream, cross the river beyond the Union right at Sulphur Springs, and march on Warrenton. Pope's orders to keep contact with Fredericksburg prevented him from extending his lines indefinitely to block Lee; instead, he assured Halleck on August 20, he would pounce on the Rebel flank and rear when able.

For the next two days, Pope matched Lee's northward movements, savagely repelling Confederate probes of crossing sites. When on August 22 he learned Stonewall Jackson had forded the river at Sulphur Springs, Pope recognized that a critical moment had arrived. He informed Halleck of his predicament and offered him two options for countering the Confederate movements: "My rear is entirely exposed if I move toward Sulphur Springs or Warrenton. I must do one of two things—either fall back and meet [Major General Samuel P.] Heintzelman behind Cedar Run [near Catlett's Station], or cross the Rappahannock with my whole force and assail the enemy's flank and rear. I must do one or the other at daylight. Which shall it be? I incline to the latter." With rare decisiveness, Halleck approved the latter course.[9]

Pope's plan had much to recommend it. Two undefended crossing sites, Kelly's Ford and Norman's Ford, offered ready access to the Rebel right and rear, and at a third, Rappahannock Station, the Federals already had a lodgment on the far bank. But Pope never had the chance to effect his plan. Sudden torrential rains swept away bridges and made the fords impassable, putting an end to the designs of both commanders for crossing the river.[10]

By opting to remain on the Rappahannock, Pope had left vulnerable his supply line, the Orange and Alexandria. Vast stores accumulated at Manassas Junction and the army's baggage train parked at Catlett's Station were only lightly guarded, and the railroad bridge over Cedar Run might be destroyed easily. Pope understood the danger but responded too late. On the night of August 22, he asked Halleck to send a brigade from Washington to protect the bridge and ordered McDowell to detach two cavalry regiments to guard the trains. But at that moment, "Jeb" Stuart's Confederate cavalry was plundering them. Pitch-black darkness and heavy rains kept Stuart from accomplishing "the great object of the expedition," the burning of the Cub Run bridge. Lee consequently credited the raid with achieving only minor advantages, and Pope dismissed the damage done as trifling.

But if the material loss was small, the injury to already weakened Federal morale was grievous. Officers and men not privy to the tactical imperatives of the withdrawal to the Rappahannock had delighted in the irony of Pope being forced to show the enemy *his* back. Said Robert Milroy, a brigade commander in Sigel's corps, "Our miserable humbug bag of gas General Pope, who said he was from the West where our armies never showed their backs and the enemy always showed theirs, in this—our first 'fall back' or retreat—made us show our backs to the rebels." Milroy and others saw in Stuart's raid confirmation of the commanding general's supposed incompetence. Said a Massachusetts soldier, "The repugnance which the army felt toward General Pope gave rise to expressions of glee at his probable discomfiture when it heard of this raid." General Patrick concurred, "This morning it is said that there was a big darky dressed up in Pope's captured clothes and paraded through the streets. [Pope] seems to be universally detested by the citizens and our troops are loud in their expressions of disgust." Perhaps the most vulgar indictment of Pope came from Samuel Sturgis, the heavy-drinking commander of a brigade in Cox's Kanawah Division, after Sturgis had appropriated a train bound for the front from Alexandria. Colonel Haupt interceded, explaining that Sturgis's actions would delay reinforcements from reaching Pope. To which Sturgis slurred, "I don't care for John Pope one pinch of owl dung!"[11]

Pope still had confidence in himself, but his judgment had become suspect. Quick to dismiss Stuart's raid as inconsequential, he neglected to consider its value as an augury. As Colonel Thomas Livermore later wrote, "Although Pope's indifference to [Stuart's raid] was creditable to his nerve, he perhaps was to blame in not recognizing it as the precursor of Jackson's coming." Nor did Pope grasp fully the danger poised by Lee's sidling movements along the Rappahannock. On the afternoon of Stuart's raid, the ubiquitous Colonel Haupt encountered General Pope sitting on a hilltop above the Orange and Alexandria Railroad. He listened as numerous reports of enemy movements up the river came to Pope. Fearing a flank march, Haupt asked Pope how far upriver he had his scouts. The distance Pope named was short, leading Haupt to ask, "Is that far enough? What is to prevent the enemy from going even as far as Thoroughfare Gap and getting behind you?" Pope dismissed his concerns. Haupt thought better than to press the point, but he left "feeling uneasy."[12]

Colonel Haupt had read the enemy's intentions correctly. Stymied by Pope at every step of his flank march up the Rappahannock, on the afternoon of August 24 Lee decided on a bold move. That day the two armies were ranged opposite one another from the Rappahannock Station to Waterloo Bridge in an uneasy stalemate partly occasioned by the rapid rise in the Rappahannock River. Pope had removed his headquarters to the Warren Green Hotel in Warrenton, there better to orchestrate a concentration of his forces at Sulphur Springs, where he erroneously believed Jubal Early's brigade of Jackson's corps, which had been stranded on the Federal side of the river by the heavy rains two days earlier, lay awaiting its destruction. But Jackson had extricated Early, and his reunited corps held the left of the Confederate line near Jeffersonton. Longstreet occupied the right between Freeman's Ford and Rappahannock Station.

Lee called upon Jackson to march his corps, twenty-four thousand strong, from Jeffersonton in a wide arc around the Union right, crossing the Rappahannock well beyond the Federal flank and marching rapidly north to Salem. From Salem, Jackson was to turn to the southeast, pass through Thoroughfare Gap into Pope's rear, and then disrupt the Federal line of supply along the Orange and

Alexandria Railroad between Bristoe Station and Manassas Junction. Until Jackson completed his mission, Longstreet was to distract Pope with bold demonstrations along the Rappahannock, then try to join Jackson by forced march. Lee's objective was to compel Pope to fall back on Washington.[13]

Jackson set off long before dawn on August 25. Prompt action by Pope almost certainly would have spoiled the end of his corps; instead, poor intelligence and vague rumors, distracting and inappropriate admonitions from Halleck, the need to make contact with reinforcements moving upriver from Fredericksburg, Pope's own muddled thinking, and the sheer audacity of Lee's plan combined to give Jackson forty-eight hours in which to march unimpeded into the rear of Pope's army.

Not that Pope was unaware of Jackson's departure from his front. At 9:30 A.M. on the twenty-fifth, Banks's aide-de-camp, Colonel John S. Clark, reported from the Waterloo Bridge signal station having seen four batteries and six to eight regiments marching hard toward Amissville. An hour earlier, McDowell's signal officer had detected Longstreet's corps moving northward to take Jackson's place opposite Sulphur Springs. Where Pope erred was in assuming Jackson's destination to be the Shenandoah Valley, rather than Pope's flank or rear.[14]

Historians have criticized Pope harshly for assuming Jackson had gone off for a second campaign in the valley. But Pope's deduction was not based merely on wishful thinking, nor was it a view he alone held. The previous morning, Brigadier General Julius White, commanding the Federal garrison at Winchester, had reported Rebel cavalry, which he believed part of Jackson's old command, marauding in his district. "This may be nothing more than a raid of bushwhackers or may indicate movements of the enemy down the valley," said White. "I give you the facts, whatever they are worth." They were worth enough to cause Halleck to instruct Pope to "ascertain, if possible, if the enemy is not moving into the Shenandoah Valley." Banks also was misled. In forwarding Colonel Clark's report, he told Pope, "It seems to be apparent that the enemy is threatening or moving upon the valley of the Shenandoah via Front Royal, with designs upon the Potomac, possibly beyond."[15]

Pope also has been condemned for doing nothing on August 25 to follow Jackson; for clinging obstinately to his Rappahannock line rather than starting his army northward. In holding fast, however, Pope believed he was complying with the wishes of Halleck, whom he not unreasonably presumed to be orchestrating the junction of the armies of Virginia and the Potomac according to some well-conceived strategic plan, rather than plodding along blindly, as Halleck was. Halleck had ordered him repeatedly to stay put and "dispute every inch of ground, and fight like the devil till we can reinforce you." When he approved Pope's movement orders for August 25, by which Pope intended to extend his line southward along the river toward Kelly's Ford to meet expected reinforcements from Burnside, rather than cut loose to chase Jackson, Halleck told him to "expect orders to recross the Rappahannock and resume the offensive in a few days."[16]

Where Pope may be open to censure is in not using his cavalry to probe for Jackson. Pope had demonstrated during the Corinth campaign and in his first days in Virginia that he understood better than most commanders how to deploy cavalry effectively beyond the army's lines. During his stay along the Rappahannock, however, he not only held the cavalry close at hand, picketing flanks and screening for the infantry, but also seems to have delegated responsibility for his two mounted brigades to General McDowell.

That the cavalry was in condition to do more is debatable. For reasons not entirely clear, the brigades of Bayard and Buford were near collapse. Buford sent scouts out toward Salem on the night of August 25 but confessed to McDowell, "If the enemy advances I can do very little. My command is almost disorganized." Colonel Alfred Duffie, commander of the First Rhode Island Cavalry, begged McDowell to allow him to go into camp, as his horses and men were worn out by "hard duties."[17]

The Yankee troopers had been worked hard, but no harder than on any other active campaign, and certainly less strenuously than their Confederate counterparts. (George Bayard later complained his brigade had been "overtasked"; a more valid explanation might have been that Federal cavalry in the East had been grossly undertasked before Pope's arrival.) What apparently did in Pope's cavalry was a lack of subsistence for man and beast. The country was barren and wells were few; the men ate green apples and unripened corn and drank muddy water, while the horses starved. Although many mounted regiments had lost contact with their trains, closer proximity would have availed them little. The problem was at the source. Herman Haupt had been straining to keep railroad trains running, but the obstacles were many. The road was a single track, and engines and cars were at a premium. Samuel Sturgis's drunken meddling closed the road for twenty-four hours. The inability of Pope's quartermaster staff to return empty trains promptly and the priority given troops rather than supplies on the cars for a time reduced to a trickle the forward flow of material. Haupt resumed regular shipments on the morning of August 25, but when he applied for forage, he found the quartermaster general's office had run out of grain.[18]

The infantry also was hungry. Recalled an officer of the Second Massachusetts, "Wagon trains had been sent to the rear. Consequently there was no regular issue of rations, and three days' issue was made to last for ten days." The colonel of the Tenth Maine allowed his men to forage freely, but "there was nothing to find but the leavings of other regiments." So the men plodded along, up and down the east bank of the Rappahannock, "damning everybody, from Pope down to our cooks, who were eating up our rations in the wagons while we starved."[19]

Had they had faith in their commanding general, the men might have borne their hunger better. But the incessant marching along the Rappahannock to no imaginable end eroded confidence in the upstart western general, who contrary to the bold promises of his July manifesto had turned his back to the enemy and quit the Rapidan with scarcely a shot fired. Complained a Maine soldier, "The men are terribly jaded, literally half-starved and in great want of meat. We are dirty, and are becoming lousy again." Subordinate commanders also were discouraged. Said the ever-critical General Patrick, "I feel that disgrace here is inevitable. This is the state of things—no order—no system—all is confusion."[20]

Certainly Franz Sigel agreed. On August 25 he was subjected to a string of orders from army headquarters so perplexing, contradictory, and seemingly capricious that he asked Pope to relieve him from command. In his original movement orders for the day, Pope had intended for Sigel to shift his corps southeastward from Waterloo Bridge and Sulphur Springs to Fayetteville. But news of Jackson's flank march caused Pope to countermand the order at noon; rather than withdraw, Sigel was told to hold firm "under all circumstances and meet the enemy if he should try to force the passage of the river." Longstreet's display on the far bank, meant to cover Jackson's departure, convinced Sigel he was about to be attacked, and at midday he asked for help from Reno and Banks, whom he thought were drawn up behind his left. Instead he found they had marched south in compliance with Pope's earlier orders. Neither were there troops on his right. Only then did Sigel receive his copy of the morning movement order. Loathe to abandon the river with the enemy threatening, Sigel searched vainly for someone to clarify matters for him. Left to his own devices, Sigel set fire to Waterloo Bridge and with deep misgivings set out for Fayetteville at dusk.

No sooner had he started than a courier from Pope brought a new order: He was to march to Warrenton. Sigel complied, only to be handed another note from Pope as his corps trudged into Warrenton at 2:00 A.M. on August 26. Sigel was to return to Waterloo Bridge and "force a passage of the river" at daylight and "see what is in front of you." After telling Sigel he thought the entire Rebel army had marched away to the northwest, Pope lashed out at the German, "I am not satisfied with your reports or your operations of today, and expect to hear tomorrow early something more satisfactory concerning the enemy." Sigel rode to headquarters to remonstrate; he had obeyed every order as received, but his men were too exhausted to march back to Waterloo Bridge. A staff officer listened as Pope berated Sigel in "such offensive language that Sigel asked to be relieved." Jesse Reno and Pope's staff intervened, and Pope relented. He permitted Sigel's corps to remain in Warrenton, but his anger with its commander simmered. "McDowell's is the only corps that is at all reliable that I have," he informed Halleck on the night of August 25. "Sigel, as you know, is perfectly unreliable, and I suggest that some officer of superior rank be sent to command his army corps.

Sigel's corps, although composed of some of the best fighting material we have, will never do much service under that officer."[21]

That Pope would call for the dismissal of a key subordinate in the midst of a campaign was incredible, the more so as his criticism of Sigel's performance was in this instance unwarranted. His nighttime tirade was the second indication Halleck had of a disturbing turn in Pope's state of mind. That morning, upon reading Halleck's simple if misguided admonition that he be ready to take the offensive, Pope had exploded. "Of course I shall be ready to recross the Rappahannock at a moment's notice," he protested. "You wished forty-eight hours to assemble the forces from the Peninsula behind the Rappahannock, and four days have passed without the enemy yet being permitted to cross." But where was the Army of the Potomac? And what were Halleck's intentions once the two armies were united? "I am not acquainted with your views, as you seem to suppose," said Pope, "and would be glad to know them as far as my own position and operations are concerned." Would Halleck take command of the combined armies, as Pope presumed? And what would his own role be? "I judge from the tone of your dispatch that you are dissatisfied with something. Unless I know what it is, of course I can't correct it. When I say these things in no complaining spirit I think you know well that I am anxious to do everything to advance your plans of campaign."[22]

Pope made no effort to conceal his ill humor. Dropping by army headquarters on the twenty-sixth, Brigadier General George G. Meade upbraided Pope with a familiarity borne of their shared Mexican War travails. "What are you doing out here?" Meade protested. "This is no place for this army. It should at once fall back so as to meet the rest of the Army of the Potomac coming up and by superior force overwhelm Lee." Meade's statement of the obvious drew a snarl from Pope. He had "orders from Washington to hold the Rappahannock as long as possible and that he should be well reinforced in forty-eight hours"; of course, Pope added querulously, well more than forty-eight hours had passed without the promised reinforcements.[23]

Brigadier General George H. Gordon also incurred Pope's wrath, though with better cause. Heartsick over the horrendous losses his brigade had suffered at Cedar Mountain, Gordon had leaked his report of the battle to an agent of the Associated Press, who had it published in Northern dailies. When Pope learned Gordon was responsible for this breach of security, he placed him under arrest (in part on the advice of Gordon's corps commander, Nathaniel Banks), notwithstanding the fact Gordon's brigade held a critical sector of the Rappahannock line. "The report was brief; it was true," remonstrated Gordon. "It made known to the public we were whipped in that battle [Cedar Mountain]; and, further than that, contained not a word from which the enemy could have received any benefit or consolation."

Gordon blamed General Banks, rather than Pope, for his troubles. Banks had caused his own, largely fictitious account of the battle to be published, and Gordon said he had done the same in self-defense. While acknowledging that Pope had been justified in arresting him, Gordon was pleased when, the following day, Pope reconsidered the wisdom of relieving a talented subordinate on such grounds and restored Gordon to his command.[24]

What had prompted these outbursts? Uncertainty over Lee's intentions played a part, as did the absence of reinforcements and the lack of direction from Washington. But what rankled Pope most of all was the chance that McClellan might be given command of both armies, to reap the rewards of a victorious offensive that Pope's holding action had made possible.

Halleck's response was as remarkable as the harangue that prompted it, and hardly reassuring to his troubled general. No one was dissatisfied with his operations along the Rappahannock, Halleck told Pope, as "the main object has been accomplished in getting troops up from the Peninsula." William B. Franklin's corps was at Alexandria waiting for its wagons; Edwin V. Sumner's and Erasmus D. Keyes's corps were "somewhere on the way." More than that, Halleck did not know. "Just think of the immense amount of telegraphing I have to do," he snapped back, "and then say whether I can be expected to give you any details as to the movement of others, even when I know them." Neither could Halleck paint a strategic canvass for Pope. "If possible to attack the enemy in flank do so. If possible to get in rear, pursue with vigor," was all he had to offer.[25]

Halleck's irascible reply was tantamount to a confession that the job of general-in-chief was too much for him. "Broken down every night with the heat, labor, and responsibility" of orchestrating the junction of two armies whose commanders detested one another, and fearing for his own military future should Lee upset the chess board, Halleck grew petulant and timorous at a time when strength of will was imperative.[26]

George B. McClellan suffered even more acutely than Pope from Halleck's moral cowardice. There is no doubt McClellan harbored a dark, private desire to see Pope humiliated by Lee, a wish that tugged at his conscience and wrestled with his sense of duty. But to say McClellan acted consciously on this impulse to bring about Pope's ruin, as Little Mac's detractors and Pope later insisted he had, is unjust. He and his corps commanders certainly felt as Secretary of the Navy Gideon Welles believed they did, "that while they did not wish the country to suffer a reverse, it would not grieve them if Pope did." Despite his private sentiments, McClellan acted responsibly. His correspondence with Pope in July was cordial, at times effusive, as when he "congratulated [Pope] heartily" on the success of Hatch's first cavalry raid, or begged him to give his "closest attention" to rumors of Jackson's departure for Gordonsville. And his letters to his wife, with whom he was most candid, suggest a depressed resignation, rather than an active effort to thwart Pope.[27]

Pope, however, went to his grave believing McClellan had worked to bring about his defeat. As evidence of McClellan's perfidy, Pope pointed to his evident delay in withdrawing the Army of the Potomac from the Peninsula: Halleck had directed McClellan to remove his sick from Harrison's Landing on July 30, and on August 3 he gave him positive orders to quit the Peninsula, yet it was August 16 before the last of the Army of the Potomac marched from Harrison's Landing to meet transports awaiting them at Yorktown and Newport News.[28]

Secretaries Stanton and Chase shared Pope's suspicions. Long of the opinion "McClellan ought not to be trusted with the command of any army of the Union," on August 28 Stanton demanded that Halleck account for Little Mac's actions on the Peninsula: Had he obeyed the recall order "with the promptness which, in your opinion, the national safety required"? No, Halleck hastened to reply, McClellan had not. While conceding that "when General McClellan's movement was begun it was rapidly carried out," Halleck said there had been "an unexpected delay in commencing it."

Having been partly responsible for McClellan's seeming lassitude, Halleck well knew the causes of delay. But fear of Stanton caused him to distort the truth. Privately, Halleck had called the proposed withdrawal from Harrison's Landing "one of the most difficult things to achieve successfully that an accomplished commander could execute." Not wishing to become like McClellan a victim of the secretary's implacable hostility, publicly Halleck minimized the difficulties of the operations and magnified his own supposed efforts to prod McClellan.[29]

Rather than mulishly resisting clear and consistent instructions from army headquarters, as Halleck maintained, McClellan had been bewildered by the general-in-chief's often paradoxical communications, beginning when Halleck visited McClellan at Harrison's Landing in late July. Ostensibly, Halleck had come to discuss with him a strategy for resuming the war effort in the East. Unbeknownst to McClellan, however, the president had sent Halleck to report on his capacity for command, with leave to dismiss him should Halleck see fit.

Halleck failed not merely to convey the administration's displeasure with McClellan, but he also reassured him of his own "friendship, confidence, [and] kindly feelings" and encouraged McClellan to express himself freely on matters of strategy. "I now ask from you that same free interchange of opinions as in former days," he wrote McClellan on the morning of July 30. "If we disagree in opinion, I know that we will do so honestly and without unkind feelings." That evening, Halleck followed his expansive telegram with two brief and enigmatic messages, both sent at 8:00 P.M. The first represented the enemy force in Richmond as small and suggested McClellan press the enemy in that direction. The second directed McClellan to remove his sick quickly, so as to be able to move in any direction.[30]

Before receiving Halleck's kindly missive, McClellan had reiterated his strategic views to the general-in-chief. "I still feel that our true policy is to reinforce the army by every available means and throw it again upon Richmond," he wrote on the morning of July 30. "Should it be determined to withdraw it, I shall look upon our cause as lost and the demoralization of the army as certain." Not surprisingly, McClellan supposed "that the order in regard to removing the sick, contemplated an offensive movement rather than a retreat, as I had no other data than the telegrams just given from which to form an opinion as to the intentions of the government." Consequently, he gave less attention to sending off his sick than to preparing to recapture Malvern Hill, which controlled the most direct approach to Richmond.

Four days later, Halleck disabused McClellan of this notion in a telegram as curt as his previous had been expansive. After complaining he had "waited most anxiously to learn the result of your forced reconnaissance toward Richmond, and also whether all your sick have been sent away," Halleck informed McClellan he was to withdraw from the Peninsula to Aquia Creek at once. Stunned and angry, on August 4 McClellan remonstrated against the order; after all, Halleck had urged him to voice his opinions. "Your telegram of last evening is received," McClellan began. "I must confess that it has caused me the greatest pain I ever experienced, for I am convinced that the order to withdraw this army to Aquia Creek will prove disastrous to our cause. I entreat that this order may be rescinded." If it was not, he would "with a sad heart obey your orders to the utmost."[31]

The order stood, and as McClellan prepared to move, relations between him and Halleck deteriorated. For the next eleven days, Halleck and McClellan snapped at one another over the telegraph wires. Halleck dismissed Little Mac's protestations that he lacked the ships needed to embark the army any faster and enjoined him to haste in messages that grew increasingly mean-spirited. McClellan bristled. "The present moment is probably not the proper one for me to refer to the unnecessarily harsh and unjust tone of your telegrams of late," he wired back on August 10. "It will, however, make no difference to my official action."

Perhaps not, but McClellan had lost a good deal of respect for Halleck. To his wife, McClellan lamented that "Halleck is turning out just like the rest of the herd. The absurdity of Halleck's course in ordering the army away from here is that it cannot possibly reach Washington in time to do any good, but will necessarily be too late. I am sorry to say that I am forced to the conclusion that Halleck is very dull and very incompetent. Alas! poor country."[32]

Contrary to McClellan's forecast, by August 26 enough of the Army of the Potomac had reported for duty to give Pope more than a fighting chance at victory. Burnside, it will be recalled, had forwarded two divisions under Jesse Reno, totaling 8,000 men, to Pope on August 14. Eight days later, Brigadier General John Reynolds arrived with his 2,500-man division of Pennsylvania Reserves from Porter's corps and was assigned to McDowell's command. On August 24 Phil Kearny's division of Heintzelman's corps reported in, Joseph Hooker's division the next morning. Together they numbered some 10,000 men. Halleck had agreed with McClellan that Keyes should remain at Yorktown, meaning only two corps of the Army of the Potomac were yet to be accounted for: Franklin's Sixth Corps, then en route from Aquia Creek to Alexandria, and Sumner's Second Corps, which had embarked from the Peninsula on August 24. Pope now commanded nearly 67,000 troops. With fewer than 55,000 men, Lee had divided his army and taken the offensive. Although Pope believed himself badly outnumbered, in truth he had men enough not merely to hold Lee at bay but also to deal the Virginian a decisive defeat.[33]

Everything Fitz John Porter had witnessed since arriving at Fredericksburg on the night of August 21 suggested Pope was not up to the task. Reporting to his friend and senior officer Ambrose Burnside, Porter had sent forward his troops as quickly as they disembarked: Reynolds's division that same night, in time to join Pope's army before it sidled northward from Rappahannock Station, Major General George Morell's division the next morning, and Brigadier General George Sykes's Regulars on the morning of August 23. Halleck had ordered Burnside to guard the lower fords of the Rappahannock and maintain contact with Pope, whose left was thought to rest near Rappahannock Station. In compliance, Porter hurried Morell and Sykes to Kelly's Ford, with supplementary orders to "do your utmost to ascertain the position of Pope's forces," an order Porter twice repeated on August 24.

Porter had not gone forward with his troops. Prostrated for three days by an acute case of dysentery, he wrote dispatches from a cot in Burnside's tent. When at last well enough to join his corps on the morning of August 25, Porter was stunned to find Pope had vanished without a trace, taking with him even his cavalry pickets. Porter supposed Pope to be at Warrenton, but having no cavalry of his own he was loathe to move farther upriver than Rappahannock Station (which he intended to do on August 26) without more precise information. "This portion of my corps would have been one day further forward had I any information of Pope's forces or the enemy," he complained to Burnside, who approved Porter's dispositions.[34]

McClellan also was angry with Pope. Not privy to Pope's plans for a concentration at Sulphur Springs, he wrote his wife from Aquia Creek on August 24 excoriating Pope. "I have seen Burnside and Porter and gained some information from them. Pope ran away from the Rappahannock last night, shamefully abandoning Porter and Burnside without giving them one word of warning. It was most infamous conduct and he deserves hanging for it. They will extricate themselves however." Protested McClellan, "I have not one word yet from Washington and am quietly waiting here for something to turn up. I presume they are discussing me now—to see whether they can get along without me. They will suffer a terrible defeat if the present state of affairs continues. I know that with God's help I can save them." Despite his own uncertain future and contempt for Pope, McClellan continued to make a good-faith attempt at cooperating with the Army of Virginia. Four times on August 24 he entreated Halleck for news of Pope's whereabouts: "Until I know that I cannot expedite Porter's movements. No certain directions can be given to those divisions until the position and intentions of Pope are ascertained, which can only be done through you." McClellan also wanted his own duties clarified. Earlier in the month, Halleck had assured him he would place Little Mac in command of "all the troops in Virginia as soon as we can get them together," but Halleck's actions since had rendered that promise suspect. "Until I know what my command and position are to be I cannot decide where I can be of most use," McClellan implored. "Please define my position and duties."

Having only sporadic telegraphic communications with Pope, Halleck was unable to tell McClellan where to find either the Army of Virginia or the enemy; neither did he clarify McClellan's responsibilities for him. Weary of McClellan's queries, he said, "There is nothing more to communicate tonight. I do not expect to hear from Pope before tomorrow. Good night."[35]

— • —

August 26 was the watershed of the short life of the Army of Virginia. Until that date, Pope handled the army commendably. He countered Lee's every move and from each fashioned opportunities of his own. But Jackson's flank march bewildered him. For the next five days, Pope planned his actions on the basis of where Jackson and Longstreet had been, or where he hoped they would be, rather than where solid information placed them.

On the night of August 25, Pope and Halleck thought Jackson headed for the Shenandoah Valley. Reports from Julius White at Winchester, who told Halleck "Union men in this region constantly inform me that the demonstration on General Pope's right is to keep the valley clear for their real attack on Maryland," seemed to confirm their suspicions. White also passed on to Pope a warning "from citizens in all directions that their secession neighbors are expecting the enemy down the valley immediately."

White's reluctance to vouchsafe the truth of these rumors forced Pope to confirm for himself the Rebels had gone. As the cavalry was too fatigued to range much beyond the Union flanks, Pope was compelled to turn to his infantry for information. Holding the remainder of the army near Warrenton and Warrenton Junction, Pope directed McDowell "as early in the morning as possible" to "make a reconnaissance with your whole corps, and ascertain what is beyond the river at Sulphur Springs."

Trying to learn something of the enemy's destination by striking at its rear with infantry was unorthodox. Not surprisingly, McDowell's efforts proved fruitless. Lee had tasked Longstreet with making enough racket along the Rappahannock on August 26 to divert Pope's attention from the threat to his flank and rear. From the heights opposite Sulphur Springs and Waterloo Bridge, Longstreet's artillery dueled with McDowell's batteries. This powerful show of force not only distracted Pope but also dissuaded McDowell from crossing the river. McDowell learned little from his sparring match with Longstreet. "What is the enemy's purpose is not easy to discover," he confessed to Pope late in the day. Apart from conveying the guesses of his staff officers, McDowell could offer Pope nothing.[36]

Pope, then, was no closer to divining Lee's intentions at nightfall on August 26 than he had been the evening before. In his first orders to Porter, issued at 8:00 P.M., Pope spoke of concentrating the army at Warrenton, and he urged Porter to bring Sykes and Morell there as early as possible on the twenty-seventh. An hour after writing Porter, Pope told McDowell he thought the decisive battle of the campaign would be fought at Warrenton, and he asked his lieutenant to try to postpone it for two days (presumably to give Franklin time to come up), after which "everything will be right."[37]

Just three hours later, Pope realized matters were far from right. Throughout the day rumors of a Confederate flanking maneuver had circulated in Sigel's corps, which lay nearest Jackson's route of march. Late that evening, Sigel forwarded reports from his scouts that placed Jackson's rear guard at Orleans, and his main body at White Plains, fifteen miles northwest of Pope's headquarters at Warrenton Junction. McDowell sent in corroborating reports from Buford's scouts at about the same time, followed by a warning from his own telegrapher that Southern cavalry apparently had rushed into Manassas. Shortly thereafter, the telegraph line with Manassas went dead.

Stonewall Jackson's infantry, and not ranging Rebel cavalry, had cut it. Rousing his command before dawn, Jackson had marched from Salem to White Plains, then onward to Thoroughfare Gap before noon. Finding the place empty of Federals, Jackson pushed his column through the gap and on to Gainesville, a village at the junction of the Warrenton Turnpike and the Manassas Gap Railroad. There the Confederates paused briefly, while Jackson decided where to cut the Orange and Alexandria Railroad. Assuming the huge Federal depot at Manassas Junction would be heavily guarded, Jackson elected to cut the road at Bristoe

Station, a minor wayside five miles southeast of Gainesville; Manassas Junction could be dealt with later.

At dusk, Major General Richard Ewell's division, proceeded by the Second Virginia Cavalry, swept into Bristoe Station. Easily dispersing the handful of Yankees guarding the place, within minutes they had torn up a quarter mile of track and caused two northbound trains to derail. Jackson, meanwhile, had learned that the immense stores five miles up the track at Manassas were also lightly guarded. With Stuart's cavalry screening, Jackson sent two regiments of infantry under Brigadier General Isaac Trimble toward the junction. In a perfectly executed night attack, Trimble routed the Federal defenders and captured the supply depot intact. More important, he had severed Pope's supply line at the cost of two dead and two wounded.[38]

Stunned by the possibility that a large enemy force had passed through Thoroughfare Gap, Pope turned initially to McDowell for answers, writing him at midnight,

> General Sigel reports the enemy's rear guard at Orleans tonight, with his main force encamped at White Plains. You will please ascertain very early in the morning whether this is so, and have the whole of your command in readiness to march; you had best ascertain tonight, if you possibly can. Our communications have been interrupted by the enemy's cavalry near Manassas. Whether his whole force, or the larger part of it, has gone round, is a question we must settle instantly, and no portion of his force must march opposite to us tonight without our knowing it. I telegraphed you an hour or two ago what dispositions I had made, supposing the advance through Thoroughfare Gap to be a column of not more than ten or fifteen thousand men. If his whole force, or the larger part of it, has gone, we must know it at once. The troops here have no artillery, and if the main forces of the enemy are still opposite you, you must send forward to Greenwich to be there tomorrow evening with the two batteries of artillery, or three if you can get them, to meet Kearny. We must know at a very early hour in the morning, so as to determine our plans.[39]

Pope's rambling, rationalizing appeal marked the first instance of what was to become a pattern with him during the remainder of the campaign. He buried his fears with wishful thinking, hid his errors by distorting the truth, and obfuscated the rest with gasconade. From Sigel's sketchy reports he somehow surmised that "not more than ten or fifteen thousand men" had passed through Thoroughfare Gap, and he accepted at face value the telegrapher's report that only Rebel cavalry had penetrated as far as Manassas. His claim to have made arrangements to meet a raid on his rear was pure fiction. What Pope referred to as dispositions was merely a request he had made to Halleck that evening to "push forward Franklin at once" and his own efforts to cajole Sturgis and Cox out of Washington.[40]

Having lied to his closest confidant at the moment of crisis, it is little wonder Pope afterward stuck to his story publicly. In his report of the campaign, written months later, he maintained he had amply provided for such an eventuality as Jackson's raid. Pope said he had asked Herman Haupt, apparently on August 26, to "direct one of the strongest divisions being sent forward to take post in the works at Manassas Junction," and that he had "requested General Halleck to push Franklin with all speed to Gainesville." Sturgis was to throw forward "strong guards along the railroad from Manassas Junction to Catlett's Station," and Kearny at Warrenton Junction was to post guards along the road to his rear. To the colonel commanding at Manassas Junction, Pope had sent orders that he dispatch cavalry "in the direction of Thoroughfare Gap, to watch any movements the enemy might make from that direction."

"After these precautions and assurances," Pope said he "thought and confidently expected that by the afternoon of the 26th Franklin would have been at or near Gainesville, one division would have been occupying the works at Manassas Junction, and that the forces under Sturgis and Cox would have been at Warrenton Junction." Certain his rear had been provided for, Pope said "Jackson's movement toward White Plains and in the direction of Thoroughfare Gap caused but little uneasiness; but on the night of the 26th it was very apparent to me that all these expected reinforcements had utterly failed me, and that upon the small force under my own command I must depend alone."[41]

The truth was far less flattering to Pope. There is no record of Pope's having ordered Haupt to deploy "one of the strongest divisions" at Manassas Junction; on the contrary, Haupt later claimed to have heard nothing from Pope after August 24. Far from having expected Franklin to be at Gainesville on the afternoon of August 26, Pope knew him to be at least two days away, as when he told Porter at 7:00 P.M. that he hoped Franklin would "by day after tomorrow night [August 28] occupy" Gainesville, or when he informed McDowell an hour later that he had only that afternoon requested Halleck to push forward Franklin. That he even intended for Franklin to halt at Gainesville is questionable; Halleck's orders to Franklin, presumably issued in response to Pope's appeal, directed him to march toward Warrenton. Pope should have known that Sturgis, whose command was awaiting transportation at Alexandria, had no means of sending guards thirty miles forward to Manassas Junction. Nor could the commander at Manassas Junction, with only 115 infantrymen and a green regiment of Pennsylvania Cavalry, be expected to scout Thoroughfare Gap. Pope was letting his "lines of retreat take care of themselves."

In the early morning hours of August 27 Pope rallied himself. As Pope then saw matters, he had two options. To preserve his army, if not his reputation, Pope could retire down the Rappahannock to Fredericksburg and join forces with Burnside. But that would leave Washington exposed. The second option offered Pope a chance to overcome his misfortune in grand style. Lee clearly had divided his army, or at least left it badly strung out on the march. Although Longstreet had started for Thoroughfare Gap himself, his rearmost division still held the heights opposite Sulphur Springs; fifty miles thus intervened between the head and the tail of the Army of Northern Virginia. Pope might turn and crush the Confederates in detail.

Given his temperament, and the probability he would be reduced to a subordinate command if he retired to Fredericksburg, Pope saw only the second option as palatable. "I determined, therefore, on the morning of the 27th of August to abandon the line of the Rappahannock and throw my whole force in the direction of Gainesville and Manassas Junction, to crush any force of the enemy that had passed through Thoroughfare Gap, and to interpose between Lee's army and Bull Run," Pope later explained. "Having the interior line of operations, and the enemy at Manassas being inferior in force, it appeared to me, and still so appears, that with even ordinary promptness and energy we might feel sure of success."

Carl Schurz speculated that "Pope, who had bragged so hastily when he took command, may have thought that he could not fall back upon the Army of the Potomac for help when the time for fighting had come." Pope himself offered a more altruistic explanation: "Of course between the two alternatives I could not hesitate in a choice. I considered it my duty, at whatever sacrifice to my army and myself, to retard, as far as I could, the movement of the enemy towards Washington, until I was certain that the Army of the Potomac had reached Alexandria."[42]

Sometime before dawn on August 27, Pope scrapped his planned crossing of the Rappahannock in favor of a withdrawal to Gainesville in three columns. McDowell was to command the left column, his own corps leading and Sigel's trailing along the Warrenton Turnpike. Jesse Reno's command and Phil Kearny's division comprised the center column, nominally led by the crotchety and only marginally competent Major General Samuel P. Heintzelman, which was to march over a meandering country road to Greenwich, a hamlet six miles southwest of Gainesville. Joseph Hooker's recently arrived division would lead the right wing in a march along the Orange and Alexandria Railroad to Manassas Junction, to force open the road. Porter was to remain at Warrenton Junction until Banks's battered corps relieved him, at which time he was to push forward in support of Hooker. Banks was to bring up the rear, shepherding the army's vast wagon train. Pope himself would travel with Hooker.[43]

Although Pope kept his head in the crisis, his plan was predicated on a false premise. From the tenor of the movement orders, and from subsequent testimony, it seems reasonably certain that Pope believed only Jackson's advance guard had reached Manassas Junction, and that the remainder of his column was still in the neighborhood of Thoroughfare Gap. By concentrating his army at Gainesville, Pope hoped to block Jackson's further progress toward the Orange and Alexandria Railroad and allow himself time to retire behind Bull Run, rather than to interpose himself between Jackson and Longstreet.[44]

Fitz John Porter was no admirer of Pope's plan. Largely through his own labors, Porter encountered Pope at Warrenton Junction on the morning of August 27. Phil Kearny had seen to it their first meeting would go badly. A notorious drinker, the one-armed general seems to have been particularly deep in his cups during the Second Bull Run campaign. With his tongue well-lubricated, Kearny spoke freely. At a council of war on the afternoon of August 26, attended by Pope, McDowell, Reno, Brigadier General Isaac Stevens, Colonel Daniel Leasure, and himself, Kearny "tried to impress upon General Pope the utter futility of hoping for any help from the Fifth Corps of the Army of the Potomac." Colonel Leasure listened in amazement. Kearny "was perfectly fierce in his denunciation of what he called the spirit of McClellanism pervading officers in high command in that army," recalled Leasure. "General Kearny insisted that cooperation on the part of [Porter] should not be looked for nor depended upon, which I thought at the time was something too monstrous to believe." Unbeknownst to Pope, that same evening Kearny buttonholed Porter to complain as harshly of Pope's management of the campaign as he ever had of McClellan.[45]

Pope had cause beyond Kearny's inebriated ravings to distrust Porter. Although Porter did not know it, his friend J. C. G. Kennedy had shared with Secretary of State William Seward a confidential letter from Porter dated July 17, in which Porter had traduced Pope to Kennedy as an ass whose plans would lead only to disaster. Seward passed the letter on to Lincoln, Stanton, and Halleck, one of whom showed it to Pope, "the origin of whose friendly feelings toward me thereafter can be imagined by the reader," conceded Porter.[46]

Porter found Pope at about 10:00 A.M., seated at a field table in a cramped, one-room telegrapher's station, writing out orders. Both were too preoccupied to talk much—Porter also had orders to draft, but what each did say failed to impress the other. Pope thought Porter apathetic: "he seemed to me to exhibit a listlessness and indifference not quite natural under the circumstances." (Pope apparently was unaware that Porter still suffered from dysentery.) Porter thought Pope edgy and disputatious. "He expressed great dissatisfaction with some of his generals, and with the plan of the campaign he had been compelled to adopt, and the way he was forced to carry it out," recalled Porter. "He said that the unfortunate position of the army was not due to him; he had been pushed, contrary to his advice, beyond the Rappahannock, and there held to draw the enemy from Richmond, in order 'to save the Army of the Potomac,'" a remark that undoubtedly offended Porter.

Apart from faultfinding, Pope had little to say to Porter. Recalled Colonel Ruggles, who was also present, "General Porter asked him the situation of affairs, and what was proposed to be done, and the future of the campaign. General Pope was rather reserved in his manner; he was reticent and uncommunicative, as it seemed to me." Ruggles remained for some ten minutes. As the interview "did not seem to progress," Ruggles inferred his presence to be inhibiting and left accordingly. Porter emerged from the tiny office a few minutes later, looking almost bereft. Pope had told him nothing; could Ruggles perhaps enlighten him as to the plan of the campaign? No, he could not. "I told him that if there was a plan of campaign it had not been communicated to me," remembered Ruggles. "I think I told him that we were to get along as best we could until the Army of the Potomac all came up."

Porter left headquarters that afternoon with Pope still professing "ignorance of the number and character of the enemy's forces in his rear, and of the damage done to his railroads and depots." Watching Porter go, Pope remarked to Colonel Ruggles that Porter had impressed him poorly. For his part, Porter left Pope convinced a general "uneasiness, arising in part from late serious disasters and from want of confidence in the plan and management of the campaign" existed at Warrenton Junction.

An exasperated Porter unburdened himself on his friend, Ambrose Burnside. In an imprudent dispatch scribbled just after he left Pope's headquarters, Porter told Burnside the Army of Virginia was demoralized, poorly supplied, and indifferently led. Pope's army "needed some good troops to give them heart, and, I think, head. We are working now to get behind Bull Run, and I presume will be there in a few days if strategy don't use us up. The strategy is magnificent, and tactics in the inverse proportions. I do not doubt the enemy have a large amount of supplies provided for them, and I believe they have a contempt for the Army of Virginia. I wish myself away from it, with all our old Army of the Potomac, and so do our companions." Pope was not entirely to blame for the wretched state of affairs, conceded Porter. "I was informed today by the best authority [Pope] that, in opposition to General Pope's views, this army was pushed out to save the Army of the Potomac, an army that could take care of itself." Begged Porter, "Most of this is private, but if you can get me away, please do so. Make what use of this you choose, so it does good."[47]

At Alexandria, George B. McClellan also felt frustrated. On the morning of August 27 he conveyed his sentiments in a hasty letter to his wife. "I have heard nothing new today and don't know what is going on in front—am terribly ignorant of the state of affairs and therefore somewhat anxious to know," he began. "Halleck is in a disagreeable situation—can get no information from the front either as to our own troops or the enemy. I shall do all I can to help him loyally and will trouble him as little as possible, but render all the assistance in my power without regard to myself or my own position."[48]

From Halleck's perspective, McClellan was very troublesome. Upon Little Mac's arrival, Halleck had assigned him to command of all troops then in and about Washington, to include the capital defenses. Understandably, McClellan wanted information commensurate with his broadened responsibilities. Between 11:00 A.M. and 3:00 P.M. on August 27, McClellan sent Halleck six dispatches, each requesting information on Pope's whereabouts and offering tentative suggestions on how best to provide for the safety of the capital. Halleck was in no mood for telegrams that simply reminded him how weak was his grasp on affairs in northern Virginia. Stanton had gotten up a petition in cabinet calling for McClellan's removal, and he and Chase were scrutinizing every message for evidence against Little Mac. Although he was not then a target, Halleck feared he would be accountable "if any disaster happens." Rather than accept the responsibility of his office, Halleck threw up his hands. "I can give you no details" on Pope's location or the state of Washington's defenses, he informed McClellan that afternoon. "As you must be aware, more than three-quarters of my time is taken up with the raising of new troops and matters in the West. I have no time for details," said Halleck. "You will therefore, as ranking general in the field, direct as you deem best; but at present orders for Pope's army should go through me."[49]

Halleck's puling letter was a remarkable confession of incompetence. McClellan and Pope both looked to Halleck for leadership; McClellan because he wanted some assurance his troops would not be slaughtered supporting Pope, Pope because he mistrusted McClellan. Porter and Burnside also might have benefited from a strong will in the War Department, capable of instilling discipline among the quarrelsome field commanders. Captain Charles Francis Adams Jr., the twenty-seven-year-old son of the United States Minister to England, certainly saw the need for a firm hand. Adams had left his regiment in South Carolina and come to Washington the day before with orders to report to Pope for duty on his staff. On August 27, over drinks at Willard's Hotel, Adams heard such a litany of woes from Halleck's staff that he feared for the very existence of the Republic. "Our rulers seem to me to be crazy," he wrote his father after hearing the bar-room confessions. "We need a head and we must have it; a man who can keep these jealousies under subordination; and we must have him or go to the wall. Is Halleck going to supply our need?" he asked rhetorically. "I hope he is, but while the question is in doubt we may lose Washington. It is my glimpse behind the scenes, the conviction that small men with selfish motives control the war without any central power to keep them in bounds, which terrifies and discourages me."

But Halleck allowed matters to drift. Largely unfettered, over the next five days McClellan and Pope would act according to the worst aspects of their natures. In the case of McClellan, that meant excessive caution. Halleck had given Little Mac liberty to do as he pleased with Franklin and Sumner at the very moment McClellan was least inclined to cooperate with Pope. McClellan's change of heart was the result of a disaster that morning near Bull Run Bridge. Anxious to prevent further damage to the Orange and Alexandria line, Herman Haupt had obtained Halleck's permission to run a wrecking and construction train, accompanied by a brigade of infantry—that of Brigadier General George W. Taylor—by rail as near to Bull Run Bridge as possible. Assuming the bridge intact and the enemy gone, Taylor was to leave a regiment at the bridge and, with the remainder of his brigade, march to Manassas Junction.[50] But the Rebels had not gone. Unloading his troops four hundred yards east of Bull Run Bridge, Taylor marched them over the bridge, along the railroad toward the old earthworks that guarded Manassas Junction, and straight into the rifle sights of A. P. Hill's Confederate division. In fifteen minutes of fighting, Taylor was wounded and a quarter of his brigade shot or captured. The leaderless remnant fled back along the track.[51]

Word of the calamity reached Colonel Haupt at Alexandria by 11:00 A.M., and he immediately sought out McClellan to request more men for a second try at reopening the railroad. Pope's army was out of forage for horses and rations for the men, Haupt pointed out; it was imperative to get supplies to them at once. But McClellan demurred, saying Haupt's plan "would be attended with risk." Haupt was incredulous. "I reminded the general that military operations were usually attended with risk, but that I did not consider the risk in this case excessive." The road was open nearly to Bull Run, Haupt explained, and if the enemy was found in force, the infantry could retire, and the train run back to safety. McClellan remained adamant. "My representations and arguments availed nothing," lamented Haupt. "The general would not give his consent, or assume any responsibility, and would give no orders, instructions, or suggestions of any kind!!"[52]

In Taylor's defeat McClellan saw his deepest fears about rash action vindicated, and he acted accordingly. Believing the enemy to be in great strength and "receiving reinforcements every minute," McClellan argued that troops should not be sent to Pope. "I think our policy now is to make these works perfectly safe and mobilize a couple of corps as soon as possible, but not to advance them until they have their artillery and cavalry." As Halleck had that morning given him leave to direct matters as he saw fit, McClellan countermanded Franklin's marching orders and told him to remain in Alexandria. With each passing hour, Mc-

Clellan would become more obdurate in his refusal to release Franklin. Pope would be left to fight with the forces he had.[53]

That evening, Charles Francis Adams Jr. also shared drinks with McClellan's staff; nearly every officer in Washington eventually found his way to Willard's. What Adams heard was most sobering—and a good reflection of McClellan's thinking. "I am ashamed at what I hear of Pope," he told his father. "[McClellan's staff] say that he is a humbug and is sure to come to grief. He has got himself into such a position that he will be crushed and Washington lost, unless McClellan saves him. He may come out with colors flying, for he is a lucky man; but if he does, he is a dangerous one, and I am advised not to connect my fortunes with his." Adams decided to return to his regiment.[54]

7 We Shall Bag the Whole Crowd

Of George B. McClellan's troubles Pope knew little and cared less; on August 27 all his attention was given over to Stonewall Jackson. A bloody afternoon clash between "Fighting Joe" Hooker's division, the vanguard of the Federal march column on the Orange and Alexandria Railroad, and Ewell's Confederate division at Bristoe Station, left behind by Jackson when he moved off to Manassas Junction, disclosed what Pope had doubted—that Jackson had reached the Orange and Alexandria with his entire command, blocking Pope's way to Bull Run.

But Pope was not dismayed. He saw instead a chance to crush Jackson before he united with Longstreet. Believing Jackson would remain at Manassas Junction, on the night of August 27 Pope issued orders designed to thwart Jackson's escape and to bring his entire strength down upon the Virginian.

The Army of Virginia was well positioned for such a movement. Apart from Hooker's rough reception near Bristoe Station, the Federals had marched easily to their destinations. Sigel was at Gainesville with his entire corps; that of McDowell was lined up along the Warrenton Pike behind him. Reno and Kearny had reached the neighborhood of Greenwich. Only Hooker was in immediate danger, but Porter's corps at Warrenton Junction was just a night's march away.

At army headquarters, the prevailing spirit was that of confident expectation.

Satisfied Jackson was trapped, Colonel Strother looked forward to "the grand denouement" the morning would bring. So too did Pope. His orders that evening were short, decisive, and certain. McDowell was to play the key role. He was to assemble Sigel's corps with its right on the Manassas Gap Railroad near Gainesville, place his own corps on Sigel's left, fronting toward the southeast, then march the entire force from Gainesville to Manassas Junction from the north, which presumably would seal off Jackson's best route of escape. "If you will march promptly and rapidly at the earliest dawn of the day," he told McDowell, "we shall bag the whole crowd." To Reno and Kearny went similar admonitions. Reno was to march on Manassas at the first blush of dawn directly from Greenwich; Kearny was to go by way of side roads to Bristoe Station, where he would relieve Hooker.[1]

Pope's orders to Porter were predicated on a gross misreading of Jackson's options and probable course of action. Pope believed Jackson had three choices: he could retire through Centreville; stage an attack against Hooker's battered division at Bristoe Station at dawn, turn the Union right, then march on Warrenton Junction and Pope's wagon trains; or stand fast at Manassas Junction and await a Federal advance against him. The first alternative Pope thought unlikely, as it would carry Jackson farther away from Longstreet. The second he would thwart in calling Kearny and Porter to Bristoe Station. The third Pope considered most likely because it was what he wanted to happen. Pope had no cavalry fit enough to feel out Jackson's intentions and perhaps delay him in whatever course he chose—Bayard's brigade was recuperating briefly back at Warrenton, and Buford's was with McDowell—and it seems never to have occurred to Pope that when McDowell and Reno descended on Manassas Junction in the morning, they might find only smoldering ruins. Wishful thinking, rather than clear reasoning, continued to dictate Pope's actions.

In ordering McDowell and Sigel to concentrate at Manassas Junction, Pope effectively turned his back on the gravest variable of the moment: what Lee and Longstreet might do. That evening, perhaps before writing the movement orders for McDowell, Reno, and Kearny, Pope received a telegram from the agitable Julius White at Winchester. White was certain the enemy was approaching his post in strength. "Signal fires have been lighted today," he reported. "A rocket from the southeast this evening and a force amounting to 300 or 400 reported in the direction of Middletown, up the valley."[2]

Undoubtedly Pope took this as evidence Longstreet had moved off toward the valley, rather than east to effect a junction with Jackson. He should not be faulted too harshly for supposing this; Halleck, McClellan, and Porter also speculated that the main Confederate push would be down the valley. But prudence dictated he also block Thoroughfare Gap, through which Longstreet must pass, should Lee decide to unite with Jackson east of Bull Run Mountain. Pope, however, gave no thought to its defense.

Not so McDowell. He understood he had been ordered to Gainesville to fore-stall a Confederate march through Thoroughfare Gap, and on the evening of August 27 he made plans to seal it off. McDowell realized Longstreet was near—Buford had kept him well apprised of the enemy's progress—and he grasped the gravity of the situation: "He had no idea of allowing a junction to be effected between the forces of Longstreet and Jackson, if it could be avoided," averred the historian John Codman Ropes. "He knew that time was all important for us; that if Jackson could be kept isolated for twenty-four hours longer, he ought to be overwhelmed." But McDowell seems not to have forwarded Buford's reports to army headquarters; instead, he contrived how best to slow Longstreet independently of Pope. Shortly before midnight, he settled on a plan: Sigel would march to Haymarket with his own corps and Reynolds's division of McDowell's corps to engage the enemy as they debouched from Thoroughfare Gap; McDowell would proceed with King's and Ricketts's divisions to Manassas Junction.

Pope's call for a concentration at Manassas interrupted McDowell's preparations. Yielding to the urgency of the summons, McDowell scrapped his own plans and told Sigel to start at once for Manassas, with his "right resting on the Manassas Railroad." Reynolds and King would follow. Loathe to leave Longstreet with a clear field, McDowell chose to diverge slightly from Pope's orders. Ricketts was to march only as far as Gainesville, where he was to halt and determine if Longstreet had come through the gap. McDowell told Reynolds to "be constantly on the lookout for an attack from the direction of Thoroughfare Gap, and in case one is threatened, he [Ricketts] will march to resist it."[3]

As it happened, Pope's orders were obsolete only minutes after they were written. Rather than accommodate Pope by staying put, Jackson slipped free of his trap, in a manner unanticipated. Lee and Jackson had been in regular contact since Stonewall started on his flanking march, so that Jackson knew to expect Longstreet at the gap by mid-day on August 28. Shortly after dark on the twenty-seventh, he started his command for the old Bull Run battlefield, just north of the Warrenton Turnpike near Groveton. There he would settle in behind the excavated trace of an unfinished railroad, fronting south, to await Longstreet's column. Should Longstreet be delayed, or if Pope found Jackson before Longstreet did, and pressed him hard, Jackson could retreat north to Aldie, from whence he might reunite with Longstreet nearer the valley. Rather than withdraw by way of Centreville, as Pope thought he must, Jackson marched due north from Manassas Junction over the Sudley Springs road. Misunderstanding the march route, A. P. Hill led his division across Bull Run and on to Centreville, a mistake that cost his men only a few hours of extra marching, but which would perplex Pope immensely. By daybreak on August 28, Jackson's men, less Hill's errant division, had broken ranks and sought slumber on the slope of Matthew's Hill, a thousand yards northwest of Groveton.

Jackson was not pleased merely to have eluded Pope's snare. He wanted Pope to find him, before the remainder of McClellan's army joined Pope. To Jackson's way of thinking, only a decisive battlefield victory would justify the gamble that his fifty-four-mile flank march had entailed; if Pope would not come to him, he would lure Pope into a fight.[4]

Pope was unaware of Jackson's departure from Manassas Junction. Rising before dawn on August 28, he walked nervously from tent to tent, bellowing at his staff, "Come, get up. Wake up. Get breakfast and get ready." Pope ate, lit a cigar, than sat down to await the opening sounds of battle. But there was only silence; no word from McDowell or Reno, and no sign of Porter or Kearny. Pope grew angry. "At intervals he nipped into delinquents of all grades, white and black," remembered Colonel Strother. His special rage he reserved for Fitz John Porter, whose absence, Pope would later claim, had invited an attack on his weak right flank.[5]

Whether Pope had good cause for outrage depends on whom one believes. Porter had received his movement orders at 10:00 P.M. the night before. They were emphatic: Porter was to march at 1:00 A.M. and reach Bristoe Station no later than daybreak, but they said nothing about a possible enemy attack on Bristoe Station. "The enemy has been driven back," the orders began; Porter was to hurry forward to help "drive him from Manassas." It was a ten-mile march from Warrenton Junction to Bristoe Station. The road was narrow and the way heavily timbered—that much was certain. Everything else was disputable. Porter said he decided to delay the march until 3:00 A.M. primarily because division commanders Sykes and Morell represented their troops as exhausted, a claim the corps historian later endorsed. "For the last two days of this march from Fredericksburg the men had been on half rations," wrote Major William Powell. "They had had no rest at Newport News, were in camp only one night at Fredericksburg, and therefore had been thirteen days and two entire nights on their continuous journey. The last day was intensely hot, and the march was over a country destitute of water; many officers and men sank down upon the road, unable to march another step, and it was near daylight the next morning before all had joined."[6]

General Pope saw matters differently. "The marches of these two divisions [Sykes and Morell] from Fredericksburg had been extremely deliberate, and involved but little more exercise than is needed for good health," he later testified. "Porter's corps was by far the freshest in the whole army, and should have been, and I believe was, in better condition for service than any troops we had." Captain Rufus Dawes of the Sixth Wisconsin, a scrupulous observer, would have agreed. Watching Porter's troops march by later that day, he thought "they appeared fresh and in good spirits, a remarkably fine body of troops. The men marched rapidly, appeared to be well fed, and there was a great contrast between them and our own exhausted troops. They showed quite a contempt for us as [being] of 'Pope's army.' They said: 'We are going to show you straw feet how to fight.'"[7]

Far more egregious than Porter's sluggishness were the missteps of Franz Sigel. Everything the German emigré general had done since receiving marching orders from McDowell at 2:30 A.M. had been wrong. Contrary to express orders, Sigel had brought with him his wagon train, which created a bottleneck in front of McDowell's divisions. Rather than move his own corps immediately as directed, Sigel waited for his trailing division to close up on the first, then permitted the men to break ranks and cook breakfast. It was mid-morning before Sigel at last started. Misconstruing the order directing the right of his line to rest on the Manassas Gap Railroad as referring to the Orange and Alexandria Railroad, Sigel arrayed his corps south of the Manassas Gap Railroad, rather than north of it, as Pope had intended. His line of march thus followed a course three miles south of that which he was to have taken. But it really mattered little. As John Codman Ropes observed, McDowell and Sigel "could not possibly, had they been at daybreak where Pope supposed they were, and marched promptly and rapidly on Manassas, have found a man of Jackson's corps near Manassas. The whole movement on Manassas was a mistake."[8]

Ironically, Pope's misguided instructions caused McDowell to miss a first-rate opportunity to engage Jackson from a direction that would have made a junction between his and Longstreet's corps problematic. Breaking free of Sigel's wagon train at 10:00 A.M., Brigadier General John F. Reynolds's division of Pennsylvania Reserves marched hard along the Warrenton Turnpike, preceded by McDowell himself, his staff, and twelve mounted scouts. A mile west of Groveton, near Pageland Lane, McDowell's entourage stumbled upon what they mistakenly conceived to be "a small body of the enemy" drawn up behind a hill north of the turnpike. As Reynolds's column came in range, the Confederates opened fire with two rifled cannon from atop a ridge near the John Brawner farm. When Rebel infantry joined the guns, Reynolds halted and deployed his lead brigade, which engaged the Southerners for nearly an hour. The Rebels suddenly vanished behind the ridge, and McDowell, Reynolds, and Brigadier General Rufus King gathered to contemplate the meaning of the brief skirmish. Concluding that Reynolds had run into nothing more than "some rear guard or cavalry party, with artillery," McDowell directed him to turn off onto Pageland Lane and resume the march toward Manassas. King's division followed.

Unbeknownst to McDowell and his generals, they had come upon Bradley Johnson's infantry brigade, which Stonewall Jackson had sent forward from the unfinished railroad to draw the Federals into a fight. Jackson's eagerness for a battle almost cost him dearly. Had McDowell taken the bait and discovered he was up against far more than cavalry, Jackson soon might have found himself contending with two Federal corps on his right flank. Undeterred by such a prospect, Jackson settled back in to await a second chance at passing Federals.[9]

— • —

Perhaps contempt had led Fitz John Porter to deviate from Pope's instructions; probably it was the darkness of the night and the congested state of the road. Whatever the reason, no harm was done. By the time Porter reached Bristoe Station at 8:00 A.M., any fear Pope may have had of an attack against Hooker had passed. Porter tried to explain why he had been delayed, but Pope was too preoccupied with chasing Jackson to care. As Pope confessed, "the necessity which made [Porter's] presence important had passed away." Rather than express displeasure with Porter's tardy arrival, Pope boasted of how he intended to go forward with Kearny's, Reno's, and Hooker's divisions "to beat up the enemy."

Together Pope and Porter rode a short distance from their staffs. Dismounting, they sat in the grass and conversed amiably. While they talked, the low rumble of distant artillery rolled through the woods from the northwest. Pope was delighted; McDowell must have found the enemy. Before leaving for the front, Pope told Porter to stay at Bristoe Station until sent for; he would "bag Jackson" with the troops at hand.[10]

Pope's mood must have darkened at least briefly as he neared Manassas. Billowing clouds of black smoke on the horizon told of the destruction Jackson had wrought the night before. When Pope's men reached the junction, they found nothing but wreckage. "Long trains of cars lately loaded with stores of all kinds were consumed as they stood on the track, smoking and smoldering, only the iron work remained entire," marveled Colonel Strother. "The whole plain as far as the eye could reach was covered with boxes, barrels, military equipment, cooking utensils, bread, meat, and beans lying in the wildest confusion." Dismounting amid the rubbish, Pope and his staff set up field headquarters in one of the old redoubts, as the distant cannonade continued. Perhaps the hot afternoon ride and the destruction he had witnessed clouded Pope's thinking. Choosing to disregard both his senses and his better judgment, Pope dismissed the battle sounds from Groveton as inconsequential and allowed a handful of dissembling Rebel prisoners convince him that Jackson had withdrawn toward Centreville and must be pursued at once. (That Jackson might have moved off to the northwest to join with Longstreet, should Lee have chosen to turn east rather than west, seems never to have entered Pope's mind.) To McDowell, sometime before 2:00 P.M., he sent instructions to halt his advance on Manassas, retrace his steps to Gainesville, and from there march rapidly down the Warrenton Turnpike toward Centreville. To Porter he sent no orders, merely news of Jackson's continued retreat; he would yet "bag" the Virginian and his elusive foot cavalry, apparently without Porter's assistance.

That was quite acceptable to Porter, who long since had stopped taking Pope at his word. Tossing aside Pope's dispatch, Porter again unburdened himself to Ambrose Burnside. "All that talk of bagging Jackson, etc., was bosh," he wrote at 2:00 P.M. "That enormous gap was left open and the enemy jumped through. The enemy have destroyed all our bridges, burned trains, etc., and made this army rush back to look after its lines of communication and find our base of subsistence. There is a report that Jackson is at Centreville, which you can believe or not."[11]

By the time Porter finished penning his missive, Pope himself no longer knew what to believe. Only minutes after he released the courier bearing his 2:00 P.M. orders to McDowell, a messenger from that general arrived with troublesome news: cavalry scouts had reported Longstreet to be closing on Thoroughfare Gap.

Acting on impulse, Pope abandoned his planned march on Centreville. Instead, he would throw his army at Longstreet, to prevent a junction with Jackson. McDowell was to suspend his march on Centreville and hold fast near Gainesville, toward which Pope would send Reno and Heintzelman that evening, "unless," Pope added, "there is a large force at Centreville, which I do not believe. Ascertain, if you can, about this." How McDowell was to confirm the presence or absence of Confederates at Centreville, when he was not to leave Gainesville, Pope failed to say. In closing, Pope begged McDowell to "give me your views fully; you know the country much better than I do."[12]

As the afternoon shadows lengthened, Pope changed his mind again. More Confederate stragglers and deserters, probably from A. P. Hill's division, as well as paroled prisoners, had come in. All insisted that Jackson had gone to Centreville. An abortive cavalry reconnaissance up the Centreville road (in this instance, Pope would have been better off without his mounted arm) somehow came to the same conclusion. On the strength of these reports, hardly conclusive by any means, Pope scrapped his plan to fight Longstreet at Gainesville. Yielding to the idea that obsessed him, at 4:00 P.M. Pope rattled off orders resuming the "pursuit" of Jackson toward Centreville. Kearny was to leave at once for Centreville. Pope hurried Reno and Hooker on through Manassas Junction to follow Kearny. He directed the hapless Franz Sigel, who was preparing to cross Bull Run just northeast of the junction, to face about and march north on the Sudley Springs road to the Warrenton Turnpike, then turn east and close on Centreville. Reynolds, then en route to Manassas, was to follow Sigel.

At 5:00 P.M. McDowell was handed his instructions: "The enemy is reported in force near Centreville. Please march immediately with your command directly upon Centreville from where you are." McDowell complied, but Pope's swings of purpose undoubtedly disturbed him. For a brief moment, it appeared that Pope at last had concluded, as McDowell himself had the day before, that Longstreet must be prevented from joining Jackson. But his latest orders set the entire army back to doing what one or two divisions alone could have accomplished: confirming the presence of Jackson at Centreville and fixing him there until reinforcements arrived. McDowell had lost any hope of reinforcing Ricketts's division, which had been struggling admirably, if futilely, since 2:00 P.M. to keep Longstreet from breaching Thoroughfare Gap. Concluding that the time had come to share his views with Pope personally, near sunset McDowell left his peripatetic corps and rode off in search of the commanding general's headquarters.[13]

What can be said of Pope's erratic course that afternoon? His dispatches reflect the fevered speculations of a man baffled and overburdened. Anxiety narrowed his focus and crowded out options, so that he could conceive of only one course of action: attack Jackson. After calling off the briefly planned concentration at Gainesville, Pope gave no further thought to Longstreet; in short, he willed him away. Wishful thinking reigned supreme at army headquarters.

Nothing, it seemed, could compel Pope to pause, take stock, and evaluate matters dispassionately, not even the near destruction of a Federal division. Marching east on the Warrenton Turnpike in compliance with Pope's latest orders, Rufus King's division collided with Jackson's corps near Groveton at sunset. Felled by an epileptic seizure only moments earlier, King was unable to direct the contest, and his brigade commanders groped about in the gathering darkness. But Jackson failed to press his advantage and the clash ended after ninety minutes—a brutal, bloody stalemate.[14]

As the fighting sputtered out, General King emerged from his seizure, dazed and uncertain. He was inclined to continue the march on Centreville, until his junior brigade commander, Brigadier General John Gibbon, dissuaded him by pointing out that the way to Centreville was obviously blocked by the enemy. When John Reynolds arrived shortly before 9:00 P.M., with a promise to bring his Pennsylvania Reserves up at daylight, King decided to hold his ground until General McDowell sent him "fresh orders to the contrary." A short time later, he learned that Ricketts's division was coming down the Warrenton Turnpike, having late that afternoon conceded Thoroughfare Gap to Longstreet. Although only McDowell had the authority to order Ricketts to Groveton—and King had no idea where to find McDowell—King gently entreated his fellow division commander to come: "I think you had better join us here, tho' that depends of course on your orders."[15]

Upon hearing the reports of garrulous Rebel prisoners, who confirmed the presence of Jackson's entire force on the field—and greatly exaggerated its strength—King again faltered. With no word from McDowell, or of his whereabouts, and with no firm idea of where the remainder of the army might be, King yielded to General Gibbon's counsel that the division take the safest course and retire toward Manassas Junction. At 1:00 A.M., King's blasted command took to the road. With Longstreet at his back, Ricketts elected to follow King to Manassas Junction. Nothing now stood between Longstreet and Jackson but ten miles of dark Virginia countryside.[16]

From a ridge beside Blackburn's Ford on Bull Run, where they paused in their ride to Centreville, John Pope and his staff watched King's fight at Groveton, eight miles distant. "We could see the smoke rising above the trees, and as it grew darker the flash of the guns and bursting of the shells could be distinctly discerned," said Colonel Strother. The meaning of it all was unclear until 9:30 P.M., when a courier from King appeared. He knew only that they had met Jackson and were holding their ground along the Warrenton Turnpike, but that was enough for Pope. "The game [is] in our hands," he exclaimed. Obviously King had encountered "the enemy retreating from Centreville, and after a severe fight had remained master of the field, still interposing between Jackson's forces and the main body of the enemy." Pope had only to crush Jackson between the corps of McDowell and Sigel and Reynolds's division, all of which he assumed to be west of Jackson near Gainesville, and the remainder of the Army of Virginia, which Pope would bring up from the east and southeast.

Messengers with marching orders were on their way from army headquarters within the hour. Pope sent word to McDowell to hold his ground. (Unaware McDowell was not with King, Pope sent no orders directly to King.) To Kearny at 9:50 P.M. went orders as ebullient as those of the night before. "General McDowell has intercepted the retreat of the enemy and is now in his front, Sigel on the right of McDowell," Pope began. "Unless he can escape by by-paths leading to the north tonight, he must be captured." To keep Jackson from slipping away in that direction, Kearny was to march west along the Warrenton Turnpike from Centreville not later than 1:00 A.M., even if he had to leave the better part of his tired troops behind. Kearny would open the battle at daybreak: "Advance cautiously and drive in the enemy's pickets tonight, and at early dawn attack him vigorously." Remembering Kearny had a corps commander, Pope also dispatched General Heintzelman, imploring him to move both Kearny and Hooker promptly. At midnight, Pope instructed Franz Sigel to "attack the enemy vigorously as soon as it was light enough to see, and bring him to a stand if it were possible to do so."[17]

Pope's orders to Porter seemed an afterthought. A "severe engagement" was likely to occur at daybreak, Pope wrote him at 3:00 A.M. Porter was to march at once to Centreville, where his "presence [was] necessary." What Porter was to do once he reached Centreville, and the role Pope envisioned for him in the coming battle, remained unstated.

To the extent Longstreet's column entered into his calculations, and it seems to have but little, Pope assumed he could destroy Jackson well before Longstreet reached the field. Pope was unaware of Ricketts's engagement at Thoroughfare Gap, and he seemed disinclined to press McDowell for information on Longstreet's probable whereabouts. With a certainty based on nothing more solid than desire, Pope "believed that we were sufficiently in advance of Longstreet, that by using our whole force vigorously we should be able to crush Jackson completely before Longstreet by any possibility could have reached the scene of action. I felt sure then that there was no escape for Jackson. The only apprehension I had was that Jackson might attempt to retreat to the north, in the direction of Leesburg."[18]

Escape was the farthest thing from Stonewall Jackson's mind. Rather than ensnared prey for Pope, Jackson saw himself as the predator. It was he who had intercepted McDowell's march; he need simply hold his strong position along the unfinished railroad until Longstreet arrived, when together they would finish off the Federals. Lee and Jackson had been in regular contact since Longstreet began his march on August 26. Nothing in Jackson's dispatches suggested alarm. On the contrary, recalled Longstreet, "as he had not expressed a wish that we should hurry, our troops were allowed to take their natural swing under the inspiration of impending battle." Longstreet bivouacked his corps on the east side of Thoroughfare Gap, ready to resume the march at dawn on August 29.[19]

The orders Pope dictated on the night of August 28 to effect Jackson's destruction were based not only on a gross misreading of the enemy's intentions, but also on a poor understanding of his own army's capabilities. Three days of marching under the hot August sun, with rations fast running out, had reduced the men to shuffling, half-starved somnambulists. Their opponents, on the other hand, were well rested, in excellent spirits, and—thanks to the stores at Manassas Junction—probably better provisioned than at any other time during the war.[20]

How the Yankees responded to the incessant marching is uncertain. One Massachusetts soldier of sanguine temperament said his comrades were hopeful withal: "Many were without blanket or blouse, some even without trousers; others with shoeless, blistered feet were marching over rough, hot, and dusty roads. Still they were full of enthusiasm for the fight; and as Pope, with a numerous staff, passed them on the road, he was loudly cheered." James Madison Stone of the Twenty-first Massachusetts saw matters differently. "It is a mistake to think that the private soldiers are not, after a certain amount of experience, able to size up their commanders in a fairly correct way," said Stone. "If there is a master mind, they know it very quickly, and it did not take the men of the Twenty-first long to discover there was no master mind at the head at that time."[21]

Phil Kearny had reached the same conclusion. Fed up with Pope's frequent changes of purpose, he reacted harshly to the orders for a 1:00 A.M. march from Centreville. "Tell General Pope to go to Hell," he snarled at the staff officer bearing the dispatch. "We won't march before morning."[22]

Colonel Strother was shaken from his sleep at 3:00 A.M. to carry orders to Fitz John Porter, but he became badly entangled among the wagon trains that choked the road to Bristoe Station. It was dawn on the twenty-ninth before he at last reached Porter's headquarters. An orderly showed the Virginian into Porter's tent, where he "found the handsome general lying on his cot covered with an elegant fancy blanket." Strother lit a candle and handed him the dispatch. Porter read it quietly. "This order surprised me," said Porter. "It carried me from the field of action." Disgusted and mystified, Porter asked for an explanation, but Strother merely shrugged. Porter looked at his watch, which showed 5:20 A.M., then sat down to write what Strother presumed were movement orders, as Pope wished Porter to march at once.

Strother soon realized he was mistaken. "While writing [Porter] looked up and asked how to spell 'chaos,'" Strother recalled. "I told him and at the same time divined what he was thinking about."[23]

Porter was writing to Burnside, excoriating Pope for not knowing where the enemy had been the night before and conveying his hope McClellan would prove able to extract his corps from Pope's army. "It would seem from proper statements of the enemy that he was wandering around loose," concluded Porter, "but I expect they know what they are doing, which is more than any one here or anywhere knows."

What McDowell may have been thinking was anyone's guess, because no one knew where to find him. He had left his corps shortly before King's evening fight, thinking General Pope needed him more than did his division commanders. McDowell certainly had expected no trouble during what he presumed would be a short absence from the front. Besides appealing for McDowell's counsel, in his last message Pope had indicated Jackson to be at Centreville, far from McDowell's corps. As McDowell later explained: "Under the belief the enemy was moving to the south of us to go entirely around and fall on our enormous wagon train under Banks, and was now on the opposite side of Manassas from where I was, and seeing from General Pope's notes that he was making mistakes as to distances and places, I wished, in order to answer his request, to give him fully my views, as I had been doing throughout the campaign—to confer with him personally, and went to Manassas Junction for that purpose."

But Pope had departed Manassas for Centreville. No sooner did McDowell and his escort reach the junction than cannon fire erupted from the direction of Groveton. McDowell set out at once for King's division. Night had fallen. Leading his party over what he thought was a shortcut, McDowell instead ran them into a dark, wooded swamp. After riding about lost for a time, McDowell's band came upon the Bethelem Church road, which they took hoping to locate Reynolds. Finding neither Reynolds nor King, at midnight McDowell and his staff dismounted to rest for the night in a bivouac of Sigel's corps.[24]

Bearing in mind his troops were exhausted, his generals querulous, and his army scattered about the Virginia countryside, one naturally asks: Why did Pope choose to fight Jackson?

Politics and personal ambition played a part. Pope had been brought east to discredit McClellan and the Democratic brand of warfare by fighting aggressively. To fall back beyond Bull Run without a struggle would vindicate McClellan's cautious approach to combat. As Halleck had shown no inclination to take the field, McClellan probably would assume command of the combined Armies of Virginia and the Potomac; under such circumstances, Pope's future would be uncertain at best.

In fairness to Pope, it must be said that he had expressed not merely a willingness but a desire to fall back behind Bull Run the week before. At Halleck's insistence, he had held the Rappahannock River line contrary to his own better judgment. An inability to subordinate his own interests to the common good did not figure decisively in Pope's calculations.

No doubt Pope believed he was making the right tactical decision. Wrong as to his own army's whereabouts, Pope thought he had Stonewall Jackson "sandwiched" between McDowell and Sigel to the west and Heintzelman, Reno, and eventually Porter to the east. But the western side of his trap was nonexistent. By 1:00 A.M. on August 29 King was in retreat to Manassas Junction and Ricketts to Bristoe Station. Sigel and Reynolds were arrayed southeast of Jackson, not west of him as Pope supposed. Kearny stood obstinately at Centreville, and Porter slumbered at Bristoe Station. Seldom was an army less prepared for battle.[25]

— ✦ —

In Washington, August 28 was a day of high anxiety and misguided activity. "Things here look badly enough and amid this atmosphere of treason, jealousy and dissension, it requires good courage not to despair of the republic," wrote Captain Charles Francis Adams Jr. from Willard's Hotel. Having heard nothing from Pope in three days and at a loss what to do, Halleck summoned McClellan to his home late on the night of August 27. They talked until 3:00 A.M.; whether they agreed how best to employ the corps of Franklin and Sumner is unknown. McClellan undoubtedly argued that Franklin should not be sent forward until his artillery and cavalry reached him, and that as the enemy probably had interposed himself between Pope and Washington, priority be given the defenses of the capital. Halleck apparently yielded to McClellan's counsel, or at least Little

Mac perceived he had. During the short return trip to Alexandria, McClellan scribbled a note to his wife that suggested he and Halleck had reached some sort of understanding. "I have a great deal of hard work before me now but will do my best to perform it," McClellan began. "I find Halleck well disposed, he has had much to contend against. I shall keep as clear as possible of the president and cabinet—endeavor to do what must be done with Halleck alone—so I shall get on better," he added. "Pope is in a bad way—his communications with Washington cut off and I have not yet the force at hand to relieve him. He has nearly all the troops of my army that have arrived. I hope to hear better news when I reach Alexandria."[26]

The first news McClellan received was anything but good. Rumors of a Confederate march on Washington were rife. A squad of New York Cavalry returned from Fall Church with word that Vienna was in enemy hands and Fairfax Court House had been seized and burned. Herman Haupt worked diligently to debunk such claims, as when he sent a train to Fairfax to bring off wounded—"I have just received the announcement, 'We are at Fairfax.' This was done by our men with a knowledge of the fact that a force of 20,000 Rebels were probably in front of them," Haupt told Halleck—but McClellan persisted in accepting them at face value.

The next dispatch handed him was even more troubling. While McClellan was en route to Alexandria, Halleck had sent orders directly to Franklin, enjoining him to move at once toward Manassas Junction. McClellan remonstrated sharply at 1:00 P.M.: "I have been doing all possible to hurry artillery and cavalry. The moment Franklin can be started with a reasonable amount of artillery he shall go."

An hour later, McClellan offered Halleck his counsel on what should be done. Discussions with Brigadier General John G. Barnard, commander of the defenses of Washington, and with Colonel E. Parker Scammon, who had supported Colonel Taylor's ill-fated expedition to Manassas the day before, convinced him that rash action was unwarranted. From Barnard, McClellan had learned of the sorry state of the capital defenses. "A serious attack would not encounter a serious resistance," confessed Barnard. He must have "experienced garrisons thrown into the works and experienced troops posted along the lines," and the only veteran troops were the division of Jacob Cox, the remnant of Colonel Taylor's brigade, and the corps of Franklin and Sumner. From his conversation with Scammon, McClellan was "satisfied that the enemy is in large force between us and Pope. It is my opinion that any movement made here must be in force, with cavalry or artillery, or we shall be beaten in detail." Better yet, Pope should fall back behind the Occoquan River, a movement Franklin and Sumner might cover from Fairfax. Concluded Little Mac, "The great object is to collect the whole army in Washington, ready to defend the works and act upon the flank of any force crossing the Upper Potomac."

Halleck offered no comment on McClellan's recommendations. Replying at 3:30 P.M., he merely repeated his insistence that "not a moment be lost in pushing as large a force as possible toward Manassas, so as to communicate with Pope before the enemy is re-enforced." Where Pope might then be, Halleck could not say. Again McClellan protested that neither Franklin nor Sumner's corps was prepared to fight. "A premature movement in small force will accomplish nothing but the destruction of the troops sent out." Concluded McClellan, "I report that I will lose no time in preparing the troops now here for the field, and that whatever orders you may give *after hearing what I have to say* will be carried out" [italics added].[27]

That final sentence held the key to McClellan's thinking. Just the day before, Halleck had abdicated the management of affairs in northern Virginia to him; "I have no time for details. You will therefore, as ranking general in the field, direct as you deem best," Halleck had told Little Mac. During their nocturnal discussion at Halleck's home, McClellan had urged Halleck to go to the front himself; that "his post as general-in-chief was with the army." Halleck demurred—he had too much office work. Less than twenty-four hours later, Halleck not only upbraided McClellan for doing what he deemed best, but also lacked the courtesy to acknowledge his recommendations.[28]

Halleck's sudden interest in details, and in Franklin's corps in particular, arose as much from fear for himself as concern for Pope's plight. That morning—probably as McClellan steamed back to Alexandria, satisfied that he and Halleck were in accord—Secretary of War Stanton handed Halleck a written query that read like a death sentence for the culpable, whomever he proved to be. He wanted Halleck to tell him four things: On what date had he first ordered McClellan to quit the James River? Was that order obeyed promptly? Had Franklin been ordered to move to Pope's relief? If so, had such orders been obeyed?

Halleck set aside his duties to write a lengthy response and clear himself of any blame. He assured the secretary he had done all he could both to prod McClellan from the Peninsula and to get Franklin started for the front. Before submitting his reply, Halleck wrote the orders necessary to make that assurance truthful, beginning with his early afternoon note to Franklin, and ending with an ultimatum that evening to McClellan to start Franklin the next morning, ready or not ready. "If we delay too long to get ready there will be no necessity to go at all, for Pope will either be defeated or be victorious without our aid. If there is a want of wagons, the men must carry provisions with them until the wagons can come to their relief."

McClellan yielded. Franklin would march at 6:00 A.M. on the twenty-ninth, he assured Halleck. Sumner would hold his corps ready to march. All other troops not on duty in the capital defenses likewise "will be ordered to hold themselves ready to march tomorrow morning, and all, except Franklin's, to await further orders," McClellan added. "If you wish any of them to move toward Manassas, please inform me." Whether Little Mac would carry through remained to be seen.[29]

8 No Place to Fight a Battle

Brigadier General John Gibbon was troubled. With each step his brigade took farther from Groveton, Gibbon became more convinced he had erred in recommending the withdrawal. A night march was always a gloomy proposition, but this one was particularly demoralizing, "a sad, tedious march," said Gibbon. "Contrary to expectations we met nobody on the road and reached the vicinity of [Manassas] Junction just as day was breaking. Here a halt was made, our poor tired men lying down alongside the road for a much-needed rest." His conscience too heavy for sleep, Gibbon left the column to seek out General Pope, that he "might inform him what had happened to us the night before."

The "scene of desolation and ruin" at the junction shocked Gibbon. He snaked his way among long trains of smoldering freight cars and heaps of spilled supplies, hoping to find army headquarters. Instead he met a lone staff officer, who told Gibbon he had last seen Pope at Blackburn's Ford. At Blackburn's Ford, Gibbon learned Pope had left for Centreville. On Gibbon rode. At 6:30 A.M., he made his report.

"Where is McDowell?" Pope interjected sharply. Gibbon did not know; McDowell had been absent during the battle.

Pope exploded. "God damn McDowell, he is never where he ought to be!"

That remark unnerved Gibbon, as "it was generally supposed in the army that Pope liked, trusted and leaned upon McDowell very much." Gibbon hastened to explain his purpose in coming: He wished to call the commanding general's attention "to the fact that our abandonment of the turnpike left no troops interposed between Jackson's and Lee's main army and consequently the two forces could join without opposition." Gibbon presumed Pope would plug the gap, but Pope ignored him, speaking only of his own plans for beating Jackson. Gibbon breathed easier when Pope turned to Colonel Ruggles and said, "Write a note to General Porter and direct him to move out with his corps on the Gainesville road and take King's division with him," adding, "Give it to General Gibbon and let him take it to General Porter at Manassas Junction."[1]

Gibbon rode off, undoubtedly perplexed at Pope's fury at McDowell. Had he known Pope better, Gibbon would have understood the commanding general was acting as he always did when under stress, lashing out randomly at those around him. Already Pope had alienated Colonel Ruggles; "I am on speaking terms with General Pope, but I would not like to serve with him as a staff officer," Ruggles later testified. "I thought several times that I was not treated as a gentleman should have been treated."[2]

Reading the order Gibbon handed him at 8:30 A.M., Fitz John Porter also felt ill-used by the commanding general. Less than six hours earlier, Pope had enjoined him to "move upon Centreville at the first dawn" with all haste; now he was to march in a different direction with equal dispatch. "Push forward with your corps and King's division, which you will take with you upon Gainesville," read his new instructions. "I am following the enemy down the Warrenton Turnpike. Be expeditious, or we will lose much."

"My orders are very conflicting," Porter complained to his assembled generals. "I first receive them from this officer, and then from that officer; officers whom I do not know and have never seen, and they are brought to me by orderlies." Porter scribbled General Pope a note, requesting him "hereafter to send all his orders to me in writing," and sent his medical director, Doctor Robert Abbott, galloping off to deliver it.[3]

Irvin McDowell also had reasons to protest Pope's order. After twelve hours of wandering about the countryside in search first of Pope and then of his own corps, McDowell finally had found King's division at Manassas Junction, only to be told Pope had given it to Porter. Reynolds was with Sigel, and Ricketts was at Bristoe Station, leaving McDowell without a command. Although his nighttime peregrination had prompted the order, McDowell nonetheless felt affronted. Porter reminded him that, as senior officer present, McDowell was in command of not only King's division but also Porter's corps, but McDowell was adamant in seeking a retraction from Pope. Ignoring Pope's entreaty for Porter to come up quickly, McDowell wrote a note to army headquarters asking that King's division be returned to him.[4]

McDowell stalled. He dismissed heavy firing from the direction of Groveton as the "usual artillery duel at long range of no importance and leading to no result." As the distant thumping continued, McDowell assured Porter "there would be no fighting at Groveton," nor any "battle that day," the intention being "to form a new line of this army [with] the reinforcements coming from the Army of the Potomac." McDowell spoke with such conviction that Porter supposed him "the ruling spirit in the operations of the Army of Virginia," and he readily acceded to McDowell's request that upon reaching Gainesville he "place King on my right, in the *new line about to be formed* [italics Porter's], so that connecting with Reynolds at Groveton, he could reclaim him at the proper time, and have his command together."

Hopeful Pope would soon restore King's division to him, at 10:00 A.M. McDowell yielded, and Porter started up the Manassas-Gainesville road toward Gainesville.

For the first time since cutting loose from the Rapidan, Pope doubted he could destroy Stonewall Jackson. His misgivings were warranted, but his reasoning was all wrong. Certain Jackson was in headlong retreat toward Thoroughfare Gap, he feared the withdrawal of King and Ricketts from Gainesville would allow Jackson to slip away. Shortages of rations and forage had become too acute for Pope to ignore; if he failed to bring Jackson to battle this day, the Army of Virginia would have to retire to Centreville. Ruling out a pursuit beyond Gainesville, Pope felt it imperative that Porter and Brigadier General John Hatch, who had assumed division command that morning from the ailing King, reach the village before Jackson.

It seems never to have crossed Pope's mind that Jackson might turn and fight by choice. Neither did the other half of the Army of Northern Virginia figure greatly in his calculations. Pope realized Longstreet was near but deemed it probable that Jackson would retreat beyond Thoroughfare Gap before Longstreet advanced too far through it. On that assumption, with all its flawed logic, he gambled everything.[5]

It was not that Pope paid Longstreet no heed, as some have asserted, but that he—and his staff—misread the warning signs. Pope had set up headquarters on a ridge near Centreville, from which were visible huge clouds of dust, raised by Longstreet's marching infantry. Colonel Strother affirmed: "Columns of dust all converging toward the battle indicated the march of ours and the enemy's supporting columns. We could even speculate upon the advance of Longstreet through Thoroughfare Gap and his repulse by Ricketts [a mistaken assumption], and then Ricketts falling back on the main body." Strother believed Longstreet was coming, but others of the staff conjectured the cause of the dust clouds to be the wagon train of Jackson's corps in retreat. With opinion divided, Pope told General Roberts to "take a position, and with a glass to observe whether troops were moving from the direction of Thoroughfare Gap to Gainesville." Climbing to higher ground, Roberts watched the horizon for some time, then told Pope what he believed he had seen. "I became convinced from the clouds of dust that arose above the Bull Run range beyond Thoroughfare Gap, toward a gap north of Thoroughfare Gap, that Longstreet was moving very rapidly to get through that northern gap and to re-enforce Jackson," recalled Roberts. "But, from the distance from the head of the column of dust to Gainesville, *I did not believe that he would be able to effect a junction before late in the evening* [italics added], and so reported to General Pope."

Pope accepted Ruggles's surmise without question. Had his own plans been progressing apace, Pope would have greeted this apparent confirmation that Longstreet was twelve hours away with greater pleasure. But by 9:00 A.M., Pope realized his three-sided trap had been reduced by two. The sounds of battle that erupted from the direction of Groveton shortly after 6:00 A.M. were too weak to suggest a major action; and the clouds of gun smoke billowing above the trees suggested the area of fighting was confined to a narrow front. Clearly Kearny had not made his presence felt from the east, and there was as yet no force near Gainesville to fix Jackson in place. Pope assumed Sigel had engaged Jackson's rear guard, and he feared Jackson would slip past Gainesville before Porter, with six miles to cover, could intervene; once beyond Gainesville, nothing could prevent his junction with Longstreet. That Jackson would of his own volition stay and fight remained unthinkable. Pope was "not a man given to over-estimating his adversary's courage or strength," observed the historian John Codman Ropes, "and he could not suppose that Jackson would voluntarily await an attack by our whole army. Pope doubtless thought it not unlikely that his army would make a promenade to Gainesville, merely picking up stragglers and some of Jackson's recently captured stores."

Pope concluded, and apparently confessed to General Roberts, that he could do no more than harass Jackson's rear guard, reunite his own army at Gainesville, and then withdraw to Centreville to receive supplies and await the inevitable advance of Lee, as well as make the hoped-for junction with the Army of the Potomac.[6]

Although based on a faulty premise—that Jackson was retreating—Pope's decision to fall back on Centreville was prudent; indeed, it was what the administration had expected him to do for some time. Unfortunately, Pope badly misstated his intentions to his subordinates. A few minutes after 9:30 A.M., Doctor Abbott reported in with Fitz John Porter's appeal for written instructions. Porter and McDowell were perplexed by Pope's order that Porter march on Gainesville with his own corps and King's division, Abbott told the commanding general. Assuming "some confusion in the orders," they wanted written clarification.[7]

What they got instead was "a masterpiece of contradiction and obfuscation,"[8] understandable only to Pope. The order Doctor Abbott returned with—known to history as the "Joint Order"—read as follows:

> You will please move forward with your joint commands towards Gainesville. I sent General Porter written orders to that effect an hour and a half ago. Heintzelman, Sigel, and Reno are moving on the Warrenton turnpike, and must now be not far from Gainesville. I desire that, as soon as communication is established between this force and your own, the whole command shall halt. It may be necessary to fall back behind Bull Run, at Centreville, tonight. I presume it will be so on account of our supplies. I have sent no orders of any description to Ricketts, and none to interfere in any way with the movements of McDowell's troops, except what I sent by his aide-de-camp last night, which were to hold his position on the Warrenton Pike until the troops from here should fall on the enemy's [Jackson's] flank and rear. I do not even know Ricketts' position, as I have not been able to find out where General McDowell was until a late hour this morning. General McDowell will take immediate steps to communicate with General Ricketts, and instruct him to rejoin the other divisions of his corps as soon as practicable.
>
> If any considerable advantages are to be gained by departing from this order, it will not be strictly carried out. One thing must be had in view, that the troops must occupy a position from which they can reach Bull Run tonight or by morning. The indications are that the whole force of the enemy [Lee] is moving in this direction at a pace that will bring them here [Centreville] by tomorrow night or the next day. My own headquarters will be for the present with Heintzelman's corps or at this place [Centreville].[9]

At noon, Porter read his copy of the Joint Order with astonishment. An hour earlier, his advance guard had run into mounted Confederates near Dawkins's Branch, a stream bisecting the Manassas-Gainesville road three miles southeast of the Warrenton Turnpike. Porter had halted the head of his march column along a ridge above Dawkins's Branch and was about to deploy Major General George Morell's lead division to dislodge the enemy when Abbott handed him the Joint Order.

At a loss what to do, Porter dismounted and called several of his generals together for their opinion of the order. While they debated its meaning, General McDowell rode up, waving his copy and yelling, "Porter, you are too far out." Before Porter could complain of Pope's latest directive, McDowell thrust upon him a message even more disturbing. After screening Ricketts's withdrawal from Thoroughfare Gap the night before, Brigadier General John Buford's cavalry

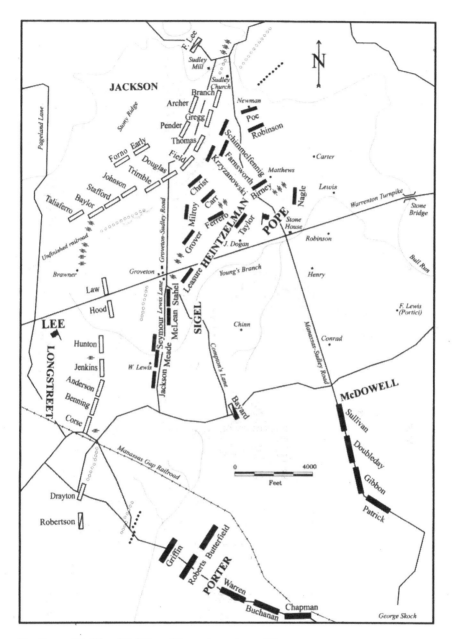

The Second Battle of Bull Run, Noon, August 29, 1862

brigade had lingered about Gainesville until 9:00 A.M.—long enough to discover Longstreet well on his way to effecting a junction with Jackson. "Seventeen regiments, one battery, 500 cavalry passed through Gainesville three-quarters of an hour ago, on the Centreville road [Warrenton Turnpike]," Buford warned McDowell at 9:30 A.M.

Porter and McDowell walked away from the gathered generals of the Fifth Corps to contemplate their predicament in private. Evidently nonplused, Porter hastened to defer to whatever McDowell might decide, citing the Sixty-second Article of War as placing him, McDowell, in command by date of rank.[10]

McDowell scanned the horizon. Before them lay several hundred yards of overgrown fields and open timber, which grew dense as the woods neared the Warrenton Turnpike. Above the most distant trees rose a thick cloud of dust. Scattered firing erupted from the same direction. To McDowell the evidence was unequivocal: Longstreet had arrived in their front, and neither they nor anyone else from the Army of Virginia were going to reach Gainesville without a lot of hard fighting along the way. Recalling Porter's long march column, which was stacked up along the Manassas-Gainesville road for nearly two miles, McDowell reflected aloud, "This is no place to fight a battle; we are too far out." Porter concurred, and McDowell concluded to act upon that portion of the Joint Order that read, "If any considerable advantages are to be gained by departing from this order it will not be strictly carried out." He would take Hatch's division and, when it returned from Bristoe, that of Ricketts, and march northward over the Manassas-Sudley road to the battlefield, where he hoped to find Reynolds's Pennsylvania Reserves and Sigel's corps. McDowell told Porter he would form on the left of Reynolds and Sigel, then try to link up with Porter's right. In the meantime, Porter should hold his ground along Dawkins's Branch; or, as General McDowell explained to Porter's chief of staff, Lieutenant Colonel Frederick T. Locke, after leaving the general, "He had better remain where he is, but if necessary for him to fall back, he can do so upon my left."[11]

That last admonition from McDowell confirmed Porter in his course, which he felt confident "did not deviate from the one of forming a line of observation, and of the necessity of 'retiring behind Bull Run to-night or by morning,' foreshadowed in General Pope's [joint] order." Certain an attack "by myself would inevitably be disastrous, my conclusions under all the circumstances were, that in the exercise of the discretion vested in me by the joint order and also, by reason of my command being a separate one, from the further fact that the condition of affairs was so different from anything supposed by General Pope in his orders to me, I should best fulfill my duty by holding the enemy in my front in check."[12]

Arriving on the battlefield shortly after noon, John Pope hardly would have disagreed with Porter that affairs were decidedly different from what Pope had understood when he drafted the Joint Order. Unfortunately, their estimates of present conditions could not have been more opposed.

Pope and his retinue had halted to make headquarters beneath a large pine tree near the John Dogan house, on a sprawling ridge just north of the Warrenton Turnpike. The day was sunny and sultry, the scene before them "grand and terrible," remembered David Strother. "The smoke was rising more than ever and the roar of the guns still more grand. The artillerymen of thirty pieces in sight worked with a fierce activity. The infantry massed in line lay behind the hills, occasionally changing position to avoid the shells which fell near or among them."[13]

For four hours, Franz Sigel had been engaged in a brutal series of attacks against Stonewall Jackson's Confederates, who were tucked behind the steep, unfinished railroad embankment a mile north of the Warrenton Turnpike. Sigel's men had fought well but accomplished nothing; Jackson's men were still in the same, well-defined position they had been at dawn. Pope, however, saw matters otherwise. Certain Jackson had been in hasty retreat toward Gainesville, rather than lying in wait for Sigel's piecemeal assaults, Pope was delighted that the German had "brought [Jackson] to a stand at the little town of Groveton." Pope dismissed Sigel's plea for reinforcements with which to resume the stalled attack; he and Heintzelman, both of whom had reported in person to Pope on Dogan Ridge, were simply to "maintain the positions they occupied." Pope assured them decisive results would come from another quarter. "I told [them] the corps of McDowell and Porter were then on the march from Manassas Junction toward the enemy's right flank, and ought, in a very short time, to be in such a position as to fall upon that portion of his line." In the meantime, they would patiently await the sound of McDowell's and Porter's guns.[14]

Either Pope did not reread the retained copy of the Joint Order or Lieutenant Colonel Smith neglected to reacquaint him with its particulars, because in his addled state Pope believed his convoluted instructions to McDowell and Porter somehow obliged them to attack Stonewall Jackson's right flank, now that the elusive Virginian had been brought to bay. Nothing in the Joint Order even hinted at an attack; on the contrary, such a step would make it impossible for McDowell and Porter "to fall back behind Bull Run, at Centreville, tonight." But, Pope must have reasoned, they surely would see the opportunity before them: a chance "to fall upon the enemy's right flank, and probably upon his rear." Certain Longstreet was miles away and Jackson's destruction was but a matter of hours, Pope rode off Dogan Ridge to inspect the army's lines and spread the word about Porter's and McDowell's impending attack.[15]

Pope had given himself over entirely to wishful thinking, and he remained under its sway until the next afternoon. The one bit of evidence that might have arrested his flight of fancy—John Buford's morning dispatch announcing the arrival of Longstreet's corps—remained on General McDowell's person, unknown to army headquarters. Why McDowell neglected to forward at once this most critical intelligence to Pope defies explanation, but not before 7:00 P.M. that evening did he share Buford's note with the commanding general.

Thrilled by the prospect of Stonewall Jackson's impending ruin, Pope probably paid scant attention to matters closer at hand, and he returned from his tour of the front satisfied with the disposition of his army. Pope had found Kearny's division on the right, its flank anchored on Bull Run, above the Sudley church. Schurz's badly cut-up division held its ground along the unfinished railroad, in uncomfortable proximity to its Confederate defenders. Two regiments each from the divisions of Stevens and Hooker had been inserted on Schurz's left, filling a gap between the German's division and the equally cut-up brigade of Brigadier General Robert Milroy. In support of Milroy was Cuvier Grover's brigade of Hooker's division. From Milroy's left to the Warrenton Turnpike ran the long line of artillery that had excited the admiration of David Strother. South of the turnpike stood the divisions of Schenck and Reynolds. Just east of Pope's field headquarters, Jesse Reno held his own division and the remainder of Hooker's in reserve.[16]

Nothing Pope saw troubled him. Had he looked more closely, he would have found good cause for fury. Phil Kearny had not simply made good on his insubordinate threat to wait until morning to march from Centreville but had contributed absolutely nothing since arriving on the battlefield at 10:00 A.M. Ignoring the admonitions of Franz Sigel and corps commander Samuel Heintzelman that he join the attack on Jackson's left, Kearny had remained inactive. His supineness, which infuriated Sigel, Schurz, and Heintzelman, who swore he had given Kearny explicit orders to attack immediately, appears to have gone unnoticed by Pope. Years later, Sigel repeated headquarters gossip to the effect that, had Kearny not been killed at Chantilly, Pope would have hauled him before a court-martial, but nothing in Pope's public or private remarks on the battle suggests displeasure with the volatile New Yorker.[17]

Also indicative of the selective nature of Pope's attention was his neglect of the cavalry. So thoroughly had horses and men been used up during the campaign that few remained fit for even the minimal—but essential—duty of watching the army's flanks when it at last joined battle. Less than a mile east of the Dogan house lay the mounted brigade of Colonel John Beardsley. It had reached the field only hours earlier, but its fitness for service may be judged by Beardsley's report: "My horses were completely worn out and almost in a starving condition. All along our route they were dropping down with their riders and dying, so that when I reported to you on the morning of the twenty-ninth most of my horses were unable to carry the rider and had to be led." George Bayard's brigade was in better condition, but it had fallen back with Ricketts's infantry to Bristoe the night before. When Bayard did report to McDowell shortly after noon, that general simply had him fall in with his march column, then snaking up the Manassas-Sudley road. Buford's cavalry also had a few miles of riding left in it, but by mid-day it was too far to the rear to be of use. Absent cavalry to apprise him of the state of affairs beyond his left, Pope was left to conjecture, unaware the eighteen thousand men of Longstreet's corps now confronted Fitz John Porter's nine thousand Federals, well positioned to contest any movement Porter might make against Jackson's right.[18]

Pope had granted the troops time to rest and replenish their ammunition, but he had no intention of waiting passively for Porter and McDowell to fall on Jackson's flank. As Pope saw matters, it was imperative to keep the army active on Jackson's front, both to prevent the Virginian from escaping and to fix his attention away from his right. Consequently, after returning from his tour of inspection Pope began a series of limited attacks to distract Jackson.

Joe Hooker, whom Pope directed to make the first effort, had little enthusiasm for a frontal attack against the unfinished railroad. To drive home his objections, Hooker led Pope to a vantage point from which he might see Jackson's artillery massed along Stony Ridge, a mile and a half west of the Dogan house, their gun tubes trained to rake the ground over which Hooker's men must pass. "I told the general that if we got possession of the woods those batteries would drive me out," Hooker later testified. He would attack but thought a joint movement with Kearny might serve Pope's purposes better, and at a lesser cost; Kearny could "get on the [Confederate] flank and perhaps agitate them a little" while he, Hooker, made the frontal assault.

Pope concurred, and he issued the necessary orders to Kearny. At 3:00 P.M., Hooker threw the lone brigade of Grover full tilt against the Confederate center, while Kearny advanced the brigade of John Robinson cautiously against the Rebel left. Remarkably, Grover was able to punch a hole briefly in Jackson's defenses, but the absence of support for what Pope had only intended as a forceful probe, combined with the failure of Robinson to make contact until Grover had been in action nearly thirty minutes, made his defeat inevitable.[19]

The repulse of Grover troubled Pope not at all. Nor should it have, if one accepts the logic of Pope's plan. What did disturb him was the unaccountable silence from the direction of Porter and McDowell. "About two o'clock in the afternoon three discharges of artillery were heard on the extreme left of our line or right of the enemy's, and I for the moment, and naturally, believed that Porter and McDowell had reached their positions and were engaged with the enemy," recalled Pope. "I heard only three shots, and as nothing followed I was at a loss to know what had become of these corps, or what was delaying them, as before this hour they should have been, even with ordinary marching, well up on our left." Growing impatient, Pope decided to stir up trouble south of the Warrenton Turnpike with Reynolds's Pennsylvania Reserves.[20]

Reynolds was no more pleased with his orders to "threaten the enemy's right and rear" than Hooker had been with his. In coming onto the field, much of Longstreet's corps had crossed Reynolds's front. Although too distant to make out the size of the enemy force, Reynolds knew there were many more Confederates on his side of the turnpike than Pope believed. Nonetheless, shortly after 3:00 P.M. he moved to comply with Pope's order, advancing the brigades of Brigadier Generals Conrad Jackson and Truman Seymour due west from near the William Lewis house. A Rebel battery posted six hundred yards to their front challenged the Federals instantly, and after some feckless maneuvering to silence it, in which Jackson's brigade took several heavy volleys of musketry from beyond its left flank—a sure sign the Southern line extended well south of the turnpike—Reynolds withdrew.

In reporting the results of his abortive attack, Reynolds told the courier, Captain H. S. Thomas, to convey the gravity of the threat to the army's left. Thomas did, telling the commanding general how many enemy battle flags he himself had counted, but Pope rejected the warning out of hand: "You are excited, young man; the people you see are General Porter's command taking position on the left of the army."[21]

Turning his attention again to the front, at 4:00 P.M. Pope sent Colonel Strother to Reno with the rather nebulous order he "put forward his division to clear a large wood from whence our artillery was annoyed by the enemy's sharpshooters." Pope was certain Reno would carry out his orders cheerfully—he had been particularly impressed with Reno's "bright and confident face and alert and hearty manner" that morning—but Reno was able to make no more of an impression on Jackson's lines than had Hooker. The 1,500-man brigade of Colonel James Nagle carried the railroad embankment briefly, but it was thrown back by a fierce Rebel counterattack that nearly fractured Pope's center and compelled him to move his headquarters 800 yards east, to Buck Hill, just north of the Stone house. No great harm was done the army, beyond the 500 men lost to this latest nudge at Jackson and the damage done the good nature of Reno, who rode directly to Pope to report the destruction of Nagle's brigade. Pope contracted his front, bringing everyone north of the Warrenton Turnpike except Reynolds's division, which was to act as the link between Porter and the remainder of the army.[22]

That Reynolds was now a half-mile from the nearest support concerned Pope little. Nor did the realization that McDowell would no longer be a part of the attack on Jackson's flank deter him. Shortly after sending Hooker forward, Pope had learned that McDowell was on his way up the Manassas-Sudley road and would be on the field with the divisions of Hatch and Ricketts within two hours. Riding ahead of his corps, McDowell and his staff reached Henry Hill at about 4:00 P.M. Rather than report to Pope, McDowell elected to await the arrival of his troops. The message from Buford remained in his pocket.

It was Pope who called on McDowell. As the survivors from Nagle's brigade and the flotsam of its supporting brigade fell back toward the Dogan house, Pope called upon McDowell for troops for a new line he was fashioning along Dogan Ridge. McDowell hastened down the Manassas-Sudley road to find them.

Gibbon's brigade led the march column. "Late in the afternoon, approaching the Henry House ahead of my brigade, I met General McDowell with his staff and mounted escort around him," remembered Gibbon. "He came forward to meet me, appearing to be laboring under great excitement and exclaiming—'Hurry forward, hurry forward, you are just in the nick of time.'" Gibbon asked him for orders. "Go right up that road," said McDowell, pointing north along the Manassas-Sudley road, toward Dogan Ridge in the distance. "To whom shall I report?" asked Gibbon. McDowell merely answered, "Go right up that road. I shall be here."[23]

For the moment, McDowell would stay on Henry Hill to deploy the remainder of his corps against what he adjudged a greater threat than the Confederate counterattack against Pope's center. Mindful of the Southern buildup south of the Warrenton Turnpike, McDowell retained Ricketts's division and the remaining brigades of Hatch's division along the Manassas-Sudley road, between Henry and Bald hills, in support of Reynolds. But while McDowell considered the Southern presence opposite Reynolds serious enough to withhold ten thousand troops from the fighting, he apparently gave no thought to informing Pope of the danger. Buford's warning was yet unknown to army headquarters.[24]

With the collapse of Nagle's assault, Pope grew weary of abiding Porter. At 4:30 P.M., he dictated to Colonel Ruggles an unequivocal order for Porter to attack. "Your line of march brings you in on the enemy's flank," Pope informed Porter. "I desire you to push forward into action at once on the enemy's right flank, and, if possible, on his rear, keeping your right in communication with

General Reynolds." A vast improvement over the Joint Order in terms of clarity, the 4:30 P.M. order was based on an assumption no less erroneous: fundamentally, Pope's continued certainty Longstreet was far from the battlefield.[25]

Although unsure precisely where Porter was, Pope assumed it would take no more than an hour for a courier "riding rapidly" to reach him. With sunset at 6:30 P.M. and nightfall less than an hour later, Porter would have little time to prepare his command to attack, unless, as Pope probably assumed, Porter's corps was already drawn up in line of battle.

General Pope entrusted the order to his aide-de-camp and nephew, Captain Douglass Pope, who had no idea how to find Porter. Colonel Ruggles suggested he take the Warrenton-Alexandria road, which ran west from the Manassas-Sudley road south of the Warrenton Turnpike. Captain Pope wisely disregarded that advice—to have followed it would have led him straight into Longstreet's lines—and instead opted to take the Manassas-Sudley road to its intersection with the Manassas Gap Railroad, as his orderly counseled, and from there search for Porter.[26]

Captain Pope and his squad of orderlies had gone perhaps two miles down the Manassas-Sudley road when they ran into General McDowell, who was bringing up Ricketts's division. Lengthening shadows whispered the need for haste, but McDowell insisted Captain Pope, who had not read the order himself, show it to him. McDowell opened the envelope and studied the order. He commented on the importance of the order but, inexplicably, said nothing to the captain of Buford's warning. Nor did he give any indication that the order could not be obeyed literally because Jackson's right flank was not in the air.

By the time Captain Pope resumed his ride, the forest lining the Manassas-Sudley road had grown dark; twilight was near. When he at last reached Porter is an open question. Captain Pope later insisted it was not later than 5:00 P.M.; one of his orderlies guessed 5:30 P.M.; Porter said it was closer to 6:30 P.M., which, given the rough state of the road much of the way and Ruggles's recollection that he *began* writing the order at 4:30 P.M., undoubtedly is closest to the truth.[27]

Captain Pope found Porter resting under a tree, still weak from the dysentery that had struck him hard at Falmouth two weeks earlier. Without rising, Porter read the order carefully. Although his manner seemed matter-of-fact, Porter intended to comply. Only a few minutes earlier, in response to an exuberant message from General Hatch that Pope had "driven the enemy into the woods" (which Porter, in turn, hopefully construed to mean Jackson was in full retreat), he had ordered Morell to reconnoiter his front. When Porter received the 4:30 P.M. order, he modified his instructions accordingly: Morell was to attack with his entire division.

Morell was incredulous. From his skirmish line had come repeated warnings of a huge Rebel presence, extending across his front and beyond his left flank.

Porter's earlier order calling for a forced reconnaissance had been troubling enough. To brigade commander Charles Griffin, who asked if he intended to comply, Morell had said, "No, it is too late; and this order has been given under a wrong impression. Colonel Marshall, who commands the pickets in front, states that the enemy are receiving reinforcements." Then Morell had dispatched a note to Porter remonstrating against the movement. Now, he repeated his fears to the bearer of the latest order, Lieutenant Colonel Frederick Locke, who in the fast-gathering twilight Morell could hardly see.[28]

Porter settled the matter a few minutes later. Morell's note had convinced him General Hatch had been wrong about the enemy retreating and Pope grossly mistaken about both Jackson's flank and, with a heavy enemy before him, Porter's ability to reach it. Galloping to the front, he told Morell to take up a strong defensive position and bed down the men for the night.[29]

Neither Porter nor his subordinates feared their inaction would compromise Pope. On the contrary, Porter thought it crucial to the very survival of the army that he hold fast: "It was, beyond peradventure, my duty to hold on to the strong position in which my front was posted, with my center and rear within close supporting distance, and thus hold in check before me the massing forces of the enemy [Longstreet's corps], which, but for my presence there, would have closed up at once upon Jackson's right, crushed our forces in front of it, outflanked General Pope on his left [and] surely doomed General Pope's whole army which was engaged that day to an inevitable and signal defeat."[30]

Despite McDowell's negligent handling of Buford's message, General Pope that afternoon did receive—but chose to disregard—reliable notice of Longstreet's presence opposite Porter. Lieutenant Stephen Weld, the clear-headed aide-de-camp to General Porter, had left the general's side at 4:00 P.M. with an urgent message for General King or McDowell that should have awakened Pope to the hazard.

Three miles of rolling fields and thick forest intervening between Porter's corps and the remainder of the army alternately distorted and deadened the crash of battle from across the Warrenton Turnpike. During much of the afternoon, neither Porter nor his generals could hear anything more than occasional artillery; rifle fire was completely lost in the timber. Consequently, when General Morell reported that the cannonading seemed to be receding in the direction of Bull Run, Porter accepted his conclusion that Pope was falling back. Having been unable to open communications with Reynolds and mindful of Pope's counsel in the Joint Order that the army might have to retire behind Bull Run before nightfall, Porter concluded to withdraw and sought to apprise King and McDowell of his decision.[31]

From General Hatch, Lieutenant Weld learned King had left the field ill.

Hatch suggested Weld deliver the message to McDowell. Weld found McDowell at army headquarters. McDowell (who had reported in at 5:00 P.M., without showing Pope the message from Buford) studied Porter's note, then protested, "I am not the man; there is the man," waving his arm in the direction of General Pope. Weld then approached the commanding general. It was probably 5:30 P.M. Distracted by heavy fighting on his own front, Pope seems not to have paid much attention to Porter's message, although Weld said he repeated it to Pope orally after the commanding general glanced at it. He dismissed Porter's fear that a large force confronted him; any troops opposite Porter's corps were merely small detachments sent out by Jackson to meet Longstreet's column, reasoned Pope, which of course had not yet come up. Nearly everyone in Pope's military family agreed, as did McDowell and his staff: Jackson was trapped, plain and simple.

Before leaving, Weld asked Pope if he had any instructions for General Porter. Undoubtedly assuming the 4:30 P.M. order borne by his nephew would arrest any rearward march of Porter, Pope merely shrugged, "Tell General Porter we are having a hard fight." Was that all he had to send to General Porter, inquired Weld? "Yes," Pope answered. Turning from the lieutenant, Pope fell into an animated discussion with McDowell. Weld withdrew a short distance, waited five minutes in case the commanding general wished to add something, then started back to corps headquarters.[32]

The commotion that had drawn Pope from Lieutenant Weld was the repulse of his third effort of the afternoon against Stonewall Jackson. After shoring up the Union center in the wake of Nagle's failed attack and ordering Porter into action at 4:30 P.M., Pope had concluded to again assault Jackson's left, the only portion of the unfinished railroad defenses where he had enjoyed any real success.

To anyone who may have questioned the wisdom of a third piecemeal attack, Pope justified it as necessary to draw Jackson's attention away from his right, which Porter—with the 4:30 P.M. order before him—would now certainly assault.[33]

Phil Kearny offered no objection; whatever disparaging remarks he may have made about Pope while in his cups, he was only too pleased to go into battle now for an aggressive commander. Following a furious shelling of the unfinished railroad that probably killed as many of Reno's wounded as it did Confederate defenders, at 5:00 P.M. Kearny unleashed two brigades against Jackson's nearly fought-out left. In two hours of brutal close combat, the Federals first swept the Confederates from the embankment and across the Groveton-Sudley road, before they were in turn thrown back into the fields from which they had come by a counterattack of Jackson's only fresh brigade, the 2,500-man command of Jubal Early. As his troops spilled out of the timber, Kearny galloped to headquarters at sunset to solicit help. He had carried the wood, Kearny told Pope breathlessly;

his loss "had been awful, but that of the enemy had been three to one. The enemy had marched on him in lines ten deep, which had been mowed down by the steady fire of his infantry."

Kearny's frenzy was contagious. Addressing McDowell, Pope enjoined, "The enemy are trying to turn our right; they have sent one or two brigades there, and I want you to send your division." McDowell demurred (it was then that Lieutenant Weld left the generals), and after some harsh words, Pope relented. Instead, he would send Reno back into the fray to bolster Kearny's line and renew the attack on the Rebel left. After writing the necessary orders, Pope and his staff rode toward the right to superintend their execution.[34]

Unlike Kearny, Reno no longer had the stomach for a fight. He had no intention of sacrificing Colonel Edward Ferrero's brigade in an effort as quixotic as that which had wrecked Nagle's two hours earlier, and he told Pope as much when they met in front of his division. Pope relented and left.

The men of Ferrero's brigade were pleased to see him go. Recalled a grateful soldier, "We thanked God that General Reno stood between us and General Pope."[35]

━ ✦ ━

John Gibbon sat pensively atop Dogan Ridge, watching the last streaks of red in the western sky fade to gray. Lost in contemplation of the carnage of attack and counterattack that profaned the fields before him, Gibbon was startled to see Generals Pope and Heintzelman and their staffs appear on the ridge. They paused a moment beside Gibbon. Scrutinizing the vista of gore, Pope commanded, "Colonel Ruggles, telegraph to Washington that we have had a severe battle and have lost ten thousand men." Then, as if shaken, he added quietly, "I think we have lost ten thousand men."[36]

Drawing rein near the Dogan house next, Pope saw a rejuvenating sight. Stretched out along the Warrenton Turnpike, rumbling westward, was a train of Confederate wagons. To Pope this could mean but one thing: "the enemy was retreating toward the pike from the direction of Sudley Springs." Colonel Ruggles begged to differ; perhaps the wagons were merely ambulances conveying wounded to the rear. No, rejoined Pope, Jackson was retreating; a pursuit must be mounted at once.[37]

A courier galloped to McDowell with orders for him to push out a division after the Confederates. Succumbing to the madness of the moment, McDowell selected Hatch's division for the "chase," assuring him and his brigade commanders that Jackson's "whole line was in great confusion, and that it was only necessary for us to move forward to render his rout complete and capture a large number of fugitives."

McDowell and his staff were on hand to encourage Hatch's Federals as they stepped off Chinn Ridge and started down the Warrenton Turnpike at the double quick. Bellowed an aide-de-camp, "The enemy is in full retreat down the Warrenton Turnpike. General Hatch will pursue, overtake, and attack him!" Another staff officer yelled out, "All you have to do is to go ahead and shoot."[38]

"As we went on, with the army watching us from the hills around, everything seemed quiet and peaceable," brigade commander Abner Doubleday remembered. "There was not even a straggler visible." For three-quarters of a mile the Federals marched unopposed, through the hamlet of Groveton and up a gentle rise beyond. Suddenly the forest in front erupted with the thunder of thousands of Southern rifle-muskets. From Buck Hill, the spectacle was bucolic in its beauty. "There occurred a very sharply contested and very beautiful combat of musketry," marveled David Strother. "The woods and meadows sparkled as with lightning bugs in July." Said Colonel Smith, "The flickering play of the musketry fire from the two lines engaged made a striking display, like a brilliant fireworks." Phil Kearny was delighted. "Look at that!" he exclaimed to Smith. "Did you ever see the like of that? Isn't it beautiful?"[39]

From headquarters the scene may have been splendid, but at the front, "the long flickering line of fire" was sinister. It "showed that we were greatly outnumbered," lamented Doubleday, whose brigade was slowly slaughtered by a foe whose front extended well beyond the Federal flanks. "The enemy," recalled a New York soldier, "were rather more combative than we presumed retreating forces usually to be." General Hatch agreed, and he sent his adjutant, Captain J. A. Judson, galloping back to Buck Hill to apprise McDowell of the calamity, in the hope he would call off the attack. Instead McDowell, as certain as Pope that the Confederates were in retreat, exploded with rage. "What! Does General Hatch hesitate?" he bellowed. "Tell him the enemy is in full retreat and to pursue him!" Mortified, Captain Judson returned to the front. "I delivered this reply to General Hatch," remembered Judson, "but it was no longer a question."[40]

During Judson's absence, the fight had deteriorated beyond the ability of anyone to direct. Gun smoke rolled over the ridge, cloaking the twilight in gray. In the forest, all was blackness and bedlam. It was fighting by feel. Opposing lines collided by chance, and friend fired on friend as often as upon foe.

Hatch kept up the struggle until nearly surrounded. It was 8:00 P.M. when the senseless affair ended and Hatch's Federals spilled back toward Chinn Ridge, having contributed two hundred more bodies to the carpet of blue that covered the fields west of Dogan Ridge.[41]

Led to believe he would encounter only the dispirited stragglers of a fleeing army, Hatch instead had run into the eager veterans of John Bell Hood's division of Longstreet's corps. Far from contemplating a withdrawal, since his arrival on the battlefield earlier that afternoon Robert E. Lee had thought only of attack. He wanted to throw Longstreet's entire command at once against the Federal left, which seemed to be protected only by Reynolds's isolated division. But Longstreet dissented; the Yankee column along the Manassas-Gainesville road looked quite capable of devastating his own right flank. After surveying the field himself at 3:00 P.M., Lee not only agreed to postpone the attack but also insisted Longstreet shore up his right. Frustrated by the presence of Porter and Hatch from either attacking himself or reinforcing Jackson's exhausted troops, Longstreet passed the next hour watching Griffin's Federal brigade maneuver along Dawkins's Branch.

By 4:30 P.M., the Yankees appeared far less menacing to Longstreet, and the dust Hatch and Ricketts raised on their march up the Manassas-Sudley road suggested a partial enemy withdrawal from his right. Longstreet again beckoned Lee, and they concluded to push Hood forward on a twilight reconnaissance-in-force, in order to gain a better position for an all-out assault along the Warrenton Turnpike at daybreak and, as Longstreet put it, perhaps find "an opening for an entering wedge" in the Federal lines.[42]

It was too dark after Hatch's retreat for Longstreet to appreciate fully just how wide a wedge he had worked into the Yankee front. When the last ragged volleys ended shortly before 9:00 P.M., nearly ten thousand Confederates lay a few dozen yards from the heart of Pope's position.[43]

To Marsena Patrick, the proximity of the enemy was all too apparent. His brigade had been hustled out the Warrenton Turnpike to cover the retreat of Doubleday and Sullivan. Scarcely had he shepherded his men into line when voices in the dark challenged him and his staff. Thinking them friendly, Patrick answered "Patrick's brigade, King's division." Came the reply: "Surrender or we fire." Patrick and his staff made a dash for it, but the Confederates fired toward the sound of beating hooves; Patrick escaped, but two of his staff fell. Patrick immediately pulled his brigade back to the Dogan house, where their safety was more illusory than real; Abner Doubleday said Patrick's pickets and those of the Rebels sank to the ground to sleep side by side, "each taking the other for friends."[44]

No sooner had Patrick escaped than Lieutenant Colonel Judson Kilpatrick, one of the army's foremost field-grade fools, sent one squadron of his Second New York Cavalry galloping down the dark turnpike, for reasons known only to him. The troopers rode straight into two Confederate brigades, which obliterated them. Only eleven horsemen survived.

In Hatch's scrape, Patrick's close escape, and Kilpatrick's suicidal charge was evidence aplenty that the enemy was astride the Warrenton Turnpike in strength. The danger should have been obvious, but at army headquarters the dominant sentiment was unguarded optimism. Confessed Colonel Strother: "It was the prevailing opinion that [Pope] had Jackson trapped, and so secure were we in our ability to handle him that we already enjoyed the victory in advance."[45]

That night, John Pope's greatest concern was that Stonewall Jackson might slip away before he was able to deliver a final, crushing blow against the Virginian. When McDowell at last handed him Buford's morning dispatch, Pope no longer could deny the presence of Longstreet on the battlefield. But from that knowledge he benefited little. Ignoring Porter's protestations that Longstreet stood opposite his corps, and refusing to consider Hood's twilight thrust against Hatch as an augury of Longstreet's plans, Pope simply willed Longstreet's twelve brigades into the place he himself would have them: in direct support to Jackson's battered lines. Of his thinking on the evening of August 29, Pope later said, "I expected that Longstreet would seek to join Jackson by the Warrenton turnpike. That would have brought Longstreet to the center of Jackson's line, as we understood it."

Dismissing the possibility Longstreet might form on Jackson's right, Pope also calculated the time of Longstreet's arrival to suit his own designs, that is, his conviction that Porter could have rolled up Jackson's flank at any time during the afternoon of August 29. Buford had reported Longstreet's column as having passed through Gainesville at 9:30 A.M. As Gainesville was a mere five miles from the battlefield and nothing stood in the way of Longstreet's Confederates, there was no reason why, marching over a broad turnpike at even a leisurely rate, they should not have come up before noon. Yet Pope refused to believe any considerable portion of Longstreet's corps had come on the field before 8:00 P.M.[46]

That none of his assumptions was founded on fact troubled Pope not at all; simply stated, he was locked in a paralysis of reason. Matters *must* be as Pope hoped they were because his plans *required* that they be so. Three weeks of sidling along the Rappahannock River opposite Robert E. Lee; of marching and countermarching after a foe as elusive as Stonewall Jackson; of indulging a general-in-chief as vacillating and mendacious as Henry Halleck, whom Pope nonetheless had expected—and hoped—would assume field command; of daily disappointments in no reinforcements and few supplies, would have severely taxed a veteran commander. For a man of Pope's mercurial temperament, who had never before led so much as a squad into battle, the strain proved unbearable. His thin veneer of composure had cracked under the comparatively benign stress of New Madrid; the bloodletting here at Bull Run stripped it off entirely. In John Pope that night, passion replaced rational thought. He clutched at tactical straws, and blind hope was his guidepost.[47]

Alternately jubilant or furious, as his emotions dictated, Pope must have frightened from the headquarters campfire all but his most intimate associates.

Not that their presence mattered. To a man, they seem to have shared in their commander's delusion. General Roberts marched in step with Pope, as did General McDowell, who bedded down early beside the ruins of the Widow Henry's house, convinced the enemy "were fast falling back." Certainly the sycophantic Thomas C. H. Smith contributed no original thoughts that night, and of the rest of the staff he later confessed, "the general feeling was one of over-elation because of our success on the enemy's left and this was added to by the fact that after Hatch's attack had failed the enemy withdrew their forces on that side of the turnpike to some distance in the rear." As chief of staff, Colonel Ruggles might have injected some sense into the proceedings atop Buck Hill, but his loathing of Pope probably kept him on the periphery.[48]

As the fury of Hatch's fight subsided, with no gain for the Federals, Pope grew angry. Perhaps forgetting he had sent Hatch forward to pursue an enemy who had no idea of leaving, Pope chose instead to blame Hatch's discomfiture on Porter's failure to attack Jackson's right flank, which he yet believed had been shored up by merely a fragment of Longstreet's corps. He remembered the missive Lieutenant Weld had handed him two hours earlier, and in it he now read a perfidious intent. By the uncertain light of a field lantern, Pope scrutinized Porter's every word. As Pope's anger mounted, McDowell slipped him another dispatch, which Porter had written him at 6:00 P.M. In it, Porter told McDowell the enemy lay between their corps. His messengers had been fired on or captured, and Rebel infantry had massed on his front. Huge dust clouds on his left suggested a major enemy movement in that direction. Porter requested instructions. "Please let me know your designs, whether you retire or not," he implored. "I cannot get water and am out of provisions. Have lost a few men from infantry firing."[49]

Pope exploded with a volley of foul epithets. *Have lost a few men from infantry firing?* Outrageous! Porter was to have attacked with his entire corps. He had had his orders. Why had he not obeyed? Pope neither knew nor probably would have cared, had he known, that Porter had written McDowell before receiving Pope's 4:30 P.M. order to attack. In Pope's mind, there could be but one explanation: Porter was a traitor.

"I'll arrest him!" thundered Pope, and he began dictating an invective-laden message to Porter. McDowell interrupted with a feeble defense of the man. Porter had not acted "from any deliberate purpose to fail in his duty" but "had probably made his military mistake from incapacity." More to the point, McDowell added, the army had won a victory; it would "produce a bad impression to cloud it by taking steps that might be considered unwarranted." Generals Roberts and Hooker endorsed McDowell's view and, after simmering a bit longer, Pope yielded. He told Colonel Smith to set aside the incomplete tirade in favor of peremptory orders for Porter to report to the main battlefield. Penned at 8:50 P.M., the message smoldered with the heat of Pope's inner rage. "Immediately upon the receipt of this order, the precise hour of receiving which you will acknowledge, you will march your command to the field of battle of to-day and report to me in person for orders," demanded Pope. "You are to understand that you are expected to comply strictly with this order, and to be present on the field within three hours after its receipt, or after daybreak to-morrow morning."[50]

Pope calmed enough to order Reynolds north of the Warrenton Turnpike, to be available for the climactic struggle on the morrow. Not for an instant did Pope contemplate withdrawing. Neither did he make firm plans to attack. Shortly after 9:00 P.M., the gathering on Buck Hill broke up. Exhausted but elated, Pope had elected to "wait until morning to decide upon what should be done."[51]

Judge Nathaniel Pope
(Illinois State Historical
Library)

Lucretia Backus Pope
(Illinois State Historical
Library)

Kaskaskia, Illinois, in the Early Nineteenth Century (Illinois State Historical Library)

Colonel John James Abert,
painted by Thomas Sully,
father of Brigadier General
Alfred Sully (United States
Military Academy Museum
Collections)

Congressman Valentine B. Horton (Ohio Historical Society)

Horton Family Home (far left), Pomeroy, Ohio (Ohio Historical Society)

Clara Horton Pope, as she appeared at middle age (United States Military Academy Museum Collections)

Brigadier General John Pope, 1861 (Massachusetts Commandery, Military Order of the Loyal Legion, and the United States Army Military History Institute)

Major General John C. Frémont (Ray D. Smith Collection, Knox College)

Brigadier General John Pope, spring 1862 (Massachusetts Commandery, Military Order of the Loyal Legion, and the United States Army Military History Institute)

General Pope's Encampment before Corinth (*Battles and Leaders of the Civil War*)

Major General and Mrs. George B. McClellan (Library of Congress)

Major General Irvin Mc-
Dowell (Ray D. Smith Col-
lection, Knox College)

Brigadier General Ben-
jamin S. Roberts (Chris
Nelson Collection, United
States Army Military History Institute)

Colonel George D. Ruggles
(Roger D. Hunt Collection,
United States Army Mili-
tary History Institute)

Major General Fitz John
Porter (Ray D. Smith Col-
lection, Knox College)

Pope's Headquarters at Warrenton (Ray D. Smith Collection, Knox College)

The Army of Virginia Entering Centreville (Mrs. Edwin Forbes, *The Life of General W. T. Sherman*)

Major General John Pope, after Second Bull Run. This photo was taken in Milwaukee less than a week after Second Bull Run, as Pope made his way to Minnesota. Compare this with the portrait of Pope taken in spring 1862; the burden of command has ravaged his features. (Milwaukee County Historical Society)

Judge Joseph Holt (*Century* magazine, October 1887)

Lieutenant General Philip H. Sheridan. A postwar view. (Ray D. Smith Collection, Knox College)

Major General John Pope, mid-1880s; photo was probably taken shortly before his retirement. (National Archives)

9 *Leave Pope to Get Out of His Scrape*

Saturday, August 30, 1862, dawned warm and fair, with the promise of a splendid summer day. "Not a warlike sound disturbed the peaceful calm," said General Doubleday's chief of subsistence, Captain George F. Noyes. "The hillsides, which yesterday echoed with fierce artillery, were now silent; the little valleys, then swarming with graybacks, were now quiet as if there was no such thing as war. The dense forest in front of us might indeed be full of treason."

Pope was up early, chewing a cigar and pacing about Buck Hill with a field glass in hand. The forest to the west was as inscrutable to him as it was to Captain Noyes. Uncertainty and the sorry state of his army reduced Pope to a perfect nonplus. "On the morning of the 30th, as may be supposed, our troops, who had been so continually marching and fighting for so many days, were in a state of great exhaustion," wrote Pope. "They had little to eat for two days previous, and artillery and cavalry horses had been in harness and saddle continuously for ten days, and had had no forage for two days previous. It may easily be imagined how little these troops, after such severe labors, and after undergoing such hardships and privation, were in condition for active and efficient service."[1]

Their commanding general was hardly better off himself. Pope had eaten little since the battle began, and this morning he either skipped breakfast or just nibbled at scraps. His chief sustenance was the string of strong cigars he sucked at furiously—which, on a nearly empty stomach, undoubtedly clouded his thinking as much as they clouded the air around him.[2]

Having appealed to Halleck for supplies two days earlier, Pope was hopeful that men and horses would soon be fed—that is, until a courier handed him a message from the telegraph station at Manassas, shortly before 5:00 A.M. As the courier withdrew, Lieutenant Colonel Thomas C. H. Smith glanced at the commanding general: "Pope was standing in plain sight of us all on Buck Hill and when he read the dispatch which the courier brought, it was evident that something terrible had happened." He read the dispatch, clutched it, crumpled it in his hand, then paced distractedly about.

Pope's demeanor troubled Colonel Louis Marshall. He had known the commanding general for many years and had served with him since the war began. "I never saw Pope get down but once," Marshall later told Smith. "That was when he got that damned dispatch from McClellan at Alexandria."

Only Benjamin Roberts had the nerve to approach Pope. "What is it, General?" he asked. Pope shoved the dispatch at him. Written by General Franklin at 8:00 P.M. the night before, it read, "I have been instructed by General McClellan to inform you that he will have all available wagons at Alexandria loaded with rations for your troops, and all of the cars, also, as soon as you will send in a cavalry escort to Alexandria as a guard to the train."

Pope was stunned. "Such a letter, when we were fighting the enemy, and Alexandria was swarming with troops, needs no comment. Bad as was the condition of our cavalry, I was in no situation to spare troops from the front nor could they have gone to Alexandria and returned within the time by which we must have had provisions or have fallen back in the direction of Washington," he later protested. "Nor do I yet see what service cavalry could have rendered in guarding railroad trains. It was not until I received this letter that I began to feel discouraged and nearly hopeless of any successful issue to the operations with which I was charged."[3]

For reasons to him equally sound, George B. McClellan felt as forlorn as Pope. Fear for the fate of the capital—a responsibility that Halleck had abdicated to him—and for the corps of Franklin and Sumner, should Pope be defeated while they were en route to him, kept McClellan up the entire night of August 28–29.

Alarmist reports from Brigadier General John Barnard, commander of the capital defenses, and Halleck's renewed dithering only compounded his frustration. Shortly after midnight, Barnard warned McClellan of reports "to headquarters that Lee is advancing on Washington to-night, probably by the Chain Bridge. I doubt whether these works can be held with the raw troops." Barnard begged McClellan for troops—at least a regiment with artillery—to hold the forts.[4]

The reports Barnard spoke of were merely unconfirmed rumors—the fabrications of stragglers, some of whom insisted Lee was on his way with 120,000 men. But they were believed, and not merely by Barnard. General Halleck not only accepted them at face value, saying his failure to confirm their veracity was due to the absence of available staff officers at his headquarters, but also directed McClellan to send every command but Franklin's to man the defenses. "I think you had better place Sumner's corps as it arrives near the fortifications, and particularly at the Chain Bridge," enjoined Halleck. "The principal thing to be feared now is a cavalry raid into this city, especially in the night-time. Use Cox's and Tyler's brigades and the new troops for the same object, if you need them."[5]

With grave misgivings that Lee might come between Pope and the capital, McClellan complied with Halleck's orders of the night before, telling Franklin to march forth from Alexandria along the Little River Turnpike. Franklin's eleven thousand men set off to the rumble of a heavy cannonade that rolled in from the west and seemed to draw steadily nearer.[6]

The cannonade troubled McClellan, as Halleck had not told him how far he wanted Franklin to go or what precisely he wished him to accomplish. At 10:30 A.M., McClellan pointedly expressed his apprehension. Franklin had started at 6:00 A.M. as instructed, Little Mac assured Halleck, with only two squadrons of cavalry to screen his advance and but forty rounds of ammunition per man. "If [Sumner] moves in support of Franklin it leaves us without any reliable troops in and near Washington, yet Franklin is too weak alone. What shall be done?" McClellan repeated his query ninety minutes later.

While Franklin's troops marched "quietly and easily" along the Little River Turnpike toward Fairfax Court House, McClellan waited for a response to his telegrams. At 1:00 P.M., he again importuned Halleck for instructions: "I anxiously await reply to my last dispatch in regard to Sumner. Wish to give the orders at once. Shall I do as seems best to me with all the troops in this vicinity, including Franklin who I really think ought not under present circumstances to advance beyond Annandale?"[7]

As the afternoon passed with no reply from the general-in-chief, McClellan's patience wore thin. When at 2:30 P.M., President Lincoln, who himself had heard little from Halleck, telegraphed asking what news Little Mac had heard from the direction of Manassas Junction in particular, and "what generally," McClellan seized the chance to present his case to the president and perhaps get guidance of the sort he had sought unsuccessfully from Halleck. With the distant pounding of artillery as a backdrop, McClellan sat down in the open air of his hilltop headquarters at Alexandria and hastily scrawled a response. Less than fifteen minutes after receiving the president's inquiry, McClellan sent a reply. "The last news I received from the direction of Manassas was from stragglers, to the effect

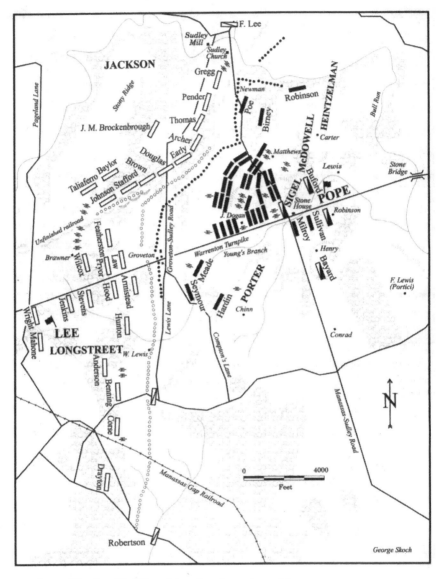

The Second Battle of Bull Run, Morning, August 30, 1862

that the enemy were evacuating Centreville and retiring through Thoroughfare Gap. This is by no means reliable," McClellan told Lincoln. "I am clear that one of two courses should be adopted: first, to concentrate all our available forces to open communication with Pope; second, to leave Pope to get out of his scrape, and at once use all our means to make the capital perfectly safe. No middle course will now answer. Tell me what you wish me to do, and I will do all in my power to accomplish it."[8]

After dashing off his missive to the president, McClellan wrote his wife, Ellen. "I have a terrible task on my hands now," he rued, "perfect imbecility to correct. No means to act with, no authority—yet determined if possible to save the country and the capital. Two of my corps will either save that fool Pope or be sacrificed for the country. I have just telegraphed very plainly to the president and Halleck what I think ought to be done—I expect merely a contemptuous silence." It was vintage Little Mac—Pope was a fool, Lincoln and Halleck imbeciles, and he the maligned savior of the nation—but not surprising under the circumstances.[9]

The words McClellan had chosen with the president also were infelicitous, noted John Codman Ropes, "but time pressed. They certainly conveyed the idea." And, as McClellan's biographer Stephen Sears has observed, to leave one to "get out of his scrape" was a pet expression of Little Mac, with no malice intended. Although the phrase would come back to haunt McClellan, particularly during the 1864 presidential election, Lincoln took no immediate umbrage at it. Rather, he simply told McClellan he thought his first alternative, "to concentrate all our available forces to open communication with Pope," to be the right one, but he did not wish to dictate a course of action; "that I wish to leave to General Halleck, aided by your counsels."[10]

Halleck, however, was incapable of decisive action. Secretary of the Navy Gideon Welles, who saw him occasionally during the late-August crisis, found him to be "heavy and irresolute" of mind and possessing "little real military talent. Destitute of originality, bewildered by the conduct of McClellan and his generals, without military resources [and, Welles might have added, terrified of Stanton], Halleck could devise nothing and knew not what to advise or do."[11]

Fifteen minutes after telling his wife he expected only "contemptuous silence" from Washington, McClellan had an answer from Halleck. It was more a note of capitulation than a statement of purpose. "Your proposed disposition of Sumner's corps seems to me judicious," Halleck began. "Of course I have no time to examine into details. The present danger is a raid upon Washington in the night-time. Dispose of all troops as you deem best." As for Franklin, he need only go far enough out to learn something of the enemy. "Perhaps he may get such information at Annandale as to prevent his going farther; otherwise he will push on toward Fairfax." In either case, Halleck seemed to say, as long as communications with Pope remained interrupted and the possibility of a strike on Washington existed, Franklin's corps was to be retained for the defense of the capital. Any news from Manassas should be gotten "by telegram or through Franklin's scouts" only.[12]

To McClellan's way of thinking, the matter was settled. He undoubtedly reasoned, as John Codman Ropes speculated he had, "Why send out Franklin at all into a region where he may have to fight a battle, unless for an object commensurate with the risk? If Franklin is required for the defense of the capital let him stay here; if he is not, let him make the best of his way to Pope and add his troops to the Army of Virginia." As McClellan had told the president, "no middle course will now answer."[13]

McClellan ordered Franklin to halt at Annandale, eight miles out of Alexandria and twelve miles short of Centreville, after Franklin forwarded him a report from the commander of his lead division, William Farrar Smith, that stragglers—one of whom was the colonel of a regiment—had said the enemy was advancing in force from Centreville. By nightfall, Franklin had more cheering news, which coincided precisely with Pope's mistaken estimate of the situation at the close of the fighting on August 29. Pope's army had fought well but was dangerously low on provisions. "From all the evidence the inference is that we have met with no disaster and that Stonewall is in a tight place," Franklin told McClellan, who forwarded the message to Halleck.[14]

Although Halleck now had the information he required of Franklin, he was hardly pleased. President Lincoln had called on Halleck late that afternoon, to show him McClellan's "Leave Pope to get out of his scrape" missive. Confronted with a note his own vacillation had compelled, Halleck dissembled, assuring the president he had ordered out Franklin's corps for the purpose of carrying out the very course of action that Lincoln had suggested to Little Mac, that is to say, to open communications with Pope. As he had the evening before in response to Stanton's interrogatory, Halleck again found it expedient to weave fiction. Halleck knew McClellan was an easy target; Secretary of the Treasury Chase had dropped by that afternoon to remind Halleck of his and Stanton's disgust with McClellan. Perhaps in the very presence of the chief executive, at 7:50 P.M. Halleck wrote McClellan a testy, obfuscating dispatch. "I have just been told that Franklin's corps stopped at Annandale, and that he was this evening in Alexandria," he began. "This is all contrary to my orders; investigate and report the facts of this disobedience. That corps must push forward, as I directed, protect the railroad, and open communications with Manassas."

Halleck had succeeded in driving deeper the wedge between Lincoln and McClellan, while deflecting blame from himself. The president returned to the White House outraged at McClellan's willingness to leave Pope to his fate, in the face of Halleck's apparent (but nonexistent) orders that he push reinforcements to him. "He has acted badly toward Pope," the president told his personal secretary, John Hay, the next morning. "He really wanted him to fail." And what of Halleck, inquired Hay, did he have any prejudices? Absolutely not, rejoined Lincoln. "Halleck is wholly for the service. He does not care who succeeds or fails, so the service is benefited."[15]

Halleck's reprimand baffled McClellan. He freely acknowledged holding Franklin at Annandale but failed to see how he had disobeyed orders. "In regard to tomorrow's movements, I desire definite instructions, as it is not agreeable to me to be accused of disregarding orders when I have simply exercised the discretion you committed to me," replied McClellan. Before retiring for the night, Little Mac cataloged his grievances to Ellen: "I am terribly crippled by the want of cavalry. I have seen neither the president nor the secretary since I arrived. I have no faith in anyone here and expect to be turned loose the moment their alarm is over." And he and Halleck had gotten into a row, which McClellan tried to interpret in the best possible light. "He sent me a telegram I did not like and I told him so very plainly. He is not a refined person at all, and probably says rough things when he don't mean them." Nothing in what McClellan said or wrote that day suggested a desire to see Pope defeated. That morning, he had sent off Franklin with the admonition, "Go, and whatever may happen, don't allow it to be said that the Army of the Potomac failed to do its utmost for the country." Now he simply told Ellen that "Pope has been in a tight place, but from the news received this evening I think the danger is pretty much over. Tomorrow will tell the story."[16]

— ◆ —

If Franklin's request for cavalry left Pope "discouraged and nearly hopeless," as he later insisted it had, he certainly hid his feelings well. Responding to a summons, Captain Noyes rode over to Buck Hill at dawn. Apart from the gathered generals, staff officers, cavalry orderlies, and inevitable gaggle of orderlies, only a few scattered cracker boxes and tents marked the spot of army headquarters. Noyes counted a dozen generals on Buck Hill beside Pope and McDowell, among them Franz Sigel, Sam Heintzelman, Phil Kearny, Joe Hooker, John Gibbon, and his own brigade commander, Abner Doubleday.

All were in remarkably fine spirits, remembered Noyes, and none more so than Pope. His generals stood in small clusters, each of which Pope visited in turn, "with the inevitable cigar in his mouth, evidently overflowing with good humor."[17]

Pope's change of temper had been abrupt. Just a few minutes before, he had been snarling to all present about the perfidy of Fitz John Porter, who had yet to report in. Porter had done nothing the day before, while the rest of the army fought for its life, Pope complained. Turning to John Gibbon, he added, "That is not the way for an officer to act, Gibbon."[18]

A visit from Marsena Patrick and the conjectures of wounded soldiers caused Pope to forget his anger at McClellan, Franklin, and Porter. Up before daybreak, Patrick had descried through the twilight a large Confederate column moving west along the Warrenton Turnpike. After calling on a battery near the Dogan house to hurry the Rebels along with a few shots, Patrick rode to McDowell with the news; together they reported to Pope.

Patrick presumed the Rebels had withdrawn only a short distance, to the woods west of Groveton. But Pope concluded they had quit the field. "You are mistaken," he told Patrick. "There is nobody in there of any consequence. They are merely stragglers."

At about the same time, reports came in from wounded Federals who, having stumbled or dragged themselves back into friendly lines, said they had overheard Southern officers speak of a withdrawal. Paroled prisoners corroborated a story Pope was all too willing to credit.[19]

Pope was at work on a letter to Halleck when these dubious bits of intelligence reached him. He excitedly added this news to his already embellished account of the action of the day before. Pope also conveyed his disgust with Franklin's request for a cavalry escort but said nothing disparaging about Fitz John Porter. The tone of the message was entirely optimistic. "Our troops behaved splendidly," Pope averred. "The battle was fought on the identical battlefield of Bull Run, which greatly increased the enthusiasm of our men. The news just reaches me from the front that the enemy is retreating toward the mountains. I go forward at once to see. We have made great captures, but I am not able yet to form an idea of their extent."[20]

Pope never said what he discerned when he went "forward at once" to watch the Rebel retreat. Presumably he rode west off Buck Hill, then up the slope of Dogan Ridge, to try and catch a glimpse of the enemy marching off down the Warrenton Turnpike. If so, he would have seen little. The movement Marsena Patrick had reported, and which Pope concluded to be part of a general Confederate withdrawal, was no more than an insignificant realignment of forces by Longstreet. Moreover, the 6,100 troops that had pulled back—a mere 1,500 yards as it turned out—were new to the battle, having arrived less than two hours earlier. Far from contemplating a retreat, Lee intended to hold fast and let Pope define the nature of the day's battle. With luck, Pope would resume his futile battering of Jackson's line. Should the Federals prove quiescent, Lee would send Jackson on another wide flanking maneuver into Pope's rear that night.[21]

By 7:00 A.M., Pope was back on Buck Hill, deliberating with his senior officers. The council was divided. Phil Kearny liked Pope's aggressive attitude and was all for renewing the fight against the Confederate left, where he had made a brief inroad the evening before. General Reynolds, whose division had been uncomfortably close to Longstreet's huge corps most of the previous afternoon, had no doubt that the enemy had been greatly reinforced, particularly opposite the Federal left. Everyone else was edgy and uncertain. After an hour of meandering discussion, Pope settled the matter: The corps of McDowell, Heintzelman, and Porter would together advance over the ground bloodied by Kearny and crush the Rebel left.[22]

At precisely 8:17 A.M., Fitz John Porter reported to Pope, while the head of his column closed on the Stone house. It was a frosty but civil encounter, with Porter doing most of the talking. He pleaded with Pope to dismiss any thought of attacking the Confederate left. Rather, their full attention should be given over to the enormous Rebel presence that extended far beyond their own left, all the way to Porter's abandoned position along the Manassas-Gainesville road. Pope listened in icy silence to the man whom he believed had derailed his plans the day before. When Porter finished, Pope spoke—just enough to convey his contempt for Porter's counsel. "I tried to convince [Pope] that there was a very large force on his left, south of the Warrenton Turnpike," Porter later lamented, "but he put no confidence in what I said."[23]

John Codman Ropes described Pope's fuzzy thinking most poignantly. "In General Pope's preoccupied mind, these facts, when stated by Porter, partook rather of the character of excuses for very culpable inactivity and disobedience of orders, than of information of the enemy's position and strength," said Ropes. "He preferred to act on the belief which his own limited observation of the field justified, and he would not listen to information coming from officers of whose good faith he chose to entertain doubts."[24]

Considered singly, there was no reason why Pope should act on Porter's report. Porter had done little to develop the enemy force along the Manassas-Gainesville road and so knew little of Rebel strength or dispositions in his former sector. What he told Pope thus was not merely vague but also represented information now more than twelve hours old. Much fresher were the reports that the enemy might be withdrawing.

But there was corroborating testimony. General Reynolds, whose division—posted now along Young's Branch, just south of the Warrenton Turnpike—was nearest Longstreet's hidden multitude, tried to intervene on Porter's behalf, but Pope dismissed his concerns just as abruptly; after all, Pope probably reckoned, Reynolds was a staunch ally of both Porter and McClellan; his word could not be accepted at face value. Perhaps to silence their concerns, Pope muttered something about sending cavalry to reconnoiter the left—a promise he never kept—then dismissed Porter and Reynolds without orders. The two departed, bewildered and bereft of faith in Pope.[25]

Porter had even greater cause for dismay when he rejoined his corps. Fearful of an attack on its exposed forward position along Dawkins's Branch, Morell had withdrawn Charles Griffin's brigade cautiously. By the time Griffin got started, the rest of the division had disappeared down the Manassas-Gainesville road. Misunderstanding his orders, and with no one to guide on, Griffin missed the turn at Bethelem Church. Rather than marching up the Manassas-Sudley road in the direction of the battlefield, he continued on toward Manassas. The brigade of Brigadier General A. Sanders Piatt, which unknown to Porter had returned from detached duty during the night, followed Griffin. Porter's combat strength was thus slashed from twelve thousand to seven thousand men before a shot had been fired.[26]

The remaining brigades of Morell's division, along with Sykes's three brigades, filed onto Dogan Ridge at 9:00 A.M. Morell relieved Patrick's brigade in the front line, and Sykes stacked his command in column behind Morell. In the absence of direction from army headquarters, Porter and Reynolds resolved to feel for the enemy themselves. Reynolds pushed his three Pennsylvania brigades south of the Warrenton Turnpike to Groveton, where they clashed briefly with Southerners from Hood's division. Morell advanced skirmishers into the Groveton Woods; they too came under fire.

Although contact had been brief and light, the activity around Groveton should have alerted Pope to at least the possibility that the Confederates were not retiring. But all his attention was given over to the extreme right. At 9:00 A.M. he instructed McDowell to move part of Ricketts's division over Matthew's Hill to replace Kearny's division in line. These movements merely riled the Rebels behind the unfinished railroad. As Kearny's exhausted troops filed off to the northeast, where Kearny was certain they would find rest along the wooded bank of Bull Run, they came under heavy fire from three enemy batteries. Ricketts's lead brigade of Abram Duryee was similarly raked with artillery fire. Duryee deployed and moved toward the railroad embankment. The woods erupted in gunfire. While Duryee struggled to extricate his brigade, at 9:30 A.M. Kearny warned Pope, "I have been relieved by Ricketts, and I now hold the country to the right of the Leesburg [Manassas-Sudley] road, and I am forced to hold this line in advance, my left in air one-fourth of a mile in advance of Ricketts's right. Besides, Ricketts's and my positions are completely enfiladed by the enemy's three or four long-range batteries. I should say," Kearny added, "that the enemy all along have intended to force us by our right, and they have the ground to do it."[27]

Kearny's admonition disturbed Pope. A three-corps assault against Jackson's left no longer seemed advisable, at least not without further reconnaissance. To that end, Pope sent Colonel Strother up the Manassas-Sudley road with orders for Ricketts to "advance and feel the enemy cautiously."

Strother found Ricketts at the edge of the woods, "looking rather dejected."

The Virginian delivered Pope's orders, to which Ricketts objected sharply that "he had already felt the enemy with his division and had been repulsed with infantry en mass and had also been shelled." General Duryee, who sat nearby, nursing a wounded hand, swore vehemently that "the enemy, instead of retreating, were in force and menacing." Ricketts asked Strother on what Pope based his belief the Confederates were retreating. Strother could only shrug. Ricketts told Strother to tell Pope he thought a second advance imprudent, but if the commanding general "peremptorily ordered it, he would go in with the certainty of having his division used up."

Colonel Strother returned to Buck Hill, his confidence in Pope rapidly dwindling. The commanding general's demeanor was hardly reassuring. Strother found Pope "walking to and fro apart and smoking, evidently solving some problem of contradictory evidence in his mind." The Virginian conveyed Ricketts's message, then asked if he should return to him with further orders. Pope thought a moment, then snarled, "No, damn it. Let him go." McDowell strode over, and the two sat down under a tree to "wait for the enemy to retreat."[28]

Brigadier General Isaac Stevens, whose chopped-up division lay opposite the railroad embankment, arrived next with contrary news. The enemy, Stevens argued, was still behind the unfinished railroad and evinced every intention of remaining there. Pope responded to Stevens's counsel as he had to Kearny's warning, by directing a limited reconnaissance.

Stevens dutifully sent forward a party from the Seventy-ninth New York, which was promptly torn to shreds. His report of the affair, lamented one of Stevens's staff officers, "had no effect on [Pope's] opinionated mind."[29]

Actually, it had, though hardly the effect Stevens would have wished. With Stevens's report, Pope now had reliable intelligence from the left, center, and right of the line that the Confederates remained on the field, apparently committed to fight. Yet he could not bring himself to act upon the counsel of Porter, Reynolds, Kearny, Ricketts, and Stevens. Fatigue and self-doubt crowded his mind, and hope blindly guided him. A paralysis settled over Buck Hill. "General Pope seemed wholly at a loss what to do and what to think," averred Lieutenant Stephen Weld. "He said that he did not know where his own men were, or where Jackson was."[30]

Pope's principal lieutenant and closest confidant, Irvin McDowell, was of no help to his tormented chief. To the extent he contributed anything, it was to second Pope in his predilections. Nor did the weak-minded Samuel Heintzelman have much to say. Although both McDowell and Heintzelman grew impatient with Pope's lack of decision and his evident abandonment of the planned attack on the extreme right, they offered no alternative plans. Instead, McDowell and Heintzelman left together to examine for themselves the ground near Bull Run.[31]

Slowly Pope emerged from his funk, more convinced than ever the Rebels were decamping. Ironically, the agent of change was Fitz John Porter. At 11:00 A.M., a Union soldier, whom Porter's skirmishers had freed from Rebel captivity, was passed to the general. The man told Porter he had "heard the rebel officers say their army was retiring to unite with Longstreet." Porter scoffed at the claim— he knew the two Confederate wings already were united—but felt duty bound to send the soldier on to Pope. However, he did so with a disclaimer: "I regard him either as a fool or designedly released to give the wrong impression, and no faith should be put in what he said."[32]

Pope disagreed. He accepted the man's story without reservation and decided to "push forward as rapidly as possible" to strike what he assumed would be Lee's rear guard. At 11:30 A.M. Pope dispatched a staff officer to tell Porter he believed the soldier and to attack, with Hatch's division in support.

McDowell and Heintzelman returned a few minutes later. Their reconnaissance, much of which they had conducted on foot, picking their way through the bushes and brambles along Bull Run, had led them also to conclude the enemy had gone. "We found all the points held by the enemy the day before beyond Bull Run abandoned, and in going over to the Sudley Springs road and west of it we saw no evidence of the enemy in force, some skirmishers and advanced posts or rear guards, as the case might be, being all that we found," said McDowell. (Fitz John Porter knew better; McDowell and Heintzelman had mistaken a contraction of Jackson's line for his retreat.) On their return ride, McDowell and Heintzelman met Franz Sigel, also afflicted with the prevailing fantasy.[33]

Dismounting on Buck Hill to report the encouraging results of their reconnaissance, McDowell and Heintzelman were silenced by Pope before they could utter a word. "I know what you are going to say," Pope interrupted confidently, "the enemy is retreating."[34]

Probably at McDowell's behest, Pope replaced his oral orders for Porter only to prod the Rebel rear guard with written instructions for a full-fledged pursuit by the entire army, which McDowell would orchestrate. Shortly before noon, Colonel Ruggles penned the necessary orders.[35]

Pope, then, was about to commit his entire command to a pursuit on the strength of an enlisted man's word.

— ◆ —

Perhaps Fitz John Porter thought he had seen the last of impossible orders from John Pope. If so, he was gravely disappointed. "No orders of this campaign," Porter later wrote of the noon pursuit order, "more erroneously stated the attitude of the opposing forces or led to more serious disaster."

Porter had been making arrangements to carry out Pope's oral instructions that he attack Jackson when the noon directive filtered its way down to him at 1:00 P.M. As part of his preparations, Porter had sent two regiments of skirmishers deep into the Groveton Woods, between Dogan Ridge and the unfinished railroad. Their advance drew "an exceedingly hot" fire from Rebel skirmishers posted along the far edge of the woods, which was supplemented by a heavy shelling from Stephen D. Lee's massed batteries as Porter moved his assaulting columns off Dogan Ridge. It was clear to Porter he could not obey Pope's order for a pursuit along the Warrenton Turnpike. With two of Morell's brigades (Morell having gone to Centreville with Griffin), Brigadier General Daniel Butterfield had gone into the Groveton Woods to see if the Rebels still held the unfinished railroad. Scarcely had Butterfield started before a withering fire stopped him. As Porter later explained, his corps was then, at 2:00 P.M., "so involved in a movement against Jackson's right that I could not make the change to push forward on the Warrenton Turnpike" without subjecting his command to a brutal enfilading fire. "Confident I was to attack a well posted and well prepared enemy, I arranged to make a strong attack, and deferred 'pushing forward' 'in pursuit of the enemy,' till I got my forces in position for this strong attack." Apprising McDowell of the true state of affairs, Porter said he would wheel to the left, take Stephen D. Lee's gun by the flank, and then approach the turnpike, should he succeed first in dislodging Jackson's infantry.[36]

McDowell already had a feeling for what Porter truly might be up against. For the first time since the battle began, his thinking would diverge from that of the commanding general. The agent of change was General Reynolds. Frustrated at the indifference with which Pope earlier that morning had received his warning of a Confederate presence near Groveton, shortly before noon Reynolds advanced his skirmish line beyond Lewis Lane, south of the Warrenton Turnpike, to gain more precise information on the enemy. Riding forward himself, Reynolds was startled to discover "a line of skirmishers covering my left flank, with cavalry formed behind them, perfectly stationary, evidently masking a column of the enemy formed for an attack on my left flank." A sharp fire sent Reynolds and his cavalcade galloping rearward.[37]

Reynolds kept riding until he reached Buck Hill, a few minutes after 1:00 P.M., his horse foaming and his eyes alive with the thrill of discovery. Jumping from the saddle, he announced breathlessly, "The enemy is turning our left!"

Pope was incredulous. Just an hour earlier he had promulgated plans for a pursuit; now he was in danger of being outflanked by an enemy presumed to be in retreat. Unwilling—or more likely unable—to comprehend the import of Reynolds's words, Pope dismissed them: "Oh, I guess not," he muttered in reply.

This time, Reynolds persisted. "I thought the information of sufficient importance to bring it to you myself and run the gauntlet of three rebel battalions. I had thought you would believe *me*," rejoined the Pennsylvanian. Pope relented slightly. Summoning John Buford, he told him, "You take your cavalry and see if the enemy *is* turning our left." Buford, who had seen Longstreet's men passing through Gainesville the previous morning, departed with an expression that seemed to say, "What an ass!"[38]

Disgusted with Pope's reception of his warning, Reynolds took his case to McDowell, who stood nearby. The Rebels "were not in retreat," Reynolds repeated, "and their right was across the pike, outflanking us." Like Pope, McDowell wanted confirmation of Reynolds's report; unlike his chief, however, he sought it himself. At 2:00 P.M., McDowell rode with Reynolds to the front. A quick reconnaissance convinced him to detach Reynolds from Porter's assaulting column and withdraw his division a thousand yards, to defensive positions along Chinn Ridge. Alert to the danger Reynolds's departure posed to the flank of Porter's column, Gouverneur Warren moved his brigade into the gap, forming line of battle along the narrow valley of Young's Branch, between the Warrenton Turnpike and Lewis Lane. To Porter, whom he had deprived of nearly one-third of his force and whose left his action had exposed, McDowell excused himself by saying King's division should suffice "to effect your purposes." A few minutes later, McDowell suggested Porter use discretion in committing even King; "as if," Porter later complained, "he had expected my 6,000 men to overcome Jackson, that which General Pope's right wing had failed to do on the previous day." Porter continued his preparations for an attack he now felt certain would fail.[39]

Franz Sigel also despaired of success. That morning, he had counted himself among those who believed Lee to be retreating; now at 2:00 P.M. Sigel, like Reynolds, was convinced the Federal left was in grave danger. Scouts had brought him disquieting reports that "the enemy was shifting his troops from the Warrenton Pike to [his] right," evidently with the intention of attacking south of the turnpike in great strength. On his own initiative, Sigel detached the Fifty-fifth Ohio Infantry to Chinn Ridge as an outpost and sent the Fourth New York Cavalry well beyond the army's left flank to make contact with the enemy, so as to confirm the movement. It did, and Sigel passed its findings on to Pope at once.[40]

Undoubtedly he did so with a feeling of repugnance. Earlier in the day, Pope had openly expressed his contempt for the German's military judgment. Learning Pope intended for Porter to attack along the Warrenton Turnpike, Sigel had hastened to Buck Hill to suggest respectfully that Pope shift Porter farther to the right and attack Jackson's left, where his lines were weaker. Pope dismissed Sigel peremptorily, snarling, "I will manage this in my own way." When Sigel asked what position he should take, Pope verbally slapped him a second time. "I will command your corps," said Pope. With that, Sigel and his staff rode back to Dogan Ridge to watch the slaughter unfold. "Ten thousand men remained inactive at Dogan's farm" while Porter's small corps made ready to advance "into the very mouth of hell," recalled a member of Sigel's staff in disgust. "Everyone knew that they could do nothing, but die—except the military imbecile sitting under the oak tree, behind the stone house on a ridge, two miles away from the enemy."

Pope responded to Sigel's warning in a manner consistent with his estimate of its author. Bestirring himself but momentarily, Pope rose from beneath the oak tree, beckoned Colonel Ruggles, and, waving his arm carelessly in the direction of Henry Hill and Chinn Ridge, told him to have Sigel place a brigade on "that bald hill." Too estranged from his commander to ask which bald hill he meant, Ruggles relayed the message exactly as it had been given. When Brigadier General Robert C. Schenck, whose division was to provide the needed brigade, asked Ruggles to be more specific, the colonel merely mimicked his chief and, his arm flailing toward the south, bellowed, "That bald hill!" Ruggles galloped away, leaving Schenck and Sigel to divine Pope's intentions for themselves.

They guessed wrong. Pope apparently wanted a brigade posted on the western slope of Henry Hill, where it would command the intersection of the Manassas-Sudley road and the Warrenton Turnpike, possession of which would prove critical in the event of a Union retreat. But Schenck instead sent Nathaniel McLean's four Ohio regiments to Chinn Ridge, where they lined up beside Reynolds's Pennsylvanians. Pope noticed the movement but supposed McLean's brigade to be part of the troops assigned to McDowell. After sending a courier to ask McDowell if he did not think his lines extended too far to the left, Pope gave the matter no further thought.

That a single brigade, regardless of where it might be posted, would prove of any use in the event of a Confederate attack south of the Warrenton Turnpike struck Sigel, Schenck, and their staffs as absurd. Said an aide-de-camp to General Hatch, "Mrs. Partington's efforts to fight the maddened waves of the ocean with a mop, was an exhibition of generalship equal to this."[41]

In actuality, there were five Federal brigades, perhaps ten thousand troops, south of the turnpike to confront the twenty-five thousand infantrymen of Longstreet's corps who rested in the fields west of Lewis Lane. That even that number was grossly insufficient troubled McDowell only slightly, and Pope not at all. The warnings of Reynolds and Sigel had convinced them the Rebels were not retreating, but neither had any idea that more than half of the Army of Northern Virginia hovered near the attenuated Union left. Although he had withdrawn the Pennsylvania Reserves to Chinn Ridge, McDowell was "yet in doubt as to the position of the enemy," thought Reynolds. Like Pope, McDowell fixed his attention firmly on the Groveton Woods. Pope had confirmed McDowell's oral approval of Porter's plan of attack by means of a cryptic note signed by Edmund Schriver, McDowell's chief of staff. As the minutes slipped quietly away, and only the occasional crack of a skirmisher's rifle broke the stillness of a hot August afternoon, Pope grew restive. A few minutes before 3:00 P.M., he told Thomas C. H. Smith to "go forward and see [Porter] and bring me word why he doesn't attack." Pope had no intention of allowing Porter's apparent lethargy to defeat his largest assault of the battle before it began.[42]

Smith went needlessly. At 3:00 P.M., the roar of artillery announced the start of Porter's attack.

Porter had not been stalling, as Pope presumed he had. Rather, he had been trying to make sense both of a tactical situation quite different from that understood at army headquarters and of a swirl of changing orders. Pope's first orders to Porter that morning had called for Hatch's division to advance on Porter's right. The noon pursuit orders substituted Ricketts for Hatch. Schriver's note said nothing of Ricketts but suggested Porter might deploy Hatch at his discretion.

Porter was confused. Expecting Ricketts to form on his right, Porter initially took no action on a request from Daniel Butterfield, whose troops suffered most from the Rebel skirmishers, that Hatch be brought forward to clear his flank. When Porter realized Ricketts was no longer in the picture, he called on Hatch to come up on his right at once and "make the attack simultaneously" with his corps. Porter enjoined Colonel Charles Roberts, commander of the right-flank brigade, to wait until Hatch arrived, "then push vigorously forward." All this took time, however, as it was 3:00 P.M. before Porter had his command arranged to his satisfaction. Behind Butterfield's two brigades and Hatch's division, Porter had stacked Sykes's division of Regulars, arranged to exploit any success. Porter's assault column came to ten thousand men, most of whom were tightly packed among the thick timber of the Groveton Woods.[43]

Although he doubted his force capable of dislodging Jackson from the railroad excavation, Porter yielded to orders. Dan Butterfield rode to the front and called for three cheers. They were given, and the Federals poured out of the woods and across Lewis Lane. While Butterfield exhorted the men in ranks, Porter penned a final appeal to McDowell, saying simply, "I fear for the result unless you push up Sigel."

When he removed Reynolds from the attack column, McDowell had assured Porter that General Pope would send up Sigel if Porter felt his command not "strong enough to effect your purpose." McDowell made the promise without consulting Pope. He compounded his negligence by inexplicably failing to inform the commanding general of Porter's call for support. Instead, he merely passed on Porter's note—without an endorsement—to Sigel, who had no idea what to do with it. There matters stood, and Porter watched his troops sweep into the Dogan pasture, with no one to support them but Sykes's Regulars.[44]

The results were precisely as Porter had feared. As Butterfield advanced, the hill to his front came alive with an enemy previously unseen, and which Pope had wished off the field. "The effect was not unlike flushing a covey of quails," said Gouverneur Warren. "From his elevated, crescent shaped position, the enemy swept with numerous artillery, every foot of ground over which we had to pass," lamented Porter. "He opposed us also by a terrible musketry fire from behind the railroad embankment, where he was driven and stood almost unharmed by us."[45]

Thick underbrush made a mockery of unit integrity. Although not directly engaged, John Gibbon's brigade broke apart so completely that Gibbon was left standing behind the Sixth Wisconsin, his only regiment in sight, while the remainder drifted toward the unfinished railroad, a bloody and confused jumble of blue. Few Yankees from front-line regiments reached the excavation alive. Those who did threw themselves against the fill for protection, "too few to even attempt to drive out the troops on the other side of it," confessed a New Yorker, and too frightened to brave the bursting shells behind them. Follow-on units only compounded the pandemonium. "Batteries on the left were shelling us— everything was in confusion," said a soldier of the Eighty-third Pennsylvania. "Regiments got mixed up—brigades were intermingled—all was one seething, anxious excited mass. In the midst of this confusion there seemed to be no competent head to bring order out of chaos."[46]

Southerners had more targets than ammunition, and many emptied their cartridge boxes during the first thirty minutes of fighting. Tossing empty rifles aside, they gathered up stones and hurled them over the embankment at the Yankees. From the western fringe of the Groveton Woods, Porter watched the destruction of Butterfield's brigades with a profound sense of hopelessness. Stephen D. Lee's massed artillery so dominated the Dogan pasture, Porter concluded, that to send Sykes into the open would be a clear violation of the military maxim, "Never reinforce failure." After forty-five minutes of pointless slaughter the survivors of Butterfield's assault spilled back into the Dogan pasture.[47]

The tide of terrified Federals nearly swept Porter away. Galloping up and down the Groveton-Sudley road, he yelled himself hoarse begging the men to "Form here! Form here!" Gibbon took a more forceful approach. "Stop those stragglers!" he shouted to the colonel of the Sixth Wisconsin. Drawing his revolver, he added, "Make them fall in! Shoot them if they don't." The men of the Sixth fixed bayonets and dropped to one knee, but most of the fugitives shoved past them nonetheless. Atop Dogan Ridge, Sigel had his brigades close ranks to receive the fugitives. Porter directed George Bayard to deploy his cavalry brigade nearby. Together, Sigel and Bayard stemmed the retreat shortly before 4:00 P.M.[48]

Nine hundred yards east of Dogan Ridge, Pope remained fixed to the lone oak tree on Buck Hill, as removed from the fighting as Porter was immersed in it. No news came from the front, and Pope evidently sent no one forward to obtain any.

McDowell had gone off to superintend Reynolds's deployment on Chinn Ridge, leaving Pope alone with his staff to speculate on the outcome of Porter's attack. When word came of his discomfiture, most on Buck Hill, remembering the bitter talk against Porter that morning, smelled treachery. Said Colonel Strother, "With this opportunity to reinstate himself and the fine reputation of his troops, much was expected from his corps today, but the impression is that it acted feebly and soon gave way."[49]

Pope's suspicion that Porter's attack had been "neither vigorous nor persistent" seemed confirmed when he saw Lieutenant Colonel William Chapman's brigade of Sykes's unbloodied division march leisurely past Buck Hill, on its way to Bull Run to draw rations. Ignorant of the circumstances that had kept the Regulars out of the fight, Pope exploded. Accosting Major George Andrews of the Seventeenth U.S. Infantry, Pope demanded to know, "What troops are these and where are you going?" Andrews told him, then withstood a verbal beating such as only the foul-mouthed Pope could deliver. Said Thomas C. H. Smith, "[Pope] soundly berated [Andrews and his men] for the example they were setting the army by this dastardly movement and ordered them at once to move up on the Henry House Hill." The Regulars shuffled dutifully off the Warrenton Turnpike by the right flank. The product of rage, Pope's placement of the Regular Brigade was, as Colonel Chapman conceded, to prove "most opportune."[50]

Regrettably, McDowell's response to Porter's defeat was to have consequences fatal to the Union cause at Second Bull Run. From his vantage point on Chinn Ridge, the collapse of Butterfield's attack looked like a general rout of the army, particularly when several hundred of Jackson's men swarmed over the railroad embankment in spontaneous pursuit. Cadmus Wilcox, whose division lay just north of the Warrenton Turnpike, near the Brawner farm, tried to orchestrate a counterattack but was dissuaded by the sight of a dozen Federal batteries arrayed along Dogan Ridge. His initial movement, however, elicited an impassioned response from McDowell. Galloping to Reynolds's side, his arm motioning in the direction of the Dogan house, McDowell screamed, "General Reynolds! General Reynolds! Get into line every man and get away there."

Reynolds obeyed with unfortunate alacrity and by 3:45 P.M. had his division marching northeast in column across the fields toward the Warrenton Turnpike. When the Pennsylvanians left, the number of Federals opposite Longstreet dropped to twenty-two hundred: a thousand men under Gouverneur Warren near Groveton, and the twelve hundred men of McLean's brigade on Chinn Ridge.[51]

The measure of a man may be taken, in part, by the manner in which he responds to crisis. In such moments arrogance is impotent, bluster is barren, and lies are transparent. Stripped of his characteristic defenses, John Pope was about to confront the supreme crisis of his life.

10 If I Could Be of Further Service, I Would Remain

James Longstreet's moment was about to come. Lee had allowed Pope to define the nature of the day's combat; he would respond accordingly. Assuming Pope would withdraw that evening, Lee had decided to send Jackson on a flanking movement by way of Sudley Springs, to cross Bull Run under the cover of darkness and fall on the Federal rear. A few minutes before 3:00 P.M., Longstreet rode forward to arrange a sunset diversion. Nearing Groveton, the Georgian was startled by Porter's sudden attack. "Evidently Pope supposed I was gone, as he was ignoring me entirely," remembered Longstreet. When the assault collapsed, Lee was ready. No better opportunity to crush Pope's army was likely to offer itself, he concluded, and the instant Jackson reported the enemy giving way in his front, Lee directed Longstreet to strike the Union left with his entire corps.

The order thrilled Longstreet. "The heavy fumes of gunpowder hanging about our ranks, as stimulating as sparkling wine, charged the atmosphere with the light and splendor of battle," he wrote. "Time was culminating under a flowing tide. The noble horses took the spirit of the riders sitting lightly in their saddles. As orders were given, the staff, their limbs already closed to the horses' flanks, pressed their spurs, but the electric current overleaped their speedy strides, and twenty-five thousand brave [men] moved in line as by a single impulse." Gouverneur Warren's isolated brigade was crushed in the onslaught; in the Fifth New York Zouaves alone, a hundred men fell in two minutes. "Not only were men wounded or killed," said a Zouave, "but they were riddled."[1]

Next in line were four Pennsylvania regiments under Colonel Martin Hardin, which McDowell had retrieved from Reynolds's column and placed on an open knoll, midway between McLean's Ohio brigade on Chinn Ridge and the scene of Warren's destruction near Groveton, to buy time—time that would be needed to fashion a defense on Henry Hill capable of stopping the Confederates. Henry Hill was the key. Seize it, and Longstreet would dominate the Warrenton Turnpike, Pope's only practical route of retreat.[2]

More than any other Union general on the field, McDowell understood the tactical significance of Henry Hill; thirteen months before, his army had met defeat on the same wooded slopes toward which Longstreet's attack was directed. After seeing off Hardin, McDowell went looking for idle units to feed into the fight. His chief's energy and courage impressed Captain Joseph C. Willard. "Through the whole of this action General McDowell and staff were at times in very exposed positions," said Willard. "I know but little of war, but I must say that never could a man try harder and with less fear of exposure to put troops forward."[3]

And what of Pope when the blow fell? The sudden crash of musketry from Young's Branch initially failed to awaken him to the horrible danger his army confronted. Encouraged by an inexperienced staff, Pope read into the fast-approaching fire a preposterous intent. Scanning the high ground west of the unfinished railroad with a field glass, Strother had noticed an aide-de-camp ride rapidly along the brow of Stony Ridge, where the Southern cannon were posted, then stop to give directions at each gun. Strother remarked to Pope that the enemy seemed to be making a noisy diversion to cover a retreat to Warrenton. The commanding general agreed heartily. As the Rebel guns limbered up, Pope exclaimed, "By God, they are taking off their artillery anyhow!" But the cannon came bounding down the forward slope of Stony Ridge, over the railroad embankment and into the Groveton Woods. Behind them marched several regiments of infantry. Then the fire grew louder on the extreme left, and both Strother and Pope at last understood what was happening.[4]

It was 4:30 P.M. when Pope came face to face with this crisis of his own creation. From that instant, said Strother, "his conduct was cool, gallant, and prompt."

Pope's first act was to send Strother galloping to the extreme right of the army, with orders to shuttle reinforcements from Ricketts's division to the imperiled left. But General Heintzelman, who exercised command of the right, demurred, saying Ricketts occupied a critical position. Instead, he offered up the two remaining brigades of Reynolds's Pennsylvania Reserves, which had ended their march behind his lines. Strother ordered them to the left at the double quick.

By the time he returned with the Pennsylvanians, matters on the left had grown desperate. "Infantry, artillery, and cavalry were breaking and hurrying off the field. The Centreville road [Warrenton Turnpike] was crowded and the whole army seemed to promise another Bull Run stampede," said Strother. "Staff officers with swords were rallying the fugitives, and a line of steady cavalry with drawn sabres were endeavoring to stem the disgraceful tide. The enemy's fire was fiercely advancing on our left and the whole position was under a storm of fire. This was evidently the crisis of the battle and the campaign, and a disgraceful defeat seemed imminent."[5]

During Strother's absence, Pope had removed army headquarters to Henry Hill. There he spoke briefly with McDowell, passing by with two brigades he had sequestered to help defend Chinn Ridge. The left was crushed, McDowell told Pope, and the very survival of the army at stake. While Pope absorbed the news, McDowell hurried off to Chinn Ridge.[6]

"As it was evident he must fight a defensive battle to secure a retreat," said Thomas C. H. Smith, the commanding general placed himself where he might do the most good: "on the summit of the hill, just in rear of the road that he lined with his troops, and under fire, so that he could watch his line and be ready to relieve any portion where the attacks of the enemy, pouring in fresh troops, should render it advisable."[7]

Despite Heintzelman's reluctance to strip his front line, Stonewall Jackson's unaccountable inactivity meant there were troops aplenty for Pope to call upon to defend Henry Hill. What he needed as badly as men was time, a commodity McDowell and Sigel bought for him with blood on the grassy slopes of Chinn Ridge. Between 4:00 P.M. and 6:00 P.M., they threw six Union brigades into the fray west of Henry Hill. Hardin's Pennsylvanians were the first to challenge Longstreet's advance. In fewer than thirty minutes of bitter fighting with Hood's Texas Brigade, the Pennsylvania brigade was shattered, its commander badly wounded and its supporting battery of artillery captured.[8]

Next into the maelstrom were the Ohioans of Colonel Nathaniel McLean's brigade, who had witnessed the massacre of the Pennsylvanians from atop Chinn Ridge. McLean held fast until the Confederates worked their way around his right flank, then gave back toward the northeast, directly in the path of Zealous Tower's brigade, which McDowell had brought over from the right. Tower deployed amid a scene of unparalleled confusion, to confront an enemy arrayed "in many lines of battle as far as could be seen. They came by the thousands, with battle flags well to the front and their officers urging them on."[9]

With victory near, Confederate infantrymen needed little encouragement. Although they suffered heavily from several well-directed volleys, the Rebels crashed into Tower's four regiments with a fury that shoved the Yankees back two hundred yards. General McDowell was on hand—"swearing like a pirate," recalled a Union enlisted man—and he immediately ordered the brigade of Colonel Robert Stiles, which he also had commandeered from the right, forward to support Tower. As Stiles's brigade came up behind Tower's disorganized firing line, it splintered. "Everything to our hasty glance seemed confusion. Wounded men were everywhere; some were being helped away, others trying with all their strength to get away a safe distance," a Massachusetts soldier wrote. "[One] wounded man begged piteously for us to take him to the rear; he was wounded in the neck, or head, and the blood flowed freely; every time he tried to speak the blood would fill his mouth and he would blow it in all directions."

The Federals of Tower and Stiles fought hard, until two fresh Confederate brigades forced them back. The opportune arrival of the brigades of colonels John Koltes and Wladimir Krzyzanowski prevented a rout but could not stay the Southern advance. At 6:00 P.M., Chinn Ridge fell to the Confederates.[10]

The fight for Chinn Ridge had cost Lee and Longstreet dearly in men, organization, and time—and Pope had put that time to good use. When Strother returned with Truman Seymour's and George Gordon Meade's brigades of Reynolds's division, Pope deployed them between the ruins of the Henry house and the Warrenton Turnpike. Seymour formed in front, and Meade held his brigade in column in reserve. Six hundred yards south of the Henry house, Colonel Chapman had formed his Regulars in line of battle along the Manassas-Sudley road. To fill the gap between Seymour and Chapman, Pope sent Colonel Ruggles after Robert Milroy's comparatively fresh brigade. Milroy shepherded his men into a long cut in the road to the right of Chapman.

By 6:00 P.M., Pope had four brigades on Henry Hill, which he supplemented with three batteries of artillery, one of which Pope positioned personally. Thirteen regiments stood shoulder-to-shoulder in the front line. The alternating cuts and fills that paralleled the roadbed made their position as strong as the unfinished railroad had been for Jackson. Leaving nothing to chance, Pope summoned the Regular Brigade of Lieutenant Colonel Robert Buchanan and the Independent Brigade of Brigadier General A. Sanders Piatt, which had just returned from its day-long detour to Centreville, to support the four brigades already deployed in defense of Henry Hill.[11]

Pope then turned to a task he would have found unfathomable three hours earlier: the dictating of withdrawal orders. Regardless of whether the Henry Hill line withstood Longstreet's inevitable attack, he felt it imperative to remove the army to Centreville. Explained Pope, "The result of the battle, the very heavy losses we had suffered, and the complete prostration of our troops from hunger and fatigue made it plain to me that we were no longer able, in the face of such overwhelming odds, to maintain our position so far to the front."[12]

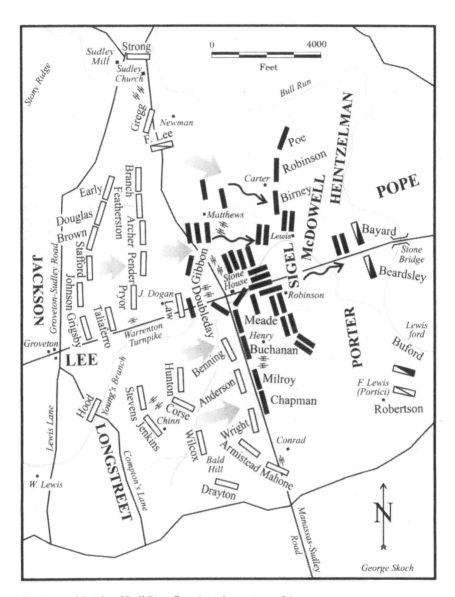

The Second Battle of Bull Run, Evening, August 30, 1862

Fitz John Porter concurred with Pope's reasoning, while adding a cause the commanding general would never accept. "In presence of an enemy vastly our superior, defeat would probably have resulted from remaining west of Bull Run, with an army dispirited by fatigue, and by scarcity of food," he conjectured. "But, be that as it may, it was hastened by uncovering the left wing and by abandoning a strong position to attack a concealed foe, whose elevated position masking his own, revealed to him all our movements, and made him master of the situation."[13]

Not everyone in the army high command conceded the need to quit the field. John Buford and David Strother both were for staying, believing victory would be theirs on the morrow. Franz Sigel remonstrated sharply against the decision to withdraw, said Colonel Strother, but "Pope curtly checked him and said that he had not sent for him to receive suggestions but to give him orders, as his mind was made up what to do."

Carl Schurz agreed with his corps commander. He and Sigel had been working out plans to fall upon Longstreet's left flank when the order to withdraw reached them. Not only did Schurz believe they could have done severe damage to Longstreet, but he also thought Pope might have "remained on the battlefield without much danger," brought up the corps of Franklin and Sumner from Centreville during the night, and renewed the battle with their fresh commands at daybreak on August 31.

Most probably shared opinions closer to those of Samuel Heintzelman, who thought the army had fought poorly, because "neither officers nor men had any confidence in Pope, nor much in McDowell"; withdrawal thus seemed the only sane alternative.[14]

No retreat could begin safely, however, until Henry Hill was secure. And at 6:00 P.M. its fate was far from certain. Three Confederate divisions struck Pope's makeshift line with a ferocity that stunned the Federal defenders. Any weakening of his line would be immediately apparent to Pope. From where he and his staff sat atop Henry Hill, said Thomas C. H. Smith, "a large part of the contested field was in sight. The battle [was] presented thus to the full compass of eye and ear and in intensest grandeur the spectacle and din."[15]

Lost in an unspeakable anguish of the mind, General Pope gave little thought to his own safety. Posted on horseback, directly behind the firing line, Pope weathered a storm of shot and shell. Colonel Strother was less phlegmatic about the peril, watching wide-eyed the odd assortment of ordnance thrown their way. When Confederate cannoneers exhausted their supply of shot and shell, they sent sections of railroad iron screeching toward Henry Hill, with gruesome effect. A nearby group of horses were eviscerated, throwing guts and dirt on Pope's staff. Minié bullets filled the air, said Strother, "as they struck in front, between, and behind us knocking up a column of dust."[16]

More vexatious to Pope than the bullets was an unexpected report that General Franklin had halted his corps at Centreville, when its presence at the front but a short time earlier might have swung the tide of battle back in favor of the Federals. Pope learned of Franklin's location a few minutes after he had issued preliminary orders to withdraw. Told Franklin had stopped at Centreville, Pope growled, "There let him stick, God damn him," and at 6:00 P.M. he sent Franklin instructions to post his command behind the fortifications there, gather whatever other troops he was able, and "hold these positions to the last extremity." Thirty minutes later, during the height of the Southern assaults on Henry Hill, in words that revealed a profound uncertainty, he ordered Banks to "destroy the public property at Bristoe and fall back upon Centreville at once."[17]

By 7:00 P.M., the situation had clarified itself. Longstreet had failed to carry Henry Hill: the Union line of retreat to Centreville was secure. Fighting would continue well into the night, but it would be fitful and purposeless, as the Confederates lacked the strength to mount another assault. North of the Warrenton Turnpike, units of the Federal right wing had fallen back to the heights east of the Manassas-Sudley road, having been nudged along by Jackson.

Atop Henry Hill, a heavy melancholy pervaded the high command of the Army of Virginia, which the eerie magnificence of nature worked to deepen. Later, those present would struggle for words to evoke the gloom. "The wind of a few hours earlier had died away and the lusterless and rifted clouds of powder smoke collected and darkened over the field," Smith recalled. Strother remembered how "the sun set red and angry behind the battle cloud, and as it grew dark the fury of the contest abated but did not entirely cease. It was now quite dark with a quarter moon only to shed its dim light."

Against this backdrop of fire and smoke, Pope played out his final battlefield act. Between 5:30 P.M. and 6:00 P.M., he had dispatched staff officers over the field with orders for commands opposing the quiescent Stonewall Jackson to fall back to high ground well east of the Manassas-Sudley road. Now, a few minutes before 8:00 P.M., by the uncertain light of a single candle he began dictating to Ruggles formal retreat orders, which told corps commanders to retire to the north side of Centreville and which enjoined Reno to cover the retreat from Henry Hill. Before Ruggles could finish, the flickering candle drew the fire of Confederate artillery. Pope told Ruggles to put out the flame. Squinting at the shadowy figures of the generals gathered about him, Pope said with unnatural diffidence, "If I could be of any further service, I would remain, but as I cannot, we will ride back to Centreville." Pope spoke briefly with McDowell, just long enough to delegate to him responsibility for the withdrawal, then swung his mount down onto the Warrenton Turnpike, to begin the somber, seven-mile ride to Centreville. A few hundred yards east of Buck Hill, Pope and Ruggles dismounted to write the formal withdrawal order. As they finished, a Rebel round shot impacted nearby, covering the commanding general with gravel and dust.[18]

Lieutenant James S. Lyon of Hatch's staff watched Pope's retinue make for the Stone Bridge over Bull Run. Having posted his rear guard, McDowell rejoined Pope for the ride across. "The turnpike was badly blocked by stragglers, wagons, and ambulances, no organized body had yet commenced to fall back. These impediments did not apparently interfere with their exit from the field. As the last of the cavalcade swept by, I involuntarily exclaimed, 'Now the Devil take the hindmost.'"[19]

The commanding general's cavalcade could hardly have "swept" past in the manner Lyon depicted. Rather, Pope and his retinue had to feel their way along. Said Colonel Ruggles, "So crowded was the road that General Pope and his staff, and I, as chief of staff, rode through the fields and other property abutting upon the road, and frequently had to leap obstructions."[20]

Phil Kearny was scarcely more sympathetic than Lieutenant Lyon, or rational. In twelve hours, Pope had tumbled in his estimation, from an aggressive, clear-headed chief to a bumbling imbecile. Drawing rein beside John Gibbon, whose brigade was calmly drawn up in line of battle near the Robinson house, Kearny let loose with a fiery tirade. "I suppose you appreciate the condition of affairs here, sir?" he asked rhetorically. Gibbon looked at him quizzically. Kearny repeated himself: "I suppose you appreciate the condition of affairs? It's another Bull Run!" "Oh!" exclaimed Gibbon. "I hope not quite as bad as that, General." "Perhaps not," conceded Kearny. "Reno is keeping up the fight. He is not stampeded. I am not stampeded, you are not stampeded. That is about all, sir, my God, that's about all!"[21]

In fact, that was not all. The Army of Virginia had been beaten but not routed. Tens of thousands of Union soldiers trudged through the darkness toward Centreville, disgusted and heartsick, but as an army, not a mob. Captain George F. Noyes, who had been sent back to Centreville earlier in the day to bring forward supplies for McDowell's corps, watched the defeated army shuffle into town. "I am bound to say that I saw very little of that panic which is said to have characterized the retreat from the First Battle of Bull Run; no break-neck driving of wagons, no cutting of traces, no headlong rushes of troops, the current set one way rapidly, but with little foam," averred Noyes. "This must be considered a retreat, not an absolute rout; and toward the last the troops moved off in good order."[22]

Pope and his staff reached Centreville at 9:00 P.M., two hours before the last of the army crossed Bull Run. After riding about in the dark for nearly an hour, they came upon the house that had been appropriated for their use. Tired but remarkably clearheaded, Pope sat down at once to inform Halleck of the campaign's grievous denouement. He had fought a "terrific battle" that day with an enemy who had been "largely reinforced." Pope had everywhere held his ground until 6:00 P.M., when the Rebels forced his left back a half mile. "Under all the circumstances," concluded Pope, "both horses and men having been two days without food, and the enemy greatly outnumbering us, I thought it best to move back to this place at dark." All was far from lost, he hastened to add: "Don't be uneasy. We will hold our own here. We have delayed the enemy as long as possible without losing the army, and I think the army entitled to the gratitude of the country. Be easy; everything will go well."[23]

It was a courageous and resolute note, an acceptance of responsibility for what had happened. As John Codman Ropes expressed it, the letter seemed "to breathe the right spirit. Whoever was demoralized after the Second Bull Run, it is certain that General Pope was not. And for this he deserves hearty commendation."[24]

Commendation hardly prevailed in Centreville that night. Outside the warming rooms of army headquarters, a spirit as dark as the sliver-mooned night engulfed the army. A fine, chilling drizzle began falling about midnight, compounding the misery of the hungry and weary Yankees. From the bivouac of Franklin's command came hoots of derision, mocking questions about "the new road to Richmond," and delight at the defeat of Pope's army. Every slur reminded Pope's men of "the arrogance, jealousy, and hatred which then was the curse of the Union armies in Virginia," said a Massachusetts soldier. "Disgusted and sick at heart, we continued our slow march."[25]

Inside army headquarters, only Pope seemed to have maintained a degree of optimism. Strother curled up in a corner; "the mortification of failure and defeat was for the time forgotten, and I slept." Gibbon received a kindly welcome from the commanding general when he reported in shortly before midnight. Pope offered him a cup of coffee and bade him remain for the night. "Tired as I was," Gibbon remembered, "I was only too glad to accept his hospitality."[26]

As the night wore on, and fatigue set in, Pope's mood darkened. After Major General William Farrar Smith's division of Franklin's corps reached Centreville, Smith, a sharp-tongued malcontent himself, called on Pope. While they talked, a courier brought word that Sumner had paused at Germantown and was awaiting orders. Smith offered that Sumner's command "had had a very long march and would be quite useless if they had to continue the march that night," to which Pope replied "with an expletive against the country and ordered Sumner forward."[27]

Sometime before dawn, Strother was awakened by the sound of "loud, excited voices." Pope and another officer were arguing about McClellan. "The officer maintained that McClellan's plans had been interfered with," Strother remembered. "Pope curtly and rudely declared it was not so; he had seen the written papers proving the contrary. He said McClellan had endeavored to screen his failures and lay the blame of his incapacity on the government and he had positive proof of the facts." The officer defending McClellan stumbled over these accusations, which a sleepy Strother found credible.

Pope's anger was aroused, the more so as he was tired beyond measure. Having exhausted the subject of McClellan's perfidy, he launched into a harangue of his favorite scoundrel, Franz Sigel. To William B. Franklin, for whom Pope felt no affection either, he berated that "damned coward" Sigel in the harshest terms to date. He had, said Pope, "an irresistible instinct to run, and manifests it on all occasions."[28]

Lacking the strength to do more than hurl epithets at high-ranking miscreants, Pope told Ruggles to send orders to the corps commanders to report to headquarters in person at dawn, then lay down for a few hours of fitful sleep.[29]

— ◆ —

President Lincoln slept poorly the night of August 30. He bombarded the War Department and General Haupt with inquiries for news from the front long after dark, while outside the White House, Washington was seized with a panic of a sort not seen since First Bull Run. Army stragglers brought rumors of treason and betrayal. All outgoing private correspondence was embargoed and telegraphic communication with the North censored. Although the War Department relaxed its ban on newspapermen at the front, there were few wagons and fewer horses available to the corps of reporters that crowded Washington saloons and hotels. The army had impressed every serviceable wagon and team to bring in wounded from the battlefield, so journalists intent on a story paid exorbitant prices for any nag they might find. Brigadier General John Sedgwick, whose division of Sumner's Second Corps had gone into camp in Alexandria that morning, marveled at the pandemonium: "Everything is in the utmost consternation, as much so as after Bull Run. Washington people seem to lose their sense at the most unfounded rumors, but there may be some cause now."[30]

Troubling to the president was McClellan's evident desire to see Pope beaten; Lincoln now found McClellan's "Leave Pope to get out of his scrape" dispatch incomprehensible and his interference with Franklin's corps suspect. McClellan must be "a little crazy," Lincoln told John Hay that evening; Hay thought "envy, jealousy, and spite [were] probably a better explanation of his present conduct." President Lincoln retired for the night, still believing in John Pope.[31]

It was a faith few at Centreville shared. Beaten Federals awoke to a gray and torn landscape, awash in suffering. Surgeons heaved amputated limbs out the windows of abandoned Rebel huts by the wagon load. Putrid reminders of yesterday's disaster mingled with grim relics of First Bull Run. "Dead animals swelled with corruption and the whitening bones of those long decayed lay beside each other. Fresh graves were beside the weed-grown sepulchers," said Strother. A Pennsylvanian remembered the whole place "had the appearance of a human slaughter house."[32]

The shock of defeat ripped the thin fabric of cooperation between Pope and his generals. All levels of command became disaffected, and each man spoke his mind. In the first hours after the battle, blame was spread liberally. Colonel Strother indicted McClellan's followers: Porter for not attacking on August 29, and Franklin and Sumner for delaying their march to the front. "Thus through the jealousy of commanders the great cause of nationality is jeopardized, if not lost," he wrote in his journal on the evening of August 31. The cause of defeat, Brigadier General Robert Milroy snarled, was "treachery and incompetency, by God!"[33]

Not everyone would concede defeat. Jesse Reno, whose division had been mangled as badly as most, told a member of McDowell's staff the battle had been a victory. "We leave because the army has no food, no supplies; we drove the enemy back—we beat them from the field—it wasn't a defeat—it was a victory!" he expostulated. But most generals saw only defeat, for which they blamed Pope and, to a lesser degree, McDowell. Though no friend of McClellan, Joe Hooker lamented to a gathering of Third Corps officers, "if they had left McClellan in command this never would have happened." Sam Heintzelman agreed, concluding that "this defeat kills Pope so dead he will have to be relieved at once." Pope was no match for Lee and must be replaced at once, said General Bayard, "or the rebels will be in Washington soon." A disappointed General Sumner dismissed his favorite subordinate of New Mexico days as a "damned blow" with no idea where his army or the enemy was. Undoubtedly echoing Fitz John Porter's sentiments, Lieutenant Stephen Weld told his father that "Pope made a complete muddle of the whole affair and ordered us into a place where we were hit hard. If we ever reach Washington in safety, it will be more than I expect."[34]

While most grumbled in the privacy of their headquarters, Franz Sigel and Carl Schurz availed themselves of the return of the press to complain publicly. They buttonholed Nathaniel Paige of the *New York Tribune,* who had been a fixture at corps headquarters until Pope expelled the press from his army, and related to him their grievances. Sigel told Paige the army had not been defeated but rather its commander out-generaled. Pope "neither knew where his enemy was nor wanted to be informed. No orders of battle were given by Pope to generals of any rank." Paige asked Sigel on what plan the battle had been fought. "Sir, there was no plan. We knew nothing but what we discovered ourselves," replied Sigel. Schurz lamented the needless loss of a thousand men in his division, telling Paige, "I dare not go into the hospital and look at the faces of those wounded men who I know have shed their blood bravely and in vain."

Having seen so many die, Schurz was sickened by the reckless campfire gasconade of the Sumner's and Franklin's generals, whom he met on the morning of August 31. "[They] expressed their pleasure at Pope's discomfiture without the slightest concealment, and spoke of our government in Washington with an affectation of supercilious contempt. Some friends informed me that they had gone through similar experiences."[35]

Regimental officers and enlisted men, for whom rumor was the main source of information, cast blame more widely. Private William Kepler listened to his comrades of the Fourth Ohio debate the causes of their defeat. "Lee and Jackson pull together, our generals don't," said some. "McClellan wanted Pope to get whipped; he thinks he is bigger than Lincoln," added others. "Our generals are a jealous, incompetent set," agreed most.

Many veterans of the Army of the Potomac thought their revered George B. McClellan, and his lieutenant Fitz John Porter, responsible for the defeat. Major Oliver Bosbyshell of the Forty-eighth Pennsylvania averred, "Fitz John Porter had it in his power to give the enemy a crushing blow and thus have [sic] made General Pope the American people's hero of the hour, but this would have cast a shadow over the bright fame of McClellan. His inaction nipped Pope's already increasing popularity in the bud." An officer of the Pennsylvania Reserves concluded the defeat was "not to be attributed to the want of generalship on the part of the commanding general or his subordinates" but rather on the conduct of Porter. "In our regiment early on [August 20], it was well known that some trouble existed between Generals Pope and Porter, and that the latter would not render a cordial cooperation." Watching the battered troops of Pope's army shuffle through Centreville, Colonel Thomas Livermore, whose Eighteenth New Hampshire belonged to Sumner's corps, felt shame at "the criminal delays of McClellan and some of his subordinates in bringing up reinforcements, seemingly bent as they were on [Pope's] ruin." Surgeon George T. Stevens, also of Sumner's corps, denounced "the foulest treachery of ambitious rivals," to which Pope had fallen victim, and he wondered who was to blame for "the criminal neglect to send the Sixth Corps to the assistance of Pope's army."[36]

Within the Army of Virginia, blame was about equally assigned among Pope, McDowell, McClellan, and Porter for the defeat. "The great mistake was want of confidence," speculated William Maxson of the Twenty-third New York. "Confidence in Pope would have made a wall of our troops, an impassable and terrible wall—a wall of fire." Major John Gould of Banks's corps was more charitable toward Pope. "I am unwilling to admit that our opinion of General Pope was generally unfavorable at the time he commanded us. The general impression is that he was more sinned against than sinning. We had a sort of confidence in him till the end."[37]

Regardless of what he might think of Pope in particular, every soldier in the Army of Virginia shared in a general malaise on the raw, rain-swept morning of August 31. Said an officer of Sykes's division, "All about were the disjecta membra of a shattered army; here were stragglers plodding through the mud, inquiring for their regiments; little squads, just issuing from their shelterless bivouac on the wet ground; wagons wrecked and forlorn; half-formed regiments, part of the men with guns and part without; wanderers driven in by the patrols; while everyone you met had an unwashed, sleepy, downcast aspect, and looked as if he would like to hide his head from all the world."[38]

In the first hours after dawn, John Pope busied himself with bringing order to the army. He charged Lieutenant Colonel Smith with distributing ammunition and gave precise instructions to corps commanders on where and how to requisition it. Pope directed Ruggles to select points of rendezvous for each division and corps and to post placards about the area directing units to their proper places. Discharging his duty skeptically, Ruggles was surprised to find Pope's method worked, as previously disorganized clusters of men moved promptly to their commands. Pope called upon Strother to ride to Fairfax Court House to see that guards posted there were permitting the sick and wounded to pass freely to Washington.[39]

Although able to attend to the army's immediate needs, Pope could not compose a tactical plan, and so he did what he had not done during the campaign—he consulted with his generals. As each corps commander arrived for the council of war Pope had called for that morning, the commanding general posed to him the question, Should the army remain at Centreville or retire to the defenses of Washington? While some declined to respond, those who ventured an opinion were of a single mind. The army was too badly cut up to contemplate offensive action, and Lee would not be so reckless as to assault the Centreville defenses directly. And as the heavily wooded, stream-laced ground south of Centreville offered no room for maneuver, Lee most probably would move by Pope's right, either north into Maryland or east along the Little River Turnpike or the Leesburg Pike into the Union. The only alternative was to fall back to Washington.[40]

How closely Pope listened to his generals is a matter of conjecture. Captain Horace H. Thomas, a paper-pushing officer from the War Department, had left his desk the previous evening to get a closer look at the face of war. He got more than he bargained for. While chatting with Colonel Ruggles on the front porch of army headquarters, Thomas happened to glance into the parlor, where General Pope sat. The general's aspect moved Thomas deeply. "He sat with his chair tipped back against the wall, his hands clasped behind his head, which bent forward, his chin touching his breast—seeming to pay no attention to the generals as they arrived, but to be wholly wrapped in his own gloomy reflections. I pitied him then. I pity him now. General Pope seems to me the most unfortunate if not the most abused officer who ever wore the American uniform."[41]

Rejecting the counsel of his generals, Pope bucked the matter of retreat to Halleck. In a note that exposed the magnitude of his mental exhaustion, Pope wrote at 10:45 A.M., "Our troops are all here, and in position, though much used up but you may rely upon our giving them as desperate a fight as I can force our men to stand up to. I should like to know whether you feel secure about Washington, should this army be destroyed. I shall fight it as long as a man will stand up to the work." But Halleck must decide where they were to fight.

The council of war resumed to no apparent end, until a wire came from Halleck. It was his reply to Pope's dispatch of the night before. "You have done nobly," Halleck began. "Don't yield another inch if you can avoid it. All reserves are being sent forward. Can't you renew the attack? I am doing all in my power for you and your noble army. God bless you and it."[42]

Pope clutched Halleck's note with the single-minded fervor of one whom fatigue and despair had robbed of rational thought. He penned a hasty letter of thanks, assuring the general-in-chief he would "fight to the last" and making extravagant claims as to the damage he had inflicted on the Rebel army. "The plan of the enemy will undoubtedly be to turn my flank. If he does so, he will have his hands full. My troops are in good heart."[43]

To the dismay of his generals, Pope announced he would remain at Centreville. Porter deplored the decision as "foolish if not criminal" and wondered if Pope had deceived Washington as to the state of the army. Lieutenant Weld thought he understood Pope's reasoning: "Pope knows he is dead if he retreats to Washington and so he keeps us here."[44]

Weld was wrong. At that moment, Pope was incapable of any action so devious. Nervous energy alone propelled him. After summarizing Halleck's letter for them, Pope dismissed all his generals except McDowell, with whom he spent the afternoon visiting the camps and inspecting the fortifications. Not only was Pope unable to plan for himself, but he also failed to take measures to prevent Lee from turning his right. The nearest and most obvious route around the Federal flank was the Little River Turnpike, a wide, macadamized road that passed four miles north of Centreville and joined the Warrenton Turnpike at Germantown, six miles behind Union lines. Prudence dictated he post a corps astride the Little River Turnpike, but Pope ignored the threat, and nobody called it to his attention. A hint of the danger came at 3:00 P.M. in the form of a dispatch from Colonel Alfred Torbert, whose cavalry brigade garrisoned Germantown, telling Pope that Southern cavalry had annihilated a Federal squadron near Chantilly. Pope's response was decidedly limited. Apart from relocating his headquarters two miles to the east and sending a brigade from McDowell's corps and a regiment of cavalry to Fairfax Court House, Pope moved no one. Nightfall found the Federals huddled behind the earthworks at Centreville.[45]

— • —

For the first time in nearly a week, John Pope had divined his foe's intentions. Lee was determined to give the beaten Yankees no rest. To distract Pope from his exposed right flank, Lee directed Longstreet to maneuver conspicuously before Centreville; then, he sent Jackson across Bull Run and down the Little River Turnpike toward Fairfax Court House, with Stuart's cavalry in the lead. After shelling a Northern supply train near Ox Hill at sunset on August 31, Stuart halted three miles west of Germantown. Jackson's corps bivouacked seven miles behind him.

Pope's mental decline continued during the night. He responded to Stuart's presence at Ox Hill with half measures. At midnight he directed McDowell to open the road from Centreville to Fairfax Court House with a force sufficient only for that purpose. Three hours later, he commanded Sumner, whose Second Corps held the right, to reconnoiter due north to the Little River Turnpike at daybreak with one or two brigades. Sumner was to recall the reconnoitering party as soon as it ascertained "whether there is any considerable movement of the enemy's infantry toward our right and rear."[46]

Dawn on Monday, September 1, found Pope quarrelsome and suspicious, more concerned with traitors in his own camp than with the developing threat beyond his right. As always, Colonel Ruggles was a convenient target for Pope's truculence. Ruggles had just sat down to breakfast with an old West Point classmate, Colonel Alexander Webb, who had come out from Alexandria to join Porter's staff, when Pope entered the room. Glaring at their guest, Pope called Ruggles from the table to scold him. Webb picked up his hat to leave. Ruggles pulled him aside and said quietly, "The truth is Webb, that General Pope don't like my asking you to breakfast. He says that he won't have any of General McClellan's staff at his table." "I pity you Ruggles, more than myself," Webb reassured his friend, "I leave at once."[47]

At 8:50 A.M. Pope took up pen, to expose once more to Halleck the shifting currents of his troubled mind. The men were near collapse, horses completely broken down, and his line of retreat uncertain, began Pope. Nevertheless, "I shall attack again tomorrow if I can; the next day certainly." But Halleck should not expect much, Pope intimated, as "many brigade and some division commanders," and one "commander of a corps," from the Army of the Potomac, have calculated by "every word and act to break down the spirits of the men and produce disaster." After reviewing Porter's failings on August 30, without accusing him by name, Pope ranted at "the demoralization among officers of high rank in the Potomac Army, arising in all instances from personal feelings in relation to changes of commander-in-chief and others. You should know these things, as you alone can stop it." Pope was powerless to act against these high-ranking "tools of parasites, [whose] example must necessarily produce very disastrous results."

Pope concluded with a doleful prognosis: The Army of Virginia was finished as an effective fighting force. "My advice to you is that, in view of any satisfactory results, you draw this army to the entrenchments in front of Washington, and set to work in that secure place to reorganize and rearrange it." In no other way could disaster be avoided. "When there is no heart in their leaders, and every disposition to hang back, much cannot be expected from the men."[48]

That the Army of Virginia could be withdrawn safely into the capital defenses became a matter of grave doubt, when at 11:00 A.M. Pope learned Sumner's reconnoitering brigade had encountered the lead elements of Jackson's corps on the Little River Turnpike, just west of Chantilly. Pope appreciated the danger. As he told Halleck, "the enemy is deploying his forces on the Little River [Turn]pike, and preparing to advance by that road on Fairfax Court House. This movement turns Centreville and interposes between us and Washington, and will force me to attack his advance, which I shall do as soon as his movement is sufficiently developed." Halleck concurred with Pope's plan but suggested he retire to Fairfax Court House or Annandale in the absence of a decisive victory.[49]

Fighting off the melancholy that had impaired his judgment over the past twenty-four hours, Pope hastened to redeploy his forces to check the Confederate thrust.

An hour after receiving Sumner's warning, he had McDowell's corps on the march toward Fairfax Court House. After taking charge of "the two brigades now there"—an evident but not explicit reference to the commands of Patrick and Torbert—McDowell was to push his combined force forward to Germantown to keep open the army's line of retreat.[50]

Although he had begun to act decisively, Pope had trouble conveying his intentions clearly. After sending McDowell his orders, with his remaining corps commanders Pope convened a brief council of war at Sumner's headquarters to select a general to assume command of any units from Washington that might have found their way to Fairfax Court House. Pope chose Hooker, who set off thinking his mission identical to that which Pope had entrusted to McDowell an hour earlier. How McDowell and Hooker reconciled their mandates is unknown, but some confusion evidently ensued, as a rumor quickly arose that Hooker had relieved McDowell.

It was the best news the men had heard since the campaign began, said Charles Davis of the Thirteenth Massachusetts, whose regiment received the report from General Ricketts personally. "The cheers that went up at this news were such as had not been heard from the boys for many a day," remembered Davis.

Soldiers jeered McDowell as he passed. Believing him guilty of collusion with the enemy at Second Bull Run—the black pith helmet he wore into battle being "a signal to the enemy to cease firing and reserve their ammunition for a more opportune moment"—many men threatened to shoot McDowell, and one regiment nearly did. The trouble arose when its colonel answered an order from McDowell that he halt at Fairfax Court House with an emphatic "Go to Hell!" Learning of his impudence, McDowell went out himself to stop the regiment and arrest its commander. But the men were no more inclined to obey McDowell than their colonel had been, and they greeted his arrival with leveled rifle muskets. McDowell raged to no avail—the regiment stood firm. McDowell slunk away, recalled a colonel who witnessed the scene, "and wept afterwards like a child."[51]

To buy time for McDowell and Hooker, Pope would fashion a textbook "defense in depth" along the Little River Turnpike, interposing forces between the advancing Confederates and the units at Germantown. He selected for the duty the Ninth Corps under Isaac I. Stevens, who had assumed command for an ill Jesse Reno. The combative, diminutive former territorial governor of Washington obeyed cheerfully his instructions to march cross-country from Centreville to Ox Hill, a hamlet on the turnpike two miles west of Germantown. Should he find Jackson, Stevens was to attack at once. Haste was imperative, Pope told Stevens; a short time earlier, two cavalrymen had told Pope they had run into Rebel infantry while foraging on the turnpike near Chantilly.[52]

Admirable as it was, Pope's response to the crisis beyond his right fell short of that which prudence dictated. Rather than withdraw the entire army from the obsolete and badly exposed position at Centreville, Pope remained there with the corps of Sigel, Porter, Sumner, and Banks, the latter having reported in after destroying the stores at Bristoe Station. Rendered pliant by defeat, Pope was incapacitated by Halleck's order that he fall back on Washington only in the "absence of a decisive victory" over Jackson. Pope also had come to doubt his instincts, which told him to quit Centreville at once. For most of the afternoon, Pope rode from the headquarters of one corps commander to another, seeking both advice and an audience for his woes.

He visited Sumner and Heintzelman first. Both counseled immediate withdrawal, but Pope decided to wait until dawn to pull them back to Germantown.[53]

Next Pope sought out Banks, whom he had not seen in nearly a week. Neither the New Englander nor his men were particularly pleased to see Pope. To their way of thinking, his attentions came two days too late. All wondered why they had not been summoned to take part in the great battle raging within earshot. It was a legitimate question, in view of Pope's stated need for reinforcements during the battle and the lack of a credible threat to the stores at Bristoe Station, but one the commanding general never answered. It looked as if they would also play no part in the fight to come, as Pope told Banks to accompany the army's trains to Fairfax Station.[54]

Pope's predicament even propelled him to Porter's headquarters. Voluble, angry, and perplexed, Pope railed at the powers in Washington. Matters were grim, Pope conceded, but the fault was not his. He had been "pushed to the front against his advice," Pope told Porter, "and had been compelled to conduct a campaign contrary to his views." Now misguided orders from Washington compelled him to hold the army at Centreville. In his letter to Halleck that morning, Pope had blamed Porter for his discomfiture; now, to Porter, Pope pointed the finger at Halleck.

Porter shared Pope's distrust of Washington, and he cautioned Pope not to "permit the government to control his movements." The army had been kept at Centreville thirty-six hours too long as it was, added Porter. Knowing the enemy's location and probable intentions, Pope should withdraw at once.

Whatever his feelings toward Fitz John Porter just then, Pope could not dispute the soundness of his advice. Returning to headquarters, Pope told his staff to pack up for a move to Fairfax Court House. At 3:30 P.M., he told Heintzelman to retire two and one-half miles on the Warrenton Turnpike, face about, and fall in on Stevens's left. That left only Porter's, Sigel's, and Sumner's corps in Centreville. "We had no orders that we would abandon Centreville," Heintzelman noted in his journal, "but I know it must be ordered."[55]

▬ ◆ ▬

That afternoon of September 1, 1862, the weather and the mood of Pope's army were equally foul. Around noon, the air turned suddenly chill. A harsh wind came up, and at 4:30 P.M. a terrific thunderstorm struck. Heads bowed against the wind and whipping rain, the men of Stevens's Ninth Corps struggled across meadows and marshy hollows toward the Little River Turnpike. At almost the same instant the storm hit, Stevens's lead division collided with elements of Jackson's corps deployed a mile south of the Little River Turnpike. A brutal, seesaw struggle ensued in which Stevens fell with a bullet in his brain. At sunset, Kearny arrived with his division, only to himself fall, shot dead after riding blindly into a regiment of Rebels. The firing sputtered out at 7:00 P.M., with both sides near their original positions. A drawn battle, the fight near Chantilly accomplished nothing— an earlier report from Jeb Stuart that the Federals held Germantown in strength already had convinced Jackson to end his march into Pope's rear. Pope's quick work in piecing together the Germantown line, and not the battle in which Stevens and Kearny lost their lives, had preserved the Union line of retreat. As far as Lee and Jackson were concerned, the campaign of Second Manassas was over.[56]

At sunset on September 1, John Pope knew he must delay his departure from

Centreville no longer. He told Sigel, Sumner, and Porter to pull back toward Fairfax Court House at once; Reno's corps and Kearny's division were to retire from Jackson's front before dawn on the second. Fearing a running battle back to Washington, Pope was unable to tell his generals where to form their commands. Hoping for guidance, Heintzelman encountered Pope and his retinue heading toward Fairfax Court House during the night. But they passed in silence, riding wearily into town at midnight. While his staff looked to their comfort elsewhere, Pope sought out McDowell, who had bedded down in the home of a hospitable Union man named Ford. Their host obliged the generals with a fine supper. Too tired to leave, Pope stayed for the night.[57]

— ♦ —

Tuesday, September 2, broke cold and dreary. Pope had slept hard, awakening only when Ruggles and Heintzelman, who was desperate for instructions, called on him two hours after dawn.

The rest had not improved Pope's mood. Learning from Heintzelman that his withdrawal order had not reached all the corps commanders, Pope flew into "a great rage," which he no doubt directed at his long-suffering chief of staff. Calming a bit, Pope told Captain Joseph C. Willard to find his staff, place a guard around the Ford house, and then take a detachment of cavalry to clear the road to Alexandria. At 7:30 A.M., Pope dictated his morning report to Halleck, in words only slightly less discouraging than those of the day before. He had defeated Lee's first effort to turn his right, but "as soon as the enemy brings up his forces again he will again turn me." Franklin's and Sumner's corps were worthless. Advised Pope, "I will give battle when I can, but you should come out and see the troops. They were badly demoralized when they joined me, both officers and men, and there is an intense idea among them that they must get behind entrenchments." Pope closed with as categorical a confession of failure as an army commander could make. "Unless something can be done to restore tone to this army it will melt away before you know it. You had best at once decide what is to be done."[58]

— ♦ —

Henry Halleck was no more capable of deciding what should be done on September 2 than he had been during the four long weeks of active campaigning. Sleepless for four nights and enfeebled by hemorrhoids, Halleck was only too pleased to abdicate real authority over the armies in northern Virginia to McClellan. "I beg of you to assist me in this crisis with your ability and experience," he pleaded. "I am utterly tired out."

President Lincoln formally relieved Halleck of responsibility for the fate of the capital that same morning when, over the vehement objections of Chase and

Stanton and without consulting Halleck, he placed McClellan in command of all troops in the fortifications of Washington. Although the president had not changed his opinion of McClellan's evident desire to see Pope defeated, he concluded there was "no one in the army who can man these fortifications and lick these troops of ours into shape half as well as [McClellan] can."[59]

Later that morning, Halleck replied to Pope's 7:30 A.M. summons with a terse directive that signaled, at least temporarily, the end of Pope's tenure in independent command. "You will bring your forces as best you can within or near the line of fortification," commanded Halleck with uncommon decisiveness. "General McClellan has charge of all the defenses, and you will consider any direction, as to disposition of the troops as they arrive, given by him as coming from me." And, no, Halleck added, he would not be coming out from Washington.

There it was, one of the few unequivocal orders Halleck had issued during the campaign. Pope offered no objection. "Your telegram of this date is just received," he responded at 11:30 A.M., "and its provisions will be carried out at once." By 2:00 P.M., the last of Pope's army had cleared Fairfax Court House.[60]

Several corps commanders were present at the Ford house when Pope received Halleck's telegram, among them a perplexed Fitz John Porter. Two hours earlier, he had received a dispatch as unexpected as that which now greeted Pope. Writing from the War Department the evening before, McClellan asked Porter "for my sake, that of the country and of the old Army of the Potomac, that you and all friends will lend the fullest and most cordial cooperation to General Pope in all operations now going on. This week is the crisis of our fate."[61]

Porter showed the telegram to Pope and asked for an explanation; had the commanding general made a complaint against him to Washington? Telling Ruggles to write up withdrawal orders, Pope retired with Porter to a sofa in the corner of the room. For twenty minutes they talked in low tones about the events of the past week. Other generals came and went, but none ventured close enough to hear what was said.

Being in a contrite frame of mind (earlier that morning, Pope had apologized to Ruggles for having treated him badly during the campaign), Pope expressed himself to Porter with less conviction than he probably felt. Yes, Pope told Porter, he was dissatisfied with certain aspects of Porter's official conduct—his tardiness in coming to Bristoe Station on August 27, his failure to attack on the twenty-ninth, and the absence of Griffin's brigade on the thirtieth—but no, he had not reported him to Washington. Pope also expressed his dismay with Porter's extra-official behavior; in particular, his carping letter to J. C. G. Kennedy of July 17, predicting disaster for the army under Pope, which the president had shown him. Unable to recall the letter, Porter answered, "if I had been unjust I would make all amends possible, and if I had predicted misfortune, he must admit the justice of the prediction."

Pope would do no such thing, but he did concede Porter's explanation of his battlefield performance to be "entirely satisfactory," with the exception of Griffin's brigade. "That can be easily explained," countered Porter. A weary Pope not only did not push the matter but also assured Porter that, as matters stood, he "should not take any action."[62]

Porter's insolent rejoinder was a trifling affront, compared to the full-dress humiliation handed Pope that afternoon on the outskirts of Washington. Riding at the head of the column, their uniforms covered with dust, their beards powdered with it, Pope and McDowell looked as forlorn as the army they led toward Washington. To Lieutenant Abner Small of the Sixteenth Maine, the whole procession seemed funereal. Rage, mortification, and disgust were etched on the grimy faces of the men. "The column passing with its ragged banners, and the long ambulance train with its awful freight of torn and battered humanity, burdened us with a crushing sense of the business we were engaged in," remembered Small, but not so heavily as to preclude jokes at Pope's expense. Observing the large, stand-up linen collar Pope wore because wool chafed his neck, one of Small's companions declaimed, "Great God! What could you expect of a man who will persist in wearing his shirt wrong end up!"[63]

During the past two days, Pope had endured more than simply jokes from the men in ranks. Recalled Ruggles, not without some satisfaction, "As we came back from Chantilly and rode along the lines of the troops, the men cursed McDowell and Pope to their faces and openly threatened to shoot McDowell on the first occasion in which they might encounter him in action."

At 4:00 P.M., Pope suffered the supreme indignity of his checkered career. On the brow of Munson's Hill, near the outer line of the capital defenses, Pope met McClellan. So self-absorbed were Pope and McDowell that they failed to notice Little Mac until someone pointed out his presence, when they at once rode to him. The contrast was painful: Pope and McDowell haggard and dirty, McClellan cocky and clean in dress uniform, complete with yellow sash and saber. Brigadier General Jacob D. Cox, who had ridden out from Alexandria with McClellan, watched the generals exchange salutes. Little Mac announced to all present his appointment to command within the fortifications, then told Pope where to place his units.

In earshot was General Hatch, whose infantry brigade led the march. Still bitter over Pope's having demoted him from command of a cavalry division, Hatch turned instantly and, riding a few paces to the head of his column, shouted, "Boys, McClellan is in command again; three cheers!" The men roared wildly, their cheers taken up by each succeeding brigade and punctuated with band music. "Warm friend of McClellan as I was, I felt my flesh cringe at the unnecessary affront to the unfortunate commander of that army," Cox wrote. "But no word was spoken. Pope lifted his hat in a parting salute to McClellan and rode quietly on with his escort."[64]

Pope awoke Wednesday, September 3, indignant and ready to resume the offensive, against both Lee's Confederates and the Army of the Potomac's caballing generals. Amid camp rumors of wholesale impending dismissals of cabinet officers and army and corps commanders, Pope wrote a friend at army headquarters, Colonel John C. Kelton, to learn something of his status and to strike out at McClellan. "Does McClellan command in chief on this side of the river or do his functions only extend to designating the positions to be occupied by the troops arriving from Centreville?" To put McClellan in general command would be a grave error, as "everybody in this army considers him responsible for the failure to send forward Sumner and Franklin and Cox or anybody else, and for the inefficient condition in which they did arrive. There is, and can be, no good feeling here under these circumstances." Pope implored Kelton to "beg [Halleck], if nothing else can be done, to command himself."[65]

Pope wrote directly to Halleck that afternoon, urging an immediate offensive down the Little River Turnpike. "We must strike again with fresh men while the enemy is weakened and broken down," Pope insisted. "I am ready to advance again to the front with the fresh troops now here. Someone ought to have the supreme command here. Let us not sit down quietly, but push forward again."

Not surprisingly, Pope's frenetic appeal fell on deaf ears. Halleck's response was both discouraging and, in terms of Pope's personal fate, enigmatic. As soon as all his troops were within the fortifications, Pope was to report in person to army headquarters. "A reorganization of an army for the field will be immediately made," Halleck informed him. "Till then General McClellan, as senior and as commanding the defenses of Washington, must exercise general authority."[66]

Although his reply confused Pope, Halleck had not played false with him. As Pope learned when he visited Lincoln that afternoon, the administration had yet to decide what to do with the armies around Washington. In the company of Secretary Chase, Pope heard the president express his "entire satisfaction with his conduct" during the recently concluded campaign. Lincoln assured him McClellan's command was only temporary and, as Chase recalled, "gave him some reason to expect that another army of active operations would be organized at once, which he (Pope) would lead." Perhaps in response to harsh words from Pope about Porter's conduct, the president showed him copies of the impolitic letters Porter had written Burnside during the campaign. To Pope, and probably to Lincoln as well, they were strong evidence of a manifest desire on Porter's part to see Pope fail. "This communication of the president to me opened my eyes to many matters which I had before been loathe to believe."[67]

Pope left the White House both encouraged and enraged. That evening, with his fury burning white, he sat down to compose a report of the Second Bull Run campaign. All bets were off. His conciliatory words to Porter at Fairfax Court

House had been naive and uninformed; now Pope would see that the miscreant corps commander got his due, even at the expense of the truth. In striking out at Porter—and McClellan as well—Pope had the full support and active encouragement of Halleck, who undoubtedly hoped to rid himself of McClellan, who coveted his job, and of Porter, who could be expected to help McClellan get it, while letting Pope take the fall for any backlash.

Whether more fully to incriminate Porter or, more probably, because anger distorted his memory, Pope portrayed his ambiguous Joint Order of August 29 as an explicit command to McDowell and Porter to "advance rapidly and attack the enemy on his flank." Exculpating McDowell by praising his decision to bring his corps "on the field in the afternoon," where it took "a conspicuous part in that day's operations," Pope went on to relate his "surprise and disappointment" at having received "late in the afternoon from Porter a note saying that his advance had met the enemy on the flank in some force, and that he was retiring upon Manassas Junction, without attacking the enemy or coming to the assistance of our other forces, although they were engaged in a furious action only two miles distant and in full hearing of him. I do not hesitate to say that if Porter had attacked the enemy on the flank on the afternoon of Friday we should have crushed Jackson before the forces under Lee could have reached him."

Pope also castigated Porter for permitting Griffin's brigade to wander off to Centreville, and he implied that weak fighting by the remainder of the Fifth Corps on August 30 had permitted Longstreet subsequently to mass his forces and crush the Federal left. Summoning aide-de-camp Speed Butler to his headquarters at Ball's [Bailey's] Cross Roads, Pope had him draft a note of a conversation he had overheard late on the thirtieth, in which Griffin allegedly traduced Pope, "spoke disrespectfully and sneeringly of other superior officers, said that he had heard that morning that General McClellan was to take command, [and] hoped it was true."[68]

President Lincoln afforded Pope the opportunity to present his report at the White House the next morning. Although Pope confessed it merely a rough draft, he showed the paper to Stanton and Chase before seeing Lincoln. In the presence of the president and of Secretary of the Navy Welles, Pope read what Welles regarded as "not exactly a bulletin nor a report, but a manifesto, a narrative, tinged with wounded pride and a keen sense of injustice and wrong." While he offered no opinion of Pope's presentation, Lincoln did promise to submit the report to his cabinet on Friday, September 5, for a decision regarding the advisability of publishing it. "It certainly needs modifying before it goes out," thought Welles, "or there will be war among the generals, who are now more ready to fight each other than the enemy." Pope's remarks as he and Welles walked together from the White House only deepened the secretary's fears. "He declares all his misfortunes are owing to the persistent determination of McClellan, Franklin, and Porter, aided by Ricketts, Griffin, and some others who were predetermined he should not be successful," recorded Welles. "They preferred, he said, that the country should be ruined rather than he should triumph."[69]

Sympathy for Pope ran strong when the cabinet met, but not strong enough to support publication of his report. Even Stanton and Chase had to confess that its release would be a mistake on "the score of policy under existing circumstances." To their eminent satisfaction, however, the president announced his intention to bring Porter, Franklin, and Griffin before courts of inquiry.[70]

Hour by hour, the mood in Washington darkened, even as the threat of a Rebel drive on the capital diminished. As early as September 4, Pope had correctly deduced Lee's intention to cross the Potomac River into Maryland, a belief Gideon Welles and most level-headed members of the cabinet shared. Supply and munitions shortages were quickly overcome, and the trusted hand of McClellan reinspired confidence among the men in ranks. But the high command seethed, and the partisan press fanned the flames of public indignation, most of which was directed at McClellan and Porter until a letter written on the battlefield of Second Bull Run by a mortally wounded Colonel Thornton F. Brodhead of the First Michigan Cavalry, then circulating on Capitol Hill, found its way into the papers. "I have fought manfully and now die fearlessly," wrote the Michigander. "I am one of the victims of Pope's imbecility and McDowell's treason. Tell the president that to save our country he must not give our flag to such hands."[71]

Public opinion, and sentiments on Capitol Hill, swung decisively against Pope and McDowell. Stanton and Chase began to cut their losses. "The outcry against McDowell is absurd beyond belief," marveled Colonel Strother. "He is charged with cowardice, treachery, and a host of other crimes too preposterous to name." On the advice of Chase, McDowell asked to be relieved, pending a court of inquiry to investigate Brodhead's charges.[72]

For John Pope, the blow fell shortly after noon on September 5, in the form of Special Orders Number 223. Porter, Franklin, and Griffin were "relieved from their respective commands until the charges against them can be investigated by a court of inquiry." The armies of the Potomac and Virginia were consolidated, and Pope was instructed to report to the secretary of war as a witness before the court. Although issued as an army directive, the decision to relieve Pope had been Lincoln's. On the way to the War Department that morning, Lincoln explained to John Hay his reasons for removing the son of old Judge Pope. "McClellan is working like a beaver," Lincoln remarked. Cabinet pressure and public opinion would eventually compel him to dismiss McClellan too, conceded Lincoln, but not yet. "He has acted badly in this matter, but we must use what tools we have.

Unquestionably he has acted badly toward Pope. He wanted him to fail. That is unpardonable. But he is too useful just now to sacrifice."[73]

Word of his removal reached Pope indirectly. Perplexed by a telegram from McClellan's headquarters that he be ready to march with three days' rations, Pope asked Little Mac's chief of staff to define for him the nature—and location— of his command, as McClellan "has ordered my troops to take post at various places, and I have never been notified in a single instance of their positions." Pope posed the same question to Halleck. As the afternoon wore on with no answer, Pope grew impatient. "I must again ask your attention to the condition of things in this army. By the present arrangement you are doing me more injury than my worst enemy could do," he remonstrated. "It is understood, and acted on, that I am deprived of my command, and that it is assigned to McClellan. An order defining his exact status here as well as my own is necessary at once."

He got it: a single-sentence directive informing Pope his army had been abolished and telling him to report for orders to the secretary of war. Halleck followed his terse telegram with an unofficial letter that oozed insincerity from every line. He had not written earlier because he did not know what would be Pope's command. But "the troops at present are under McClellan's orders, and it's evident that you cannot serve under him willingly. More over, your testimony is required by the Court of Inquiry ordered on Generals Porter, Franklin, and Griffin." Pope's report had been read to the cabinet members, Halleck continued, who "were unanimously of opinion that it ought not to be published," a view the president shared. "Do not infer from this that any blame attaches to you. On the contrary, we think you did your best with the material you had. I have not heard any one censure you in the least. You know that I am your friend and will never see any injustice done to you if I can help it," Halleck added, "but there are matters of such great importance to be decided that individual preferences must yield. We must do what seems best to reconcile the differences which exist in the two armies. I will explain to you more fully as soon as you come over to report."[74]

With his staff, Pope set out for Washington at once. As they crossed the Long Bridge into Georgetown, Pope buttonholed his long-suffering chief of staff, Colonel Ruggles, to request he appear as principal witness in the trial of Fitz John Porter. Despising Pope as he did, Ruggles resisted, reminding the commanding general of his congenial talk with Porter at Fairfax Court House. When they reached army headquarters, a troubled Ruggles submitted the matter to Colonel Kelton.[75]

Whatever words Halleck had for Pope scarcely mollified him. Neither did it help to learn the next day that the official pretense for his dismissal had effectively been rescinded less than twenty-four hours after its promulgation. One of McClellan's first acts in command had been to ask Halleck to restore Porter, Franklin, and Griffin for the impending campaign against Lee in Maryland, a request to which Halleck acceded.[76]

What do to with Pope then became the question. Although evident to Lincoln he could no longer command the respect of eastern troops or cooperate with their generals, the president still believed in the military capacity of the problematic Pope. He had been defeated, but not routed, by the South's best; certainly he deserved at least a corps—the despised Irvin McDowell had fared far worse at First Bull Run yet had retained a considerable command. While his reputation may have been forever ruined in the East, Pope remained a popular figure in the West. William T. Sherman was outraged at the treatment accorded him. "I see the people have made a clear sacrifice of Pope and McDowell," he told his brother, "and are now content with having killed two of their own generals. This is a glorious war!" For Lincoln, the principal problem would have been deciding who to remove in the West to make room for Pope.[77]

But the president's dilemma was solved for him before he truly had time to ponder it. From far-off Minnesota in late August came a startling appeal: The state must receive a stay of its military-draft obligations, Governor Alexander Ramsey implored President Lincoln. An "Indian outbreak has come upon us suddenly. Half the population of the state are fugitives. It is absolutely impossible that we should proceed. No one not here can conceive the panic in the state."

From Private Secretary John G. Nicolay, whom Lincoln had sent to the Northwest to meet with the Chippewa Indians, came confirmation of Ramsey's claims. "The Indian War grows more extensive. Sioux, mustering perhaps 2,000 warriors, are striking along a line of scattered settlements of 200 miles, having already massacred several hundred whites, and the settlers of the whole border are in a panic and in flight, leaving their harvest to waste in the fields as I myself have seen even in neighborhoods where there is no danger. Against the Sioux it must be a war of extermination."

Governor Edward Salomon of Wisconsin added his voice to the clamor, writing Secretary Stanton on September 2, "There is very great apprehension in the northwestern and central portions of the state on account of the Indians. Families are leaving their homes for fear of the wandering bands. The people must be protected." Reports from Indian agents caused the secretary of the interior to warn Stanton the conflict also threatened to spill over into the Nebraska Territory.[78]

Distracted by the crisis in northern Virginia, both Lincoln and Stanton paid scant attention to the Northwest. On the morning of September 6, a frustrated Governor Ramsey reminded the president "those Indian outrages continue. This is not our war; it is a national war." Lincoln reluctantly agreed. The Northwest was an important source of fighting men and food. Minnesota politicians such as Henry Rice of the Senate Committee on Military Affairs were capable of embarrassing the administration, should nothing be done. Then, too, Confederate complicity in the outrages could not be discounted. Southern agents were widely believed to be fomenting trouble with the tribes of the south-central Plains, and Richmond already had made an effort to seize control of the Colorado Territory and the Southwest. With one stroke, the president would demonstrate his concern for the Northwest and rid himself of a two-star liability: on September 6, John Pope received orders to proceed to Minnesota as commander of the newly formed Department of the Northwest.[79]

The encomia in the orders from Stanton read as plastic as Halleck's words of reassurance had the day before. "The Indian hostilities now prevailing require the attention of some military officer of high rank, in whose ability and vigor the Government has confidence, and you have therefore been selected for this important command." Stanton could offer little beyond platitudes; having "no detailed information respecting the extent of the outrages that have been committed or of the force engaged in their perpetration, [he] therefore must leave to [Pope's] judgment and discretion the measures to be taken."[80]

Although rapid, the decision to exile Pope clearly had been difficult for Lincoln, and he probably realized its injustice. As General Jacob D. Cox later remarked, "Between Halleck, McClellan, and Pope, the only one who had fought like a soldier and maneuvered like a general was sent to the northwestern frontier to watch Indian tribes, carrying the burden of others' sins into the wilderness. Mr. Lincoln's sacrifice of his sense of justice to what seemed the only expedient in the terrible crisis, was sublime. McClellan commanded the army, and Porter and Franklin each commanded a corps. If the country was to be saved, confidence and power could not be bestowed by halves."[81]

A startled Pope stumbled about Washington seeking solace. He went first to the bar at Willard's Hotel, a favorite watering place of generals. Present were Banks, Sumner, Heintzelman, Reno, Schurz, and a host of lesser officers. Sigel walked in later to a hearty round of cheers; Pope had met only silence.[82]

That night Pope called on Salmon P. Chase. As a simple act of justice the secretary must have Pope's report published. Chase objected; the moment was inopportune. However, he conceded Halleck should issue a general order of thanks to the army. That would be satisfactory, said Pope, but Halleck would not consent to it. Chase promised to speak to the president, and Pope left for the evening, his orders from Stanton in hand.

Certain he had been conspired against and his twenty-year army career blighted beyond repair, Pope nonetheless acted like a soldier. On September 9, he boarded a train for the Northwest.[83]

11   *I Could Tell a Sad Story*

     Perhaps, in the course of the long ride west, Pope contemplated the irony of his Minnesota exile. Thirteen years earlier, as a brash young brevet captain out to make a name for himself, he had extolled the remarkable richness and potential of the Minnesota Territory. Now that land, much of it ravaged by unspeakable horrors, was to be home to his disgrace.

     The journey itself was an ordeal. At stops in Baltimore on September 11 and in Philadelphia a day later, Pope spoke little. "He looked tired and careworn," said a journalist who saw him; Pope believed, however, "his generalship would be vindicated when the true account of the battle of Second Bull Run was published." A friendly greeting from the citizens of Lancaster, Pennsylvania, helped revive his spirits. He thanked them warmly for their "kind reception" and complimented the conduct of Pennsylvania regiments at Second Bull Run. "They did all men could do, but we were not supported by the government as we should have been."[1]

     With friends in Cincinnati, Pope spoke bluntly. During an interview with Murat Halstead of the *Cincinnati Daily Commercial,* Pope launched into a tirade against that "damned coward" Sigel and members of the McClellan clique. He repeated his defamatory remarks to prominent Republicans around town.

Publicly, Pope was circumspect. From Cincinnati, where he remained a few days with Clara and her family, Pope traveled to Chicago. The *Chicago Tribune* gratified him with a series of unflinchingly supportive editorials—"there is but little doubt," announced the *Tribune,* "that there was a conspiracy of a certain clique of pro-slavery West Pointers to be beaten, and [to] disgrace and ruin [Pope]"—and a crowd of several thousand turned out to greet him. Addressing the cheering throng from his hotel balcony, Pope spoke sincerely: "My friends— I am glad to see you tonight. I am glad to be back to breathe again the pure air of the State of Illinois. It has been for many years my home, and I am glad to return to it. God Almighty only knows how sorry I am I ever left it."

Pope was equally sorry he had left his western army. He had neither sought nor desired higher position. "My friends," Pope concluded cryptically, "I could tell a sad story to you tonight, of recent events, but it is wiser and better that I should not tell it. I am a soldier and recognize a soldier's duty. My services and my life are at the disposal of the Government, and God knows how gladly I will render up both in its behalf. My record is before the people. The popular voice is the best judge, and with them I am willing to leave it."[2]

As reflected in the nation's press, public opinion concerning Pope's record divided along party lines. Upon learning of his Minnesota appointment, the *New York World* of Manton Marble, himself a close friend of Porter, had a good deal of cheap fun at Pope's expense. "The Indians never trouble themselves about bases of supply or lines of retreat, and the country they make war on must support them," taunted the *World.* "They agree also with General Pope, Secretary Stanton, and the Radicals in scorning a rose-water or kid-glove style of conducting a war. A stern policy is their delight and hence they rob, murder all non-combatants in their line of march, which it will be remembered was the very spirit of Pope's famous orders."

The pro-administration *Boston Evening Transcript* was quick to scold the *World.* "A more unjust attack or cruel slander upon a loyal general was never penned by the most malignant secessionist sheet in Rebeldom," opined the Boston daily.[3]

The unexpected publication in the *New York Times* on September 8 of Pope's draft report of the Second Bull Run campaign gave friendly editors heavy ammunition for their defense of the beleaguered general. Despite Pope's desire to see "the true account of the battle published," no evidence exists he leaked the document himself, or sanctioned its divulgence. Most probably Thomas C. H. Smith or Benjamin Roberts did so in a misguided effort to help him.

The *Chicago Tribune* called the report a "revelation [that] will startle the country. Officers who betray their country in battle should be shot as soon as the facts are made known." That McClellan withheld supplies and reinforcements and

Porter withdrew from the battlefield in defiance of Pope's orders had yet to be proven, but "Pope's statements have an air of probability to say the least, agreeing with those of numerous witnesses who have written from the field."

The best rebuttal to pro-Pope dailies came from the *Washington Star,* which lamented the report's release as "singularly ill-timed" and noted Pope had written it before receiving a single report from his subordinates. The *New York Evangelist* got in the best swipe at Pope himself, quoting Commodore Foote as saying the general was "a good man for a dash. Give him 10,000 men to carry a position and it is done promptly. He has courage, energy, and enterprise, and in a smaller field was remarkably successful, but in a large theatre of action he is out of his place and nothing but failure could be expected."[4]

Publication of his report may have helped Pope marginally with public opinion, but it cost him much goodwill with the administration. Its release coincided with Robert E. Lee's crossing of the Potomac River into Maryland, so that the president was too preoccupied to punish those responsible. He was angry, however, and told the cabinet Pope must be held accountable, should the leak be traced to him. But, Lincoln added, Pope was cunning; the report, he concluded, "can never, by any skill, be traced to him." Montgomery Blair hastened to agree. "That is the man," he nodded. "Old [Judge] Pope, his father, was a flatterer, a deceiver, a liar, and a trickster; all the Popes are so." Stanton and Chase kept silent.[5]

On the afternoon of September 16, 1862, General Pope arrived in St. Paul, Minnesota, with a small party that included Thomas C. H. Smith, Louis Marshall, and Douglass Pope. Brigadier General Benjamin S. Roberts was due in the next morning. Coming from Virginia, Pope's staff could offer no insights into the troubles in Minnesota. Nearly alone, Pope had to make sense of the "consternation and dismay" he encountered everywhere.

Not that he was unwelcome in St. Paul. The *St. Paul Daily Press* reminded its readers "the government in assigning General Pope to the direction of the Indian campaign, has selected a brave and accomplished officer, whose former experience and peculiar fitness designate him as the proper person for the work to be performed." His reverse in Virginia should be no cause for alarm, the *Daily Press* continued. "In command of the Army of Virginia he did all he could do under the circumstances and it is no slight praise to say he was instrumental in delivering the Army of the Potomac from its imprisonment."

Prominent Minnesotans bombarded Pope with lurid stories of Indian atrocities, but the prevailing panic was hardly conducive to a true accounting of affairs. Letters to the editor of the *Daily Press* reflected a people gone berserk. "We must do one of two things: either kill every Sioux Indian within our borders or drive the tribe out of the state," said one letter writer. "Let it be a war of extermination," agreed another. Governor Alexander Ramsey was equally strident in his official correspondence: "The Sioux Indians must be exterminated or driven forever beyond the borders of the state," he told the state militia. We whites are blameless, he and other Minnesotans seemed to say, for the outrages of the Sioux.[6]

The truth was far less flattering. Hostilities with the Sioux stemmed from a familiar pattern of perfidy and encroachment. As Pope had predicted a decade earlier, the lovely and fertile Minnesota Territory drew thousands of settlers. From barely six thousand inhabitants in 1849, Minnesota grew in a decade to a population of nearly two hundred thousand. Breaking treaties, white settlers pushed the region's six thousand Sioux inhabitants into a fifteen-mile-wide ribbon of land along the southern bank of the Minnesota River, from Lake Traverse 150 miles south to Fort Ridgely. The federal government divided the area into an Upper Reservation, comprised of the Sisseton and Wahpeton bands, and a Lower Reservation, comprised of the Mdewakanton and Wahpekuta Sioux. The Redwood Indian Agency was established near Fort Ridgely to manage the Lower Reservation, and the Yellow Medicine Agency was built at the mouth of the Yellow Medicine River to administer the Upper concern. Around these places clustered missions for proselytizing the Indian and white villages for supplying earthly wants.

Because it encompassed several of their traditional village sites, the Upper Sioux regarded the land assigned them by treaty in 1851 as adequate; but the Lower Sioux, removed from their woodlands home to open prairie, accepted the reservation reluctantly. For the next ten years, they and their northern cousins endured efforts of white missionaries to Christianize them, of Indian agents to make farmers of them, and of Indian traders to cheat them. When in 1861 Federal troops were drawn away to fight Confederates, disgruntled Sioux saw a chance to reclaim their lands. Autumn witnessed widespread crop failure, and the winter of 1862 brought the Sioux to the edge of starvation. Then the annual spring disbursement of annuity goods and cash was delayed. By August, the Lower Agency Sioux had grown tired of waiting. When agency traders refused Chief Little Crow's demand for credit—one trader reputedly rebuked Little Crow, "If they are hungry, let them eat grass or their own dung"—his warriors exploded in an orgy of violence.

On August 17, a small hunting party murdered two families of settlers at Acton after a trivial quarrel. The act had not been premeditated, but for the Sioux it marked a turning point. Concluding that their tribes would be punished for the homicides, that evening a council of chiefs decided to wage all-out war, under the leadership of a reluctant Little Crow, to drive the whites from the Minnesota Valley. What followed was the bloodiest Indian uprising in American history.[7]

The Sioux moved swiftly. On the morning of August 18, they attacked the Redwood Agency, killing twenty. Later that day, they slaughtered 50 settlers in Milford Township and ambushed a 46-man relief column from Fort Ridgely, killing 27 at a loss of but one brave. Finding they could "kill white men like sheep," the Lower Agency Indians attacked Fort Ridgely itself and the heavily defended town of New Ulm, while also falling upon isolated homesteads. The Upper Agency Sioux joined the uprising reluctantly, but once committed, they matched Little Crow's bands in brutality and thoroughness. Spreading out along the frontier, ravaging Indians from both agencies killed hundreds. Isolated bands marauded to within thirty miles of St. Paul. Panic gripped the state, and settlers by the thousand fled to the capital.

Determined resistance at New Ulm and Fort Ridgely stalled Little Crow's advance and gave Governor Ramsey time to organize a response. Placing the public welfare over political expediency, he called upon his old political rival, former governor Henry Hastings Sibley, to lead a relief expedition into the beleaguered counties as colonel of whatever state troops he could muster. Ramsey appointed Charles E. Flandrau, the defender of New Ulm, to build a line of forts along Minnesota's southwestern frontier.[8]

In Sibley, Ramsey had chosen wisely. Long a resident of the Minnesota frontier, Sibley had been a fur trader and the first territorial delegate to Congress. He knew the Sioux intimately and spoke their tongue. A decade earlier, Captain John Pope had appealed to Sibley to promote his Pembina report in Congress.

At the head of 1,400 volunteers, Sibley set out for the Lower Agency on August 26. He relieved Fort Ridgely, then went after the four warring tribes, with nearly disastrous results. At Birch Coulee, 150 of his men were surprised by 500 warriors. At Acton on September 3, a second detachment was stampeded, after which Sibley decided to halt operations until the Third Minnesota Infantry arrived from the South.

Apart from the ongoing siege of Fort Abercrombie by the Upper Agency Sioux, the clashes at Birch Coulee and Acton marked the end of concerted Indian offensive action. Little Crow's failure to take Fort Ridgely caused dissension among his chiefs, a growing number of whom dreaded white retribution. Although raids continued along the frontier, Sibley and Flandrau were relatively unhindered in implementing Governor Ramsey's plan to exterminate or drive the Sioux from Minnesota. Flandrau was to hold his chain of forts while Sibley marched against the Indians.

Minnesotans waited, but Sibley's first clashes with Little Crow had rendered him overcautious, and his deliberate preparations infuriated the revenge-crazed populace. Newspaper editors called him a "snail," a coward, the "State undertaker," and worse. Demoralized, Sibley submitted his resignation. Ramsey returned it, and Sibley stayed on. He refused, however, to march without sufficient rations, ammunition, and clothing, experienced infantry to give battle, and cavalry to give chase.[9]

At this juncture, Pope reached St. Paul. Knowing Sibley as he did, Pope prudently ignored the calls for his dismissal. But he shared in the general alarm. "From all indications and information we are likely to have [an] Indian war all along the frontier," Pope told Halleck. "Unless immediate steps are taken to put a stop to it, Wisconsin and Minnesota will be half depopulated before the winter begins." Although anxious to punish the Sioux, Pope conceded the need for Sibley's punitive force to be properly fitted out. "I am rejoiced to find you in command of the expedition against the Sioux," Pope told Sibley on September 17, "and assure you that I will push forward everything to your assistance as fast as possible." Whatever Sibley's needed, Pope would work vigorously to supply.

Pope also acquainted Sibley with his own plans for chastising the Sioux. With the sure hand of a veteran, he had acted quickly and confidently. While en route to Minnesota, he had asked the governor of Wisconsin to forward four recently recruited regiments for Indian fighting. Convinced like Sibley that only cavalry could corral Little Crow, Pope purchased 2,500 horses, with which he intended to mount half the Wisconsin troops. He would distribute the Wisconsin regiments in contingents throughout the threatened area: 1,000 men at Fort Abercrombie, 500 at Otter Trail, 1,000 at Fort Ripley, and 1,000 at Crystal Lake, as a buffer between the Sioux and the Winnebago, whom both Pope and Sibley feared would join the uprising.

Governor Ramsey believed guilty Sioux must be exterminated or driven beyond Minnesota; Pope took his proposals a step further: to prevent future troubles, he would send expeditions deep into Dakota Territory to attack Yankton Sioux who had taken arms against settlers there. "I do not think it best to close the campaign until the very last moment, even should our men suffer much," he advised Sibley. "Confidence and safety will at once be restored among the settlers when they find you are driving the Indians."

Pope counseled celerity not merely out of concern for the welfare of Minnesotans. He wanted to get back into the military mainstream as quickly as possible and doubted the administration intended his exile to be permanent. Most western soldiers, to whom Pope was yet a first-class general, hoped for his return. Lamented an Ohio private who had served under him at Island No. 10, "Pope, the best general in our Army, has been sent to the West to fight a squad of Indians. It's a shame, there is too much jealousy amongst our leading men. When will our rulers learn wisdom?" Charles Wills, an Illinoisan, wondered the same. "We're in hopes that Pope will be sent back to us after he finishes hanging those Indians. I don't believe there is a regiment in this army that would not cheer him as its corps commander," he wrote home from Tennessee. "Everybody seems to be willing to bet something on Pope."[10]

But Pope did little to further his own cause. He was too angry with Lincoln and Halleck to pen the sort of measured prose that might win him reassignment, and he was honest enough with himself to confess that a rest from the sort of "severe labor of mind and body" he had endured in Virginia would do him good. Also, Pope was anxious to be reunited with Clara, who after the death of their first-born child had returned to Pomeroy to stay with her parents. He begged Congressman Horton to convince the headstrong Clara to come to Minnesota. St. Paul was "a most delightful town, with a very agreeable population," Pope assured him. He had taken a large furnished house, well-suited for Clara and for her mother and sisters, should they wish to accompany her. With the Confederate Army of Mississippi marching north through Kentucky, a border town on the Ohio River was no place for women to be. "You have no idea whatever of the insult and outrage that would be visited upon them should any of the enemy succeed in occupying Pomeroy even for a short time," Pope warned, apparently regarding St. Paul as safe from Indian depredations. Pope sent a similar telegram directly to Clara.[11]

While he awaited her reply, Pope unburdened himself to Governor Yates and William Butler of Illinois in language most infelicitous, but with conviction no doubt sincere. On September 21, Pope addressed Yates his most forceful expression to date of his feelings about the administration, the McClellan clique, and the state of the nation. Rather than dwell directly on the "sad and shameful story" of his own travails in Virginia, occasioned by McClellanites, Pope emphasized the threat they posed to the nation. It was his "conviction that the country (by which I mean our institutions) is in more danger of destruction if McClellan be successful in his present campaign than if he be defeated." Much of what Pope wrote was hyperbole, but the apprehensions he voiced were shared by many, Republicans and Democrats alike, who feared the ascendancy of the eastern military establishment in public affairs. Drawing an analogy to Republican Rome in its death throes, Pope declared, "the Praetorian system is as fully developed and in active operation in Washington as it ever was in Ancient Rome. Today the thirty or forty officers who clamor about the White House of disaffection in the Army only seek the removal of one general [Pope] and the replacement of another [McDowell]." By consenting to Pope's banishment, Lincoln had sealed his own fate and with it gravely endangered the Republic. "With success in their clamor, the demands will not be slow to increase in extent and importance, and under the present system and practice as soon as they demand the removal of Lincoln and the substitution of someone else, whether citizen or soldier, he cannot in view of his antecedent practice refuse to abdicate."

In words that presaged William T. Sherman's iron policy of 1864, Pope concluded, "Our government and our institutions must at all hazards be preserved, and this Rebellion put down. No halfway measures will answer for this purpose.

We must make war with this sole and only purpose, and we must use all means, whether black or white[,] to accomplish this object. War means desolation and death, and it is neither humanity nor wisdom to carry it on upon any other theory. The more bitter it is made to the delinquents the sooner it will end."

To William Butler, who probably already had heard similar complaints from his son and former Pope staff officer Speed Butler, Pope was more pointed in his criticism of the president. The "feeble, cowardly, and shameful" conduct of Lincoln shocked him. His obeisance to McClellan had debased the office of the presidency, and Pope concluded caustically that Lincoln had "sold himself or given himself away to the Devil."

Pope also traduced Halleck—and with good reason. Halleck had been right to unite the western armies under his command in the spring of 1862, Pope said, but the instant he came to Washington he reversed himself. He divided the West into several independent departments so as better to control subordinates whose talent he envied and whose ambition he feared. Pope saw Halleck's actions as those of a timorous man intent on self-preservation. "Halleck feels that his position in Washington is insecure. He is trying to play trimmer and keep on the fence, which no man can do in times like these."

What was to be done? The Western Theater must again be united in one department and commanded by a western man, Pope told Butler. Until then there would be "neither harmony of council nor unity of action." Of course Pope coveted the job for himself, but he had the good sense not to trumpet his own candidacy, instead recommending Don Carlos Buell, Grant, and Samuel Curtis as qualified.

The more Pope brooded, the greater his indignation became. Unable to contain himself, Pope let fly on September 30 with a titanic and menacing unofficial letter to Halleck. That "which I am about to address you had perhaps better have been left unwritten," he began. "You will excuse a little plain speaking, since it will no doubt be for our mutual benefit."

Having helped Halleck become general-in-chief, Pope expected that "every sense of justice and fair dealing, as well as a sense of deep personal obligation, should have impelled you to sustain me against the machinations of McClellan and his parasites." Despite their treachery, McClellan and Porter retained important commands, while he, who had "endeavored to carry out [Halleck's] program in Virginia" with "constancy, energy, and zeal," had been "banished to a remote and unimportant command." To keep McClellan at the head of the Army of the Potomac was bad both for the country and for Halleck. Sneered Pope, "By yielding to and advancing McClellan you have only put into the hands of an enemy a club to beat your own brains out with."

Pope demanded redress. He would push to have the investigation against

Porter resumed, if not in a military court then in Congress. To rectify the "degradation" of his exile, Pope insisted Halleck place him in command of a united western department. With that Pope closed, assuring Halleck he would "not again address [him] a letter on such a subject."[12]

Rather than cultivate Halleck's goodwill, Pope antagonized him almost daily through official channels. Integrity and duty compelled Pope to do everything within his power to support Colonel Sibley in the field and to bring the Sioux uprising to not merely a speedy but also a permanent end. It was clear from Halleck's first letter on the subject (dated September 19) that the general-in-chief neither understood nor cared much about the Northwest. He demanded Pope release newly recruited Iowa regiments that had been ordered to Missouri; "it is not believed, that you will require a very large infantry force against the Indians, as their numbers cannot be very great."

Pope was incredulous. He held two recent telegrams from Sibley predicting failure should he not receive cavalry or such basics as bread, pork, forage, blankets, and wagons. Counseled Sibley, "this Indian war is a formidable one, and will tax the resources of the states within your military district if it is to be brought to a speedy close."

To the great annoyance of both Halleck and Stanton, Pope championed Sibley's cause before Washington. When Halleck ignored him, Pope took his case to the secretary of war, from whom Minnesota senator Henry Rice of the Committee on Military Affairs had also demanded action. Both Rice and Pope agreed hostile Sioux must be extirpated, in Dakota and Nebraska if necessary, and not merely defeated in a single campaign. Halfway measures would only encourage future uprisings. The situation was perilous; Stanton must realize this. "The mass of the settlers west of the Missouri are abandoning everything and precipitating themselves on the river towns." Halleck did "not seem to be aware of the extent of the Indian outbreaks." Twenty-six hundred Sioux stood ready to give battle to Sibley's poorly equipped force of 1,600; farther west, the Indians had nearly depopulated the Dakota Territory with their murderous raids.

In florid prose, Pope wrote of "the wide, universal, and uncontrollable panic everywhere in this country. Over 500 people have been murdered in Minnesota alone and 300 women and children now in captivity." The most unspeakable outrages have been perpetrated, he told Washington, "children nailed alive to trees and houses, women violated and then disemboweled—everything that horrible ingenuity could devise." Only a large force and much time could prevent everyone from leaving the state. "I am acting as vigorously as I can, but without means. There is positively nothing here." He must have experienced quartermaster and commissary officers, veteran troops, and 500 wagons.[13]

Pope had conveyed the danger as most Minnesotans saw it. Nevertheless,

Stanton dismissed his requests as abruptly as had Halleck. The problem was that Pope competed for the War Department's attention and for scarce resources at precisely the moment when the Northern war effort was at its nadir. McClellan had blunted Lee's invasion of Maryland along Antietam Creek, but the initiative remained with the Virginian. The same Confederate army that caused Pope to fear for Clara in southern Ohio was then threatening Louisville and Lexington, Kentucky. Further west, two Confederate armies under Sterling Price and Earl Van Dorn appeared poised to reverse Union gains in northern Mississippi and western Tennessee. With so much at stake elsewhere, neither Stanton nor Halleck could be bothered by a few hundred Indians in the Northwest.

On September 25, Stanton told Halleck to clarify for Pope the limit of Washington's indulgence. "I am informed that it will be impossible to give you all the supplies you ask for," wrote Halleck. Pope must move "very light and keep down the transportation," contracting wagons from displaced settlers (there were few to be had; searching three days, Pope turned up only eleven wagons) and employing mountain howitzers instead of heavy field pieces (Pope had neither). Concluded Halleck, "it is hoped that the campaign will be a short one, and that temporary expedients will be resorted to for moving your supplies. The most rigid economy must be enforced."[14]

The campaign did prove brief. On September 23, Sibley's command stumbled upon a thousand warriors near Wood Lake. In a two-hour fight, Sibley broke the back of Sioux resistance. Friendly Sioux secured most of the white hostages, and Little Crow and his most ardent followers fled to Devil's Lake, in northeastern Dakota Territory. The remaining chiefs opened negotiations with Sibley, who demanded and on September 26 gained the release of the white captives.

Although pleased, Pope saw in Little Crow's discomfiture but a partial victory; every hostile Sioux must be captured, whatever the cost. One hundred well-armed cavalry were on the way, Pope assured Sibley, and more would be forwarded shortly. Under no circumstances should Sibley withdraw, nor make any treaty with the Sioux, "even should the campaign against them be delayed until the summer. It is idle and wicked," he admonished Sibley, "in view of the atrocious murders these Indians have committed, in the face of treaties and without provocation, to make treaties or talk about keeping faith with them."

After ten days in the Northwest, Pope had formulated a cogent, if cruel, program for dealing with hostile Indians that recognized their disdain for weakness, even as it ignored their grievances. His purpose, Pope told Sibley, was to "utterly exterminate" the warring Sioux, "even if it requires a campaign lasting the whole of next year." They were to be forced out onto the Plains and there hunted down like wild beasts.[15]

While he agreed with Pope, Sibley lacked the wherewithal to press the campaign to its logical conclusion. Food was scarce—"the camp would be in a starving state but for the potatoes found in the Indian fields," he told Pope—and forage nonexistent. Little Crow and 200 of his adherents already were at least 120 miles from Sibley's camp, heading west to join restless Yankton Sioux in the Dakotas. Under these circumstances, pursuit was pointless; the campaign had best be considered closed.

In poor health and suffering financially from the extended absence from his businesses, Sibley applied to Governor Ramsey and to Pope to be relieved of further duty. But an order from Halleck came appointing him a brigadier general for his service to date and, to Pope's great satisfaction, Sibley relented. Unable to accomplish more in the field, however, he returned with the freed whites and some 1,500 captive Sioux to Fort Ridgely, where he at once appointed a military tribunal to identify and punish those Indians guilty of atrocities.

Reluctantly, Pope consented to Sibley's actions and on October 4 told Halleck the campaign was over. Pope expected no further trouble from the Sioux that winter and would accordingly release his Wisconsin regiments for duty in the South. He insisted, however, that he be reinforced for the inevitable spring campaign with regiments paroled by their Confederate captors. And in his first, tentative display of compassion for and comprehension of Indian grievances, Pope asked that the permits of traders be rescinded and that no white men except Indian agents be permitted among the Sioux. He told Halleck, "There will not long be trouble as soon as the government renders it impossible for white men to make money out of the Indians."[16]

Henry Halleck had something to say to his problematic subordinate on quite a different matter. Regretting the "spirit and threatening tone" of Pope's letter on the Virginia campaign, the general-in-chief set forth a feeble-sounding—but generally honest—defense of his own behavior. Not only had he not sent Pope into exile, but he also had advised strongly against it. And the decision to restore McClellan had been the president's alone. Pleaded Halleck, "I have done everything for you that I could have done for a brother; but you have wished me to do for you impossibilities. You have asked me to do for you what my superiors and yours would not authorize me to do."

"I never charged you with unfriendly feeling nor acts toward me," Pope answered on October 20. Luring Halleck into a rhetorical trap, Pope then asked that he merely "acknowledge publicly, as has been done privately, by the whole administration, that I did my duty bravely and skillfully in Virginia, and I have nothing further to say about what you do with the criminals who betrayed the country." Reminding Halleck he had "endeavored in all fidelity to accomplish" his program in Virginia, Pope wondered why the general-in-chief had not done so. "Why do you refuse to do me this simple act of justice? Who is to be shielded by unjustly ruining, or allowing to be ruined, my reputation and my honor as a soldier?" In the next breath, Pope answered himself: "I am informed that you object to publishing such an order; that the cabinet and president are willing." As the season for a court of inquiry against McClellan, Porter, or Griffin would soon pass—snow generally closed the Mississippi River by November 25, making it unlikely Pope would be able leave St. Paul to testify after that date—the least the government could do was to acknowledge his good service.

Halleck's terse response merely confirmed Pope's suspicions of culpability. Halleck excused his public silence with a stumbling reference to his late-August letter to Stanton on McClellan's slow movements from the Peninsula. As the secretary might wish to make that letter the basis of a court of inquiry, it would be improper for Halleck to write publicly on the Virginia campaign. Characteristically, Halleck portrayed himself as the victim. "There is an evident intention to blame me for bringing any of McClellan's army from the Peninsula. That is to be made the real point of attack. You will soon hear the opening of the newspaper batteries on me. We must both be patient; it will all come right in the end." Meanwhile, silence was the best course.[17]

From the tenor of Halleck's second telegram Pope concluded the general-in-chief had failed to act on Pope's behalf not from malice but rather because he—and Stanton—were powerless to do otherwise. Abandoning any hope of being ordered south before the year's end, an eventuality he had expected for a brief time in late October, Pope told Congressman Horton the true villain was Lincoln. "Bound in chains" to the McClellanites, he "degraded himself and his office even to the point of deceiving his cabinet." The president's "disregard of all the principles of common honesty and fair dealing with everybody connected with the government is one of the saddest features of our condition."

Pope's sense of betrayal was the greater because he knew the president still entertained a high regard for his skill as a soldier. Governor Samuel J. Kirkwood of Iowa told Pope that both Lincoln and Halleck had privately assured him and other members of a visiting deputation of Republican governors that the Virginia campaign "was not only faultless but was conducted by [Pope] with consummate ability." Why in God's name, Pope thundered to his father-in-law, would they not say so publicly? It was because Halleck was feeble and Lincoln compromised.[18]

On November 20, Pope closed his correspondence with Halleck by reciting the wrongs done him and pledging to "wait the action of the government with all the patience that is in my nature."

As Pope was among the least patient of Northern generals, Halleck probably put little stock in his pledge—nor should he have. One of Brigadier General Benjamin S. Roberts's chief duties upon arriving at St. Paul was to prepare a pamphlet containing those official letters and orders pertaining to the Virginia campaign that the president would not permit be made public for fear, as Pope put it, of offending McClellan with the truth. Should Lincoln continue to deny him the chance to vindicate himself publicly, Pope would have a copy of the pamphlet placed on the desk of every member of Congress.[19]

Roberts apparently had a second clandestine duty at headquarters, one far more important to Pope than his official functions, which were largely nil. Although evidence is circumstantial, it would seem Pope had charged Roberts with drafting an elaborate set of charges and specifications of misconduct by Fitz John Porter during the Second Bull Run campaign, then sent him to Washington to pressure Halleck into appointing a tribunal to review them.

Carrying a carpetbag full of his pamphlets and a bulky indictment of Porter, Roberts set out for Washington on November 13 as, to use Pope's words, "a witness in the case of Fitz John Porter." Four days later, the Adjutant General's Office announced that a military commission was to assemble at the capital on November 20 to "examine and report on charges preferred against Major General Fitz John Porter, U.S. Volunteers, by Major General John Pope, U.S. Volunteers." The military commission proved a bust, however, meeting only four times and taking no action of note.

Whether Pope was aware of the commission's brief tenure is uncertain, but he was in any case spared the need to make good his threat to expose Lincoln's duplicity. On November 25, the deadline Pope had set for the convening of a meaningful court of inquiry, General Halleck did him one better, replacing the military commission with a general court-martial for the trial of Fitz John Porter and calling Pope to Washington to testify.[20]

Halleck's summons found Pope quite able to absent himself from the Department of the Northwest, as there remained little to do in St. Paul before winter. With the assignment in October of Brigadier Generals John Cook and Washington L. Elliott—the former a boyhood acquaintance and the latter a loyal subordinate in Missouri and at Second Manassas—the department had begun to assume a more businesslike form. Staff and organization emerged, and the arrival of Colonel Robert E. Clary, a career soldier of thirty years' service, as chief quartermaster brought order to that troubled branch. In late November, a War Department General Order formally divided the fledgling department into administrative districts. Pope gave Sibley command of the all-important District of Minnesota, Cook the District of Iowa, and Elliott the District of Wisconsin. Nebraska was detached from Pope's department and placed in the Department of the Missouri.

Of more immediate concern than bureaucratic improvements, Henry Sibley's military commission had completed its deliberations on November 5, condemning 303 Indians and mixed-bloods to death for outrages committed against soldiers and civilians during the uprising. Although both Sibley and Pope were for hanging the guilty at once—primarily to prevent vengeful Minnesotans from slaughtering innocent Sioux—neither felt he had clear authority to carry out the sentence. As early as October 13, Pope had asked Halleck if he needed permission to execute Indians the commission had condemned. Having received no answer, Pope telegraphed the names of the condemned to President Lincoln on November 7, for his review. Under pressure from eastern humanitarians to grant clemency where possible, the president asked Pope to forward by mail "the full and complete record of the convictions." With that, all action locally was put on hold, and the condemned were imprisoned under heavy guard near Mankato.[21]

Pope availed himself of the president's request to explain more fully why he felt all the guilty should be executed without delay. "I desire to represent to you that the only distinction between the culprits is as to which of them murdered most people or violated most young girls," he wrote bluntly. "The people of this state, most of whom had relations or connections thus barbarously murdered and brutally outraged are exasperated to the last degree, and if the guilty are not all executed, I think it nearly impossible to prevent the indiscriminate massacre of all the Indians—old men, women, and children. The soldiers guarding them are entirely new and raw, and are in full sympathy with the people on this subject. I will do the best I can, but fear a terrible result." Pope also thought "the effect of letting them off from punishment will be exceedingly bad upon all other Indians along the frontier, as they will attribute it to fear and not to mercy."[22]

It was not merely military men like Pope and Sibley, or furious settlers and enraged newspapermen, who argued against clemency. Governor Ramsey urged Lincoln to uphold the sentences on grounds similar to those Pope articulated. So too did Stephen Riggs, a missionary of the Upper Agency whose many years among the Sioux and knowledge of their ways and language had qualified him to be the commission's chief interrogator. While he derived no pleasure in their punishment, Riggs took as a "terrible necessity the demand of public justice that the great majority of those condemned be executed as an atonement [and] to secure the protection and proper treatment of the women and children and innocent men who remain."[23]

Regardless of what course the president adopted, Pope knew a spring campaign would be needed. As the scope of operations might well depend on how many Sioux hung, he could not begin detailed planning until Lincoln made known his decision. But Pope did assure the people of Minnesota he would settle the Indian problem in the Northwest in 1863. Although Governor Ramsey questioned the need for a spring campaign, most Minnesotans applauded Pope's pronouncement, as they had his actions to date. Said the *St. Paul Daily Press,* "Since his arrival in St. Paul his time has been assiduously devoted to his duties, with results highly satisfactory to the people of the state. We are glad to be assured that his disposition of troops and other arrangements for vigorous hostilities against the Sioux are so complete that most thorough work will be expected next spring. Upon the Indian policy demanded by the interests of Minnesota, General Pope's views have been those of a statesman [and] will associate his name permanently and honorably with the future welfare of the state."[24]

Enjoying a warm send-off, John and Clara Pope left St. Paul by boat on November 25. Their immediate destination was not Washington but rather Madison, Wisconsin. The court-martial of Porter had yet to be called. Independent of any consideration of Pope's testifying in Washington, Halleck had agreed with Pope that departmental headquarters should be at a place accessible year round. Consequently, he directed Pope to remove himself and his staff to Madison, which had good rail links to Milwaukee, Chicago, and points east. Only after he reached Madison did Pope learn of Porter's impending trial and of a separate court of inquiry called to review Irvin McDowell's actions in the Virginia campaign. Lodging Clara in a rented home, Pope hastened by train to Washington with Thomas C. H. Smith, to testify against Porter and on behalf of his friend McDowell.[25]

— ♦ —

Pope arrived in Washington on the blustery winter evening of Monday, December 1, 1862, and checked in at Willard's Hotel. The Porter court had met twice the week before, but it had adjourned on both occasions without conducting any business, to await the arrival of a tardy judge.

On December 3, the court convened in earnest. At about 9:00 A.M. the doors of the court were thrown open, and the judge advocate read the two charges against Porter and specifications thereupon, based upon the Articles of War of 1789 and 1806.

The first charge accused Porter of violating the Ninth Article of War, which held, in part, that "any officer or soldier who shall disobey any lawful command of his superior officer, shall suffer death, or such other punishment as shall, according to the nature of his offense, be inflicted upon him by the sentence of a court-martial."

Five specifications were read against Porter under the Ninth Article: First, that he disobeyed Pope's order of 6:30 P.M. on August 27, to march at 1:00 A.M., August 28, to Bristoe Station; second, that he disregarded the Joint Order of August 29; third, that he ignored Pope's 4:30 P.M. attack order of the same day; fourth, that he disobeyed the letter of Pope's 8:50 P.M. order of August 29 by permitting Griffin's brigade to wander off to Centreville; and fifth, that he further disobeyed that order by allowing Piatt's brigade to stray as well.

The second charge held Porter to have violated the Fifty-second Article of War, which said, in part, "Any officer or soldier, who shall misbehave himself before the enemy, run away, or shamefully abandon any fort, post, or guard, which he or they may be commanded to defend, or speak words inducing others to do the same, shall suffer death, or such other punishment as shall be ordered by the sentence of a general court-martial."

In this regard, Porter was charged on three specifications (a fourth, that he had delivered a feeble attack on August 30, was read into the record and dropped). The first specification alleged Porter to have flouted Pope's 4:30 P.M. order of August 29 by retreating "from advancing forces of the enemy without any attempt to engage them, or to aid the troops who were already fighting greatly superior numbers, and were relying on the flank attack he was thus ordered to make to secure a decisive victory, and to capture the enemy's army, a result which must have followed from said flank attack."

The second specification deemed Porter guilty of criminal inertia, in that on August 29, "within sound of the guns and in the presence of the enemy, and knowing that a severe action of great consequence was being fought, and that the aid of his corps was greatly needed, [Porter] did fail all day to bring it on the field, and did shamefully fall back and retreat from the advance of the enemy, without any attempt to give them battle, and without knowing the forces from which he shamefully retreated."

The third specification derived from the second, in that Porter, "being in the belief that the troops of the said General Pope were sustaining defeat and retiring from the field, did shamefully fail to go to the aid of the said troops and general, and did shamefully retreat away and fall back with his army to the Manassas Junction."

To each charge and specification, Porter entered a plea of not guilty, and the court adjourned until 11:00 the following morning, when John Pope was to be sworn in and examined as the prosecution's principal witness.[26]

Pope strode into the large, Spartan courtroom on the morning of December 4 in full-dress uniform and sporting a formal sword, clearly pleased with the prospects for convicting the man whom, after McClellan, he held most responsible for his Northwest exile. A newspaper reporter caught Pope's public persona of smug self-confidence and condescension. In Minnesota Pope had regained much of the weight he had shed during the Virginia campaign, so that he struck the reporter as a "singularly round and heavy little man. His face is round—round as an apple—and surrounded by a heavy growth of beard and hair; his head is round—his body is round." Everything in his demeanor suggested self-satisfaction. "His voice is a tolerable tenor, with a streak of harshness in it, over which his words, uttered pleasantly enough, have to be rasped as they go," continued the reporter. "His smile commences pleasantly, but subsides into a sneer, or, rather, perhaps, into quick indifference. His whole appearance would indicate that he is on good terms with self, morally and physically, and that if he should do anything wrong, he would not be unlikely to suspect someone else was chiefly to blame. He talks rapidly, and is fond of it, as an exercise or diversion. He uses language with good discrimination."[27]

Pope had good cause for optimism. Whether Secretary Stanton or Halleck selected the members of the court is uncertain, but Pope could take heart as he studied them.[28] Seated at the head of the large, long wooden table at the front of the courtroom was the court president, Major General David Hunter, a friend of Pope and a favorite of Radical Republicans.

To Hunter's right sat Major General Ethan Allen Hitchcock, an aging Regular who had incurred the displeasure of Stanton; one further misstep, and he might very well find himself on the retirement list. On Hitchcock's right sat Brigadier General Benjamin M. Prentiss, who the year before had bested Pope in the election for command of the first brigade of Illinois volunteers. A hero of Shiloh and a man of real integrity, Prentiss could be expected to render an impartial judgment. Not so the officer to his right, Brigadier General Silas Casey, who nurtured a deep animus toward Porter. Several months earlier, Porter had rejected Casey for service in his corps, thinking him too old for field duty. On Casey's right sat Brigadier General Napoleon Bonaparte Buford, one of the oldest, least competent, and most malleable generals in the service.

Those to Hunter's left were no better disposed to Porter. Brigadier Generals Rufus King and James Ricketts were both under a cloud for errors committed during the Second Bull Run campaign—unfriendly wags suggested King had been drunk throughout the battle itself. Their performance was the subject of intense scrutiny by the McDowell court of inquiry, then holding session in the same building. Both were anxious to deflect blame for the defeat away from themselves, and both needed to please the War Department. The youngest officer on the board, thirty-one-year-old Brigadier General James Garfield, sat to the left of Ricketts. He was an Ohio Republican and a protégé of Salmon P. Chase, to whom he owed his rapid rise through the ranks. No less determined to see a conviction than Stanton, Chase purportedly told Garfield, "Great things are expected from you on the court." The last of the nine judges, Brigadier General John P. Slough, was a new volunteer officer whose appointment the secretary of war had not yet forwarded to the Senate.[29]

To ensure the judges were properly informed of the circumstances of Porter's treachery, General Roberts surreptitiously gave each a copy of his pamphlet. He also gave prosecution witnesses copies to guide their testimony.

Although ethically dubious, Roberts's actions were technically permissible, as the charges against Porter had been brought under his signature, in his former capacity as inspector general of the Army of Virginia. That procedure quite possibly was a device cooked up by Stanton and Pope, to give to the latter's testimony a greater air of credibility. Also, by having Roberts front for him, Pope avoided the legal requirement that the president himself appoint judges in a court-martial called on charges brought by an army commander. Lincoln undoubtedly would have exercised greater discretion in choosing judges than had Halleck, who was merely Stanton's inquisitory instrument.[30]

Pleased with the composition of the court and the surreptitious activities of Chase and Roberts, Pope also felt at ease with the judge advocate in the case, Joseph Holt. Two years earlier, as secretary of war in the Buchanan administration, Holt had saved Pope from a court-martial; now he was back to prosecute the government case against General Pope's malefactor.

Military law of the day trifurcated the obligations of the judge advocate. First, he acted as the clerical officer of the court. Second, he advised the judges on point of law. Third, he was the public prosecutor. In that capacity he was to be studiously impartial, so as not to compromise his first two functions. In the event the defendant lacked counsel, the judge advocate was accorded a fourth duty, that of public defender.

A staunch War Democrat and friend of Stanton, whom he served as judge advocate general of the army, Holt could hardly be expected to act without bias. Nor did he probably feel obliged to, as Porter had as his counsel Reverdy Johnson, one of the most eminent attorneys in the nation.[31]

Pope testified from a rocking chair, provided to ease what was sure to be a long examination. Holt questioned Pope about each specification under the first charge in the order in which it had been preferred. With respect to Porter's alleged failure to obey the 6:30 P.M. march order of August 27, which had endangered Hooker's isolated command at Bristoe Station, Pope declared the night to have been clear and the road to the station only partly obstructed. "But even had the roads been entirely blocked up, the railroad track was clear, and along that track had passed the larger portion of Hooker's infantry. There was no obstruction in the advance of infantry," averred Pope. Holt then asked Pope, "Whatever obstacles, in point of fact, may have existed to the execution of this order, I ask you, as a military man, was it, or not, the duty of General Porter, receiving this command from you as his superior officer, to have made efforts, and earnest efforts, to obey?" "Undoubtedly," said Pope, "it was his duty."

Perhaps because Pope had trouble answering them, Holt asked few questions about the Joint Order of August 29. When asked if Porter had obeyed the enigmatic order, Pope stumbled. "I do not know whether he obeyed it," he conceded. "He did not obey it fully; how far he obeyed it, I am not able to say; he certainly did not obey the order fully." Holt helped Pope back on track: "If [Porter] had obeyed it, would it not have brought him up with the enemy before half-past four in the evening?" "Yes, sir."

Holt turned next to the most damning specification: Porter's alleged disobedience of the 4:30 P.M. attack order. "Will you state to the court, and describe the condition of the battle-field at that hour, and the importance of his obedience of that order to the success of your troops?"

Pope had been "rocking assiduously" in his chair while Holt articulated the question; pausing, he leaned forward to reply: "Late in the afternoon of the 29th, about the time that I hoped that General Porter would be in his position, and he assaulting the enemy on the flank, and when General McDowell had himself arrived with his corps on the field of battle—I directed an attack to be made on the left of the enemy's line, which was handsomely done by Heintzelman's corps and Reno's corps. The enemy was driven back in all directions. Had General Porter fallen upon the flank of the enemy, as it was hoped, at any time up to 8 o'clock that night, it is my firm conviction that we should have destroyed the army of Jackson."

Holt concluded his examination by asking Pope about the 8:50 P.M. order of August 29. Porter had violated it, Pope said, by coming onto the field with only part of his command; the absence of Griffin's brigade, he added, had had "a very great effect" on the fortunes of battle on the thirtieth.[32]

From his seat to the right and rear of Holt, Reverdy Johnson rose to begin the cross-examination. Then a senator-elect from Maryland, Johnson had won for Cyrus McCormick a decision upholding his patent of the reaper, had defended the runaway slave Dred Scott, and had been attorney general in Zachary Taylor's administration; his interrogatories reflected an astuteness born of long experience. Trying to establish Pope's attitude toward Porter during the campaign, Johnson asked him if he had expressed displeasure to Porter over his tardy arrival at Bristoe Station on August 28. Pope said he had not.

Johnson turned next to Pope's conversation with Porter at Fairfax Court House on September 2. Had Pope voiced dissatisfaction with Porter's performance then? He had, in a brief conversation of no more than three minutes duration, mentioned to Porter "the disobedience of orders at Bristoe Station, and his failure on the field of battle on the twenty-ninth. I also mentioned to him the absence of Griffin's command, and its remaining the whole day at Centreville as being among the reasons I had for being dissatisfied."

Questioned next about McClellan's September 1 telegram to Porter, in which Little Mac begged his generals to extend their fullest cooperation to Pope, Pope recalled the message had perplexed Porter. "He asked me why I supposed such a dispatch had been sent to him, seeming to apprehend that I had reported his conduct to Washington." Pope had assured him he "had not reported him to Washington; and that, as matters stood, I thought I should not take any action in reference to his case."

Reverdy Johnson pounced on this answer. Could the general explain "if, as you have stated, you were of the opinion that the army under your command had been defeated, and in danger of still greater defeat, and the capital of the country in danger of capture by the enemy, and you thought that these calamities could have been obviated if General Porter had obeyed your orders, why was it that you doubted, on the second of September, whether you would or would not take any action against him."

Pope refused to answer the question as irrelevant, but even the most sympathetic onlookers realized the defense had, as the correspondent of the *Chicago Tribune* put it, "got Pope in a contradiction." Johnson looked to the judges, who cleared the room and retired to deliberate. When they returned, it was to announce their agreement with Pope. Johnson submitted a written protest, and the court adjourned for the day.[33]

Retiring to his room at Willard's, Pope realized he had been outwitted. He implored Holt to put General Roberts on the stand the next morning, both to distance himself temporarily from Johnson's fire and so that Roberts would afterward be free to help Holt in court. "Many little points important in a military view may escape your attention, while Roberts having been in action in all the scenes involved has the very details stored away in his mind," Pope told Holt. "He may be of much assistance to you by reminding you on occasion of small matters of this kind."[34]

When Holt waffled, Pope reconsidered. The next morning he startled the defense, and the judges, by asking the court's permission to answer Johnson's question. The court concurred, the question was read from the record, and Pope proceeded to respond, at length. "I would state that on the night of the twenty-ninth of August, when I found that General Porter did not make his appearance upon the field, and when I had received the dispatch which he wrote to Generals McDowell and King, stating that he was about to fall back to Manassas Junction, I determined to arrest him, and had commenced to dictate the order. I was persuaded not to do so by several officers."

After that revelation, Pope related a portion of his conversation with Porter at Fairfax Court House he had forgotten the day before. "I now remember I said to General Porter that I had received information from friends of mine in Washington that he had written letters to General Burnside, dated before he had joined me, which criticized my conduct, my military capacity, and the campaign which I was conducting, very seriously, and which exhibited an exceedingly unkind spirit." Pope said he asked Porter if he did not think it unfair to so prejudge Pope's plans, before he knew anything about them. "He seemed surprised and stated that it was a private letter to General Burnside, which he had never intended to go further. He expressed his regret that he had written the letter." That satisfied Pope that Porter never meant to "hold back from any proper co-operation with me; that it was merely an expression of his private opinion," and he so told Porter. Explaining his unusual magnanimity, Pope said, "I am a frank, open man, and slow to entertain suspicions of so grave a character against an officer. Although I had been warned by several officers a day or two previously that he would fail me, I did not believe so at Fairfax Court House."

Then Pope explained his change of opinion. "It was not until I came to Washington on the fourth or fifth of September, that I was informed by the President of the United States that he had seen several dispatches or letters from General Porter to General Burnside, dated a day or two previous to these battles, which had occasioned him very grave apprehensions that General Porter would fail to do his duty. This communication of the president to me opened my eyes to many matters which I had before been loathe to believe, and which I cannot bring myself now to believe." Despite this disclosure by the president, Pope had taken no action against Porter beyond setting forth the facts of the campaign in his report. "This is all I have yet done," Pope reminded the court. "I have not preferred charges against him."

Pope had hit Porter hard. Apart from the names of the officers who had told Pope that Porter would fail him—Benjamin S. Roberts and Thomas C. H. Smith—Reverdy Johnson's cross-examination elicited little of substance.[35]

The next morning, Saturday, December 6, Johnson explored one of the fundamental underpinnings of the government's case: the relative locations of Porter and Longstreet on the afternoon of August 29. Again Pope was the sole witness. Pope testified that, when he issued the 4:30 P.M. order, he assumed Porter's corps to be "somewhere on the road between Manassas Junction and Gainesville, and by that time far advanced toward Gainesville," well positioned to strike Jackson's right flank. Although he "feared the junction" of Jackson and Longstreet was imminent, Pope did not believe that "at that time any considerable portion of Longstreet's corps had reached the field."[36]

After a Sunday recess, the proceedings resumed on Monday, December 8. Defense questioning was desultory and unrevealing, except for one admission drawn from Pope. Calling the court's attention to John Buford's 9:30 A.M. warning of a heavy Confederate presence near Gainesville, Johnson asked Pope whether, had Longstreet been in Gainesville as late as 1:00 P.M., he could have closed on Jackson's right by 4:30 P.M. "According to my opinion as to the capacity of troops for marching," conceded Pope, "they would have had more than time."[37]

The examination of John Pope ended that afternoon, and Lieutenant Drake

De Kay, a strongly anti-McClellan aide-de-camp of Pope, took the stand. Roberts testified on December 9, Pope's nephew, Captain Douglass Pope, was examined the following day, and Smith was scheduled to appear December 11.

The case was going nicely for the prosecution. The same reporter who had written of Pope's smugness in court also confessed "his cross-examination has been a very severe ordeal, and he has stood fire well." Pope had also given his testimony in the McDowell court of inquiry.

Under the circumstances, he saw no reason to remain in Washington. Besides, Pope informed Judge Holt, "I have important business in my department which requires my immediate attention and the interests of the service are affected by my longer detention here." In the event he was needed later, Pope could return to Washington in two days' time.[38]

If Generals Sibley and Elliott were correct, Pope was needed back in the department to save the captive Sioux. On the night of December 4, they reported, some two hundred angry citizens had assaulted the prison guards at Camp Lincoln, intent on murdering the condemned prisoners. The story later proved false, but Sibley warned Elliott that "combinations, embracing thousands of men in all parts of the state, are said to be forming, and in a few days our troops, with the Indian prisoners, will be literally besieged." Elliott relayed the news to Halleck, who passed it on to Pope. At the same time he heard of the trouble in Minnesota, Pope learned President Lincoln had decided to execute only those Indians shown to have been "guilty of individual murders and atrocious abuse of their female captives." Thirty-nine Sioux were to hang on December 19; the remaining 264 were to be held until further notice.[39]

Apparently Judge Holt dissuaded Pope from leaving immediately, because he lingered in Washington until December 15. Smith testified on the eleventh, and McDowell was examined on December 13. McDowell's testimony was particularly beneficial to the government's case. Had Porter attacked in compliance with the 4:30 P.M. order, McDowell maintained, the battle would have turned decisively in their favor; even had Porter been repelled, the large enemy force needed to halt his corps would have "so much relieved the front as to have gained a success for the army generally."[40]

On Sunday, December 14, Pope, Roberts, Smith, and Holt met at Willard's Hotel to review the testimony for the prosecution and, as Pope put it, "see what yet remains to be proved of the charges." All were pleased with McDowell's testimony, and Holt consented to release Pope. In his absence, General Roberts would assist the prosecution.[41]

Although objecting to clemency for the condemned Indians, Pope set about to see that order was maintained in Mankato, where the warriors were imprisoned. Governor Ramsey begged the people, as "good citizens," not to upset the public order, and the press, though disgusted with Lincoln's magnanimity, also urged restraint.[42]

The president agreed to a one-week postponement of the execution to allow more time for the grim arrangements. A huge, diamond-shaped gallows of heavy oak timbers, twenty-four feet on each side and twenty-feet high, went up opposite the Indian prison. On Christmas day, the condemned were permitted visitors. The next morning, arms tied, faces painted, and draped in blankets, the thirty-eight (one having been reprieved) quietly awaited the hour of execution. At 10:00 A.M., they were led to the scaffold, around which stood 1,400 soldiers in solid ranks. Pope had authorized martial law. Saloons were closed, and the hotels of Mankato were packed. Despite the wet and cold of a Minnesota winter, people crowded the streets, rooftops, and windows for a good view of the proceedings. On the scaffold, as the Sioux sang their death song, the platform rope was cut, the floor fell away, and a cheer went up from the crowd.[43]

Fifteen hundred miles to the east and three weeks later, the trap door was sprung on Fitz John Porter. On January 21, 1863, the president approved the court-martial's findings and recommendation, which had been made eleven days earlier but kept secret until Holt and Lincoln could review them.

After deliberating three hours, the court had found the accused guilty of the first charge and of three of its five specifications, and guilty of the second charge and of its three specifications. "And the court [did] therefore sentence him, Major General Fitz John Porter, *'To be cashiered, and to be forever disqualified from holding any office of trust or profit under the Government of the United States.'*"[44]

12 *I Confine Myself to My Duty*

Porter's demise was a mixed blessing for Pope. It gratified him but brought no transfer from Minnesota. The Democratic press, which saw the verdict as "a deliberate conspiracy at Washington against all that still remains to us of conservatism and constitutional principle in the army and the state," unleashed another barrage at Pope. Criticism of Pope's conduct of the "short and unfortunate" Virginia campaign even appeared in the normally nonpartisan *Army and Navy Journal.*[1]

For much of this, Pope had only himself and his supporters to blame. Roberts's pamphlet demanded a reply, as did a tract gotten up and paid for by Thomas C. H. Smith immediately after the prosecution had rested its case. Smith's pamphlet contained the evidence given by him, Roberts, Pope, and other government witnesses under, as Reverdy Johnson later argued, "a title page which, as evidently intended, would lead the reader to suppose that it contained either all the evidence in the case, or that the evidence that it did contain, was in no particular rebutted by other proof."

Perhaps most infuriating to Johnson, Manton Marble of the *New York World,* and Porter's other influential, conservative allies was Holt's summation of the court-martial proceedings. Not only had it been composed "as if in defense of the decision," said Gideon Welles, but it also advanced ideas not brought out in court, a most unusual tact for a judge advocate to take. Holt emphasized Porter's "animus" toward Pope, although this had not been proven, and urged Lincoln to bear it in mind as he reviewed the judgment of the court. With respect to events of August 27, Holt cited only government witnesses, and in reviewing Porter's actions of the twenty-ninth, he assumed the veracity of government over defense witnesses.[2]

Throughout the storm of truculence battering what remained of Pope's reputation, President Lincoln kept silent. It was little wonder, then, that Pope continued to bear a grudge against him. After listening to the discordant explanations of Lincoln and Halleck in December as to who had put McClellan back in command, Pope had become more angry and his sense of betrayal had grown. When Valentine B. Horton wrote from the capital in early March that the president's feelings for Pope were "of a most friendly character," he received from his son-in-law a most uncharacteristic verbal lashing.

"Let us consider the matter a little," began Pope. "In what respect or in fact in what one instance has Mr. Lincoln ever exhibited such a feeling? Granting, however, that Mr. Lincoln's feeling for me is what you believe, how sad a price have I paid for his friendship. He has suffered me to be traduced and maligned for months, he has allowed the falsest and grossest slanders to be circulated to the discredit of my personal and professional character, knowing all the while how false it was, yet how much it was injuring me." No, Pope concluded, Lincoln was no friend of his, nor did Pope "desire that anyone should be under the impression that any friendly relations exist between us. I cannot afford such a friend."[3]

Yet Pope was not so demoralized as his letter to Horton had made it seem. While still insisting the president "by his deeds [is] the worst enemy I ever had in my life," Pope confessed in a subsequent letter to Horton that life in Milwaukee (the new seat of department headquarters) was "very pleasant, and if Clara were with me I should be perfectly satisfied. The people are very kind and hospitable and I have made many acquaintances among the ladies, whom I am sure Clara would like." The prospect of an early visit from Clara, who had passed part of the winter with relatives in New York, also cheered him, as did letters of support from prominent generals and politicians, among them his old friend William Starke Rosecrans, then commander of the Army of the Cumberland, and Senator Zachariah Chandler of Michigan, who pledged to Pope "that justice should be done to him and to his campaign in Virginia, even though I were called upon to vindicate him from my seat in the Senate."[4]

Especially gratifying were continued expressions of esteem from Salmon P. Chase, who wrote Pope in April, asking what he thought of the war effort and what command he might wish for himself.

Pope replied thoughtfully. "Further removed from the scene of action, and with less occupation to distract me from anxious thoughts upon the condition of our military operations, perhaps I feel, if not more strongly, at least more constantly than even yourself, apprehension and uneasiness for the result of our immediate military movements." He lamented "the great *unwisdom* of attempting so much at so many different places, of scattering our forces to remote points from which they could not, by any possibility, co-operate with each other; of landing at various points of the coast without force sufficient to advance into the interior, and with no power except to protect from their neighbors, a few Union men who would not try to protect themselves; in short, of so frittering away our strength that it was not felt by the enemy, and, of consequence, was greatly underrated by them and by ourselves." He pointed out, "We sought secondary and not primary objects. As well we seek to kill a strong man by sticking pins into him as to attempt to subdue this rebellion in the South by such operations."

The primary objective of Federal operations, said Pope, should be "to divide the rebellious states by interposing in some way between the Southeastern and the Southwestern states, so as to render concerted action impossible; to occupy the producing districts, the region whence subsistence for their armies is drawn so to place ourselves that *we* instead of *they,* shall be operating upon interior lines."

The "true theater of action in which the decisive operations must find their solution" was the West; more specifically, the Chattanooga, Atlanta, and Montgomery corridor into the Deep South. Grant should abandon his operations against Vicksburg and join with Rosecrans at Murfreesboro for a rapid march against Chattanooga, which would force the Confederate Army of Tennessee back upon Atlanta. After securing Chattanooga as a base of supply, the combined armies of Grant and Rosecrans should continue on to Atlanta. At the same time, forty thousand troops from the East should disembark at Pensacola and march on Montgomery.

The success of such an operation, added Pope, depended on there being a supreme commander in the West, "untrammeled by instructions. Quick, decided, and bold action alone can accomplish these great results."

Pope was circumspect as to his own ambitions. Although he had not lobbied for it, Pope had hoped to be appointed commander of the Department of Missouri in March, after Edwin V. Sumner died en route to the post. When the job went to Samuel R. Curtis, Pope resigned himself to a long stay in Milwaukee; or at least he became less vocal in demanding a change. He declined Chase's "friendly request" that he suggest an appropriate command for himself, saying, "It is my firm conviction, that the practice of indulging the ambition of officers, of whatever merit, by giving them separate commands, has led to that very dispersion of our forces, and that want of harmonious and concerted action, which have rendered our operations abortive. I am not willing to put my personal advancement in the way of our military success."[5]

Matters less profound than grand strategy, but pressing nonetheless, demanded more of Pope's attention in 1863 than he let on to Chase. From the Dakota Territory came reports of unrest among the Brulé and Uncpapa Sioux, and of efforts by the belligerent Minnesota Sioux to stir up the Yanktonai. The Yankton agent and a Dakota judge warned Lincoln that Little Crow had gathered a thousand warriors on the upper Missouri River in anticipation of an early spring campaign against the whites. Lincoln passed their letter on to Halleck, who in turn admonished Pope to watch for trouble on the Dakota frontier.[6]

Pope had been doing precisely that for several weeks. Incursions of white miners and settlers had aroused the seven Teton tribes west of the Missouri River, and reliable reports placed 7,000 Sioux warriors near Devil's Lake, at the mouth of the Minnesota River. Although he thought the numbers inflated, Pope had no doubt the Sioux intended to attack settlements along the Missouri and James Rivers in the spring. His plan, as he explained to Sibley and the War Department in mid-February, was to launch a preemptive strike against the Devil's Lake stronghold "as soon as the grass is sufficiently advanced to subsist animals," and to overawe the Tetons along the Missouri River.

He would send three columns into Dakota: one up the Minnesota River, a second along the Big Sioux River from the Iowa border, and a third up the Missouri River from Fort Randall. As Sibley had under his command 5,500 of the 8,900 troops in the department, Pope expected him to lead the first two columns. Speed was essential, Pope reminded Sibley; presaging tactics used against the Plains Indians a decade later, he suggested Sibley mount his infantry and keep his supply train to a minimum.

As he neither expected nor asked for reinforcements, Pope requested that the Department of the Interior assume responsibility for the nearly 2,000 Indian prisoners in Sibley's district, in order to free their military guards for field duty. To his astonishment, the department not only refused to take charge of them but also declined to feed them. Halleck apologized, saying, "We, therefore, have no alternative but to guard them and feed them until the president sees fit to otherwise dispose of them."

As the long Northwest winter drew to a close, other obstacles arose to Pope's plans. The Minnesota press leaked details of the impending campaign, which British American sympathizers passed on to the Sioux. Henry Sibley demanded more troops to protect the Minnesota frontier, which the spring offensive would leave unprotected. Pope rebuked him sharply, "So far from thinking you have too little force, my impression is, and has been, that there are more troops in Minnesota than are needed there. Surely now, when the country is in the most pressing need of troops at Murfreesboro and Vicksburg, you should consider carefully before you apply for additional troops."

Pope did agree with Sibley that the success of their campaign depended on denying the Sioux sanctuary in British America, where renegade white traders sold them arms and ammunition. On April 4, he told the War Department that, unless instructed otherwise, he would permit Sibley to pursue hostile Indians into Canada.

Military necessity guided Pope's thinking. If not followed across the border, Pope explained to Halleck, "the Indians, having a secure place of refuge, will be at liberty to resume hostilities whenever a favorable occasion presents itself, and all expeditions against them must fail of success. The result will involve the necessity of keeping the large force in this department constantly on the frontier until the Indians choose to close their hostilities."[7]

Concerned solely with Indian affairs, Pope ignored the risk of war with neutral Great Britain. But Lincoln did not. The president, not military commanders, made foreign policy; "under no circumstances," Halleck told Pope, "will our troops cross the boundary line into British territory without his authority."

Pope persisted. In May, he asked Halleck to raise the subject with the president again. The Hudson's Bay Company and most British Americans along the frontier wanted badly to keep the wild Indians in check, insisted Pope, but lacked the military means to do so. Authority must be granted to cross the border; if not, he reiterated, "it is nearly certain that the Indian campaign will be fruitless of results." President Lincoln agreed to submit Pope's request to the British ambassador, Lord Lyons, who in turn referred it to London, which effectively killed the subject for the time being.[8]

Other irritants arose as the spring passed. Pope had wanted Benjamin S. Roberts to replace the hopelessly inept General Cook in command of the expedition up the Missouri River, but Stanton—who regarded Roberts's loyalty to Pope as his sole qualification for command—insisted he instead take Brigadier General Alfred Sully. A good soldier who had seen prewar service in the Dakotas and Minnesota, Sully had also compiled an enviable record in the early campaigns in Virginia. Pope acceded to Stanton's wish and created for Sully the District of Dakota, four regiments strong, shunting Roberts off to the Department of Iowa.[9]

Pope had hoped to open the campaign before May 10, but low water on the Missouri River delayed Sully. Sibley delayed because he was reluctant to strip Minnesota of its frontier defenses. To prod him, Pope traveled to St. Paul.[10]

If Minnesotans shared Sibley's misgivings, it was not evident from the reception they accorded Pope. Scores of prominent Minnesotans wished to pay him tribute. On May 28, a deputation delivered to him a letter of thanks from the people of St. Paul "for the manner in which you have managed the affairs of the Northwest department" and invited him to a public dinner in his honor at the International Hotel the following evening. "As Western men, General," the letter concluded, "we feel more than ordinary interest in your welfare and hope you will accept our invitation." Pope replied with words of high praise for Minnesota but was compelled to turn down the dinner invitation. For no sooner had he reached St. Paul than a new crisis interrupted his preparations for the Indian campaign.[11]

Faced with declining manpower and a cooling of patriotic ardor, on March 3, 1863, Congress had adopted conscription. The presence in Iowa and Wisconsin of a small but highly vocal antiwar element, known as Copperheads, prompted Pope to caution Halleck that a well-considered system of meeting opposition to the conscription law throughout the Northwest should be worked out soon. His warning went unheeded; on May 27, two days after enrollment for the draft lottery began, trouble flared up in Iowa and Wisconsin. "Difficulties on account of enrollment which by prudence I hope may be avoided" forced Pope to curtail his stay in St. Paul.

Returning to Milwaukee, Pope found the situation tense but manageable. Several Wisconsin counties resisted enrollment. An irate Copperhead from Dodge County shot an enrolling officer, and others blew up the county courthouse. In Iowa, a Davis County Copperhead convention announced that its members would "resist to the death attempts to draft any of our citizens and will permit no arbitrary arrests."

Copperhead agitation against unjust detention was not unprovoked. Heavy-handed provost marshals were nearly as prevalent in the loyal states of the Northwest as Pope had found them in Missouri, and a habit of giving way to them threatened to weaken civil institutions. A quick resort to military force, at the expense of legitimate civil authority, was the watchword of far too many Federal department commanders during the Civil War. But Pope stood as strongly now for the sanctity of civil preeminence as he had in Missouri, when he opposed Frémont's imposition of martial law. Being "very unwilling that the military should be brought into collision with either the civil authorities or the people," Pope refused appeals from the mayors of Madison and Milwaukee for troops to enforce draft enrollment. His belief that "with ordinary prudence the enrollment can be made throughout this department without any sort of resistance or difficulty" proved correct, as the police of the two towns proved fully able to squelch what little trouble arose.[12]

As department commander, Pope could check renegade provost marshals more effectively than he had been able while under Frémont's thumb in Missouri. Far too many district provost marshals, he told the War Department, were "rash, imprudent men, whose zeal outruns all discretion, and who, acted upon by extreme men, who rather desire to stir up a riot, in order to rid themselves of offensive opponents, may probably get the authorities into difficulty."

During June, Pope lectured both the provost marshal general in Washington, Colonel James B. Fry, and the governor of Wisconsin on the larger evils of army intervention in civil affairs: "The habit of resorting to military force in every trifling case of resistance or opposition to the laws is becoming sufficiently common to be alarming. Such a practice entirely supplants the civil authorities, sets aside time-honored means for the enforcement of the laws of this country, destroys in the citizen that feeling of personal interest in their execution and prepares the public mind for the abdication of civil rule."[13]

One of the most egregious transgressions against civil law in the Northwest department was committed by Pope's crony Benjamin S. Roberts. Alarmed at Copperhead activity in Iowa, Roberts had seized arms and personal property belonging to suspected members of the organization. Pope reprimanded him for his rash act: "I don't desire you to have anything to do with such matters. I confine myself strictly to my military duty. I hope you will do the same. Surely the seizure of personal property on suspicion merely that it might hereafter be used in resisting the laws was out of place by a military commander in loyal States, and can only lead to ill-feeling which it has been my steady purpose to avoid." Roberts desisted at once.[14]

At a Fourth of July celebration in Milwaukee, Pope urged unity of purpose among the people of the Northwest. Taking the podium amid hearty cheers, Pope avowed, "I know nothing about and care nothing for political parties. My only desire is to see the rebellion crushed and I sympathize with all whose hearts are in this work. I can only appeal to you as patriots and men to stand by those in the field and to support the government no matter what your views of particular measures."[15]

Before departing St. Paul, Pope had secured Sibley's promise to march on June 12 for Devil's Lake. The Sioux were still there, in lesser numbers, apparently prepared to resist what had slipped from a spring to a summer campaign. Pope conceded two crucial points to the recalcitrant Minnesotan: he would permit Sibley to advance in one, rather than two columns; and he allowed Sibley to garrison 3,000 men in small posts among the outermost Minnesota settlements, even though Pope felt this number "more than sufficient, even if the whole of the Indians should disperse themselves for such desultory warfare" as raiding.[16]

On June 16, Sibley moved out from Camp Pope, his staging area just upriver from New Ulm. With him were six Minnesota regiments totaling 3,300 men—most of whom were on foot, despite Pope's admonition that Sibley mount his infantry—and a 300-wagon supply train. Progress was slow, conditions appalling.

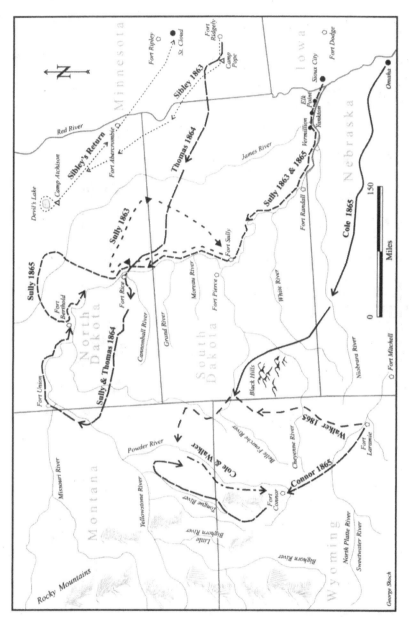

The Sioux Campaigns of 1863 and 1864, and the Powder River Campaign of 1865

Dusty prairie, heat, locust swarms, and alkaline water "having the appearance of clean soapsuds" conspired against the Minnesotans. "The noon hour usually found us at the end of our allotted score of miles, hungry and always thirsty. Palatable drinking-water seemed to have been forgotten in the make-up of Dakota," complained one volunteer. In five weeks, Sibley's column covered barely 200 miles.[17]

Despite their differences, Pope defended Sibley against those who questioned the Minnesotan's conduct. Particularly troublesome were Henry Rice, Democratic senator from Minnesota, and his maverick Republican colleague, Morton Wilkinson. Rice coveted Sibley's job, and Wilkinson was a mere conduit for complaints of his rural constituents, who saw an Indian behind every tree stump. Both wanted Sibley's command reduced, and they convinced Halleck to ask Pope to reduce his column by two-thirds. But Pope refused to bend to political pressure, telling Halleck, "I have no information which leads me in any way to the belief that General Sibley will encounter any less force of Indians than was supposed from the beginning. Sibley has passed his whole life in Minnesota, and knows Indian character well. He conducted the successful campaign of last autumn in the midst of the same carping. Surely it may be fairly presumed that General Sibley understands his business as well at least as anybody else does."[18]

Sibley proved worthy of Pope's continued confidence. Leaving his wagon train under guard at a temporary depot forty miles south of Devil's Lake, on July 20 he started with 2,300 men in pursuit of 600 Sioux lodges, which had left the lake and were making for the Missouri River, presumably to scalp settlers and river travelers. Four days later, he surprised a hunting party of 1,500 Sisseton, Wahpeton, Yanktonai, Cutheads, Blackfoot, and Uncpapa Sioux near a spot called Big Mound. In the ensuing melee, he inflicted nearly 100 casualties at a cost of one man killed. Pursuing the Indians toward the Missouri, Sibley destroyed huge quantities of dried meat, tallow, buffalo hides, and "other indispensable articles." Against the combined strength of the Plains Sioux, nearly 2,500 warriors by his own estimate, he fought and won two more battles—at Dead Buffalo Lake on July 26, and at Stony Lake two days later—before the supply shortage compelled Sibley to call off the chase. On August 1, he began the return march to Minnesota.[19]

And what of Sully? According to Pope's plan, he was to have been far up the Missouri River by late July, in position to intercept the Sioux as they fled Sibley's advance. Instead, he languished at Fort Pierre, waiting in vain for the water to rise enough to float his supply boats. As the summer passed with no movement, Pope's patience grew thin. "I never dreamed you would consider yourself tied to the boats," he prodded Sully on August 5. "It seems to me impossible to understand how you have stayed about the river, delaying from day to day, when time of all things was important, and when you had wagons enough to carry at least two months' subsistence for your command. Your force consists entirely of cavalry, and there can be no reason why you should not be able to execute the object of your expedition."

When he learned the Sioux had escaped across the Missouri, Pope criticized Sully harshly. Sibley and his infantrymen had covered 600 miles on foot and fought three engagements; Sully had moved by boat only 160 miles—from Fort Randall to Fort Pierre—with his cavalry and had not fired a shot in anger. "It is painful for me to find fault but I feel bound to tell you frankly that your movements have greatly disappointed me, and I can find no satisfactory explanation of them."

Nor did Sully offer one, although many of the problems he faced were inherited from General Cook. Instead, stung into action by Pope's censure, he marched from Fort Pierre on August 13. Three days later, he broke free of the Missouri and ascended the Little Cheyenne River to search for Sioux. On September 3, a small detachment of the Sixth Iowa Cavalry stumbled upon a war party of 1,500 warriors near White Stone Hill. While the Indians taunted the trapped Iowans and prepared for a ceremonial slaughter, Sully hurried ten miles with the remainder of his command and surprised the Sioux. In a short fight, Sully killed 150 Indians and took 156 prisoners, destroyed tons of buffalo meat and supplies, and burned the hostile camp. Satisfied the survivors had scattered, Sully returned to Fort Pierre three days afterward.[20]

Fitz John Porter would have been surprised to learn that Pope could forgive a subordinate's honest missteps. Gratified that Sully had accomplished something, in late September Pope wrote him a public, conciliatory message: "Whilst I regret that difficulties and obstacles of a serious character prevented your cooperation with General Sibley at the time hoped, I bear willing testimony to the distinguished conduct of yourself and your command and to the important service you have rendered to yourself and to the government—to yourself and your command, I tender my thanks and congratulations."[21]

Pope's charitable words of praise masked a greater disappointment. Sibley and Sully had won victories, but the Indians had escaped, and from their winter camps in the Dakotas they announced their intent to resist any further white encroachment, be it military or civilian. Come spring, they would block navigation of the Missouri, close the overland Northern Emigrant Route, and raid existing white settlements in the Dakotas. What the 1863 campaign had accomplished was to bring the war to the Sioux homeland and destroy food and supplies needed for the harsh Plains winter. Faced with starvation, many less defiant tribes sued for peace. Pope refused, however, to conclude the sort of hasty and temporizing treaty to which the Indians were accustomed, preferring to launch a campaign deep into the heart of Sioux country in 1864.

Minnesotans and Dakotans alike applauded Pope's resolve. Said the *St. Paul*

Weekly Press, "It will require another season of vigorous and active operations to reduce the fierce and haughty tribes of the Missouri Valley to submission. The snake is scotched but not killed. Subjugation is one of those things that cannot be half done." The *Yankton Dakotan* agreed "the Sioux Nation is still hostile, and until every nose on each of its many heads is tweaked, and they bear the humiliation without a murmur, we shall not admit that the Indian war is ended. They must be conquered, and when they are, and our benevolent old Uncle gets them under his capacious thumb, we trust our Indian affairs will be managed with more wisdom and sagacity than heretofore."[22]

Pope intended to do his part to see they were. In the months that followed, reform of Federal Indian policy would become for him a religion.

━ ✦ ━

The year 1863 ended pleasantly for Pope. For several months Clara had been with him in Milwaukee, and together they spent an enjoyable Christmas at the home of a staff officer, where General Pope delighted in a large, festively decorated model of Fort Sumter. He also was back in the good graces of Halleck and Stanton, both of whom recommended him to replace Major General John M. Schofield as commander of the Department of Missouri. Lincoln seemed inclined to agree, until Senators B. Gratz Brown and John B. Henderson objected on the grounds Pope's 1861 law-and-order decrees had prejudiced the people of Missouri against him. No matter, Pope wrote a friend on New Year's Day, 1864; all in all, "we are in a state of tolerable quiet."[23]

For Pope, the quiet and dreary Wisconsin winter was a season of planning and contemplation. In a rare instance of like thinking, Pope agreed with Commissioner of Indian Affairs William Dole, who in his annual report argued "the urgent necessity for military posts on the Upper Missouri" and for an early spring campaign against hostile Sioux. Pope studied the problem; consulted with General Sibley, who had come to admire the accuracy of Pope's "knowledge and experience" in Indian affairs; and on February 6 proposed to the War Department that four posts be built in the Dakota Territory.

It was a chance for Pope to put into practice what he had recommended to Colonel Abert while serving in New Mexico a decade earlier: the dispersal of troops in small posts throughout the Indian country, thus compelling Indians "who may be disposed to commit depredations upon the inhabitants to pass a military post both in going and returning." In the present instance, Pope intended his posts to keep hostile Indians northwest of the line of garrisons he would draw along the Missouri River.

The first post was to be built at Devil's Lake; the second would go up on the James River, west of Fort Abercrombie. Both were to have eight-company garrisons. The third post was to be located on the Missouri River, near the mouth of either the Heart or the Cannonball River, and garrisoned with four companies of infantry and a battalion of cavalry. The fourth post would be built somewhere on the Yellowstone River, as operations dictated. While troops marched from Minnesota to garrison these posts and to reinforce Sully, the Minnesota Mounted Rangers would scour the region east of the Missouri and drive any remaining fragments of Indian bands beyond the proposed line of posts; this process would be repeated in the summer. Concurrent with the construction of the third fort, General Sully was to march from Fort Pierre with a regiment of infantry and battalion of cavalry, through the Black Hills and along the upper Yellowstone River. There, in the heart of Uncpapa Sioux country, Sully was to construct the proposed Yellowstone River post at a site of his choosing.[24]

Pope doubted his efforts would avert bloodshed. He knew he could only make the Northern Emigrant Route less hazardous for travel, and he cautioned the War Department, "The wonderful accounts of gold found in [Idaho] Territory have greatly inflamed the minds of the people throughout the Northwest, and a very heavy emigration will begin in the spring. Of course there will be much suffering and perhaps not infrequent massacres of the emigrants by Indians. Such people are proverbially careless and imprudent, but, notwithstanding, the government will be held responsible for any repetition of the sufferings which marked the early overland travel to California."

To his proposals for the spring campaign, Pope appended a long letter to Secretary of War Stanton calling for radical reform of Federal Indian policy. Fourteen months of service in the Northwest convinced him reform was needed urgently. The prospect of capturing, in the forthcoming Badlands campaign, more Sioux who had been directly or indirectly involved in the 1862 Minnesota uprising, and of confronting in battle tribes with which treaties had never been concluded, required immediate decisions in Washington to prevent a repetition of past mistakes.

Pope had come to see the causes of the Minnesota uprising, as of other native unrest, to be white perfidy and fraud, rather than Indian blood lust or bad faith. He conducted a searching investigation of Federal Indian policy from its beginnings, with especial attention to its probable impact on his own operations. Foremost in Pope's calculations was the need for a policy that would ensure a just peace with tribes defeated in battle.[25]

As Pope saw matters, there was little in past practice worth repeating. "The system of Indian policy hitherto pursued seems to have been the result of temporary expedients," he observed, "and not of well-considered examination of the subject." Inheriting precedents from the colonial era, the new Federal government had tried to obtain title to Indian lands through treaties and had in a small way supported philanthropic efforts at educating, Christianizing, and civilizing treaty Indians. The government envisioned a gradual and orderly progression of the frontier, but restless whites repeatedly grabbed land with no regard for treaties. In response, a "removal" policy was introduced in the 1830s. Indians were forced west and a "permanent" Indian frontier was created on the edge of the Great Plains. Scarcely had the ink on these treaties dried than the California Gold Rush and Mormon migration shattered the frontier boundary. By the 1860s, the chimera of a permanent frontier had been irrefutably exposed.

Created in 1824 and transferred from the War Department to the Department of the Interior in 1849, the Bureau of Indian Affairs had proved not merely unable to repair the damage but, as was evident to any intelligent critic, had also created explosive new tensions with the Indian. Bureau representatives often misinformed Indian chiefs regarding the contents of treaties under negotiation, as when the Santee Sioux consented unwittingly in 1851 that their debts to Indian traders be subtracted from their treaty payments, which came in the form of regular annuities. To the Indians, annuities were a sign of government weakness; they were being paid to be peaceful. A few select depredations might increase the payments, reasoned the Indians, so that, as Pope observed, annuities "lead necessarily to the very hostilities they are intended to prevent."

No less incendiary than the annuities themselves were the ruffians they lured. Citing the example of the tribes of Minnesota, Pope explained,

> The money and goods annually furnished them under treaty, through the Indian agent, necessarily attracted all the gamblers, whiskey sellers, Indian traders, and other unprincipled characters who infest the frontier, whilst the purchase and transportation of large quantities of goods brought also into the Indian system a horde of contractors.
>
> The Indian was thus provided with the worst possible associations and surrounded by the most corrupt influences, and became a gambler, a drunkard, and a vagabond, plundered and wronged on all sides.
>
> The Indians on these reservations, surrounded by such influences and forced into association with so depraved a class of white men, were completely fortified against any efforts to educate or Christianize them. Even in their wild state they were not so entirely withdrawn from any hope of civilization. In his wild condition the Indian possesses at least many noble qualities.

Contact with white men had created four classes of Indians, said Pope, each requiring a distinct policy. The first class consisted of semicivilized tribes "surrounded by white settlements and living on small reservations," namely the annuity Sioux and Winnebago; the second was comprised of roving Indians who maintained relations with wild tribes, such as the Teton Sioux and Comanche, but were also connected with whites through annuities paid for land surrendered, and who kept their treaties; the third consisted of those who had violated their treaties; and the fourth was comprised of the wild tribes themselves.

Pope proposed that Indians of the first two classes be disarmed and removed to a point far behind the frontier settlements. Money annuities should be halted, tribal organization gradually broken up, schools built, and Christianity taught. Surrounded by American farmers rather than unscrupulous frontiersmen, the Indian might feel such "humanizing influences" that the second generation would become, if not good citizens, at least "harmless member[s] of any community in which [their] lot might be cast." Assimilation was the only alternative to extermination.

Wild tribes and treaty violators demanded different treatment. Broken treaties should be discarded and no new ones concluded until the hostiles had been thoroughly subdued. Trade laws would be enforced, rapacious whites kept away, and the Indians collected near military posts where missionaries might set to work preparing them for removal and assimilation. All this should occur under the exclusive jurisdiction of the War Department. "I ask that the military be left to deal with these Indians without the interposition of Indian agents. I ask it because I believe that any permanent peace with the Indians depends on it, and because I am convinced that the condition of the Indian in his wild state is far better than his status under present Indian policy." Concluded Pope, "Either a radical change in our Indian policy should be made, or, in justice to the government as well as to the Indian and to the cause of humanity, he should be left in his native state, only subject to the condition that he shall not molest the emigrants who pursue their journey through his vast domain."[26]

In normal times, such a sweeping indictment of Federal policy would have rocked official Washington, but in early 1864, with the nation fighting for its very survival, Pope's paper caused hardly a stir. Henry Halleck embraced both Pope's campaign plans and his proposals for reform, approving the former and forwarding the latter to Stanton with an admonition that "the change of policy is well worth the attention of those charged with the management of the Indians in the Northwest." But Stanton did not push the matter, and the Bureau of Indian Affairs ignored Pope's plan.[27]

Perhaps anticipating such a reception, Pope had written to Senator James R. Doolittle, a Republican from Wisconsin, privately on the matter. He urged Doolittle to call for his letter to Stanton, so that its merits might be openly discussed in Congress and in the press. "Much very useful information would be thus elicited and many crying evils exposed," Pope insisted. "The remodeling of our Indian system would inevitably result from any public exposé of facts connected with its present management and any such radical change could not fail to be of great benefit to the Indian, the bona fide white settler and emigrant, and to the cause of humanity."[28]

Support came to Pope from an unexpected source: Henry Halleck. Service on the frontier and the influence of his cousin, the reform-minded Bishop Henry Whipple of Minnesota, who had long championed missionary efforts among the tribes of the Northwest, had led Halleck to recognize the need for fundamental change in United States Indian policy. Disgusted with the manner in which corrupt Interior Department officials and others "interested in perpetuating the present system of frauds" had misrepresented Pope's proposal, Halleck obtained Stanton's permission to publish it in the influential *Army and Navy Gazette.* Bishop Whipple also approved of Pope's recommendations, and when he came to Washington in April, Halleck cleverly sent him to the Interior Department to call attention to the "Pope Paper."

Unable to ignore the issue any longer, Commissioner of Indian Affairs William Dole chose instead to distort what Pope had written. Dole claimed Pope intended to disarm and exile 300,000 Indians to the barren high Plains, where they either would starve or provoke a general war with the United States. Pope, of course, had proposed no such thing. The last thing he wished to do was increase the barrier to travel by moving more Indians to the Plains. Dole, however, succeeded in clouding the issue, and his Bureau of Indian Affairs refused to consider any reform that threatened its prerogatives.[29]

Secretary Stanton was not much help either. Learning Bishop Whipple planned to call on him, Stanton asked Halleck, "What does Bishop Whipple want? If he has come here to tell us of the corruption of our Indian system and dishonesty of Indian agents, tell him that we know it. But the government never er reforms an evil until the people demand it. Tell him that when he reaches the heart of the American people, the Indians will be saved."[30]

While Pope's program of reform languished in Washington, he strove from Milwaukee for a prompt start to the spring military campaign. Determined to avoid the delays of the year before, Pope pressed his commanders to get their columns into the field early. Neither low water on the Minnesota and Missouri Rivers nor a shortage of wagons would be acceptable excuses; Sibley and Sully must be prepared to move. Demands for troops by the new general-in-chief, Ulysses S. Grant, to support operations against the Confederacy disrupted Pope's timetable, but he accepted the diminutions to his already small command philosophically, telling Sully, "We must do the best we can."

Only when the War Department threatened to deprive him of the Sixth Minnesota Infantry did Pope complain. Minnesotans who insisted troops be sent south were those who profited most from the corrupt Indian system—agents, traders, whiskey sellers, contractors—and Democratic politicians like Henry Rice, who hoped to embarrass the administration by prolonging hostilities with the Indians. "The military operations in this department during the coming season promise to separate the Indians entirely from any communication with Minnesota, and to place them far beyond reach of the people of that state," said Pope. "Hence the persons I have mentioned are opposed to the operations which promise so complete a success, and seek to bring the military purposes to an unsuccessful issue. This can now be done only by inducing the War Department to order off a sufficient number of troops to prevent success. . . . You may rely confidently on my not retaining a man in this department more than is needed, nor a moment after he can be spared."[31]

Halleck found Pope's argument compelling. He convinced Stanton to suspend the transfer of the Sixth Minnesota, and relations between the generals had warmed sufficiently for Halleck to praise Pope for the alacrity with which he had answered every previous request for troops.[32]

Pope took every possible precaution to ensure that the 1864 campaign would be decisive. A heavy migration to the Idaho gold mines by way of the Missouri River and the upper Plains was expected to begin with the spring. As he had no troops to spare to guard emigrant trains, Pope warned travelers to postpone their journeys until Sully's expedition had cleared the region of hostile Uncpapa and Teton Sioux. If they must proceed, Pope cautioned them to travel in parties of at least three hundred well-armed men and to bulletproof their river boats.[33]

As far as possible, Pope also meant to deny the Indians the means to make war. He prevailed upon the Bureau of Indian Affairs to delay the disbursement of annuity payments, supplies, arms, and ammunition to the Sioux of the upper Missouri until after the campaign. Pope drafted detailed trade regulations intended to force whites to deal justly with the Indian. He cautioned Sully to permit no treaties to be made with any tribes he might defeat, and he advised Halleck of his intentions. "I shall have small hope of a successful result to operations against Indians this summer unless the military are left to deal with the Indians exclusively. I shall not permit any sort of interference or interposition from Indian agents until this campaign is over, unless I receive contrary orders from proper authority." Halleck authorized him to proceed as he deemed best.[34]

On June 6, to the tune of "The Girl I Left Behind Me," a force of 1,550 men under the command of Colonel Minor T. Thomas marched from Fort Ridgely to rendezvous with Sully's column at the mouth of the Cannonball River, the site settled upon for the third of Pope's planned forts. Three weeks later, Sully started up the east bank of the Missouri River.

The campaign opened ominously. On the second day out, Sully's topographical engineer was killed after straying from the main column. Alert cavalry captured the three Sioux perpetrators. So there would be no mistaking his resolve,

Sully had the captives beheaded. The bloody trophies were mounted on poles as a warning to others. News of the atrocity "flew as upon the wings of the wind to every Dakota camp from the Oglalas on the Platte to those in farthest Canada," averred a Sioux historian, precipitating a general retreat into the Badlands, "where the white men could not come."[35]

The columns of Sully and Thomas met at the mouth of the Cannonball River in early July. As construction commenced on Fort Rice, Sully set out westward up the Cannonball River Valley with his combined command of slightly more than 2,600 troops, expecting to find a camp of 1,500 Sioux lodges. But the Indians had moved on. Sully pursued northward, to the Heart River and beyond. On July 28 he came upon the Indian camp, nestled in a chain of high hills called Killdeer Mountain. Sully claimed to have given battle to at least 5,000 warriors of the Uncpapa, Sans Arcs, Blackfoot, Minneconjou, Yanktonai, and Santee Sioux; Indian sources place the figure at 1,600. Whatever the true count, the warriors were so confident of victory they left their village standing and assembled their squaws and children on the hills to watch the massacre. But Sully's artillery swept the Sioux from the field, and in their haste to escape, the Indians left behind valuable supplies and some 100 dead.

Low on rations, Sully felt obliged to cross the Badlands, a rough and dismal region he described as "hell with the fires put out," in order to meet transports with much-needed supplies on the Yellowstone River. Pushing on through blistering heat and clouds of locusts, and skirmishing with Indians every step of the way, Sully's column reached the river on August 12. There they found only two of an expected four supply boats: the third had struck a snag and sunk with all the forage for Sully's half-starved horses, and the fourth had become disabled downriver. Under the circumstances, Sully thought it best to abandon plans for a post on the Yellowstone and return instead to Fort Rice.[36]

In his report, Sully called the expedition a success "in every respect as far as it was in the power of any one or any body of troops to make it so." More could have been accomplished had the Missouri risen earlier and supply boats not been lost. Nevertheless, his command had "met the combined forces of the Sioux nation at points they chose to give us battle, and in these engagements completely routed them, destroying a large portion of their camps and baggage, and scattered them in all directions."[37]

Although the 1864 campaign had fallen short of his expectations, Pope was generally pleased with the results. For the second consecutive year the Sioux had lost most of their camp equipage and supplies; the prospect of starvation might drive many to surrender before winter. Fort Rice had been built on the Missouri, and garrisons were left at Fort Berthold, near Killdeer Mountain, and at Fort Union on the Yellowstone. The military frontier had been pushed nearly to the border of the Montana Territory, rendering Minnesota and the settlements of eastern Dakota as safe as military arms could make them. On October 20, Pope recommended Sully for brevet promotion to major general.[38]

The close of 1864 brought Pope other cause for cheer, both personal and professional. On November 14, Clara gave birth to a son in Milwaukee. She and John named the child Horton. Nine days later, Pope received a cryptic telegram summoning him to the War Department at once. Placing Sully in temporary command of the department, Pope departed the next day. He arrived in Washington on November 26, 1864, much as he had two-and-a-half years before—with no idea why he had been called.[39]

Perhaps Pope expected the worst. In October he had complained formally to Halleck of troublesome inspectors whom Grant had sent to Milwaukee to find troops, and who had impugned the veracity of Pope's official strength returns. "It is not believed that the War Department will take action implying so insulting a charge . . . without furnishing [me] . . . the statements and the names of [my] maligners," protested Pope. But Halleck had defended him to Grant, assuring the general-in-chief that Pope had done everything possible to cooperate with the war effort. "It is a very great mistake to suppose that General Pope has retained an unnecessarily large force in his department," wrote Halleck. "On the contrary I have found him the most ready of all the department commanders to give assistance to others when asked."[40]

No sooner did he reach Washington than Pope was ordered to report in person to General Grant at his field headquarters at City Point, Virginia. There, on November 30, he learned from Grant why he had been called east. Grant had for some time contemplated a wholesale discharge of department commanders. Unlike Pope, Major General William Starke Rosecrans had resisted every effort to take troops from his Department of Missouri, and Grant wanted him replaced. Grant also wanted to relieve the commander of the Department of Kansas, Major General Samuel R. Curtis, for gross inefficiency. A fall from his horse had left the commander of the Department of the South, Major General John Foster, unfit for duty, and Grant wanted him retired.[41]

Pope, however, stood high in Grant's estimation. He appreciated his good service in the Northwest and had read with interest his recommendations on Indian affairs. Memories of Pope's kindness three years earlier in Missouri, and of his aggressiveness before Corinth, may also have entered into Grant's thinking. In any event, he offered Pope command of the Department of the South, which consisted of occupied portions of Georgia, South Carolina, and eastern Florida.[42]

Here was a chance to return to the war, but Pope declined. Frontier service was more attractive to him than occupation duty, and he knew his Virginia farragoes had made him obnoxious to the South. Then too, there was Clara and the baby. Pope wished to remain as close to both as possible; taking Clara, with her chronic poor health, to the malarial Carolina coast was unthinkable.[43]

Not only did Grant accept Pope's arguments for refusing the command, but he also offered Pope a far more appealing alternative. He decided, perhaps on the spot, to merge the Departments of Missouri, Kansas, and the Northwest into a military division, with headquarters at St. Louis and Pope in command. Pope accepted, and Grant asked Halleck to lay the proposal before Secretary Stanton at once. "I wish you would urge that the change be immediately made," Grant told Halleck on November 30. "With Pope in command we secure at least two advantages we have not heretofore had, namely, subordination, and intelligence of administration." Grant followed up with an appeal to the president, in which he praised Pope's disinterested management of the Department of the Northwest.[44]

The wheels of War Department bureaucracy turned slowly, but on February 3, 1865, Pope assumed command of the Military Division of the Missouri, and he and Clara once again took up residence in St. Louis, near his aging mother, who had moved there after the death of his father. A month later, Pope was brevetted major general in the Regular Army for meritorious service in the capture of Island No. 10.

As commander of the Department of the Northwest, Pope had directed a mere 5,600 troops on the periphery of the war; now he had at his disposal 41,000 men, deployed throughout what was, after William T. Sherman's Military Division of the Mississippi, the largest geographic command in the United States service. Ulysses S. Grant had restored much of the luster to John Pope's tarnished reputation.[45]

13 *Posterity Will Bless Your Name*

Command of the Military Division of the Missouri presented Pope with a wider array of problems than that faced by any other regional commander in the Union army; its magnitude gave him more responsibility than any general in the United States, excepting Grant and Sherman.

Each problem seemed exigent. Encompassing nearly the entire Plains region, Pope's new division brought all the great western tribes—Sioux, Cheyenne, Kiowa, Arapaho, and Comanche—under his sway. Here was a chance to implement his Indian policy on a grand scale. But first, Pope had to deliver the Plains from the worst outbreak of Indian violence ever seen west of the Mississippi River. On November 29, 1864, while Pope conferred with Grant at City Point, a ruthless colonel named John M. Chivington, intent on getting up an Indian war, had massacred a peaceful Cheyenne village at Sand Creek in eastern Colorado.

Retribution was swift. In January, the Southern Cheyenne and their Sioux and Arapaho allies struck hard along the Arkansas and Platte River emigrant routes, burning wagon trains, wrecking ranches, cutting a hundred miles of telegraph lines, and slaughtering men, women, and children indiscriminately. Troops along the routes of travel retreated into their stockades, and the Indians gained control of the Overland Mail Route (also known as the Platte Route) from

Julesburg to Denver, isolating the capital and throwing the state's mining camps into turmoil. Old-timers would call 1865 "the bloody year on the Plains." Every tribe from Texas to the Yellowstone River was at war with the whites, and friendly Indians were leaving reservations by the hundreds to join the hostiles. General Halleck's first instructions to Pope were that he reopen the Overland Mail Route and restore order to the emigrant roads to New Mexico, Colorado, Utah, and Idaho.[1]

Much closer to Pope's St. Louis headquarters there was turmoil nearly as absolute as that which gripped the Plains. Three and a half years before, Pope had predicted Frémont's martial-law edict would plunge the state into a maelstrom of fratricide and military despotism. He had been right. Upon assuming command of the Department of the Missouri in December 1864, a horrified Major General Grenville M. Dodge observed that "the greater portion of the state was in a state of confusion approaching anarchy, continually fomented by marauders, guerrilla bands, and roving Confederates, who were murdering, robbing, plundering, and committing all the outrages known to crime or barbarous warfare." Missouri had a provisional government loyal to the Union, but in most counties the provost marshal reigned, fettered only by the decisions of overburdened military courts. Soldiers and civilians, men and women, crowded the military prisons, awaiting trial on vague charges. Restoring order and the primacy of civil authority was imperative.

But first, the borders of Missouri had to be secured from marauding guerrillas and invading Confederates. The ubiquitous Sterling Price had been severely punished at the Battle of Westport in October 1864, which ended his most recent raid into Missouri; the ensuing retreat into Arkansas claimed the greater part of his army. Although his command had disintegrated, Price was still viewed as a serious threat by Dodge and other nervous Federal commanders in Missouri, most of whose own troops were to be mustered out in the spring of 1865. "The Rebels are making extensive preparations to commence their work so soon as the leaves come," Dodge advised Secretary Stanton in January. "Price's men, many of them, are coming back for that purpose, and I am confident it will require from 12,000 to 15,000 troops to hold our border. At the present rate of expiration of service I shall by the 1st of May have only between 3,000 and 4,000 men."[2]

Besides the remnants of Price's army, brigade-sized irregular forces under M. Jeff Thompson and Jo Shelby hung about the Missouri border, as did a force of nearly 7,000 mixed-bloods and stragglers from Price's army under the Cherokee Stand Watie. Lying just beyond the southern limit of Pope's military division but capable of far greater mischief than the commands of Price, Thompson, Shelby, or Watie was the trans-Mississippi army of General Edmund Kirby Smith, which the Federals variously estimated at from 50,000 to 100,000 strong. Smith claimed as his domain virtually all of Texas, that portion of Louisiana west of the Mississippi, all of southern Arkansas beyond a few miles' radius of Federal military posts, and the Indian Territory. Navigation of the White and Arkansas Rivers was hazardous, and the Red River was closed to Federal ships. A member of Pope's staff averred, "From Southern Missouri to the Gulf our hold on the vast country between, enough in extent for a great empire, was nominal."[3]

To meet the challenges of his new command, Pope would work through two department commanders. Major General Samuel R. Curtis would be around but a short time. Having first defended Chivington for the Sand Creek affair, Curtis had proven incapable of arresting the bloodshed that followed. At his own request, he was relieved of command of the turbulent Department of Kansas and reassigned to the relatively quiet Department of the Northwest. Pope had as his second department commander the thirty-three-year-old Dodge, a talented Iowan whom he and Grant regarded highly. Upon Curtis's transfer, the Department of Kansas was merged into Dodge's Department of the Missouri.[4]

Pope arrived at his St. Louis headquarters on February 5, 1865, weakened by a lingering winter illness. A round of dispatches announcing new Indian depredations along the Overland Mail Route greeted him. Territorial governors hectored him to guarantee the safety of emigrant and freight trains. Pope made a quick study of the situation, calling to his headquarters anyone with personal knowledge of, and a direct interest in, the region. He found everyone united in the belief that Brigadier General Patrick Edward Connor—the impetuous commander of the District of Utah, who a month earlier had submitted to Washington a plan to punish the northern Plains tribes and clear the mail line—was the best man to restore order. Pope endorsed their view, and on February 8 he asked General Halleck to create for Connor a Department of the Plains, consisting of the territories of Colorado, Nebraska, and Utah and embracing the beleaguered Platte Route. As he explained to Halleck, "in all arrangements for defense against Indians it is, of course, very desirable to accommodate matters as far as reasonable to the wishes of the people most interested, both to give them confidence in the plans and purposes of the government and to preclude them from any captious complaints afterward." Halleck concurred, but Stanton felt a new department excessive; instead, he authorized for Connor a district. In March, the District of the Plains was added to Grenville Dodge's department.

Pope instructed Dodge and Connor to secure the Overland Mail Route and other lines of travel by April 1, as it was "essential to the subsistence of the people of Colorado and Idaho that the freight trains for those regions should go through with the earliest grass." Connor did not disappoint. Making good use of two regiments of former Rebel prisoners of war, known as "Galvanized Yankees," that Pope sent him, Connor soon had the telegraph line open from Fort Kearny to Denver, and detachments posted along six hundred miles of road.[5]

No sooner had Pope cleared away the distressing dispatches from the Plains than he received an urgent appeal from President Lincoln to curb the "outrageous and ridiculous" excesses of Missouri provost marshals, which Lincoln's private secretary, John Hay, after a visit to Missouri some months earlier, had brought to the president's attention. "Dispatch received," Pope hastened to reply the next morning, February 13. "Provost-marshal system in Missouri is oppressive and absurd. I am examining into and will correct the whole matter."

What he discovered both startled and dismayed Pope. Prior to assuming command, Pope had assumed the "anomalous and anti-American" intrusion of the military in the civil affairs of Missouri to be on the wane. With the defeat of Price there was no longer an organized Confederate presence in the state. The Radical Party of Missouri had made a clean sweep in the fall 1864 elections. Radical gubernatorial candidate Thomas C. Fletcher, who triumphed by a margin of forty thousand votes, had promised a policy of magnanimous reconstruction. The general assembly had ratified the Thirteenth Amendment, ending slavery in Missouri, and a Radical-dominated state convention had drafted a new constitution. Nevertheless, Pope found the military more entrenched in civil affairs than it had been when he left Missouri three years before.

After studying the matter for two weeks, Pope asked Governor Fletcher to come to St. Louis, before either of them acted. Conferring for nearly a week, Pope and Fletcher found themselves in near perfect accord on the need and methods for restoring civil rule to Missouri. Undoubtedly to help shape public opinion, the governor asked Pope to submit in writing his "views as to the best uses of the military forces of the United States in this department and their relation as to the present and prospective condition of this state."

Pope obliged with a long and passionate appeal to the people of Missouri to "resume their civil rights and privileges, administer civil government, and set to work to execute their own laws," so that he might end the military administration.

It was imperative, Pope told Fletcher in the same letter, that steps be taken at once to reassert civil authority, not merely for benefit of Missouri, but for the sake of "civil liberty and free institutions" nationwide. "The example of Missouri," said Pope, "is of the last importance in re-establishing the Union."

Pope's proposal to Governor Fletcher was sound. He understood some counties were better prepared to resume their civic responsibilities than were others, and he suggested a "gradual and careful" reduction in the military role as most desirable; nevertheless, the first steps must be taken immediately. Pope agreed with Fletcher that bushwhackers were the greatest threat to a smooth transition but thought their very presence could be used to good advantage. "A single example of the trial of one of these outlaws before your courts, and his execution by your civil authorities, would do more to put an end to bushwhacking in Missouri than a thousand military executions," predicted Pope. "Strip these rogues of respectability borrowed from the notion that they are armed enemies and Southern soldiers, and reduce them, by actual trial and punishment before your courts, to their true status as outlaws and ruffians, guilty of theft and arson, and you will deal them and their sympathizers such a blow as will go far to end the business. In this undertaking you shall have all the assistance the military can render you," Pope promised. "The military forces shall act under the direction of your civil officers, according to law and the practice in times past."

Published in the St. Louis press, Pope's program garnered the enthusiastic support of most Missourians, including Governor Fletcher, who in turn demanded that judges and justices of the peace hold regular terms of court and exercise their authority to arrest and bind over offenders of both state and Federal laws.

In the weeks that followed, Fletcher and Pope worked together closely to implement their policies. To give teeth to the governor's March 7 proclamation, Pope promulgated Special Orders Number 15, which immediately relieved provost marshals of their extramilitary duties in all counties in which civil courts had been reestablished. If called upon by civil officers to enforce their judgments, military personal should comply promptly but under no circumstances supersede them.

Welcome and necessary as were Pope's pronouncements, in pledging his support to Governor Fletcher, Pope had exceeded his authority. He had forwarded to President Lincoln his proposals on March 8 but then acted upon them before receiving a reply. Walking a political tightrope of disingenuousness, he told Fletcher that Lincoln had approved his plan and Lincoln that Fletcher had endorsed it, before either had done so formally. But Pope believed strongly in the justice of his program and on the need to move swiftly; fortunately, on March 19, Lincoln approved his plan without change. The next day, Pope reiterated his unconditional pledge to help Fletcher restore civil rule.

Having himself been a provost marshal in Missouri, and later a brigade commander in the Union service, Governor Fletcher well understood the moral courage Pope had demonstrated. His gratitude was enormous. "I can appreciate fully the importance of the services you have rendered in this crisis in the history of our state," Fletcher told Pope. "I have assurances from every part of the state that thousands of persons who have heretofore given no assistance whatever to the cause of the Union, of peace, and of quiet will actively and heartily cooperate with us in an earnest effort to enforce the civil law."

The reconstruction of Missouri depended also on keeping out the Confederates. Although Sterling Price had been crippled badly, it was widely believed in Missouri he could yet muster enough troops in southwestern Arkansas and the Indian Territory to raid the state, should the Union army not take the offensive against him. Price's pro-Union son warned Grenville Dodge privately that his father intended to strike north in April, either for Missouri or southern Kansas. Other reports added elements of Smith's large army to the raiding force. While not entirely convinced of the threat himself, Pope felt it important to take preemptive action. He proposed to Halleck that all available troops from the Departments of the Missouri and of Arkansas be concentrated along the Arkansas River to intercept both regular Confederate forces and bushwhackers heading north. The trouble was, Pope told Halleck, that he neither knew what troops were available in the Department of Arkansas nor could count on cooperation from that quarter. Common sense, said Pope, dictated the Department of Arkansas be added to his geographic division. Pope made a similar appeal directly to Grant.[6]

Grant agreed with Pope. On March 22, the Department of Arkansas was added to Pope's sprawling military division. From his headquarters in St. Louis, Pope now held sway over a region nearly half the size of the United States, ranging from the Red River north to the border with Canada, and from the Mississippi River west to the Humboldt Mountains of Nevada.

Now that Arkansas had been added to Pope's command, Grant expected him to act quickly against Price. He left the details to Pope but hoped him able to break up Price's army and to launch a subsequent campaign into Smith's northeast Texas bread basket, a rich country largely spared the ravages of war. Grant accorded Pope enormous discretionary authority, just as he promised him huge reinforcements. "Movements now in progress may end in such results within a few weeks as to enable me to send you forces enough for any campaign you may want to make, even to the overrunning of the whole of Texas." Grant advised him. "If so, and you want them, they will be promptly sent." All Grant asked was that Pope let him know what he intended to do, and what he might do if he had 25,000 more troops.

Pope set out at once for Arkansas to confer with the department commander, Major General Joseph J. Reynolds. After a week there, Pope returned to St. Louis to draft campaign plans, which he submitted to Grant on April 8.

With nearly all the troops in the Department of Missouri committed to duty on the Plains, or about to be mustered out, Pope found he had only the 17,000 troops of Reynolds's department—nearly 7,000 of whom were dismounted cavalry—available for service against Price and Smith. Smith was thought to have 60,000 men, posted across northeastern Texas and southern Arkansas.

For the moment, Pope could only stand on the defensive, along the Arkansas River. But with 30,000 reinforcements—western men, accustomed to long and hard marches, not pampered eastern soldiers—he would undertake the invasion of northern Texas contemplated by Grant. Pope proposed to move in three columns from the Arkansas toward the Red River. Two columns were to converge and turn Smith's left near Clarksville, Texas, then march rapidly in his rear to the port of Galveston; the third column was to divert Smith with a demonstration toward Camden, Arkansas. Pope would personally command the expedition; Grenville Dodge would relinquish his department to lead a corps. As Grant expected the army to live off the land, Pope thought it best to delay his offensive until June 1, when Texas corn and wheat crops would be nearly ripe. But the war, it seemed, would not wait for Pope's reappearance on the stage of conflict. Two days after Pope submitted his campaign plans, Robert E. Lee surrendered at Appomattox. Perhaps, Pope suggested to Grant, Smith might be induced to surrender under terms similar to those accorded Lee; should he not try to so convince Smith?[7]

While awaiting Grant's reply, Pope learned of the assassination of President Lincoln on Good Friday, April 14, the day before Pope was to deliver a celebratory address on Appomattox to the people of St. Louis. Pope's grief was real. He had overcome his feelings of betrayal and, like the rest of the nation, could lament the passing of one whose goodness and sagacity he had only just come to appreciate.[8]

Grant agreed the time was right for an approach to Smith, but he also ordered Pope to push campaign preparations aggressively. Pope in turn urged Reynolds to make haste and to collect all possible information on northern Texas and its resources. At the same time, he sent his chief of staff, Colonel John T. Sprague, and an aide, Lieutenant J. M. Bundy, to the Red River on a confidential peace mission. They carried a letter from Pope, offering Smith the same terms as those to which Lee had agreed. Pope appealed to Smith's better judgment. "By accepting the terms proposed you will preserve Western Louisiana and Texas from the devastation and misery which have been the lot of nearly every Southern state east of the Mississippi, and you will aid in restoring peace to this distracted country. . . . Wisdom and humanity alike require that this contest be brought to an end without further suffering or shedding of blood."[9]

Sprague and Bundy left St. Louis on April 20. It took them nearly three weeks to reach Smith's headquarters at Shreveport, Louisiana, and when they did, Smith rejected Pope's offer as insulting to his sense of duty and honor. Negotiations might have ended then and there but for the intervention of Governor Henry Allen of Louisiana, who proposed a conference of the Confederate governors of Texas, Missouri, Arkansas, and Louisiana to consider Pope's terms. Smith agreed, the governors convened on May 10, and Sprague and Bundy awaited their decision.

Confident Smith would capitulate, on May 1 Grant had ordered Pope to suspend preparations for a campaign in northern Texas; should Smith hold out, he would send a force to "overrun the whole country west of the Mississippi." In the days that followed, General Joseph E. Johnston surrendered his Army of Tennessee to Sherman in North Carolina, and Lieutenant General Richard Taylor yielded the Departments of Alabama and Mississippi to Major General E. R. S. Canby. Confederate resistance east of the Mississippi River had ended, but still Smith refused to submit. He and the governors demanded terms far more generous than those granted Lee. Not authorized to exceed Pope's written offer, Sprague and Bundy started home, and Smith set off for Houston, to marshal Confederate forces in Texas.

Sprague had kept Pope apprised of his efforts in Shreveport. Smith's recalcitrance did not trouble Pope. On May 17, he assured Grant that a campaign into Texas would most likely be unnecessary. "As every day will render it more and more clear that the rebellion and the rebel government are at an end, I think [Smith] will very shortly agree to the terms. . . . His men are altogether demoralized, and will leave him in large numbers."

Pope had also been encouraged by the ease with which he and Grenville Dodge had convinced the colorful and ardent secessionist M. Jeff Thompson to surrender the 7,500 men he commanded in northern Arkansas. But Grant had become less sanguine about a negotiated settlement. The same day Pope wired his reassurances, Grant appointed Major General Philip H. Sheridan to command the region west of the Mississippi and south of the Arkansas rivers. Sheridan was not to replace Pope but rather to lead field operations against Smith. With 25,000 men from Canby's division, which was broken up to accommodate Sheridan, 17,000 from Reynolds, and reinforcements from Nashville, Sheridan was to sweep through Texas to the Rio Grande.

Although disappointed he would not be returning to the field, Pope understood Grant's actions reflected no loss of confidence in him. On the contrary, Grant was most impressed with Pope's management of his vast command. He had endorsed Pope's plans for ending military rule in Missouri, had approved his actions to date against the Plains Indians, and had read with interest Pope's views on restoring civil rule to Arkansas. The appointment of Sheridan was rather a reward to Grant's most able subordinate in the Virginia campaigns, who since the surrender of Lee had nothing to occupy his talents. Also, Grant had a second motive for sending Sheridan into Texas, beyond simply compelling the capitulation of Smith, one incompatible with the larger duties of a geographic division commander. With the encouragement of the Confederacy, Napoleon III of France had invaded Mexico three years before. By 1865, the French presence had grown tenuous; nonetheless, Stanton and Grant still feared French intervention in the Civil War and hoped a show of force along the Rio Grande would forestall any effort by Napoleon III to resuscitate the dying trans-Mississippi Confederacy. Until Congress or the president decided upon a plan of reconstruction, Pope would be busy enough administering civil affairs in Arkansas.[10]

That was a task to which Pope already had given considerable thought. During his visit to Arkansas in early April, Pope had availed himself of a delay in meeting with General Reynolds to examine the civil affairs of the state. Finding state and local government in even greater disarray than in Missouri, upon his return to St. Louis he addressed President Lincoln a long and urgent letter, advising him that "speedy measures should be adopted to preserve [Arkansas] from abandonment to utter lawlessness."

Pope laid before the president a policy similar to that which he had proposed for Missouri. First and foremost, Pope told Lincoln, the military administration of Arkansas must end, except as was necessary to enforce federal law. "All local matters, political or judicial, had best be left to the state government, and to the action of the people," suggested Pope. "The people and the state government will act and react upon each other so as to produce a healthy condition of civil administration as soon as it becomes manifest that the latter is permanently established, exercises jurisdiction over civil affairs independent of military control, and is in fact as well as in theory the final appeal of the people in all matters pertaining to local civil questions." Military authorities might intervene only as requested by state officers "in the execution of state laws and their own proper functions." Pope intended, "in other words, to confine the military to the duty of defending the state against insurrection and against invasion from the enemy and to other proper military business."

Moved by the suffering of Arkansan noncombatants, and of civilians throughout the Mississippi River Valley, Pope urged that restrictions on trade be lifted. As the Union controlled all western river ports and railroad termini, it was difficult for Pope to "conceive that the country wagons and carts over country roads can carry supplies that are likely to be of much service to the enemy at any considerable distance." Humanity demanded a prompt redress. "It has, I think, long been plain that those who suffer most by suspension of trade are not the rebel armies and soldiers, but old men, women, and children."

Forbearance was a crucial element in Pope's conception of Reconstruction. Left to itself, the state government of Arkansas undoubtedly would do things objectionable to the military, or which might even jeopardize military operations; but this was a price that must be paid. "It is far better, in view of the future," concluded Pope, "for the military commander to counteract the effect of such measures by additional precautions and for the government to employ some thousands of additional soldiers to secure military operations against such a danger than by arbitrary orders to overrule or set aside the action of the civil authorities."

Pope took care to act as he advised. On April 12, two days after writing Lincoln on Arkansas, Pope told Governor Fletcher he intended "quietly and without any published orders" to withdraw all provost marshals from northern Missouri, and to allow "the whole administration [there] to drift quietly into the hands of the civil authorities." Pope implored Fletcher to support him. Lee had surrendered; the rebellion was all but dead. "Be the first in this reconstruction. The longer you wait the less originality and force there will seem to be in your policy."

Governor Fletcher concurred with all Pope recommended. "From every circuit in the state the reports are that courts are being held and an improved condition of things is observable everywhere." Pope had been right. "We shall have peace in Missouri," exalted Fletcher, "and our posterity will bless your name for the noble part you have acted toward us."[11]

Having encouraged the governor to reassert civil authority, Pope would brook no backsliding on his part. He refused a request for troops to enforce the banishment of former bushwhackers and Confederate soldiers, resident in Missouri, to states further south, telling Dodge that Missouri had no right to pass her problems off to her southern brethren. She must herself deal with such people, properly residents and citizens of the state. Petition denied.

Pope also would not permit Federal troops to enforce Governor Fletcher's ordinance removing objectionable state officers. With a loyal executive and a majority of forty thousand loyal voters, Pope told Grant, Missouri was abundantly able to enforce its own laws. Fletcher had no right to call upon Federal troops before using its own civil and militia power. Grant agreed, and Governor Fletcher conceded the wisdom of Pope's counsel.[12]

As Missouri inched its way toward normalcy, Pope was able to devote more attention to a second great challenge of his command: the pacification of the Plains Indians. In March, he fashioned plans for a concerted offensive against all warring tribes south of the Arkansas and north of the Platte rivers (the narrow strip between was comparatively free of hostiles). His objectives were twofold: to prevent a repetition of the previous winter's depredations and to secure for immigrant travel the principal land and water routes through the department. In the south, Pope hoped to clear the Arkansas River road and the Santa Fe Trail and expel hostile tribes from Kansas and the Nebraska Territory. In the north, Pope faced the dual problem of clearing the Platte Route of marauding bands and of helping to secure a new trail that John M. Bozeman and John Jacobs had blazed through the Powder River Country to the Montana gold fields two years earlier. With the coming of spring, emigrants in droves would gather at Fort Laramie, the trail head. Because the Bozeman Trail passed through the last great hunting grounds of the Plains Sioux, conflict was inevitable.

In his planning Pope was ably seconded by the commander of the Department of the Missouri, Grenville Dodge. The two generals held similar views on every aspect of Indian policy. Together they evolved a strategy for smashing the

Great Plains tribes in the early spring, before grass returned to the Plains and the Indians resumed their raids on the emigrant routes. Three expeditions were to strike simultaneously, one in the south and two in the north. From Fort Larned, Brigadier General James H. Ford was to march with 1,200 cavalry against the Southern Cheyenne, Comanche, Kiowa, Kiowa-Apache, and Arapaho, whose principal villages lay in the Wichita Mountains, south of the Arkansas River. The northern campaign would be a joint pincer movement, similar to that attempted by Sully and Sibley in the Dakotas the year before. Marching north from Fort Laramie into the Powder River country, General Connor was first to build a fort and supply station, then strike at Sioux and Cheyenne wintered near the Bighorn Mountains. General Sully would approach the Powder River from Sioux City with 1,200 cavalry. He was to punish the Sioux who had attacked Forts Rice and Berthold during the winter, then turn west to fight several hundred lodges of hostile Sioux, Northern Cheyenne, and Arapaho, believed to be in the Black Hills. Driving this band before him, Sully was to press on to the Powder River country, establish a fort on the river, and trap any remaining Indians between him and Connor.[13]

The plans of Pope and Dodge were constructed on two premises: that Civil War veterans in large numbers would be available for duty in the West, and that Pope and Dodge would be left to treat with hostile tribes as they saw fit. Like Pope, Dodge regarded the existing treaty system, and the civilian agents of the Interior Department who administered it, with contumely. Both believed the bad policies of the past had precipitated present troubles. "In my opinion there is but one way to effectually terminate these Indian troubles," Dodge told Pope, "to push our cavalry into the heart of their country from all directions, to punish them whenever and wherever we find them, and force them to respect our power and to sue for peace. Then let the military authorities make informal treaties with them for a cessation of hostilities." No annuities that rewarded depredations, and no civilian traders to corrupt the Indians. Pope could not have stated his purpose better himself.[14]

When Pope and Dodge first discussed a spring offensive, there were 52,000 troops in the Military Division of the Missouri. Dodge calculated his needs for the campaign at 12,000 troops: 5,000 men to protect existing stations and guard trains, and 7,000 men for active operations. But what originally appeared a surfeit rapidly turned into a dire shortage of troops. Circumstances conspired to delay the campaign; April, then May, passed with no movement. Heavy rains, overflowing waterways, tardy supplies, inadequate transportation, and a lack of cavalry mounts prevented Connor, Sully, and Ford from starting on schedule. Neither Pope nor Dodge could do much to assist them. The logistical needs of frontier commands were met by civilian contractors, whose contracts were let in

Washington by quartermaster officers unfamiliar with western conditions. Not signed until May 1, 1865, the annual supply contracts permitted contractors until December 1 to meet their obligations.[15]

While his field commanders struggled with nature and logistics, Pope watched his forces unexpectedly melt away. At first, it seemed the end of the Civil War would free up vast reserves of volunteers for service on the frontier. But no sooner did units arrive at their western duty stations than they demanded to be sent home. The Northern volunteer had enlisted to fight Rebels, not Indians. Governors and state legislators echoed these demands. Regiments were released rapidly; fourteen regiments sent to Dodge under orders from Washington were mustered out before they reached him. Those that remained were sullen and mutinous. Dodge complained that one-fourth of his troops deserted. Sully found both his own troops and those from the East to be "fast mustering [themselves] out by desertion." Connor had to suppress a mutiny "with grape and canister." By June, Dodge had fewer than seven thousand officers and men in his entire department; to undertake the planned campaign he had to strip troops from guard duty along the overland routes.[16]

The second pillar of Pope's planning also fell before the campaign had begun. Public revulsion over the Sand Creek affair caused Congress to enact two measures, both inimical to the army's interests. The first created a joint congressional committee chaired by Senator James R. Doolittle of Wisconsin to investigate "the condition of the Indian tribes and their treatment by the civil and military authorities of the United States." The second, gotten up by Governor Newton Edmunds of the Dakota Territory, added $20,000 to the Indian Appropriations Act to finance a new treaty with the Sioux of the upper Missouri, which Edmunds himself would negotiate.[17]

Although upset at the prospect of congressional meddling in his military division, Pope was less hostile toward the Doolittle committee than might be expected. He and Doolittle had long been on good terms. A year earlier, Pope had asked the senator to bring before Congress his letter to Secretary of War Stanton on Indian policy. Before setting out for the southern Plains in early May, Doolittle and his colleagues met with Pope at his St. Louis headquarters. They seemed receptive to his views and agreed with Pope that conquered tribes should be settled far from the overland routes. Doolittle also acceded to Pope's request that Major General Alexander M. McCook accompany the committee.[18]

Pope's hopes of winning over the committee were short lived. At Fort Larned in late May Doolittle fell under the sway of Jesse H. Leavenworth, a former volunteer colonel who was then Indian agent for the Upper Arkansas Agency. Leavenworth was convinced he could achieve "a full and complete burying of the hatchet" with the southern Plains tribes, if only the military were prevented from provoking them further. Generals Dodge and Ford dismissed Leavenworth as a deluded visionary, but Doolittle and McCook yielded to his persuasion. Pretending to speak for Pope, on May 31 McCook ordered Ford to suspend his expedition. Two weeks later, Doolittle won from President Andrew Johnson authority to negotiate formal treaties with the tribes of the southern Plains. Pope's intention was that hostile Indians be dealt with solely by the military, which would protect those who surrendered themselves from "outrages by whites"; that no presents be given hostile tribes; and that no treaty be made with them, beyond "the mere understanding to be had with them by the military authorities, that so long as the Indians keep the peace they will not be molested by U.S. troops." But that approach was now stillborn south of the Arkansas River. Instead, Doolittle and Leavenworth would launch an unconditional peace offensive grounded in nothing firmer than goodwill.[19]

Not long after Doolittle wrested presidential authority to treat for peace, the objects of his attention unleashed a series of brutal raids along the Santa Fe Trail. A disgusted General Dodge begged Pope's permission to start punitive columns from Fort Larned. "There is not a leading officer on the plains who has had any experience with Indians who has faith in peace made with any of these Indians unless they are punished for the murders, robberies, and outrages they have committed for over a year," Dodge told Pope. "Unless we have a settled policy, either fight and allow the commanding officer of the department to dictate terms of peace to them, or else it be decided that we are not to fight, but make some kind of peace at all hazards, we will squander the summer without result."[20]

This was precisely what Pope wanted to prevent. His priorities, however, were different than Dodge's. Perhaps because of his long and frustrating experience with the Sioux, Pope was more concerned with resolving matters north of the Platte River than in subduing tribes south of the Arkansas. Consequently, he tried to accommodate Doolittle and had tolerated Jesse Leavenworth's earlier attempts at peace making. Pope refused, however, to concede anything to Governor Edmunds. In denying the governor's request for military protection for his peace commission, Pope informed Edmunds, "There are no Sioux Indians in Dakota Territory with whom it is judicious to make such treaties of peace as you propose." They were all hostile and, as such, were "public enemies" under the sole jurisdiction of the military. "When they choose to have peace instead of war the commanding officers on the frontier are instructed as to the terms, which do not involve giving of presents or making of treaties, nor any expenditure of public money."

Edmunds protested to Secretary of the Interior James Harlan, who took up the matter with Stanton. When Stanton sustained Pope's orders, Governor Edmunds and territorial newspapers friendly to him resorted to libel. The Yankton *Union and Dakotaian* informed its readers that "the military ornament at St. Louis who commands this department has issued orders prohibiting treaties with the Indians." Because of Pope's "imbecile administration of affairs," the paper added, Dakota was to be left open to Indian attacks. Ridiculing Pope's misfortunes at Second Bull Run, the *Union and Dakotaian* concluded, "As well might we rely upon the Army of the Potomac—as upon the Army of the Yellowstone." General Sully and his staff also came under fire from the territorial press, and the *Union and Dakotaian* drew upon leaked Bureau of Indian Affairs correspondence to suggest army malfeasance in the letting of department contracts.[21]

Although he had abundant cause for outrage, Pope's response was dignified and well argued. Rather than wrestle in the mud with Edmunds, he appealed directly to Secretary Harlan's sense of fair play. Differences of opinion between officers of the War and Interior departments were inevitable, Pope conceded in a letter written June 19, and should be encouraged—but through official channels, so that the secretaries of war and the interior might make informed decisions. Maintained Pope, "If the views of the army on this question of Indian policy be unwise they will not, of course, be adopted, but it is surely proper that the mere expression of them to the War Department, or in official communications to officers of the Indian Department, should be received courteously and not made the subject of coarse abuse in the newspapers. If the officer of the Indian Department is right, it needs no such abuse of another, and no articles in the newspapers to sustain his position. He has only to convince the Secretary of the Interior that he is so, and he will, without doubt, have his way." Measured prose and sound logic had replaced the public bombast of the "Proclamation Pope" of 1862, and it succeeded. Not only did Harlan apologize formally to Pope, but he also issued a circular prohibiting Indian agents and superintendents from vilifying their opponents in the press.[22]

With his letter Pope enclosed for Harlan's consideration several official documents that reflected his views on Indian policy. "If true, some correction of the evils set forth should be applied," urged Pope. "If I am found to be mistaken I shall submit very cheerfully and bend all my efforts to carry out successfully the present or any other policy adopted by the government." It was an easier pledge for Pope to make than he let on. Four days before writing Harlan, Pope had received the unqualified approval of General Grant to conduct the summer campaign as he had proposed.[23]

Grant's ringing endorsement had come in response to a lengthy and impassioned letter from Pope on Indian policy. Occasioned by the machinations of Edmunds and the Doolittle committee, Pope's June 14 letter was the most comprehensive, compelling, and heartfelt statement on Indian matters he had penned since his February 1864 missive to Stanton.

Enumerating the Indian outrages committed since Edmunds and Doolittle announced their peace offensives, Pope commented wryly, "If these things show any desire for peace, I confess I am not able to perceive it." Buying peace with gifts and annuities, as both Edmunds and Doolittle proposed, was not the answer. Reiterating arguments he had made with Stanton, Pope told Grant, "It is a common saying with the Sioux that whenever they are poor and need powder and lead they have only to go down to the overland routes and murder a few white men and they will have a treaty to supply their wants." Such a treaty they kept but a short time. "Of one thing we may be sure," predicted Pope, "and that is that they will now demand a higher price for signing such a promise than they did before, and in six months or less will be ready for another treaty at a still higher price," Pope predicted. "It seems idle to pursue the subject." Instead, Pope had directed his subordinates to make "an explicit understanding with the Indians that so long as they keep the peace the United States will keep it, but as soon as they commit hostilities the military forces will attack them, march through their country, establish military posts in it, and as a natural consequence their game will be driven off or killed. . . . Indians will keep the peace when they fear the consequences of breaking it, and not because they are paid (and badly paid, too) for keeping it."

Sounding the first note of a clarion call that Grant, Sherman, John M. Schofield, and others in the army high command would soon come to trumpet with equal conviction, Pope suggested an end to the confusion and inefficiency stemming from the present, bifurcated administration of Indian policy. His solution: return the Bureau of Indian Affairs to the War Department. "Whenever Indian hostilities or massacres occur on the frontier the military are held responsible for them, and by none are they so held more promptly and violently than by the officials of the Indian Department who have made the treaties with the very Indians concerned which could not fail to lead to an outbreak," said Pope. "Either the War or the Interior Department should have the sole management of Indian affairs," he concluded. From divided jurisdiction arose inevitable evils. The single-minded desire of Indian officials to make remunerative treaties (from which many benefited financially) clashed with the awareness of military commanders that they would be held accountable for breaches of the bribing treaties. Pope held that differences of opinion and conflicts of jurisdiction could be avoided only in one of two ways: "First, to return to the War Department the whole management of Indian affairs, or, second to provide for making treaties without the expenditures of money or goods. Having no power to effect the former arrangement, I am endeavoring to effect the latter." By his early outspokenness on the matter of divided jurisdiction, Pope became the first advocate of what was to be a primary objective of army politicking on Indian affairs.

Unlike many who called for stern measures in dealing with recalcitrant Indians, Pope held a genuine interest in their welfare. Not mere expediency, argued Pope, but "wisdom and humanity alike dictate a change in the present system of Indian management." Pope concluded with an eloquent and perspicacious lament of the Indian's plight:

> The development of the mining regions has attracted such a horde of emigrants that the Indian country is penetrated in every direction, highways are made through it, and the game driven off or destroyed. The Indians are more and more confined by circumscribed areas, where they are less able every day to subsist by hunting. A few years more and they will be driven to extremities.
>
> No one can say what outrages are committed upon Indians by these irresponsible crowds of white men flocking through their country. It is only what the Indian does to the white man that is published to the country; never what the white man does to the Indian. I have not a doubt that the Indians could be pacified if they did not hope from day to day that by keeping up hostilities they would secure a treaty such as has always before been made with them, and which will supply their wants. By sending troops enough the Indians can of course be exterminated, but surely such cruelty cannot be contemplated by the government. The question is now squarely before us. Either the extermination of the Indian tribes or a humane policy which shall save them from so cruel a fate, and at the same time secure from danger white emigrants.

Pope wrote frankly and with no conspiratorial intent. He thought Secretary Harlan would "examine and consider his views courteously" and asked Grant to share the letter with him.[24]

Although welcome, Grant's approval of his plans did not end Pope's woes. Not only was he no closer to getting his three columns off than he had been before Doolittle and Edmunds interfered, but interference from an unexpected direction also derailed part of the campaign altogether. In early May, a wandering band of sixteen Santee Sioux, thought by nervous Minnesotans to be part of a huge "hive of hostile Sioux" concentrated at Devil's Lake, had slipped through the Minnesota defenses and raided as far south as Mankato. They murdered a family and threw the state into a panic, to which Generals Sibley and Curtis succumbed. Sibley saw the raid as the harbinger of a general Sioux and Chippewa onslaught, and both he and Curtis demanded that Pope divert Sully's expedition to Devil's Lake, to attack Sioux camps there and build a permanent post.

Seeing the commotion for what it was—an effort by Minnesota business interests to draw more troops and another post to the state—Pope refused to help Curtis and Sibley, both of whom he chastened for having joined in the "stampedes" that occurred in Minnesota every spring and autumn. He regarded their present command of eighteen cavalry companies and four infantry companies as ample protection for Minnesota and doubted any force able to corral whatever hostile Sioux might be at Devil's Lake, so long as the British continued to permit the Sioux a sanctuary in Canada. He changed his mind only after Sully, whose judgment he trusted far more than Curtis's, forwarded what he deemed credible reports from the upper Missouri that three thousand Sioux lodges were coming to Fort Rice to make peace. Assuming the danger in the northern Black Hills to be ended, Pope instructed Sully to suspend his march toward the Powder River and instead go first to Fort Rice to treat with the Sioux coming in; afterward, he might pursue the Devil's Lake Indians. Curtis and Sibley lost no time in making the change in plans public.[25]

Within a week, it became clear to Pope he had acted prematurely. On June 2, a large party of Sioux attacked the garrison at Fort Rice. Shortly thereafter, reports reached Pope that several hundred lodges of Tetons, Cheyennes, and Arapahos had assembled at Bear Butte, on the northeastern edge of the Black Hills, anxious for a fight. Congressman Asahel W. Hubbard of Iowa, who had sponsored a bill appropriating funds for a wagon road to Montana from Sioux City, voiced concern that the road-building expedition would be massacred as it neared Bear Butte. General Sully also expressed doubts about the wisdom of his marching north while such a huge party of hostile Indians lay off his western flank. Rather than redirect Sully to the Black Hills, Pope bowed to political pressure from Minnesota and, against his better judgment, gave Sully's former mission to Dodge and Connor, telling Dodge he "must deal with these Indians in the Black Hills and establish the post at Powder River."[26]

Not all Pope's attention was given over to Indian troubles. In June, he decided to settle an old score with Henry Halleck. Henry Heth, a former major general in the Confederate army and a prewar acquaintance of Pope, happened to be in St. Louis at the time visiting friends. As a paroled ex-Confederate, Heth had been enjoined by Federal authorities to remain at home until further notice. Having traveled to St. Louis without permission, Heth became worried when a soldier appeared at his hotel-room door saying General Pope wished to see him. Heth packed his bag and followed the soldier to Pope's office, all the while wondering "to what jail I would be consigned." But Pope greeted him warmly, extending his hand and telling Heth he wanted to show him a letter he had been writing to Halleck. A much-relieved Heth listened as Pope explained, "You doubtless remember how unmercifully your papers pitched into me on account of an alleged dispatch of mine to General Halleck when I was in command near Corinth, saying I had driven the enemy twenty miles, captured 10,000 prisoners, artillery, etc.?" "Yes," said Heth, "I remember that very well, and that our papers gave you hail Columbia." "That dispatch was a fabrication of Halleck's," retorted Pope. "I never sent such a dispatch to him. I did not propose to have any controversy with Halleck during the war, but determined to wait until it was ended and then to put myself right; so I wrote him this note."

Heth read the draft, in which Pope reminded Halleck of the incident, denied having sent him such a dispatch, and asked Halleck to produce a copy of any such report Pope may have made. As he left Pope's headquarters, Heth mused at the irony of Pope then ascribing to Halleck the reputation he had enjoyed before the war: that of the biggest liar in the army.[27]

Pope telegraphed Halleck the letter on July 3—but from Washington, D.C., not St. Louis. Under mounting pressure from President Andrew Johnson and the cabinet to reduce military expenditures, particularly on the Plains, just four days after giving Pope the go-ahead for his planned campaign General Grant had been compelled to order him to "cut down the expeditions all you can and direct that [cavalry animals] be grazed as far as possible." Neither the president nor Grant yet understood that frontier expenses were high for reasons beyond the control of regional commanders. Reliance on civilian contractors, the dispersal of units in company-sized garrisons, the great distances involved, and the absence of ready sources of supply all worked to wrench logistical costs upward. The figures were indeed dizzying; quartermaster department expenditures in support of operations against the Plains Indians in 1865 alone would exceed $19,000,000, exclusive of pay.

Pope appreciated the pressures on Grant but was at a loss how to reduce expenses. He also saw in the administration's evolving policy a false economy. "I think the government will find it true economy to finish the Indian war this season so that it will stay finished," he hastened to reply to Grant, adding that he hoped to conclude his campaign and muster out the remaining volunteers by September 1. "We have troops enough now on the plains to do it and can do it now better than hereafter. If I could only get legislation or a determined resolution of the government to do away with the present system of Indian policy everything would go right."[28]

Contemplating the matter further, Pope concluded that only by a personal conference with Grant, the president, and the secretaries of war and the interior could he properly impart his views, which he hoped might lead to a "satisfactory understanding between all concerned." Grant agreed and on June 26 ordered Pope to the capital.[29]

The results of his nine-day stay in Washington were mixed. On the one hand, Secretary Harlan agreed he and Pope should "communicate freely on the subject of Indian affairs" in the future. Although he doubted reservations could be placed far enough from bad whites to prevent "this returning evil," Harlan pledged to effect Pope's suggestions with those of the southern Plains tribes as might capitulate and for whom suitable lands might be found. In the case of warring tribes, he would also remind his agents and commissioners to subordinate their actions to War Department directives. The trouble was, as Pope soon discovered, the War Department was not at all pleased with his plans, even though Pope had cut the number of troops participating in half, from slightly over ten thousand cavalry to some five thousand troopers. Ignorance of frontier conditions, combined with an overriding desire to both demobilize the volunteers and reduce the standing army, made President Johnson openly hostile to his designs and Stanton a reluctant ally at best. Pope simply had expected too much, too soon, in the way of military effort and policy reform from a government weary of war and of painful decisions. In his zeal to reform federal Indian policy, Pope also had neglected a fundamental point, which Secretary Harlan pointed out to him: that "whether this policy is wise or unwise is not now a practical question" for Harlan, Stanton, or the president. "Treaties made and ratified must be enforced until abrogated by the same power which made them." Only congressional action could bring about the changes Pope desired.[30]

While at the capital, Pope was handed an additional, startling bit of news: he would no longer command the Military Division of the Missouri. The very day Pope reached Washington, Grant issued orders expanding Pope's command and giving it to Major General William T. Sherman, on leave in Ohio. Pope would stay on as commander of the Department of the Missouri, Dodge as commander of all forces in the field, except Sully's. Both Sherman and Pope would make their headquarters at St. Louis; Dodge would direct matters on the ground from Fort Leavenworth.

Pope probably took the news in stride. After all, General Sherman was second only to Grant in popularity in the North, and with the end of Southern hostilities, a place had to be made for him commensurate with his stature. That he was given the Military Division of the Missouri was a testimony to the importance of the command Pope had wielded since February rather than any indication of a loss of confidence in Pope. If Pope's vanity had been wounded, it was probably assuaged when Pope learned his department would be no smaller than his division had been. Although Arkansas, Illinois, and the Indian Territory were taken from him, Grant transferred Colorado to his jurisdiction; upon assuming command Sherman recommended, and Grant concurred in, the transfer of the Districts of Utah and New Mexico to Pope's department as well.[31]

Before leaving Washington, Pope wrapped up a piece of unrelated business. To Pope's query about the phantom prisoners at Corinth, Henry Halleck had replied tersely, "As my papers are all boxed up for transportation to California, I am not able to refer to the dispatches to which you allude, nor can I trust my memory in regard to communications made more than three years ago further than to say that I never reported to the secretary of war dispatches received from you which were not so received." Pope angrily denied submitting such a dispatch and accused Halleck of having tampered with pertinent records. "In almost any other case the question could be easily and conclusively decided by a reference to the official files at the headquarters of the department which you then commanded," snarled Pope, "but I have ascertained, General, that when you left the west you ordered that portion of the dispatches and reports concerning the operations around Corinth, which bore upon this question, to be cut out of the official books and brought with you to Washington, leaving the official records in St. Louis mutilated and incomplete." Pope offered that "my main purpose in writing to you on the subject was to give you the opportunity to explain the matter in a manner that, while it would relieve me from the misconception arising from your dispatch, would leave unimpaired the personal relations which have always existed between us." When Halleck ignored Pope's rejoinder, Pope had their correspondence printed and made public. Like nearly everyone who had held high command during the Civil War, Pope would not let old wounds heal. Because his record had been so controversial, and because it suited his temperament, Pope succumbed more readily than most to the postwar pastime of refighting old battles.[32]

From the capital Pope traveled to Ohio, where he spent ten days, visiting Clara's family in Pomeroy and perhaps conferring with Sherman. Shortly after Pope returned to St. Louis, Sherman pressed him to reduce expenses and muster out the volunteers quickly. Although everything in his experience told him such actions were shortsighted and wrong, Pope did his best to comply. He instructed Dodge to "reduce everything at once to the lowest possible necessity, and . . . muster out every man you can," and he insisted that supply requisitions to Washington (where all supply contracts were let) be submitted through department headquarters for his review.

Dodge reacted angrily. He defended General Connor, whose expedition was proving the most costly, and demanded Pope make the government "understand that it has either got to abandon the country west entirely to the Indians or meet the war issue presented." But Pope's visit to Washington had convinced him he could not silence the swelling clamor for retrenchment. While he permitted Connor, whose columns had barely begun to move as July drew to close, to go ahead as planned, he set October 1 as a deadline for all operations to cease, come what may. After that date, all units would return to a defensive posture, as the War Department demanded. Faced with the prospect of losing all influence over Indian policy in his division if he did not soften his uncompromising stance on civilian treaties, on August 4 Pope ordered Dodge to call off Sanborn's expedition. He further authorized Sanborn to cooperate with Plains agent Jesse Leavenworth, who was confident he could bring the southern tribes to a peace conference if the army stayed away. On August 15, Sanborn and Leavenworth signed an agreement with the chiefs of the Kiowa, Apache, Comanche, and Arapaho nations, calling for a mutual suspension of hostilities until October 4, when all would meet with Indian commissioners to arrange a "perpetual peace."[33]

Not that Pope held out any real hope of peace, either from Leavenworth's dealings or Connor's Powder River expedition. He revealed his doubts in another long epistle on Indian affairs, this one written on August 1 to Colonel Roswell M. Sawyer, adjutant of the new Military Division of the Mississippi, as Sherman's command was first called, in response to Sherman's first cost-cutting call. Pope himself considered the letter one of his seminal treatises on the subject. Much merely reiterated what he had written Grant in June and had said in Washington, but the tone was more pessimistic, and not a little insolent. Pervading the letter too were a growing despair over the tasks before him and a deepening sympathy for the Plains Indian.

"The Indian question is the most difficult, and I confess I do not see how it is to be solved without an entire change of the Indian policy." Government schizophrenia encouraged the very hostilities Pope was charged with preventing. On the one hand, Washington negotiated treaties guaranteeing the sanctity of Indian lands; on the other, it encouraged the very emigration that overran them. Pope realized, "of course, neither the movements nor the conduct of [immigrants] can be controlled. No man except themselves can say what wrongs they do to the Indians by robbing, by violence, or by dispossessing them of [their] country." Seeing his lands vanish, the buffalo slaughtered, and his family starved, what choice did the Indian have but to make war on the white man? "Driven to desperation . . . there is not a tribe of Indians on the great plains or in the mountain regions . . . which is not now warring on the whites." Question followed upon question, and a tragic end loomed certain:

> Lately large reinforcements have been organized which are now moving against the Indians in the hope to restore peace, but in my judgment with little prospect of doing so. The first demand of the Indian is that the white man shall not come into his country. How can we promise this, with any purpose of fulfilling the obligation, unless we prohibit emigration west or south of the Missouri River? So far from being prepared to make such engagements with the Indian, the government is every day stimulating emigration and its resulting wrong to the Indian. Where under such circumstances is the Indian to go, and what is to become of him?
>
> My duties require me to protect the emigration, the mails, and the settlements against hostile acts of the Indians. I have no power under the laws of the United States to do this except by force. As the Indians are more and more driven to desperation, the end is sure and dreadful to contemplate.

Pope indicted the false economy that compelled him to muster out the volunteers rapidly when future hostilities loomed certain. Cautioned Pope: "It is proper for the government to realize that owing to the changed condition of affairs on the plains, arising from the rapid development of the mining regions and the great emigration, a much larger force will for a long time be required in that region than we have heretofore considered necessary."[34]

For the moment, Pope's words of warning were ignored, both at division headquarters and at Washington, where, through no fault of his own, his standing had dropped sharply. It was simply that no one wanted, or had the time for, problems on the Plains. Weary of capital politics, Grant spent most of the summer touring the North and enjoying the accolades of a grateful populace. What thought he did give national affairs was mostly in regard to troubles on the Texas-Mexico border, where war with France seemed imminent. President Johnson and Secretary Stanton were preoccupied with matters in the South, where Reconstruction had gotten off to a tempestuous start.[35]

Stanton's principal sources of information on western matters seem to have been the quartermaster general of the army and members of the Doolittle committee. Neither was reliable. Angered over General Connor's unorthodox practice of buying supplies directly from local civilians, rather than submitting requests through staff channels, the army quartermaster for Denver and Fort Laramie lodged a protest with Quartermaster General Montgomery Meigs, alleging commanders and line officers had usurped his duties. Jealous of department prerogatives, Meigs fed Stanton wildly exaggerated figures of expenditures throughout Pope's entire command. Despite prior claims of goodwill, at heart Secretary of the Interior Harlan saw Pope as a troublesome rival; now he assured Stanton that Pope was "an improper man, extravagant and wasteful."

The Doolittle committee was disingenuous in its reports, labeling the Powder River expedition a failure before it had begun. Doolittle and his colleagues also insisted that only defensive measures and monetary treaties were needed to pacify the Indians.[36]

On August 8, the matter came before the cabinet. Stanton informed his colleagues that three columns of twenty-two thousand troops were moving into the Indian country. Where he got such a figure is unknown; in truth, the combined strength of units then converging on the Powder River region was less than twenty-five hundred officers and men. On learning of Stanton's claim, Grenville Dodge wrote, "It is no wonder that with such ignorance in the cabinet as to the condition of the country, that the administration at Washington was so incompetent in the Civil War."

The cabinet was appalled, the more so as Stanton claimed not to have authorized so huge an expedition. Stanton also said Quartermaster General Meigs had assured him the campaign would cost at least $50,000,000, a revelation that brought a stunned Secretary of the Treasury Hugh McCulloch to his feet.

Three days later, the subject again came up in cabinet. Saying Grant had denied ordering an expedition of such magnitude, Stanton implicitly blamed the fictitious enterprise on Pope. On August 18, Senator Doolittle addressed the cabinet. He denounced "the folly and wickedness of [an] expedition which has been gotten up by somebody without authority or the knowledge of the government," another thinly veiled indictment of Pope. Only Stanton's assurances that he would sharply scale down the expedition prevented further cabinet action.[37]

For the remainder of the month, Stanton harangued Grant, who was still touring northern cities, about Pope's operations. Seeming to forget he had told Pope two months earlier to "push out your expeditions against the Indians in your own way," Grant informed Stanton he had neither ordered them nor had been "posted as to the necessity of them." Promising to go to St. Louis himself in September to rectify matters, Grant in the meantime wrote Sherman, suggesting he reign Pope in.[38]

But Pope had been practicing restraint for some time. On August 2, six days before Stanton caused a cabinet panic, Pope had instructed Dodge to reduce his already depleted command to seven thousand men the moment Connor's expedition returned, regardless of the outcome. Five days later, he urged Dodge to "hurry on your expeditions." Then he ordered Dodge to "break up every post in southern Kansas not absolutely necessary." Denying a request for more horses for Connor's expedition, Pope told Dodge, "If you cannot accomplish results with what you have they must be left undone." Pope also remained critical of Connor, whom three months earlier he had touted to Grant as "the very best and most active officer I have." When he learned Connor had ordered the commanders of his supporting columns, Colonel Nelson Cole and Lieutenant Colonel Samuel Walker, to receive no "overtures of peace or submission from Indians, but attack and kill every male Indian over twelve years of age," Pope exploded. "These instructions are atrocious, and are in direct violation of my repeated orders. You will please take immediate steps to countermand such orders. If any such orders as General Connor's are carried out it will be disgraceful to the government."[39]

Not that there was any real chance of their being put into practice. Far from showing any disposition to submit, the Powder River tribes lashed at the columns of Cole and Walker with unprecedented ferocity. Neither had gotten started until late July, Cole marching from Omaha with 1,108 men, Walker with some 600 troops from Fort Laramie. Connor, who left Fort Laramie himself on July 30 with 475 men, had planned to rendezvous with Cole and Walker on September 1 along Rosebud Creek, a tributary of the Yellowstone River running north of the Bozeman Trail, presumably with all hostile warriors either dead or trapped between their converging columns. Instead, Connor lost track of Cole and Walker, not gaining the first hint of their whereabouts until September 11. By then, both their commands were exhausted and starving. "Vulture like," said Cole, the Sioux hovered around his flanks as he struggled up the Powder River. Only Connor had been able to bring the Indians to battle, on August 29 near the head of the Tongue River, but all he had to show for the encounter were a few dozen Indian dead and wounded. Cole and Walker, moving together after August 18, fought several running skirmishes with nearly 3,000 warriors in the face of gale-like winds and pelting snow, always on ground of the Indians' choosing. They lost 500 animals and several troopers, but, confessed Walker, "I cannot say as we killed one [Sioux]."[40]

When at last Connor met Cole and Walker on September 24 at Fort Connor, a "rather rude affair" Connor had constructed at the Powder River crossing of the Bozeman Trail and named for himself, they found the expedition had been ended for them. A courier brought orders from Pope dated August 22, breaking up Connor's sprawling District of the Plains into four smaller districts and directing Connor to return to his old command, the District of Utah, "at the earliest practical moment." Brigadier General Frank Wheaton, whose new District of Nebraska now encompassed the Powder River country, had been told by Pope to "return to a purely defensive arrangement for the security of the overland routes" and "reduce troops and expenditures without delay." Similar admonitions went out to the commanders of the Districts of Colorado and Kansas. Dodge and Connor protested, asking Pope to permit a second strike at the Sioux. If not, warned Dodge, "the entire Indian tribes will be down on our lines, and we will have our hands full, and more too." Pope did not necessarily disagree with Dodge's prediction, but the wishes of the War Department, however ill-advised he might find them, must be obeyed: Request denied.[41]

It was a harder pill for Pope to swallow than Dodge or Connor probably imagined. The failure of the Powder River campaign to do more than exacerbate Sioux hostility discredited the aggressive policies Pope had championed. Nor had Pope's dogmatic stand with Governor Edmunds yielded much. When Sully marched to Fort Rice in July he encountered only a handful of blanket Sioux, rather than the three thousand lodges desirous of peace he had been led to expect, and at Devil's Lake he found no Indians at all.

In the wake of the army's discomfiture, civilians stepped forward. On the Little Arkansas River in October, Jesse Leavenworth and the peace commissioners signed annuity treaties in October with the southern Plains tribes. At Fort Sully that same month, Generals Curtis and Sibley joined Governor Edwards and the commission he had been laboring to assemble over Pope's obstructionism since spring in concluding a series of treaties with the Teton and Yanktonai Sioux, binding the signatories to quit the emigrant routes and promising annuity payments.

Although the October 1865 treaties assuaged national guilt over Sand Creek and pleased eastern humanitarians, Pope doubted they would endure much beyond the winter, as did Sherman, who joined Pope in pressing Grant to hurry Regulars to the Plains before spring.[42]

— ♦ —

As 1865 drew to a close, Pope had much with which to be pleased. He might balance the Powder River debacle and his rough handling in Washington against the fact that he had returned from near obscurity to a command of great importance. Despite Stanton's dissembling before the cabinet that summer, he still held Pope in high esteem. And in August, the president had awarded him the rank of brevet major general in the Regular Army. John Pope the family man also had cause for thanks. Clara enjoyed good health, as did their infant son, Horton. At forty-five, Pope himself settled into a more sedentary middle age. He shaved his beard close and watched his waistline grow so quickly he had to have $138 worth of uniform pants and vests, ordered in August, altered in September.[43]

— ♦ —

John Pope was not one to give up easily. He knew continual warfare would be the normal state of affairs on the Great Plains, the October treaties notwithstanding. While the bitter Plains winter buried his vast department in snow, keeping soldier and Indian alike off the overland trails, Pope busied himself with letters and memoranda to educate Grant and Sherman better on changing conditions on the Plains and to convince them that a transfer of Indian affairs to the War Department was the necessary precursor to needed reform.

To buttress his arguments, Pope gathered corroborating testimony from Indian experts outside the army. Two who endorsed Pope's views were William Bent, the famous Plains trader and friend of the Cheyenne, and Kit Carson, the legendary mountain man, Indian agent, and volunteer officer. As both had participated in the Little Arkansas treaty negotiations, their support would be particularly convincing. Calling Bent and Carson to St. Louis in the late fall, Pope asked them to submit a written report on Indian policy.[44]

They complied in a manner that delighted Pope. Both indicted the present system, which offered "no security, either to the Indian or government, against the rapacity and cupidity of the agents," who were a principal cause of unrest. To Bent and Carson military control of Indian affairs offered the only solution to the Indian problem. They also agreed with Pope that, until the Indian could be civilized, the only chance of saving him from extermination was to place him on reservations run by the army.

The report of Carson and Bent catalyzed Pope into pressing hard for War Department control of Indian affairs. Recalling Secretary Harlan's counsel that only Congress could effect policy change, Pope asked Sherman to forward the report to Grant, so that the general-in-chief might furnish copies to the Joint Congressional Committee on Indian Affairs. Important legislation was pending, and the opinions of Carson and Bent should be heard. "It is unnecessary to say that Carson and Bent are men of standing and reliability, thoroughly acquainted with Indians and Indian management by the experience of their whole lives and that what they have herein stated may be entirely relied on in any measures adopted by Congress," said Pope. "Their statements simply reiterate with uncommon forbearance, the experience and opinions of all honest persons in the army or out of it, who have ever served on the frontier." As one of the faithful, Pope bundled up for Sherman copies of his own letters and reports on Indian matters with that of Bent and Carson.[45]

Finding himself in accord with his department commander, Sherman forwarded the correspondence to Secretary Stanton, calling his attention to "the recommendation for the transfer of the control of Indian affairs from the Department of the Interior to the War Department, which is entirely concurred in." Sherman also commended Pope for "the spirit he displays, in endeavoring to carry out the well known wishes" of Grant to muster out volunteers and cut costs.

Before receiving Bent's and Carson's report, Pope had written Grant directly on the transfer question. Similarly impressed with Pope's judgments, Grant also recommended Stanton consider "the necessity of Indian affairs being under control of the War Department." When no action was forthcoming, Pope asked Sherman to "press matters in the proper quarter." Decisions were needed quickly, he explained, as "our Indian affairs on the plains are now in favorable condition for final and general pacification provided the military authorities are authorized to control them and regulate the treaties." As much as they might agree with Pope, Grant and Sherman were not yet ready to become embroiled in a debate over Indian policy, nor was Secretary Stanton then disposed to push the question, and for the moment at least, the matter died.[46]

Pope's next missive was to have a far greater, and more immediate, impact. As he contemplated his mandate for 1866, which was to undertake no offensive operations, muster out remaining volunteers rapidly, and get the Regulars onto the Plains as soon as the weather allowed, Pope realized he lacked the guidance needed to make adequate plans. How many troops were to be assigned him? Would he be expected to open or protect new travel routes, or to construct new posts? He needed answers before the spring thaw, Pope told Sherman on February 2. So that he and Grant might better understand what Pope faced, and so make informed decisions, on February 25 Pope presented Sherman with a "Report of the Condition and Necessities of the Department of the Missouri." His most comprehensive exposition to date on the Indian question and its meaning for the military, Pope's report showed an appreciation of the West that members of Congress and officials of the Indian Bureau lacked, and it reflected thinking that was national in scope.[47]

His department was "divided by nature" into three, great geographic belts, explained Pope, the well-settled agricultural region along the Mississippi and Missouri rivers, the largely uninhabited High Plains, and the eastern range of the Rocky Mountains, fast filling with miners. Migrants to the latter region depended on supplies from the agricultural district, which must pass across a Plains populated with hostile Indians. How to keep open communications with the mining territories and protect new settlements there "is the question of absorbing interest in this department, and one in which, directly or indirectly, the government of the United States and large classes of the people are equally concerned."

Critical to the army's task on the Plains was the rapid construction of the transcontinental railroad. Rail transport would greatly reduce the cost of supplying the mining district and eliminate the need for costly military garrisons on the Plains. Every effort should thus be bent toward completing the Pacific lines. In addition to what was needed to guard existing overland routes, adequate numbers of troops should be assigned to protect railroad workers and surveying parties. Pope warned that "it would be false economy to suffer the construction of these lines of communication to be delayed or embarrassed for the want of a few troops, and the temporary expense they would occasion." The only enduring way to secure lines of travel, continued Pope, was to collect the Plains tribes and place them on reservations along the Missouri and Mississippi rivers, where they could be cheaply fed, civilized, and taught to support themselves. The other possibility, that of restricting travel to selected routes, was unrealistic, because "the American emigrant cannot and will not be restricted in either the direction or extent of his movements." Although the October 1865 treaties had created "a general pacification in this department," Pope predicted they would not long endure. However much the Indian might desire peace, the rapid overrunning of his country by white travelers would force him to go to war simply to protect himself. Assuming the treaties held through 1866, Pope estimated he would need 12,000 troops, or a third more than he presently had. To replace the volunteers, 5,350 Regulars should be hurried to the department before mid-April.[48]

Sherman found Pope's report of incomparable value in understanding his new command. He heartily commended it to Grant's attention as "the best, most clear and satisfactory condensed description" of the region, and he asked that Grant withhold any decisions on Indian matters until he had read it. Unless Grant instructed him otherwise, Sherman would act according to Pope's recommendations, both in terms of "the general policy proposed, and the distribution of troops for the coming year."[49]

Grant was also impressed with Pope's "very admirable" report, which he confessed to be the only reliable information he had on the West. Not only did Grant endorse Pope's operational proposals, but the report also roused him to discuss the question of War Department control with members of Congress. Secretary Stanton shared Grant's regard for Pope's opinions, and he transmitted both the report and a batch of Pope's earlier letters to the House Committee on Indian Affairs.[50]

Both Grant and Sherman agreed with Pope that Indian troubles could be minimized if emigrants were compelled to travel on established routes. Though less sanguine than they that this could be accomplished, Pope made an effort. On February 28, he promulgated General Order Number Twenty-seven, which required all wagon trains to rendezvous at designated points and organize for their own defense. Travel was restricted to trains of twenty or more wagons and no fewer than thirty armed men. Although often ignored as travelers straggled westward in small groups, heedless of the dangers, the order brought at least a degree of order and safety to the westward movement that year.[51]

In light of the praise he had received, Pope was startled to learn, just a week after submitting his report, that Sherman intended to reduce his command drastically. Concluding the Department of the Missouri to be too vast to be managed by any single commander, no matter how capable, Sherman proposed dividing it into two departments. Pope objected, but Grant concurred. In late March, Pope found himself in command of a Department of the Missouri that consisted of Kansas, Colorado, Utah, and New Mexico, with headquarters to be at Fort Leavenworth. The Montana and Dakota territories, Minnesota, Iowa, and Nebraska were consolidated in the new Department of the Platte, commanded by Brigadier General Philip St. George Cooke.[52]

Pope suffered this setback well. Pleased when Sherman instructed Cooke to pay close attention to his recommendations for the northern Plains, Pope continued to offer suggestions for managing affairs in the new department that were well received by Sherman and Grant, the more so as Cooke quickly showed himself unsuited to the command. Pope mustered out the remaining volunteers and got Regular replacements onto the Plains in April, then tended to the defense of the Smoky Hill Road south of the Platte River, over which most of the season's wagon trains were expected to pass. Apart from scattered raids on unwary travelers, the Plains tribes remained at peace.[53]

Sherman availed himself of the relative quiet to conduct an inspection of the division. With Pope's report to guide him, he left St. Louis in May for a two-month journey, mostly through the Department of the Platte and the Great Lakes region.

On June 1, Pope set out on a tour of his own. As he informed Grant, he planned to "be absent about four months . . . to inspect all the posts on the Platte, go to Salt Lake, and thence down into New Mexico." No doubt Pope went because Sherman wanted him to. He had resisted even moving his headquarters from St. Louis to Fort Leavenworth, officially because of the difficulty in moving the huge stock of military records gathered in St. Louis since 1861, but really for family reasons. His mother was in poor health, and Clara was then three months pregnant. Before leaving for the Plains, Pope asked Grant to consider transferring him to command of the Department of the East upon his return from the Plains in October, as he "had served in the West all my life and would be glad to see a year or two of service in the East."[54]

The next four months were for Pope the most physically demanding since the Second Bull Run campaign. He rode from post to post on the arid Plains, pausing to inspect each. What he found disgusted him. The posts generally were small, company-sized affairs constructed by the men who garrisoned them. Not being laborers, the troops did the job poorly. As Sherman told Grant of Pope's inspection of Colorado posts, "Some are really enough to make men desert, built years ago, of upright cottonwood poles, daubed with mud, and covered with mounds of earth, as full of fleas and bedbugs as a full sponge is of water. Were it not for the intensely bitter winds of winter which force men to go in such holes, or perish, no human being, white man, Indian, or Negro, would go inside." Pope was frustrated with his inability to alleviate the soldiers' discomfort. For posts in areas barren of trees, Pope thought boards and other building materials should be hauled out from the larger forts to the east, regardless of the cost. But department quartermasters opposed him, insisting that only they could decide where and how the troops were to be quartered. Sherman agreed with Pope that "this is all wrong. We who command the troops must station them, and we must be the judge of the kind of structures needed." But the quartermasters prevailed. It was Pope's first exposure to a problem that was to confound department commanders for years to come: the virtual autonomy of army staff departments in Washington, who reported to the secretary of war rather than to the commanding general of the army, and of their representatives in the field, who operated outside the authority of troop commanders.[55]

Not all Pope's time was spent inspecting dismal, flea-infested frontier posts. He also visited the leading towns of the region, speaking with prominent civilians about his Indian policy at every opportunity. Pope passed through Julesburg and Denver, Colorado, and lingered several days longer than was probably necessary in Santa Fe and Albuquerque, enjoying the fine southwestern climate he had come to appreciate during his artesian-well experiments on the Llano Estacado a decade before.[56]

While Pope was on the Plains, important decisions bearing on his career were being made in Washington. On July 28, President Andrew Johnson signed the "Act to Increase and Fix the Military Peace Establishment of the United States" (also known as the Army Reorganization Act), which determined the shape of the postwar Regular Army. Of most concern to Pope, the act provided for five major generals and ten brigadier generals of the line. Competition for the latter appointments was intense, as scores of volunteer generals sought a permanent place in the military. But Pope's record (and perhaps his Republican politics) prevailed, and Congress confirmed him as a permanent brigadier general in the Regular Army.[57]

Although assured a career for two decades more, until the mandatory retirement age of sixty-five, Pope faced uncertain immediate prospects. The Army Reorganization Act engendered a realignment of geographical commands. The West continued as two military divisions, separated roughly by the Continental Divide—Sherman, now a lieutenant general, remained in command of the Division of the Missouri from St. Louis, and Halleck, a major general in the Regular establishment, commanded the Division of the Pacific from San Francisco. A new command was created within Sherman's division, as Montana and the Dakotas were taken from the ineffectual Cooke and given to Brevet Major General Alfred H. Terry as the Department of Dakota. Halleck's division consisted of the Department of California (California, Nevada, and Arizona), commanded by Irvin McDowell, and the Department of the Columbia (Oregon, Washington, and Idaho), under Frederick Steele. Next to occur that summer was a reshuffling of commanders among the geographic departments. President Johnson selected Major General Winfield Scott Hancock, a favorite of his, to replace Pope in command of the Department of the Missouri. Unbeknownst to Pope, he was to go to Oregon as the new commander of the Department of the Columbia, an assignment Grant assumed Pope would find acceptable.[58]

Riding into Fort Dodge, Kansas, the last week of August, after his "long and wearisome journey," Pope found the orders assigning him to the Northwest coast. He was horrified. Command in Oregon not only would mean serving under Henry Halleck, with whom his personal relations were "unpleasant," but also would entail a long separation from Clara, who was expecting their second child in December. Pope also understood, if Grant did not, that he was to be exiled for having publicly disapproved of President Johnson's reconstruction policy. While yet at Fort Dodge, Pope dashed off letters to Stanton and Grant, begging them to rescind the transfer. He also asked Orville H. Browning, newly installed as secretary of interior, to intercede with President Johnson. What he really wished, Pope told Grant and Browning—now that it was clear Joe Hooker would stay on as commander of the Department of the East in consideration of his poor health—was the superintendency of the United States Military Academy.[59]

Twenty-four years earlier, Pope had left West Point an angry young second lieutenant, mortified before his father at not having graduated higher in his class. Pope's low opinion of the Military Academy faculty, whom he blamed for his middling class rank, had not improved with time. To begin with, the curriculum was inadequate. Teaching only "the science of mathematics and the science of war," West Point turned out graduates poorly prepared for proper society and not much better prepared for war. The military curriculum had not improved much since Pope's day, when it consisted of Napoleon's art of war, in preparing cadets for command. As Pope discovered during the Civil War, volunteer officers made better generals: "The best school of generals is war and whatever of value is found in the teachings of the military schools is greatly modified by preconceived theories of war taught there[,] which much interfere with the rapid acquirement of the lessons learned in actual campaigns by the intelligent volunteer." The same could be said of service on the Plains, where conventional tactics taught at West Point were irrelevant to chasing down Indians.[60]

Pope also judged the academic board to be inept and the faculty myopic. "It has always been and no doubt still is the theory of West Point professors, that after a young fellow has passed one year at the academy, they can solve his equation," Pope charged. "Whatever he does or fails to do when he leaves there, in no respect shakes their estimate of him. To these worthy professors, with their inflexible opinions about the men whom they had taught, the career of such men as Grant and Sheridan was a fountain of wonder, and perplexity, and they felt themselves much in the predicament of Balaam when his ass began to talk so wisely."[61]

In lobbying for the job of West Point superintendent, Pope was careful to use more dignified language. The Army Reorganization Act had included provisions for overhauling the academy's curriculum in order, Pope conjectured, "to place West Point upon a different footing in all respects . . . and establish such military character for the institution as has been lacking whilst it was only a school under charge of engineer officers." Change was imperative and must be thorough. To effect it, a high-ranking officer should be appointed superintendent. "More than ever," Pope reminded Grant, "the tone and character of the army will depend upon the graduates now in service and those who will graduate from the academy. I need not tell you either how many things purely military but most essential to a young officer are omitted at West Point because neither superinten-

dent nor professors have ever served with the army." Too many new second lieutenants had been ruined because the academy had failed to prepare them for
army life.[62]

Pope concluded his business as department commander quickly. At Fort Leavenworth in early September, he briefed Hancock on his tour of inspection, then
set out for the Horton family home in Pomeroy, Ohio, to await Grant's reply.[63]

Grant tried to accommodate Pope, recommending to Secretary Stanton he
be permitted to choose any department command he wished, consistent with
his rank, except those of Hooker and Edward R. S. Canby. But as nothing was
available in the East, Grant suggested Pope apply for a six-month leave of absence.

Pope considered the matter carefully. On the one hand, he disliked "to be idle
for such a length of time and would prefer to be on some sort of duty." On the
other, he cherished the thought of spending time with relatives and friends and
wanted Clara comfortable. With a second child on the way, more children hoped
for, and only twenty years until forced retirement, Pope grew concerned about
providing for his family's future, beyond what an army paycheck offered. He
needed time for business ventures that he hoped to undertake with Valentine B.
Horton. Pope also wanted time to refight Second Bull Run, which had never been
far from his mind. In early 1866, former *New York Times* war correspondent William Swinton had published *Campaigns of the Army of the Potomac,* in which he
blamed Pope for the defeat and claimed Pope had lost control of the army before
the battle opened. In May, an outraged Pope had asked Thomas C. H. Smith, who
had begun work on his own book about Second Bull Run, to pen a reply. Nothing had yet come of either that request or Smith's book, and Pope hoped to meet
with Smith at length on the matter. "I have been so much misrepresented, traduced in many ways, and so unjustly dealt with that I begin to feel discouraged,"
he confided to Smith. "It is a trial for a man not conscious of having failed in any
respect to perform his duty to find himself so persistently followed by calumny."
Having served the country for twenty-four years with no real leave of absence,
Pope concluded to accept Grant's offer. On October 1, 1866, he hung up the army
blue for six months.[64]

14 I Find the Situation Very Perplexing

For John Pope the year 1866 closed on a bittersweet note. On December 16, Clara gave birth to their second child, a boy, whom they named John Horton. A week later, reading the newspapers at the Horton family home, Pope saw realized the grim prognosis of a Plains war made in his February report and repeated that summer to Sherman. Commenting in August on recently concluded peace talks at Fort Laramie, Pope had warned Sherman, "I do not consider the treaties lately made with the Sioux worth the paper they are written on. I have myself no doubt that hostilities will again break out before the beginning of winter." On December 21, Captain William J. Fetterman and a ninety-two-man detachment were slaughtered near Fort Kearny by Teton Sioux.

The Fetterman disaster stunned and outraged the army. Making perhaps the most infelicitous public utterance of his career, Sherman told Grant, "We must act with vindictive earnestness against the Sioux, even to their extermination, men, women, and children." Besides a call for genocide, the Fetterman affair also occasioned the army's first real effort to have the Bureau of Indian Affairs returned to the War Department, just as Pope had championed for three years. Grant now became the most vocal proponent of a transfer. He lobbied members of Congress and had his Seneca Indian aide, Colonel Ely S. Parker, draft a transfer bill. To buttress Parker's legislation, Grant asked Pope to restate for the record "the leading reasons why the Indian bureau should be transferred to the War Department" and to explain them to Congress.[1]

Never one to pass up a chance to be heard, Pope was pleased to interrupt his leave of absence for a brief trip to the capital. On January 25, 1867, he handed Grant his report. It was a cogent, if smug, justification for an immediate end to divided jurisdiction over Indian affairs. Conflict was inevitable between two departments whose interests were so divergent. Explained Pope, "As soon as the military forces, after a hard campaign, have succeeded in forcing the Indians into such a position that punishment is possible, the Indian, seeing the impossibility of avoiding it, immediately proclaims his wish to make peace. The Indian agent, anxious, for manifest reasons, to negotiate a treaty, at once interferes 'to protect' (as he expresses it) the Indians from the troops, and arrests the further prosecution of the military expedition, and the whole labor and cost of the campaign are lost," he complained. "While the army is fighting the Indians at one end of the line, Indian agents are making treaties and furnishing supplies at the other end, which supplies are at once used to keep up the conflict."

Indian agents profited handsomely from this recurring cycle of war and treaties. Unlike civilian agents, army officers, whose "first and great interest is to preserve peace," could be counted on to distribute annuities honestly; were an officer to do otherwise, argued Pope, he would risk the lifelong odium of dishonorable discharge. "The Indian agent, on the other hand, accepts his office for a limited time and for a specific purpose, and he finds it easy when he has secured his ends (the rapid acquisition of money) to account for his removal from office on political grounds."

Military control over Indian affairs would permit the army to take preventive measures, rather than merely to respond after the Indians "have devastated many miles of settlements, or massacred parties of emigrants or travellers." Because the army had no jurisdiction over Indians officially at peace, by the time military commanders learned of an uprising, "the worst has been accomplished, and the Indians have escaped from the scene." Finally, by eliminating the vast army of civilian Indian superintendents, agents, jobbers, and other assorted hangers-on who infested the frontier, exclusive military jurisdiction "would save the government annually a sum of money which I will not venture to estimate." Army officers performing these duties would receive no extra compensation.

Secretary of War Stanton circulated Pope's letter in cabinet, where it made an impression. Gideon Welles, who had condemned the military in general for Indian hostilities and Pope in particular for the Powder River debacle, now conceded Indian agents—"political party adventurers and speculators, without conscience or principles"—to be a root cause of Indian troubles. On January 28,

Stanton submitted copies of Pope's letter to the House and Senate Committees on Military Affairs. Pope's arguments helped ease Parker's transfer bill out of committee and onto the floor of Congress, where it carried in the House of Representatives. But Senate peace proponents offered Sherman's harsh words about exterminating the Sioux as proof the army could not be trusted with Indian management, and the measure was defeated in the upper chamber. Secretary of the Interior Browning, who also read Pope's report, persuaded President Johnson to appoint another peace commission to conciliate the Sioux, rather than approve the "crude" policies Grant and Pope urged.[2]

Although of great moment to John Pope, legislation on Indian matters was but a distraction to members of the Thirty-ninth Congress, for whom Southern reconstruction was the overriding concern. Having triumphed in the fall 1866 congressional elections, Radical Republicans set about to dismantle the conservative policies of President Johnson, who had encouraged the Southern electorate to reject the Fourteenth Amendment and nodded approvingly as the former Confederate states enacted black codes that made the condition of freedpersons more deplorable than had slavery. A welter of proposals relating to Southern reconstruction filled legislative hoppers, but the bill that survived a presidential veto to emerge on March 2, 1867, as law was the First Reconstruction Act, known also as the "Military Bill." A stunning capitulation of civil prerogatives, the act divided the former Rebel states into five military districts and called upon the president to appoint a Regular Army general as commander of each, with sufficient military power to enforce his authority, which was sweeping. Labeling existing Southern state governments illegal and detrimental to "peace and good order," the act assigned district commanders the duty "to protect all persons in their rights of person and property, to suppress insurrection, disorder, and violence, and to punish, or cause to be punished, all disturbers of the public peace and criminals." How this was to be done was left to a commander's discretion: he might allow civil courts to retain jurisdiction or might supplant them with military tribunals; in either case, "all interference under color of state authority with the exercise of military authority under this act shall be null and void."

Military rule would cease when Congress readmitted a state to representation, which could occur only after the people of the state had elected a constitutional convention, framed a new state constitution in conformity with the United States Constitution, and ratified the Fourteenth Amendment. Until then, existing state governments were provisional only, subject to "the paramount authority of the United States at any time to abolish, modify, control, or supersede" them. A supplemental act passed over presidential veto on March 23 set forth the particulars of electing delegates to the conventions. District commanders were to effect a state-by-state registration of voters by September 1, in accordance with a prescribed oath, and apportion delegates in proportion to registration figures. All adult males—white and black—who were not disfranchised for having partici- pated in the rebellion were eligible to vote for delegates. Commanders were to appoint as many three-man boards of registration as they deemed necessary, publish election results, and, if a majority of votes cast favored a state constitu- tional convention, order the elected delegates (chosen in the same election) to convene within sixty days.[3]

On March 11, a general order announced the five generals selected for recon- struction command. Virginia, the First District, was given to Brevet Major Gen- eral John M. Schofield; the Carolinas, the Second District, went to Major Gener- al Daniel E. Sickles; the Third District, consisting of Alabama, Georgia, and Florida, went to Major General George H. Thomas; Mississippi and Arkansas, comprising the Fourth District, were placed under Brevet Major General E. O. C. Ord; and the Fifth District—Louisiana and Texas—went to Major General Philip H. Sheridan.

Stanton had made the selections, but Grant availed himself of them to help Pope. Thomas's assignment to the Third District opened up his Department of the Cumberland, which Grant promptly gave Pope. Pope was delighted—department headquarters were in Louisville, which would put him among paternal relatives and near his own mother in St. Louis, Clara's family in Pomeroy, and his emerg- ing business interests in Cincinnati. But Thomas, who outranked Pope, protest- ed his assignment to the South, and the order was revoked. Thomas was to remain in Louisville, and Pope would go to Montgomery, Alabama, in his place.

The change pleased neither President Johnson nor Pope. None too enthusi- astic about executing a law he had vetoed, the president had permitted Secretary Stanton to select the district commanders. When Thomas, probably the least objectionable of all to Johnson on political grounds, objected to his assignment, Stanton was pleased to give the Third District command to Pope. For some time the unsympathetic feelings of most Regular Army generals toward Republican political objectives, particularly party plans for raising the black to the ballot box in the South, had troubled Stanton. Pope strongly and vocally supported these aims; in fact, while on leave that fall he had hazarded his career on their behalf.

Events in the South during 1866 had revealed growing disagreement between the president and the Supreme Court on one side, and Congress and the army on the other, regarding the army's role in the postwar South and the general course of reconstruction. Southern courts reborn under Johnson's auspices were hearing suits against army personnel for damages arising under martial law, and the Supreme Court had questioned the army's very right to invoke martial law. On neither score was President Johnson helpful to the military. He countenanced outrages against soldiers and blacks by unreconstructed rebels, whom his lenient policies had returned to power, and opposed black suffrage, which most generals thought necessary to break the strength of the old secessionist class. One by one during the last months of 1866, the army's leaders entered the political struggle. Stanton, Grant, Sheridan, Sickles, Ord, and Pope aligned themselves—openly or otherwise—with Republicans in Congress, while Sherman, Winfield Hancock, and George Meade favored President Johnson.

Pope found himself the first spokesman of the pro-Congress clique. In the late summer of 1866, city police in New Orleans had killed 156 black delegates to a Union convention. Trouble had been predicted, but President Johnson had prohibited the military from involving itself. The New Orleans riot infuriated Stanton and Grant, both of whom believed a clear statement of army prerogatives imperative. They asked Pope, then on leave in Pomeroy, to make a speech defending martial law. As a captain five years earlier, Pope had risked a court-martial for publicly challenging President Buchanan's management of the secessionist crisis; he now proved no less willing to incur the wrath of President Johnson. Speaking in Cincinnati, he argued that the suspension of military power in the South would immediately allow "the old political and personal influences [to] resume their activity. Northern Copperheads would flock to the aid of these Southern Bourbons, tearing the Republic asunder and plunging the nation again into war."[4]

Such sentiments made Pope a favorite of congressional Radicals. The powerful Republican congressman James G. Blaine spoke for his colleagues when he welcomed Pope to the South, as Pope's "political convictions were of a very positive character, and not at all in sympathy" with the president's. While displeased, Johnson did not "interpose any serious objection," and Pope was sent his new orders on March 15.[5]

Northern public opinion generally approved of his selection—one journal praised him as "a moderate Republican and an excellent administrator," but Pope himself was crestfallen. He received word of the change while at the home of his friend, attorney Lewis E. Mills, in St. Louis, attending the funeral of his mother, Lucretia. Saddened by her death, Pope fell ill, and he scribbled his reply from bed. "The first assignment was very agreeable and satisfactory," he told Grant; "of the last I had best perhaps say nothing." Although "still far from well," Pope set out for Montgomery on March 25, but not before thanking Grant for the commanding general's efforts on his behalf. "Whilst the assignment to the Third or in fact any other military district under the Reconstruction Act is not pleasant I trust you will believe that I shall go very cheerfully and do the best I can," he assured Grant. "I know you intended and arranged to give me a much more satisfactory command and I am greatly obliged to you for it."[6]

Armed with a copy of the First Reconstruction Act and its supplement, but lacking "any interpretation of those acts, or any orders whatever, touching on the performance of my duties," Pope arrived in Montgomery on April 1, 1867. As did his fellow military governors, Pope made one of his first official acts the promulgation of general orders explaining his basic policies. He and his colleagues reminded Southerners that existing civil governments were provisional and subject to absolute military control. They exhorted officials to carry out their duties and see that justice was administered faithfully and impartially, and they called upon the people to cooperate. Pope added a note of warning to his pronouncement. Left to place his own construction upon the First Reconstruction Act, Pope deduced its "manifest design [was] to free the southern people from the baleful influence of old political leaders, and of the bitterness and hostility to the United States government with which those leaders were industriously and persistently tormenting the less intelligent portion of the community." As most of the provisional state governments were composed of these unrepentant secessionists, Pope cautioned civil authorities in his district to "confine themselves strictly to the performance of their official duties [and] not use any influence to deter or dissuade the people from taking an active part in reconstructing their state governments." Pope and Phil Sheridan both promised to remove no local officials unless they hindered reconstruction; he and Ord said they would fill civil vacancies by appointment. Pope also prohibited any elections not called for in the First Reconstruction Act.[7]

Just two days into his governorship, Pope realized district headquarters were in the wrong place. Alabamans seemed resigned to Reconstruction, and the governor and most state officers pledged their full cooperation. Pope found the commanding general in Alabama, Wager Swayne, "intelligent, earnest," and as committed to congressional policy as he. Georgia, however, was a different matter. The state senate had rejected the Fourteenth Amendment unanimously, the house with only two dissenting voices. Popular antipathy toward reconstruction was nearly as absolute. The military commander there was indifferent toward reconstruction; Governor Charles J. Jenkins had yet to declare himself on the subject; and the few prominent Unionists in the state urged Pope to come to Georgia at once. Also, General Thomas had suggested to Pope, when the two conferred in Louisville five days earlier, that he might wish to relocate to Atlanta, as that city offered better communications with Washington and a healthier climate in the summer. Now Pope had both compelling political and practical causes for requesting the change, which Grant endorsed and Stanton approved on April 13.[8]

His presence in Georgia was imperative, more so than Pope had assumed. No sooner had he settled into Atlanta's National Hotel than Pope found himself a defendant in an original proceeding in the United States Supreme Court, brought by Governor Jenkins on behalf of the state of Georgia. Determined to thwart what he regarded as a "palpably unconstitutional and grievously oppressive" measure, Jenkins asked the Supreme Court to enjoin Secretary Stanton, General Grant, and General Pope from enforcing it in Georgia. His legal demand—which the court later dismissed—recited what one supporter termed a "quaint anomaly": that the failure of Georgia to secede fixed her status in the Union under the very philosophy by which the North had waged the war; that status was confirmed when Congress had submitted the Fourteenth Amendment to Georgia for ratification. From Washington, Governor Jenkins on April 10 issued an address to the people of Georgia, advising "a firm but temperate refusal of acquiescence in the adoption of the [Military] Bill, and a patient, manly endurance of military government, until better counsels shall prevail at the Federal capital—we, meantime, strictly observe law and order, and vigorously addressing ourselves to industrial pursuits."[9]

What Governor Jenkins counseled was passive resistance; nonetheless, any effort by a public official to dissuade the people from cooperating with Reconstruction was a violation of Pope's general orders. Consequently, on April 17 Pope drew up an order removing Jenkins and submitted it to Grant for his information. Exercising a restraint inconceivable for him in younger days, Pope decided to withhold the removal order until Jenkins had a chance to explain himself. Summoned to district headquarters, Jenkins pleaded ignorance of the general orders, which had been issued during his absence, and promised to abide by them in the future. He supposed he had been "using such freedom in the public expression of opinion relative to public matters as seems still to be accorded to the citizens of the republic, not imagining that it was abridged by the accident of the speaker or writer holding office." Unwilling to let the remark pass and wishing to set the record straight publicly, on April 22 Pope wrote Jenkins an open letter reminding him that his tenure was provisional and explaining the differences between private and public expressions of opinion. "I only require that the civil machinery of the state of Georgia be not perverted so as to frustrate the laws of the United States," asserted Pope. "It is manifestly impossible for me to perform the duties required of me by the acts of Congress while the provisional governor of the state is openly denouncing them and giving advice to the public in his official capacity." The next day, he promulgated an order restating the ban on such public utterances by civil officials, which he said would be interpreted in the broadest possible sense.[10]

Pope was frustrated with his duties, and it showed. Like his fellow district commanders, he needed help in charting the murky waters of constitutional law and civil administration. To Grant's endorsement of Pope's abortive order to remove Jenkins, in which the commanding general suggested it might be better to suspend Jenkins and bring him before a military trial, rather than remove him outright, Pope responded candidly, "I am much gratified to know that my course thus far has met your approval—I find the situation here very perplexing and it is not always easy to decide what is best to be done." Sometimes his temper got the best of him, and the old Pope family arrogance surfaced more frequently, as when he refused to speak with two of Grant's trusted aides, Horace Porter and Orville Babcock, who called on him at his quarters to discuss how matters were progressing in Georgia. But in the main, he showed moderation in the discharge of his duties. While he shared their political convictions, Pope refused to entertain a petition from Savannah Republicans who urged he remove Mayor Edward C. Anderson, a Democrat, and appoint a Republican in his place. He also rebuffed efforts of the Republican Club of Jacksonville—perhaps his best allies in Florida— to obtain the dismissal of that state's Democratic governor. Similarly, Pope rejected a petition from Florida Unionists asking for a wholesale removal of state officers so as to speed the work of reconstruction. Such an act, Pope told Grant, would simply make them "martyrs to military despotism" and allow them to stir further unrest; "retained in office and silenced on these questions they are harmless." The Union men of Florida must understand that "over zeal or the indulgence of feelings naturally well-warranted and to be respected as they deserve to be, will lead to difficulty if not indeed to disaster in the attempt to secure a great and final result." Although he wished to be circumspect, Pope told Grant he would not hesitate to remove officials for malfeasance, gross incompetence, or dereliction of duty.[11]

That resolve was tested three weeks later, when a crisis broke out in Alabama. On the night of May 14, Congressman W. D. Kelley of Pennsylvania tried to deliver a pro-reconstruction speech in Mobile. A Yankee harangue was more than the crowd could bear, and it grew restive. Several rowdies taunted Kelley with shouts of "Put him down," "Give that dog a bone," and "How many Negroes and pianos did you steal?" For good measure, a heckler fired a pistol shot at the podium. With that, a riot broke out. No police were on hand—although violence had been feared before the meeting began—and by the time they arrived, one man lay dead and several others were wounded.[12]

Pope responded swiftly. He removed Mayor Jones M. Withers, who happened to have been a former Confederate general, and also the chief of police, for "not taking proper measures to suppress" the riot. On the recommendation of General Swayne, he later dismissed the board of aldermen and the city council. To prevent any future misunderstanding as to the responsibilities of local officials, Pope issued General Orders Number Twenty-five. It required both mayors and chiefs of police to be present at "every public political meeting" held in their jurisdictions, with enough police on hand to prevent disturbances; at meetings outside town limits, county sheriffs would be expected to keep order. The edict included a standard threat: if a riot occurred and it could not be shown that the proper civil officials "were present and did actively and faithfully perform their duties," they would be removed and held criminally liable. Army officers, detailed from local commands to observe all political meetings, would decide their guilt or innocence.

The Mobile riot resonated in Washington, where the attorney general was preparing an opinion as to whether the First Reconstruction Act empowered military district commanders to remove civil officials. Assuming his removals would meet with some objection from President Johnson, who hoped to curb military authority, Pope wrote Grant a lengthy defense of his actions. Should the president interfere to restore the removed officials, Pope told Grant, he would be compelled to impose absolute martial law. That, Pope assured Grant, was an outcome he hoped to avoid. Concluded Pope, "The fact that I have interfered not at all with the civil administration in any other place, ought to be good evidence that when I do interpose I do so reluctantly, and only because I think it cannot be avoided, in view of the security of person and property to citizens, for whose safety I am held responsible by the law."

Both Grant and Stanton sustained Pope. The secretary of war availed himself of the Mobile riot to offer the president his written opinion that the First Reconstruction Act gave district commanders the power to remove civil officers; in this instance, Pope was warranted in doing so. Stanton "respectfully recommended" that the president let the action stand.[13]

Besides the Jenkins petition and the Mobile affair, there was much other business to occupy Pope's attention. Not since Second Bull Run had he been so overtaxed; never before had he felt so acutely the burdens of administration, the more so as the whole notion of military government was noxious to him. Pope was gratified to learn Johnson approved of his dismissal of the Mobile municipal government and relieved when the Supreme Court dismissed Jenkins's suit. But vexing problems remained. How should he deal with former Rebel officers who agitated against Reconstruction, Pope asked Grant; did their paroles preclude such activity? Where were the staff officers he so desperately needed? Until mid-April Pope worked alone. Should he regulate commerce, as Sickles had done in the Second District? Pope opted to keep clear of the matter; he did not "think himself warranted" in making "violent and radical changes in the ordinary course of civil business." How to respond when, in early April, the town of Tuscumbia, Alabama, held municipal elections in violation of the First Reconstruction Act? Pope elected to annul the elections and appoint a mayor himself.

Filling vacant offices seemed incessant. Apart from the twenty-seven appointments Pope made in the wake of the Mobile riot, in May alone he filled fifty-seven vacancies by appointment, including mayors, tax collectors, sheriffs, justices of the peace, and school superintendents. Whenever possible, Pope appointed men who favored congressional Reconstruction. Pope also answered countless appeals from officials and ordinary citizens that he intercede in civil matters. Most he refused, as when one of Georgia's first black state senators, Tunis Campbell, asked him to purge the city government of Darien for "unjust and partial administration of the civil laws," or when his old West Point classmate and battlefield foe, James Longstreet, now turned Radical sympathizer, asked the military to intervene in a civil case in Alabama.[14]

Of the myriad problems confronting them, that which gave Pope and his fellow district commanders their greatest and most persistent headaches was the registration of eligible voters before the September 1 deadline laid down in the First Reconstruction Act. Apart from the deadline and the requirement that local boards of registration be composed of three loyal citizens, little regarding registration was clearly established in the act. The act was unacceptably vague on the most vexing question of all: precisely what antebellum office-holding and wartime activities caused disfranchisement? Congress had said only that a prospective registrant must swear he had never been "an executive or judicial officer of any state" before the war and subsequently had not "engaged in insurrection or rebellion against the United States, or given aid or comfort to the enemies thereof." Both John Schofield and Phil Sheridan requested clarification from Attorney General Henry Stanbery, who evinced no disposition to act quickly on the matter. Each district commander then worked out a registration plan to suit himself.[15]

Concerning registration, Pope believed the Reconstruction Act made "manifest" three requirements: "First, that the work should be done with the greatest dispatch in order to complete it by September 1; Second, that the registration should be as thorough as it could possibly be made, and should include every man not disqualified by the acts themselves; [and] Third, that it should be done with the least expense to the government." To these, Pope added two personal imperatives: to give Republicans as much time as possible, consistent with the law, to organize, and to get out the black vote to the greatest extent possible. Northern Republican and (often self-styled) philanthropic groups already were educating blacks as to their rights and could be counted upon to get black males registered. To their efforts, Pope added a few devices of his own. He decreed that each three-man registration board should contain a black member. Publicly Pope termed this arrangement an act "of simple justice to the colored race, enfranchised by the reconstruction acts." It was that, and more. The presence of a black registrar not only would encourage the freedman vote, but also would discourage disloyal whites from registering. As Pope told Grant, "I think this arrangement will keep many of the 'dignity party' who would otherwise register and vote against a convention entirely aloof. They will not be willing to be questioned and cross-examined by and compelled to take an oath administered by a darkey." Ostensibly to foster a wide and impartial registration, but really, as Pope confessed privately to Grant, better to ensure the black vote, he also decreed that registrars would be paid on the basis of the number of persons registered. Fifteen cents was paid for each urban voter registered, forty cents apiece for those in the most distant and sparsely settled counties, with compensation for more accessible rural areas graduated between those limits. Finally, Pope enjoined registrars to "explain to all persons who have not heretofore enjoyed the right of suffrage what are their political rights and privileges, and the necessity of exercising them upon all proper occasions."[16]

There was nothing improper in Pope's actions—he had been given wide authority to implement the demands of Congress, which happened to coincide with his own political convictions, and he intended to do so as aggressively as the law and the dictates of conscience permitted. Others took more questionable steps: Sheridan, for instance, had army officers directly supervise the boards of registration, whereas Pope tried to keep the military removed from the process. With respect to disfranchisement, he also interpreted "executive and judicial officers" far more broadly than did Pope, to include even auctioneers and sextons of cemeteries. Schofield established six-man boards, composed of an equal number of whites and blacks, each of whom had the power to declare a person disfranchised.[17]

Fearful that President Johnson and Attorney General Stanbery would succeed in watering down Congress's reconstruction laws by interpreting them narrowly, Stanton and Grant encouraged district commanders to enforce the measures of Congress "according to the spirit of their acts." Both were particularly pleased with the aggressive work of Sheridan and Pope.[18]

A crisis of authority threatened in June, when Stanbery made known his opinions on registration and on the general powers of district commanders. As to the former, Stanbery ruled that antebellum municipal officers and those state employees whose duties had been function-specific, such as bank examiners and road commissioners, were not disfranchised. He also determined that registration boards could not reject any prospective applicant who insisted on taking the oath. With respect to the latter, Stanbery ruled that the Reconstruction Act did not give district commanders the power to alter state governments or dismiss civil authorities. On June 20, the Adjutant General's Office transmitted Stanbery's opinion on registration to district commanders.

Pope and his fellow military governors appealed to Grant for guidance. Were they to regard Stanbery's ruling as binding? As Pope complained to Grant on June 27, "Ten days ago I had made and published instructions to registers [sic] which will have to be dropped if the attorney general's opinion is enforced." Because Congress had "imposed on me alone" responsibility for registration in his district, Pope told Grant he would ignore Stanbery's "opinion" unless positively instructed otherwise. No, Grant hastened to assure Pope, he should enforce his own construction of the Military Bill. "The opinion of the attorney general has not been distributed to district commanders in language or manner entitling it to the force of an order, nor can I suppose that the president intended it to have such force," Grant added. Actually, Johnson had intended Stanbery's ruling to have the force of an order, but apparently he was unwilling to press the point over the objections of Grant and Stanton, both of whom rejected the attorney general's interpretations.[19]

Congress came swiftly to the support of the beleaguered district commanders with the passage on July 19 of a second supplement to the First Reconstruction Act, known as the Third Reconstruction Act. Drafted by Stanton, with the help of Grant, the law granted district commanders the express authority to remove civil officials, subject to the approval of the general-in-chief, rather than the president, and confirmed all removals already made. The act also overruled Stanbery's narrow interpretation of disfranchisement. Most significant, Congress ordained that district commanders and those they appointed would in no way be bound "by any opinion of any civil officer of the United States."[20]

For Pope, this expanded power came none too soon. Southern opponents of congressional reconstruction were becoming increasingly strident, particularly in Georgia. Robert Toombs, an ardent secessionist and former Confederate general, had returned from European exile in June to organize an anti-Reconstruction party and to fulminate against the military regime. Former governor Herschel Johnson told whites to register but "never to embrace [congressional] despotism." Former Confederate senator Benjamin H. Hill, only recently pardoned by the president, indulged in an orgy of righteous indignation over the "Hellish dynasty" Congress had imposed on Georgia. His anti-Reconstruction newspaper articles and speeches made him the darling of white supremacists and the bane of Pope, whom Hill included with congressional Radicals as among the "perjured assassins of liberty," and "hell-born rioters of sacred things." Perhaps hoping to provoke a sharp response, such as would make him a political martyr, Hill went out of his way to torment Pope. Despite an injunction to avoid incendiary subjects, in a speech at Davis Hall in Atlanta on July 16, at which Pope was present, Hill denounced the Radical Congress with some of his most inflammatory rhetoric to date. He advised Georgians to register but otherwise not cooperate with Reconstruction.[21]

Although invested with the indisputable authority to silence Hill and those of his sort, Pope acted cautiously. To Grant, whom he sent a newspaper clipping of Hill's Davis Hall speech, Pope complained that Hill's actions made a mockery of government clemency and reflected "the hopelessness of any satisfactory reconstruction of the southern states while such men retain influence." Nonetheless, Pope would allow Hill and other reactionaries not then holding public office "the widest latitude of speech consistent with law and the public peace," so that "the battle may be fought out now and openly."

With rare prescience, Pope cautioned Grant, "These politicians are wily and sagacious. They will make no laws which are not equal on their face to all men. It is in the execution of these laws, which seem to bear equally on all, that wrong will be done and a condition of things produced which bears no resemblance to free government except in name." Candor compelled Pope to say a tendency toward violence and intimidation prevailed among Southern whites of all political shades, including the reconstructionists. The condition of blacks he found far more encouraging. "The earnest and touching anxiety of the freed people to learn, cannot but make a profound impression upon the mind of anyone who has had the opportunity to observe it," Pope told Grant, who shared Pope's hopes for the freedpersons. "It may safely be said that the marvelous progress made in education and knowledge by these people finds no parallel in the history of mankind. It becomes us, therefore, to guard jealously against any reaction which may and will check this most desirable progress of the colored race." Himself increasingly at odds with the president, Grant advised district commanders to ignore restrictive opinions emanating from the White House, as he had those of Stanbery. Thus he applauded Pope's views as sound, "both in the construction which you give to the laws of Congress and to the duties of the supporters of good government."[22]

Pope backed up his rhetoric with action that cost him what little popularity he yet enjoyed among conservative Southern whites. Because the black population of his district was very much unsettled, Pope was afraid changes of residence might deprive freedmen of their vote. Consequently, with the strong concurrence of General Grant, on August 15 he issued General Order Number Fifty, which directed boards of registration to provide a duly registered voter about to depart their precinct with a certificate of registration, which would enable him to vote elsewhere in the state. Four days later, Pope mandated that jurors for both civil and criminal cases be drawn solely and without racial discrimination from lists of voters registered under the Reconstruction Acts. Jurists were required to swear under penalty of perjury that they were duly registered.[23]

A furor of protest arose from Southern Democrats, particularly in Georgia, where an 1866 statute had barred blacks from jury service. One of the state's most prominent jurists, Superior Court Judge Augustus Reese of the Ocmulgee Circuit, led the opposition. He refused to comply with the "Jury Order" on the grounds that it conflicted with the laws and constitution of Georgia. Loathe to remove one so popular, Pope tried to reason with Reese, reminding him in a public letter of the primacy of federal over state laws and imploring him to carry out the order. Reese refused, and Pope was compelled to remove him.[24]

Most obnoxious to Southern whites was General Order Number Forty-nine. Issued on August 12, it prohibited official patronage of newspapers that opposed congressional reconstruction or sought to intimidate civil officials appointed by Pope through "threats of future penalties for their official acts," the latter a very real problem that had rendered it difficult to find qualified whites willing to accept office. Governor Jenkins protested that the order was unrealistic: only six papers in Georgia met Pope's criteria, and state law required that all official notices be published in newspapers throughout the state, otherwise they were invalid; furthermore, notices of county officers must be published in a paper of the same county. Pope reminded Jenkins, as he had Judge Reese, that federal law took precedence over state statutes. To the "hideous outcry" that went up charging him with abridging the freedom of the press, Pope replied sardonically, "I was surprised to learn, for the first time, that in Georgia and Alabama freedom of the press is inseparably connected with the possession of official patronage. I am under the belief that the very opposite opinion is entertained everywhere else." He reflected on the irony that the newspapers that complained the loudest were the very ones that had forced loyal papers out of existence during the Civil War, aided by a Confederate state government that had patronized only the secessionist press. As was often the case, Pope's words proved harsher than his acts, and he enforced the "Newspaper Order" only sporadically.[25]

Employing the same logic to official patronage and freedom of speech, in mid-August Pope ordered the state endowment for the University of Georgia suspended at Athens after a student, who happened also to be a member of the Georgia general assembly and a protégé of Benjamin H. Hill, closed the commencement exercises with an incendiary, anti-Reconstruction speech. As a school trustee and professor of law, Hill was on hand to whip up the crowd, which "cheered rapturously and showered bouquets upon" the student. Pope interpreted the event as a veiled effort by Hill, in his capacity as trustee, to bring the university to "the support of his political course." Governor Jenkins protested to President Johnson, and the matter was discussed in cabinet, where Grant declared himself unwilling to revoke the order "unless peremptorily ordered to do so." After Hill offered to resign from the university board, Pope settled the matter himself by reinstating the grant.[26]

Pope had taken his most aggressive steps to enforce congressional reconstruction during a time of great apprehension among the army high command. Furious over Stanton's role in drafting the Third Reconstruction Act and fed up with his obstreperousness in cabinet, on August 5 President Johnson demanded the secretary's resignation, but he had to content himself with Stanton's suspension. In Stanton's place, Johnson appointed Grant interim secretary of war, while permitting him to retain his status as commanding general. Privately, Grant continued Stanton's uncompromising support of congressional reconstruction; publicly, however, he wore an aspect of circumspection, which annoyed his Republican friends and no doubt troubled his vulnerable district commanders. Grant was confident he could protect them from presidential retaliation until on August 17 Johnson removed Phil Sheridan from the Fifth District over the strong protest of the entire cabinet. A few days later, Johnson dismissed Dan Sickles from Second District command.[27]

Among district commanders, after Sheridan and Sickles, Pope was most closely associated in the public mind with congressional reconstruction. Rumors spread among hopeful Democrats that he would be the next to fall. Republican stalwarts like the *Chicago Tribune* editor Joseph Medill were outraged that Pope might be "put out" for having "done [his] duty and carried out the laws of Congress." Pope himself felt exceedingly vulnerable: Secretary Stanton, his sole advocate in a cabinet aligned against Congress, was gone, and Grant had proven incapable of sustaining his favorite subordinate, Phil Sheridan. On September 7, Pope asked Grant to advise him, "if consistent with propriety[,] whether there is any probability of my being relieved from this command. I am about to rent a house for the winter and don't wish to commit myself to the bargain unless I am to retain command." Three days later, Pope again telegraphed Grant confidentially to say he hoped to remain in command at least until the elections were over. "Two months ago I should have been rejoiced to be relieved from these duties," confided Pope. "But now having completed the registration which has been the hardest work of all, and being just on the eve of elections which will show the result of this work, I should be very unwilling to jeopard[ize] the certain result of being replaced by some one else less familiar with the situation." In the meantime, he would act cautiously, so as to give the president no grounds for dismissing him.

Grant hardly knew how to answer Pope. He too had heard rumors that Pope might be relieved but was unable to assess their credibility. He had "not a word of this from official sources," but then again, he had not been consulted in advance of the removals of Sheridan and Sickles. Confessed Grant, "All I can say is that I would not involve myself in any contract which would be burdensome if removal takes place, were I you."[28]

Amid the general opprobrium heaped upon him in the South, one piece of news heartened Pope. Governor Robert M. Patton of Alabama had written Grant on September 3 to lobby against any dismissal of Pope. "The general has uniformly manifested the most anxious solicitude for the execution of the reconstruction laws in a perfectly fair and impartial manner, with a view of a speedy and satisfactory accomplishment of the objects for which those laws were enacted," said Patton of Pope's administration. "General Pope's rule has been mild, and free from all semblance of tyranny or even harshness. He has in no way interfered with freedom of speech or freedom of the press." As for himself, Grant approved fully of Pope's official conduct, and he promised to wave Patton's letter before the cabinet before acceding to any order for his removal.[29]

Besides seeking Grant's help in divining the future, in September 1867 Pope also looked to the commanding general to help prevent a rewriting of the past. Nine months earlier, Fitz John Porter had written President Johnson requesting he appoint a court to reconsider the proceedings that had resulted in his dismissal. Not until September 12 did Johnson forward it to Grant for his opinion. Pope had gotten wind of Porter's appeal, and on September 13 he remonstrated with Grant against a reopening of the case. Were Grant to feel compelled to appoint a commission to study the new testimony Porter claimed to have, Pope hoped the commanding general, knowing as he did "the bitter personal and official controversies which this case occasioned," would select "officers of the highest rank who have never had any connection with the Army of the Potomac."

Apparently well informed of one another's intentions, over the next several days Pope and Porter competed for Grant's regard. On September 16, Porter told Grant he had conclusive testimony from Longstreet and other Confederate generals showing he could not have made the attack Pope had requested on August 29, 1862, without his corps having certainly been annihilated. Pope telegraphed Grant that same day. As for Porter's contention his attack would have failed, Pope reasoned, "If in a general battle a corps or division commander receiving a positive order to attack a portion of the enemy's line has the right to disobey this order on the ground that he does not believe the attack would be successful I cannot see how any combinations can be made by the commanding general or how he can expect that his orders will be obeyed. How can a corps commander know his attack is not intended to prevent the enemy's troops in front of him from reinforcing other parts of their line upon which an attack is being made?"

Pope couched the latter point in terms Grant would appreciate, as he had won one of his most signal victories in that very manner. Asked Pope, "Had Sherman failed to attack the enemy's right at Chattanooga on the grounds that the enemy was in strong force and he would be repulsed (as indeed was the fact) what would have become of Hooker, what indeed of the entire victory at Chattanooga?"

Pope's arguments told. Firmly convinced of Porter's guilt, Grant declined to endorse Porter's appeal. Rather than refuse it outright, however, he suggested to the president the matter be referred to the attorney general for his opinion as to the legality of a second trial for one convicted by court-martial. He also asked the judge advocate general of the army, who happened to be Joseph Holt, for his views. Not surprisingly, given his role in the original court-martial, Holt concluded a retrial "would be a measure wholly opposed to principle and precedent and to sound public policy."[30]

Not only could Pope take satisfaction in seeing Porter's first appeal to the president and the War Department rebuked, but he also might be encouraged by the efforts of congressional supporters on his behalf. Representative James A. Garfield introduced a measure prohibiting presidential reappointment of any cashiered officer without Senate confirmation. After the bill passed the House, Radical senators Zachariah Chandler and Benjamin F. Wade orchestrated Senate approval.[31]

Close upon the "Jury Order" controversy came a new wave of Southern censure to torment Pope. Muted complaints of "sharp political practice" in the drawing of election districts were heard in Florida, and to a lesser degree in Alabama. But from Georgia came loud and blistering condemnation of Pope's handiwork. As Pope complained to Grant in late October, "The inexpressibly vile newspapers of this state, I doubt not aided and encouraged by the Ben Hills of the state[,] are circulating and will doubtless represent to the authorities, that I have as they term it, gerrymandered the state in apportioning delegates so as to give a majority of the districts to the colored voters." Governor Jenkins added his voice in protest, telling President Johnson that Pope had selected election districts so that "an undue advantage is given to the colored race over the white race."[32]

Pope denied categorically that any "idea of Negro or other majorities entered my head in this apportionment," and he dismissed the allegations as a good indication of "rebel" desperation. But the evidence seemed to sustain the charges. Voter registration had yielded a slender white majority: 95,214 white voters as against 93,457 blacks. However, the election districts in which blacks predominated controlled 104 of 169 seats in the proposed convention, giving blacks and Unionist whites such an advantage that the convention could not have a conservative majority even if every white man in the state had so voted, an impossible outcome as most conservatives planned to boycott the election.[33]

To his defamers, Pope also pointed out he had merely adopted districts "of their own making." He had not, after all, created new districts but rather had used existing senatorial districts—in Florida and Alabama as well as in Georgia—to which he apportioned delegates according to their voting population. Any fault in the arrangement was not his own. "The truth is that the state senatorial districts of Georgia were purposely arranged in times past so as to give the planting aristocracy the control of the state legislature," Pope explained to Grant. "For this purpose every three counties were made a district entitled to one senator in the state legislature so that in the planting counties a white population however small would have equal representation with a county of five times the white population but in which there were few or no slaves." Unlike the "slave aristocracy" before the war, he had done his best to be fair. "If anyone can do it [better] I will cheerfully acknowledge that I have been wrong, but I must protest against any such charges as those made by Governor Jenkins and his friends ostensibly in behalf of the poor whites whom they have always wronged on such matters."[34]

Where Pope did openly and unabashedly interfere to aid black voters was in extending the duration of the election. He had called for three days of voting, beginning on October 28. But when rural boards of registration reported to him on October 30 that blacks were finding it hard to reach polling places on time, he extended the polling until 6:00 P.M. on November 2.

The extra time was needed less to win a positive vote for the constitutional convention than to ensure that a majority of registered voters cast ballots, as the law required to validate the results. As Pope had expected, voter apathy among Georgia whites was general. By October 30, only two whites had voted in Albany, none in Macon, and none in Columbus. The final tally showed that fewer than 37,000 of the more than 100,000 registered whites had voted. But blacks came out in strength and voted overwhelmingly for a convention. Fifty-six percent of the total electorate participated, with 102,283 affirmative votes cast to 4,127 against a convention. Similar results were had in Florida and Alabama. Registration in Florida had yielded a black majority of nearly 5,000 voters, making an affirmative vote inevitable, so most whites stayed home on election day. Two-thirds of Alabama whites also boycotted the election.[35]

Although nearly all white Democrats had stayed away from the polls in Georgia, 31 percent of eligible white voters cast ballots in favor of a convention. Most probably were Union League members, Southern whites disaffected with the old secessionist and planter leadership. Rather than cast negative votes themselves, the Democrats used economic intimidation to discourage freedmen from going to the polls, as Democratic employers across the state fired black workers who voted.

After the referendum, Democrats turned to attacking the convention and its delegates. Howell Cobb termed the whole concern "an infamous farce," the consequence of General Pope's "unscrupulous purpose of putting us under Negro rule." Isaac W. Avery, a Ku Klux Klansman and *Atlanta Constitution* editor, denounced the "new and odious" convention as "a menagerie ransacked for its stock of puppets and harlequins." Ignoring the fact that half the delegates were native Georgians, and only a fifth were black, the Milledgeville *Southern Recorder* termed the convention "a miserable mulatto concern—the bastard of Abolition policy, begotten of Negro ignorance and prejudice." Allegations of voter fraud and renewed charges of gerrymandering also appeared in the conservative press. Pope tolerated the calumny, but when Milledgeville hotel owners threatened to deny rooms to black delegates, he intervened, ordering the convention moved to Atlanta. There it opened on December 9, to frame a constitution that would restore Georgia to the Union.

Among the first acts of the convention was to petition General Pope to remove Governor Jenkins, in order to "restore loyalty, harmony, and tranquility, and to secure for our state her proper place in the Union." Apart from their political differences with Jenkins, the delegates were angered over the governor's refusal to authorize the state treasurer to release $40,000 to pay them for their per diem expenses. Pope entered the fray on behalf of the delegates, demanding that Jenkins direct the requested payment. When he refused, Pope referred the matter to Grant for the consideration of the cabinet.[36]

Although he had acted with calm in this latest crisis of authority, Pope continued to be the subject of unrelenting attack by the Democratic press of his district. From Alabama came protests that he and General Swayne had manipulated the vote count in Montgomery. Similar charges were leveled against them elsewhere in the state. Northern Democrats repeated the allegations, and word reached Pope that Johnson seemed to believe them. Utterly frustrated, Pope unburdened himself to Grant in a letter dated December 27: "The perplexities and difficulties of a military commander in the South are such that he must have the support of the government to execute the laws. If he cannot have that it is next to impossible for him to discharge the duties of his office. If the president has not confidence in the officers commanding in the South it would be best to send others at once who can rely upon his support and whom he will support." President Johnson agreed. The very day Pope wrote Grant, Johnson replaced him with Major General George G. Meade. By the same order General Swayne was removed from command in Alabama. Pope was to proceed to Washington for further orders.[37]

No reason was given officially for the dismissal. Press speculation varied. In an article headed "Who Killed Cock Robin?" the *New York Herald* suggested the U.S. Attorney for Georgia, a pro-Johnson man named H. S. Fitch, had argued personally to the president for Pope's removal on behalf of conservative Georgians. Others guessed Pope had been removed because of Johnson's dissatisfaction with the "Jury Order." The White House itself insinuated Pope and Swayne had fallen because they had permitted registration fraud in Alabama. Gideon Welles thought Johnson simply had grown fed up with Pope's Radicalism.[38]

The proximate cause of his removal was of little interest to Pope. He knew he had been immolated for having too faithfully administered the reconstruction laws. Far from troubling him, the knowledge was cause for satisfaction. As Pope told Grant before leaving Atlanta, "It is a misnomer to call this question in the South a political question. It is *War* pure and simple. The question is not whether Georgia and Alabama will accept or reject reconstruction. It is, shall the Union men and Freedmen, be the slaves of the old Negro rebel aristocracy or not? Or rather shall the former be permitted to live in these states at all or the Negroes as free men?"[39]

Meade saw at once that Pope had been right. As Meade was a Democrat himself, his appointment had raised conservative hopes in the South. Petitions calling for a reversal of many of Pope's policies greeted Meade, and the *Savannah Daily Morning News* rejoiced that a high-minded soldier had replaced a military satrap. But Meade meant to enforce the law. As his first order of business he demanded Governor Jenkins and the state treasurer pay the constitutional convention. When they declined, Meade tidied up Pope's unfinished business by dismissing them both.[40]

15 *I Speak Not Now of Myself*

John Pope's assignment after Reconstruction duty represented a compromise of sorts between his long-held desire for an East Coast post and his dread of serving on the Pacific Coast under Henry Halleck: on February 1, 1868, Pope assumed command of the Department of the Lakes, with headquarters in Detroit.

Duty in Detroit proved less demanding than any other work Pope had done during his nearly twenty-six years of active service. There were no real challenges and only a handful of minor irritants. For a while in 1868, rumors circulated that a breakaway faction of the Fenians, an organization of Irish-Americans dedicated to freeing Ireland from British rule, would invade Canada from the Michigan border in order to involve the United States in its quarrel with Great Britain. Pope engaged Allan Pinkerton's detective agency to investigate the matter. After several weeks of rummaging through the basements of Catholic churches looking for weapons and infiltrating Fenian meetings from Chicago to Port Huron, Pinkerton's detectives turned up no evidence of Fenian activity along the Great Lakes.[1]

Apart from watching for Fenians, Pope largely occupied himself by endorsing reports on Civil War deserters and forwarding pension claims. Pope's complaints were few and trivial. He would have preferred to have made his headquarters in Milwaukee, disliked the Democratic politics of Detroit, had a hard time finding a suitable house for Clara and the children, and lamented the fact that he had only sixteen of an authorized one hundred civilian employees in the department. Most troublesome to him was Clara's health, which was poor throughout the winter of 1868–69.[2]

A little excitement came his way in March, when Pope addressed Michigan's Republican state convention. Heartily endorsing congressional reconstruction, Pope assured his listeners that "physical force is the only way by which southern leaders are influenced." The delegates, in turn, nominated Pope as Michigan's vice presidential candidate.[3]

To Georgia's former wartime governor, Joseph E. Brown, now an advocate of congressional reconstruction and a personal friend, Pope expressed sentiments less vitriolic. "I rejoice to hear that you have much confident expectation of success in the approaching campaign for the ratification of your constitution," he wrote, "as such of the southern states as shall reject the propositions of Congress are likely to have a hard fate for the next four years. That Georgia may escape is my earnest hope."[4]

With little to fill his time or to challenge his restless intellect, Pope seemed almost to welcome another round with Fitz John Porter, which came in the autumn of 1869 when Porter submitted a second appeal to clear his name. This time Porter framed his appeal in the form of a letter to the recently installed commanding general of the army, William T. Sherman, for referral to the new president, Ulysses S. Grant. General George H. Thomas, a close friend of Sherman, added a word on Porter's behalf, telling Sherman that those who knew Porter had been "utterly astounded when the decision of the court was published" in January 1863. Sherman himself seemed well disposed to Porter. On November 3, he told Secretary of War William W. Belknap he intended to recommend the president remit that part of Porter's sentence prohibiting him from holding civil office.

Being on friendly terms with Pope, Secretary Belknap at once informed him of Porter's latest gambit. Pope acted with craft and dispatch to counter it. Before writing Grant or Sherman on the matter, in November he composed a document calculated to discredit any Confederate testimony Porter might invoke on his behalf. "In order that we may arrive at a clear understanding of the conduct for which Fitz John Porter was tried, convicted, and cashiered, I shall proceed to give a brief statement of the facts, stripped of the clouds of witnesses and words in which such cases are always enveloped when tried by military or civil courts," began Pope in his *Brief Statement of the Case of Fitz John Porter.* "The only testimony I shall refer to as to Porter's guilt in this brief review, is his own; the only testimony as to the consequences of that guilt to the Union army and to the country will be the written testimony of the three rebel officers highest in rank and command in front of us on that day." Pope then presented extracts from the reports of Longstreet, Stuart, and Jackson, which General McDowell transcribed for him from War Department files, to show that Porter was wrong in assuming Longstreet to have been in his front during the day on August 29, 1862. Quoted as they were out of context, the words of the three Confederate generals appeared to damn Porter. As for his pledge to allow Porter's own words to reconfirm his guilt, Pope reproduced the note Porter had sent McDowell and King late on the afternoon of August 29, in which Porter had speculated on the defeat of the army beyond his right and had announced his intention to withdraw toward Manassas. After briefly restating the government's original case against Porter, Pope concluded the "plain statement of facts" to have established, "on Porter's own testimony, one of the most enormous military crimes ever committed in this country, and Porter stands as clearly responsible for every life lost on that field as if he had murdered the men with his own hands."[5]

To preempt Porter in the press, Pope enlisted the help of former subordinates and Republican friends. Don Piatt, who had been a major during the Second Bull Run campaign and now was the Washington correspondent of the *Cincinnati Commercial,* ran the *Brief Statement* in that paper under his personal byline. Another partisan of Pope, former aide-de-camp J. M. Bundy, published the statement under his name in the *New York Mail.* And Pope's attorney, Lewis E. Mills, set about preparing a lengthy treatise on the 1862 Virginia campaign, in which he blamed Porter, McClellan, and Franklin for the defeat. Mills presented his paper before the Cincinnati Literary Club, saw it widely quoted in the press, and had it published in pamphlet form.[6]

During the month of December, Pope wrote long and impassioned letters to Grant, Sherman, and Secretary Belknap, imploring them, for "the honor of the army," to remit no portion of Porter's sentence without first considering carefully both the voluminous evidence presented to the court-martial and that contained in his *Brief Statement,* copies of which he enclosed with his letters. Pope reserved his strongest rhetoric for Sherman. "I speak not now of myself whose life has been embittered and whose hopes of service to the country blasted by Porter's shameful conduct on the field of battle, nor of the thousands of gallant men whom his desertion consigned to bloody graves"; rather, Pope wished to remind Sherman that remitting any part of Porter's sentence would both cast doubt upon the integrity of the court-martial board and be manipulated by the Democratic press for partisan purposes.[7]

Pope made similar arguments to friendly congressmen. Having been a member of the court-martial, James A. Garfield was particularly sympathetic to Pope, assuring him "no public act with which I have ever been connected was ever made clearer to me than the righteousness of the findings of that court that convicted Fitz John Porter." Senator Zachariah Chandler spoke out on Pope's behalf. Responding to Porter's appeal on the floor of the Senate on February 21, 1870, Chandler reminded his colleagues that, as a former member of the Joint Congressional Committee on the Conduct of the War, he had been in a good position to know what had occurred during Pope's campaign. After recounting the government version of events, Chandler turned to the Porter court-martial and announced, "During this very trial Fitz John Porter said in the presence of my informant, who is a man that most of you know, and who is today in the employment of Congress, and whose word I would take as soon as I would most men's—though I told him I would not use his name, but I will give his sworn testimony, taken down within two minutes after the utterance was made—Porter said in his presence, 'I was not true to Pope, and there's no use in denying it.'" Chandler's source, William B. Lord, formerly stenographer to the joint committee, stuck by his story when his identity was revealed; W. L. Orsmby, a *New York Times* reporter who also had overheard the remark, corroborated Lord's statement.

Chandler's speech shut the door on Porter's appeal. Grant had been disinclined to consider the matter all along, but now Sherman also turned against Porter. In an abrupt reversal of sympathy, in late February he assured Pope that Porter's case could not be reopened nor the verdict challenged. Sherman agreed Porter was guilty and denied having advocated removing his civil disability. He also made clear Porter should address no further appeals through him.

In vain did Porter attempt to stem the new tide of opprobrium Chandler's revelation had released. He tried to call attention to two serious errors—perhaps maliciously introduced—in Pope's *Brief Statement:* First, Pope had omitted a key sentence in Porter's note to King and McDowell, that which had read, "I am now going to the head of the column to see what is passing and how affairs are going, and will communicate with you"; second, the excerpt quoted from Stonewall Jackson's report referred to the events not of the first day's battle but rather of August 30. Porter leveled both charges in a published reply to the *Brief Statement.* Pope ignored the accusation that he had tampered with Porter's message and excused away the second, saying General McDowell had copied the extracts from the Confederate reports for him, and that both the adjutant general and inspector general of the army had attested to their correctness. No matter that Pope's defense was weak; public sentiment had turned sharply against Porter, and, as he lamented, no one "took the trouble to examine" the record closely.[8]

Pope was jubilant. He believed Porter had played his last card and lost for good. Pope assured his sister that "there is no sort of likelihood that the present or any other administration will ever touch" the Porter case again. "The tall structure of falsehood and slander erected by McClellan and his partisans in 1862 and

1863 during a condition of the public mind favorable to anything which might be invented against me and my military operations is tottering to its fall and McClellan and his friends have no material to repair it."

From his friend Governor Rutherford B. Hayes of Ohio came wonderful words of reassurance. Pope had sent Hayes the *Brief Statement* and other documents on the case; now, on April 6, Hayes wrote "to thank you for the papers and heartily to congratulate you on the posture of this matter." In his demand for a rehearing Porter inadvertently had caused the truth concerning Pope's "masterful campaign" in Virginia to be revealed. "Now the whole matter, with the new light now shed upon it, is spread before the public and is made an interesting topic of discussion for some months, and the truth is made clear and unquestionable, vindicating your whole conduct and character in a way that is exceedingly gratifying to all your friends. It is good—very good," mused Hayes. "I know nothing that would be legal testimony in the case except what is known by everybody," Hayes wrote, "but in the subordinate position I held at Alexandria and Upton's Hill on those dreadful August days I saw and heard things which settle my own opinions against Porter and his confederates in the most decided way."[9]

Still more gratifying news came to Pope when on April 30, 1870, he learned he had once again been assigned to command the Department of the Missouri, with headquarters at Fort Leavenworth. Evidently Pope had availed himself of the untimely death of George H. Thomas in March to do a bit of lobbying for the job. During the first week of April, he and Phil Sheridan accompanied the general's remains by train from Chicago to the home of Thomas's widow in Troy, New York. Besides swapping army yarns, they undoubtedly discussed future command vacancies. At Thomas's funeral were assembled Grant, Sherman, Sheridan, and all the department commanders. Despite the somber circumstances, talk of reassignments was inevitable. John M. Schofield, looking to assume the now vacant Division of the Pacific, endorsed Pope as his successor to the Department of the Missouri. Sheridan also recommended to President Grant that Pope be returned to his former command.

John and Clara were delighted with the assignment, the more so when they learned headquarters had been returned temporarily to St. Louis to make room at Fort Leavenworth for the Seventh Cavalry, which had been drawn in from the Plains to winter there. Not anxious to expose Clara to the rigors of the Plains any sooner than necessary, Pope was also pleased to accept Schofield's invitation for Clara to summer with Mrs. Schofield in the Schofields' rented cottage in St. Louis. Having accumulated little wealth and less property during Pope's long years of service, John and Clara consented to buy the Schofields' furniture "at the prices you name."[10]

Pope arrived at department headquarters in early May to a greatly changed state of affairs on the frontier. When Grant was elected president in 1868, General

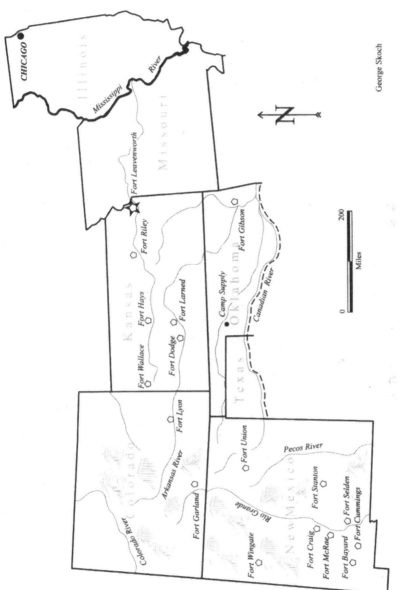

The Department of the Missouri, 1869–83

George Skoch

Sherman had gone east to replace him as commanding general of the army. Phil Sheridan, who as commander of the Department of the Missouri had recently concluded a brutally effective winter campaign against the southern Plains Indians, had been elevated to command of the Division of the Missouri.

Sheridan took a decidedly hard approach to Indian affairs. Reservation Indians were to be treated fairly but with a firm hand—any who strayed must be punished severely. Total war should be waged against hostile Indians—they must be made to conform to the government's wishes or be destroyed. Understanding that whites often precipitated Indian troubles, Sheridan nonetheless sided emphatically with his own race and the inevitable, and to him highly desirable, Christian civilizing of the West. Shortly after assuming command, Sheridan had remarked to Sherman that the Indian problem seemed merely a matter of who would live on the Plains—red man or white—and he had made his choice.

Subordinates whose views did not coincide with those of Sheridan were made to suffer. Always quick to pick a fight with his brother officers, Sheridan had grown more headstrong since coming west. He tended to see a sinister motive behind any action, or even suggestion, not in accord with his own wishes. His relationship with subordinate commanders ranged from strained to stormy. Sheridan broke with General George Crook when he found his old friend too sympathetic to the plight of the Apache, and he resented Colonel Benjamin H. Grierson's flirtations with humanitarian reformers. Pope's views on Indian matters were closer to those of Crook and Grierson than to those of Sheridan, and his temper was equal to that of his new commander. It seemed inevitable that Pope and Sheridan should clash.[11]

For the moment, however, Sheridan was stymied in his aggressive designs against the Plains tribes by a new federal Indian policy in which he had little confidence and which, conversely, was more congenial to Pope's views than any policy previously attempted. Receptive to the reform impulses of eastern humanitarians, disgusted with the corrupt management of Indian affairs, and anxious to clear the paths of westward expansion as humanely as possible, President Grant promoted a series of measures that came to be known as "Grant's Peace Policy." Much of the peace policy bore the mark of Pope's thinking on Indian affairs, as conveyed in letters and reports to Grant and Sherman shortly after the war. The reform-minded Jacob D. Cox, Grant's secretary of the interior and a friend of Pope, told Congress in 1869 that the "sincere cultivation of peaceful relations with the tribes" was to be attempted. All nomadic tribes were to be placed on large, fixed reservations, where they would be educated and taught Christianity preparatory to citizenship and instructed in farming so as to become self-supporting. The old treaty system would be scrapped and the payment of annuities phased out. In their place would come a system of land severalty and territorial government.

Although the Bureau of Indian Affairs would maintain control of reservation tribes, its activities were to be closely scrutinized by a watchdog committee of ten philanthropic citizens appointed by the president in June 1869. To improve further the moral tone of the Indian service, Grant acceded to a recommendation of the Orthodox Society of Friends that religious men be appointed Indian agents. "If you can make Quakers out of the Indians it will take the fight out of them," Grant is said to have replied, and he permitted the Friends to nominate members of their congregations to run the Central and Southern Superintendencies—the former lying within Pope's department—on a trial basis.[12]

Initially, the peace policy clarified the role of the army in a manner that even Sheridan found satisfactory. Indians who defied settlement on reservations or who left them without Indian Bureau authorization came under the sole jurisdiction of the army, which might take such action against recalcitrant bands as the generals deemed appropriate. In the summer of 1869, Indian agents and military commanders received identical instructions from Washington: The Indian Bureau had "exclusive control and jurisdiction" of Indians on their reservations, the army of those off them. The army was to treat all Indians off their reservations as hostile but was not permitted to interfere with Indians on their reservations unless requested by the agent or his superiors.

By clearly delineating the responsibilities of each service, for a brief time the peace policy inspired harmony between the army and the Bureau of Indian Affairs. The promise of civil-military cooperation also eased the antipathy humanitarian groups naturally felt for the military. Eastern philanthropists spoke optimistically of a "new order of things," in which the Indian would benefit from the fruits of "justice, freedom, and humanity."[13]

The hopes of humanitarian reformers were dashed abruptly on January 23, 1870, when two squadrons of cavalry under Major Eugene M. Baker wiped out a village of Piegans in Montana. Although the Piegans had been guilty of depredations against white settlements, humanitarians branded the affair a deliberate and unprovoked massacre of men, women, and children. The eastern press accepted sensational, though largely unfounded, accounts of army brutality. Efforts of Sherman and Sheridan to defend Baker's actions antagonized not only the humanitarians, but also Congress and the general eastern public. A bill to transfer Indian affairs to the War Department had been on the verge of passing both houses, but it died quickly. Members of Congress joined with churches and reformers in demanding church control be extended to all Indian agencies and greater restrictions be placed on the military. The element of coercion that the framers of the peace policy envisioned as necessary to compel Indian compliance was lost in a wave of antimilitarism.[14]

Unpropitious for army commanders in the West in general, circumstances were even more problematic for General Pope. Because three of the most warlike

and intractable of the Plains tribes—the Kiowa, Comanche, and Southern Cheyenne—fell under his jurisdiction, the Department of the Missouri was certain to
become the principal testing ground for the peace policy.

Pope's command embraced the states of Illinois, Missouri, Kansas, Colorado,
New Mexico, and the Indian Territory. Railroads, which Pope had four years earlier advised as critical to the rapid movement of troops and supplies, the department now had aplenty. The Kansas Pacific had edged to within a few miles of
Denver and was only a few months away from building a connecting link from
Denver northward to the Union Pacific. Further south, the Atchison, Topeka, and
Santa Fe was nearing the southern border of Colorado. Pope had at his disposal
three regiments of cavalry, four regiments of infantry, and three batteries of artillery—just under four thousand men in all.[15]

Whether Pope would be permitted to use either the railroads or his troops was
doubtful. By the time he assumed departmental command, the Quakers had
been installed in the Central Indian Superintendency for nearly a year. Enoch
Hoag, a headstrong idealist from Iowa with a long interest in Indian matters, was
superintendent, with his headquarters at Lawrence, Kansas, uncomfortably close
to Pope's. Another Iowan, Lawrie Tatum, an honest farmer with no Indian experience, ran the Kiowa and Comanche Agency, located near Fort Sill in the Indian Territory. Brinton Darlington was agent to the Cheyenne and Arapaho, whose
reservation lay some eighty miles to the northeast, near Fort Reno.[16]

Neither Hoag nor his agents needed the Piegan affair to convince them that
moral suasion, generosity, and kindness, rather than military force, were the true
means to solving the Indian problem; these precepts were fundamental to Quaker
pacifism. Loathe to call upon the military to return straying Indians to their reservations or prevent raiding parties from leaving them, the Quakers resorted to
the very sort of bribery that Pope had so long opposed and which the peace policy had intended to halt: the payment of annuities to ensure good behavior. "It
is the opinion of all the chiefs that we have conversed with," wrote an ingenu-
ous Quaker delegation of inspectors in 1869, "that much difficulty will be experienced in retaining the Indians on their reservations without such an issue."[17]

Having taken heart at the appointment of agents who were at least honest,
Pope was disappointed with the restoration of annuity payments. Aware that the
present political climate rendered the military's opinion on any aspect of Indian affairs suspect, Pope muted his criticism of Quaker policy. "Speaking generally," he said in his annual report for 1870, "there has been little trouble with the
Indians in this department during this season. This result is mainly due to the
fact that these Indians have been fed and furnished with nearly everything they
asked for. It may be safely said, however, that if the Indians are to be kept quiet
by feeding them, there are much cheaper and safer places to do it than their
present reservations."

Pope believed it exceedingly foolish to place the Kiowa and Comanche on reservations near the very frontier settlements they had been in the habit of raiding for decades. Doing so, Pope observed, merely gave marauding parties "what alone they have needed in the past to secure success in their hostile expeditions, or security to themselves, in case of failure: First, a depot of supplies furnished by the government, and second, a place of safety where they are protected by an agent of the government from the consequences of any crimes they choose to commit." That they would go on committing crimes against Texas settlements Pope had no doubt. He had come to know both the Kiowa and their Comanche allies well during his work on the Pacific railroad surveys and his drilling expeditions on the Llano Estacado two decades earlier. Pope understood, as Tatum would come to learn, that farming was beneath the dignity of the Kiowa, whom Pope rather unfairly termed the "most faithless, cruel, and unreliable of all the Indians on the plains." Raiding was at the center of tribal society; the wealth of a Kiowa or Comanche man was measured in the number of horses he had stolen and his status in the tribe determined by how many coups he had counted. What Pope seemed to forget—as did every other Plains commander—were the very real grievances the Comanche and allied Kiowa had against the Texans, dating from March 1840, when the Republic of Texas lured twelve chiefs and their families to their deaths on the pretense of making peace.[18]

The prospect of troubles with the southern tribes led Pope to call first the attention of staff officers at division headquarters (Phil Sheridan was in Europe observing the Franco-Prussian War), and later that of the War Department, to a conundrum of the peace policy: How could the Indians be kept from using their reservations as sanctuaries from which to raid? Having no jurisdiction on the reservations, and confronted with Indian agents who refused to believe their charges responsible for depredations already occurring along the Texas frontier, Pope could do little to avert bloodshed. A month after assuming command, he protested bitterly to division headquarters, "The Indians having the power to nurture their plans and make their preparations unmolested, and the choice of points to strike along an extensive frontier but scantily supplied with troops, must of course always be successful on their first move." Such raiding parties, Pope noted in his annual report, "could be wholly prevented by arresting for the time the active parties engaged in getting them up, or by seizing and keeping for awhile the ponies of the tribe or tribes concerned."[19]

That was impossible so long as the Quaker policy prevailed. Not only Lawrie Tatum, but also the commander at Fort Sill, Benjamin Grierson, believed Kiowa protestations that frontier raids—which grew in frequency and intensity in 1871—had been instigated by the Quahadi Comanche, who roamed the Llano Estacado beyond the reservation, and they correctly noted that many supposed Indian raids were actually conducted by disguised whites. Grierson was so enamored of the peace policy that he sometimes withheld reports of Kiowa and Co-manche misbehavior from Sheridan. Pope defended his friend and subordinate, however, for the generally good judgment he exercised in "his delicate and critical relations with the Kiowas and Comanches."

In Washington, the warnings of Pope were blunted by humanitarians like Samuel F. Tappan, a member of the Peace Commission that had negotiated the abortive Indian treaties of 1867, who insisted that the clamor about Indian depredations was merely a subterfuge to draw troops away from protecting freedpersons in the Reconstruction South—a strange charge to level, directly or otherwise, against John Pope.[20]

With Sheridan in Europe, it fell to Sherman, as commanding general, to sort out for himself the situation in the Indian Territory. Touring the Texas frontier in May 1871 with a small escort, Sherman saw little evidence that Indian troubles were as extensive as Texans had portrayed them or as Pope had predicted in his reports. His doubts were abruptly erased when he reached Fort Richardson. There Sherman learned that a large civilian supply train following a few hours behind his entourage had been ambushed near Jacksboro by a Kiowa raiding party; indeed, the Indians had permitted Sherman to pass unmolested only because a larger prize awaited. Continuing on to Fort Sill, Sherman found Lawrie Tatum wavering in his commitment to nonviolence. By then it had not only become clear to Tatum that some of his own Kiowa were participating in the Texas raids, but he knew by their own boasts that the war chiefs Satanta, Satank, and Big Tree were responsible for Sherman's near brush with death at Jacksboro. Tatum asked Sherman to have them arrested; in the ensuing melee, Sherman was nearly shot.[21]

Although Sherman's inspection and the arrest of the war chiefs neither stopped the raids in Texas nor signaled a tougher application of the peace policy—Superintendent Hoag chastised Tatum for having called upon the military and explained away Kiowa depredations as simply their way of asserting their rights to Texas homelands of which they had been defrauded (actually, a fairly accurate view of matters)—it did free Pope from further responsibility for the mess. Deciding a change in division and department boundaries was needed to deal more effectively with both the agency troublemakers and the Staked Plains Comanche, Sherman transferred Fort Sill, the Kiowa-Comanche Agency, and the southern half of the Indian Territory to the Department of Texas (Camp Supply, an important logistical depot on the upper Canadian River, and the Cheyenne-Arapaho Agency would remain under Pope's jurisdiction), then moved that department from the Division of the South to Sheridan's division. Sherman recalled Sheridan from Europe and placed the capable Brigadier General Christopher C. Augur in command of the Department of Texas.[22]

With the redrawing of department boundaries, Pope gave greater attention to the Cheyenne and Arapaho, who frequently strayed north from their agency, usually to hunt buffalo but occasionally to raid settlements in eastern Colorado and southwestern Kansas. Pope believed himself better able to prevent periodic raids by wandering Cheyenne and Arapaho than he had the savage and constant ravages of the Kiowa against the Texas frontier. The strategy he fashioned blended the military advantages of new railroads with unceasing congressional pressure to cut military expenditures. The completion of the Kansas Pacific Railroad to Denver across the southern reaches of Pope's department permitted a more reliable flow of supplies, more rapid concentration of troops, and, most important, a means of early warning against approaching Cheyenne or Arapaho who, Pope noted, "cannot reach the settlements exposed to them without crossing or very nearly approaching the line of the railroad, where their appearance and number can be rapidly communicated by telegraph, and the necessary force sent by rail."[23]

Shortly after assuming command in May 1870, Pope had quelled Sioux raids in northwestern Kansas by ordering six troops of the Seventh Cavalry under George A. Custer to set up a summer camp near Fort Hays, from which detachments continually patrolled the most extreme settlements. The success of this endeavor and the advantages offered by the railroad led Pope to replicate the practice along the southern borders of Kansas and Colorado, and in the New Mexico Territory, where small bands of Apache presented a persistent but manageable threat. As the Plains Indians raided only in warm weather, when there was grass to subsist their ponies, and kept to their reservations during the long winter, Pope proposed limiting the army's presence in threatened areas to the temperate months, and then only in mobile camps and constantly roving patrols. Explained Pope of his purpose: "Summer camps of cavalry and infantry sent out in early spring to important points from some large central posts accomplish all the objects to be expected from small posts kept up all the year at the same points, and I am satisfied that they can accomplish these objects much more completely and at vastly less cost." In a reversal of his long-held preference for numerous, small posts in the heart of Indian lands, Pope now argued that troops could also be fielded more efficiently from large posts. "With 1,000 men at one post it is easy to put into the field, on the shortest notice, 850 men. Distribute the thousand men in four small posts and it will not be found practicable to put into the field 600 men." He also insisted that concentrating troops at a few large posts—such as Fort Hays and Fort Leavenworth in Kansas—would also improve discipline, morale, and the quality of training.[24]

Phil Sheridan disagreed with Pope on the merits of concentration and did not care for his defensive use of cavalry (seeming to forget that the Quaker interpretation of the peace policy largely precluded any other such use), but he did permit Pope to close down four far-flung posts in 1871 and three more the following year.[25]

While taking steps to protect the white settlers in his department, Pope also strove to avoid conflict whenever possible and to ameliorate some of the causes. Pope understood that most of the Cheyenne and Arapaho who left their reservation did so with the permission of their agent, simply to follow the rapidly dwindling herds of buffalo. Pope resisted calls from frightened Kansas authorities in 1872 to attack them, and he similarly dismissed an appeal from the secretary of the interior in the fall of 1873 to make war on hunting parties of Cheyenne then roaming over eastern Colorado. In both instances, Pope saw the Indians safely returned to their reservations and urged Superintendent Hoag, whose sympathy for the Indian blinded him to the fears—and rights—of settlers, to keep them there. "It is far better policy and wiser economy, if game be absolutely essential to Indian diet," entreated Pope, "to hire white hunters to furnish it from lands subject to white men's occupancy, than to allow Indians to intrude upon white men's lands, while white men are prohibited from setting foot on an Indian reservation."[26]

One potential source of conflict upon which both Pope and the Indian Bureau agreed was the booming, illicit trade in whiskey. Not only did whiskey debauch the reservation Indians—agent John Miles claimed to have seen twelve hundred of his Cheyenne charges "drunk as loons" at a single time—but it also bred war. Whiskey traders as often dealt in weapons, and drunken, well-armed Indians could spark a conflagration unwittingly. Licensed traders and white buffalo hunters were important sources of whiskey, but by far the most pernicious were the *comancheros,* ruffians from New Mexico who crossed the Llano Estacado to deal arms and whiskey to blanket Indians in exchange for captives and stolen livestock. Pope did what he could to destroy this illicit trade, but with his 1,558 cavalry already stretched thin guarding railroads and settlements, results were disappointing.[27]

On the balance, Pope was satisfied with the state of Indian affairs during the first four years of his second tenure as commander of the Department of the Missouri. Perhaps Pope should have read in the wanton slaughter of the buffalo by white hide-hunters, in the whiskey and arms trade, and in the cultural proclivity of the southern tribes toward war the portents of an inevitable, major uprising. But the prevailing, if uneasy, peace made him sanguine. Pope was pleased not only with his own accomplishments in averting war and exercising economy, but also with the good work of the Quakers. Despite frequent disagreements with Superintendent Hoag, Pope gave the peace policy and its civilian administrators high marks. Before the House Committee on Military Affairs in January 1874, Pope testified:

> Seven or eight years ago I was very much in favor of the transfer of the Indian Bureau to the control of the War Department. . . . Since that time, however,

the larger part, if not all of the dishonest agents and their followers who infested the frontier . . . have been gotten rid of. While such a condition of
things obtained on the plains I was in favor of having the Indian Bureau transferred to the War Department; but since the present policy has been in operations I have noticed a very decided improvement in the condition of things
on the frontier, both as to peacefulness with the Indian tribes and as to honesty in the administration of the Indian Bureau. . . . I therefore believe that it
is better to leave the Indian Bureau to be managed as it has been managed for
the last four years.[28]

In fewer than seven months, Pope would have abundant cause to rue that hopeful testimony.

— ◆ —

For John Pope the early 1870s were satisfying years, generally speaking, both pro-
fessionally and personally. Although he had returned department headquarters
to Fort Leavenworth from St. Louis in the summer of 1870 reluctantly and was
even less disposed to subject his family to life there, within a very short time Pope
found he had been mistaken about the place.

From reluctant resident Pope became the post's greatest booster in the army
high command and the first to recognize its long-term value to the army. "The
military reservation of Fort Leavenworth is one of the most valuable and most
useful possessed by the government," Pope attested in his annual report for 1870.
"It embraces about 6,000 acres of good land. It lies on the Missouri River, at a
point where steamers can reach it for eight or nine months of the year, is connected by railroad with all points southeast and south, and from it the Kansas
Pacific Railroad extends westward to the Rocky Mountains. For years to come it
must be the most suitable place for the headquarters of a department embracing
the whole region of country as far west as the eastern line of California, and as
far south as the northern boundary of Texas." He might also have mentioned that
nearby Leavenworth City had grown to a population of over eighteen thousand—
nearly five times greater than that of Kansas City. Pope was sincere about cutting
costs in his department, but not where Fort Leavenworth was concerned. To reduce the reservation would be false economy of the worst kind. The acreage,
much of which was farmed profitably to the government's benefit, was "the
cheapest and best possession for the military service to be had in all this country," said Pope. "So far from selling any part of it, it would clearly be for the interests of the government to appropriate every year, for some years to come, a
considerable sum of money to enlarge and increase the accommodations." To a
parsimonious Congress, Pope had the temerity to suggest an immediate appropriation of $300,000 to replace the rotting log buildings erected in 1829, into

which he had been compelled to move department headquarters and officers' billets, with modern brick structures.[29]

There was strong sentiment in Congress to sell off the entire reservation, and Phil Sheridan was indifferent to the fate of Fort Leavenworth. General Sherman, however, embraced Pope's recommendations enthusiastically. He lobbied the Senate on Pope's behalf, arguing that, "though the amount asked for may seem large, it is in fact small as compared to the sums expended on our seacoast forts, which are not half as important." The Senate favored Pope's plan of expansion, but for no more than $200,000; the House, however, refused to appropriate a single cent. Two years later, with the warm support of Congressman James A. Garfield, Sherman and Pope tried to secure a $200,000 appropriation. They again failed in Congress, but owing to Pope's persistence, the post gained, little by little, with each passing year. A War Department allotment of $50,000 permitted the construction of new officers' quarters in 1871, and funds were allocated to build an arsenal the following year. Working through Kansas legislators, Pope also secured $15,000 from Congress to build a macadamized road from the post to the business district of Leavenworth City.[30]

Pope also orchestrated the construction of the first United States military prison (today known as the United States Military Disciplinary Barracks) in 1875. Past practice had been to confine army prisoners, both long-term inmates and minor offenders, in local post stockades and in state penitentiaries. Pope argued for a single military prison, located at Fort Leavenworth. Rather than expending $3,000 a year to support each army prisoner in state penitentiaries, the federal government would be able to make money from the labor of long-term convicts confined under centralized army control.[31]

Although many problems remained—including poor sanitation in the enlisted quarters and a general overcrowding—living conditions at Fort Leavenworth improved markedly after Pope's arrival. General Nelson A. Miles fondly remembered the early 1870s as a time of enhanced "social civilities and recreation" on post. Dances and theatricals enlivened the post, a race track and grandstands went up, and the two hundred saloons and bawdy houses in Leavenworth offered plenty of distraction off-post. The general appearance of Fort Leavenworth improved as trees were planted along post roads and officers were enjoined to landscape their quarters. "General Pope took a personal interest in every member of his command and had friendly acquaintances with every officer in it," averred a regular visitor to headquarters. "His annual visits to the remoter posts were gala days; and every officer esteemed himself fortunate when opportunity gave him a visit to headquarters. Life at Leavenworth was the ideal of military life."[32]

Certainly life had improved for John Pope. Among the first of the new buildings to go up was Pope's quarters, a large, comfortable house with indoor plumbing, hot and cold running water, a copper boiler, expensive bathroom fixtures, and—before the end of the decade—a telephone. On November 16, 1871, Clara gave birth at Fort Leavenworth to a daughter, Lucretia, bringing the family to five. Apart from a brief bout with malaria in the spring of 1873, Clara was in good health, and John felt better than he had in years. He had grown a bit more paunchy and had shaved off his beard, but at age fifty-one Pope still appeared vigorous and alert.[33]

The Popes enjoyed entertaining. William T. Sherman and Senator James G. Blaine were frequent visitors, as were Pope's friends Thomas C. H. Smith and Manning F. Force, particularly during the summer months, when Smith, Force, and Pope would "take a run on the Plains."

Thomas C. H. Smith could be cantankerous and uncommunicative for long stretches of time, but Force proved steady and faithful, perhaps the closest friend Pope ever had. Their friendship became a family affair when Force married Clara's sister, Frances Dabney Horton, in 1874. A lawyer before the Civil War, Force ended the conflict a brevet major general, having fought under Sherman, from Vicksburg to the Carolinas, winning his final brevet for "especial gallantry before Atlanta." Sherman thought highly enough of Force to offer him the colonelcy of a Regular regiment after the war, but Force declined and returned to his law practice in Cincinnati, where he was elected judge of the common pleas court and became active in state Republican politics. Like Pope, Force was a man of keen intellect and fine literary taste, and he wrote books on such diverse topics as Darwinism, Amerigo Vespuccui, and the Forts Henry and Donelson campaign.[34]

Sherman and Force remained warm friends after the war. Force also was a lifelong, intimate friend of Rutherford B. Hayes, which of course helped further Pope's own friendship with Ohio's governor. Pope and Hayes, however, got along well on their own account. Hayes was sufficiently impressed with Pope's addresses to veterans' groups and his papers on Indian affairs to suggest he take up writing. "I can't help feeling that you owe the world a book or two," wrote Hayes a few days before ending his second term as governor. He himself was glad to be "out of bondage of office and the ruts of politics. I do not mean to take any prominent part in public affairs again," Hayes declared to Pope. "My family, friends, books, and happiness will I hope hereafter be the aims of life."

As Hayes encouraged Pope to write, so did Pope urge Hayes not to give up politics for good. Sherman admonished his generals to stay clear of partisan politics, but Pope ignored him; he was, and always would be, a Republican. More to the point, Hayes's reformist ideals appealed to Pope's notions of what a public servant should represent. "Men like you are too much needed in public affairs to be permitted thus to escape the bondage of public life," Pope told Hayes. In begging him to close no door prematurely, Pope revealed something of his own ambivalence about public service, saying, "Of all exacting matters in this world, the American public is conspicuous, and if their gratitude for service performed were in any respect in proportion to these exactions, public life in this country would have charms which it now very much lacks."[35]

Public life lost some of its residual charm for Pope later that year. On November 6, Major General George G. Meade died, leaving vacant one of the three major-general slots authorized under the Army Act of 1869. All ten brigadier generals lobbied President Grant hard for the promotion. Pope's strongest support came from Ohio. Governor Edward F. Noyes, who had commanded a regiment under Pope at Island No. 10, former governor Hayes, and Manning Force all urged Pope's elevation; Congressman Matthew H. Carpenter argued that Pope merited it as compensation for the bad treatment accorded him during the war. In the end, the relentless operation of the seniority system won out, and Grant selected Irvin McDowell, distinguished principally for his age and time in service, for advancement.[36]

During the summer of 1874, Pope unexpectedly found himself at odds with his commanding officer, with a ruthlessly ambitious subordinate, and with much of the Kansas public and press.

As the bitter Plains winter receded and the grass that sustained buffalo and Indian ponies returned, the latent discontent of the southern Plains tribes erupted in violence. Conditions had become intolerable for the reservation Indians. With the coming of spring, Kansas buffalo hunters had crossed into the Indian Territory, stipulated by treaty as exclusive Indian hunting grounds, to decimate the last of the great herds. Horse thieves from Kansas and Texas were even more audacious, robbing Indian ponies from the reservations themselves. The scourge of whiskey traders, rations that arrived late and were inevitably poor, and government surveys of Indian lands rounded out the list of Indian grievances. Although the Arapaho remained at peace, large war parties of Kiowa, Southern Cheyenne, and Comanche broke from their reservations to mete out revenge, feed their starving families, and, as many perceived, make one final fight for their old way of life.[37]

War came to the Department of the Missouri with the first thaw in March, as small raiding parties struck along the Medicine Lodge Creek, in southern Kansas, burning ranches and killing several white hunters and herders. Pope deployed additional troops to the area, attempting, as in years past, to throw up a protective cordon around the northern and western boundaries of the Indian Territory in an effort to contain the hostilities. Clashes were inconclusive, as the soldiers were prohibited from pursuing the raiders onto their reservations, but the integrity of the line of settlements below the Arkansas River and of the railroads was protected, which was Pope's immediate priority. In spite of Pope's efforts, panic spread along the Kansas frontier. "There was never in my experience," he wrote Governor Thomas Osborn to allay his fears, "a frontier so fully guarded as the frontier of Kansas."

That guarantee appeared dubious when, on June 19, a war party attacked a squadron of the Sixth Cavalry and a company of infantry along the road from Fort Dodge to Camp Supply. Two days later, a column led by Fort Dodge's commander, Major C. E. Compton, was attacked on its return from Camp Supply. A larger war party attacked Compton's force on June 24 but was driven back with four dead.[38]

On June 27, the Cheyenne launched their most ambitious strike to date, sending a huge war party against an illegal trading post set up in the Texas panhandle by Dodge City buffalo hunters and whiskey and gun merchants near Adobe Walls, the site of a former Indian fight. In a daylong fight, the twenty-eight well-armed whites on hand managed to keep the Cheyenne at bay, and with nightfall the Indians broke off the assault. Meanwhile, hunter Henry Lease had sneaked away from Adobe Walls to appeal for help from the army. When he found that no one at Dodge City had authority to send troops to rescue the hunters, Lease appealed to Governor Osborn, who promised to intercede at once with General Pope.

Osborn's efforts were unavailing. Apart from the fact that Adobe Walls was not in his department, Pope had no intention of rescuing the very scoundrels whose illegal forays into the Indian Territory had helped precipitate the present crisis. "They have justly earned all that may befall them," Pope had his adjutant inform Governor Osborn; if he "were to send troops to the locality of these unlawful trading establishments, it would be to break them up and not to protect them." As Pope explained in his annual report:

> A trading post, as is understood, not with any permit or license from the Indian Bureau, or other United States authority, was established by some persons in business in Dodge City, at Adobe Walls, in the Pan-Handle of Texas and far beyond the limits of this department, to trade with the Cheyennes and Arapahos, and such other Indians as might come there mainly to supply the buffalo hunters, whose continuous pursuit and wholesale slaughter of the buffalo, both summer and winter, had driven the great herds down into the Indian reservations. This trading post sold arms and ammunition, whiskey, etc., not only to the hunters, but the Indians, and the very arms and ammunition thus furnished the Indians they afterward used to attack and break up this trading post, which was put there to enable the white hunters to invade unlawfully the Indian reservation. There can be no doubt the present difficulties with the Cheyennes were mainly caused by the unlawful intrusion and illegal and violent acts of the white hunters.[39]

That Pope had laid the fault for the uprising where it belonged won him few friends on the Kansas frontier. The press execrated him, particularly in Dodge City. "The merchants and business men of Dodge City have survived the anathemas of General Pope, who seems to think they are fit subjects for total extermination," said the *Kansas Daily Commonwealth*. "If the general would take the trouble to visit the frontier, and become acquainted with the real facts, he would find that the business men of Dodge, or any other town, are in no manner responsible for the outbreak. They are shrewd, go-ahead business men, and the imputations of the general are unwarranted to say the least." (These same shrewd, go-ahead businessmen, it was later found, had scalped and decapitated the thirteen Indians killed at the Adobe Walls fight and spiked their heads on corral gateposts as decoration, an act, said Colonel Nelson Miles, that only bore witness to "the depravity of these men.")[40]

Pope's refusal to aid the buffalo hunters at Adobe Walls enraged Phil Sheridan, who not only believed all white men deserved the army's protection, regardless of their character, but also thought the buffalo hunters were doing the nation a great service by depleting the Indian commissary—the sooner the buffalo was exterminated, the easier it would be to keep the Indians on their reservation, went Sheridan's thinking. He also differed fundamentally with Pope as to the cause of the Red River uprising. "This outbreak does not look to me as being originated by the action of bad white men, or the sale of whiskey to Indians by the traders," he asserted in his annual report. "It is the result of the restless nature of the Indian, who has no profession but arms, and naturally seeks for war and plunder when the grazing gets high enough to feed his ponies."[41]

An angry Phil Sheridan went after Pope with acrimonious vigor but little real cause. During the first two weeks of July, Pope had been left to meet the Indian outbreak with no clear guidance from above. When both the agent at the Cheyenne-Arapaho (Darlington) Agency and Superintendent Hoag appealed for the army's help to keep peaceable bands from joining the war parties and to protect supply trains carrying rations for the reservations, Pope responded decisively. He dispatched a strong column from Fort Dodge to Darlington's agency, ordered out three cavalry troops to patrol the length of the Darlington-Wichita road, a key supply route; increased the garrison at Camp Supply; and stationed more men along Medicine Lodge Creek.

Pope assumed he had acted as higher authority wished; on July 7, Sherman had wired him to waylay the Sixth Cavalry, then en route to Arizona, and employ it to help protect the border settlements of Kansas and keep the roads open. Having received no instructions from Sheridan, Pope wrote him on July 10. After explaining the disposition of his troops, Pope expressed his confidence that he could protect the frontier and assured Sheridan "we shall act vigorously and use everything we have." Although he preferred to wait until winter rendered the Indians immobile, Pope also wanted to go over to the offensive and attack the hostiles on their reservations. As Superintendent Hoag refused to permit this, Pope urged Sheridan to use his influence to obtain authorization for an offensive campaign in the Indian Territory. Rather than acknowledge Pope's appeal, Sheridan merely criticized Pope for not acting more aggressively.[42]

Frustrated with Hoag's intransigence and Sheridan's displeasure with his performance—even though no official policy or plan had yet been handed down—Pope wired Sheridan on July 16 for specific instructions. While asking that his duties be clarified, Pope also reiterated his own desire to assume the offensive. He wanted to attack without warning, to prevent hostile bands from withdrawing to the agencies. Absent Indian Bureau permission to enter the Indian Territory, Pope thought the army should wait until winter to strike, when Indians off the reservation would be most vulnerable—precisely the tactics Sheridan employed so successfully in the winter of 1868.

Still angry over Adobe Walls, Sheridan read Pope's request for instructions as a stall for time. He used the occasion of a telegram from Sherman, which offered only vague suggestions as to the conduct of a campaign, to fulminate against Pope. "I coincide with you fully that General Pope should make the Sixth Cavalry take the offensive," Sheridan wired Sherman. "I asked him to do so about a week ago, but he asked further time. He is so taken with the idea of defense that he does not see the absurdity of using cavalry in that way."[43]

When some fool at army headquarters leaked Sheridan's telegram to the Kansas press, it was Pope's turn to explode. He demanded a retraction; what he got was a halfhearted apology—"I shall deeply regret that a friendship on my part existing during the last twelve or thirteen years, and which was often agreeably taxed in your defense, should be jeopardized by the blunder of some clerk in letting my dispatch be published," said Sheridan—along with a written rebuke for not having succored the buffalo hunters at Adobe Walls.

"Very greatly chagrined" over the episode, Pope refused to let the matter rest, and Sherman was compelled to intervene. While agreeing with Sheridan's right to criticize a subordinate in "confidential communications," Sherman urged him to go easy on Pope: "We have a fine good set of general officers now, and I hope and pray we may all be friends—If I can do nothing else I can try to be Peace Maker, and if General Pope makes allusions to it I know you will meet him more than half way."[44]

Despite their harsh words with one another, Sheridan and Pope held strategic views that were essentially the same, which became evident when tempers cooled. One historian of the Red River War suggested Sheridan's "fulminations against his department commander were based on confusion, ignorance, and a quick tongue." Both men were quick to anger, but neither bore the other any lasting ill will from the affair. An Interior Department decision on July 20 helped soothe their rancor: all hostiles were to be punished, declared the secretary of the interior, wherever they may be found. Friendly Indians were to gather at their agencies for enrollment; after a suitable time, those who had not reported in would be regarded as hostile.[45]

Despite his displeasure with Pope, Sheridan permitted him and Brigadier General Christopher C. Augur to plan the campaign as they saw fit. Beyond a desire that operations unfold along the general lines of his own 1868 offensive, with a combination of aggressive converging movements by separate mounted columns, Sheridan offered no guidance.

Lacking direction from above, Pope and Augur adopted similar strategies independently of one another. Although Pope continued to doubt the efficacy of a summer campaign, he nonetheless got his troops in motion quickly. To enroll friendly Cheyennes at the Darlington Agency, a government-dictated first step to separate hostile from presumably peaceful Indians, Pope detailed Lieutenant Colonel Thomas H. Neill with a detachment of cavalry. On July 27, six days after he received permission from the interior department to move troops on the reservations, Pope ordered Colonel Nelson A. Miles, commander of the Fifth U.S. Infantry, to proceed to Fort Dodge and assume command of the eight companies of cavalry and four of infantry gathering there for an expedition south into the Indian Territory toward Fort Sill, by way of Camp Supply on the North Canadian River. Pope gave Miles wide discretionary authority, permitting him to assume temporary command of Fort Dodge if he found it necessary, and he enjoined the quartermaster and subsistence departments to "promptly comply with all requisitions for supplies" Miles might make. To act in conjunction with the main body under Miles, Pope instructed Major William R. Price to march east from Forts Union and Bascom in the New Mexico Territory along the South Canadian River as far as Antelope Hills, on the rugged eastern fringe of the Llano Estacado. There he was to join Miles's column or act independently, as circumstances might dictate. Although he well understood from his own service on the barren and tortuous Llano Estacado two decades earlier that precise timetables were meaningless, the more so as the Indians might take refuge in any of a number of deep and nearly impenetrable canyons carved into its eastern edge, Pope nonetheless hoped the two columns would move so as to meet no later than the end of August.[46]

Meanwhile, at Department of Texas headquarters in San Antonio, General Augur was busy orchestrating three expeditions of his own. Colonel John W. Davidson was to strike westward from Fort Sill with his Tenth Cavalry; Colonel George P. Buell would move northeastward from Fort Griffin with the Eleventh

Cavalry; and the fiery and gifted Colonel Ranald Mackenzie, from whom Augur expected the most, would sweep northward from Fort Concho with his crack Fourth Cavalry. All five columns were to operate with minimal restrictions; department boundaries were to be ignored in the interest of chasing down hostile Indians.[47]

From Fort Leavenworth, Pope watched the campaign unfold. "I trust the Indian campaign may turn out better than I expect," he wrote Secretary of War Belknap in September. "I have done all I can to make it a success. You probably know that it was against my judgment to make it at this season of the year, and I am sorry to say that the results so far have confirmed my views."[48]

Pope's doubts had as much to do with the character of his principal lieutenant as with the season of the year. Perhaps the most unpleasant and nakedly ambitious field grade officer on the frontier, Nelson Miles never hesitated to disparage anyone, superior officers included, whom he saw as coming between him and a promotion. For Miles, the summer campaign was simply a means of winning recognition. To ensure that the nation learned of his exploits, Miles employed a correspondent of the stridently anti-Indian (and anti–John Pope) *Kansas Daily Commonwealth* as a scout. Miles railed against Pope for not having given him command of all department forces in the field. "Price should really be under my orders," he assured his wife. "The idea of anyone presuming to direct movements against Indians five hundred miles away and ten days away from telegraph communications!"[49]

Intent on reaching the Indian strongholds along the base of the Llano Estacado ahead of his principal rival, Ranald Mackenzie, Miles pushed his men relentlessly over the most inhospitable terrain imaginable. "The march has been rapid and the heat intense, the unusually dry season has left the country almost destitute of water," Miles told Pope in one of his few dispatches from the field. Supplies also grew low, as Miles's march had taken him over a hundred miles from his depot at Camp Supply.

Rather than slow the pace, when Miles saw the Indians' trail freshen and grow larger, he accelerated the march. On August 30, he struck the principal Cheyenne encampment near the entrance of Palo Duro Canyon, at the headwaters of the Red River. An eight-day running fight ensued. Only three warriors were killed, but Miles succeeded in destroying large amounts of Indian property and provisions before the hostiles dispersed over the Llano Estacado. Practically out of supplies himself, Miles halted and sent his wagons back to Camp Supply.[50]

Appreciative of Miles's talent, if not his nature, Pope praised his efforts on the Red River. Although correctly fearing the Indians were now "hopelessly scattered until the cold weather forces them into the wooded country where fuel and food can be had," Pope told Sheridan that "Colonel Miles has acted with great vigor and persistency and has done the best that could be expected at this time of year according to my opinion." His good opinion of Miles soured, however, when the egotistical colonel explained away his failure to accomplish more by accusing Pope of having withheld supplies and transportation. Miles also falsely charged Pope's chief quartermaster officer, Stewart Van Vliet, not only with "bad management" but also with corruption, alleging he had skimmed off supplies destined for the field. By not investigating Van Vliet, Miles complained to his wife and to his staff, Pope had subverted the expedition—accusations that the Dodge City press prudently declined to repeat.[51]

An infuriated Pope defended his actions to Sheridan. Miles seemed to "want wagons enough to haul supplies and forage to great distances which it is impractical to furnish him and impracticable for him to get along with if he had them. For anything like efficient service, or rapid movement," concluded Pope, "Miles has all the transportation he can use advantageously, and to buy more mules and fit up wagons would be a long tedious and unnecessary labor and expense as it seems to me." Pope's ire was the greater because Miles had neglected his rear, permitting hostile Kiowa and Comanche from the Anadarko Agency, driven west by Davidson, to cut his supply line; they were joined by some of the very Cheyenne whom Miles had encountered in Palo Duro Canyon. On September 9, the Anadarko renegades attacked Miles's supply train on the bank of the Washita River. Only the opportune arrival of Price's cavalry prevented a massacre. At the same time, small war parties swept through southwestern Kansas, which had been stripped of troops to support Miles. Among those killed was a party of surveyors, whom Miles had refused a military escort on the grounds no Indians could have slipped through his lines. Utterly exasperated, Pope ordered Miles to withdraw to the Washita River, a directive with which Sheridan concurred. Miles did so, but not before complaining to the press that he was hurt and baffled as to why the department commander should hold him back.[52]

Although he expected Miles to protect his own trains, Pope tried to meet his supply needs. He ordered Van Vliet to comb the countryside for wagons and to set up a supply camp for Miles on the Washita before October 1, and he promised to send Miles fresh mounts. Miles condemned Pope's orders as "coldblooded" and continued to snarl over treachery in the quartermaster department. He went so far as to suggest to General Sherman, whose nephew he was by marriage, that the "whole Indian region" be organized as a separate department, with himself in command.

While Miles ranted about Pope's "lack of sympathy" for his command, Colonel Mackenzie engaged the Cheyenne at Tule Canyon on September 26, and again at Palo Duro Canyon two days later. In the most decisive action of the campaign, Mackenzie overran the Indian camp, burning lodges and food stores and slaughtering the Cheyenne pony herd of some one thousand animals. Buell, Price, and Davidson also destroyed large amounts of Indian provisions, and a resupplied detachment from Miles's command whipped the Cheyenne decisively at McClellan Creek on November 8. Harsh, early-winter blizzards compounded the Indians' suffering, and as the winter wore on, defectors from the hostile camps streamed into the agencies to surrender in ever greater numbers. Supply difficulties engendered by bad weather and civilian contractors unable to meet their obligations prevented the winter campaign that Pope had wanted and Sheridan had come to believe necessary, but an offer from Pope of amnesty and small-scale operations after the first spring thaw sufficed to cause the remaining hostile bands to capitulate. On June 2, 1875, the last of the renegades filed sullenly into Fort Sill and threw down their arms, ending what came to be called the Red River War.[53]

Phil Sheridan was thrilled with the outcome. The Red River War had far surpassed his own campaign of six years before, he conceded. Stripped of the means of making war, the southern Plains tribes had been subjugated forever. "This campaign was not only very comprehensive," Sheridan averred in his annual report for 1875, "but was the most successful of any Indian Campaign in this country since its settlement by the whites; and much credit is due to the officers and men engaged in it." Pope concurred. Forgetting their differences, Pope praised Miles—whose stubborn persistence had done much to demoralize the Indians—warmly in his own report.[54]

16 A Life for the Nation

The collapse of Cheyenne, Kiowa, and Comanche resistance on the southern Plains gave John Pope an occasion to demonstrate just how profound were his concerns for the welfare of the Indian. As early as October 1874, Pope had expressed his displeasure with the Indian Bureau's cavalier treatment of the friendly tribes. Despite the presence of troops under orders to attack all Indians not at their agencies, in that month Commissioner of Indian Affairs Edward P. Smith permitted four hundred unsuspecting Pawnee to hunt buffalo in the Indian Territory. An incredulous Pope protested, "When it is considered that the Indian Territory is everywhere now the theatre of active hostilities, and that troops, as well as hostile bands of Indians, are to be met anywhere, this action of the Indian Department seems most extraordinary."

More extraordinary still was the neglect of the agency Indians, whom Pope in late December reported to be "well nigh starving, the Indian agent being unable to feed or clothe them." Pope met with Sheridan on the matter, and the latter was appalled. "These peaceful Indians have behaved so admirably," Sheridan wrote the War Department, "that they should not be allowed to suffer."[1]

But they did suffer. Unable to feed them during the winter months, Indian agents throughout the territory permitted their charges to hunt buffalo off their reservations; many other friendly bands wandered off without permission. Again Pope protested angrily. From the hunting parties the hostile Indians were supplied with ponies, ammunition, and the weapons needed to keep up their fight. Wrote Pope, "As long as their agents neglect to provide the Reservation Indians with the necessary food, and allow them to roam at will through the country in which the troops are operating against hostile Indians, or, in other words, so long as divided authority exists over these Indians, as is now the case, it is idle to expect that the operations of the troops against the Indians who are hostile will accomplish any satisfactory result."

Pope had been guilty of hyperbole—army operations against the hostiles proved quite successful, but their very success compounded the difficulties Pope faced. In February, Pope received orders from Washington to stop issuing military supplies to Indians surrendering as prisoners of war. What alternative to their starvation existed, asked Pope? Conditions at the agencies were so bad that the Indians were slaughtering their ponies for food. Constrained by congressional guidelines that prohibited the issuance of foodstuffs to Indians who had been hostile during the previous fiscal year, the Indian Bureau was unable to feed the sixteen hundred Southern Cheyennes who had given themselves up. Pope could of course rearm them and send them back into the war zone to hunt, but he doubted Washington wanted that. Absent explicit instructions to the contrary, Pope would continue to feed them.

It was incomprehensible to Pope that Indians should be compelled to suffer once they had been forced back onto their reservations. The prospect of starvation, he feared, might lead to a renewal of the war. "Who can blame them," he wrote the War Department, "if, rather than starve to death and see their women and children suffering the pangs of hunger in slow process of starvation, they break away and get food for them in any manner and as soon as they can?"[2]

To prevent such an eventuality, which he feared would lead inexorably to the "final extermination of the Indian race by violence," in late February Pope proposed moving the Southern Cheyenne east to Fort Leavenworth. "We are bound by every law, human and Divine, to feed these prisoners," he insisted. Appealing to the government's economizing instincts, Pope added, "There is good ground and plenty of timber and the Indians can shelter themselves comfortably and be fed at one half the expense which would be incurred at their present agency. I have no doubt that the annual appropriation for these Indians will maintain them here, and deprived of horses and arms and unable to leave the place, they can be subjected under the best conditions to all the influences of civilization and Christianity." Pope also proposed to sell the tribe's ponies and use the proceeds to buy cattle to feed them.

Both General Augur and Colonel Miles, as well General Sherman, who met with Pope and Sheridan in St. Louis in March 1875 to discuss the problem, endorsed Pope's views. Said Sherman to his brother, "The Indian troubles we could settle in an hour, but Congress wants the patronage of the Indian Bureau, and the bureau wants the appropriations without any of the troubles of the Indians themselves."

President Grant initially subscribed to Pope's recommendation to relocate the Cheyennes, but eastern humanitarians, opposed to military control of the Indians under any circumstances, protested vigorously. The corrupt Secretary of the Interior, Columbus Delano, and peculators in the Indian Bureau took up the standard for more selfish reasons. Delano prevailed upon Congress to thwart Pope's plan, and the Cheyennes were left upon their reservation, slowly to starve.[3]

Hunting parties were able to bring in just enough buffalo to subsist the Southern Plains tribes during the remainder of 1875, but the rapid decimation of the few remaining herds convinced Pope a better remedy must be found, and quickly. Colonel Mackenzie, who with the addition of Fort Sill and its neighboring Indian agency to the Department of the Missouri late that year had come under Pope's jurisdiction, agreed. The efforts of Quaker humanitarians to make farmers of the Indians had proved unavailing, as Pope had expected. It was as futile, he argued in his annual report for 1876, to expect the nomadic Plains hunters "to undergo the daily toil of such plowing and hoeing and reaping as are necessary for the cultivation of a farm, as it would be to force an Arab or a Tartar to adopt so artificial a mode of life."

Teach them to be stock raisers, maintained Pope, and the first major step toward assimilation would be accomplished. Acting on their convictions, Pope and Mackenzie arranged to dismount and disarm the Comanche and Kiowa, sell their ponies, and retain most of the proceeds to buy them cattle for livestock. The results were dramatic, conceded Agent James Haworth, who praised the army for its work and endorsed the "peculiar fitness of the Indians for stock-raising." Sadly, little was done in the coming months by the Indian agents to buy enough cattle to have a lasting impact, and as rations again grew scarce, the Indians slaughtered their cattle for food.[4]

Pope continued to demand a more humane, and consistent, government policy toward the Plains Indians, but his words were lost in the storm of scandal that darkened the final months of the Grant administration. With the election of his close friend Rutherford B. Hayes to the White House in November 1876, it looked for a time as if Pope's recommendations might at last be implemented. Pope had been thrilled by Hayes's nomination as the Republican presidential candidate that summer. "My heart is too full today to undertake to write you what I feel," he wrote Hayes friend in unabashedly partisan terms. "You need not be told that I have been for you from the first, no doubt largely influenced by personal attachment, but also and in a larger sense, because I believed and believe that the salvation of the party and the best interests of this country demanded it."[5]

After his election, Hayes repaid Pope's loyalty with an invitation for him to submit through their mutual friend, Judge Manning Force, his opinions on public matters for the president elect's consideration. Pleased as always to have a forum for his views, regardless of the topic, Pope expounded at length on what he saw to be Hayes's obligations to the nation. Sickened by the excesses of the Grant cabinet, Pope insisted, "It is the mission of Hayes to restore the authority and responsibility of the Executive Department of the government; to confine Congress to its legitimate function of legislation; and to conduct the business affairs of the government on business principles." Purity of government and integrity of administration were imperative; to achieve them, Hayes should appoint to his cabinet men new to politics, "young, vigorous, and earnest, who have a future to make and not a past to protect or cover up." No longer an unconditional Republican, Pope believed both parties had "outlived their time"; an emerging populist, he hoped Hayes would form a direct allegiance with the common voter to wipe away the stain of machine politics.

Warming to the subject, Pope wrote Force again two months later to reiterate the need for Hayes to "stand firm on the policy of reform," particularly of the patronage-plagued civil service. "I never felt more anxious about anything in my life than about Hayes's success in administration," he averred. "Everything is at stake—the destiny of this country depends now on Hayes. How many of us are ready and willing to fight against corruption and venality which seem to many necessary to their personal or political interests?"[6]

Hayes seemed ready to give battle. Before leaving Ohio, he broke with the party's elder statesmen and, partly as a consequence of the recommendations of Force and Pope, selected several reformists for his cabinet, among them Carl Schurz as Secretary of the Interior. As a division commander in the Army of Virginia, Schurz had been among the more outspoken critics of Pope after Second Bull Run. But he was determined to cleanse both his department and the Bureau of Indian Affairs, and he now consulted openly with Pope on the subject of Indian policy. At the secretary's request, Pope provided him with his salient papers on the subject, written during the preceding fifteen years. Schurz was particularly taken with Pope's experiments in selling Indian ponies for cattle, and he made that a fundamental tenet of his administration of Indian affairs. He also agreed with Pope on the need to expose the Plains Indians to the better elements of American society, "to see and watch civilization at work in its own atmosphere." However, rather than removing the agencies to the east, as Pope advocated, Schurz preferred educating Indian young at schools in the rural northeast.[7]

As president, Hayes was interested in Pope's views on both Indian and army affairs. To hear them firsthand, he invited Pope to Washington in April.[8]

During the 1870s, Pope had come to fear the effects upon society of the army's growing isolation, which service on the harsh and remote frontier exacerbated. Still a strong proponent of absolute civilian primacy over the military (except in the management of Indian affairs), Pope insisted that "the well-being of the people equally with the well-being of the army requires a common sympathy and a common interest between them." Addressing a reunion of the Society of the Army of the Tennessee in October 1873, Pope asked, "Shall we especially of the Regular Army be willing to contemplate without sorrow the certainty that the strong affection which unites us to so many comrades who have returned to civil life will perish, and that the unhappy and well-nigh fatal divorce which for years had separated the Regular Army from the people and which required a great civil war to reconcile, shall again be pronounced upon our descendants?"

Perilous for the Republic too, said Pope, were the effects the isolation and monotony of frontier army life had on the attitudes of the individual soldier. "So long as the soldier remains one of the people; so long as he shares their interests, takes part in their progress, and feels a common sympathy with them in their hopes and aspirations, so long will the army be held in honorable esteem and regard," he told his listeners. "When he ceases to do this; when officers and soldiers cease to be citizens in the highest and truest sense, the army will deserve to lose, as it will surely lose, its place in the affections of the people, and properly and naturally become an object of suspicion and dislike." Pope reiterated his fears in a well-publicized speech before the Society of the Army of the Tennessee a year later, entitled "The Regular Army: Our Teachers in War; Our Defenders in Peace." President Grant attended the meeting and endorsed Pope's words of caution, and Hayes, then governor, read the address with great interest.[9]

Society and the soldier would remain at odds, Pope told President Hayes during their April 1877 meetings, until the army underwent a thoroughgoing reorganization. "I have radical ideas on this subject," Pope told Hayes. Thirty-five years of service had convinced him the Regular establishment was hopelessly unsuited to the demands of American democracy. Patterned after the British military, which Pope termed the most aristocratic system in the world, the Regular Army reflected social and other distinctions "abhorrent to the sentiments of our people and to the spirit of our institutions, an army consisting of a certain number of gentlemen who are officers, and a large number of menials who are the soldiers."

Among the officer corps, rued Pope, "tenacity of life is the only qualification for promotion," while the capable enlisted man was rarely advanced; if he should be promoted, "he is as a rule so demoralized by the social ostracism of years of service as a soldier that he is practically incompetent to adapt himself to the new station." Why was it, Pope asked, "that service in the ranks of the army should be so degraded that we can enlist in the army only the dregs of the slums and alleys of our large cities, and the great railroad or other corporations can commend the very best material in all the conditions of life and society," even though they paid less than the army? Why also was "the soldier so discontented in the army and so anxious to get out of it whilst the officer is so unwilling to be discharged?" These considerations, maintained Pope, must underscore any plan for reorganizing the army.

Pope indicted the army high command candidly. "The trouble with us and especially with our higher officers in the army is that we cannot emancipate ourselves from the monkey state in which imitation is the rule," he wrote. "Because an army organization of a particular sort has proved very efficient in Germany, we immediately jump to the conclusion that we ought to adopt it, and the result is that all of our army papers on organization are simply compilations from foreign sources without the slightest consideration of the enormous difference of circumstance and condition which exist in this country."

The American army must reflect American values. Pope insisted, "When we have organized an army in this country, in which we can command the services of the best men for the work as the railroads now do, and from which the soldier will be as unwilling to be discharged as the officer, we shall have constructed an army in harmony with our free institutions and with the feelings and habits of the people."

And who should determine the shape of the army? Not army officers, said Pope, but rather the civilian leaders of the land. "It is altogether a mistake to suppose that there is any mystery about the conduct of military business," he confessed. "It is subject to the same rules of common sense and especially business sense as any other business and the violation of these rules is as injurious in military as in civil affairs." Although he had not served in the Civil War, George Washington McCrary, the Iowa jurist whom Hayes had appointed secretary of war, impressed Pope as up to the task.[10]

While awaiting whatever action the president might take on his proposals, Pope tried to push several lesser measures for the soldier's welfare through the War Department. To combat desertion, which he attributed partly to the drudgery of frontier duty, Pope made a novel suggestion: use half the amount collected in court-martial sentences to buy books, magazines, and newspapers and to build post libraries and reading rooms. As the Indian threat diminished, he also vigorously championed the closing of remote posts and the concentrating of units in regimental strength at larger installations. The money thus saved, argued Pope, could be used to build more modern quarters and provide better training.[11]

━ ◆ ━

Undoubtedly John Pope felt, with the advent of the Hayes administration, that his day had arrived. Not only was Hayes deeply interested in Pope's views on national affairs, but the new president could be expected to look out for Pope's professional welfare, perhaps even obtaining for him the next available major general's billet.

Pope expectations were shattered, however, when in April 1878 he learned that the same spirit of justice and impartiality that motivated Hayes's reformist policies had also led him—after repeated applications by the chairman of the Senate Military Affairs Committee, Theodore F. Randolph—to appoint a board of senior army officers to review the findings in the Fitz John Porter case. Brigadier General John M. Schofield, whose relations with both Pope and Porter were cordial but lukewarm, was named chairman. Brigadier General Alfred H. Terry and Colonel George W. Getty rounded out the board. The board convened on June 20, 1878, at West Point, where Schofield served as superintendent.

For Porter, the board hearing was the hopeful culmination of sixteen years of incessant appeals; for Pope and his friends, a stunning reversal. Judge Force at once wrote Hayes to question the propriety of rehearing the case, in view of President Grant's refusal to reopen the matter. Pope lamented to Joseph Holt that the appointing of the review board implied nothing less than an effort "to try the court-martial and all connected with it." To his intimate friend James A. Garfield, Pope confided his fear the board would reverse the 1863 decision.[12]

Commanding General of the Army William T. Sherman urged Pope to remain calm and not give the board cause for hostility toward him. "I would fail in a friendly duty were I to remain passive, and for this reason I venture to advise you not to contest further what has been done and to conform as gracefully as you can, and as you so well know how to do," counseled Sherman. Should the board call upon Pope to testify, Sherman recommended he comply "cheerfully and thoroughly," particularly as the board was empowered merely to make recommendations to the president, who Sherman believed held a continuing kindly regard for Pope.[13]

Sound advice, but on the matter of Fitz John Porter, Pope was beyond the appeal of reason. For sixteen years he had believed Porter's culpability to be "perfectly clear and beyond mistake or misunderstanding." When in 1876 the Comte de Paris, Louis-Philippe d'Orleans, a former member of McClellan's staff turned military historian, published in the English translation of the second volume of his widely read history of the Civil War an exculpatory account of Porter's actions at Second Bull Run, based on new evidence in the form of Confederate reports, Pope had a public duel of letters with him.

Pope spoke out reluctantly. He had expected Thomas C. H. Smith already to have published his long-awaited (by Pope at least) work on the Second Bull Run campaign. "For my children's sake and the place I am to hold in their minds in the future," Pope had told Smith in 1875, "I am painfully anxious about the publication of your book. You will understand and appreciate what I feel and say and I beg you if it be possible to do this for me."

Two years later, with Smith's opus still incomplete, Pope told Judge Force he despaired of ever seeing the work in print. Smith had grown despondent after losing his considerable wealth in the 1871 Chicago fire, and what began as a well-documented, judicious narrative deteriorated into a disjointed collection of opinionated drafts. Smith had amassed enough evidence to refute everything Porter and the Comte de Paris had published, Pope complained to Force, "but he is so touchy that I don't like to say anything to him about the long delay in getting his book ready and the injury such delay is doing me by allowing false and unfair statements and books to crystallize into history."

Between May 1876 and April 1877, Pope exchanged letters with the Comte de Paris, whom he felt had taken Porter's side on the subject of Second Bull Run without examining all the evidence, in particular the testimony of General McDowell given at the court-martial. The Comte de Paris resented Pope's questioning of his version of events, and in rebutting Pope he also exposed the emptiness of Pope's arguments against Porter. Faced with the force of a logic he could not concede, Pope terminated their correspondence in disgust.[14]

Nothing in Porter's most recent appeal changed Pope's perspective on the campaign. "Neither Porter nor any of his friends, so far as I know (and I have seen all his papers), undertake to deny any of the allegations set forth in the charges and specifications on which he was tried and cashiered," Pope assured Judge Force. "His papers merely attempt to set forth *justification* of his conduct. This justification is based solely on letters from Confederate officers and others that the enemy was in strong force in front of him and that he would have been defeated if he had attacked."[15]

Beginning in late June, the Schofield board heard witnesses from the original court-martial, as well as former Confederate General James Longstreet, whom the government's counsel could not shake from his conviction that Porter would have been slaughtered, had he attacked any time after noon on August 29, 1862. Counsel for Porter was more effective, tripping up both Thomas C. H. Smith and Douglass Pope on more than one occasion. Most significant, Douglass Pope was compelled to admit he really had not known at what hour he had delivered to Porter the 4:30 P.M. attack order. By mid-October, only John Pope remained to be heard from. Counsel for Porter insisted Pope's presence was necessary in justice to its client. The government counsel, Major Asa B. Gardner, told Porter's lead attorney, John C. Bullitt, to summon Pope as its witness. Bullitt refused, saying he wished Pope called as a witness for the government, in order that he might be cross-examined on his testimony of sixteen years before. Not surprisingly, Gardner declined, as such an act would be contrary to all law and prejudicial to

Pope's rights as a witness. At that Schofield intervened, promising to call Pope as a witness for the board.

Pope was outraged. Besides being illegal, Pope told Schofield, to appear before the board without knowing whether he had been called explicitly for the petitioner or the government would put him in a false position. Not that he was unwilling to testify: "To a subpoena regularly issued to appear as a witness for either side, I will cheerfully and promptly respond."

In reply, Schofield took it upon himself to summon Pope on behalf of the government. Pope was incredulous, and he passed Schofield's demand on to the secretary of war for his opinion. "For General Schofield to subpoena me now, in spite of the refusal of the counsel for government to do so, as a witness for the government simply to accommodate the wish of petitioner's counsel, is wholly inconsistent with the proceedings of the civil or military tribunals of the country as well as with justice," Pope complained to Secretary McCrary. Why, Pope asked, should he be compelled to undergo cross-examination on direct evidence given in 1862, and about which he was then thoroughly questioned by Porter's counsel? Pope also doubted that the board, convened as it was to consider new evidence presented by Porter and only such other testimony "as might be presented to it," had the legal authority to subpoena witnesses. Pope concluded: "I wish to do exactly what is right, and if I can avoid it will not submit to wrong." Indignant but unsure of the correctness of his legal interpretation, Pope also asked Judge Force for his opinion.[16]

Force concurred with Pope. So too did Secretary McCrary, who admonished Schofield for having exceeded his authority. Pope could be called only as a witness for the petitioner, and he must not be cross-examined except upon matters brought out on direct examination in the present proceedings.

Although Pope heard nothing further from the board, Porter's partisans availed themselves of Pope's seeming intransigence to pummel him in the Democratic press. "On a mere quibble, Pope avoids appearing before the Porter board of inquiry," the *Washington Post* told its readers on October 31. "He dares not confirm, under oath, the wild stories that he and his friends dinned into the public ear sixteen years ago. His failure to appear, when invited by the board, will be construed as an admission that he cannot support his old charges." The *New York World* agreed that, by refusing to appear, Pope had "given very strong evidence against himself."[17]

Comments of that sort caused Pope to despair that "I am the person on trial apparently." Why should he "rush eagerly forward of his own volition to prostrate himself" before the Schofield board, he asked Force, when attendance before it was purely voluntarily? Pope marveled, "I am at a loss to know sometimes whether I am insane myself or whether I am dealing with people who have lost their senses."[18]

That impression was confirmed in Pope's mind when the Schofield board made public its report on April 2, 1879. Not only did Schofield and his colleagues exculpate Porter from wrongdoing during the campaign, but they also obliquely chastised Pope for having been misinformed about the state of affairs on August 29, 1862. This misapprehension, they speculated, had colored the findings of the court-martial because its members had taken Pope's account of events at face value. In submitting its report to President Hayes, the board recommended he annul the findings and sentence of the court-martial and restore Porter to duty.

General Schofield always insisted he had entered into the West Point proceedings presuming Porter's guilt, but that the evidence of his innocence that emerged had been incontrovertible. "The cold terms of an official report," Schofield wrote Porter after the report was published, "could but faintly express the feeling which my associates fully shared with me when we fully realized the magnitude of the wrong under which you had so long suffered, since your conduct had been not only free from fault but deserving of high commendation and praise."[19]

Pope thought otherwise. He was sure Schofield had been enlisted for duty on the board because of his undisguised "bias and partisanship." Major Gardner told Pope that Schofield had made up his mind before the proceedings began; Schofield also submitted the report before Gardner had concluded his summary arguments. The board, Pope told Force, was nothing but a whitewash of Porter. "It is hard to know what to do or to say in such a matter," Pope confided in exasperation. "For myself, I shall say or do nothing." He would not object, however, if Judge Force worked the press on his behalf.[20]

Fitz John Porter was enormously pleased with the outcome. "May God bless you and yours as he has me and mine through you," he wrote Schofield. Congratulatory letters came to Porter from, among others, George B. McClellan, Gouverneur K. Warren, Winfield Scott Hancock, John Gibbon, Montgomery Blair, and the Comte de Paris. The Democratic press trumpeted the board findings and condemned the testimony of Thomas C. H. Smith and other Pope partisans.[21]

Pope, however, was not without his advocates. Republican senators John A. Logan, Zachariah Chandler, and Matthew H. Carpenter opposed the verdict, as did Congressmen James A. Garfield and Jacob D. Cox and Indiana Republican stalwart Benjamin Harrison. Robert Todd Lincoln also deplored it. Brigadier General Benjamin H. Grierson offered Pope his support. Secretary of War McCrary and presidential private secretary William K. Rogers read the report with disgust. And, Rogers told Pope, President Hayes evidently regretted "he had ever taken such an elephant [as the Porter case] on his shoulders." If he accepted the board's verdict, Hayes would in effect be repudiating Abraham Lincoln, a dangerous act for a Republican, and offending many of his own most powerful supporters. Pope recognized Hayes's dilemma and divined he would neither sign nor approve the report. Instead, Hayes sent it without comment to Congress, where in the coming decade it would provoke an abiding controversy.[22]

Besides savoring Hayes's predicament, Pope also enjoyed a small victory over Schofield. In April, he was called to New York City to serve on a court-martial board himself. While there, Pope was startled to receive a call at his hotel from Schofield. Only two weeks had elapsed since the board report had been made public. Pope contemplated declining to see him, but as Logan was standing nearby when the desk clerk told him of the general's visit, Pope concluded "it would appear childish to refuse to recognize him." Schofield strode forward and extended his hand; Pope returned the courtesy with "rigid politeness." Schofield had come to invite Pope to present the diplomas and give an address to the graduating West Point class in June. Pope deferred a reply until Schofield should send him a written invitation. "Now what do you think?" Pope chuckled to Force. "I know it must be a bitter pill to him, that it obliges him to eat dirt in the face of the whole corps of cadets as well as of the army and that to Porter and his friends it will be an aggravation beyond expression." Nevertheless, Pope was not sure he should attend; his presence might be construed as a compromise of sorts on the Porter case. He left the decision to Force, who urged Pope to go.[23]

Pope enjoyed another public moment that fall. On the evening of November 13, he was a principal guest and speaker at the most lavish reunion of the Army of the Tennessee to date. Six hundred guests attended the banquet dinner at the Palmer House in Chicago. Among those at the head table were Grant, Sherman, Sheridan, Logan, Augur, and Pope. Schofield sat elsewhere.[24]

— ◆ —

Aggravating though they were, the Fitz John Porter proceedings were not Pope's sole concern as the decade drew to a close. No sooner had the southern Plains tribes been pacified than trouble broke out with the Ute of southwestern Colorado. Although nominally located on a sprawling reservation some seventy-five miles west of Denver, the thirty-five hundred Ute continued to roam much as they always had. Pope had little sympathy for the Ute, whom he dismissed in a February 1879 letter as "worthless, idle vagabonds, who are no more likely to earn a living where they are by manual labor than by teaching metaphysics." For several years he had seen the potential for an outbreak, as wandering Utes annoyed lawful settlers, burned forests, killed cattle, and stole horses. The discovery of silver in the San Juan Mountains compelled the Ute to cede one-quarter of their land in 1873; the prospect of more riches buried elsewhere on the reservation, as well as the rich agricultural potential of its western reaches, caused Coloradans to mount a strident campaign to have the tribe removed to the Indian Territory.

White depredations grew apace until, by the autumn of 1879, Pope had come to view the Ute as the true victims. In his annual report, Pope begged the government to give early attention to the problem. While he did not believe a general war likely, Pope insisted that, "as the relations between the emigrants and the Indians are becoming every day more critical it is quite out of the question that things can be left long as they are without serious troubles and collisions."[25]

Particularly troublesome to Pope were the two bands of Ute on the White River Agency. They had declined to treat with government commissioners the year before; worse yet, from Pope's perspective, their new agent, Nathan C. Meeker, was an eccentric old fool who demanded the Ute relinquish their customs and instantly become farmers. When they resisted, Meeker demanded Pope send troops to compel their compliance. Reluctantly, Pope dispatched a troop of cavalry to the vicinity of the reservation—but only to investigate reports of Ute setting forest fires. From the Department of the Platte, George Crook sent an infantry column under Major Thomas T. Thornburgh north toward the agency. For the White River Ute, the summoning of soldiers by Meeker was the last straw; a rumor spread among them that they were to be removed in chains to the Indian Territory. On September 29, a war party ambushed Thornburgh's column, killing the major and ten soldiers and touching off a bloody uprising that next claimed the lives of Meeker and nine of his employees. Availing themselves of the railroads, which a decade earlier Pope had predicted would change the nature of Plains warfare, he and Crook poured thirty-two hundred troops into the region within two weeks of the Meeker massacre. Hostilities ended shortly thereafter.[26]

The Ute War impressed upon Pope the critical need for judicious Indian agents in his department. In the spring of 1880 it appeared that Galen Eastman, the Indian agent at Fort Defiance, New Mexico, was about to provoke an uprising among the normally peaceful Navajo by his "absurd and injudicious efforts to control them in their amusements by withholding supplies unless they conformed to his ideas about holding Sunday and observing other religious requirements which he deemed essential to a healthy religious life." Pope acted quickly. He sent Colonel George P. Buell with all the troops in southern Colorado by forced march to remove Eastman. In his place, Pope installed Captain Frank Bennett of the Ninth Cavalry, whom the Navajo liked and trusted. Bennett readily defused the situation.

The War Department sustained Pope, but the Indian Bureau reinstated Eastman shortly thereafter. Tensions mounted as soon as Eastman returned. At the same time, full-scale war threatened to break out with the Apache in Arizona. Fearful that the angry Navajo might make common cause with Apache renegades under Victorio, Pope again replaced "the psalm-singing hypocrite" Eastman with Captain Bennett.[27]

Pope had a high regard for the Navajo, of whom he wrote:

They are partly civilized, having had for many years constant intercourse and commingling with the whites. They are consequently quite intelligent and know perfectly well what are their rights as well as their wrongs, in dealing with their agents and with the people around them. To keep them peaceful and contented requires that they have an agent of unusual intelligence, force of character, and knowledge of Indians as well as of frontier whites. . . . The Navahoes are rich in herds and powerful in numbers, courageous and sensitive of wrong, and make as formidable warriors as any Indians on this continent.[28]

Less threatening than the discontent of the Navajo but more poignant was the suffering of the subjugated southern Plains tribes. Since the end of the Red River War, Pope had been forced to watch them degraded and starved. Speaking before the Social Science Association of Cincinnati on May 24, 1878, Pope gave his most impassioned and eloquent defense of Indian rights ever. As Pope told his listeners, "It is a most painful duty to be forced to witness suffering and privation day after day, and to see whole tribes of Indians so destitute that it makes the heart sick to witness it. The military authorities have not even the right to relieve the hungry and the destitute from the public stores in their charge, but whatever goes on, they must remain silent and on no account interfere with the transactions of the Indian agent, whatever he does or fails to do."[29]

Particularly galling to Pope was the habit of Indian agents to withhold food when their charges misbehaved. On August 16, 1880, the Southern Cheyenne nearly went to war when Agent Miles refused to release back rations due them. A mob of three hundred hungry Indians yanked Miles from his horse and threatened to sack the agency if he failed to open the stores. "Certainly some better and less exasperating method than this can be found to compel the Indians to work in the field, send their children to school, and other things that the Indian Bureau may consider for the benefit of the Indian," Pope complained in his 1881 report.[30]

Only slightly less infuriating to Pope was the steadily growing number of white intrusions onto Indian lands. Led by the likes of David Payne, an unscrupulous Kansan, and Charles Carpenter, who delighted in taunting "General Bull Run Pope," droves of land-hungry settlers called "Boomers" lined up along the southern Kansas border. Pope set up a cavalry cordon to protect the sanctity of the Indian Territory and did his best to remove those squatters who got through it. The frontier press condemned Pope, but President Hayes sustained him, proclaiming on April 26, 1879, and again on February 12, 1880, that any white invaders of Indian lands would be removed by force.

Hayes's well-intentioned proclamations accomplished little. No sooner were Payne and his indigent followers arrested than they were released, being too poor to pay their fines. Better legislation and steeper penalties, Pope argued to both Sheridan and Sherman, were needed urgently, but Congress refused to act, and the Boomers gradually succeeded in opening the Indian Territory to settlement.[31]

A third source of concern to Pope was the trespassing on Indian lands of cattle herds from the Chisholm Trail and from Texas and Kansas border ranches. By the spring of 1882, some 150,000 head of cattle had spilled onto the reservations, destroying the Indians' best range and spreading disease among their own small herds. The secretary of the interior demanded the War Department remove the illicit herds, but Pope protested that such a task was beyond the capability of his small command. General Sheridan endorsed Pope's views, as did most subordinate officers in the field. In an odd instance of like thinking, Pope recommended the government adopt a proposal by Agent Miles, who suggested cattle be permitted on remote parts of the Cheyenne-Arapaho Reservation in exchange for a grazing tax, which he would in turn use to supplement the Indians' meager rations. The commissioner of Indian affairs denied Miles's petition, but Pope persisted. Phil Sheridan forwarded his letters to the War Department, which in turn pressed the matter with the Department of the Interior. Finally, in April 1883, the Indian Bureau relented, with the caveat that payment for grazing privileges be made in cattle. In eighteen years of personal struggle for reforms in the Indian system, Pope could count precious few other victories over his bureaucratic adversaries in Washington.[32]

But he made new and influential friends, among them Jacob D. Cox. A reformist Republican and close friend of Hayes and Garfield, Cox had left the Ohio state senate at the start of the Civil War to raise volunteer regiments. He served with distinction during the war, rising to command of the Twenty-third Corps during the Atlanta campaign. After the war, Cox was elected governor of Ohio; later he served as secretary of the interior in the Grant administration. Cox always maintained a deep interest in military affairs. Generally recognized as an elegant and forceful writer, of fine critical ability and impartial judgment, he wrote widely on the Civil War and was *The Nation's* military book critic.

Long after the war, Cox came to know Pope through their mutual friend, Judge Force. Remembering how he had shrunk from service under Pope during the Second Bull Run campaign, because of the general's reputation of being "vehement and positive in character, choleric and even violent toward those who displeased him," Cox was surprised to find the John Pope of the early 1880s a very different man, "broken in health and softened by personal afflictions." They met often at the home of Judge Force, and the tall, graceful, and courteous Cox became a devoted friend of the aging general.[33]

The decline Cox witnessed in Pope was due in no small measure to the continuing strain of the Porter case. Porter and his partisans were hard at work in the

Senate, trying to gather Republican support for a bill to set aside the 1863 court-martial decision and restore Porter to the army. John A. Logan remained vehemently opposed to Porter's redemption, as did Senators Garfield and John Sherman. Together they defeated the first two relief bills.

Public opinion, however, was turning in Porter's favor. On July 2, 1881, Pope lost perhaps his greatest ally in the fight when an assassin's bullet felled the newly elected president, James A. Garfield. Also that summer, the distinguished historian John Codman Ropes came out with *The Army under Pope,* which, although not openly hostile to Pope, generally approved of Porter's conduct at Second Bull Run. Most devastating to Pope was the appearance in the April issue of the prestigious *North American Review* of an article by Ulysses S. Grant exculpating Porter of any misconduct. Not only did Grant find the report of the Schofield board compelling, but he also publicly apologized for having failed to act on Porter's behalf himself while president. Logan fought back with a letter to the *Chicago Tribune,* in which he asserted that any vindication of Porter implied the condemnation of Garfield and Lincoln. Equating opposition to Porter with Republicanism, in December Logan delivered a titanic, vituperative speech on the Senate floor that succeeded in killing the third Porter relief bill in the House of Representatives.

Undeterred, Porter's congressional allies introduced yet another relief bill in February 1883. Logan again led the opposition. Despite his mammoth stature in the Senate, Logan was unable to stay the tide of congressional opinion, and the bill passed both houses. At this juncture, President Chester Arthur stepped in with a veto, which the House overrode but the Senate confirmed. No one was more disgusted with the outcome than Grant. "You can scarcely believe the pain it caused me to read the veto of your bill by the president," Grant told Porter. "I was not prepared for it. His message was the merest sophistry."[34]

During the congressional debate over the relief bills, Pope had written little and said less. He deeply appreciated the constancy of Logan and the support of his new friend, Jacob Cox. In February 1882, Cox had spoken against Porter before the Army and Navy Society; later that year, he expanded upon that address in a book entitled *The Second Battle of Bull Run, as Connected with the Fitz-John Porter Case.*[35]

Where Pope did speak up was in regard to his own military future. The impending retirement of Irvin McDowell meant a vacancy in one of the Regular Army's three major-general billets. As senior brigadier, with forty years service, Pope felt eminently entitled to the promotion. Scratching out a cable from Fort Leavenworth on October 16, 1882, Pope told President Arthur in no uncertain terms, "If there be any purpose or question of promoting anyone over my head I ask respectfully that I be first permitted as a matter of justice to appear personally before [you] at such time as [you] may designate with senators and military friends to represent my case." Letters of recommendation followed from, among others, former generals Manning F. Force, Andrew Hickenlooper, and John W. Fuller; Judge David Davis; former Supreme Court justice William Strong; Walter Q. Gresham, United States District Court judge for Indiana; and William Howard Taft, then collector of internal revenue for Cincinnati. Secretary of War Robert Todd Lincoln probably also spoke up on Pope's behalf. On October 26, 1882, Pope learned of his promotion to McDowell's billet.[36]

Promotion meant a change of duty stations. Pope coveted command of the Military Division of the Missouri, which Sheridan could be expected to relinquish when Sherman retired as commanding general of the army, and lobbied hard to gain it. Senator Philetus Sawyer of Wisconsin, Governor George Washington Glick of Kansas, Congressman Dudley A. Haskell of the Leavenworth district, and nearly all the leading citizens of Leavenworth City implored the president to grant Pope the promotion. Haskell wrote, "General Pope has greatly endeared himself to our people, and they would rejoice to have him remain with them" in the enhanced capacity of division commander. Governor Glick agreed, telling Arthur, "The general has commanded in our Indian troubles, knows completely our ways, so that our people have unbounded confidence in him."[37]

Aware he faced mandatory retirement himself in four years, Pope was reluctant to move his family any farther from the Midwest than was necessary. Division headquarters in Chicago would place him close to both St. Louis, where he and Clara hoped to retire, and Pomeroy, Ohio, where Pope had considerable business interests. And neither he nor Clara was in the best of health. Then too, their family had grown with the birth of a third son, Francis Horton Pope, in 1876. As the sixty-year-old father of a six-year-old, and with eldest son Horton off to Harvard University, Pope was troubled about his ability to provide for his family after retirement. On the advice of Judge Force and of Clara's nephew, the eminent economist Dana Horton, Pope had invested heavily in Horton family enterprises in Pomeroy, particularly the Pomeroy Coal Company and Horton salt furnaces. In the spring of 1883 a horrendous flood of the Ohio River submerged Pomeroy, sweeping away hundreds of thousands of dollars in property and industry. A second flood followed the next spring. Close on the heels of the 1884 deluge came a tremendous fire, which destroyed an entire block in the business district in one night. When the Pomeroy Coal Company, the largest employer in the county, collapsed, most townspeople thought a death blow had been dealt to the area's capital and public enterprise.[38]

It certainly seemed so to Pope, who suddenly found himself badly overextended. Only with the floods and fire did he learn that Dana Horton had squandered so much of his own and Pope's money on bad investments that he was unable to meet the coal company's vast indebtedness. "I have read carefully Dana's statement. To me it is simply a record of debt, debt on all sides and nothing else," Pope wrote bitterly to Force that June. "I see no outcome and I cannot in justice to my family borrow money which I should not be able to pay back, merely to throw it into that maelstrom of debt. I cannot make out what was in his mind when he was loading himself with all manner of liabilities for concerns and business not his own. Perhaps I don't understand matters as I am no businessman, but I think I do comprehend enough of the subject not to be willing to risk all I have in the world to support my family and educate my children upon enterprises of this sort."[39]

Pope was disappointed but not surprised when on November 1, 1883, he was assigned command of the Military Division of the Pacific, with headquarters at the Presidio in San Francisco; Sheridan and Sherman both had been evasive on the matter of the Missouri command.[40]

Much to their delight, Pope and Clara both found the temperate climate of northern California agreeable, although she was occasionally troubled by rheumatic gout in her arms during the rainy months. Their quarters at the Presidio were elegant and the view of the bay spectacular. Although he doubted he "could ever become domesticated here," Pope enjoyed the city of San Francisco and its society. He was guest of honor at the annual dinner of the Harvard Club, held at the sumptuous Palace Hotel on October 16, 1884. Rising to offer a toast, Pope was "heartily applauded," said the San Francisco Examiner. Pope spoke with a pleasant humility and warm humor. He stood before them, he said, "with the greatest diffidence," as he was "almost afraid to tell Harvard men anything." His son Horton, a Harvard sophomore, had visited for the summer, Pope went on, and he had found it "almost impossible to tell that Harvard sophomore anything that he did not know." Pope went on to speak of West Point, expressing a hope that "the day would come when that institution gave her sons a little more liberal training." Pope wanted to see literature taught, along with all things a gentleman should know. The applause that followed, observed the Examiner, was as hearty as that which had preceded Pope's talk.[41]

With all the Indians of the division except the Apaches in Arizona long since pacified, duty was easy, and Pope had plenty of time on his hands. He filled it with reading, becoming something of an authority on the exploration and early history of San Francisco, and with entertaining family and friends. His sisters visited, as did Senator John Sherman and Judge and Mrs. Force. Pope tried to convince Thomas C. H. Smith to come out to California, only to learn from his daughter that his old friend had become "a hermit with no special interest in anything." An unexpected renascence in steamboat traffic on the Ohio River, a vigorous rebirth of the Pomeroy coal and salt industries, and the discovery of oil on Horton property eased Pope's financial worries. All things considered, Pope wrote Force, "we are all happy as people can expect in this life."[42]

Not even the inauguration of Democratic president Grover Cleveland in March 1885 or his signing into law in July of a relief bill reinstating Porter to the army with the rank of colonel (Porter was placed on the retired list the same day) dampened Pope's spirits. Rutherford B. Hayes, who spent some time with Pope that year, thought him of "a different spirit now," no longer contentious or particularly interested in the old rivalries. Clara's health, the welfare of his children and dearest friends, and his own imminent retirement occupied nearly all of Pope's attention. Apart from letters to contest Porter's appeals, Pope had said nothing publicly about Second Bull Run in eight years. But in the spring of 1885, devious maneuvering by the editors of the monthly *Century* magazine compelled him to revisit that painful topic.

The year before, *Century* had begun featuring papers written by leading participants in the Civil War, North and South, under the title *Battles and Leaders of the Civil War.* The editors had staked much on the series' success and so were unwilling to accept a polite no to their request that John Pope contribute a paper on Second Bull Run. If he would not write a history of the campaign, they would find someone "who might not possibly be friendly" to the general.

Pope wrote the paper, which was published in the January 1886 issue of *Century.* Former Confederate general James Longstreet, who had dealt Pope the fatal blow at Second Bull Run, contributed a paper from the Southern perspective.[43]

Surprisingly temperate in tone, Pope's article nonetheless repeated the same arguments against Porter he had made for the past twenty-four years. The response to it was partisan but generally favorable; Pope had written a second article for *Century,* to be published only if "the attacks on the first should go beyond temperate and fair criticism," but there was no need to run it. The press greeted Pope's article politely, and friends such as Force, Hayes, Cox, and Grierson applauded the paper. Supporters of Porter deplored it. Brigadier General John Gibbon assured Porter that "as a contribution to history this paper of Pope's is utterly worthless, except in a negative way. He reminds me of the cuttle fish which . by clouding the water about him succeeds in eluding, for a time, his enemies."[44]

Pope himself was pleased with the response to the article. From the Presidio, where he was about to relinquish command of the Military Division of the Pacific prior to retiring, Pope wrote Judge Force merrily, "We are in the midst of packing up for our move east and I've time this morning to write you a few lines as I must go home immediately to help Clara who is not in condition to over[see] matters though she won't let anyone else do it. My article seems to have been received with almost universal praise. I am quite surprised at the reception of the article by many papers which heretofore have been very hostile."[45]

Pope had enjoyed writing war history. His retirement on March 16, 1886, gave him time to do more of it. He, Clara, and their three younger children settled into the family home in St. Louis, at 3223 Lucas Street. Clara's health grew increasingly fragile, and Pope himself suffered periodically from lumbago. When they did venture out, the Popes found St. Louis society wanting. Hoping to indulge his forensic and literary interests in retirement, Pope was disappointed to find St. Louis had become, to him at least, a city of money-grubbing philistines. With little outside the home to engage him, Pope welcomed a request from the editors of the *National Tribune* that he contribute his war memoirs to its pages.[46]

Headquartered in Washington, D.C., the *National Tribune* was an ideal venue for Pope. Intended as an advocatory forum for Union army veterans, the *National Tribune* was a weekly newspaper that kept its 300,000 readers informed about congressional debates on war pensions and veterans' benefits, and on the activities of the Grand Army of the Republic. By the time Pope began setting down his own recollections in the autumn of 1886, the *National Tribune* already had run the serialized memoirs of Generals Oliver Otis Howard and William P. Carlin.

Pope made his debut in the February 17, 1887, issue of the *National Tribune* with a piece on Missouri at the outbreak of the Civil War. Three more installments were devoted to his service in Missouri, followed at irregular intervals over the next eighteen months by articles on the Island No. 10 campaign and the Siege of Corinth, as well as six consecutive installments on the Second Bull Run campaign.[47]

Pope's writing ranged well beyond his own wartime experiences. He penned a laudatory biographical sketch of George Gordon Meade for later use by the *National Tribune,* and in June 1887 he contributed a thoughtful article on the legacy of the Civil War to the *North American Review.*

Pope also ruminated about the sorry state of Indian affairs. To his friend Benjamin H. Grierson, still on active duty in the New Mexico Territory, he complained about the forced removal of the Jicarilla Apache from their old reservation, something he had resisted while commander of the Department of the Missouri. Summing up two decades of thankless efforts on behalf of Indian reform, in December 1887 Pope wrote sadly, "There is no rest for the Indian on this continent except in the grave to which he is being driven with accelerated speed every day. I used to think something in accordance with the ordinary dictates of humanity might be devised for him and carried into execution by the government but that hope has long been abandoned and death alone appears to offer relief from an outrage which will be a stain on this government and this people forever."[48]

Personal tragedy brought Pope's thoughts squarely back to family matters. On January 18, 1888, Valentine B. Horton died quietly in his Pomeroy, Ohio, home just eleven days short of his eighty-sixth birthday. Horton had appointed Pope as an executor of his will, but he and Clara were too ill themselves even to attend the funeral. Six months after her father's passing, Clara Horton Pope died at the Popes' Lucas Street home of what doctors called a "hemorrhage of the bowels." She was fifty-three years old.[49]

With the death of Clara, remembered Judge Force, "much of the light" went out of Pope's life. Despite the loss of Clara and his own poor health, Pope was determined to keep living, if only for his children's sake. As he told Force, whose own failing health troubled Pope profoundly, "It is so important both to you and to me for plain reasons, that we should live on and be reasonably well for some time yet that we ought to pay a good deal of care to our health and do so now."[50]

By 1890, Pope had rallied enough to resume work on his memoirs. For his earlier articles, he had drawn on testimony he had given during and just after the war before the Joint Congressional Committee on the Conduct of the War, as well as reports and correspondence found in Frank Moore's twelve-volume *Rebellion Record*. With the December 11 issue of the *National Tribune*, there began a series of fifteen colorful, highly personal articles, all under the rubric "War Reminiscences: Personal Recollections of Conspicuous People, Civil and Military," in which Pope sized up for posterity the leading figures of the war, North and South, with whom he had come in contact, while also relating his experiences with them. These he probably penned from a still-sharp memory, buttressed by his own letters and the published accounts of others. In addition to a compelling portrait of Secretary Stanton, Pope offered readers of the *National Tribune* an intimate glimpse at Lincoln's rail journey as president-elect to Washington, D.C., in February 1861; a stirring account of the Mexican War battles of Monterrey and Buena Vista; and a trenchant critique of the West Point system.

A spirit of conciliation and goodwill pervaded Pope's recollections. There was none of the angry settling of scores found in many other war memoirs of the day. Rather, Pope forgave where he felt able and dispatched his enemies, including McClellan, with understated wit. The final installment of Pope's memoirs appeared in the March 19, 1891, issue of the *National Tribune*.[51]

Pope ventured out little in the years following Clara's death. His children, whom Force considered the most devoted he had ever known, remained by his side at home. Their company, and that of Judge Force and his wife, Francie, was all Pope wished. In September 1892, he made a rare trip from St. Louis to visit Force, who had retired as judge of the superior court of Cincinnati to accept a quiet position as commandant of the Ohio Soldiers' and Sailors' House in Sandusky, on the bank of Lake Erie. On the evening of September 23, after a pleasant dinner with Force, Pope passed away in his sleep. The surgeon of the home termed the cause of death "a complete breaking down of his nervous system; a letting loose of all vital force, which has been very properly styled nervous prostration."

Pope was buried beside his wife in St. Louis's Bellefontaine Cemetery on September 28, 1892, with full military honors. In informing the military community of his death, a spokesman for the War Department said, "General Pope's death closes an eminently useful, patriotic and distinguished career of nearly half a century in the service of his country. This service, covering two wars and a large diversity of other duties, coupled with his life-long habit of study had stored his mind with a wealth and variety of knowledge and information on professional and very many other subjects; his discriminating judgment and ready facility with voice and pen in using his knowledge gave him a commanding influence during a larger portion of his career. The many acts promoted by his thoughtful and generous nature have endeared him to those with whom he was associated."

"Military critics may dispute as to General Pope's capacity as a general in command of armies in the field," offered the editors of the *Army and Navy Journal;* "none, however, can deny that he was a faithful servant of his country, a patriot, and a scholar, deserving of the fullest commendation, and a place in the hearts of his countrymen with those whose ultimate success make them the foremost of the leaders of their time."[52]

A fitting tribute to a man who, in the truest sense, had lived his life for the nation.

Notes

Abbreviations

ACPB	Appointments, Commissions, and Personal Branch
AGO	Adjutant General's Office
ALBS	Abraham Lincoln Book Shop, Chicago
ARSW	*Annual Report of the Secretary of War*
B&L	*Battles and Leaders of the Civil War*
BU	Boston University
CCW	U.S. Congress, *Conduct of the War: Report of the Joint Committee on the Conduct of the War*
CHS	Chicago Historical Society
CWSR	*Conduct of the War: Supplemental Report of the Joint Committee on the Conduct of the War*
DAB	*Dictionary of American Biography*
DMo	Department of Missouri
H. Ex. Doc.	House Executive Document
HA	Headquarters of the Army
HL	Huntington Library
HPL	Rutherford B. Hayes Presidential Library
HSP	Historical Society of Pennsylvania
ISHL	Illinois State Historical Library
LR	Letters Received
LS	Letters Sent
MDMo	Military Division of the Missouri
MHSMC	Military Historical Society of Massachusetts Collection
MnHS	Minnesota Historical Society
MOLLUS	Military Order of the Loyal Legion of the United States
NA	National Archives
NT	*National Tribune*
NYHS	New-York Historical Society
OHS	Ohio Historical Society
OR	*War of the Rebellion: A Compilation of the Official Records of the Union and Confederate Armies* (unless otherwise stated, all references are to Series 1)

PMHSM	Papers of the Military and Historical Society of Massachusetts
RG	Record Group
S. Ex. Doc.	Senate Executive Document
TB	Topographical Bureau
USMA	United States Military Academy Library
UW	University of Washington
WRHS	Western Reserve Historical Society

Prologue

1. John Pope (hereafter, JP), "War Reminiscences, XI," *NT,* Feb. 19, 1891; David S. Stanley, *Personal Memoirs of Major-General D. S. Stanley, U.S.A.* (Cambridge, Mass., 1917), 85, 104; *OR* 17, pt. 3, 17.

Chapter 1: The Approbation of My Own Conscience

1. Paul M. Angle, "Nathaniel Pope, 1784–1850, a Memoir," *Illinois State Historical Society: Transactions for the Year 1936,* Publication No. 43 (Springfield, 1936), 111–12; *DAB,* 15:77.

2. *DAB,* 15:77–78; Merlin G. Cox, "John Pope, Fighting General from Illinois" (Ph.D. diss., University of Florida, 1956), 4–8; Angle, "Nathaniel Pope," 111–12.

3. Thomas Hoyne, "The Lawyer as a Pioneer," in *Chicago Bar Association Lectures, Part One,* Fergus Historical Series No. 22 (Chicago, 1882), 72–73; Ninian W. Edwards, *History of Illinois, from 1778 to 1833; and Life and Times of Ninian Edwards* (Springfield, Ill., 1870), 254–55; John Moses, *Illinois: Historical and Statistical,* 2 vols. (Chicago, 1889), 1:237, 242, 276–82; *DAB,* 15:78.

4. *DAB,* 15:78; Hoyne, "Lawyer as Pioneer," 73–74.

5. Angle, "Nathaniel Pope," 150–51, 158, 163–64; *Illinois State Journal,* Jan. 23, 1850; Daniel H. Brush, *Growing Up with Southern Illinois, 1820–1861,* ed. Milo M. Quaife (Chicago, 1944), 113; Gustave Koerner, *Memoirs of Gustave Koerner, 1809–1896,* 2 vols. (Cedar Rapids, Iowa, 1909), 1:391; Edwards, *History of Illinois,* 255; Isaac M. Arnold, "Recollections of Early Chicago," in *Chicago Bar Association Lectures, Part One,* Fergus Historical Series No. 22 (Chicago, 1882), 11–12.

6. M. Cox, "Pope," 11–12; Nathaniel Pope to JP, Sept. 3, 1837, Nathaniel Pope Papers, ISHL.

7. Edwards, *History of Illinois,* 255; Angle, "Nathaniel Pope," 159–60; John Reynolds, *The Pioneer History of Illinois* (Chicago, 1887), 331; M. Cox, "Pope," 12–13.

8. M. Cox, "Pope," 13.

9. Manning F. Force, "John Pope, Major General U.S.A.: Some Personal Memoranda," in *Sketches of War History, 1861–1865: Papers Prepared for the Ohio Commandery, MOLLUS,* 6 vols. (Cincinnati, 1888–1919), 4:355; Thomas C. H. Smith, "Memoir and Review of Pope's Campaign in Virginia, July, August, September 1862," 29, Smith Papers, OHS; Arnold, "Recollections," 13; Usher F. Linder, *Reminiscences of the Early Bench and Bar of Illinois* (Chicago, 1879), 216–17; Joseph Gillespie, *Recollections of Early Illinois and Her Noted Men,* Fergus Historical Series No. 13 (Chicago, 1880), 15.

10. M. Cox, "Pope," 6, 10; Angle, "Nathaniel Pope," 177.

11. Angle, "Nathaniel Pope," 178; Linder, *Reminiscences,* 216.

12. Reynolds, *Pioneer History,* 331–32; *DAB,* 15:78; Wallace J. Schutz and Walter N. Tren-

erry, *Abandoned by Lincoln: A Military Biography of General John Pope* (Urbana, Ill., 1990), 7; M. Cox, "Pope," 16. When John graduated from West Point in 1842, Judge Pope was short of money and had to arrange for his son to borrow funds from a family acquaintance to pay for his army uniforms. JP to R. H. Nevins, Apr. 27, 1842, JP Papers, USMA.

13. "Recent Deaths: Major General John Pope," *Army and Navy Journal*, Oct. 1, 1892. For a detailed treatment of the travails of the summer encampment, see James L. Morrison Jr., "The United States Military Academy, 1833–1866: Years of Progress and Turmoil" (Ph.D. diss., Columbia University, 1973), 98–108.

14. Angle, "Nathaniel Pope," 164–65; Koerner, *Memoirs*, 1:391; Nathaniel Pope to JP, Sept. 3, 1837, Nathaniel Pope Papers, ISHL; Lloyd Lewis, *Letters from Lloyd Lewis, Showing Steps in the Research for His Biography of U. S. Grant,* ed. Angus Cameron (Boston, 1950), 64, 66; Morrison, "United States Military Academy," 324–26; JP to Lucretia Pope, July 7 and Sept. 17, 1838, JP Papers, USMA.

15. James Longstreet, "Our March against Pope," *Century* 31, no. 4 (Feb. 1886): 613; JP to Lucretia Pope, Nov. 24, 1839, JP Papers, USMA.

16. Schutz and Trenerry, *Abandoned by Lincoln*, 38; JP, "War Reminiscences, III," *NT,* Dec. 25, 1890.

17. JP to John James Abert, Feb. 24, 1851, LR, TB, RG 77, NA; David A. White, ed., *News of the Plains and Rockies, 1803–1865,* 4 vols. (Spokane, 1996–   ), 2:437; Hazard Stevens, *Life of General Isaac Ingalls Stevens,* 2 vols. (Boston, 1901), 1:257.

18. The Corps of Topographical Engineers was a small branch, having a full strength of only thirty-six officers, which meant Colonel Abert was able to keep a close eye on Pope. Schutz and Trenerry, *Abandoned by Lincoln*, 18–19; Allan Nevins, *Frémont: The West's Greatest Adventurer,* 2 vols. (New York, 1928), 1:132. For an excellent biography of Long, which is also instructive for the state of the Corps of Topographical Engineers at the time, see Richard G. Wood, *Stephen Harriman Long: Engineer, Explorer, Inventor* (Glendale, Calif., 1966).

19. Schutz and Trenerry, *Abandoned by Lincoln*, 20–21; Curran Pope to Nathaniel Pope, Jan. 27, 1845, Ozias M. Hatch Papers, ISHL.

20. Schutz and Trenerry, *Abandoned by Lincoln*, 21–22.

21. George Meade, *The Life and Letters of George Gordon Meade, Major-General, United States Army,* 2 vols. (New York, 1913), 1:111.

22. Ibid.; K. Jack Bauer, *The Mexican War, 1846–1848* (New York, 1974), 92; JP, "War Reminiscences, XV," *NT,* Mar. 19, 1891.

23. The Fort of the Tannery.

24. JP, "War Reminiscences, XV"; George C. Furber, *The Twelve Months Volunteer; or, Journal of a Private in the Tennessee Regiment of Cavalry, in the Campaign in Mexico, 1846–1847* (Cincinnati, 1848), 99; Bauer, *Mexican War,* 89–95.

25. Justin H. Smith, *The War with Mexico,* 2 vols. (New York, 1919), 1:250–51; N. C. Brooks, *A Complete History of the Mexican War* (Chicago, 1965), 31; M. Cox, "Pope," 21; JP, "War Reminiscences, XV"; Furber, *Twelve Months Volunteer,* 105; George W. Smith and Charles B. Judah, eds., *Chronicles of the Gringos: The U.S. Army in the Mexican War, 1846–1848; Accounts of Eyewitnesses and Combatants* (Albuquerque, 1968), 80–82; Ulysses S. Grant, *Memoirs and Selected Letters,* ed. Mary D. McFeely (New York, 1990), 81.

26. Bauer, *Mexican War,* 95; JP, "War Reminiscences, V," *NT,* Jan. 8, 1891; Samuel G. French, *Two Wars: An Autobiography* (Nashville, 1901), 61–62.

27. Furber, *Twelve Months Volunteer,* 103–4; Bauer, *Mexican War,* 95–99.

28. Schutz and Trenerry, *Abandoned by Lincoln*, 26.

29. M. Cox, "Pope," 23; Meade, *Life and Letters*, 1:166; *Sangamon Journal*, Jan. 14, 1847.

30. Italics are Meade's.

31. Meade, *Life and Letters*, 1:166. In point of fact, it was Meade and another engineer officer who discovered the gorge through the Saltillo road, and Pope happened to be with the vanguard in the attack only because Mansfield was there. U. S. Grant, *Memoirs and Letters*, 75.

32. Meade, *Life and Letters*, 1:147; Braxton Bragg to Samuel G. French, Oct. 13, 1847, French Papers, USMA. Seen in context, Pope's behavior was less egregious than Bragg would have it. Lawlessness was rampant among the American volunteers, who regarded Mexicans as scarcely human. Taylor's army behaved disgracefully in Monterrey, plundering and killing residents. Most American soldiers doubted Mexican women had any virtue worth protecting. Mexican highwaymen in turn waylaid unwary soldiers. Bauer, *Mexican War*, 101–2, 202–3; William P. Rogers, "Diary and Letters of William P. Rogers, 1846–1862," *Southwestern Historical Quarterly* 22 (1928/29): 269.

33. Bauer, *Mexican War*, 204–12; JP, "War Reminiscences, XIV," *NT*, Mar. 12, 1891; idem, "War Reminiscences, XV."

34. M. Cox, "Pope," 23; JP, "War Reminiscences, XIV."

35. JP, "War Reminiscences, XIV."

Chapter 2: The Most Ridiculous Assumption of Position

1. William H. Goetzmann, *Army Exploration in the American West, 1803–1863* (Austin, Tex., 1991), 153.

2. 31st Congress, 1st sess., House Executive Document 51, *Report of Brevet Major Samuel Woods*, 1; "Minnesota as Seen by Travelers: A Dragoon on the March to Pembina in 1849," *Minnesota History* 8 (1927), 61, 63.

3. 31st Cong., 1st sess., 1850, H. Ex. Doc. 51, *Report of Brevet Major Samuel Woods*, 12, 19; 31st Congress, 1st session, Senate Executive Document 42, *Report of the Secretary of War, Communicating the Report of an Exploration of the Territory of Minnesota, by Brevet Captain Pope, March 21, 1850*, 13, 27–29; JP, "Field Notes of Capt. Pope's Expedition from Fort Snelling to Pembina, Made in 1849, Land Route (Outward)," 18–20, vol. 25, Alfred J. Hill Papers, MnHS; "Minnesota by Travelers," 67; Thomas C. H. Smith, "Memoir and Review of Pope's Campaign," 29, Smith Papers, OHS; R. Wood, *Long*, 128–30, 235.

4. "Field Notes of a Reconnaissance of the Red River and of the North, Leaf, and Crow Wing Rivers, Made by Capt. J. Pope, in 1849," 2, vol. 23, Hill Papers, MnHS; 31st Cong., 1st sess., H. Ex. Doc. 51, *Report of Brevet Major Samuel Woods*, 19; 31st Cong., 1st sess., S. Ex. Doc. 42, *Report of Exploration of Minnesota*, 31, 34–40; "Minnesota by Travelers," 74; *Illinois State Journal*, Nov. 7, 1849.

5. 31st Cong., 1st sess., S. Ex. Doc. 42, *Report of Exploration of Minnesota*, 2–4, 6; *Illinois State Journal*, Nov. 7, 1849; JP to Henry H. Sibley, Feb. 5, 1850, Henry S. Sibley Papers, MnHS; JP to John James Abert, Feb. 7, 1850, LR, TB, RG 77, NA.

6. Goetzmann, *Army Exploration*, 66–71; Thomas C. H. Smith, "Memoir and Review of Pope's Campaign," 28, Smith Papers, OHS; JP to Abert, Dec. 28, 1849, and Feb. 14, 1850, LR, TB, RG 77, NA; Wallace J. Schutz to Walter N. Trenerry, Feb. 20, 1982, Schutz-Trenerry Papers, HPL; William F. Smith, *Autobiography of Major General William F.*

Smith, 1861–1864, ed. Herbert M. Schiller (Dayton, 1990), 51. The quality and detail of Pope's sketch maps varied but generally were thorough; they were certainly better than Colonel Abert would concede. Pope's sketch maps are to be found in his field notes of the expedition, which were copied by Alfred J. Hill for the Minnesota Historical Society in 1860.

7. JP to Franklin Steele, Mar. 29 and Apr. 16, 1851, Sibley Papers, MnHS.

8. *Illinois State Journal,* Oct. 31, 1849.

9. 31st Cong., 1st sess., S. Ex. Doc. 42, *Report of Exploration of Minnesota,* 41; JP to Abert, Aug. 16 and Sept. 3, 1850, LR, TB, RG 77, NA.

10. Abert to JP, Nov. 27, 1850, and Apr. 8, 1851, LS, and Joseph Johnston to Abert, Feb. 17, 1851, and JP to Abert, Feb. 24, 1851, LR, TB, RG 77, NA.

11. JP to Abert, Apr. 16 and Sept. 18, 1851, LR, TB, RG 77, NA; JP to Franklin Steele, Apr. 16, 1851, Sibley Papers, MnHS; JP to Benjamin H. Grierson, Jan. 16, 1888, Grierson Papers, ISHL; "Captain John Pope's Plan of 1853 for the Frontier Defense of New Mexico," ed. Robert M. Utley, *Arizona and the West* 5, no. 2 (Summer 1963): 151, 154–55.

12. JP to Abert, May 25 and Aug. 12, 1851, LR, TB, RG 77, NA; Goetzmann, *Army Exploration,* 247.

13. Leo E. Oliva, "The Aubry Route of the Santa Fe Trail," *Kansas Historical Quarterly* 5, no. 2 (Spring 1973): 20–21; Edwin V. Sumner to JP, Aug. 6, 1851, and JP to Abert, Sept. 18, 1851, LR, TB, RG 77, NA; Edward M. Kern to "Dear Dick," Aug. 22, 1851, in Kern, "Notes of a Military Reconnaissance," HL.

14. Nevins, *Frémont,* 1:207; Donald Chaput, *François X. Aubry: Trader, Trailmaker, and Voyageur in the Southwest, 1846–1854* (Glendale, Calif., 1975), 114; Kern to "Dear Dick," Aug. 22, 1851, in Kern, "Notes," HL; JP to Abert, Sept. 18, 1851, LR, TB, RG 77, NA. Pope failed to mention that the movement of troops from the towns to frontier posts was precisely the mission the secretary of war had given Sumner before he left Fort Leavenworth. "Captain Pope's Plan," 150–51.

15. Abert to JP, Oct. 2, 1851, LS, TB, RG 77, NA.

16. JP to Abert, Oct. 11, 1851, LR, TB, RG 77, NA. Abert apparently mistook Pope's route for a well-publicized trail opened that same year by the celebrated French-Canadian trailmaker and trader, François-Xavier Aubry. Known as the "Aubry Cut-off," or "Aubry Route," it was a completely different trail, running some fifty miles east of that claimed by Pope. Pope also thought the routes were one and the same. He accused Aubry of having taken credit for his discovery; Aubry returned the compliment with a sharp editorial in the *Santa Fe Gazette.*

Colonel Abert's defense of Frémont's map was unwarranted. Also a friend of Frémont, François Aubry nonetheless dismissed his and all military maps of the Santa Fe Trail as worse than worthless. Chaput, *Aubry,* 101, 113–14; Oliva, "Aubry Route," 24–25.

17. Abert to JP, Oct. 27, 1851, LS, TB, RG 77, NA.

18. Stanley, *Personal Memoirs,* 31–32.

19. H. Stevens, *Life of Isaac Stevens,* 1:257–59; JP to Abert, July 28, 1852, and Sumner to Abert, Oct. 27, 1852, LR, TB, RG 77, and JP "Statement of Service," LR, ACPB, AGO 1871–1894, RG 94, NA; Goetzmann, *Army Exploration,* 262–63.

20. "Captain Pope's Plan," 149–50, 153.

21. Ibid., 162.

22. Schutz and Trenerry, *Abandoned by Lincoln*, 43.

23. Goetzmann, *Army Exploration*, 262–65.

24. Ibid., 272–78, 290–91.

25. 33d Cong., 2d sess., Sen. Ex. Doc. 78, *Report of Exploration of a Route for the Pacific Railroad Near the Thirty-second Parallel of North Latitude from the Red River to the Rio Grande*, 1; Stanley, *Personal Memoirs*, 32.

26. 33d Cong., 2d sess., S. Ex. Doc. 78, *Report of Exploration of Route for Pacific Railroad*, 3; Goetzmann, *Army Exploration*, 291.

27. 33d Cong., 2d sess., S. Ex. Doc. 78, *Report of Exploration of Route for Pacific Railroad*, 9–10, 21, 28, 35–38; Rupert T. Richardson, *The Frontier of Northwest Texas, 1846–1876* (Glendale, Calif., 1964), 124–26.

28. Goetzmann, *Army Exploration*, 275, 346–47; Lee Myers, "Pope's Wells," *New Mexico Historical Review* (Oct. 1963): 282. Pope's report had a second, enduring consequence. His praise of the thirty-second-parallel course led to its being chosen as the route of the Butterfield Overland Mail, an important factor in the development of northwest Texas. Richardson, *Frontier*, 215–16, 219.

29. L. Myers, "Pope's Wells," 283–84; Goetzmann, *Army Exploration*, 366–67.

30. John B. Floyd to JP, May 22, 1857, JP Papers, USAMHI; Estella Weeks to William W. McCullough Jr., Apr. 1, 1960, McCullough Papers, Rosenberg Library; Goetzmann, *Army Exploration*, 367; Schutz and Trenerry, *Abandoned by Lincoln*, 51–53, 57; T. M. Eddy, *The Patriotism of Illinois*, 2 vols. (Chicago, 1865), 1:14; JP, "Statement of Service," LR, ACPB, AGO, RG 94, NA.

Chapter 3: A Favorite Son of Illinois

1. *Meigs County (Ohio) Telegraph*, Sept. 20, 1859, and June 13, 1888; Stillman C. Larkin, *The Pioneer History of Meigs County* (Columbus, Ohio, 1908), 179; *DAB*, 9:238; JP to Valentine B. Horton, June 24, 1861, JP Papers, NYHS; Edgar Ervin, *Pioneer History of Meigs County, Ohio, to 1949, Including Masonic History of the Same Period* (Columbus, Ohio, 1949), 303–4.

2. *DAB*, 9:238–39; Ervin, *Pioneer History*, 303; Larkin, *Pioneer History*, 179–80; JP to George W. Cullum, Mar. 1, 1860, JP Papers, USMA.

3. JP to Abraham Lincoln, Jan. 27, 1861, Robert Todd Lincoln Papers, DLC.

4. John G. Nicolay and John Hay, *Abraham Lincoln: A History*, 10 vols. (New York, 1890), 3:290; Henry Villard, *Memoirs of Henry Villard, Journalist and Financier, 1835–1900*, 2 vols. (Boston, 1904), 1:149–50.

5. JP, "War Reminiscences, VIII," *NT*, Jan. 29, 1891.

6. Ibid.; George Alfred Townsend, *Rustics in Rebellion: A Yankee Reporter on the Road to Richmond, 1861–1865* (Chapel Hill, N.C., 1950), 192.

7. Nicolay and Hay, *Lincoln*, 3:303; JP, "War Reminiscences," *NT*, Dec. 11, 1890; JP, "War Reminiscences, VIII"; JP, "War Reminiscences IX," *NT*, Feb. 5, 1891.

8. Nicolay and Hay, *Lincoln*, 3:296–98.

9. Ibid., 298–300; JP, *A Military View of the Southern Rebellion: Our National Fortifications and Defenses* (Cincinnati, 1861), 1–4; JP to Manning F. Force, Sept. 29, 1883, JP Papers, OHS.

10. JP, *Military View*, 1; "Major-General Pope," *Portrait Monthly* (July 1863): 7.

11. JP, "War Reminiscences, VIII"; Nicolay and Hay, *Lincoln*, 3:313–15; JP, "War Reminiscences, IX."

12. Special Order 60, Feb. 19, 1861, ACPB, AGO, RG 94, NA. The Fifth Article of War reads in part: "Any officer or soldier who shall use contemptuous or disrespectful words against the President of the United States . . . if a commissioned officer, shall be cashiered, or otherwise punished as a court-martial shall direct."

13. JP to Ward Hill Lamon, Mar. 19, 1861, John P. Nicholson Papers, HL; JP to Lamon, Apr. 11, 1861, Robert Todd Lincoln Papers, DLC; Thomas C. H. Smith, "Memoir and Review of Pope's Campaign," 30, Smith Papers, OHS; Robert H. Jones, *The Civil War in the Northwest* (Norman, Okla., 1960), 7; Abraham Lincoln, *The Collected Works of Abraham Lincoln,* ed. Roy P. Basler, 8 vols. (New Brunswick, N.J.), 4:327.

14. JP to Richard Yates, Apr. 12, 1861, Yates Papers, ISHL; M. Cox, "Pope," 43; Lincoln, *Collected Works,* 4:344–45; JP to Abraham Lincoln, Apr. 20, 1861, Robert Todd Lincoln Papers, DLC.

15. JP, "War Reminiscences."

16. Frederick H. Dyer, *A Compendium of the War of the Rebellion,* 3 vols. (New York, 1959), 3:1046–49; Daniel C. Smith to James Flagg, May [8], 1861, Smith Letters, ISHL; Cyrus Dickey to Ann Dickey, Apr. 24, 1861, Wallace-Dickey Papers, ISHL; Charles Wills, *Army Life of an Illinois Soldier, Including a Day-by-Day Record of Sherman's March to the Sea* (Washington, D.C., 1906), 8; George L. Paddock, "The Beginnings of an Illinois Volunteer Regiment in 1861," in *Military Essays and Recollections; Papers Read before the Commandery of the State of Illinois, MOLLUS,* 4 vols. (Chicago, 1891–1907), 2:258.

17. JP, "War Reminiscences"; Dyer, *Compendium,* 3:1046–49; JP to Lyman Trumbull, May 8, 1861, Trumbull Family Papers, DLC; JP to Abraham Lincoln, May 15, 1861, Robert Todd Lincoln Papers, DLC.

18. JP to Orville H. Browning, June 23, 1861, Browning Papers, ISHL; JP to Abraham Lincoln, June 16, 1861, Robert Todd Lincoln Papers, DLC; JP to Lyman Trumbull, June 16, 1861, Trumbull Family Papers, ISHL; JP to Valentine B. Horton, June 24, 1861, JP Papers, NYHS; Frank Moore, ed., *The Rebellion Record: A Diary of American Events,* 12 vols. (New York, 1861–68), 1:185 (docs.); OR, series 3, 1:154–56; Lewis, *Letters,* 83.

19. Lincoln, *Collected Works,* 4:369–70, 463.

20. JP to Orville H. Browning, June 23, 1861, Browning Papers, ISHL.

21. Clark E. Carr, *The Illini* (New York, 1905), 364; William Butler, Jesse Dubois, and Ozias M. Hatch to Abraham Lincoln, June 16, 1861, and Richard Yates to Abraham Lincoln, June 15, 1861, both in Robert Todd Lincoln Papers, DLC; Lincoln, *Collected Works,* 4:407, 411.

22. Lincoln, *Collected Works,* 4:411.

23. JP to Abraham Lincoln, June 16, 1861, Robert Todd Lincoln Papers, DLC; Lincoln, *Collected Works,* 4:411.

24. JP to Valentine Horton, June 24, 1861, JP Papers, NYHS; John Y. Simon, ed., *The Papers of Ulysses S. Grant,* 20 vols. (Carbondale, Ill., 1967–   ), 2:11, 22–23; Augustus Chetlain, *Recollections of Seventy Years* (Galena, Ill., 1899), 75; JP to Lyman Trumbull, June 16 and 23, 1861, Trumbull Family Papers, ISHL; JP, "War Reminiscences, IV," *NT,* Jan. 1, 1891.

25. U. S. Grant, *Memoirs and Letters,* 157–58.

26. JP, "War Reminiscences, IV"; JP to George B. McClellan, June 20 and 29, 1861, ACPB, AGO, RG 94, NA. Grant's account of his conversation with Pope seems less plausible than Pope's, when one considers the lengths to which Grant ultimately went to secure a commission. Chetlain, *Recollections of Seventy Years,* 75–77.

27. Augustus L. Chetlain, "Recollections of General U. S. Grant," in *Military Essays,* 1:15; JP to Valentine B. Horton, June 24, 1861, JP Papers, NYHS; *OR* 3, 390.

28. Charles Morton, "Early War Days in Missouri," *War Papers, Being Papers Read before the Commandery of the State of Wisconsin, MOLLUS,* 4 vols. (Milwaukee, 1891–1903), 2:147.

29. JP, "Missouri in 1861, I," *NT,* Feb. 17, 1887; *OR* 3, 394-99; 39th Congress, 1st sess., "Report of General Pope," *CWSR,* 2 vols. (Washington, D.C., 1866), 2:4. Both in his memoirs and in his postwar testimony before the Joint Congressional Committee on the Conduct of the War, Pope said he assumed command in northern Missouri on July 17; contemporaneous correspondence indicates he did not cross into Missouri until July 19.

30. 39th Cong., 1st sess., "Report of General Pope," *CWSR,* 2:5-7; James L. Foley, "With Fremont in Missouri: Part I—General Review of Fremont's Campaign," in *Ohio MOLLUS,* 6 vols. (Cincinnati, 1888-1903), 5:486; *OR* 3, 402.

31. 39th Cong., 1st sess., "Report of General Pope," *CWSR,* 2:6; JP, "Missouri in 1861, I."

32. *OR* 3, 403-4.

33. John B. Sanborn, "Reminiscences of the War in the Department of the Missouri," in *Glimpses of the Nation's Struggle: A Series of Papers Read before the Minnesota Commandery, MOLLUS,* 6 vols. (St. Paul, Minn., 1887-1909), 2:230; *OR* 3, 405-6; 39th Cong., 1st sess., "Report of General Pope," *CWSR,* 2:7-8.

34. Moore, *Rebellion Record,* 2:474 (docs.).

35. JP to Trumbull, July 6, 1861, Trumbull Family Papers, ISHL.

36. 39th Cong., 1st sess., "Report of General Pope," *CWSR,* 2:9-10; *OR* 3, 417-19; JP to Robert T. Van Horn, Van Horn Papers, Missouri Historical Society, Columbia.

37. *OR* 3, 415, 420-21; JP to John C. Kelton, Sept. 18, 1861, ACPB, AGO, RG 94, NA.

38. Simon, *Papers of Grant,* 2:86, 124.

39. U. S. Grant, *Memoirs and Letters,* 165-66; Foley, "With Fremont in Missouri," 488-89; John C. Frémont, "In Command in Missouri," in *B&L,* vol. 1, pt. 2, 284-85.

40. *OR* 3, 457-61; Wiley Britton, *The Civil War on the Border,* 2 vols. (New York, 1899), 1:145-47; JP, "Missouri in 1861, II," *NT,* Feb. 24, 1887.

41. *OR* 3, 145.

42. Nevins, *Frémont,* 2:500-501; Nicolay and Hay, *Lincoln,* 4:416-17; *OR* 3, 456-57.

43. William E. Parrish, *Turbulent Partnership: Missouri and the Union, 1861-1865* (Columbia, Mo., 1963), 54; William Pittinger diary, Sept. 14, 1861, OHS; JP to Valentine B. Horton, Aug. 22, 1861, JP Papers, NYHS; JP, "War Reminiscences"; John James Abert to JP, Oct. 27, 1851, LS, TB, RG 77, NA.

44. Nevins, *Frémont,* 2:493-94; John C. Kelton to JP, Aug. 5, 1861, ACPB, AGO, RG 94, NA; Nicolay and Hay, *Lincoln,* 4:412; JP, "War Reminiscences."

45. JP, "War Reminiscences"; Albert Shumate, *The Notorious I. C. Woods of the Adams Express* (Glendale, Calif., 1986), 107; Francis Grierson, *The Valley of Shadows* (Boston, 1909), 233-34.

46. 39th Cong., 1st sess., "Report of General Pope," *CWSR,* 2:13.

47. JP, "Missouri in 1861, III," *NT,* Mar. 3, 1887; Oliver W. Nixon, "Reminiscences of the First Year of the War in Missouri," in *Military Essays,* 3:413-36; *OR* 3, 167.

48. JP to Valentine B. Horton, Aug. 22, 1861, JP Papers, NYHS; *OR* 3, 511-13.

49. 39th Cong., 1st sess., "Report of General Pope," *CWSR,* 2:14; *OR* 3, 166-67, 474-75, 487.

50. James Monaghan, *The Civil War on the Western Border* (Boston, 1955), 184–87; James A. Mulligan, "The Siege of Lexington, Mo.," in *B&L*, vol. 1, pt. 2, 307–8.

51. *OR* 3, 172–75, 491, 494–95, and vol. 53, 437; Alfred W. Gilbert, *Colonel A. W. Gilbert, Citizen Soldier of Cincinnati,* ed. William E. Smith and Ophia D. Smith (Cincinnati, 1934), 57.

52. 39th Cong., 1st sess., "Report of General Pope," *CWSR,* 2:14–15; JP, "Missouri in 1861, III"; Manning F. Force, *From Fort Henry to Corinth* (New York, 1881), 8; *OR* 3, 176; Erasmus Gest to William Dennison, Oct. 12, 1861, State Archives Series 147, OHS.

53. Orville H. Browning, *The Diary of Orville Hickman Browning, 1850–1884,* ed. Theodore C. Pease and James G. Randall, 2 vols. (Springfield, Ill., 1925), 1:507–8; *Chicago Tribune,* Sept. 25, 1862; *Leavenworth (Kansas) Conservative,* Oct. 3, 1862; *Missouri Democrat,* Sept. 26, 1862; *Missouri Republican,* Sept. 26, 1862; Gest to Dennison, Oct. 12, 1861, State Archives Series 147, OHS.

54. Jefferson C. Davis, "Campaigning in Missouri: Civil War Memoirs of General Jefferson C. Davis," *Missouri Historical Review* 54 (1959–60): 40–41.

55. *OR* 53, 439; Nixon, "Reminiscences," 420–21; JP, "Missouri in 1861, III"; Moore, *Rebellion Record,* 3:142–45 (docs).

56. Nicolay and Hay, *Lincoln,* 4:428; Britton, *War on the Border,* 1:144; Nevins, *Frémont,* 2:529.

57. JP to John C. Frémont, Aug. 21, 1861, ACPB, AGO, RG 94, NA; JP to Valentine B. Horton, Oct. 1, 1861, JP Papers, NYHS.

58. Butler's son, Captain Speed Butler, served as aide-de-camp to Pope. JP to William Butler, Butler Papers, Sept. 22, 1861, CHS.

59. JP to Valentine B. Horton, Oct. 1, 1861, JP Papers, NYHS; Albert A. Pomeroy, *History and Genealogy of the Pomeroy Family, Collateral Lines in Family Groups* (Pomeroy, Ohio, n.d.), 515.

60. *OR* 3, 504; Nevins, *Frémont,* 2:529–30; JP, "Missouri in 1861, III"; Britton, *War on the Border,* 1:149.

61. Nevins, *Frémont,* 2:531–36; JP, "Missouri in 1861, III"; 39th Cong., 1st sess., "Report of General Pope," *CWSR,* 2:16; Monaghan, *War on the Western Border,* 200.

62. Nicolay and Hay, *Lincoln,* 4:429–30.

63. JP, "Missouri in 1861, III."

64. Nicolay and Hay, *Lincoln,* 4:431–34; *Philadelphia Inquirer,* July 4, 1862; John R. Howard, *Remembrance of Things Past: A Familiar Chronicle of Kinsfolk and Friends Worth While* (New York, 1925), 157, 188; Jessie Benton Frémont, *The Letters of Jesse Benton Frémont,* ed. Pamela Herr and Mary Lee Spence (Urbana, Ill., 1993), 29; *OR* 3, 544–45.

65. Monaghan, *War on the Western Border,* 200–203; Pope, "Missouri in 1861, III"; U.S. Congress, "Pope's Testimony," *CCW,* 2:247–48; Jessie Benton Frémont, *Letters,* 288–90; Nevins, *Frémont,* 535–36. Pope was mistaken about Price's whereabouts but not his intentions. Price remained at Neosho until the end of October, before retiring to the state line for the winter. *OR* 3, 727–28, 730–32; Albert Castel, *General Sterling Price and the Civil War in the West* (Baton Rouge, 1968), 59.

66. Britton, *War on the Border,* 1:155–56; Frémont, "In Command in Missouri," 287; JP, "Missouri in 1861, III"; *OR* 3, 559; 39th Cong., 1st sess., "Report of General Pope," *CWSR,* 2:16–17; J. H. Eaton to JP, Nov. 2, 1861, ACPB, AGO, RG 94, NA; Jessie Benton Frémont, *Letters,* 290.

67. JP, "Missouri in 1861, III"; Nixon, "Reminiscences," 422.

68. JP, "Missouri in 1861, IV," *NT,* Mar. 10, 1887; idem, "War Reminiscences, XIII,"

NT, Mar. 5, 1891; Stephen E. Ambrose, *Halleck, Lincoln's Chief of Staff* (Baton Rouge, 1962), 12–14; Edward Wright to JP, Nov. 7, 1861, ACPB, AGO, RG 94, NA; *OR* 3, 369; *Report of the Military Services of Gen. David Hunter, U.S.A., during the War of the Rebellion, Made to the U.S. War Department, 1873* (New York, 1873), 9; Shumate, *Notorious I. C. Woods,* 107.

69. *OR* 3, 382, 390–91; Ambrose, *Halleck,* 15; 39th Cong., 1st sess., "Report of General Pope," *CWSR,* 2:20.

70. Britton, *War on the Border,* 1:186; Moore, *Rebellion Record,* 3:478, 481 (docs.); Charles I. Adkins, "Service Observations from the Standpoint of a Private Soldier," *National Tribune Scrap Book* (Washington, D.C., n.d.), 55.

71. Moore, *Rebellion Record,* 3:479 (docs.); Britton, *War on the Border,* 1:188–91; 39th Cong., 1st sess., "Report of General Pope," *CWSR,* 2:20–23; Adkins, "Service Observations," 55–56; *Cincinnati Enquirer,* Dec. 19, 1861; JP, "Missouri in 1861, IV"; *OR* 8, 447; Joanne C. Eakin, *Battle at Blackwater River* (Independence, Mo., 1995), 2, 11.

72. Moore, *Rebellion Record,* 3:480 (docs.); *OR* 8, 461–68; Castel, *Price,* 66–65; Britton, *War on the Border,* 1:191; Force, *Fort Henry to Corinth,* 11–12; JP, "Missouri in 1861, IV"; 39th Cong., 1st sess., "Report of General Pope," *CWSR,* 2:23; John M. Schofield, *Forty-six Years in the Army* (New York, 1897), 358–59; JP to John C. Kelton, Dec. 30, 1861, ACPB, AGO, RG 94, NA.

Chapter 4: You Deserve Well of Your Country

1. Pomeroy, *History and Genealogy,* 515; JP to Valentine B. Horton, Feb. 14, 1862, JP Papers, NYHS.

2. Force, *Fort Henry to Corinth,* 66; Larry J. Daniel and Lynn N. Bock, *Island No. 10: Struggle for the Mississippi Valley* (Tuscaloosa, Ala., 1996), 22.

3. JP, "Island Number Ten, I," *NT,* May 3, 1887; *OR* 8, 79, 559–61; Charles W. Davis, "New Madrid and Island No. 10," in *Military Essays,* 1:70; Daniel and Bock, *Island No. 10,* 36.

4. JP to Valentine Horton, Feb. 14, 1862, JP Papers, NYHS; C. W. Davis, "New Madrid," 78–79; Adkins, "Service Observations," 59; Daniel and Bock, *Island No. 10,* 38.

5. *OR* 8, 564–65, 570; JP, "Island Number Ten, I."

6. *OR* 8, 80, 570; C. W. Davis, "New Madrid," 79; JP, "Island Number Ten, I"; Adkins, "Service Observations," 59; Pittinger diary, undated entry, 91–93, OHS.

7. Ezra Warner, *Generals in Blue: Lives of the Union Commanders* (Baton Rouge, 1964), 199–200, 358–59; *OR* 8, 571–72; John M. Palmer to his wife, Feb. 22, 24, and 28, 1862, John M. Palmer II Papers, ISHL; Adkins, "Service Observations," 59.

8. Adkins, "Service Observations," 59–60; *OR* 8, 80–81; JP, "Island Number Ten, I"; Pittinger diary, undated entry, 93, OHS; Wellington Eldred to "Dear Sir," Mar. 25, 1862, Eldred Letters, MoU.

9. *OR* 8, 81, 125–26, 141–42, 582; Nixon, "Reminiscences," 431; C. W. Davis, "New Madrid," 80; Benjamin T. Smith, *Private Smith's Journal: Recollections of the Late War,* ed. Clyde C. Walton (Chicago, 1963), 26. While at New Madrid, McCown was promoted to major general. Ezra Warner, *Generals in Gray: Lives of the Confederate Commanders* (Baton Rouge, 1959), 199–200; Daniel and Bock, *Island No. 10,* 53.

10. *OR* 8, 81, 167, 582, 587; Nixon, "Reminiscences," 428. The Confederate strength at New Madrid probably was closer to 3,500. JP, "Island Number Ten, I"; C. W. Davis, "New Madrid," 80–82.

11. *OR* 8, 583, 587–88, 592–98.

12. Adkins, "Service Observations," 60–61; Daniel Smith to his wife, Mar. 8, 1862, Smith Letters, ISHL; Charles H. Smith, *History of Fuller's Ohio Brigade* (Cleveland, 1909), 50; Nixon, "Reminiscences," 429; Joseph Strickling reminiscences, 12, OHS.

13. *OR* 8, 599–602, 604–9; *DAB*, 16:500–501; Adkins, "Service Observations," 61; Nixon, "Reminiscences," 430.

14. *OR* 8, 82, 98, 99; John M. Palmer to his wife, Mar. 14, 1862, John M. Palmer II Papers, ISHL; Strickling reminiscences, 12–13, OHS; Luther Bradley to his wife, Mar. 31, 1862, Bradley Papers, USAMHI.

15. *OR* 8, 82–83, 613; David T. Stathem diary, Mar. 13, 1862, Stathem Papers, OHS; C. W. Davis, "New Madrid," 83–84.

16. *OR* 8, 127, 185, 613–14; JP, "Island Number Ten, II," *NT,* May 10, 1887.

17. *OR* 8, 619–20; Moore, *Rebellion Record,* 4:439 (docs.); JP, "Island Number Ten, II."

18. *OR* 8, 529–31, 619–29, 634–35, 643–46; Schuyler Hamilton, "Who Projected the Canal at Island Number Ten?" *Century* 32, no. 8 (July 1885): 776–77; JP, "Island Number Ten, I"; J. W. Bissell, "Sawing Out a Channel above Island Number Ten," *Century* 30, no. 8 (June 1885), 325; Daniel and Bock, *Island No. 10,* 104–6.

19. B. T. Smith, *Private Smith's Journal,* 24; Wellington Eldred to "Dear Sir," Mar. 25, 1862, Eldred Letters, MoU.

20. Bissell, "Sawing Out a Channel," 325–26; *OR* 8, 86–87, 650; JP, "Island Number Ten, II."

21. C. W. Davis, "New Madrid," 87–89; *OR* 8, 123, 660–61, 666; Henry Walke to JP, Apr. 6, 1862, Walke Papers, CHS.

22. *OR* 8, 88–89, 649, 669–70; Bissell, "Sawing Out a Channel," 326–27.

23. C. W. Davis, "New Madrid," 90–91; *OR* 8, 109, 133, 671.

24. Bissell, "Sawing Out a Channel," 327; C. W. Davis, "New Madrid," 91; *OR* 8, 110; Nixon, "Reminiscences," 433.

25. Nixon, "Reminiscences," 433; Stathem diary, Apr. 8, 1862, OHS; B. T. Smith, *Private Smith's Journal,* 32.

26. Nixon, "Reminiscences," 433–34; R. Waters, "Surrender at Tiptonville," *NT,* Oct. 2, 1913; *OR* 8, 111–12.

27. Nixon, "Reminiscences," 434; *OR* 8, 90, 93, 674–76; Alfred W. Gilbert to his wife, Mar. 18, 1862, Gilbert Papers, Miami University of Ohio; Lyman Needham to his friends, Apr. 9, 1862, Needham Papers, ISHL; Henry Halleck to JP, Apr. 8, 1862, ACPB, AGO, RG 94, NA; JP to William Butler, Apr. 8, 1862, Butler Papers, CHS.

28. Richard Yates and William Butler to Abraham Lincoln, Apr. 9, 1862, Robert Todd Lincoln Papers, DLC; Abraham Lincoln, *Collected Works,* 5:186.

29. JP to Major Allen, Apr. 10, 1862, JP to Lewis B. Parsons, Apr. 19, 1862, and Speed Butler to Parsons, Apr. 22, 1862, all in Parsons Papers, ISHL; JP, "Siege of Corinth, I," *NT,* May 17, 1888; *OR* 10, pt. 2, 112–17; 39th Cong., 1st sess., "Report of General Pope," *CWSR,* 2:70–71.

30. Ambrose, *Halleck,* 45–48; U. S. Grant, *Memoirs and Letters,* 251. Corinth's strategic value stemmed from its location at the junction of the Mobile and Ohio Railroad and the Memphis and Charleston Railroad, two vital Southern arteries.

31. *OR* 10, pt. 1, 664, 673, and pt. 2, 123, 138, 143; Pittinger diary, undated entry, 121, OHS; Villard, *Memoirs,* 1:266.

32. 39th Cong., 1st sess., "Report of General Pope," *CWSR,* 2:71–72; *OR* 10, pt. 2, 158; U. S. Grant, *Memoirs and Letters,* 251, 255; William T. Sherman, *Memoirs of General W.*

T. Sherman, 2 vols. (New York, 1875), 1:272; Edward Bouton, *Events of the Civil War* (Los Angeles, 1906), 38; JP, "Siege of Corinth, I."

33. *OR* 10, pt. 2, 169–76; 39th Cong., 1st sess., "Report of General Pope," *CWSR,* 2:72; Force, *Fort Henry to Corinth,* 186; Strickling reminiscences, 15, OHS.

34. *OR* 10, pt. 1, 807–9; Strickling reminiscences, 15, OHS.

35. JP, "Siege of Corinth, I"; Strickling reminiscences, 15, OHS; 39th Cong., 1st sess., "Report of General Pope," *CWSR,* 2:72–73, vol. 2; *OR* 10, pt. 1, 674, 806–9, and pt. 2, 176–77, 180–81; Memphis *Appeal,* May 17, 1862.

36. J. Cutler Andrews, *The North Reports the Civil War* (Pittsburgh, 1955), 183–85; Villard, *Memoirs,* 1:272; Moore, *Rebellion Record,* 4:117, 119 (docs.).

37. U. S. Grant, *Memoirs and Letters,* 252; Grenville M. Dodge, "Some Characteristics of General U. S. Grant," *Annals of Iowa,* ser. 3, no. 10 (1913): 576; JP, "War Reminiscences, IV."

38. Force, *Fort Henry to Corinth,* 187; *OR* 10, pt. 1, 862–63, and pt. 2, 202, 208–9, 211; JP, "Siege of Corinth, I."

39. Strickling reminiscences, 16–17, OHS; Theodore S. Bowers to his family, June 13, 1862, author's collection; Force, *Fort Henry to Corinth,* 190; Moore, *Rebellion Record,* 5:149 (docs.); Stanley, *Personal Memoirs,* 100; JP, "War Reminiscences, VI," *NT,* Jan. 15, 1891.

40. *OR* 10, pt. 2, 232–452, 255, 286–87; 39th Cong., 1st sess., "Report of General Pope," *CWSR,* 2:74; JP, *Correspondence between Generals Pope and Halleck in Relation to Prisoners Captured at Corinth* (N.p., n.d.), 1.

41. *St. Paul Daily Press,* Sept. 24, 1862; 39th Cong., 1st sess., "Report of General Pope," *CWSR,* 2:75, 79; Julia Dent Grant, *The Personal Memoirs of Julia Dent Grant,* ed. John Y. Simon (New York, 1975), 101; William P. Carlin, "Military Memoirs, V," *NT,* Feb. 19, 1885; Bouton, *Events,* 46–48; Thomas W. Knox, *Camp Fire and Cotton Field: Southern Adventure in Time of War* (New York, 1865), 170–71; JP, *Correspondence between Pope and Halleck,* 1; *New Albany (Indiana) Ledger,* July 3, 1862; *OR* 17, pt. 2, 17.

42. *OR* 17, pt. 2, 18, 20; JP to John C. Kelton, June 15, 1862, ACPB, AGO, RG 94, NA; *Pomeroy Weekly Telegraph,* July 25, 1862; JP, "War Reminiscences X," *NT,* Feb. 12, 1891.

43. JP, "Army of Virginia," *NT,* Aug. 2, 1888; Marshall P. Thatcher, *A Hundred Battles in the West* (Detroit, 1884), 43; Thomas C. H. Smith, "Memoir and Review of Pope's Campaign," 37, Smith Papers, OHS; Stanley, *Personal Memoirs,* 85; John M. Palmer to his wife, Mar. 9, 11, and 28, 1862, John M. Palmer II Papers, ISHL.

44. Fitz John Porter to John P. Nicholson, Oct. 26, 1874, Nicholson Papers, HL; JP, "War Reminiscences X."

45. Stanley, *Personal Memoirs,* 104; Byron C. Bryner, *Bugle Echoes: The Story of Illinois 47th* (Springfield, Ill., 1905), 35; *History of the Forty-sixth Regiment Indiana Volunteer Infantry* (Logansport, Ind., 1888), 26; Mildred Throne, *Cyrus Clay Carpenter and Iowa Politics, 1854–1898* (Iowa City, 1974), 59–60; Robert G. Ingersoll to Ebon Clark Ingersoll, Sept. 10, 1862, Robert G. Ingersoll Papers, ISHL; *Philadelphia Public Ledger,* Sept. 15, 1862.

46. David T. Stathem to his family, n.d., Stathem Papers, OHS; Oscar L. Jackson, *The Colonel's Diary: Journals Kept before and during the Civil War* (Sharon, Pa., 1922), 60–61; Thatcher, *A Hundred Battles,* 44; Henry Eby, *Observations of an Illinois Boy in Battle, Camp, and Prison* (Mendota, Ill., 1910), 41; Lyman B. Pierce, *History of the Second Iowa Cavalry* (Burlington, Iowa, 1865), 15; Henry Clay McNeil to his sister, Nov. 29, 1862, McNeil Papers, Sioux City Public Museum, Sioux City, Iowa.

Chapter 5: A Moral Odor of Sewer Gas

1. *Philadelphia Inquirer,* June 26, 1862; George W. Richards, *Lives of Generals Halleck and Pope* (Philadelphia, 1862), 24; JP, "War Reminiscences, X"; 39th Cong., 1st sess., "Report of General Pope," *CWSR,* 2:104.

2. Clara Horton Pope to JP, June 26, 1862, Fitz John Porter Papers, DLC.

3. JP, "War Reminiscences, X."

4. Ibid.; Joseph P. Cullen, "Five Cent Pope," *Civil War Times Illustrated* (Apr. 1980): 7; Force, "Pope," 359.

5. Salmon P. Chase, *Inside Lincoln's Cabinet: The Civil War Diaries of Salmon P. Chase,* ed. David Donald (New York, 1954), 90–91; JP, "The Second Battle of Bull Run," *Century* 31, no. 3 (Jan. 1886): 441–42, "War Reminiscences X," and "Army of Virginia"; JP to Henry Halleck, Sept. 30, 1862, JP Papers, CHS; John J. Hennessy, *Return to Bull Run: The Campaign and Battle of Second Manassas* (New York, 1992), 8; *Fitz John Porter—Pope's Campaign, Speech of Hon. Zachariah Chandler, of Michigan, in the United States Senate, February 21, 1870* (Washington, D.C., 1870), 2; *General Orders No. 1, Headquarters, Army of Virginia, June 27, 1862,* Thomas C. H. Smith Papers, OHS.

6. Kenneth P. Williams, *Lincoln Finds a General,* 5 vols. (New York, 1949–58), 1:135; Ambrose, *Halleck,* 60; Hennessy, *Return to Bull Run,* 5; Nicolay and Hay, *Lincoln,* 6:23; D. Taylor to Valentine B. Horton, Aug. 30, 1871, Thomas C. H. Smith Papers, OHS; Cullen, "Five Cent Pope," 8; See Chase, *Inside Lincoln's Cabinet,* 90–95; Gideon Welles, *The Diary of Gideon Welles,* 3 vols. (Boston, 1911), 1:91–118; Benjamin P. Thomas and Harold M. Hyman, *Stanton: The Life and Times of Lincoln's Secretary of War* (New York, 1962), 150, 204, 385, 643; George B. McClellan, *The Civil War Papers of George B. McClellan,* ed. Stephen W. Sears (New York, 1989), 354–55.

7. Chase, *Inside Lincoln's Cabinet,* 96–97; *New York Tribune,* June 27, 1862; *Philadelphia Public Ledger,* June 30, 1862; David H. Strother, *A Virginia Yankee in the Civil War: The Diaries of David Hunter Strother,* ed. Cecil D. Eby Jr. (Chapel Hill, N.C., 1961), 19, 67.

8. McClellan, *Papers,* 368; Jacob D. Cox, *Military Reminiscences of the Civil War,* 2 vols. (New York, 1900), 1:241; Chase, *Inside Lincoln's Cabinet,* 97–98; *New York Daily Tribune,* June 26, 1862; *Missouri Democrat,* June 26, 1862.

9. 39th Cong., 1st sess., "Report of General Pope," *CWSR,* 2:104–5; JP, "Second Bull Run," 444–45, and "Army of Virginia"; Chase, *Inside Lincoln's Cabinet,* 97; Cullen, "Five Cent Pope," 8.

10. *OR* 11, pt. 3, 296–97; 39th Cong., 1st sess., "Report of General Pope," *CWSR,* 2:106.

11. *OR* 11, pt. 3, 306; Cullen, "Five Cent Pope," 8; James Fry, "McClellan and His 'Mission,'" *Century* 48, no. 5 (Sept. 1894): 941.

12. Chase, *Inside Lincoln's Cabinet,* 97; JP, "Second Bull Run," 445; J. Cox, *Military Reminiscences,* 1:249–50; JP to Halleck, Sept. 30, 1862, JP Papers, CHS; *OR* 12, pt. 2, 22; Townsend, *Rustics in Rebellion,* 191–92.

13. Robert K. Krick, *Conquering the Valley: Stonewall Jackson at Port Republic* (New York, 1996), 499; Thomas C. H. Smith, "Memoir and Review of Pope's Campaign," 58, Smith Papers, OHS.

14. Hennessy, *Return to Bull Run,* 6–7; Strother, *Virginia Yankee,* 65–66; Alpheus S. Williams, *The Civil War Letters of General Alpheus S. Williams: From the Cannon's Mouth,* ed. Milo M. Quaife (Detroit, 1959), 107; Captain Gaines and George D. Ruggles, "Statements in Regards to Gen. Pope's Language in Regard to Gen. Sigel," n.d., George G.

Lyon to Sigel, Oct. 10, 1862, and draft of a letter from Sigel to Ambrose Burnside, [Dec. 1862], all in Sigel Papers, NYHS; Franz Sigel, manuscript notes on Federal generals, Sigel Papers, WRHS.

15. George H. Gordon, *A History of the Campaign of the Army of Virginia under John Pope* (Boston, 1889), 11; Sigel, manuscript notes on Federal generals, Sigel Papers, WRHS.

16. Strother, *Virginia Yankee*, 65; JP, "Army of Virginia, II," *NT*, Aug. 9, 1888; Robert K. Krick, *Stonewall Jackson at Cedar Mountain* (Chapel Hill, N.C., 1990), 5.

17. Thomas C. H. Smith, "Memoir and Review of Pope's Campaign," 58, Smith Papers, OHS; JP, "Second Bull Run," 442–43; Samuel J. Bayard, *The Life of George Dashiell Bayard* (New York, 1874), 219; *Philadelphia Inquirer*, July 12, 1862; *OR* 12, pt. 3, 417, 423, 437, 439, 441, 447, 451, 455; Charles D. Rhodes, *History of the Cavalry of the Army of the Potomac, Including That of the Army of Virginia* (Kansas City, Mo., 1900), 31.

18. *OR* 12, pt. 3, 421–23, 425, 427–30, 462; Thomas C. H. Smith, "Memoir and Review of Pope's Campaign," 58, Smith Papers, OHS.

19. *Pomeroy Weekly Telegraph*, July 19, 1862.

20. Edwin C. Fishel, *The Secret War for the Union: The Untold Story of Military Intelligence in the Civil War* (Boston, 1996), 186; *OR* 12, pt. 3, 456, 472–73.

21. Thomas C. H. Smith, "Memoir and Review of Pope's Campaign," 58–59, Smith Papers, OHS.

22. Charles E. Davis, *Three Years in the Army: The Story of the Thirteenth Massachusetts Volunteers* (Boston, 1894), 90; C. W. Boyce, *A Brief History of the Twenty-eighth Regiment New York State Volunteers* (Buffalo, 1896), 34; Rufus R. Dawes, *Service with the Sixth Wisconsin Volunteers* (Marietta, Ohio, 1930), 51; J. Cox, *Military Reminiscences,* 1:247.

23. Hennessy, *Return to Bull Run*, 12; John M. Gould, *History of the First–Tenth–Twenty-ninth Maine Regiment* (Portland, 1871), 163; Boyce, *Twenty-eighth New York*, 34; Alonzo H. Quint, *The Potomac and the Rapidan* (Boston, 1864), 174; C. E. Davis, *Three Years in the Army*, 90–91; Benjamin F. Cook, *History of the Twelfth Massachusetts Volunteers* (Boston, 1892), 58; James P. Sullivan, *An Irishman in the Iron Brigade: The Civil War Memoirs of James P. Sullivan,* ed. William J. K. Beaudot and Lance J. Herdegen (New York, 1993), 42.

24. Dawes, *Service with the Sixth Wisconsin*, 51; Marsena R. Patrick, *Inside Lincoln's Army: The Diary of Marsena Rudolph Patrick, Provost Marshal General, Army of the Potomac,* ed. David S. Sparks (New York, 1964), 108; Robert Gould Shaw, *Blue-Eyed Child of Fortune: The Civil War Letters of Robert Gould Shaw,* ed. Russell Duncan (Athens, Ga., 1992), 224–25; George H. Gordon, *Brook Farm to Cedar Mountain in the War of the Great Rebellion* (Boston, 1883), 274; Carl Schurz, *The Reminiscences of Carl Schurz,* 3 vols. (New York, 1907), 2:352.

25. J. Cox, *Military Reminiscences,* 1:222–23; Thomas C. H. Smith, "Memoir and Review of Pope's Campaign," 60, D. Taylor to Valentine B. Horton, Aug. 30, 1871, and Salmon P. Chase to Horton, Dec. 5, 1871, all in Smith Papers, OHS; Force, "Pope," 359; Gordon, *Brook Farm to Cedar Mountain,* 273; Shaw, *Blue-Eyed Child,* 225.

26. McClellan, *Papers,* 368; Hennessy, *Return to Bull Run,* 13, 476; FitzJohn Porter to J. C. G. Kennedy, July 17, 1862, Porter Papers, DLC; Philip Kearny to Cortlandt Parker, July 24, 1862, Kearny Papers, DLC; *OR* 12, pt. 2 (Suppl.), 1005.

27. John Watts De Peyster, *Personal and Military History of Philip Kearny, Major Gen-*

eral United States Volunteers (New York, 1869), 389; J. Cox, Military Reminiscences, 1:248; Philadelphia Public Ledger, July 18, 1862.

28. General Orders, No. 5, dated July 18, 1862, No. 7, dated July 10 [sic] 1862, and No. 11, dated July 23, 1862, all issued by Headquarters, Army of Virginia, Washington, Thomas C. H. Smith Papers, OHS.

29. Wilder Dwight, Life and Letters of Wilder Dwight (Boston, 1868), 60; Quint, Potomac and Rapidan, 174, 181; Pomeroy Weekly Telegraph, Aug. 22, 1862; Gould, First-Tenth-Twenty-ninth Maine, 162–63.

30. James M. Stone, Personal Recollections of the Civil War (Boston, 1918), 57; Shaw, Blue-Eyed Child, 52; Pomeroy Weekly Telegraph, Aug. 22, 1862.

31. William T. Lusk, War Letters of William Thompson Lusk (New York, 1911), 177; H. Stevens, Life of Isaac Stevens, 2:426; James S. Lyon, War Sketches, from Cedar Mountain to Bull Run (Buffalo, 1882), 6; Patrick, Inside Lincoln's Army, 109; Hennessy, Return to Bull Run, 15–16.

32. Chase, Inside Lincoln's Cabinet, 95–96; Hennessy, Return to Bull Run, 16–17; J. Cox, Military Reminiscences, 1:222–23; New York Daily Tribune, July 19, 1862; [Edward A. Pollard], The Second Battle of Manassas, with Sketches of the Recent Campaign in Northern Virginia and on the Upper Potomac (Richmond, 1862), 9; 39th Cong., 1st sess., "Report of General Pope," CWSR 2:111. In testimony before the Joint Congressional Committee on the Conduct of the War in 1865, Pope left the question of authorship unclear, saying merely that the orders "set out very fully the policy which I considered advisable, and which at the time received the sanction of the government." Shortly after coming east, General Halleck told McClellan he regretted Pope's general orders, but "as I understand they were shown to the President before they were issued I felt unwilling to ask him to countermand them." OR 11, pt. 3, 359.

33. Pomeroy Weekly Telegraph, July 25, 1862.

34. 39th Cong., 1st sess., "Report of General Pope," CWSR, 2:114–15.

35. Hennessy, Return to Bull Run, 21.

36. Ibid., 10, 26–27; 39th Cong., 1st sess., "Report of General Pope," CWSR, 2:115; JP, "Army of Virginia" and "Second Bull Run," 445.

37. Strother, Virginia Yankee, 64–66, 71–73.

38. De Peyster, Kearny, 402; George C. Gorham, Life and Public Services of Edwin M. Stanton, 2 vols. (Boston, 1899), 2:21.

39. William Allan, "Strength of the Forces under Pope and Lee in August 1862," in The Virginia Campaign of General Pope in 1862, PMHSM (Boston, 1886), 2:195–220; Charles P. Horton, "The Campaign of General Pope in Virginia—First Part: To the 19th of August, 1862," in Virginia Campaign, 2:46.

40. George L. Andrews, "The Battle of Cedar Mountain, August 9, 1862," in Virginia Campaign, 2:398–404; JP to E. A. Carman, Feb. 16, 1877, JP Papers, HL; OR 12, pt. 2, 24; Noah Jones to Thomas C. H. Smith, n.d., Smith Papers, OHS; Townsend, Rustics in Rebellion, 216; Fishel, Secret War, 188; Bayard, Bayard, 227; JP, "Army of Virginia, III," NT, Aug. 16, 1888; Joseph C. Willard diary, Aug. 8, 1862, Willard Family Papers, DLC.

41. Strother, Virginia Yankee, 74–75; Willard diary, Aug. 8, 1862, Willard Family Papers, DLC; G. Andrews, "Cedar Mountain," 404; 39th Cong., 1st sess., "Report of General Pope," CWSR, 2:116–17; Thomas C. H. Smith, "Memoir," 71, Smith Papers, OHS; Krick, Jackson at Cedar Mountain, 21.

42. *OR* 12, pt. 2, 25–26; 39th Cong., 1st sess., "Report of General Pope," *CWSR*, 2:118; Gordon, *Brook Farm to Cedar Mountain*, 282; JP, "Army of Virginia, III."

43. Charles P. Horton, "Campaign of General Pope," 46–47; Quint, *Potomac and Rapidan*, 196; G. Andrews, "Cedar Mountain," 405; U.S. Congress, "Miscellaneous Papers: Battle of Cedar Mountain," *CCW*, 3:45, 55.

44. D. D. Jones to John Jordon Jr., Aug. 11, 1862, Jones Papers, HSP; Charles P. Horton, "Campaign of General Pope," 51; *OR* 12, pt. 3, 462, 466–67, 470; Chase, *Inside Lincoln's Cabinet*, 108; Gordon, *Brook Farm to Cedar Mountain*, 338–56; idem, *History of the Second Mass. Regiment of Infantry, Third Paper . . .* (Boston, 1875), 214–20.

45. U.S. Cong., "Miscellaneous Papers: Battle of Cedar Mountain," *CCW*, 2d Series, 3:45; Thomas C. H. Smith, "Memoir and Review of Pope's Campaign," 71–75, Smith Papers, OHS; Gordon, *Second Mass.*, 214, 218.

46. Krick, *Jackson at Cedar Mountain*, 99–104; Fitz John Porter, "Memorandum: The Campaign in Northern Virginia under Major-General John Pope," folio 1025, Porter Papers, DLC; G. Andrews, "Cedar Mountain," 422–23; U.S. Cong., "Miscellaneous Papers: Battle of Cedar Mountain," *CCW*, 2d Series, 3:46, 51–52; Gordon, *Second Mass.*, 221–22.

47. G. Andrews, "Cedar Mountain," 405–7, 440; D. D. Jones to John Jordon Jr., Aug. 11, 1862, Jones Papers, HSP; Lyon, *War Sketches*, 9; Strother, *Virginia Yankee*, 76; Noah Jones to Thomas C. H. Smith, n.d., and Thomas C. H. Smith, "Memoir and Review of Pope's Campaign," 72, Smith Papers, OHS; Willard diary, Aug. 9, 1862, Willard Family Papers, DLC; JP, "Army of Virginia, III"; 39th Cong., 1st sess., "Report of General Pope," *CWSR*, 2:120; Gordon, *Brook Farm to Cedar Mountain*, 214.

48. Thomas C. H. Smith, "Memoir and Review of Pope's Campaign," 72, Smith Papers, OHS; Krick, *Jackson at Cedar Mountain*, 219; Gordon, *Brook Farm to Cedar Mountain*, 315.

49. *OR* 12, pt. 2, 27; Strother, *Virginia Yankee*, 76; George L. Wood, *The Seventh Regiment: A Record* (New York, 1865), 129.

50. *OR* 12, pt. 2, 239; Noah Jones to Thomas C. H. Smith, n.d., Smith Papers, OHS; Krick, *Jackson at Cedar Mountain*, 316–17; JP, "Army of Virginia, III"; Strother, *Virginia Yankee*, 77; *Washington Star*, Aug. 11, 1862; A. S. Williams, *Letters of Alpheus Williams*, 101.

51. Strother, *Virginia Yankee*, 79–80; Willard diary, Aug. 10, 1862, Willard Family Papers, DLC.

52. Hennessy, *Return to Bull Run*, 28–29; *New York Herald*, Aug. 13, 1862; *Chicago Tribune*, Aug. 12, 1862; *OR* 12, pt. 2, 132, and pt. 3, 560.

53. Samuel M. Quincy, "General Halleck's Military Administration in the Summer of 1862," in *Virginia Campaign*, 2:6–11, 24, 28; *OR* 12, pt. 3, 560–61; JP, "Army of Virginia, III."

Chapter 6: The Enemy's Purpose Is Not Easy to Discover

1. Hennessy, *Return to Bull Run*, 35–37; Thomas C. H. Smith, "Memoir and Review of Pope's Campaign," 82, Smith Papers, OHS.

2. Hennessy, *Return to Bull Run*, 38; Franz Sigel, manuscript notes on John Pope, Sigel Papers, WRHS; Patrick, *Inside Lincoln's Army*, 120.

3. *OR* 12, pt. 3, 573; Gordon, *History of Army of Virginia*, 79–80; Willard diary, Aug. 2, 17, and 26, 1862, Willard Family Papers, DLC.

4. Patrick, *Inside Lincoln's Army*, 122–23; Hennessy, *Return to Bull Run*, 38–39; T. Fitzgerald to Thomas C. H. Smith, Sept. 7, 1865, Smith Papers, OHS; Herman Haupt, *Reminiscences of General Herman Haupt* (Washington, D.C., 1901), 69–70.

5. Hennessy, *Return to Bull Run*, 40–42; *OR* 12, pt. 3, 439; John D. Stevenson, "Pope's Virginia Campaign," in *War Papers and Personal Reminiscences, 1861–1865, Read before the Commandery of the State of Missouri, MOLLUS* (St. Louis, 1892), 336; *Philadelphia Inquirer*, July 12, 1862; William Gardiner, "Incidents of Cavalry Experiences during General Pope's Campaign," *Personal Narratives of Events in the War of the Rebellion, Being Papers Read before the Rhode Island Soldiers and Sailors Historical Society*, ser. 2, no. 20 (Providence, 1883), 420–21.

6. In *The Secret War for the Union* (191–94), Edwin C. Fishel characterizes Halter's report to Pope as "the timeliest single product of espionage received by any Union commander during the entire war," a direct consequence of Pope's "energetic direction of the army."

7. Thomas C. H. Smith, "Memoir and Review of Pope's Campaign," 82–83, Smith Papers, OHS; Haupt, *Reminiscences*, 70–71; Thomas L. Livermore, "The Conduct of Generals McClellan and Halleck in August, 1862; and the Case of Fitz John Porter," in *Virginia Campaign*, 2:320–21; Patrick, *Inside Lincoln's Army*, 124; Allan, "Strength of Forces," 202, 207–8.

8. Thomas C. H. Smith, "Memoir and Review of Pope's Campaign," 84–85, Smith Papers, OHS; Lyon, *War Sketches*, 13; Hennessy, *Return to Bull Run*, 52; 39th Cong., 1st sess., "Report of General Pope," *CWSR*, 2:123–25.

9. 39th Cong., 1st sess., "Report of General Pope," *CWSR*, 2:123, 127; Hennessy, *Return to Bull Run*, 61; Lyon, *War Sketches*, 14; Thomas C. H. Smith, "Memoir and Review of Pope's Campaign," 86, Smith Papers, OHS.

10. Hennessy, *Return to Bull Run*, 73; John C. Ropes, "Campaign of General Pope—Second Part," in *Virginia Campaign*, 2:58–59.

11. Hennessy, *Return to Bull Run*, 53, 74, 80–81; Thomas C. H. Smith, "Memoir and Review of Pope's Campaign," 90, Smith Papers, OHS; C. E. Davis, *Three Years in the Army*, 103–4; Edwin E. Bryant, *History of the Third Regiment of Wisconsin Veteran Volunteer Infantry* (Madison, 1891), 102–3; Patrick, *Inside Lincoln's Army*, 128; Haupt, *Reminiscences*, 82–83.

12. Livermore, "Conduct of McClellan and Halleck," 321; Haupt, *Reminiscences*, 73.

13. Hennessy, *Return to Bull Run*, 71–92; Gordon, *History of Army of Virginia*, 78.

14. *OR* 12, pt. 3, 655; Livermore, "Conduct of McClellan and Halleck," 321–22.

15. Livermore, "Conduct of McClellan and Halleck," 327; Hennessy, *Return to Bull Run*, 103, 108; *OR* 12, pt. 3, 652–55.

16. Hennessy, *Return to Bull Run*, 110; Pope, "Second Battle of Bull Run," 446; Thomas C. H. Smith, "Memoir and Review of Pope's Campaign," 95–96, Smith Papers, OHS; *OR* 12, pt. 2, 57, and pt. 3, 641–42, 647–48; Livermore, "Conduct of McClellan and Halleck," 324; Gordon, *History of Army of Virginia*, 94–95.

17. *OR* 12, pt. 2, 90, and pt. 3, 644, 656–58.

18. Frederic Denison, *Sabres and Spurs: The First Regiment Rhode Island Cavalry in the Civil War, 1861–1865* (Central Falls, R.I., 1876), 130–35; Bayard, *Bayard*, 230–36, 238, 240; Gardiner, "Incidents," 420–21; Haupt, *Reminiscences*, 83–93.

19. Charles F. Morse, "From Second Bull Run to Antietam," in *Missouri MOLLUS*, 269; Gould, *First-Tenth-Twenty-ninth Maine*, 200, 202.

20. Bryant, *Third Wisconsin*, 102–3; Gould, *First-Tenth-Twenty-ninth Maine*, 207; C.

E. Davis, *Three Years in the Army,* 103; Ropes, "Campaign of General Pope—Second Part," 61–62; Patrick, *Inside Lincoln's Army,* 128.

21. Ropes, "Campaign of General Pope—Second Part," 61–62; Hennessy, *Return to Bull Run,* 104–5; *OR* 12, pt. 2, 263–64, 653, and pt. 3, 641; 39th Cong., 1st sess., "Report of General Pope," *CWSR,* 2:131–35; Franz Sigel, manuscript notes filed with typescript "McDowell's Defense," Sigel Papers, WRHS.

22. *OR* 12, pt. 2, 65–66.

23. John Gibbon, *Personal Recollections of the Civil War* (New York, 1928), 47.

24. Gordon, *History of Army of Virginia,* 38–40; JP, "Army of Virginia," IV, *NT,* Aug. 23, 1888.

25. *OR* 12, pt. 2, 666.

26. Ambrose, *Halleck,* 70; idem, "Henry Halleck and the Second Bull Run Campaign," *Civil War History* 6 (1960): 238–49; Hennessy, *Return to Bull Run,* 101–2; Anson D. F. Randolph, *General H. W. Halleck's Report Reviewed in the Light of Facts* (New York, 1862), 3–4.

27. *OR* 11, pt. 3, 328, 330, 333, and 12, pt. 3, 739; McClellan to his wife, Aug. 10, 18, 23, 27, and 28, 1862, in McClellan, *Papers,* 390, 395, 399–400, 404, 406, 411.

28. JP, "Army of Virginia, V," *NT,* Aug. 30, 1888; *OR* 11, pt. 1, 76, 80–81.

29. Chase, *Inside Lincoln's Cabinet,* 115–16; Welles, *Diary,* 1:83, 112–13, 119–21; *OR* 12, pt. 3, 706, 739; Nicolay and Hay, *Lincoln,* 6:2–3; Ambrose, "Halleck and Second Bull Run," 244.

30. Fry, "McClellan and His 'Mission,'" 942; Nicolay and Hay, *Lincoln,* 6:3; Stephen W. Sears, *To the Gates of Richmond: The Peninsula Campaign* (New York, 1992), 351–52; *OR* 11, pt. 1, 76–77, and pt. 3, 342–43.

31. *OR* 11, pt. 1, 77, 80–81, and pt. 3, 342; Sears, *To the Gates,* 353–54; McClellan, *Papers,* 385, and *McClellan's Own Story* (New York, 1887), 491–92.

32. *OR* 11, pt. 1, 81–86, and pt. 3, 353–55, 359–60, 372–73; Fry, "McClellan and His 'Mission,'" 943; Livermore, "Conduct of McClellan and Halleck," 320.

33. Hennessy, *Return to Bull Run,* 81, 89–90; John C. Ropes, *The Army under Pope* (New York, 1881), 194–98; Thomas Livermore, *Numbers and Losses in the Civil War* (Bloomington, Ind., 1959), 88–89.

34. Fitz John Porter, *Gen. Fitz John Porter's Statement of the Services of the Fifth Army Corps, in 1862, in Northern Virginia* (New York, 1878), 8–13; *OR* 12, pt. 2 (Suppl.), 1006, and pt. 3, 647–48.

35. McClellan, *Papers,* 404–5; *OR* 12, pt. 3, 645–46; Gordon, *History of Army of Virginia,* 90–91.

36. Hennessy, *Return to Bull Run,* 105, 107–9; *OR* 12, pt. 2, 68, 348–49, and pt. 3, 665–66; 39th Cong., 1st sess., "Report of General Pope," *CWSR,* 2:137–39; Ropes, "Campaign of General Pope—Second Part," 62.

37. Hennessy, *Return to Bull Run,* 109; Livermore, "Conduct of McClellan and Halleck," 322; Francis J. Lippitt, "Pope's Virginia Campaign, and Porter's Part in It," *Atlantic Monthly,* Sept. 1878, 357.

38. Schurz, *Reminiscences,* 2:359–60; *OR* 12, pt. 3, 668; 39th Cong., 1st sess., "Report of General Pope," *CWSR,* 2:140–42; Hennessy, *Return to Bull Run,* 106–15.

39. *OR* 12, pt. 2, 70.

40. 39th Cong., 1st sess., "Report of General Pope," *CWSR,* 2:140–41.

41. Hennessy, *Return to Bull Run,* 109–10; *OR* 12, pt. 2, 33–34. In testimony before the Joint Congressional Committee on the Conduct of the War in 1865, Pope offered the

same version of events. He repeated it twenty-one years later in his *Century* article on Second Bull Run and served it up in abbreviated form to the readers of the *National Tribune.*

42. Haupt, *Reminiscences*, 92–97; 39th Con., 1st sess., "Report of General Pope," *CWSR*, 2:140, 142; Porter, *Statement of Services*, 14; Hennessy, *Return to Bull Run*, 110, 113; Livermore, "Conduct of McClellan and Halleck," 322–23; JP, "Second Bull Run," 448; Schurz, *Reminiscences*, 2:361.

43. Historians have praised Pope's decision to go after Jackson. John Hennessy said Pope evinced "precisely the type of positive attitude . . . needed to get out of his unfortunate fix; indeed it is not difficult to postulate that Lee would have pursued the same response had the roles been reversed." William Swinton, an early historian of the Army of the Potomac, called the plan "not only correct," but "brilliant." The Comte de Paris, while generally critical of Pope, also approved. Hennessy, *Return to Bull Run*, 117–19; JP, "Second Bull Run," 449; 39th Cong., 1st sess., "Report of General Pope," *CWSR*, 2:142–43; *OR* 12, pt. 3, 684; Ropes, "Campaign of General Pope—Second Part," 63.

44. 39th Cong., 1st sess., "Report of General Pope," *CWSR*, 2:142; Ropes, "Campaign of General Pope—Second Part," 63–64; Livermore, "Conduct of McClellan and Halleck," 325–26. Although on the morning of August 27 Pope told Halleck a "strong column penetrated by way of Manassas Railroad last night to Manassas," he believed most of the Rebel army to be at White Plains and felt he could break up the force presumably still at Manassas Junction with Hooker's division alone. *OR* 12, pt. 3, 684.

45. Porter, *Statement of Services*, 16; Porter to John Page Nicholson, Oct. 26, 1874, Nicholson Papers, HL; Daniel Leasure, "Personal Observations and Experiences in the Pope Campaign in Virginia," in *Minnesota MOLLUS*, 147–48; JP to Mrs. Philip J. Kearny, Oct. 30, 1862, Philip J. Kearny Papers, New Jersey Historical Society. Kearny presumably was drunk when he railed against Pope, because Porter later confessed to Pope that Kearny had spoken well of his conduct of the campaign, and Kearny also wrote his wife of his satisfaction with Pope's leadership. *OR* 12, pt. 2 (Suppl.), 840, 980; Kearny to his wife, Aug. 30, 1862 Kearny Papers, DLC.

46. Fitz John Porter, "Kennedy Correspondence," 1, and J. C. G. Kennedy to William Seward, July 22, 1862, both in Porter Papers, DLC.

47. JP, "Second Bull Run," 447–48; 46th Cong., 1st sess., S. Ex. Doc. 37, *Proceedings and Report . . . Case of Fitz John Porter*, 2:307–8; Porter, *Statement of Services*, 16–20; *OR* 12, pt. 2 (Suppl.), 830, 981.

48. McClellan, *Papers*, 406.

49. Franklin Haven Jr., "The Conduct of George McClellan at Alexandria in August, 1862," in *Virginia Campaign*, 2:270–71; *OR* 12, pt. 3, 689–91; Welles, *Diary*, 1:97–98; Ambrose, "Halleck and Second Bull Run," 244.

50. Charles Francis Adams, *A Cycle of Adams Letters*, ed. Worthington C. Ford, 2 vols. (Boston, 1920), 2:177–78; Hennessy, *Return to Bull Run*, 119–20; Haupt, *Reminiscences*, 97–103.

51. George H. Gordon, "The Twenty-seventh Day of August, 1862," in *Virginia Campaign*, 2:104–5.

52. Haupt, *Reminiscences*, 98.

53. *OR* 12, pt. 3, 690–92; Hennessy, *Return to Bull Run*, 128–29; Gordon, "Twenty-seventh Day of August," 114–20.

54. Adams, *Cycle of Letters*, 1:181.

Chapter 7: We Shall Bag the Whole Crowd

1. Ropes, "Campaign of General Pope—Second Part," 64–65; 39th Cong., 1st sess., "Report of General Pope," *CWSR*, 2:144–46; JP, "Second Bull Run," 451; *OR* 12, pt. 3, 704.

2. 39th Cong., 1st sess., "Report of General Pope," *CWSR*, 2:144, 146; JP, "Second Bull Run," 450; Hennessy, *Return to Bull Run*, 139–40; *OR* 12, pt. 2, 334–35, 354, and pt. 3, 706; Ropes, "Campaign of General Pope—Second Part," 64, and *Army under Pope*, 73; Livermore, "Conduct of McClellan and Halleck, 326–27.

3. *OR* 12, pt. 2, 335, and pt. 3, 689–90, 699–70; Ropes, "Campaign of General Pope—Second Part," 64; idem, *Army under Pope*, 67, 360.

4. Hennessy, *Return to Bull Run*, 143–46.

5. Strother, *Virginia Yankee*, 90; JP, "Second Bull Run," 450.

6. Porter, *Statement of Services*, 22–23; Livermore, "Conduct of McClellan and Halleck," 327–28; William H. Powell, *The Fifth Army Corps (Army of the Potomac); A Record of Operations during the Civil War . . .* (New York and London, 1896), 195–96. Franz Sigel dismissed as absurd the idea that Porter delayed the march through some treacherous intent: "If it had been the intention of General Porter to defeat the order of his commander, he could have made the effort to march at 1 o'clock to cover his treachery, and retarded his march on the road." Sigel, manuscript notes on the Second Bull Run campaign, Sigel Papers, WRHS.

7. JP, "Second Bull Run," 450; 39th Cong., 1st sess., "Report of General Pope," *CWSR*, 2:147; Dawes, *Service with the Sixth Wisconsin*, 69.

8. *OR* 12, pt. 2, 335–36; Ropes, *Army under Pope*, 69–70.

9. Ropes, *Army under Pope*, 70; Hennessy, *Return to Bull Run*, 149–51; *OR* 12, pt. 1, 212–13, and pt. 2, 336.

10. Strother, *Virginia Yankee*, 90; JP, "Second Bull Run," 450; *OR* 12, pt. 2 (Suppl.), 836–37; Porter, *Statement of Services*, 23–24; 46th Cong., 1st sess., S. Ex. Doc. 37, *Proceedings and Report . . . Case of Fitz John Porter*, 3:291.

11. JP, "Second Bull Run," 451; *OR* 12, pt. 1, 203, and pt. 3, 717, 732; Porter, *Statement of Services*, 24; Ropes, *Army under Pope*, 71–73, 79.

12. *OR* 12, pt. 2, 74, 337; Hennessy, *Return to Bull Run*, 162.

13. Hennessy, *Return to Bull Run*, 155–63; Ropes, *Army under Pope*, 74; *OR* 12, pt. 2, 337, 361.

14. *OR* 12, pt. 1, 213; William H. Harries, "Gainesville, Virginia, August 28, 1862," in *Minnesota MOLLUS*, Sixth Series, 166; Gibbon, *Personal Recollections*, 54–55.

15. Harries, "Gainesville," 166; Hennessy, *Return to Bull Run*, 191; Gibbon, *Personal Recollections*, 57; Charles King, "In Vindication of General Rufus King," *Century* 31, no. 6 (Apr. 1886), 935; *OR* 12, pt. 1, 208.

16. Gibbon, *Personal Recollections*, 55–57. For a compelling discussion of how King was wrongly indicted (by Pope in particular) for his decision to quit the field, see Hennessy, *Return to Bull Run*, 192–93, and King, "In Vindication of General King," 935.

17. King, "Gainesville, 1862," *Wisconsin MOLLUS*, 3:258; idem, "In Vindication of General King," 936; 39th Cong., 1st sess., "Report of General Pope," *CWSR*, 2:150–51; *OR* 12, pt. 2, 39, 266.

18. Hennessy, *Return to Bull Run*, 194; 39th Cong., 1st sess., "Report of General Pope," *CWSR*, 2:150–51; Strother, *Virginia Yankee*, 91; *OR* 12, pt. 1, 205.

19. Ropes, *Army under Pope*, 79–80; Longstreet, "Our March against Pope," 606–7; idem, *From Manassas to Appomattox*, 177.

20. Warren L. Goss, "Recollections of a Private—VI; Two Days of the Second Battle of Bull Run," *Century* 31, no. 3 (Jan. 1886): 468–69; Franz Sigel, manuscript notes on John Pope, Sigel Papers, WRHS.

21. Goss, "Recollections—VI," 468; Stone, *Personal Recollections*, 64.

22. A. E. Voglebach to Fitz John Porter, Aug. 22, 1878, Porter Papers, DLC; Fitz John Porter to John Page Nicholson, Oct. 26, 1874, Nicholson Papers, HL.

23. Strother, *Virginia Yankee*, 91–92; Porter, *Statement of Services*, 25.

24. *OR* 12, pt. 2, 191, 316–17; Willard diary, Aug. 28, 1862, Willard Family Papers, DLC.

25. Schurz, *Reminiscences*, 1:361; Gibbon, *Personal Recollections*, 47; Hennessy, *Return to Bull Run*, 196; Thomas C. H. Smith, "Memoir and Review of Pope's Campaign," 127–28, Smith Papers, OHS.

26. Adams, *Cycle of Letters*, 1:181; *OR* 12, pt. 3, 707; McClellan, *Papers*, 411.

27. *OR* 12, pt. 3, 705–12; Haupt, *Reminiscences*, 107; Stephen M. Weld, "The Conduct of General McClellan at Alexandria in August, 1862," in *Virginia Campaign*, 2:301–2. That night, Barnard repeated his fears to Halleck, who waved him away saying, "I have no time for these details, and don't come to me until you exhaust other resources."

28. Weld, "Conduct of McClellan," 302.

29. *OR* 12, pt. 3, 710; Gorham, *Stanton*, 2:37–38. Previous to August 28, Halleck's orders regarding Franklin had been discretionary in nature.

Chapter 8: No Place to Fight a Battle

1. Gibbon, *Personal Recollections*, 58–59; *OR* 12, pt. 2 (Suppl.), 832–33. Pope incorrectly thought Porter was at Manassas, when in fact he was at Bristoe Station.

2. *OR* 12, pt. 2 (Suppl.), 978–80; Hennessy, *Return to Bull Run*, 197; John Gibbon, "Pope at Bull Run," 1–3, undated manuscript in Porter Papers, DLC.

3. *OR* 12, pt. 2 (Suppl.), 884, 987, and pt. 3, 730; Porter, *Statement of Services*, 27.

4. Gibbon, *Personal Recollections*, 60; *OR* 12, pt. 2 (Suppl.), 902; Porter, *Statement of Services*, 28; John Piatt to Fitz John Porter, June 28, 1878, Porter Papers, DLC.

5. *OR* 12, pt. 1, 241, and pt. 2 (Suppl.), 832; Hennessy, *Return to Bull Run*, 198; Porter, *Statement of Services*, 28; JP, "Second Bull Run," 454; [Thomas C. H. Smith], "General Pope's Campaign in Virginia," *Army and Navy Journal*, Feb. 6, 1864.

6. *OR* 12, pt. 2 (Suppl.), 832, 851, 867, 870, 1094; Strother, *Virginia Yankee*, 92; Ropes, "Campaign of General Pope—Third Part," 82–83.

7. *OR* 12, pt. 2 (Suppl.), 867, 885; John Hay, *Letters of John Hay and Extracts from Diary*, 3 vols. (Washington, D.C., 1908), 1:59; Willard diary, Aug. 29, 1862, Willard Family Papers, DLC; Ropes, "Campaign of General Pope—Third Part," 83.

8. Hennessy, *Return to Bull Run*, 232.

9. *OR* 12, pt. 1, 76.

10. Ropes, *Army under Pope*, 93; *OR* 12, pt. 2 (Suppl.), 903–4, 983; Porter, *Statement of Services*, 29; 46th Cong., 1st sess., S. Ex. Doc. 37, *Proceedings and Report . . . Case of Fitz John Porter*, 2:427–28.

11. Porter, *Statement of Services*, 30–31; *OR* 12, pt. 2, (Suppl.), 904, 955–56; Willard

diary, Aug. 29, 1862, Willard Family Papers, DLC; Henry Gabler, "The Fitz John Porter Case: Politics and Military Justice" (Ph.D. diss., City University of New York, 1979), 128–29; Hennessy, *Return to Bull Run*, 233–34.

12. Porter, *Statement of Services*, 33–34.

13. Thomas C. H. Smith, "Memoir and Review of Pope's Campaign," 132, Smith Papers, OHS; 46th Cong., 1st sess., S. Ex. Doc. 37, *Proceedings and Report . . . Case of Fitz John Porter*, 3:303; Strother, *Virginia Yankee*, 92; Lyon, *War Sketches*, 26; OR 12, pt. 2, 39, and pt. 2 (Suppl.), 853.

14. OR 17, pt. 2 (Suppl.), 832; 46th Cong., 1st sess., S. Ex. Doc. 37, *Proceedings and Report . . . Case of Fitz John Porter*, 3:887, 892.

15. JP, "Second Bull Run," 454–55; OR 12, pt. 2 (Suppl.), 832; Hennessy, *Return to Bull Run*, 236.

16. Hennessy, *Return to Bull Run*, 236–37, 514; OR 12, pt. 2, 39.

17. Sigel, "McDowell Notes," filed with tyescript "McDowell's Defense," Sigel Papers, WRHS. For a penetrating discussion of Kearny's odd behavior and the reasons for it, see Hennessy, *Return to Bull Run*, 219–23.

18. OR 12, pt. 2, 272; Hennessy, *Return to Bull Run*, 229–30; Longstreet, "Our March against Pope," 610.

19. Hennessy, *Return to Bull Run*, 244–45, 250–58.

20. JP, "Second Bull Run," 455; OR 12, pt. 2, 394.

21. OR 12, pt. 2, 38, 394; John J. Hennessy, *Second Manassas Battlefield Map Study* (Lynchburg, Va., 1986), 145; Captain H. S. Thomas to Fitz John Porter, July 13, 1878, Porter Papers, DLC. Pope evidently thought so little of the episode—or else was so anxious to squelch it—that he made no mention of his conversation with Captain Thomas, or of Reynolds's abortive attack, in his report of the battle.

22. Strother, *Virginia Yankee*, 93; JP, "Second Bull Run," 455; Willard diary, Aug. 29, 1862, Willard Family Papers, DLC; Hennessy, *Return to Bull Run*, 268.

23. Thomas C. H. Smith, "Memoir and Review of Pope's Campaign," 138, Smith Papers, OHS; OR 12, pt. 2 (Suppl.), 851; JP, "Second Bull Run," 455; Gibbon, *Personal Recollections*, 60–61.

24. Hennessy, *Return to Bull Run*, 268.

25. 46th Cong., 1st sess., S. Ex. Doc. 37, *Proceedings and Report . . . Case of Fitz John Porter*, 2:303–4; JP, "Second Bull Run," 455; Porter, *Statement of Services*, 39; OR 12, pt. 2 (Suppl.), 852.

26. OR 12, pt. 2 (Suppl.), 852, 860, 879, 882, 1031, 1034; 46th Cong., 1st sess., S. Ex. Doc. 37, *Proceedings and Report . . . Case of Fitz John Porter*, 2:304.

27. OR 12, pt. 2 (Suppl.), 879, 949, 957, 1031, 1033, 1085; Porter, *Statement of Services*, 39, 41; Porter, manuscript calculations of times on the battlefield, Porter Papers, DLC; 46th Cong., 1st sess., S. Ex. Doc. 37, *Proceedings and Report . . . Case of Fitz John Porter*, 3:1095, 1097; Richard Robins, "The Battle of Groveton and Second Bull Run," in *Military Essays*, 3:92.

28. OR 12, pt. 2 (Suppl.), 950, 968, 984, 1012, 1032; Porter, *Statement of Services*, 38, 40; Porter, manuscript calculations of times on the battlefield, Porter Papers, DLC; 46th Cong., 1st sess., S. Ex. Doc. 37, *Proceedings and Report . . . Case of Fitz John Porter*, 2:294, 325. Colonel E. G. Marshall, who had been on the picket line all afternoon, told Morell an attack would mean "certain destruction" for the entire division.

29. OR 12, pt. 2 (Suppl.), 1094–96; Porter, *Statement of Services*, 41–42.

30. *OR* 12, pt. 2 (Suppl.), 1095; Porter to George B. McClellan, May 22, 1878, McClellan Papers, DLC.

31. Minutes after dispatching Lieutenant Weld, Porter abandoned the idea of withdrawing. "On going to the head of the column, I found I had been misinformed," recalled Porter. "The opening of an artillery fire beyond Groveton toward Sudley Springs on General Pope's extreme right, and the cessation temporarily of that near Groveton, had created the erroneous impression that 'the firing of the enemy had advanced and ours retired.' No action was taken to carry out the determination expressed, and there was no withdrawing to Manassas, or falling back of any kind." Porter, *Statement of Services,* 34–37, 42; *OR* 12, pt. 2 (Suppl.), 950. For a superb treatment of the phenomenon of "acoustic shadows" on Civil War battlefields, see Charles Ross, "SSH! Battle in Progress!" *Civil War Times Illustrated* 35, no. 6 (Dec. 1996): 56–62.

32. *OR* 12, pt. 2, 30, 527, and pt. 2 (Suppl.), 832, 834, 849–52, 950; 39th Cong., 1st sess., "Report of General Pope," *CWSR,* 2:154–55; 46th Cong., 1st sess., S. Ex. Doc. 37, *Proceedings and Report . . . Case of Fitz John Porter,* 2:295; Strother, *Virginia Yankee,* 94; Franz Sigel to Fitz John Porter, Nov. 2, 1867, Sigel Papers, WRHS; Willard diary, Aug. 29, 1862, Willard Family Papers, DLC.

33. 39th Cong., 1st sess., "Report of General Pope," *CWSR,* 2:154; JP, "Second Bull Run," 457; Strother, *Virginia Yankee,* 93; Thomas C. H. Smith, "Memoir and Review of Pope's Campaign," 138, Smith Papers, OHS.

34. Philip Kearny to his wife, Aug. 30, 1862, Kearny Papers, DLC; Strother, *Virginia Yankee,* 93; Hennessy, *Return to Bull Run,* 270–85; Jubal A. Early, *War Memoirs: Autobiographical Sketch and Narrative of the War between the States,* ed. Frank E. Vandiver (Bloomington, Ind., 1960), 123–28; *OR* 12, pt. 2 (Suppl.), 950; Thomas C. H. Smith, "Memoir and Review of Pope's Campaign," 138, 142, Smith Papers, OHS.

35. Thomas C. H. Smith, "Memoir and Review of Pope's Campaign," 142, Smith Papers, OHS; Stone, *Personal Recollections,* 66; Charles F. Walcott, *History of the Twenty-first Regiment Massachusetts Volunteers* (Boston, 1882), 144.

36. Gibbon, *Personal Recollections,* 61–62; 46th Cong., 1st sess., S. Ex. Doc. 37, *Proceedings and Report . . . Case of Fitz John Porter,* 2:194.

37. *OR* 12, pt. 2, 40; 46th Cong., 1st sess., S. Ex. Doc. 37, *Proceedings and Report . . . Case of Fitz John Porter,* 2:198, 312; Thomas C. H. Smith, "Memoir and Review of Pope's Campaign," Smith Papers, OHS, 142.

38. *OR* 12, pt. 2, 369; Abner Doubleday journal, Aug. 29 1862, Generals' Books and Papers, RG 94, NA; Willard diary, Aug. 29, 1862, Willard Family Papers, DLC; Gordon, *History of Army of Virginia,* 333–34; George F. Noyes, *The Bivouac and the Battlefield* (New York, 1863), 128.

39. Doubleday journal, Aug. 29, 1862, Generals' Books and Papers, RG 94, NA; Strother, *Virginia Yankee,* 93–94; Thomas C. H. Smith, "Memoir and Review of Pope's Campaign," 143, Smith Papers, OHS.

40. Doubleday journal, Aug. 29, 1862, Generals' Books and Papers, RG 94, NA; Hennessy, *Return to Bull Run,* 294–95; J. A. Judson to Fitz John Porter, May 9, 1878, Porter Papers, DLC.

41. Judson to Porter, May 5, 1878, Porter Papers, DLC; *OR* 12, pt. 2, 367; Gordon, *History of Army of Virginia,* 335–36.

42. Hennessy, *Return to Bull Run,* 288–89; James Longstreet, *From Manassas to Ap-*

pomattox: *Memoirs of the Civil War in America* (Philadelphia, 1912), 183; idem, "Our March against Pope," 608–9.

43. Hennessy, *Return to Bull Run,* 299.

44. Ibid., 300; 46th Cong., 1st sess., S. Ex. Doc. 37, *Proceedings and Report . . . Case of Fitz John Porter,* 2:231; Doubleday journal, Aug. 29, 1862, Generals' Books and Papers, RG 94, NA.

45. Hennessy, *Return to Bull Run,* 301; Strother, *Virginia Yankee,* 94.

46. *OR* 12, pt. 2 (Suppl.), 834, 851–52; Strother, *Virginia Yankee,* 94.

47. John Hennessy reaches similar conclusions in his *Return to Bull Run,* 305–8.

48. *OR* 12, pt. 2, 870; Willard diary, Aug. 29, 1862, Willard Family Papers, DLC; Porter, *Statement of Services,* 47; JP, "Second Bull Run," 461; Thomas C. H. Smith, "Memoir and Review of Pope's Campaign," 144, Smith Papers, OHS.

49. *OR* 12, pt. 2, 525.

50. Thomas C. H. Smith, "Memoir and Review of Pope's Campaign," 144, Smith Papers, OHS; Incomplete dispatch from Pope to Porter, 8:45 P.M., Aug. 29, 1862, John C. Ropes Papers, Military Historical Society of Massachusetts Collection, Boston University; George D. Ruggles to Fitz John Porter, Oct. 14, 1887, Porter Papers, DLC; Hennessy, *Return to Bull Run,* 306; *OR* 12, pt. 2, 525, and pt. 2 (Suppl.), 832, 840–41; 39th Cong., 1st sess., "Report of General Pope, *CWSR,* 2:154; JP, "Army of Virginia, VI," *NT,* Sept. 6, 1888.

51. *OR* 12, pt. 3, 724; Thomas C. H. Smith, "Memoir and Review of Pope's Campaign," 145, Smith Papers, OHS.

Chapter 9: Leave Pope to Get Out of His Scrape

1. Noyes, *Bivouac and Battlefield,* 134–35; Charles A. Page, *Letters of a War Correspondent, 1862–1865* (Boston, 1899), 28; 39th Cong., 1st sess., "Report of General Pope," *CWSR,* 2:155.

2. Willard diary, Aug. 30, 1862, Willard Family Papers, DLC.

3. Thomas C. H. Smith, "Memoir and Review of Pope's Campaign," 145–46, Smith Papers, OHS; *OR* 12, pt. 2, 17, 41; 39th Cong., 1st sess., "Report of General Pope," *CWSR,* 2:156.

4. McClellan, *Papers,* 415; Haven, "Conduct of McClellan," 277; Weld, "Conduct of McClellan," 293; *OR* 11, pt. 1, 97, and 12, pt. 3, 724–25.

5. Ropes, *Army under Pope,* 164; McClellan, *Papers,* 414.

6. Weld, "Conduct of McClellan," 297; Comte de Paris, Louis-Philippe-Albert d'Orleans, *History of the Civil War in America,* 4 vols. (Philadelphia, 1875–88), 2:287, 294; Franklin Sawyer, *A Military History of the 8th Regiment Ohio Vol. Inf'y* (Cleveland, 1881), 64; *OR* 11, pt. 1, 99.

7. McClellan, *Papers,* 415–16; *OR* 11, pt. 1, 99. George T. Stevens, *Three Years in the Sixth Corps* (Albany, N.Y., 1866), 129.

8. J. Cox, *Military Reminiscences,* 1:236; McClellan, *Papers,* 416.

9. McClellan, *Papers,* 417.

10. *"Leave Pope to Get Out of His Scrape," McClellan's Dispatches* (Washington, D.C., 1864), 5; Ropes, *Army under Pope,* 161; McClellan, *Papers,* 254; Lincoln, *Collected Works,* 5:399.

11. Welles, *Diary,* 1:118, 122.

12. *OR* 12, pt. 3, 722; Ropes, *Army under Pope,* 160.

13. Ropes, *Army under Pope,* 160.

14. Weld, "Conduct of McClellan," 299; *OR* 12, pt. 3, 723–24.

15. Ropes, *Army under Pope,* 162; Chase, *Inside Lincoln's Cabinet,* 116; *OR* 12, pt. 3, 723; Nicolay and Hay, *Lincoln,* 6:19, 23; Hay, *Letters and Diary,* 1:60–61.

16. McClellan, *Papers,* 418–19; Weld, "Conduct of McClellan," 301; Ropes, *Army under Pope,* 163–64; J. Cox, *Military Reminiscences,* 1:236.

17. Noyes, *Bivouac and Battlefield,* 135–36; Gibbon, *Personal Recollections,* 62; C. Page, *Letters,* 28; Heintzelman journal, Aug. 30, 1862, Heintzelman Papers, DLC; Franz Sigel to Fitz John Porter, Nov. 2, 1867, Sigel Papers, WRHS.

18. Gibbon, *Personal Recollections,* 62.

19. 46th Cong., 1st sess., S. Ex. Doc. 37, *Proceedings and Report . . . Case of Fitz John Porter,* 2:232–33; *OR* 12, pt. 2, 41, 340; Schurz, *Reminiscences,* 2:352.

20. Noyes, *Bivouac and Battlefield,* 135; *OR* 12, pt. 3, 741.

21. Hennessy, *Return to Bull Run,* 309, 314–15.

22. Philip Kearny to his wife, Aug. 30, 1862, Kearny Papers, and Samuel P. Heintzelman journal, Aug. 30, 1862, Heintzelman Papers, both in DLC; Porter, *Statement of Services,* 65; Gouverneur K. Warren to Porter, May 20, 1878, Porter Papers, DLC.

23. Robins, "Groveton and Second Bull Run," 94; *OR* 12, pt. 2 (Suppl.), 854; Porter, *Statement of Services,* 64–65; idem, "Memorandum: The Campaign in Northern Virginia under Major-General John Pope," folios 1040–42, Porter Papers, DLC.

24. Ropes, *Army under Pope,* 129–30.

25. Hennessy, *Return to Bull Run,* 312–13; Gouverneur K. Warren to Fitz John Porter, May 20, 1878, Porter Papers, DLC; Porter, *Statement of Services,* 65; Porter to Ropes, Sept. 7, 1897, Ropes Papers, MHSMC, BU; Porter to John P. Nicholson, Oct. 26, 1874, Nicholson Papers, HL.

26. Porter, *Statement of Services,* 64; *OR* 12, pt. 2 (Suppl.), 854.

27. Hennessy, *Second Manassas Map Study,* 233–43; *OR* 12, pt. 3, 755.

28. Strother, *Virginia Yankee,* 94–95.

29. Hennessy, *Return to Bull Run,* 321–22; Pope, "Second Battle of Bull Run," 465.

30. Stephen M. Weld, *War Diary and Letters of Stephen Minot Weld* (Boston, 1979), 81; Hennessy, *Return to Bull Run,* 322–23.

31. Porter, "Memorandum: The Campaign in Northern Virginia under Major-General John Pope," folio 1027, Porter Papers, and Heintzelman journal, Aug. 30, 1862, both in DLC; 46th Cong., 1st sess., S. Ex. Doc. 37, *Proceedings and Report . . . Case of Fitz John Porter,* 2:238–39; *OR* 12, pt. 2, 340; Willard diary, Aug. 30, 1862, Willard Family Papers, DLC.

32. Porter, *Statement of Services,* 65; Stephen M. Weld to Porter, Nov. 11, 1862, Porter Papers, DLC; Weld, *Diary and Letters,* 81.

33. Hennessy, *Return to Bull Run,* 324; Porter, *Statement of Services,* 65–66; *OR* 12, pt. 2, 340; Heintzelman journal, Aug. 30, 1862, Heintzelman Papers, DLC.

34. Gibbon, *Personal Recollections,* 62–63; Hennessy, *Second Manassas Map Study,* 228, 261.

35. Porter, *Statement of Services,* 66; Hennessy, *Return to Bull Run,* 325; Gordon, *History of Army of Virginia,* 348.

36. Porter, *Statement of Services,* 66–67; Hennessy, *Return to Bull Run,* 326–27; *OR* 12, pt. 3, 959–60.

37. Hennessy, *Return to Bull Run,* 328; E. M. Woodward, *Our Campaigns: The Second Regiment Pennsylvania Reserve Volunteers* (Philadelphia, 1865), 140–41.

38. George Ruggles to Fitz John Porter, June 10, 1877, Porter Papers, DLC; Porter to John C. Ropes, Sept. 7, 1897, Ropes Papers, MHSMC, BU; 46th Cong., 1st sess., S. Ex. Doc. 37, *Proceedings and Report . . . Case of Fitz John Porter,* 2:311.

39. *OR* 12, pt. 2, 340, 963–64; Willard diary, Aug. 30, 1862, Willard Family Papers, DLC; Porter, *Statement of Services,* 67–68.

40. *OR* 12, pt. 2, 268; Hennessy, *Second Manassas Map Study,* 261–62.

41. Thomas C. H. Smith, "Memoir and Review of Pope's Campaign," 147, 151–52, Smith Papers, OHS; Lyon, *War Sketches,* 30–31; *OR* 12, pt. 2, 281–82, 340–41.

42. *OR* 12, pt. 2, 964; 46th Cong., 1st sess., *Proceedings and Report . . . Case of Fitz John Porter,* 2:384; Pope, "Second Battle of Bull Run," 462; Porter, *Statement of Services,* 68.

43. Hennessy, *Second Manassas Map Study,* 271–72.

44. Hennessy, *Return to Bull Run,* 337, 340; Porter, *Statement of Services,* 68.

45. Gordon, *History of Army of Virginia,* 363; Porter, *Statement of Services,* 68–69.

46. Gibbon, *Personal Recollections,* 63; Theron W. Haight, "Gainesville, Groveton, and Bull Run," *Wisconsin MOLLUS,* 2:367; Hennessy, *Second Manassas Map Study,* 297.

47. Hennessy, *Return to Bull Run,* 348–56.

48. Porter, *Statement of Services,* 69; Hennessy, *Return to Bull Run,* 358; Dawes, *Service with the Sixth Wisconsin,* 71; Schurz, *Reminiscences,* 2:372–73.

49. Strother, *Virginia Yankee,* 95.

50. 39th Cong., 1st sess., "Report of General Pope," *CWSR,* 2:157; *OR* 12, pt. 2, 496, 501; Thomas C. H. Smith, "Memoir and Review of Pope's Campaign," 150–51, Smith Papers, OHS.

51. Hennessy, *Return to Bull Run,* 358–61; Gordon, *History of Army of Virginia,* 363–65; Woodward, *Our Campaigns,* 141–42.

Chapter 10: If I Could Be of Further Service, I Would Remain

1. Longstreet, "Our March against Pope," 609; idem, *Manassas to Appomattox,* 188; Hennessy, *Return to Bull Run,* 370.

2. Ropes, *Army under Pope,* 140.

3. *OR* 12, pt. 2, 340–41; Hennessy, *Second Manassas Map Study,* 318; idem, *Return to Bull Run,* 374–75; Gordon, *History of Army of Virginia,* 371–73; Willard diary, Aug. 30, 1862, Willard Family Papers, DLC.

4. Strother, *Virginia Yankee,* 95.

5. Ibid., 95–96; Ropes, *Army under Pope,* 136.

6. Hennessy, *Return to Bull Run,* 393–94.

7. Thomas C. H. Smith, "Memoir and Review of Pope's Campaign," 157, Smith Papers, OHS; 46th Cong., 1st sess., *Proceedings and Report . . . Case of Fitz John Porter,* 2:385.

8. Martin Hardin, *History of the Twelfth Regiment Pennsylvania Reserve Volunteer Corps* (New York, 1890), 100.

9. Gordon, *History of Army of Virginia,* 368; Hennessy, *Second Manassas Map Study,* 344; John D. Vautier, *History of the Eighty-fifth Pennsylvania Volunteers in the War for the Union* (Philadelphia, 1894), 55.

10. Hennessy, *Second Manassas Map Study,* 354; Austin C. Stearns, *Three Years with Company K* (Rutherford, N.J., 1976), 108; Comte de Paris, *Civil War in America,* 2:299.

11. 39th Cong., 1st sess., "Report of General Pope," *CWSR,* 2:157; Thomas C. H. Smith, "Memoir and Review of Pope's Campaign," 157–58, Smith Papers, OHS; Hennessy, *Return to Bull Run,* 409–10.

12. *OR* 12, pt. 2, 43.

13. Porter, *Statement of Services,* 70.

14. Strother, *Virginia Yankee,* 100; Schurz, *Reminiscences,* 2:366–67; Heintzelman journal, Aug. 30, 1862, Heintzelman Papers, DLC; Charles S. Wainwright, *A Diary of Battle: The Personal Journals of Colonel Charles S. Wainwright, 1861–1865,* ed. Allan Nevins (New York, 1962), 90.

15. Thomas C. H. Smith, "Memoir and Review of Pope's Campaign," 160–61, Smith Papers, OHS.

16. Strother, *Virginia Yankee,* 96.

17. Pope, "Second Battle of Bull Run," 463; Thomas C. H. Smith, "Memoir and Review of Pope's Campaign," 164, Smith Papers, OHS; *OR* 12, pt. 2, 77–78.

18. Gibbon, *Personal Recollections,* 67; Thomas C. H. Smith, "Memoir and Review of Pope's Campaign," 160, 163, Smith Papers, OHS; Strother, *Virginia Yankee,* 96–97; 46th Cong., 1st sess., S. Ex. Doc. 37, *Proceedings and Report . . . Case of Fitz John Porter,* 2:310–11; Franklin Haven to John C. Ropes, Jan. 24, 1897, Ropes Papers, MHSMC, BU; Hennessy, *Second Manassas Map Study,* 375; Heintzelman journal, Aug. 30, 1862, Heintzelman Papers, and Willard diary, Aug. 30, 1862, Willard Family Papers, DLC.

19. Lyon, *War Sketches,* 33; Franklin Haven to John C. Ropes, Jan. 24, 1897, Ropes Papers, MHSMC, BU.

20. George D. Ruggles to William R. Livermore, May 10, 1897, MHSMC, BU.

21. Fitz John Porter to John P. Nicholson, n.d., Nicholson Papers, HL; Gibbon, *Personal Recollections,* 66–67; Dawes, *Service with the Sixth Wisconsin,* 74–75.

22. Ropes, *Army under Pope,* 144–45; Pope, "Second Battle of Bull Run," 463–64; "William H. Powell to the Editors, March 12, 1885," *Century* 31, no. 3 (Jan. 1886), 473; Theodore M. Nagle, *Reminiscences of the Civil War* (New York, 1923), 37; Noyes, *Bivouac and Battlefield,* 139; William B. Franklin, "The Sixth Corps at Second Bull Run," *B&L,* vol. 2, pt. 2, 540.

23. Pope, "Second Battle of Bull Run," 464; Strother, *Virginia Yankee,* 464; *OR* 12, pt. 2, 78–79; 46th Cong., 1st sess., S. Ex. Doc. 37, *Proceedings and Report . . . Case of Fitz John Porter,* 311–12.

24. Ropes, *Army under Pope,* 145.

25. G. Stevens, *Three Years in the Sixth Corps,* 129; Hennessy, *Return to Bull Run,* 437; Thomas L. Livermore, *Days and Events, 1860–1866* (Boston, 1920), 110.

26. Strother, *Virginia Yankee,* 97; Gibbon, *Personal Recollections,* 68–69.

27. W. F. Smith, *Autobiography,* 51.

28. Strother, *Virginia Yankee,* 97; Captain Gaines and George D. Ruggles, "Statements in Regard to Gen. Pope's Language in Regard to Gen. Sigel," n.d., and Joseph Hooker to Franz Sigel, Dec. 7, 1862, both in Sigel Papers, NYHS.

29. 39th. Cong., 1st sess., "Report of General Pope," *CWSR,* 2:161; *St. Paul Daily Press,* Sept. 24, 1862.

30. Haupt, *Reminiscences,* 135; *Chicago Times,* Sept. 4, 1862; J. C. Andrews, *North Reports,* 268; John Sedgwick, *Correspondence of John Sedgwick, Major General,* 2 vols. (New York, 1902–3), 2:78–79.

31. Hay, *Letters and Diary,* 1:61–62.

32. Strother, *Virginia Yankee*, 99; Hennessy, *Return to Bull Run*, 439.

33. Strother, *Virginia Yankee*, 99; Sawyer, *8th Ohio*, 66; Horace H. Thomas, "What I Saw under a Flag of Truce," *Military Essays*, 1:136–37.

34. Franklin Haven to John C. Ropes, Jan. 24, 1897, Ropes Papers, MHSMC, BU; Wainwright, *Diary of Battle*, 90; Heintzelman journal, Aug. 31, 1862, Heintzelman Papers, DLC; Bayard, *Bayard*, 240; Henry L. Abbott, *Fallen Leaves: The Civil War Letters of Major Henry Livermore Abbott*, ed. Robert Garth Scott (Kent, Ohio, 1991), 140; [Thomas C. H. Smith], "General Pope's Campaign in Virginia," *Army and Navy Journal*, Feb. 6, 1864; Weld, *Diary and Letters*, 132.

35. *New York Daily Tribune*, Sept. 3, 1862; *Philadelphia Inquirer*, Sept. 5, 1862; Schurz, *Reminiscences*, 2:382.

36. William Kepler, *History of the Three Months' and Three Years' Service, from April 16th, 1861, to June 22d, 1864, of the Fourth Regiment Ohio Volunteer Infantry in the War for the Union* (Cleveland, 1886), 78; Oliver C. Bosbyshell, *The Forty-eighth in the War, Being a Narrative of the Campaigns of the 48th Regiment, Infantry, Pennsylvania Veteran Volunteers, during the War of the Rebellion* (Philadelphia, 1895), 70–71; Woodward, *Our Campaigns*, 146–47; Livermore, *Days and Events*, 110; G. Stevens, *Three Years in the Sixth Corps*, 132–33.

37. Pound Sterling [William P. Maxson], *Camp Fires of the Twenty-third: Sketches of the Camp Life, Marches, and Battles of the Twenty-third Regiment, N.Y.V.* (New York, 1863), 81; Gould, *First–Tenth–Twenty-ninth Maine*, 219–20. For more on the matter of blame, see Charles Barber, *The Civil War Letters of Charles Barber, Private, 104th New York Volunteer Infantry*, ed. Raymond G. Barber and Gary E. Swinson (Torrance, Calif., 1991), 85; M. T. V. Bowman, "My Experience on 'Pope's Retreat,'" in *War Sketches and Incidents as Related by the Companions of the Iowa Commandery, MOLLUS*, 2 vols. (Des Moines, 1893–98), 2:56; Bryant, *Third Wisconsin*, 118; Dawes, *Service with the Sixth Wisconsin*, 76; Leasure, "Personal Observations and Experiences," 166.

38. "William H. Powell to Editors," 473.

39. *St. Paul Daily Press*, Sept. 24, 1862; Thomas C. H. Smith, "Memoir and Review of Pope's Campaign," 170–72, Smith Papers, OHS; 39th Cong., 1st sess., "Report of General Pope," *CWSR*, 2:161; George D. Ruggles to William L. Livermore, May 10, 1897, Ropes Papers, MHSMC, BU; Strother, *Virginia Yankee*, 98.

40. Hennessy, *Return to Bull Run*, 440; *OR* 12, pt. 2 (Suppl.), 843; John G. Moore, "The Battle of Chantilly," *Military Affairs* 28, no. 2 (Summer 1966), 50.

41. H. H. Thomas, "What I Saw," 137.

42. *OR* 12, pt. 2, 79–80; Heintzelman journal, Aug. 31, 1862, Heintzelman Papers, DLC.

43. 39th Cong., 1st sess., "Report of General Pope," *CWSR*, 2:163.

44. Fitz John Porter to William B. Franklin, July 6, 1876, George B. McClellan Papers, DLC; Weld, *Diary and Letters*, 132.

45. Moore, "Battle of Chantilly," 50–52; *St. Paul Press*, Sept. 24, 1862; Willard diary, Aug. 31, 1862, Willard Family Papers, DLC; *OR* 12, pt. 3, 770–71; Strother, *Virginia Yankee*, 99.

46. Moore, "Battle of Chantilly," 50–52.

47. Weld, *Diary and Letters*, 132–33; 46th Cong., 1st sess., S. Ex. Doc. 37, *Proceedings and Report . . . Case of Fitz John Porter*, 3:972–73.

48. *OR* 12, pt. 2, 82–83.

49. Moore, "Battle of Chantilly," 54–55.

50. *OR* 12, pt. 2, 84; Charles F. Walcott, "The Battle of Chantilly," in *Virginia Campaign*, 2:149.

51. Moore, "Battle of Chantilly," 56–57; *OR* 12, pt. 2, 538; C. E. Davis, *Three Years in the Army*, 119; Hennessy, *Return to Bull Run*, 466; Franz Sigel, manuscript notes on Irvin McDowell at Second Bull Run, Sigel Papers, WRHS.

52. Hennessy, *Return to Bull Run*, 447; H. Stevens, *Life of Isaac Stevens*, 2:480–81.

53. Strother, *Virginia Yankee*, 99; Heintzelman journal, Sept. 1, 1862, Heintzelman Papers, DLC; *OR* 12, pt. 2, 415.

54. 39th Cong., 1st sess., "Report of General Pope," *CWSR*, 2:165; Quint, *Potomac and Rapidan*, 206; Marvin, *Fifth Connecticut*, 232.

55. Hennessy, *Return to Bull Run*, 447–48; *OR* 12, pt. 3, 788; Weld, *Diary and Letters*, 136; Heintzelman journal, Sept. 1, 1862, Heintzelman Papers, DLC.

56. Moore, "Battle of Chantilly," 59–61; Walcott, "Battle of Chantilly," 153–55; H. Stevens, *Life of Isaac Stevens*, 2:483–94; Hennessy, *Return to Bull Run*, 450.

57. 39th Cong., 1st sess., "Report of General Pope," *CWSR*, 2:169; Walcott, "Battle of Chantilly," 160; Strother, *Virginia Yankee*, 99; Willard diary, Sept. 1 and 2, 1862, Willard Family Papers, DLC.

58. Willard diary, Sept. 2, 1862, Willard Family Papers, DLC; *OR* 12, pt. 3, 796–97.

59. Hennessy, *Return to Bull Run*, 451; J. Cox, *Military Reminiscences*, 1:244, 257; *OR* 12, pt. 3, 809; Gorham, *Stanton*, 2:44–47; Chase, *Inside Lincoln's Cabinet*, 118–19; Nicolay and Hay, *Lincoln*, 6:23; Henry Halleck to JP, Oct. 10, 1862, Halleck Papers, CHS; Hay, *Letters and Diary*, 2:64–65.

60. *OR* 12, pt. 3, 797; Samuel P. Heintzelman Journal, Sept. 2, 1862, Heintzelman Papers, DLC.

61. Porter, *Statement of Services*, 74.

62. *OR* 12, pt. 2 (Suppl.), 838, 976; Porter, *Statement of Services*, 75–76.

63. J. Cox, *Military Reminiscences*, 1:245; Abner R. Small, *The Road to Richmond: The Civil War Memoirs of Major Abner R. Small*, ed. Harold A. Small (Berkeley, 1939), 42–43.

64. George D. Ruggles to William L. Livermore, Apr. 24, 1897, Ropes Papers, MHSMC, BU; B. W. Richmond to Salmon P. Chase, Sept. 14, 1862, Chase Papers, DLC; Strother, *Virginia Yankee*, 99–100; J. Cox, *Military Reminiscences*, 1:243, 245; Dawes, *Service with the Sixth Wisconsin*, 76; Gibbon, *Personal Recollections*, 70; Willard diary, Sept. 2, 1862, Willard Family Papers, DLC.

65. Strother, *Virginia Yankee*, 100; Gabler, "Porter Case," 163; *OR* 12, pt. 3, 808.

66. *OR* 12, pt. 3, 808–9.

67. Gabler, "Porter Case," 168; Chase, *Inside Lincoln's Cabinet*, 120; Thomas C. H. Smith, "Memoir and Review of Pope's Campaign," 184, Smith Papers, OHS; *Boston Evening Transcript*, Sept. 2, 1862; Porter, *Statement of Services*, 77; *OR* 12, pt. 2, 840; JP to Henry Halleck, Oct. 20, 1862, Pope Papers, CHS. Pope testified at Porter's trial that the president informed him of the dispatches on either September 4 or 5, but the tenor of Pope's report suggests Lincoln showed them to him on the third.

68. *OR* 12, pt. 2, 15–18; JP to Halleck, Sept. 30, Oct. 10, and Nov. 20, 1862, Pope Papers, and Halleck to JP, Oct. 10, 1862, Halleck Papers, all in CHS.

69. Welles, *Diary*, 1:109–10; Gabler, "Porter Case," 169.

70. Welles, *Diary*, 1:110–11; Chase, *Inside Lincoln's Cabinet*, 120.

71. *OR* 12, pt. 3, 809–10; Welles, *Diary*, 1:111, 113; Weld, *Diary and Letters*, 137; *Chica-*

go Tribune, Sept. 4, 1862; *Philadelphia Inquirer,* Sept. 3, 1862; Schurz, *Reminiscences,* 2:381–82; Hennessy, *Return to Bull Run,* 466.

72. *Boston Evening Transcript,* Sept. 6 and 8, 1862, *Philadelphia Inquirer,* Sept. 8, 1862; Chase, *Inside Lincoln's Cabinet,* 121; J. Cox, *Military Reminiscences,* 1:258; Schurz, *Reminiscences,* 2:383; Hennessy, *Return to Bull Run,* 466–67; *OR* 19, pt. 2, 197.

73. *OR* 12, pt. 3, 811, and 19, pt. 2, 188; Hay, *Letters and Diary,* 2:64–65.

74. *OR* 12, pt. 3, 811–13.

75. *OR* 12, pt. 2 (Suppl.), 976–78; Strother, *Virginia Yankee,* 100.

76. Gabler, "Porter Case," 187; *OR* 19, pt. 2, 189–90; Weld, *Diary and Letters,* 82–83. Although McClellan's request of September 6 was not formally granted until September 11, Porter, Franklin, and Griffin never ceased to exercise their commands.

77. Welles, *Diary,* 116, 126; Wills, *Army Life,* 144; William T. Sherman, *Home Letters of General Sherman,* ed. M. A. DeWolfe Howe (New York, 1909), 233.

78. *OR* 13, 597, 599, 644; *Civil War Messages and Proclamations of Wisconsin War Governors,* ed. Robert G. Thwaites (Madison, Wis., 1912), 138–39.

79. R. Jones, *Civil War in the Northwest,* 6, 36; *OR* 13, 617; Richard N. Ellis, *General Pope and U.S. Indian Policy* (Albuquerque, 1970), 6–7.

80. *OR* 13, 617.

81. Welles, *Diary,* 122–26; J. Cox, *Military Reminiscences,* 1:259; JP to Richard Yates, Sept. 21, 1862, Pope Papers, CHS.

82. *Boston Evening Transcript,* Sept. 6, 1862.

83. Chase, *Inside Lincoln's Cabinet,* 123; *Chicago Tribune,* Sept. 11, 1862.

Chapter 11: I Could Tell a Sad Story

1. *Chicago Tribune,* Sept. 11, 1862; *Philadelphia Public Ledger,* Sept. 12, 1862.

2. Henry Villard to Franz Sigel, Dec. 1, 1862, Franz Sigel to Joseph Hooker, Dec. 2, 1862, and Murat Halstead to Franz Sigel, Dec. 5, 1862, all in Sigel Papers, NYHS; *Chicago Tribune,* Sept. 10, 1862; James G. Wilson, *Biographical Sketches of Illinois Officers Engaged in the War against the Rebellion of 1861* (Chicago, 1862), 92.

3. *New York World,* Sept. 9, 1862; *Boston Evening Transcript,* Sept. 10, 1862.

4. *New York Times,* Sept. 8, 1862; *Boston Evening Transcript,* Sept. 10, 1862; Gabler, "Porter Case," 174; *Washington Star,* Sept. 11, 1862; *Philadelphia Public Ledger,* Sept. 13 and 15, 1862.

5. Welles, *Diary,* 1:125–27.

6. *OR* 13, pt. 1, 642; *St. Paul Daily Press,* Aug. 30, Sept. 10, 13, and 16, 1862; 39th Cong., 1st sess., "Report of General Pope," *CWSR,* 1:191; Thomas C. H. Smith, "Memoir and Review of Pope's Campaign," 28, 186, Smith Papers, OHS; Kenneth Carley, *The Sioux Uprising of 1862* (St. Paul, Minn., 1962), 54.

7. William F. Morse, "The Indian Campaign in Minnesota in 1862," in *Personal Recollections of the War of the Rebellion; Addresses Delivered before the Commandery of the State of New York, MOLLUS* (New York, 1891–1912), Fourth Series, 184; Isaac V. D. Heard, *History of the Sioux War and Massacres of 1862 and 1863* (New York, 1864), 14; R. Jones, *Civil War in the Northwest,* 14–24; Robert M. Utley, *Frontiersmen in Blue: The United States Army and the Indian, 1848–1865* (New York, 1967), 262, 264; Nathaniel West, *The Ancestry, Life, and Times of Hon. Henry Hastings Sibley* (St. Paul, Minn., 1889), 263; R. Jones, *Civil War in the Northwest,* 16–24; Henry H. Sibley journal, Sept. 8, 1862, Sibley Papers, MnHS.

8. W. F. Morse, "Indian Campaign in Minnesota," 189–92; Carley, *Sioux Uprising*, 25–36, 52–53; West, *Sibley*, 254.

9. Daniel Buck, *Indian Outbreaks* (Mankato, Minn., 1904), 162–63; West, *Sibley*, 255–65; Carley, *Sioux Uprising*, 55; *St. Paul Daily Press*, Sept. 6 and 9, 1862; Utley, *Frontiersmen in Blue*, 267–68.

10. *OR* 13, pt. 1, 642, 648; *St. Paul Daily Press*, Sept. 17, 1862; Ellis, *Pope and Indian Policy*, 7; JP to Valentine B. Horton, Sept. 25, 1862, JP Papers, NYHS; *OR* 13, pt. 1, 649; Wills, *Army Life*, 144.

11. JP to Valentine B. Horton, Sept. 25, 1862, JP Papers, NYHS.

12. JP to Richard Yates, Sept. 21, 1862, JP to William Butler, Sept. 26, 1862, and JP to Halleck, Sept. 30, 1862, all in JP Papers, CHS; [R. N. Arpe], *Stanton and Halleck in the Civil War; Fitz-John Porter and 2nd Bull Run, by a Veteran* (New York, 1905), 10–11.

13. *OR* 13, pt. 1, 650–51, 662–68; Ellis, *Pope and Indian Policy*, 9–10.

14. R. Jones, *Civil War in the Northwest*, 145–46; Ellis, *Pope and Indian Policy*, 10–11; *OR* 13, pt. 1, 664, 668–69.

15. W. F. Morse, "Indian Campaign in Minnesota," 194–96; Carley, *Sioux Uprising*, 57–59; Utley, *Frontiersmen in Blue*, 269; *OR* 13, pt. 1, 685–86.

16. West, *Sibley*, 273–79; *OR* 13, pt. 1, 680, 685–87, 706, 709, 716; Sibley journal, Sept. 27, 1862, Sibley Papers, MnHS; W. F. Morse, "Indian Campaign in Minnesota," 195.

17. Halleck to JP, Oct. 10, 1862, Halleck Papers, CHS; *OR* 13, pt. 1, 821–24; [Arpe], *Stanton and Halleck*, 11.

18. JP to Horton, Nov. 1, 1862, JP Papers, NYHS; Sibley journal, Oct. 25, 1862, Sibley Papers, MnHS.

19. *OR* 13, pt. 1, 825; JP to Horton, Nov. 1, 1862, JP Papers, NYHS; Fitz John Porter to John P. Nicholson, July 11 [1870?], Nicholson Papers, HL.

20. JP to Halleck, Nov. 13, 1862, Nathaniel Banks Papers, DLC; JP to Horton, Nov. 1, 1862, JP Papers, NYHS; JP to Manning F. Force, Jan. 15, 1878, Force Papers, UW; Gabler, "Porter Case," 201, 217; *OR* 12, pt. 2, 506; [Arpe], *Stanton and Halleck*, 12; *OR* 12, pt. 2, 506–7, and pt. 2 (Suppl.), 821.

21. R. Jones, *Civil War in the Northwest*, 55, 100–101; Carley, *Sioux Uprising*, 63–64; *OR* 13, 733, 787; West, *Sibley*, 280–81, 286.

22. *OR* 13, 788, and 22, pt. 1, 790–91.

23. *OR* 13, 787; *St. Paul Daily Press*, Nov. 29, 1862, St. Paul *Pioneer*, Oct. 23, 1862; Ellis, *Pope and Indian Policy*, 16.

24. Ellis, *Pope and Indian Policy*, 16; *St. Paul Daily Press*, Nov. 23, 1862.

25. *Chicago Tribune*, Nov. 20, 1862; *St. Paul Daily Press*, Nov. 23, 25, and Dec. 2, 1862; Louis H. Pelouze to JP, Nov. 28, 1862, ACPB, AGO, RG 94, NA; Fitz John Porter to John P. Nicholson, July 11 [1870], Nicholson Papers, HL.

26. Gabler, "Porter Case," 212–13; *OR* 12, pt. 2 (Suppl.), 824–27.

27. Gabler, "Porter Case," 204–5; *Milwaukee Sentinel*, Dec. 17, 1862.

28. Alexander K. McClure, *Colonel Alexander K. McClure's Recollections of Half a Century* (Salem, Mass., 1902), 432; Otto Eisenschiml, *The Celebrated Case of Fitz John Porter: An American Dreyfuss Affair* (Indianapolis, 1950), 81; Thomas and Hyman, *Stanton*, 260.

29. Gabler, "Porter Case," 207–10; Eisenschiml, *Celebrated Case*, 77–80.

30. Porter to Nicholson, July 11, [1870?], Nicholson Papers, HL; Gabler, "Porter Case," 215–16; Eisenschiml, *Celebrated Case*, 326. In a postwar letter to the Comte de Paris, Pope implied he himself had brought the charges against Porter. JP to M. Le

Comte de Paris, May 29, 1876, printed copy in Papers Concerning the Second Battle of Bull Run, USMA.

31. Gabler, "Porter Case," 211–12; *DAB*, 9:182–83; JP, "War Reminiscences, XIV."

32. *OR* 12, pt. 2 (Suppl.), 829–35; *Milwaukee Sentinel*, Dec. 17, 1862, quoted in Schutz and Trenerry, *Abandoned by Lincoln*, 169.

33. *DAB*, 10:113; *OR* 12, pt. 2 (Suppl.), 836–38; *Chicago Tribune*, Dec. 5, 1862.

34. JP to Joseph Holt, Dec. 4, 1862, Holt Papers, DLC.

35. *OR* 12, pt. 2 (Suppl.), 840–41.

36. Ibid., 850–51.

37. Gabler, "Porter Case," 234–35; *OR* 12, pt. 2 (Suppl.), 855.

38. Drake De Kay to Thomas C. H. Smith, Mar. 28, 1863, Smith Papers, OHS; *Milwaukee Sentinel*, Dec. 17, 1862, quoted in Schutz and Trenerry, *Abandoned by Lincoln*, 169; JP to Holt, Dec. 10, 1862, Holt Papers, DLC.

39. West, *Sibley*, 284–86; Buck, *Indian Outbreaks*, 223–25; Lincoln, *Collected Works*, 5:542–43.

40. *Extracts from the Testimony of General McDowell in the Case of Fitz John Porter*, printed copy in Second Bull Run Papers, USMA.

41. JP to Holt, Dec. 13, 1862, and Roberts to Holt, Dec. 15, 1862, both in Holt Papers, DLC.

42. *St. Paul Daily Press*, Dec. 7–11, 1862; *Milwaukee Sentinel*, Dec. 10, 1862; West, *Sibley*, 286.

43. West, *Sibley*, 290–91; Buck, *Indian Outbreaks*, 267–69.

44. Gabler, "Porter Case," 285; *OR* 12, pt. 2, 511–12.

Chapter 12: I Confine Myself to My Duty

1. *New York World*, Jan. 23, 1863; *Milwaukee Sentinel*, Feb. 12, 1863; Drake De Kay to Thomas C. H. Smith, Mar. 28, 1863, Smith Papers, OHS.

2. Gabler, "Porter Case," 285–96; JP to Joseph Holt, Sept. 24, 1863, Holt Papers, DLC.

3. JP to Valentine B. Horton, Mar. 9, 1863, JP Papers, NYHS.

4. JP to Horton, Mar. 29, 1863, JP Papers, NYHS; *Fitz John Porter—Pope's Campaign; Speech of Hon. Zachariah Chandler, of Michigan, in the United States Senate, February 21, 1870* (Washington, D.C., 1870), 1.

5. JP to Salmon P. Chase, Apr. 22, 1863, in JP, *Letters of General Pope to Hon. S. P. Chase, Proposing Plan of Military Operations for 1863* (N.p., n.d.), 1–3; De Kay to Thomas C. H. Smith, Mar. 28, 1863, Smith Papers, OHS; Albert B. Hart, *Salmon Portland Chase* (Boston, 1899), 297.

6. Ellis, *Pope and Indian Policy*, 16–17.

7. *OR* 22, pt. 1, 90, 115–20, 176, 198–99, 289; Utley, *Frontiersmen in Blue*, 270–71.

8. Ellis, *Pope and Indian Policy*, 20; *OR* 22, pt. 2, 211; Alvin C. Gluek Jr., "The Sioux Uprising: A Problem in International Relations," *Minnesota History* 34 (Winter 1955), 317–19.

9. Langdon Sully, *No Tears for the General: The Life of Alfred Sully, 1821–1879* (Palo Alto, Calif., 1974), 113–27; *OR* 22, pt. 2, 288; *Sioux City Register*, Oct. 4, 1863.

10. *OR* 22, pt. 2, 186, 294.

11. *St. Paul Daily Press*, May 27 and 31, 1863.

12. *OR* 22, pt. 2, 160, 303; R. Jones, *Civil War in the Northwest*, 104–5.

13. *OR* 22, pt. 2, 303, 395–96; 39th Cong., 1st sess., "Report of General Pope," *CWSR*, 2:208–9.

14. *OR* 22, pt. 2, 398–99.

15. *St. Paul Daily Press*, July 12, 1863.

16. Ibid.; JP to John C. Kelton, June 1, 1863, JP Papers, HL.

17. *OR* 22, pt. 2, 381–82; *St. Paul Daily Press*, July 10, 1863; L. W. Collins, "The Expedition against the Sioux Indians in 1863, under General Henry H. Sibley," in *Minnesota MOLLUS*, Second Series, 182–83.

18. Ellis, *Pope and Indian Policy*, 24–25; *OR* 22, pt. 2, 381–82.

19. Carley, *Sioux Uprising*, 72–73; *OR* 22, pt. 2, 382–83.

20. *OR* 22, pt. 1, 555–61, and pt. 2, 434; *Sioux City Register*, Oct. 24, 1863; Ellis, *Pope and Indian Policy*, 23; *St. Paul Weekly Press*, Sept. 17, 1863.

21. Sully, *No Tears for the General*, 179; *St. Paul Weekly Press*, Nov. 19, 1863.

22. R. Jones, *Civil War in the Northwest*, 75; Ellis, *Pope and Indian Policy*, 28; *St. Paul Weekly Press*, Nov. 19, 1863.

23. Undated family reminiscences, 545, Lambert Naegele and Family Papers, MnHS; Parrish, *Turbulent Partnership*, 175; JP to W. A. Nichols, Jan. 1, 1864, JP Papers, HL.

24. *St. Paul Weekly Press*, Dec. 25, 1863; *OR* 22, pt. 2, 152–56, 250, 256, 257–58; JP to Abert, Sept. 18, 1851, LR, TB, RG 77, NA.

25. Ellis, *Pope and Indian Policy*, 33–34; *OR* 34, pt. 2, 259–60.

26. Ellis, *Pope and Indian Policy*, 31–32, 37–42; Robert W. Mardock, "The Humanitarians and Post–Civil War Indian Policy" (Ph.D. diss., University of Colorado, 1958), 2–11; *OR* 34, pt. 2, 260, 260–64.

27. *OR* 34, pt. 2, 303, 330; Ellis, *Pope and Indian Policy*, 46.

28. JP to James R. Doolittle, Feb. 16, 1864, JP Letters, ALBS.

29. *OR* 34, pt. 3, 159; Cullen, "Five Cent Pope," 47; Henry B. Whipple, *Lights and Shadows of a Long Episcopate* (New York, 1899), 521–24; Ellis, *Pope and Indian Policy*, 48–51.

30. Whipple, *Lights and Shadows*, 144.

31. Ellis, *Pope and Indian Policy*, 56; R. Jones, *Civil War in Northwest*, 81–82; *OR* 34, pt. 2, 700, 713, 792–93, 805, and pt. 3, 263, 579–80.

32. *OR* 34, pt. 3, 33, 44–45.

33. Ibid., pt. 2, 608–9.

34. Ellis, *Pope and Indian Policy*, 59–60; *OR* 34, pt. 2, 688–89, 735, and pt. 3, 447–48, 565–67.

35. Ellis, *Pope and Indian Policy*, 60–61; R. Jones, *Civil War in the Northwest*, 84–85.

36. R. Jones, *Civil War in the Northwest*, 87; *OR* 41, pt. 1, 145–47, 154.

37. *OR* 41, pt. 1, 154.

38. Ellis, *Pope and Indian Policy*, 65; Utley, *Frontiersmen in Blue*, 280; *OR* 41, pt. 4, 151.

39. Pomeroy, *History and Genealogy*, 515; *OR* 41, pt. 4, 672.

40. R. Jones, *Civil War in the Northwest*, 189–90; *OR* 41, pt. 2, 29–30, 662, 676, 736–37, 739, 754–55.

41. *OR* 41, pt. 2, 739, and pt. 4, 709; Simon, *Papers of Grant*, 13:27–29.

42. Cullen, "Five Cent Pope," 47; Utley, *Frontiersmen in Blue*, 304; *OR* 41, pt. 4, 717.

43. Ellis, *Pope and Indian Policy*, 66.

44. Simon, *Papers of Grant*, 13:35–36, 78.

45. *OR* 48, pt. 1, 714; JP to Samuel R. Curtis, Feb. 4, 1865, and JP to Clara Pope, Feb. 6, 1865, both in ACPB, AGO, RG 94, NA.

Chapter 13: Posterity Will Bless Your Name

1. Utley, *Frontiersmen in Blue*, 307; *OR* 48, pt. 1, 331, 694, 714; Grenville M. Dodge, *The Battle of Atlanta and Other Campaigns* (Council Bluffs, Iowa, 1911), 63–64; D. Alexander Brown, *The Galvanized Yankees* (Urbana, Ill., 1963), 4; Brigham D. Madsen, *Glory Hunter: A Biography of Patrick Edward Connor* (Salt Lake City, 1990), 121.

2. Samuel J. Crawford, *Kansas in the Sixties* (Chicago, 1911), 181–82; Monaghan, *War on Western Border*, 343; *OR* 48, pt. 1, 329–30, 695.

3. J. M. Bundy, "The Last Chapter in the History of the War, *Galaxy* 8, no. 1 (1869): 112; *OR* 48, pt. 1, 851, 858.

4. *OR* 48, pt. 1, 686, 694, 748, and pt. 2, 176; Monaghan, *War on Western Border*, 344.

5. *OR* 48, pt. 1, 760, 778, 793, 795, 816, 849, 947, 996–98, 1254; Eugene F. Ware, *The Indian War of 1864* (Topeka, Kans., 1911), 427–28; Brown, *Galvanized Yankees*, 16–19.

6. *OR* 48, pt. 1, 828, 834, 848–49, 1009, 1060, 1070–77, 1101–10, 1114–15, 1122–26, 1131–32, 1181, 1202–3, 1214, 1219–20, 1243–44; Parrish, *Turbulent Partnership*, 191–92, 198–202.

7. *OR* 48, pt. 1, 1236, 1248, and pt. 2, 20, 44, 48, 50–53, 64, 77; Simon, *Papers of Grant*, 14:187–88, 192–95; Bundy, "Last Chapter," 114.

8. James S. Thomas, et. al. to JP, Apr. 14, 1865, JP Personal File, ACPB, AGO, RG 94, NA; JP, "War Reminiscences, IX."

9. Simon, *Papers of Grant*, 14:394, 403–4; *OR* 48, pt. 1, 110, 186–87; Bundy, "Last Chapter," 114.

10. *OR* 48, pt. 1, 191–92, 236, and pt. 2, 283, 481–82; Bundy, "Last Chapter," 114–17, 120–21; Simon, *Papers of Grant*, 15:59; Philip H. Sheridan, *Personal Memoirs of P. H. Sheridan*, 2 vols. (New York, 1888), 2:208–10.

11. *OR* 48, pt. 2, 80–81, 99, 125–31.

12. Ibid., 224, 244, 682–83, 685–86, 797.

13. Dorothy M. Johnson, *The Bloody Bozeman: The Perilous Trail to Montana's Gold* (New York, 1971), 3, 139; Utley, *Frontiersmen in Blue*, 307–8; Dodge, *Battle of Atlanta*, 79, 80, 85; *OR* 48, pt. 1, 1295–96, and pt. 2, 237–38.

14. Ellis, *Pope and Indian Policy*, 74; Dodge, *Battle of Atlanta*, 84–85.

15. *OR* 48, pt. 1, 1308; Dodge, *Battle of Atlanta*, 79; Utley, *Frontiersmen in Blue*, 308–9.

16. Ellis, *Pope and Indian Policy*, 77; Dodge, *Battle of Atlanta*, 80.

17. Utley, *Frontiersmen in Blue*, 309–10.

18. JP to James R. Doolittle, Feb. 16, 1864, ALBS; *OR* 48, pt. 2, 157, 708.

19. *OR* 48, pt. 2, 492–93, 708, 895–96; Dodge, *Battle of Atlanta*, 80–81.

20. Utley, *Frontiersmen in Blue*, 312; Dodge, *Battle of Atlanta*, 81–82.

21. *OR* 48, pt. 2, 357–38; Ellis, *Pope and Indian Policy*, 99–100.

22. *OR* 48, pt. 2, 934–35; Ellis, *Pope and Indian Policy*, 100–101.

23. *OR* 48, pt. 2, 935; Simon, *Papers of Grant*, 15:142.

24. *OR* 48, pt. 2, 879–82; Robert Wooster, *The Military and United States Indian Policy, 1865–1903* (New Haven, 1988), 77–79; Simon, *Papers of Grant*, 15:142.

25. *OR* 48, pt. 2, 391, 412–14, 486, 493, 557–58, 576–79, 764.

26. Utley, *Frontiersmen in Blue*, 323; Ellis, *Pope and Indian Policy*, 92–93.

27. Henry Heth, *The Memoirs of Henry Heth,* ed. James L. Morrison Jr. (Westport, Conn., 1974), 199-200.

28. Dodge, *Battle of Atlanta,* 105-7; Welles, *Diary,* 2:357; *OR* 48, pt. 2, 860; Utley, *Frontiersmen in Blue,* 336-37; Simon, *Papers of Grant,* 15:161.

29. Grant to JP, June 26, 1865, and *Headquarters of the Army, Special Orders 356, July 7, 1865,* both in JP Personal File, ACPB, AGO, RG 94, NA.

30. *OR* 48, pt. 2, 1056-57, 1218; 39th Cong., 1st sess., "Report of General Pope," *CWSR,* 2:204; Wooster, *Military and Indian Policy,* 112-13.

31. *OR* 48, pt. 2, 1027, 1052; Ellis, *Pope and Indian Policy,* 106-7.

32. *Correspondence between Pope and Halleck,* 1-3.

33. JP to Grenville M. Dodge, July 7, 1865, and to Joseph M. Bell, July 19, 1865, both in JP Personal File, ACPB, AGO, RG 94, NA; *OR* 48, pt. 1, 350-53, 360-63, and pt. 2, 1122, 1124, 1154-58; Utley, *Frontiersmen in Blue,* 331, 337.

34. *OR* 48, pt. 2, 1150-53; 39th Cong., 1st sess., "Report of General Pope," *CWSR,* 2:203.

35. Brooks D. Simpson, *Let Us Have Peace: Ulysses S. Grant and the Politics of War and Reconstruction, 1861-1868* (Chapel Hill, N.C., 1991), 111-12; Thomas and Hyman, *Stanton,* 446-49.

36. Dodge, *Battle of Atlanta,* 106-7; *OR* 48, pt. 2, 1127; Madsen, *Glory Hunter,* 135-37; Welles, *Diary,* 2:357.

37. Welles, *Diary,* 2:355-62; Dodge, *Battle of Atlanta,* 106-8; *OR* 48, pt. 2, 1178-79.

38. *OR* 48, pt. 2, 1178-79, 1196-99.

39. Ibid., pt. 1, 352-53, 356, and pt. 2, 565.

40. Madsen, *Glory Hunter,* 139-52; Dodge, *Battle of Atlanta,* 89-90; Utley, *Frontiersmen in Blue,* 324-30.

41. Madsen, *Glory Hunter,* 153; *OR* 48, pt. 2, 1201-7; Dodge, *Battle of Atlanta,* 96-97.

42. Utley, *Frontiersmen in Blue,* 333-39; *OR* 48, pt. 2, 1240.

43. George Townsend to JP, Aug. 9, 1865, JP Personal File, ACPB, AGO, RG 94, NA; Welles, *Diary,* 2:361; JP to Spence and Thompson, Sept. 18, 1865, ALBS.

44. Ellis, *Pope and Indian Policy,* 115-17.

45. JP to William T. Sherman, Nov. 6, 1865, LR, HA, RG 108, NA.

46. Simon, *Papers of Grant,* 15:622-23, 16:429; Ellis, *Pope and Indian Policy,* 116; Robert G. Athearn, *William Tecumseh Sherman and the Settlement of the West* (Norman, Okla., 1956), 34-35.

47. Simon, *Papers of Grant,* 16:428-29, 450; "General Pope's Report on the West, 1866," ed. Richard N. Ellis, *Kansas Historical Quarterly* 35, no. 4 (Winter 1969): 346-48; Ellis, *Pope and Indian Policy,* 120.

48. "Pope's Report," 354-71; Ellis, *Pope and Indian Policy,* 110-20. For sentiments regarding white provocation of the Indian similar to those Pope expressed, see Sherman to John A. Rawlins, Feb. 17, 1886, LR, HA, RG 108, NA.

49. Sherman to Grant, Mar. 7, 1866, and Sherman to Rawlins, Mar. 8, 1866, both in LR, HA, RG 108, NA.

50. Simon, *Papers of Grant,* 16:116-18.

51. 40th Cong., 1st sess., S. Ex. Doc. 2, *Protection to Trains on the Overland Route,* 2-4; Ellis, *Pope and Indian Policy,* 122-23.

52. Sherman to Rawlins, Feb. 17, 1866, and Sherman to Grant, Mar. 7, 1866, both in LR, HA, RG 108, NA; Simon, *Papers of Grant,* 16:92.

53. Simon, *Papers of Grant,* 16:97, 479–80; Sherman to Grant, Apr. 13 and May 17, 1866, both in LR, HA, RG 108, NA; Athearn, *Sherman and Settlement,* 39.

54. Wooster, *Military and Indian Policy,* 116; Pope to Grant, May 8, 1866, LR, HA, RG 108, NA.

55. JP to Orville H. Browning, Aug. 28, 1866, Browning Papers, ISHL; Simon, *Papers of Grant,* 16:388; Sherman to Grant, LR, HA, RG 108, NA; J. P. O'Neil to H. E. Maynadier, June 18, 1866, JP Personal File, ACPB, AGO, RG 94, NA; Russell R. Weigley, *The History of the United States Army* (New York, 1967), 290–91.

56. J. P. O'Neil to H. E. Maynadier, June 16, 1866, JP Personal File, ACPB, AGO, RG 94, NA; Missouri *Democrat,* Aug. 29, 1866; Andrew Johnson, *The Papers of Andrew Johnson,* ed. Paul H. Bergeron, 16 vols. (Knoxville, Tenn.: 1967–99), 11:4–5.

57. Robert M. Utley, *Frontier Regulars: The United States Army and the Indian, 1866–1890* (New York, 1973), 12–13; Schutz and Trenerry, *Abandoned by Lincoln,* 182.

58. Utley, *Frontier Regulars,* 15–16; James E. Sefton, *The United States Army and Reconstruction, 1865–1877* (Baton Rouge, 1967), 116, 177; Simon, *Papers of Grant,* 16:248, 508; JP to Orville H. Browning, Aug. 28, 1866, Browning Papers, ISHL.

59. JP to Browning, Aug. 28, 1866, Browning Papers, ISHL; JP to Thomas C. H. Smith, Sept. 14, 1866, Smith Papers, OHS; Simon, *Papers of Grant,* 16:508.

60. JP, "War Reminiscences"; "Harvard's Annual Dinner," undated newspaper clipping enclosed in JP to Manning F. Force, Oct. 22, 1884, Force Papers, UW; Koerner, *Memoirs,* 1:391; JP to Henry L. Kendrick, Oct. 24, 1863, JP Papers, NYHS.

61. JP to Rutherford B. Hayes, Apr. 12, 1878, Pope Letter Books, HPL; JP, "War Reminiscences." Balaam was an Old Testament prophet who was commanded to curse the Israelites but who blessed them instead after being rebuked by the ass he rode. Pope's views about West Point were not unique. Erasmus D. Keyes, a corps commander during the Civil War who had taught at West Point in the 1840s, expressed similar sentiments. "During my service at West Point my opportunities enabled me to observe the qualities and to estimate the promise of a great number of cadets, of whom several afterwards became known to the public," wrote Keyes. "Subsequent success has not in all cases corresponded with class standing, nor could that be expected, since the number of a cadet in his class is chiefly determined by the acquisitions in the exact sciences, of which the foundation is mathematics." Keyes, *Fifty Years' Observation of Men and Events, Civil and Military* (New York, 1884), 197.

62. JP to Grant, Sept. 14, 1866, LR, HA, RG 108, NA.

63. Simon, *Papers of Grant,* 16:250; JP to Thomas C. H. Smith, Sept. 14, 1866, Smith Papers, OHS.

64. JP to Grant, Sept. 14, 1866, LR, HA, RG 108, NA; JP to Thomas C. H. Smith, May 9, Sept. 14 and Dec. 9, 1866, and Daniel E. Sickles to L. S. Doty, Feb. 19, 1866, all in Smith Papers, OHS; Gabler, "Porter Case," 335–36.

Chapter 14: I Find the Situation Very Perplexing

1. Pomeroy, *History and Genealogy,* 515; 39th Cong., 2d sess., H. Ex. Doc. 1, *ARSW* (1866), 30; *Reports of the Secretary of War and Interior . . . in Relation to the Massacre at Fort Phil. Kearny . . .* (Washington, D.C., 1867), 28; Utley, *Frontier Regulars,* 116–18; Welles, *Diary,* 3:30; JP to Grant, Jan. 25, 1867, LR, HA, RG 108, NA.

2. JP to Grant, Jan. 25, 1867, LR, HA, RG 108, NA; Simon, *Papers of Grant,* 17:23; *Reports in Relation to Massacre at Fort Kearny,* 47, 56; Utley, *Frontier Regulars,* 117.

3. Harold M. Hyman, ed., *The Radical Republicans and Reconstruction, 1861–1870* (Indianapolis, 1967), 377–78; Alan Conway, *The Reconstruction of Georgia* (Minneapolis, 1966), 139; Sefton, *Army and Reconstruction,* 113.

4. Thomas and Hyman, *Stanton,* 530; Simon, *Papers of Grant,* 17:83–84; Harold M. Hyman, "Johnson, Stanton, and Grant: A Reconsideration of the Army's Role in the Events Leading to Impeachment," *American Historical Review* 66 (Oct. 1960): 86–93; Sefton, *Army and Reconstruction,* 94–95.

5. Thomas and Hyman, *Stanton,* 451, 530–31; Welles, *Diary,* 2:64–65; James G. Blaine, *Twenty Years of Congress,* 2 vols. (Norwich, Conn., 1886), 2:297–98; Simon, *Papers of Grant,* 17:84.

6. JP to Grant, Mar. 17 and Mar. 25, 1867, LR, HA, RG 108, NA.

7. 40th Cong., 2d sess., H. Ex. Doc. 1, vol. 2, pt. 1, *ARSW,* 321, and H. Ex. Doc. 342, *General Orders—Reconstruction,* 100; Sefton, *Army and Reconstruction,* 118–19; JP to Grant, Apr. 2, 1866, LR, HA, RG 108, NA.

8. Isaac W. Avery, *The History of the State of Georgia from 1850 to 1881* (New York, 1881), 358–59; JP to Grant, Mar. 28 and Apr. 2, 1866, LR, HA, RG 108, NA; Simon, *Papers of Grant,* 17:100–102.

9. [Lewis E. Mills], *Supreme Court of the United States; In Equity; The State of Georgia, vs. Edwin M. Stanton, Ulysses S. Grant, and John Pope; Brief for the Defendant, John Pope* (Cincinnati, 1867), 1–3; Wallace J. Schutz and Walter N. Trenerry, *John Pope: The Professional Soldier as Unwilling Servant of Party Politics, 1861–1865; A Paper Presented at the Fourth Annual Illinois History Conference* (Springfield, Ill., 1983), 16–17; Avery, *History of Georgia,* 366–67.

10. Simon, *Papers of Grant,* 17:120–21; Avery, *History of Georgia,* 370; 40th Cong., 2d sess., H. Ex. Doc. 1, vol. 2, pt. 1, *ARSW,* 323–25, and H. Ex. Doc. 342, *Reconstruction,* 101–2.

11. Elizabeth S. Nathans, *Losing the Peace: Georgia Republicans and Reconstruction, 1865–1871* (Baton Rouge, 1968), 51; 40th Cong., 2d sess., H. Ex. Doc. 1, vol. 2, pt. 1, *ARSW,* 370–74; William W. Davis, *The Civil War and Reconstruction in Florida* (1913; rpt., Gainesville, 1964), 464, 472; Simon, *Papers of Grant,* 17:117–18, 120, 127.

12. 40th Cong., 2d sess., H. Ex. Doc. 1, vol. 2, pt. 1, *ARSW,* 329, and H. Ex. Doc. 342, *Reconstruction,* 108; Sefton, *Army and Reconstruction,* 125.

13. 40th Cong., 2d sess., H. Ex. Doc. 1, vol. 2, pt. 1, *ARSW,* 329–30; Sefton, *Army and Reconstruction,* 125–26; Simon, *Papers of Grant,* 17:121–22; Thomas and Hyman, *Stanton,* 537.

14. Simon, *Papers of Grant,* 17:102; 40th Cong., 2d sess., H. Ex. Doc. 1, vol. 2, pt. 1, *ARSW,* 364–74; Nathan, *Losing the Peace,* 51; Sefton, *Army and Reconstruction,* 146; Russell Duncan, *Entrepreneur for Equality: Governor Rufus Bullock, Commerce, and Race in Post-Civil War Georgia* (Athens, Ga., 1994), 20.

15. Sefton, *Army and Reconstruction,* 128–29.

16. 40th Cong., 2d sess., H. Ex. Doc. 1, *ARSW,* 334–35, and H. Ex. Doc. 342, *Reconstruction,* 42–43, 102–4; Simon, *Papers of Grant,* 17:102, 119; Duncan, *Entrepreneur for Equality,* 18.

17. Sefton, *Army and Reconstruction,* 129–30, 137.

18. Thomas and Hyman, *Stanton,* 537–38; Adam Badeau, *Grant in Peace, from Appomattox to Mount McGregor* (Hartford, Conn., 1887), 62, 71, 102.

19. Welles, *Diary,* 3:111–13; Martin E. Mantell, *Johnson, Grant, and the Politics of Reconstruction* (New York, 1973), 32–33; Simpson, *Let Us Have Peace,* 180–82; Simon, *Papers of Grant,* 17:204–6.

20. Sefton, *Army and Reconstruction*, 142; Hyman, *Radical Republicans*, 402–6, 546.

21. C. Mildred Thompson, *Reconstruction in Georgia: Economic, Social, Political, 1865–1872* (1913; rpt., Gloucester, Mass., 1964), 174; Avery, *History of Georgia*, 370–71; Benjamin H. Hill Jr., *The Life, Speeches, and Writings of Benjamin H. Hill* (Atlanta, 1891), 304–5; Conway, *Reconstruction of Georgia*, 141, 144.

22. 40th Cong., 2d sess., H. Ex. Doc. 1, *ARSW*, 349–51; Hyman, *Radical Republicans*, 397–98; Thomas and Hyman, *Stanton*, 545; Simon, *Papers of Grant*, 17:256.

23. Thompson, *Reconstruction in Georgia*, 176–77; Conway, *Reconstruction of Georgia*, 146; 40th Cong., 2d sess., H. Ex. Doc., 342, *Reconstruction*, 110; Simon, *Papers of Grant*, 17:262.

24. Thompson, *Reconstruction in Georgia*, 177–78; *Augusta Constitutionalist*, Sept. 25, 1867; Simon, *Papers of Grant*, 17:323.

25. 40th Cong., 2d sess., H. Ex. Doc. 1, *ARSW*, 324–29; Charles J. Jenkins to JP, Aug. 20, 1867, Governor's Letter Books, Georgia Department of Archives and History; Conway, *Reconstruction of Georgia*, 147; Nathans, *Losing the Peace*, 52–53.

26. Simon, *Papers of Grant*, 18:10–13, 22; Avery, *History of Georgia*, 372; Robert Manson Myers, *The Children of Pride: A True Story of Georgia and the Civil War* (New Haven, Conn., 1972), 1393; Browning, *Diary*, 1:164.

27. Thomas and Hyman, *Stanton*, 555–56; Sefton, *Army and Reconstruction*, 154–58; Simon, *Papers of Grant*, 17:520; Mantell, *Johnson, Grant, and Politics*, 35–36.

28. Nathans, *Losing the Peace*, 53; Fitz John Porter to William G. Moore, Oct. 16, 1867, Nicholson Papers, HL; Simon, *Papers of Grant*, 17:321–22, 521.

29. Simon, *Papers of Grant*, 17:321–22, 520.

30. Ibid., 327–28; Gabler, "Porter Case," 340–41; Ulysses S. Grant, "An Undeserved Stigma," *North American Review* 135 (Apr. 1882): 545.

31. Gabler, "Porter Case," 343–44; Simon, *Papers of Grant*, 17:338–39.

32. 40th Cong., 2d sess., H. Ex. Doc. 1, *ARSW*, 346–49; W. W. Davis, *Reconstruction in Florida*, 465–66; Simon, *Papers of Grant*, 17:367.

33. Sefton, *Army and Reconstruction*, 165–66; Simon, *Papers of Grant*, 17:366–67.

34. Simon, *Papers of Grant*, 17:368, 370.

35. 40th Cong., 2d sess., H. Ex. Doc. 342, *Reconstruction*, 113–17, 118; Edward McPherson, *Political History of the United States during the Period of Reconstruction, 1865–1870* (Washington, D.C., 1871), 374; Duncan, *Entrepreneur for Equality*, 28; Nathans, *Losing the Peace*, 54–55; W. W. Davis, *Reconstruction in Florida*, 469, 492; Simon, *Papers of Grant*, 17:366.

36. Conway, *Reconstruction of Georgia*, 149–50; Duncan, *Entrepreneur for Equality*, 28–29; Simon, *Papers of Grant*, 18:92–93.

37. Simon, *Papers of Grant*, 18:87–88, 94.

38. Mantrell, *Johnson, Grant, and Politics*, 75; Thompson, *Reconstruction in Georgia*, 178; Sefton, *Army and Reconstruction*, 169; Welles, *Diary*, 3:248–49.

39. Simon, *Papers of Grant*, 18:95–96.

40. Thompson, *Reconstruction in Georgia*, 178–79; Simon, *Papers of Grant*, 18:97; JP, "Meade under Grant," *NT*, Dec. 13, 1900.

Chapter 15: I Speak Not Now of Myself

1. 40th Cong., 3d sess., H. Ex. Doc. 1, pt. 2, *ARSW*, 287–91.

2. Ibid., 286; JP to Ulysses S. Grant, Feb. 19, 1868, Cyrus B. Comstock Papers, DLC;

JP to William W. Belknap, Apr. 29, 1871, JP Letters, HL; JP to Thomas C. H. Smith, Feb. 12, 1869, Smith Papers, OHS.

3. M. Cox, "Pope," 294.

4. JP to Joseph E. Brown, Mar. 29, 1868, Brown Family Papers, University of Georgia, Athens.

5. Gabler, "Porter Case," 351–52; JP to William W. Belknap, Jan. 3 and Nov. 23, 1871, JP Letters, HL; JP to "My Dear Sister," Feb. 15, 1870, ALBS; JP, *Brief Statement of the Case of Fitz John Porter*, N.p., [1869], 1–4; 46th Cong., 1st sess., S. Ex. Doc. 37, *Proceedings and Report . . . Case of Fitz-John Porter*, 3:1138.

6. JP to "My Dear sister," Feb. 15, 1870, ALBS; Fitz John Porter, "Incidents in the History of the 'Brief Statement' Prepared by Maj. Gen. John Pope in the Case of Genl. Fitz John Porter," 1, unpublished manuscript in Porter Papers, DLC; Lewis Este Mills to John P. Nicholson, Jan. 2, 1877, Nicholson Papers, HL; Lewis E. Mills, *General Pope's Virginia Campaign of 1862; Read before the Cincinnati Literary Club, February 5, 1870* (Cincinnati, 1870).

7. 46th Cong., 1st sess., S. Ex. Doc. 37, *Proceedings and Report . . . Case of Fitz-John Porter*, 3:1129–30; JP to Thomas C. H. Smith, Feb. 22, 1870, Smith Papers, OHS; JP to Ulysses S. Grant, Dec. 3, 1869, copy in JP Papers, NYHS; JP to William T. Sherman, Dec. 10 and 16, 1869, Sherman Papers, DLC.

8. James A. Garfield to JP, Dec. 24, 1869, Garfield Papers, DLC; Gabler, "Porter Case," 354–58; JP to Estes Hines, Mar. 2, 1870, JP Papers, NYHS; William T. Sherman to JP, Feb. 24, 1870, Sherman Papers, DLC; Porter, "Incidents," 4, Porter Papers, DLC; 46th Cong., 1st sess., S. Ex. Doc. 37, *Proceedings and Report . . . Case of Fitz-John Porter*, 3:1138.

9. JP to "My Dear Sister," Feb. 15, 1870; Charles R. Williams, *The Life of Rutherford Birchard Hayes, Nineteenth President of the United States,* 2 vols. (Columbus, Ohio, 1938), 2:421; Rutherford B. Hayes to JP, Apr. 6, 1870, Hayes Papers, HPL.

10. "Statement of the Military Service of John Pope . . . ," 2, JP Personal File, ACPB, AGO, RG 94, NA; JP to G. L. Hartsfull, Apr. 11, 1870, and JP to Sheridan, Apr. 26, 1870, both in LS, Department of the Lakes, RG 393, NA; JP to John M. Schofield, Apr. 19, 22, 26, 1870, Schofield Papers, DLC; M. Cox, "Pope," 296; Marvin H. Garfield, "The Military Post as a Factor in the Frontier Defense of Kansas, 1865–1869," *Kansas Historical Quarterly* 1 (Nov. 1931), 53; Schofield, *Forty-six Years,* 427–29.

11. Paul A. Hutton, *Phil Sheridan and His Army* (Lincoln, Nebr., 1986), 121–29, 180–85, 228–30; Thomas C. Leonard, "Red, White and the Army Blue: Empathy and Anger in the American West," *American Quarterly* (May 1974): 177–78.

12. Wooster, *Military and Indian Policy,* 146; Robert M. Utley, "The Celebrated Peace Policy of General Grant," *North Dakota History* 20, no. 3 (July 1953): 121, 124–26; Mardock, "The Humanitarians," 67–70.

13. Utley, *Frontier Regulars,* 197; Ellis, *Pope and Indian Policy,* 133; Mardock, "The Humanitarians," 80–81.

14. Mardock, "The Humanitarians," 82–88; Utley, *Frontier Regulars,* 198–99.

15. "Statement of the organization of . . . the command of Brigadier General John Pope," War Department document dated Jan. 2, 1884, JP Personal File, ACPB, AGO, RG 94, NA; Hutton, *Sheridan and His Army,* 120–21.

16. Lawrie Tatum, *Our Red Brothers and the Peace Policy of President Ulysses S. Grant* (Lincoln, Nebr., 1970), 24–25; Lee Cutler, "Lawrie Tatum and the Kiowa Agency, 1869–1873," *Arizona and the West* 13 (Autumn 1971): 226–27.

17. Utley, "Celebrated Peace Policy," 128.

18. Cutler, "Tatum and the Kiowa Agency," 232–33; 41st Cong., 3d sess., H. Ex. Doc. 1 *ARSW*, 8, 10, 18; 33d Cong., 2d sess., S. Ex. Doc. 78, *Report of Exploration of Route for Pacific Railroad*, 15–16; James L. Haley, *The Buffalo War* (New York, 1976), 6.

19. JP to George Hartsuff, June 1, 1870, LS, DMo, RG 393, NA; 41st Cong., 3d sess., H. Ex. Doc. 1, pt. 2, *ARSW*, 9.

20. Hutton, *Sheridan and His Army*, 233–34; idem, *Soldiers West: Biographies from the Military Frontier* (Lincoln, Nebr., 1987), 162–63; John F. Marszalek, *Sherman: A Soldier's Passion for Order* (New York, 1993), 391, 394.

21. Marszalek, *Sherman*, 394–96; Tatum, *Our Blood Brothers*, 116–17; Hutton, *Sheridan and His Army*, 234–35.

22. Cutler, "Tatum and Kiowa Agency," 239–40; Hutton, *Sheridan and His Army*, 237.

23. Wooster, *Military and Indian Policy*, 145; 41st Cong., 3d. sess., H. Ex. Doc. 1, pt. 2, *ARSW*, 11.

24. 41st Cong., 3d sess., H. Ex. Doc. 1, pt. 2, *ARSW*, 11–12; JP to William W. Belknap, Aug. 18, 1873, JP Letters, HL; 43d Cong., 1st sess., H. Ex. Doc. 275, *Reduction of the Military Establishment*, 189.

25. Wooster, *Military and Indian Policy*, 145–46; 42d Cong., 2d sess., H. Ex. Doc. 1, pt. 2, *ARSW*, 35; 42 Cong., 3d sess., H. Ex. Doc. 1, pt. 2, *ARSW*, 48.

26. Richard N. Ellis, "The Humanitarian Generals," *Western Historical Quarterly* 3 (1972), 174; idem, *Pope and Indian Policy*, 158; 43d Cong., 1st sess., H. Ex. Doc. 1, pt. 2, *ARSW* 46; 42 Cong., 1st sess., H. Ex. Doc. 1, pt. 2, *ARSW*, 46–47.

27. Ellis, *Pope and Indian Policy*, 170–73; 42 Cong., 3d sess., H. Ex. Doc. 1, pt. 2, *ARSW*, 47; 43d Cong., 1st sess., H. Ex. Doc. 275, *Reduction*, 192.

28. 43d Cong., 1st sess., H. Ex. Doc. 275, *Reduction*, 190–91.

29. 41st Cong., 3d sess., H. Ex. Doc. 1, pt. 2, *ARSW*, 17–18; George Walton, *Sentinel of the Plains: Fort Leavenworth and the American West* (Englewood Cliffs, N.J., 1973), 159; 43d Cong., 1st sess., H. Ex. Doc. 275, *Reduction*, 190.

30. Elvid Hunt, *History of Fort Leavenworth, 1827–1937* (Fort Leavenworth, Kans., 1937), 123–25; 42d Cong., 3d sess., H. Ex. Doc. 1, pt. 2, *ARSW*, 48; JP to John A. Halderman, Feb. 3, 1875, Halderman Papers, KHS.

31. Walton, *Sentinel of the Plains*, 175; Hunt, *Fort Leavenworth*, 125; 42d Cong., 3d sess., H. Ex. Doc. 1, pt. 2, *ARSW*, 50.

32. Walton, *Sentinel of the Plains*, 151–54; Hunt, *Fort Leavenworth*, 128; Force, "Pope," 362.

33. Hunt, *Fort Leavenworth*, 128; JP to Rutherford B. Hayes, May 26, 1872, Hayes Papers, HPL; JP to Thomas C. H. Smith, Mar. 22, 1873, Smith Papers, OHS.

34. Hunt, *Fort Leavenworth*, 128; JP to Hayes, July 16, 1872, Hayes Papers, HPL; *DAB*, 6:511–12.

35. James Grant Wilson, "Recollections of General Sherman," *NT*, Feb. 27, 1902; Hayes to JP, Dec. 29, 1871, and JP to Hayes, Jan. 2, 1872, both in Hayes Papers, HPL; C. R. Williams, *Life of Hayes*, 1:365–66, 2:321; Marszalek, *Sherman*, 426.

36. Schutz and Trenerry, *Abandoned by Lincoln*, 192; M. Cox, "Pope," 300.

37. Haley, *Buffalo War*, 38–44.

38. Ibid., 95–96; 44th Cong., 1st sess., H. Ex. Doc. 1, pt. 2, *ARSW*, 29–30; Ellis, *Pope and Indian Policy*, 182.

39. H. K. Dunn to Thomas Osborn, July 8, 1874, LS, DMo, RG 393, NA; 43d Cong., 2d sess., H. Ex. Doc. 1, pt. 2, *ARSW*, 30.

40. Haley, *Buffalo War,* 77, 130–31; J. T. Marshall, *The Miles Expedition of 1874–1875: An Eyewitness Account of the Red River War* (Austin, Tex., 1971), 5.

41. Sheridan to Pope, Aug. 21, 1874, LS, MDMo, RG 393, NA; Hutton, *Sheridan and His Army,* 246; 43d Cong., 2d. sess., H. Ex. Doc. 1, pt. 2, *ARSW* (Sheridan's Report), 27.

42. Haley, *Buffalo War,* 98–99; Ellis, *Pope and Indian Policy,* 182–83; JP to William W. Belknap, Sept. 23, 1874, JP Letters, HL; JP to Sheridan, July 10, LS, DMo, RG 393, NA; Joe F. Taylor, ed., "The Indian Campaigns on the Staked Plains, 1874–1875: Military Correspondence from File 2815-1874, Adjutant General's Office, War Department," *Panhandle-Plains Historical Review* 34 (1961), 10.

43. Pope to Sheridan, July 16, 1874, LS, DMo, Sheridan to Sherman, July 16 and 18, LS, MDMo, all in RG 393, NA; Haley, *Buffalo War,* 103.

44. Haley, *Buffalo War,* 103; Hutton, *Sheridan and His Army,* 247–48; Sheridan to Sherman, Sept. 7, 1874, Sheridan Papers, DLC.

45. Haley, *Buffalo War,* 103; Ellis, *Pope and Indian Policy,* 186.

46. Utley, *Frontier Regulars,* 225, 227; Haley, *Buffalo War,* 104, 124; JP to Belknap, Sept. 23, 1874, HL; Taylor, "Indian Campaign," 14–15; 44th Cong., 1st sess., H. Ex. Doc. 1, pt. 2, *ARSW,* 30.

47. Utley, *Frontier Regulars,* 226–27.

48. JP to Belknap, Sept. 23, 1874, JP Letters, HL.

49. Haley, *Buffalo War,* 126–27; Marshall, *Miles Expedition,* 3–4; Virginia W. Johnson, *The Unregimented General: A Biography of Nelson A. Miles* (Boston, 1962), 48.

50. Taylor, "Indian Campaign," 24, 27; Brian C. Pohanka, ed., *Nelson A. Miles: A Documentary Biography of His Military Career, 1861–1903* (Glendale, Calif., 1985), 81; Haley, *Buffalo War,* 132–37.

51. Taylor, "Indian Campaign," 25; Pohanka, *Miles,* 80; 44th Cong., 1st sess., H. Ex. Doc. 1, pt. 2, *ARSW,* 31; Utley, *Frontier Regulars,* 237; Haley, *Buffalo War,* 137, 166.

52. Taylor, "Indian Campaign," 40–42; Pohanka, *Miles,* 81; Jerry L. Rogers, "The Indian Territory Expedition," *Texas Military History* 4 (1970), 241; Haley, *Buffalo War,* 137, 147–48, 153, 156–61, 165–67.

53. Utley, *Frontier Regulars,* 232–37; Johnson, *Unregimented General,* 57–61; Paul A. Hutton, ed., *Soldiers West: Biographies from the Military Frontier* (Lincoln, Nebr., 1987), 217; Haley, *Buffalo War,* 183, 195, 209; Taylor, "Indian Campaign," 101; Charles Robinson, *The Indian Trial: The Complete Story of the Warren Wagon Train Massacre and the Fall of the Kiowa Nation* (Glendale, Calif., 1997), 179.

54. J. Rogers, "Indian Territory Expedition," 246–47; Pohanka, *Miles,* 83–86.

Chapter 16: A Life for the Nation

1. Richard N. Ellis, "General Pope and the Southern Plains Indians, 1875–1883," *Southwestern Historical Quarterly* 72 (Oct. 1968): 154; Taylor, "Indian Campaign," 142.

2. Ellis, "Pope and Plains Indians," 156–57; Taylor, "Indian Campaign," 167–69.

3. Taylor, "Indian Campaign," 167–69, 182–86, 215; Ellis, *Pope and Indian Policy,* 194–95.

4. 44th Cong., 2d sess., H. Ex. Doc. 1, pt. 2, *ARSW,* 449–50; Ellis, "Pope and Plains Indians," 168; 45th Cong., 2d sess., H. Ex. Doc. 1, pt. 2, *ARSW,* 59–60.

5. Ellis, "Pope and Plains Indians," 164; JP to Rutherford B. Hayes, June 17, 1876, Hayes Papers, HPL; Theodore F. Randolph to Fitz John Porter, Mar. 8, 1878, Porter Papers, DLC.

6. JP to Manning F. Force, Dec. 31, 1876, Feb. 22 and 26, 1877, all in Hayes Papers, HPL.

7. JP to Hayes, May 3, 1877, and JP to W. K. Rogers, May 5, 1877, both in Hayes Papers, HPL; C. R. Williams, *Life of Hayes,* 2:16–22; Carl Schurz, "Present Aspects of the Indian Problem," *North American Review* 133 (July 1881): 12–17.

8. JP to John M. Schofield, Mar. 24, 1877, Schofield Papers, DLC; JP to Rogers, May 5, 1877, Hayes Papers, HPL.

9. JP quoted in Weigley, *History of the Army,* 270–72; JP to Thomas C. H. Smith, Smith Papers, OHS; JP to Hayes, Oct. 29, 1875, Hayes Papers, HL; "Address of General Pope at the Reunion of the Society of the Army of the Tennessee at Des Moines, Iowa, September 29 and 30, 1875," handwritten transcript in Schutz-Trenerry Papers, HPL.

10. JP to Hayes, May 3, 1887, and JP to W. K. Rogers, May 8, 1877, both in Hayes Papers, HPL. Pope had his letter to Hayes printed and circulated among Congress and the cabinet. Future president James A. Garfield was particularly taken with Pope's views, on both army reorganization and administration (the latter as expressed in a February 1876 letter to then Secretary of War Alphonso Taft), and he repeated them in an April 1878 article on army reform. James A. Garfield, "The Army of the United States, Part II," *North American Review* 262 (Apr. 1878): 442–65.

11. Pope made these appeals in every one of his annual reports, from 1876 to 1881. 44th Cong., 2d sess., H. Ex. Doc. 1, pt. 2, *ARSW,* 452; 45th Cong., 2d sess., H. Ex. Doc. 1, pt. 2, *ARSW,* 61–64; 46th Cong., 2d sess., H. Ex. Doc. 1, pt. 2, *ARSW,* 83–84; 46th Cong., 3d sess., H. Ex. Doc. 1, pt. 2, *ARSW,* 91–92; 47th Cong., 2d sess., H. Ex. Doc. 1, pt. 2, *ARSW,* 123–24.

12. 46th Cong., 2d sess., S.R. 158, *Report of Senator Randolph in the Case of Fitz John Porter,* 1; Gabler, "Porter Case," 384–85; JP to John M. Schofield, July 13, 1878, Schofield Papers, DLC; JP to Manning F. Force, Jan. 15, 1878, Force Papers, UW; Force to Hayes, Apr. 21, 1878, Hayes Papers, HPL; JP to Joseph Holt, Apr. 27, 1878, Holt Papers, DLC; JP to Garfield, Apr. 16, 1878, Garfield Papers, DLC.

13. William T. Sherman to JP, July 2, 1876, Sherman Papers, DLC.

14. JP to Thomas C. H. Smith, Oct. 23 and 28, 1875, and Jan. 30, 1877, Smith Papers, OHS; JP to G. W. Mindil, Apr. 26, 1877, ALBS; Peter Cozzens and Robert I. Girardi, eds., *The Military Memoirs of General John Pope* (Chapel Hill, N.C., 1998), xxii–xxiii. The last-named work contains the complete text of the Pope–Comte de Paris correspondence.

15. JP to Force, Jan. 15, 1878, Force Papers, UW.

16. Gabler, "Porter Case," 386–404; "Porter and Pope, the Investigation at West Point," *NT,* July 13, 1878; JP to Manning F. Force, Nov. 2 and 3, 1878, Force Papers, UW; 46th Cong., 1st sess., S. Ex. Doc. 37, *Proceedings and Report . . . Porter Case,* 3:1018.

17. JP to Force, Nov. 2 and 3, 1878, Force Papers, UW; Washington *Post,* Oct. 31, 1878; *New York World,* Oct. 31, 1878.

18. JP to Force, Nov. 3, 1878, Force Papers, UW.

19. Schofield, *Forty-six Years,* 461–62; Gabler, "Porter Case," 413–15.

20. JP to Force, Mar. 22 and 31, and Apr. 12 and 15, 1879, Force Papers, UW.

21. Gabler, "Porter Case," 415–16; Porter to Schofield, Apr. 7, 1879, Schofield Papers, DLC.

22. Mrs. John A. Logan, *Reminiscences of a Soldier's Wife: An Autobiography* (New York, 1913), 396; *Cincinnati Commercial,* Mar. 1, 1882; JP to Benjamin H. Grierson, Oct. 10, 1879, Grierson Papers, Texas Tech University; JP to Force, Apr. 11 and Oct. 10, 1879, Force Papers, UW; JP to Zachariah Chandler, Feb. 15, 1879, Chandler Papers, DLC;

Gabler, "Porter Case," 426; JP to John A. Logan, Mar. 8, 1880, and Robert Todd Lincoln to Logan, Apr. 8, 1880, both in Logan Memorial Collection, ISHL.

23. JP to Force, Apr. 18, 1879, Force Papers, UW; JP to Schofield, Apr. 28 and June 10, 1879, Schofield Papers, DLC; JP to William T. Sherman, May 22, 1879, JP Personal File, ACPB, AGO, RG 94, NA.

24. Mrs. John A. Logan, *Reminiscences,* 388–89.

25. 46th Cong., 2d sess., H. Misc. Doc. 38, *Ute Indian Outbreak,* 101–3; Utley, *Frontier Regulars,* 341–42; 46th Cong., 2d. sess., H. Ex. Doc. 1, pt. 2, *ARSW,* 81–82.

26. Utley, *Frontier Regulars,* 346–47; 46th Cong., 3d sess., H. Ex. Doc. 1, pt. 2, *ARSW,* 82–83.

27. 46th Cong., 3d sess., H. Ex. Doc. 1, pt. 2, *ARSW,* 85; Ellis, *Pope and Indian Policy,* 226–28.

28. 47th Cong., 1st sess., H. Ex. Doc. 1, pt. 2, *ARSW,* 119.

29. JP, *The Indian Question; Address by General Pope, before the Social Science Association, at Cincinnati, Ohio, May 24, 1878* (Cincinnati, 1878), 19–20.

30. 47th Cong., 1st sess., H. Ex. Doc. 1, pt. 2, *ARSW,* 89–90.

31. Ellis, *Pope and Indian Policy,* 221–22; 46th Cong., 3d sess., H. Ex. Doc. 1, pt. 2, *ARSW,* 91; 47th Cong., 1st sess., H. Ex. Doc. 1, pt. 2, *ARSW,* 114–15; JP to William T. Sherman, Feb. 12 and Mar. 6, 1880, JP to W. D. Whipple, Feb. 25, 1880, and Samuel Breck to JP, July 12, 1880, all in Rutherford B. Hayes Papers, HPL.

32. Edward Dale, "Ranching on the Cheyenne-Arapaho Reservation, 1880–1885," *Chronicles of Oklahoma* (Nov. 1928): 35–47; Ellis, *Pope and Indian Policy,* 241.

33. DAB, 4:476–78; J. Cox, *Military Reminiscences,* 1:247.

34. Gabler, "Porter Case," 439–49; Grant, "An Undeserved Stigma."

35. *Cincinnati Commercial,* Mar. 1, 1882; Jacob D. Cox, *The Second Battle of Bull Run, as Connected with the Fitz-John Porter Case* (Cincinnati, 1882); JP to John A. Logan, Mar. 8, 1880, Logan Memorial Collection, ISHL; Cozzens and Girardi, *Pope Memoirs,* xxiv.

36. JP to Chester Arthur, Oct. 16, 1882, David Davis to Chester Arthur, Oct. 20, 1882, Robert Todd Lincoln to Manning F. Force, Oct. 25, 1882, William Strong to Robert Todd Lincoln, Oct. 25, 1882, John W. Fuller to Robert Todd Lincoln, Oct. 26, 1882, William Howard Taft, Andrew Hickenlooper, et. al., to Chester Arthur, Oct. 26, 1882, Walter Q. Gresham to Robert Todd Lincoln, Oct. 27, 1882, and JP to the Adjutant General of the Army, Oct. 30, 1882, all in JP Personal File, ACPB, AGO, RG 94, NA.

37. Citizens of Leavenworth to Dudley A. Haskell, May 11, 1883, Dudley A. Haskell to Chester Arthur, May 13, 1883, Philetus Sawyer to Robert Todd Lincoln, May 26, 1883, and Governor Glick to Chester Arthur, Sept. 13, 1883, all in JP Personal File, ACPB, AGO, RG 94, NA; Cozzens and Girardi, *Pope Memoirs,* xix–xx.

38. *Pomeroy Telegraph,* Dec. 15, 1886; JP to Force, Sept. 28, 1883, Force Papers, UW; R. E. Banta, *The Ohio* (New York, 1949), 508–9.

39. JP to Force, June 4 and 16, 1883, and Jan. 14, 1885, all in Force Papers, UW.

40. JP to Force, Oct. 9, 1883, Force Papers, UW.

41. JP to Force, July 3, Aug. 21, and Oct. 22, 1884, Apr. 15, 1885, Force Papers, UW; *San Francisco Examiner,* Oct. 20, 1884.

42. Pope left the prosecution of the Apache campaign to the capable commander of the Department of Arizona, Brigadier General George Crook. George Crook to JP, June 6, July 3, and Dec. 26, 1885, Crook Papers, HPL; JP to Benjamin H. Grierson, Mar. 12, 1885, Grierson Papers, ISHL; 49th Cong., 1st sess., H. Ex. Doc. 1, pt. 2, *ARSW,* 166;

JP to Force, July 3, 1884, Jan. 14, Apr. 15, June 3, Sept. 30, and Oct. 29, 1885, Force Papers, UW; JP to Thomas C. H. Smith, June 10, 1885; Banta, *Ohio*, 512–13; *Pomeroy Telegraph*, Dec. 15, 1886; Ohio Coal Company balance sheet dated Mar. 1, 1886, Charles W. Dabney Papers, OHS.

43. Gabler, "Porter Case," 464–67; Rutherford B. Hayes, *Diary and Letters of Rutherford Birchard Hayes, Nineteenth President of the United States*, ed. Charles R. Williams, 6 vols. (Columbus, Ohio, 1924), 4:264–65; JP to Force, June 3 and July 22, 1885, Force Papers, UW; Cozzens and Girardi, *Pope Memoirs*, xxiv.

44. Cozzens and Girardi, *Pope Memoirs*, xxiv; John Gibbon, "Pope at Bull Run," 2–3, undated manuscript in Porter Papers, DLC.

45. JP to Force, Feb. 25, 1886, Force Papers, UW.

46. R. C. Drum, memorandum announcing the retirement of Major General John Pope, Mar. 16, 1886, JP Personal File, ACPB, AGO, RG 94, NA; JP to Force, Sept. 13, 1886, Jan. 1, 14, and 29, 1887, Force Papers, UW.

47. Cozzens and Girardi, *Pope Memoirs*, xxvi.

48. JP to Force, Jan. 29, 1887, Force Papers, UW; JP, "Some Legacies of the Civil War," *North American Review* 367 (June 1887); JP to Grierson, Dec. 16, 1887, Grierson Papers, ISHL.

49. *Pomeroy Telegraph*, Jan. 18 and 25, and June 20, 1888.

50. JP to Force, Feb. 16, 1889, Force Papers, UW.

51. For a detailed discussion of the character and merits of Pope's work, see my introduction to Cozzens and Girardi, *Pope Memoirs*.

52. JP to Force, Feb. 16, 1889; Force, "Pope," 362; Headquarters of the Army, Washington, Sept. 24, 1892, Announcement of the death of John Pope, and J. T. Haynes to Force, Oct. 4, 1892, both in JP Personal File, ACPB, AGO, RG 94, NA; *Army and Navy Journal*, Oct. 1, 1892.

Bibliography

Manuscripts

Abraham Lincoln Book Shop, Chicago
    John Pope Letters
Author's Collection
    Theodore S. Bowers Letter
Boston University
    Military Historical Society of Massachusetts Collection, John C. Ropes Papers
Chicago Historical Society
    William Butler Papers
    Henry Halleck Papers
    John Pope Papers
    Henry Walke Papers
Henry E. Huntington Library, San Marino, California
    Edward Meyer Kern, "Notes of a Military Reconnaissance"
    John Page Nicholson Papers
    John Pope Letters
Historical Society of Pennsylvania, Philadelphia
    D. D. Jones Papers
Illinois State Historical Library, Springfield
    Orville H. Browning Papers
    Charles H. Floyd Letters
    Benjamin H. Grierson Papers
    Ozias M. Hatch Papers
    Robert G. Ingersoll Papers
    John A. Logan Memorial Collection
    Lyman Needham Letters
    John M. Palmer Papers
    Lewis B. Parsons Papers
    John Pope Papers
    Nathaniel Pope Papers
    Daniel C. Smith Letters
    Lyman Trumbull Family Papers

Wallace-Dickey Family Papers
Richard Yates Papers
Kansas State Historical Society, Topeka
John Adams Halderman Papers
Library of Congress, Washington, D.C.
Nathaniel Banks Papers
Blair Family Papers
Zachariah Chandler Papers
Salmon P. Chase Papers
Samuel P. Heintzelman Papers
Joseph Holt Papers
Philip Kearny Papers
Robert Todd Lincoln Papers
George B. McClellan Papers
Fitz John Porter Papers
John M. Schofield Papers
Philip H. Sheridan Papers
William T. Sherman Papers
Lyman Trumbull Papers
Willard Family Papers
Miami University of Ohio, Oxford
Alfred W. Gilbert Letters
Minnesota Historical Society, St. Paul
Alfred J. Hill Papers
Lambert Naegele and Family Papers
Henry H. Sibley Papers
National Archives, Washington, D.C.
Record Group 77: Records of the Topographical Bureau, Office of the Chief of
Engineers, Letters Sent and Received
Record Group 94: Records of the Adjutant General's Office, 1871–94, Appoint-
ment, Commission, and Personal Branch (Personnel File of John Pope)
Record Group 94: Records of the Adjutant General's Office, Civil War Generals'
Papers and Books
Record Group 108: Records of the Headquarters of the Army
Record Group 393: Records of Geographical Commands
New Jersey Historical Society, Newark
Philip Kearny Papers
New-York Historical Society, New York, New York
John Pope Papers
Franz Sigel Papers
Oberlin College, Oberlin, Ohio
Jacob D. Cox Papers
Ohio Historical Society, Columbus
Charles W. Dabney Papers
William Pittinger Diary
John Pope Papers
Thomas C. H. Smith Papers

David T. Stathem Papers
State Archives Series 147 (Correspondence to the Governor and Adjutant General of Ohio, 1861–66)
Joseph Strickling Reminiscences
Rosenberg Library, Galveston, Texas
William Wallace McCullough Papers
Rutherford B. Hayes Presidential Library, Fremont, Ohio
George Crook Papers
Rutherford B. Hayes Papers
Wallace J. Schutz–Walter N. Trenerry Papers
Sioux City Public Museum, Sioux City, Iowa
Henry Clay McNeil Letters
Texas Tech University, Lubbock
Benjamin H. Grierson Papers
United States Army Military History Institute, Carlisle Barracks, Pennsylvania
Luther Bradley Letters
John Pope Papers
United States Military Academy, West Point, New York
Samuel G. French Papers
Papers Relating to the Second Battle of Bull Run
John Pope Papers
University of Georgia, Athens
Brown Family Papers
University of Washington, Seattle
Manning F. Force Papers
Western Historical Manuscripts Collection, Missouri Historical Society, Columbia
Robert T. Van Horn Papers
Western Historical Manuscripts Collection, University of Missouri, Rolla
Wellington Eldred Letters
Western Reserve Historical Society, Cleveland
Franz Sigel Papers
Yale University, Sterling Memorial Library, New Haven, Connecticut
Logan Family Papers

Newspapers

Army and Navy Journal
Atlanta Constitution
Augusta Constitutionalist
Boston Evening Transcript
Chicago Times
Chicago Tribune
Cincinnati Commercial
Cincinnati (Daily) Gazette
Cincinnati Enquirer
Illinois State Journal (Springfield)
Leavenworth (Kansas) Conservative

Meigs County (Ohio) Telegraph
Memphis *Appeal*
Milledgeville (Georgia) Federal Union
Milledgeville *Southern Recorder*
Milwaukee Sentinel
Missouri Democrat (St. Louis)
Missouri Republican (St. Louis)
New Albany (Indiana) Ledger
New York Daily Tribune
New York Herald
New York Mail
New York World
Philadelphia Inquirer
Philadelphia Public Ledger
Pomeroy (Ohio) Weekly Telegraph
San Francisco Examiner
Sangamon (Illinois) Journal
Savannah Daily Morning News
Savannah Daily Republican
Sioux City (Dakota Territory) Register
St. Paul Daily Press (Minnesota)
St. Paul Pioneer
St. Paul Weekly Press
St. Louis Democrat
St. Louis Post-Dispatch
Sunday Herald and Weekly National Intelligencer (Washington, D.C.)
Washington Post
Washington Star (Washington, D.C.)

Official Documents

Civil War Messages and Proclamations of Wisconsin War Governors. Edited by Robert G. Thwaites. Madison, Wis., 1912.

Report of the Military Services of Gen. David Hunter, U.S.A., during the War of the Rebellion, Made to the U.S. War Department, 1873. New York, 1873.

Reports of the Secretary of War and Interior, in Answer to Resolutions of the Senate and House of Representatives in Relation to the Massacre at Fort Phil. Kearny, on December 21, 1866; with the Views of Commissioner Lewis V. Bogy, in Relation to the Future Policy to Be Pursued by the Government for the Settlement of the Indian Question; also Reports of Gen. John Pope and Col. Eli S. Parker on Same Subject. Washington, D.C., 1867.

31st Congress, 1st Session, House Executive Document 51. *Report of Brevet Major Samuel Woods, Relative to His Expedition to the Pembina Settlement, and the Conditions of Affairs on the Northwestern Frontier of the Territory of Minnesota.*

31st Congress, 1st Session, Senate Executive Document 42. *Report of the Secretary of War, Communicating the Report of an Exploration of the Territory of Minnesota, by Brevet Captain Pope, March 21, 1850.*

33d Congress, 2d Session, Senate Executive Document 78. *Report of Exploration of a Route for the Pacific Railroad Near the Thirty-second Parallel of North Latitude from the Red River to the Rio Grande.*

37th Congress, 3d Session, Executive Document 81. *Letter from the Secretary of War, in Answer to Resolution of the House of 18th ultimo, Transmitting Copy of Report of Major General John Pope.*

39th Congress, 1st Session. *Conduct of the War: Supplemental Report of the Joint Committee on the Conduct of the War.* 2 vols. Washington, D.C.: Government Printing Office, 1866.

39th Congress, 2d Session, House Executive Document 1. *Annual Report of the Secretary of War* (1866).

40th Congress, 1st Session, Senate Executive Document 2. *Protection to Trains on the Overland Route.*

40th Congress, 2d Session, House Executive Document 1, *Annual Report of the Secretary of War* (1867).

40th Congress, 2d Session, House Executive Document 342. *General Orders—Reconstruction.*

40th Congress, 3d Session, House Executive Document 1, Pt. 2. *Annual Report of the Secretary of War* (1868).

41st Congress, 3d Session, House Executive Document 1, Pt. 2. *Annual Report of the Secretary of War* (1870).

42d Congress, 2d Session, House Executive Document 1, Pt. 2. *Annual Report of the Secretary of War* (1871).

42d Congress, 3d Session, House Executive Document 1, Pt. 2. *Annual Report of the Secretary of War* (1872).

44th Congress, 1st Session, House Executive Document 1, Pt. 2. *Annual Report of the Secretary of War* (1874).

44th Congress, 2d Session, House Executive Document 1, Pt. 2. *Annual Report of the Secretary of War* (1876).

45th Congress, 2d Session, House Executive Document 1, Pt. 2. *Annual Report of the Secretary of War* (1877).

46th Congress, 1st Session, Senate Executive Document 37. *Proceedings and Report of the Board of Army Officers, Convened by Special Orders No. 78, Headquarters of the Army, Adjutant General's Office, Washington, April 12, 1878. In the Case of Fitz-John Porter. Together with the Proceedings in the Original Trial and Papers Related Thereto.* 3 parts. Washington, D.C., 1879.

46th Congress, 2d Session, House Executive Document 1, Pt. 2. *Annual Report of the Secretary of War* (1878).

46th Congress, 2d Session, House Miscellaneous Document 38. *Ute Indian Outbreak.*

46th Congress, 2d Session, Senate Report 158. *Report of Senator Randolph in the Case of Fitz John Porter.*

46th Congress, 2d Session, Senate Report 158, Pt. 2. *Views of the Minority: Case of Fitz John Porter.*

46th Congress, 3d Session, House Executive Document 1, Pt. 2. *Annual Report of the Secretary of War* (1880).

47th Congress, 1st Session, House Executive Document 1, Pt. 2. *Annual Report of the Secretary of War* (1881).

47th Congress, 2d Session, House Executive Document 1, Pt. 2. *Annual Report of the Secretary of War* (1882).

48th Congress, 1st Session, House Executive Document 1, Pt. 2. *Annual Report of the Secretary of War* (1883).

49th Congress, 1st Session, House Executive Document 1, Pt. 2. *Annual Report of the Secretary of War* (1885).

U.S. Congress. *Conduct of the War: Report of the Joint Committee on the Conduct of the War.* 8 vols. Washington, D.C.: Government Printing Office, 1863–66.

The War of the Rebellion: A Compilation of the Official Records of the Union and Confederate Armies. 70 vols. Washington, D.C.: Government Printing Office, 1880–1901.

Addresses, Articles, and Essays

Adkins, Charles I. "Service Observations from the Standpoint of a Private Soldier." In *National Tribune Scrap Book,* 54–62. Washington, D.C., n.d.

Allan, William. "Strength of the Forces under Pope and Lee in August 1862." In *The Virginia Campaign of General Pope in 1862: Papers Read before the Military Historical Society of Massachusetts in 1876, 1877, and 1880,* vol. 2, 195–220. Boston, 1886.

Ambrose, Stephen E. "Henry Halleck and the Second Bull Run Campaign." *Civil War History* 6 (1960): 238–49.

Andrews, George L. "The Battle of Cedar Mountain, August 9, 1862." In *The Virginia Campaign of General Pope in 1862: Papers Read before the Military Historical Society of Massachusetts in 1876, 1877, and 1880,* vol. 2, 387–442. Boston, 1886.

Angle, Paul M. "Nathaniel Pope, 1784–1850, a Memoir." *Illinois State Historical Society: Transactions for the Year 1936,* Publication No. 43, 111–82. Springfield, 1936.

Arnold, Isaac N. "Recollections of Early Chicago." In *Chicago Bar Association Lectures, Part One. Fergus Historical Series No. 22,* 1–15. Chicago, 1882.

[Arpe, R. N.]. *Stanton and Halleck in the Civil War: Fitz-John Porter and 2nd Bull Run, by a Veteran.* New York, 1905.

Bissell, J. W. "Sawing Out a Channel above Island Number Ten." *Century* 30, no. 8 (June 1885): 324–27.

Bowman, M. T. V. "My Experience on 'Pope's Retreat.'" In *War Sketches and Incidents as Related by the Companions of the Iowa Commandery, Military Order of the Loyal Legion of the United States,* vol. 2, 48–56. Des Moines, 1898.

Boynton, Henry V. "A Just Man and a Great Historical Work." *Century* 34, no. 3 (July 1887): 467–68.

Bundy, J. M. "The Last Chapter in the History of the War." *Galaxy* 8, no. 1 (1869): 112–21.

"Captain John Pope's Plan of 1853 for the Frontier Defense of New Mexico." Edited by Robert M. Utley. *Arizona and the West* 5, no. 2 (Summer 1963): 149–63.

Carlin, William P. "Military Memoirs V." *National Tribune,* Feb. 19, 1885.

Chetlain, Augustus L. "Recollections of General U. S. Grant." In *Military Essays and Recollections: Papers Read before the Commandery of the State of Illinois, Military Order of the Loyal Legion of the United States,* vol. 1, 9–32. Chicago, 1891.

Collins, L. W. "The Expedition against the Sioux Indians in 1863, under General Henry H. Sibley." In *Glimpses of the Nation's Struggle: A Series of Papers Read before the Minnesota Commandery of the Military Order of the Loyal Legion of the United States,* Second Series, 173–203. Minneapolis, 1890.

Cullen, Joseph P. "Five Cent Pope." *Civil War Times Illustrated* (Apr. 1980): 4-11, 46-47.

Cutler, Lee. "Lawrie Tatum and the Kiowa Agency, 1869-1873." *Arizona and the West* 13 (Autumn 1971): 221-44.

Dale, Edward. "Ranching on the Cheyenne-Arapaho Reservation, 1880-1885." *Chronicles of Oklahoma* (Nov. 1928): 35-59.

Davis, Charles W. "New Madrid and Island No. 10." In *Military Essays and Recollections: Papers Read before the Commandery of the State of Illinois, Military Order of the Loyal Legion of the United States*, vol. 1, 75-92. Chicago, 1891.

Davis, Jefferson C. "Campaigning in Missouri: Civil War Memoirs of General Jefferson C. Davis." *Missouri Historical Review* 54 (1959-60): 39-45.

Dodge, Grenville M. "Some Characteristics of General U. S. Grant." *Annals of Iowa*, ser. 3, no. 10 (1913): 570-89.

Ellis, Richard N. "After Bull Run: The Later Career of General John Pope." *Montana: The Magazine of Western History* 19 (Autumn 1969): 46-57.

———. "General Pope and the Southern Plains Indians, 1875-1883." *Southwestern Historical Quarterly* 72 (Oct. 1968): 152-69.

———. "The Humanitarian Generals." *Western Historical Quarterly* 3 (1972): 169-78.

Fitz John Porter—Pope's Campaign; Speech of Hon. Zachariah Chandler, of Michigan, in the United States Senate, February 21, 1870. Washington, D.C., 1870.

Foley, James L. "With Fremont in Missouri: Part I—General Review of Fremont's Campaign." In *Sketches of War History, 1861-1865: Papers Prepared for the Ohio Commandery of the Military Order of the Loyal Legion of the United States*, vol. 5, 484-521. Cincinnati, 1903.

Force, Manning F. "John Pope, Major General U.S.A.: Some Personal Memoranda." In *Sketches of War History, 1861-1865: Papers Prepared for the Ohio Commandery of the Military Order of the Loyal Legion of the United States*, vol. 4, 355-62. Cincinnati, 1896.

Franklin, William B. "The Sixth Corps at Second Bull Run." In *Battles and Leaders of the Civil War. Grant-Lee Edition*, vol. 2, pt. 2, 539-40. Edited by Clarence C. Buell and Robert U. Johnson. New York, 1884-87.

Frémont, John C. "In Command in Missouri." In *Battles and Leaders of the Civil War. Grant-Lee Edition*, vol. 1, pt. 2, 278-88. Edited by Clarence C. Buell and Robert U. Johnson. New York, 1884-87.

Fry, James. "McClellan and His 'Mission.'" *Century* 48, no. 5 (Sept. 1894): 931-46.

Gardiner, William. "Incidents of Cavalry Experiences during General Pope's Campaign." *Personal Narratives of Events in the War of the Rebellion, Being Papers Read before the Rhode Island Soldiers and Sailors Historical Society*, ser. 2, no. 20. Providence, 1883.

Garfield, James A. "The Army of the United States, Part II." *North American Review* (Apr. 1878): 442-65.

Garfield, Marvin H. "The Military Post as a Factor in the Frontier Defense of Kansas, 1865-1869." *Kansas Historical Quarterly* 1 (Nov. 1931): 50-62.

"General Pope's Report on the West, 1866." Edited by Richard N. Ellis. *Kansas Historical Quarterly* 35, no. 4 (Winter 1969): 345-72.

Gillespie, Joseph. *Recollections of Early Illinois and Her Noted Men. Fergus Historical Series No. 13.* Chicago, 1880.

Gordon, George H. *History of the Second Mass. Regiment of Infantry: Third Paper. Deliv-*

ered by George H. Gordon . . . at the Second Mass. Infantry Association, on May 11, 1875. Boston, 1875.

———. "The Twenty-seventh Day of August, 1862." In *The Virginia Campaign of General Pope in 1862: Papers Read before the Military Historical Society of Massachusetts in 1876, 1877, and 1880,* vol. 2, 99–132. Boston, 1886.

Goss, Warren L. "Recollections of a Private—VI; Two Days of the Second Battle of Bull Run." *Century* 31, no. 3 (Jan. 1886): 467–74.

Grant, Ulysses S. "An Undeserved Stigma." *North American Review* 135 (Apr. 1882): 536–46.

Haight, Theron W. "Gainesville, Groveton, and Bull Run." In *War Papers Read before the Commandery of the State of Wisconsin, Military Order of the Loyal Legion of the United States,* vol. 2, 357–72. Milwaukee, 1896.

Hamilton, Schuyler. "Who Projected the Canal at Island Number Ten?" *Century* 32, no. 8 (July 1885): 776–77.

Hampton, H. D. "The Powder River Indian Expedition of 1865." *Montana: The Magazine of Western History* 14 (Autumn 1964): 2–15.

Harries, William H. "Gainesville, Virginia, August 28, 1862." In *Glimpses of the Nation's Struggle: A Series of Papers Read before the Minnesota Commandery of the Military Order of the Loyal Legion of the United States,* Sixth Series, 157–68. Minneapolis, 1909.

Haven, Franklin, Jr. "The Conduct of General McClellan at Alexandria in August, 1862." In *The Virginia Campaign of General Pope in 1862: Papers Read before the Military Historical Society of Massachusetts in 1876, 1877, and 1880,* vol. 2, 263–86. Boston, 1886.

Horton, Charles P. "The Campaign of General Pope in Virginia—First Part: To the 19th of August, 1862." In *The Virginia Campaign of General Pope in 1862: Papers Read before the Military Historical Society of Massachusetts in 1876, 1877, and 1880,* vol. 2, 31–54. Boston, 1886.

Hoyne, Thomas. "The Lawyer as a Pioneer." In *Chicago Bar Association Lectures, Part One, Fergus Historical Series No. 22.* Chicago, 1882.

Hyman, Harold M. "Johnson, Stanton, and Grant: A Reconsideration of the Army's Role in the Events Leading to Impeachment." *American Historical Review* 66 (Oct. 1960): 85–100.

King, Charles. "Gainesville, 1862." In *War Papers Read before the Commandery of the State of Wisconsin, Military Order of the Loyal Legion of the United States,* vol. 3, 258–83. Milwaukee, 1896.

———. "In Vindication of General Rufus King." *Century* 31, no. 6 (Apr. 1886): 935.

Leasure, Daniel. "Personal Observations and Experiences in the Pope Campaign in Virginia." In *Glimpses of the Nation's Struggle: A Series of Papers Read before the Minnesota Commandery of the Military Order of the Loyal Legion of the United States,* 135–66. St. Paul, Minn., 1887.

"Leave Pope to Get Out of His Scrape": McClellan's Dispatches. Washington, D.C., 1864.

Leonard, Thomas C. "Red, White and the Army Blue: Empathy and Anger in the American West." *American Quarterly* (May 1974): 176–90.

Lippitt, Francis J. "Pope's Virginia Campaign, and Porter's Part in It." *Atlantic Monthly,* Sept. 1878, 349–66.

Livermore, Thomas L. "The Conduct of Generals McClellan and Halleck in August, 1862; and the Case of Fitz John Porter." In *The Virginia Campaign of General Pope* in *1862: Papers Read before the Military Historical Society of Massachusetts in 1876, 1877, and 1880*, vol. 2, 315–48. Boston, 1886.

Longstreet, James. "Our March against Pope." *Century* 31, no. 4 (Feb. 1886): 601–14.

Lyon, James S. *War Sketches, from Cedar Mountain to Bull Run; Consisting of Personal and Historical Incidents of the Campaign under Major General Pope, in the Summer of 1862. By a Staff Officer.* Buffalo, 1882.

"Major General Pope." *Portrait Monthly* (July 1863): 7.

Mills, Lewis E. *General Pope's Virginia Campaign of 1862; Read before the Cincinnati Literary Club, February 5, 1870.* Cincinnati, 1870.

[———]. *Supreme Court of the United States; In Equity; The State of Georgia, vs. Edwin M. Stanton, Ulysses S. Grant, and John Pope; Brief for the Defendant, John Pope.* Cincinnati, 1867.

"Minnesota as Seen By Travelers: A Dragoon on the March to Pembina in 1849." *Minnesota History* 8 (1927): 61–74.

Moore, John G. "The Battle of Chantilly." *Military Affairs* 28, no. 2 (Summer 1966): 44–61.

Morse, Charles F. "From Second Bull Run to Antietam." In *War Papers and Personal Reminiscences, 1861–1865; Read before the Commandery of the State of Missouri, Military Order of the Loyal Legion of the United States*, vol. 1, 268–77. St. Louis, 1892.

Morse, William F. "The Indian Campaign in Minnesota in 1862." In *Personal Recollections of the War of the Rebellion; Addresses Delivered before the Commandery of the State of New York, Military Order of the Loyal Legion of the United States*, Fourth Series, 184–96. New York, 1912.

Morton, Charles. "Early War Days in Missouri." In *War Papers Being Papers Read before the Commandery of the State of Wisconsin, Military Order of the Loyal Legion of the United States*, vol. 2, 145–58. Milwaukee, 1892.

Mulligan, James A. "The Siege of Lexington, Mo." In *Battles and Leaders of the Civil War. Grant-Lee Edition*, vol. 1, pt. 2, 307–13. Edited by Clarence C. Buell and Robert U. Johnson. New York, 1884–87.

Myers, Lee. "Pope's Wells." *New Mexico Historical Review* (Oct. 1963): 281–82.

Nixon, Oliver W. "Reminiscences of the First Year of the War in Missouri." In *Military Essays and Recollections: Papers Read before the Commandery of the State of Illinois, Military Order of the Loyal Legion of the United States*, vol. 3, 413–36. Chicago, 1899.

Oliva, Leo E. "The Aubry Route of the Santa Fe Trail." *Kansas Historical Quarterly* 5, no. 2 (Spring 1973): 18–31.

Paddock, George L. "The Beginnings of an Illinois Volunteer Regiment in 1861." In *Military Essays and Recollections: Papers Read before the Commandery of the State of Illinois, Military Order of the Loyal Legion of the United States*, vol. 2, 253–68. Chicago, 1894.

Pope, John. *Address of General John Pope to the Army of the Tennessee, in Response to the Toast, "Our County," October 15, 1874.* N.p., n.d.

———. *Address of General John Pope to the Army of the Tennessee, in Response to the Toast, "Our Soldiers," October 16, 1873.* N.p., n.d.

———. "Army of Virginia." *National Tribune*, Aug. 2, 1888.

———. "Army of Virginia, II." *National Tribune*, Aug. 9, 1888.

———. "Army of Virginia, III." *National Tribune*, Aug. 16, 1888.

———. "Army of Virginia, IV." *National Tribune*, Aug. 23, 1888.

———. "Army of Virginia, V." *National Tribune*, Aug. 30, 1888.

———. "Army of Virginia, VI. *National Tribune*, Sept. 6, 1888.

———. *Brief Statement of the Case of Fitz John Porter*. N.p., [1869].

———. *The Indian Question; Address by General Pope, before the Social Science Association, at Cincinnati, Ohio, May 24, 1878*. Cincinnati: N.p., 1878.

———. "Island Number Ten, I." *National Tribune*, May 3, 1887.

———. "Island Number Ten, II." *National Tribune*, May 10, 1887.

———. "Meade under Grant." *National Tribune*, Dec. 13, 1900.

———. *A Military View of the Southern Rebellion: Our National Fortifications and Defenses*. Cincinnati, 1861.

———. "Missouri in 1861, I." *National Tribune*, Feb. 17, 1887.

———. "Missouri in 1861, II." *National Tribune*, Feb. 24, 1887.

——— "Missouri in 1861, III." *National Tribune*, Mar. 3, 1887.

———. "Missouri in 1861, IV." *National Tribune*, Mar. 10, 1887.

———. "The Second Battle of Bull Run." *Century* 31, no. 3 (Jan. 1886): 441–66.

———. "The Siege of Corinth, I." *National Tribune*, May 17, 1888.

———. "Some Legacies of the Civil War." *North American Review* 367 (June 1887).

———. "War Reminiscences." *National Tribune*, Dec. 11, 1890.

——— "War Reminiscences, III." *National Tribune*, Dec. 25, 1890.

———. "War Reminiscences, IV." *National Tribune*, Jan. 1, 1891.

———. "War Reminiscences, V." *National Tribune*, Jan. 8, 1891.

———. "War Reminiscences, VI." *National Tribune*, Jan. 15, 1891.

———. "War Reminiscences, VIII." *National Tribune*, Jan. 29, 1891.

———. "War Reminiscences, IX." *National Tribune*, Feb. 5, 1891.

———. "War Reminiscences, X." *National Tribune*, Feb. 12, 1891.

———. "War Reminiscences, XI." *National Tribune*, Feb. 19, 1891.

———. "War Reminiscences, XIII." *National Tribune*, Mar. 5, 1891.

———. "War Reminiscences, XIV." *National Tribune*, Mar. 12, 1891.

———. "War Reminiscences, XV." *National Tribune*, Mar. 19, 1891.

"Porter and Pope, the Investigation at West Point." *National Tribune*, July 13, 1878.

Quincy, Samuel M. "General Halleck's Military Administration in the Summer of 1862." In *The Virginia Campaign of General Pope in 1862: Papers Read before the Military Historical Society of Massachusetts in 1876, 1877, and 1880*, vol. 2, 1–30. Boston, 1886.

Randolph, Anson D. F. *General H. W. Halleck's Report Reviewed in the Light of Facts*. New York, 1862.

Robins, Richard. "The Battle of Groveton and Second Bull Run." In *Military Essays and Recollections: Papers Read before the Commandery of the State of Illinois, Military Order of the Loyal Legion of the United States*, vol. 3, 69–96. Chicago, 1899.

Rogers, Jerry L. "The Indian Territory Expedition." *Texas Military History* 4 (1970): 233–50.

Rogers, William P. "Diary and Letters of William P. Rogers, 1846-1862." *Southwestern Historical Quarterly* 22 (1928/29): 259–99.

Ropes, John C. "Campaign of General Pope—Second Part." In *The Virginia Campaign of General Pope in 1862: Papers Read before the Military Historical Society of Massachusetts in 1876, 1877, and 1880*, vol. 2, 55–70. Boston, 1886.

———. "Campaign of General Pope—Third Part." In *The Virginia Campaign of General*

Pope in 1862: Papers Read before the Military Historical Society of Massachusetts in 1876, 1877, and 1880, vol. 2, 73–97. Boston, 1886.

Ross, Charles. "SSH! Battle in Progress!" *Civil War Times Illustrated* 35, no. 6 (Dec. 1996): 56–62.

Sanborn, John B. "Reminiscences of the War in the Department of the Missouri." In *Glimpses of the Nation's Struggle: A Series of Papers Read before the Minnesota Commandery of the Military Order of the Loyal Legion of the United States,* Second Series, 224–57. Minneapolis, 1887.

Schurz, Carl. "Present Aspects of the Indian Problem." *North American Review* 133 (July 1881): 1–24.

[Smith, Thomas C. H.] "General Pope's Campaign in Virginia." *Army and Navy Journal,* Feb. 6, 1864.

Stevenson, John D. "Pope's Virginia Campaign." In *War Papers and Personal Reminiscences, 1861–1865, Read before the Commandery of the State of Missouri, Military Order of the Loyal Legion of the United States,* 323–53. St. Louis, 1892.

Suppeger, Joseph. "Lincoln and Pope." *Lincoln Herald* 77 (1973): 218–22.

Taylor, Joe F., ed. "The Indian Campaign on the Staked Plains, 1874–1875: Military Correspondence from War Department File 2815-1874, Adjutant General's Office, War Department." *Panhandle-Plains Historical Review* 34 (1961): 7–216.

Thomas, Horace A. "What I Saw under a Flag of Truce." In *Military Essays and Recollections: Papers Read before the Commandery of the State of Illinois, Military Order of the Loyal Legion of the United States,* vol. 1, 135–46. Chicago, 1899.

Utley, Robert M. "The Celebrated Peace Policy of General Grant." *North Dakota History* 20, no. 3 (July 1953): 121–42.

Walcott, Charles F. "Battle of Chantilly." In *The Virginia Campaign of General Pope in 1862: Papers Read before the Military Historical Society of Massachusetts in 1876, 1877, and 1880,* vol. 2, 133–94. Boston, 1886.

Waters, R. "Surrender at Tiptonville." *National Tribune,* Oct. 2, 1913.

Weld, Stephen M. "The Conduct of General McClellan at Alexandria in August, 1862." In *The Virginia Campaign of General Pope in 1862: Papers Read before the Military Historical Society of Massachusetts in 1876, 1877, and 1880,* vol. 2, 287–302. Boston, 1886.

Wiggins, Sarah W. "The 'Pig Iron' Kelley Riot in Mobile, May 14, 1867." *Alabama Review* 23, no. 1 (Jan. 1970): 45–55.

"William H. Powell to the Editors, March 12, 1885." *Century* 31, no. 3 (Jan. 1886): 473.

Wilson, James Grant. "Recollections of General Sherman." *National Tribune,* Feb. 27, 1902.

Personal Narratives, Memoirs, Diaries, Letters, and Collected Works

Abbott, Henry L. *Fallen Leaves: The Civil War Letters of Major Henry Livermore Abbott.* Edited by Robert Garth Scott. Kent, Ohio, 1991.

Adams, Charles Francis. *A Cycle of Adams Letters.* Edited by Worthington C. Ford. 2 vols. Boston, 1920.

Barber, Charles. *The Civil War Letters of Charles Barber, Private, 104th New York Volunteer Infantry.* Edited by Raymond G. Barber and Gary E. Swinson. Torrance, Calif., 1991.

Bates, Edward. *The Diary of Edward Bates, 1859–1866. Volume IV of the Annual Report of the American Historical Association for the Year 1930.* Edited by Howard K. Beale. Washington, D.C., 1933.

Blaine, James G. *Twenty Years of Congress.* 2 vols. Norwich, Conn., 1886.

Bouton, Edward. *Events of the Civil War.* Los Angeles, 1906.

Browning, Orville H. *The Diary of Orville Hickman Browning, 1850–1864.* Edited by Theodore C. Pease and James G. Randall. 2 vols. Springfield, Ill., 1925.

Brush, Daniel H. *Growing Up with Southern Illinois, 1820–1861.* Edited by Milo M. Quaife. Chicago, 1944.

Chase, Salmon P. *Inside Lincoln's Cabinet: The Civil War Diaries of Salmon P. Chase.* Edited by David Donald. New York, 1954.

Chetlain, Augustus. *Recollections of Seventy Years.* Galena, Ill., 1899.

Civil War Messages and Proclamations of Wisconsin War Governors. Edited by Robert G. Thwaites. Madison, 1912.

Cox, Jacob D. *Military Reminiscences of the Civil War.* 2 vols. New York, 1900.

Cozzens, Peter, and Robert I. Girardi, eds. *The Military Memoirs of General John Pope.* Chapel Hill, N.C., 1998.

Crawford, Samuel J. *Kansas in the Sixties.* Chicago, 1911.

Dodge, Grenville M. *The Battle of Atlanta and Other Campaigns.* Council Bluffs, Iowa, 1911.

Dwight, Wilder. *Life and Letters of Wilder Dwight.* Boston, 1868.

Early, Jubal A. *War Memoirs: Autobiographical Sketch and Narrative of the War between the States.* Edited by Frank E. Vandiver. Bloomington, Ind., 1960.

Eby, Henry. *Observations of an Illinois Boy in Battle, Camp, and Prison.* Mendota, Ill., 1910.

Frémont, Jessie Benton. *The Letters of Jessie Benton Frémont.* Edited by Pamela Herr and Mary Lee Spence. Urbana, Ill., 1993.

French, Samuel G. *Two Wars: An Autobiography.* Nashville, 1901.

Furber, George C. *The Twelve Months Volunteer; or, Journal of a Private in the Tennessee Regiment of Cavalry, in the Campaign in Mexico, 1846–1847.* Cincinnati, 1848.

Garfield, James A. *The Diary of James A. Garfield.* Edited by Harry James Brown and Frederick D. Williams. 4 vols. East Lansing, Mich., 1967.

General Grant's Unpublished Correspondence in the Case of Gen. Fitz-John Porter. N.p., n.d.

Gibbon, John. *Personal Recollections of the Civil War.* New York, 1928.

Gilbert, Alfred W. *Colonel A. W. Gilbert, Citizen Soldier of Cincinnati.* Edited by William E. and Ophia D. Smith. Cincinnati, 1934.

Gordon, George H. *Brook Farm to Cedar Mountain in the War of the Great Rebellion.* Boston, 1883.

———. *A History of the Campaign of the Army of Virginia under John Pope in 1862.* Boston, 1889.

Grant, Julia Dent. *The Personal Memoirs of Julia Dent Grant.* Edited by John Y. Simon. New York, 1975.

Grant, Ulysses S. *Memoirs and Selected Letters.* Edited by Mary D. McFeely. New York, 1990.

Grierson, Francis. *The Valley of Shadows.* Boston, 1909.

Haupt, Herman. *Reminiscences of General Herman Haupt.* Washington, D.C., 1901.

Hay, John. *Letters of John Hay and Extracts from Diary.* 3 vols. Washington, D.C., 1908.

Hayes, Rutherford B. *Diary and Letters of Rutherford Birchard Hayes, Nineteenth President of the United States.* Edited by Charles R. Williams. 6 vols. Columbus, Ohio, 1924.

Heth, Henry. *The Memoirs of Henry Heth.* Edited by James L. Morrison Jr. Westport, Conn., 1974.

Hill, Benjamin H., Jr. *The Life, Speeches, and Writings of Benjamin H. Hill.* Atlanta, 1891.

Howard, John R. *Remembrance of Things Past: A Familiar Chronicle of Kinfolk and Friends Worth While.* New York, 1925.

Hyman, Harold M., ed. *The Radical Republicans and Reconstruction, 1861–1870.* Indianapolis, 1967.

Jackson, Oscar L. *The Colonel's Diary: Journals Kept before and during the Civil War.* Sharon, Pa., 1922.

Johnson, Andrew. *The Papers of Andrew Johnson.* 16 vols. Vol. 11, edited by Paul H. Bergeron. Knoxville, Tenn., 1967–99.

Keyes, Erasmus D. *Fifty Years' Observation of Men and Events, Civil and Military.* New York, 1884.

Knox, Thomas W. *Camp Fire and Cotton Field: Southern Adventure in Time of War.* New York, 1865.

Koerner, Gustave. *Memoirs of Gustave Koerner, 1809–1896.* 2 vols. Cedar Rapids, Iowa, 1909.

Lewis, Lloyd. *Letters from Lloyd Lewis, Showing Steps in the Research for His Biography of U. S. Grant.* Edited by Angus Cameron. Boston, 1950.

Lincoln, Abraham. *The Collected Works of Abraham Lincoln.* Edited by Roy P. Basler. 8 vols. New Brunswick, N.J., 1953.

Linder, Usher F. *Reminiscences of the Early Bench and Bar of Illinois.* Chicago, 1879.

Livermore, Thomas L. *Days and Events, 1860–1866.* Boston, 1920.

Logan, Mrs. John A. *Reminiscences of a Soldier's Wife: An Autobiography.* New York, 1913.

Longstreet, James. *From Manassas to Appomattox: Memoirs of the Civil War in America.* Philadelphia, 1912.

Lusk, William T. *War Letters of William Thompson Lusk.* New York, 1911.

Marshall, J. T. *The Miles Expedition of 1874–1875: An Eyewitness Account of the Red River War.* Austin, Tex., 1971.

McClellan, George B. *The Civil War Papers of George B. McClellan.* Edited by Stephen W. Sears. New York, 1989.

———. *McClellan's Own Story.* New York, 1887.

McClure, Alexander K. *Colonel Alexander K. McClure's Recollections of Half a Century.* Salem, Mass., 1902.

Meade, George. *The Life and Letters of George Gordon Meade, Major-General, United States Army.* Edited by George Gordon Meade. 2 vols. New York, 1913.

Moore, Frank G., ed. *The Rebellion Record: A Diary of American Events.* 12 vols. New York, 1861–68.

Nagle, Theodore M. *Reminiscences of the Civil War.* New York, 1923.

Noyes, George F. *The Bivouac and the Battlefield.* New York, 1863.

Page, Charles A. *Letters of a War Correspondent, 1862–1865.* Boston, 1899.

Patrick, Marsena R. *Inside Lincoln's Army: The Diary of Marsena Rudolph Patrick, Provost Marshal General, Army of the Potomac.* Edited by David S. Sparks. New York, 1964.

Pope, John. *Correspondence between General Pope and the Comte de Paris, Concerning the Second Battle of Bull Run.* N.p., 1876.

———. *Correspondence between Generals Pope and Halleck in Relation to Prisoners Captured at Corinth.* N.p., n.d.

———. *Correspondence in Relation to Gen. Franklin's Charges, with Gen. Thomas's Disclaimer.* Detroit, 1870.

———. *John Pope to J. Bright Smith, August 3, 1866.* N.p., 1866.

———. *John Pope to the Comte de Paris, April 19, 1877.* N.p., n.d.

———. *Letters of General Pope to Hon. S. P. Chase, Proposing Plan of Military Operations for 1863.* N.p., n.d.

Porter, Fitz John. *Gen. Fitz John Porter's Statement of the Services of the Fifth Army Corps, in 1862, in Northern Virginia.* New York, 1878.

Quint, Alonzo H. *The Potomac and the Rapidan.* Boston, 1864.

Schofield, John M. *Forty-six Years in the Army.* New York, 1897.

Schurz, Carl. *The Reminiscences of Carl Schurz.* 3 vols. New York, 1907.

Sedgwick, John. *Correspondence of John Sedgwick, Major General.* 2 vols. New York, 1902–3.

Shaw, Robert Gould. *Blue-Eyed Child of Fortune: The Civil War Letters of Robert Gould Shaw.* Edited by Russell Duncan. Athens, Ga., 1992.

Sheridan, Philip H. *Personal Memoirs of P. H. Sheridan.* 2 vols. New York, 1888.

Sherman, William T. *Home Letters of General Sherman.* Edited by M. A. DeWolfe Howe. New York, 1909.

———. *Memoirs of General W. T. Sherman.* 2 vols. New York, 1875.

Simon, John Y., ed. *The Papers of Ulysses S. Grant.* 24 vols. Carbondale, Ill., 1967– .

Small, Abner R. *The Road to Richmond: The Civil War Memoirs of Major Abner R. Small.* Edited by Harold A. Small. Berkeley, 1939.

Smith, Benjamin T. *Private Smith's Journal: Recollections of the Late War.* Edited by Clyde C. Walton. Chicago, 1963.

Smith, George W., and Charles B. Judah, eds. *Chronicles of the Gringos: The U.S. Army in the Mexican War, 1846–1848; Accounts of Eyewitnesses and Combatants.* Albuquerque, 1968.

Smith, William F. *Autobiography of Major General William F. Smith, 1861–1864.* Edited by Herbert M. Schiller. Dayton, 1990.

Stanley, David S. *Personal Memoirs of Major-General D. S. Stanley, U.S.A.* Cambridge, Mass., 1917. Reprint, Gaithersburg, Md., 1987.

Stearns, Austin C. *Three Years with Company K.* Rutherford, N.J., 1976.

Sterling, Pound [William P. Maxson]. *Camp Fires of the Twenty-third: Sketches of the Camp Life, Marches, and Battles of the Twenty-third Regiment, N.Y.V.* New York, 1863.

Stone, James M. *Personal Recollections of the Civil War.* Boston, 1918.

Strother, David H. *A Virginia Yankee in the Civil War: The Diaries of David Hunter Strother.* Edited by Cecil D. Eby Jr. Chapel Hill, N.C., 1961.

Sullivan, James P. *An Irishman in the Iron Brigade: The Civil War Memoirs of James P. Sullivan.* Edited by William J. K. Beaudot and Lance J. Herdegen. New York, 1993.

Tatum, Lawrie. *Our Red Brothers and the Peace Policy of President Ulysses S. Grant.* Lincoln, Nebr., 1970.

Townsend, George Alfred. *Rustics in Rebellion: A Yankee Reporter on the Road to Richmond, 1861–1865.* Chapel Hill, N.C., 1950.

Villard, Henry. *Memoirs of Henry Villard, Journalist and Financier, 1835–1900.* 2 vols. Boston, 1904.

Wainwright, Charles S. *A Diary of Battle: The Personal Journals of Colonel Charles S. Wainwright, 1861–1865.* Edited by Allan Nevins. New York, 1962.

Ware, Eugene F. *The Indian War of 1864.* Topeka, Kans., 1911.

Weld, Stephen M. *War Diary and Letters of Stephen Minot Weld.* Boston, 1979.

Welles, Gideon. *The Diary of Gideon Welles.* 3 vols. Boston, 1911.

Whipple, Henry B. *Lights and Shadows of a Long Episcopate.* New York, 1899.

White, David A., ed. *News of the Plains and Rockies, 1803–1865.* 4 vols. Spokane, 1996– .

Williams, Alpheus S. *The Civil War Letters of General Alpheus S. Williams: From the Cannon's Mouth.* Edited by Milo M. Quaife. Detroit, 1959.

Wills, Charles. *Army Life of an Illinois Soldier, Including a Day-by-Day Record of Sherman's March to the Sea.* Washington, D.C., 1906.

Unit Histories

Bosbyshell, Oliver C. *The Forty-eighth in the War, Being a Narrative of the Campaigns of the 48th Regiment, Infantry, Pennsylvania Veteran Volunteers, during the War of the Rebellion.* Philadelphia, 1895.

Boyce, C. W. *A Brief History of the Twenty-eighth Regiment New York State Volunteers.* Buffalo, 1896.

Bryant, Edwin E. *History of the Third Regiment of Wisconsin Veteran Volunteer Infantry.* Madison, 1891.

Bryner, Byron C. *Bugle Echoes: The Story of Illinois 47th.* Springfield, Ill., 1905.

Cook, Benjamin F. *History of the Twelfth Massachusetts Volunteers.* Boston, 1892.

Davis, Charles E. *Three Years in the Army: The Story of the Thirteenth Massachusetts Volunteers.* Boston, 1894.

Dawes, Rufus R. *Service with the Sixth Wisconsin Volunteers.* Marietta, Ohio, 1930.

Denison, Frederic. *Sabres and Spurs: The First Regiment Rhode Island Cavalry in the Civil War, 1861–1865.* Central Falls, R.I., 1876.

Gould, John M. *History of the First–Tenth–Twenty-ninth Maine Regiment.* Portland, 1871.

Hardin, Martin. *History of the Twelfth Regiment Pennsylvania Reserve Volunteer Corps.* New York, 1890.

History of the Forty-sixth Regiment Indiana Volunteer Infantry. Logansport, Ind., 1888.

Kepler, William. *History of the Three Months' and Three Years' Service, from April 16th, 1861, to June 22d, 1864, of the Fourth Regiment Ohio Volunteer Infantry in the War for the Union.* Cleveland, 1886.

Pierce, Lyman B. *History of the Second Iowa Cavalry.* Burlington, Iowa, 1865.

Powell, William H. *The Fifth Corps (Army of the Potomac): A Record of Operations during the Civil War in the United States of Army, 1861–1865.* New York and London, 1896.

Quint, Alonzo H. *The Record of the Second Massachusetts Infantry.* Boston, 1867.

Rhodes, Charles D. *History of the Cavalry of the Army of the Potomac, Including That of the Army of Virginia.* Kansas City, Mo., 1900.

Sawyer, Franklin. *A Military History of the 8th Regiment Ohio Vol. Inf'y.* Cleveland, 1881.

Smith, Charles H. *History of Fuller's Ohio Brigade.* Cleveland, 1909.

Stevens, George T. *Three Years in the Sixth Corps.* Albany, N.Y., 1866.

Thatcher, Marshall P. *A Hundred Battles in the West, St. Louis to Atlanta, 1861–1865, the Second Michigan Cavalry.* Detroit, 1884.

Vautier, John D. *History of the Eighty-fifth Pennsylvania Volunteers in the War for the Union.* Philadelphia, 1894.

Walcott, Charles F. *History of the Twenty-first Regiment Massachusetts Volunteers.* Boston, 1882.

Wood, George L. *The Seventh Regiment: A Record.* New York, 1865.

Woodward, E. M. *Our Campaigns: The Second Regiment Pennsylvania Reserve Volunteers.* Philadelphia, 1865.

Secondary Sources: Books and Pamphlets

Ambrose, Stephen E. *Halleck, Lincoln's Chief of Staff.* Baton Rouge, 1962.

Andrews, J. Cutler. *The North Reports the Civil War.* Pittsburgh, 1955.

Athearn, Robert G. *William Tecumseh Sherman and the Settlement of the West.* Norman, Okla., 1956.

Avery, Isaac W. *The History of the State of Georgia from 1850 to 1881.* New York, 1881.

Badeau, Adam. *Grant in Peace, from Appomattox to Mount McGregor.* Hartford, Conn., 1887.

Banta, R. E. *The Ohio.* New York, 1949.

Bauer, K. Jack. *The Mexican War, 1846–1848.* New York, 1974.

Bayard, Samuel J. *The Life of George Dashiell Bayard.* New York, 1874.

Britton, Wiley. *The Civil War on the Border.* 2 vols. New York, 1899.

Brooks, Nathan C. *A Complete History of the Mexican War.* Chicago, 1965.

Brown, D. Alexander. *The Galvanized Yankees.* Urbana, Ill., 1963.

Buck, Daniel. *Indian Outbreaks.* Mankato, Minn., 1904.

Carley, Kenneth. *The Sioux Uprising of 1862.* St. Paul, Minn., 1962.

Carr, Clark E. *The Illini.* New York, 1905.

Castel, Albert. *General Sterling Price and the Civil War in the West.* Baton Rouge, 1968.

Chaput, Donald. *François Aubry: Trader, Trailmaker, and Voyageur in the Southwest, 1846–1854.* Glendale, Calif., 1975.

Comte de Paris, Louis-Philippe-Albert d'Orleans. *History of the Civil War in America.* 4 vols. Philadelphia, 1875–1888.

Conway, Alan. *The Reconstruction of Georgia.* Minneapolis, 1966.

Cox, Jacob D. *The Second Battle of Bull Run, as Connected with the Fitz-John Porter Case.* Cincinnati, 1882.

Daniel, Larry J., and Lynn N. Bock. *Island No. 10: Struggle for the Mississippi Valley.* Tuscaloosa, Ala., 1996.

Davis, William W. *The Civil War and Reconstruction in Florida.* 1913. Reprint. Gainesville, Fla., 1964.

De Peyster, John Watts. *Personal and Military History of Philip Kearny, Major General United States Volunteers.* New York, 1869.

Dictionary of American Biography. Edited by Dumas Malone. 21 vols. New York, 1928–44.

Duncan, Russell. *Entrepreneur for Equality: Governor Rufus Bullock, Commerce, and Race in Post–Civil War Georgia.* Athens, Ga., 1994.

Dyer, Frederick H. *A Compendium of the War of the Rebellion.* 3 vols. New York, 1959.

Eakin, Joanne C. *Battle at Blackwater River.* Independence, Mo., 1995.

Eddy, T. M. *The Patriotism of Illinois.* 2 vols. Chicago, 1865.

Edwards, Ninian W. *History of Illinois, from 1778 to 1833; and Life and Times of Ninian Edwards.* Springfield, Ill., 1870.

Eisenschiml, Otto. *The Celebrated Case of Fitz John Porter: An American Dreyfuss Affair.* Indianapolis, 1950.

Ellis, Richard N. *General Pope and U.S. Indian Policy.* Albuquerque, 1970.

Ervin, Edgar. *Pioneer History of Meigs County, Ohio to 1949, Including Masonic History of the Same Period.* Columbus, Ohio, 1949.

Fishel, Edwin C. *The Secret War for the Union: The Untold Story of Military Intelligence in the Civil War.* Boston, 1996.

Force, Manning F. *From Fort Henry to Corinth.* New York, 1881.

Ford, Thomas. *A History of Illinois, from Its Commencement as a State in 1818 to 1847.* 2 vols. Chicago, 1945–46.

Goetzmann, William H. *Army Exploration in the American West, 1803–1863.* Austin, Tex., 1991.

Gorham, George C. *Life and Public Services of Edwin M. Stanton.* 2 vols. Boston, 1899.

Haley, James L. *The Buffalo War.* New York, 1976.

Hart, Albert B. *Salmon Portland Chase.* Boston, 1899.

Heard, Isaac V. D. *History of the Sioux War and Massacres of 1862 and 1863.* New York, 1864.

Hennessy, John J. *Return to Bull Run: The Campaign and Battle of Second Manassas.* New York, 1992.

———. *Second Manassas Battlefield Map Study.* Lynchburg, Va., 1986.

Hine, Robert V. *In the Shadow of Frémont: Edward Kern and the Art of American Exploration, 1845–1860.* Norman, Okla., 1982.

Hunt, Elvid. *History of Fort Leavenworth, 1827–1937.* Fort Leavenworth, Kans., 1937.

Hutton, Paul A. *Phil Sheridan and His Army.* Lincoln, Nebr., 1986.

———, ed. *Soldiers West: Biographies from the Military Frontier.* Lincoln, Nebr., 1987.

Johnson, Dorothy M. *The Bloody Bozeman: The Perilous Trail to Montana's Gold.* New York, 1971.

Johnson, Virginia W. *The Unregimented General: A Biography of Nelson A. Miles.* Boston, 1962.

Jones, Robert N. *The Civil War in the Northwest.* Norman, Okla., 1960.

Krick, Robert K. *Conquering the Valley: Stonewall Jackson at Port Republic.* New York, 1996.

———. *Stonewall Jackson at Cedar Mountain.* Chapel Hill, N.C., 1990.

Larkin, Stillman C. *The Pioneer History of Meigs County.* Columbus, Ohio, 1908.

Livermore, Thomas L. *Numbers and Losses in the Civil War.* Bloomington, Ind., 1959.

Madsen, Brigham D. *Glory Hunter: A Biography of Patrick Edward Connor.* Salt Lake City, 1990.

Mantell, Martin E. *Johnson, Grant, and the Politics of Reconstruction.* New York, 1973.

Marszalek, John F. *Sherman: A Soldier's Passion for Order.* New York, 1993.

McPherson, Edward. *Political History of the United States during the Period of Reconstruction, 1865–1870.* Washington, D.C., 1871.

Monaghan, James. *The Civil War on the Western Border.* Boston, 1955.

Moses, John. *Illinois: Historical and Statistical.* 2 vols. Chicago, 1889.

Myers, Robert Manson. *The Children of Pride: A True Story of Georgia and the Civil War.* New Haven, Conn., 1972.

Nathans, Elizabeth S. *Losing the Peace: Georgia Republicans and Reconstruction, 1865–1871.* Baton Rouge, 1968.

Nevins, Allan. *Frémont: The West's Greatest Adventurer.* 2 vols. New York, 1928.

Nicolay, John G., and John Hay. *Abraham Lincoln: A History.* 10 vols. New York, 1890.

Pohanka, Brian C., ed. *Nelson A. Miles: A Documentary Biography of His Military Career, 1861–1903.* Glendale, Calif., 1985.

[Pollard, Edward A.] *The Second Battle of Manassas, with Sketches of the Recent Campaign in Northern Virginia and on the Upper Potomac.* Richmond, 1862.

Reynolds, John. *The Pioneer History of Illinois.* Chicago, 1887.

Richards, George W. *Lives of Generals Halleck and Pope.* Philadelphia, 1862.

Richardson, Rupert T. *The Frontier of Northwest Texas, 1846–1876.* Glendale, Calif., 1964.

Robinson, Charles. *The Indian Trial: The Complete Story of the Warren Wagon Train Massacre and the Fall of the Kiowa Nation.* Glendale, Calif., 1997.

Ropes, John Codman. *The Army under Pope.* New York, 1881.

Schutz, Wallace J., and Walter N. Trenerry. *Abandoned by Lincoln: A Military Biography of General John Pope.* Urbana, Ill., 1990.

———. *John Pope: The Professional Soldier as Unwilling Servant of Party Politics, 1861–1865; A Paper Presented at the Fourth Annual Illinois History Conference, Springfield, December 2–3, 1983.* Springfield, Ill., 1983.

Sears, Stephen W. *To the Gates of Richmond: The Peninsula Campaign.* New York, 1992.

Sefton, James E. *The United States Army and Reconstruction, 1865–1877.* Baton Rouge, 1967.

Shumate, Albert. *The Notorious I. C. Woods of the Adams Express.* Glendale, Calif., 1986.

Simpson, Brooks D. *Let Us Have Peace: Ulysses S. Grant and the Politics of War and Reconstruction, 1861–1868.* Chapel Hill, N.C., 1991.

Smith, Justin H. *The War with Mexico.* 2 vols. New York, 1919.

Stevens, Hazard. *The Life of Isaac Ingalls Stevens.* 2 vols. Boston, 1901.

Sully, Langdon. *No Tears for the General: The Life of Alfred Sully, 1821–1879.* Palo Alto, Calif., 1974.

Thomas, Benjamin P., and Harold M. Hyman. *Stanton: The Life and Times of Lincoln's Secretary of War.* New York, 1962.

Thompson, C. Mildred. *Reconstruction in Georgia: Economic, Social, Political, 1865–1872.* 1913. Reprint. Gloucester, Mass., 1964.

Throne, Mildred. *Cyrus Clay Carpenter and Iowa Politics, 1854–1898.* Iowa City, 1974.

Utley, Robert M. *Frontier Regulars: The United States Army and the Indian, 1866–1890.* New York, 1973.

———. *Frontiersmen in Blue: The United States Army and the Indian, 1848–1865.* New York, 1967.

Walton, George. *Sentinel of the Plains: Fort Leavenworth and the American West.* Englewood Cliffs, N.J., 1973.

Warner, Ezra. *Generals in Blue: Lives of the Union Commanders.* Baton Rouge, 1964.

———. *Generals in Gray: Lives of the Confederate Commanders.* Baton Rouge, 1959.

Weigley, Russell R. *The History of the United States Army.* New York, 1967.

West, Nathaniel. *The Ancestry, Life, and Times of Hon. Henry Hastings Sibley.* St. Paul, Minn., 1889.

Williams, Charles R. *The Life of Rutherford Birchard Hayes, Nineteenth President of the United States.* 2 vols. Columbus, Ohio, 1938.

Williams, Kenneth P. *Lincoln Finds a General.* 5 vols. New York, 1949–58.

Wilson, James G. *Biographical Sketches of Illinois Officers Engaged in the War against the Rebellion of 1861.* Chicago, 1862.

Wood, Richard G. *Stephen Harriman Long: Engineer, Explorer, Inventor.* Glendale, Calif., 1966.

Wooster, Robert. *The Military and United States Indian Policy, 1865–1903.* New Haven, Conn., 1988.

Ph.D. Dissertations

Cox, Merlin G. "John Pope, Fighting General from Illinois." University of Florida, 1956.

Gabler, Henry. "The Fitz John Porter Case: Politics and Military Justice." City University of New York, 1979.

Mardock, Robert W. "The Humanitarians and Post–Civil War Indian Policy." University of Colorado, 1958.

Morrison, James L., Jr. "The United States Military Academy, 1833–1866: Years of Progress and Turmoil." Columbia University, 1973.

Index

Peter Cozzens is a Foreign Service Officer with the U.S. Department of State. A summa cum laude graduate of Knox College, Illinois, Cozzens served as a captain in the United States Army before joining the Foreign Service in 1983. His books include *No Better Place to Die: The Battle of Stones River; This Terrible Sound: The Battle of Chickamauga; The Shipwreck of Their Hopes: The Battles for Chattanooga; The Darkest Days of the War: The Battles of Iuka and Corinth;* and *The Military Memoirs of General John Pope.*

University of Illinois Press
1325 South Oak Street
Champaign, IL 61820-6903
www.press.uillinois.edu